CW01082961

THE LOSS OF NORMANDY

The Loss of Normandy

1189—1204

Studies in the History of the Angevin Empire

BY

SIR MAURICE POWICKE

MANCHESTER
UNIVERSITY PRESS

First published by Manchester University Press 1913 (first edition),
1960 (second edition)
Special edition for Sandpiper Books Ltd, 1999

Published by Manchester University Press
Oxford Road, Manchester M13 9NR
http://www.man.ac.uk/mup

British Library Cataloguing-in-Publication Data
A catalogue record for this book is available from the British Library

05 04 03 02 01 00 99   7 6 5 4 3 2

ISBN 0 7190 5740 X

Printed in Great Britain by
Bookcraft (Bath) Ltd, Midsomer Norton

PREFACE TO THE FIRST EDITION (1913)

THE following studies are based upon researches which I began some years ago as Langton Fellow in the University of Manchester. They were inspired by the teaching which I received in that university, and I am glad to think that they have been considered worthy of a place in the historical series published by the University Press.

The studies cover a great deal of ground, and I am conscious that many of them are of a tentative nature. At the same time a twofold aim is common to all the chapters in this book. I desire, in the first place, to call attention to the importance of the extensive materials for the study of Norman history, more especially in the twelfth century. Secondly, I hope to show how a fuller use of our neglected Chancery records may illustrate the actual operations of early institutions in war and peace. In the course of the description I have had to deal with several matters which await treatment by more qualified students. For example, I should like to think that the second chapter will encourage some French scholar to write a book which will fill the gap between the studies, on the one hand, of Halphen on Anjou, Latouche on Maine, and Lasteyrie on Limoges, and, on the other, of Boutaric upon Alfonse of Poitiers; or, again, that the appendix upon the division in the Norman baronage will attract some trained genealogist to a neglected field of research.

The reaction of Norman upon English studies must increase in the future. In the third, eighth and tenth chapters I have tried to point out some ways in which the history of England under Henry II and his sons is modified or assisted by an examination of Norman evidence. In particular I have found, in studying the loss of Normandy that much light is thrown upon the origin in England of a sense of nationality, and upon the relations between feudal and national ideas. This important problem has been discussed at some length by recent writers, especially in America.[1] It lies behind the long discussion upon Magna Carta, and I feel that much recent criticism of that famous document would have been written rather differently, if its authors had been students of Norman and Angevin, as well as of English, history.

From one point of view, all that I have written is a commentary upon Thomas Stapleton's *Observations on the Great Rolls of the Exchequer of Normandy*. I join with Mr. Round in admiration for that great antiquary. His work was taken up and carried on by the young

---

[1] *e.g.*, in C. H. McIlwain's *The High court of Parliament* (1910).

v

Léopold Delisle more than fifty years ago; and the frequent references to their work in the following pages testify both to the value of
their labours and to the later neglect of Norman history.[2] I owe most
to Professor Haskins of Harvard, amongst modern scholars. He has
kindly read several of the early chapters and given me much valuable
criticism. Moreover, his essays upon the history of Normandy in the
eleventh and early twelfth centuries are a sure foundation for any
work upon a later period. The knowledge that he was continuing his
elaborate labours upon Norman charters has justified me in limiting
the scope of the chapter upon Norman administration. My friends
and teachers, Professor Tout, Professor Tait and Mr. H. W. C. Davis
have added to a long series of kindnesses by reading and advising me
upon various parts of the book. To Mr. Tout's unwearying encourage-
ment I feel especially that I could never do justice in a preface. My
friend Professor Weaver, of Trinity College, Dublin, has also been
good enough to read one or two chapters; and my friends Mr. S. O.
Moffet, of the John Rylands Library, Manchester, and Mr. V. H.
Galbraith, of Balliol College, Oxford, have helped me constantly by
searching for information and verifying references.[3] My special
thanks are due to Mr. H. M. McKechnie, the Secretary to the Publications Committee in the University of Manchester, for his continual
help in supervising the progress of the proofs through the press.

Finally, I must express my gratitude to the Council of the London
Society of Antiquaries for permission to reprint Stapleton's *Tabula
Normanniae*; and to Mr. R. L. Poole the editor, and Messrs. Longman
& Co. the publishers of the *English Historical Review*, for allowing me
to make free use in the text of my articles in that periodical, and to
reprint almost entire the essay upon King John and Arthur of
Brittany.

Although this is a Manchester book, I have put it together, in the
exercise of my privileges, in Oxford and Belfast. These privileges
have been very great; in particular, I can never forget the kindly
influences of Merton, *domus placida*,—of the Fellows' Quadrangle,
and, most of all, of Bishop Rede's Library.

F. M. POWICKE

THE QUEEN'S UNIVERSITY,
   BELFAST,
      January, 1913

[2] On the work of Stapleton and Delisle, see *Quarterly Review* (1911), pp.
486–9.

[3] In quoting from original sources, I have, in nearly all cases, retained the
medieval spelling and grammatical peculiarities. Note also, that, unless otherwise stated, reference to Norman finances are made in terms of Angevin money,
according to official usage.

PREFACE TO THE SECOND EDITION

THIS book has been out of print for a long time, and I am grateful to the Manchester University Press for this second edition, mainly a reprint of the first with revisions, omissions and additions here and there. I am told that, although much has been written since 1913, the book as a whole stands firm. I have not tried to deal with the extensive literature upon the origins of ducal authority in Normandy, for this problem is a subject in itself, and one merely incidental to the present volume; but I know how much we owe to D. C. Douglas here in England, and to the French scholars M. de Bouard, L. Musset, J. Yver and others. My hope that the appendix upon the division in the Norman baronage, especially between 1204 and 1244, might attract some trained genealogist to study the connection between genealogy and the social history of England and Normandy after their separation, has not been fulfilled. I have left this tentative appendix and the last chapter of the book as they were first written, with such corrections as the late L. C. Loyd and the editors of *The Complete Peerage* have happened to make.

The nature of this new edition has been discussed with such good friends of mine as C. N. L. Brooke, C. R. Cheney, John le Patourel and Lady Stenton. Professor Brooke very kindly sent me a number of notes on the first three chapters, and Mr. Allen Brown most generously prepared a list of corrections and suggestions for the text and footnotes of chapters IV to IX. My own revision has been made much easier by their help.

F. M. P.

OXFORD, 1960

CONTENTS

CHAPTER VII

THE NORMAN DEFENCES

CHAPTER VIII

WAR AND FINANCE

MAPS

All the maps appear at the end of the volume

INTRODUCTORY NOTE ON AUTHORITIES

THE loss of Normandy has only once been the subject of a separate work—in A. Poignant's inadequate *Histoire de la Conquête de la Normandie par Philippe Auguste en 1204* (Paris, 1854). The political histories of Miss Norgate and Sir James Ramsay, Lehmann's *Johann ohne Land* (Berlin, 1904), and the half-volume written by M. Luchaire for Lavisse's *Histoire de France* (III, i) contain scholarly narratives; and, at greater length, so does A. Cartellieri's *Philipp II August* (Leipzig, 1899–1922). Since M. Poignant wrote, the materials for a survey of Norman society at the close of the twelfth century have been completely revised or re-edited, and many additions have been made to our knowledge. It is unnecessary to describe the French and Anglo-Norman chronicles of the period.[1] Nor is it needful to attempt a critical survey on a large scale of the authorities for Norman history, since the appearance of M. Henri Prentout's studies in Norman bibliography included in his contributions to the excellent series, *Les Régions de la France*, first published in the *Revue de Synthèse Historique*.[2] At the same time, it may be useful to refer the reader to the more important or more recent contributions to the subject. References to special books and articles upon points of detail or of interest foreign to Norman history will be found in the course of the essay.

It is doubtful whether certainty will ever be reached about the origin and nature of the Norman state in the tenth century. M. Ferdinand Lot's studies on the abbey of Saint-Wandrille (Paris, 1913)

---

[1] See Charles Gross, *The sources and literature of English history from the earliest times to about 1485* (2nd edition, 1915); and A. Molinier, *Les Sources de l'histoire de France* (1901–6). Note, in addition, M. Delisle's edition of the fourth part of a *Chronique française des rois de France par un anonyme de Béthune* in the *Recueil des Historiens de France*, t. xxiv, pt. ii, p. 751: compare *Histoire Littéraire*, xxxii, 222; also a new text for the year 1154 onwards of the *Chronicon Universale Anonymi Laudunensis*, prepared by Dr. Wolf Stechele and Dr. Cartellieri (Leipzig and Paris, 1909). Cf. my remarks upon the contemporary chroniclers in general (*English Historical Review*, xxi (1906), 630–3) and upon the relations between the Coggeshall chronicle and Roger of Wendover (*ibid.*, p. 286).

[2] M. Prentout's articles commenced in the *Revue de Synthèse historique* for August, 1909. They have been separately published as *Les Régions de la France*, vii (Paris, 1910). [For recent literature see the notes to C. H. Haskins, *Norman Institutions*, Cambridge (Mass.), 1918, D. C. Douglas, 'The Rise of Normandy', in the *Proceedings of the British Academy*, xxxiii (1947), 101–30, and the bibliography in J. Boussard, *Le Gouvernement d'Henri II Plantagenêt*, Paris, 1956.]

began a new revision;[3] yet even Mr. Haskins, who has made the early history of the duchy his own, practically gives up the study of the 'interaction of Frankish and Scandinavian elements in the tenth century'. On the other hand, researches into later periods have reacted upon the problems of the earlier and in some degree reduced their importance. The exact nature of ducal authority, the precise amount of Scandinavian law in Normandy after the settlement of 912, become questions of less moment when it is proved that before the conquest of England Normandy had become a highly centralised feudal State, with financial, judicial and military institutions well defined. We can stand on firm ground and await with patience the solution or surrender of the questions which vexed Waitz and Palgrave.[4]

The lead in these inquiries was taken by Charles H. Haskins. The first fruits of his labours appeared in the *American Historical Review* and the *English Historical Review* between 1903 and 1909. These were collected with revisions and additions in his *Norman Institutions* (1918).

The reconstruction of the Norman State in the eleventh and early twelfth centuries by Haskins, together with the help of such important works as the *Essai sur l'origine de la noblesse* of M. Guilhiermoz (Paris, 1902) and Dr. Boehmer's *Kirche und Staat in England und der Normandie in XI und XII Jahrundert* (Leipzig, 1899), gives point and meaning to the insistence of earlier writers upon the solidarity of the Norman State. Their writings may now be used with more confidence, since their conclusions can be checked and the errors excluded, by reference to known facts. Chief among these suggestive if disputable works are Steenstrup's well-known *Inledning i Normannertiden* (Kjoebenhavn, 1876), of part of which the author published a French translation, *Etudes preliminaires pour servir à l'histoire de Normands et de leur invasions* (Caen, 1880). Steenstrup's later work *Normandiets Historie under de syv første hertuge* (1925), should now be added. Cf. also M. Flach's pages upon Normandy in his *Origines de l'ancienne France* (vols. ii and iii, *passim*, 1893, 1904).

As was shown by that great pioneer Dr. Heinrich Brunner in his *Enstehung der Schwurgerichte* (1872), it is impossible to separate the

[3] See also the new edition of William of Jumièges by J. Marx (Soc. de l'histoire de Normandie, 1914).
[4] For the older theories, see Stubbs, *Constitutional History of England*, i, 270–1, and especially the summary of literature in Karl v. Amira's valuable review of Steenstrup in Sybel's *Historiche Zeitschrift*, 1878, Neue Folge, iii, 240: 'Die Anfänge des normannischen Rechts.' Prentout discussed the whole question in his *Essai sur les origines et la fondation du duché de Normandie* (Paris, 1911). See now Douglas, noted above.

study of Norman institutions from the study of Norman law. Of recent years the critical examination of the earliest Norman law books has done much for Norman history; some success, for example, has been achieved in separating custom from ordinance in the *Statuta et Consuetudines*, the oldest custumal of Normandy, which, as M. Ernest Joseph Tardif showed in his excellent edition, included in his *Coutumiers de Normandie* (Société de l'histoire de Normandie; the first volume published in two parts, 1881 and 1903) was put together in the last months of 1199 or early in 1200, probably by a clerk of the seneschal, William Fitz Ralf (i, pp. lxv–lxxii, lxxxi).[5] The best comparative studies in Norman law are contained in Pollock and Maitland's *History of English Law* (2nd edition, vol. i, 64–78 and elsewhere) in the works of Brunner and Guilhiermoz, and especially in M. Paul Viollet's article on the Norman custumals in the *Histoire Littéraire de la France* (1906, vol. xxxiii, pp. 40–190). Dr. Brunner has recently republished his critical bibliography, useful for an account of administrative records as well as of the custumals, in an appendix to his study of the English sources—*Geschichte der Englischen Rechtsquellen im Grundriss* (Leipzig, 1909, pp. 62–75).

Besides the earliest custumal, the official records of the Angevin dukes of Normandy survive for some of the later years of the twelfth century. In any case the numerous charters, the English Pipe Rolls, and the chronicles of Robert of Torigni and the author known as Benedict of Peterborough, but now shown to have been Roger of Howden himself,[6] would enable us to be more familiar with the Norman State in the second than in the first part of the century. The charters of the dukes and their subjects have been worked over by several generations of scholars, notably by the great English antiquary Stapleton, and the Norman Lechaudé d'Anisy. They have been used by the editors of the well-known collections of ecclesiastical documents, the *Neustria Pia* and *Gallia Christiana*. Mr. Round has summarised a valuable collection in his *Calendar of Documents preserved in France*, 918–1206 (1899). Finally, in his essay upon the acts of Henry II, published in the new and important series of *Chartes et diplômes relatifs à l'histoire de France* (the introductory volume, 1909), M. Léopold Delisle crowned the labours of over half a century.[7]

---

[5] In the light shed by the Vatican MS., Viollet argues against Tardif for a revision in 1203–4 (*Hist. litt.*, xxxiii, 48).

[6] Cf. D. M. Stenton in *English Historical Review*, lxviii (1953), 574–82, and below, p. 84, note 18.

[7] For a fuller account of the work which has been done upon the chartularies, scattered charters, etc., of Normandy, cf. Haskins, *Norman Institutions*, pp. 341–9. [See now the texts of Henry's charters etc., relating to the continental fiefs and to France in the *Recueil des actes de Henri II*, edited by Delisle and Berger, Paris, 1909–27.]

But, in addition to the charters which have been brought together from the departmental archives of France, the student has a few important official rolls at his disposal. The various Chancery rolls which survive for England since John's reign had their Norman counterparts. Of these Norman rolls the charter roll for the second year of King John, the contra-brevia rolls for the second and fourth years, the oblate roll for the second year, and a fragment of a roll for the fifth year remain, and were edited by Sir Thomas Duffus Hardy in 1835. With their help and with the help of the charters and letters of Philip Augustus (edited by Delisle under the title *Catalogue des Actes de Philippe Auguste*, 1856), it is possible to follow in detail the advance of the French power in Normandy. Supplemented by the charters and records of Norman administration of the thirteenth century, and by the Exchequer rolls, they also enable us to form a picture of Norman government in its most developed state. Of these records, Delisle edited the charters and judgments of the thirteenth century.[8] Stapleton produced his classical edition of the exchequer rolls so long ago as 1840-4. It is probable that the financial records commenced early in the twelfth century, if not earlier. It is certain that some official records of the sums due to the ducal fisc from local officials must have been used even in the eleventh century,[9] and the advocate De la Foy, who published a work on the constitution of the duchy in 1789, says that he possessed a fragment of an old exchequer roll for 1136.[10] There is even evidence for the existence of Norman chancery rolls at the beginning of Henry II's reign.[11] Unfortunately the exchequer rolls survive in a fragmentary condition, fairly complete for the years 1180, 1195, 1198, partially for the years 1184 [12] and 1203.

This varied material has been used in the following chapters to

[8] *Cartulaire Normand de Philippe Auguste, Louis XIII, Saint Louis et Philippe le Hardi* (1852); *Jugements de l'Echiquier de Normandie. Notices et extraits*, xx, pt. ii (1862).

[9] This follows from the facts proved by Mr. Haskins, *American Historical Review*, xiv, 467. *Norman Institutions*, p. 44.

[10] See the reference in Delisle's introduction to the Norman edition of the exchequer rolls, *Mémoires de la Société des Antiquaires de Normandie*, xvi, pt. i, xxx, xxxi.

[11] Delisle, *Introduction* to the *Recueil des Actes de Henri II*, p. 194 and note. Assize rolls also existed in the time of the Angevin dukes; they are referred to in the custumal (Tardif, *Coutumiers*, I, i, 24). See also Delisle's *Mémoire sur les recueils de jugements rendus par l'échiquier de Normandie*, in the memoirs of the Académie des Inscriptions et Belles-Lettres, vol. xxiv, pt. ii, pp. 352-67. See also below, p. 54, note 89.

[12] One fragment has been edited by M. Delisle in the introductory volume to his *Actes de Henri II* (pp. 334-44). It was unknown to Stapleton, who published another fragment of the same roll (*Rotuli Scaccarii Normanniae*, I, 109-23).

illustrate the working of a mediæval state in time of war. References to the special monographs and articles which I have used will be found in their proper places. Only those who have tried to cope with the records can know how much they owe to M. Delisle's famous articles on the public revenues of Normandy in the *Bibliothèque de l'Ecole des Chartes* (vols. x, xi, xiii), and to his equally well-known *Etudes sur la condition de la classe agricole et l'état de l'agriculture en Normandie au moyen âge* (Evreux, 1851; re-issued, Paris, 1903). The latest contribution to the constitutional history of Normandy before 1204 has been made by a Norman jurist, M. Lucien Valin, in his study *Le Duc de Normandie et sa Cour* (912–1204), Paris, 1910. M. Valin has been led into some needless investigations through his ignorance of the papers of Mr. Haskins, and of M. Ferdinand Lot's *Fidèles ou Vassaux?* (Paris, 1904). His essay, however, which is based upon a careful study of the charters and records to which he has had access, contains much that is suggestive and useful.

It is hardly necessary to remind my readers that the *Histoire de Guillaume le Maréchal*, re-discovered in 1881 by M. Paul Meyer and edited by him between 1891 and 1901, has shown the way to a more intimate knowledge of the reigns of Henry II and, more especially, of his sons than could ever have been hoped for before its appearance in print.

Much bibliographical revision will be required in the following pages, although, as this book was designed to be an account of the struggle for Normandy in the days of Richard and John, and to be preceded by a general sketch of Angevin administration, it is unnecessary to give a full account of the work done since 1913 on the origin, nature and development of the so-called Angevin Empire. It is only just, however, to call attention to a few basic works, in addition to Haskins' *Norman Institutions*, J. Boussard's comprehensive book and the essay of D. C. Douglas (one of many papers written by him on the problem of Norman history). For example, the late Ch. Petit-Dutaillis, an assiduous student of English as well as of French history, expounded his views clearly in his book *La monarchie féodale en France et en Angleterre* (Paris, 1933); a preliminary study by J. Boussard was devoted to *Le comté d'Anjou sous Henri Plantagenêt et ses fils* (1151–1204) (Paris, 1938). Ten years earlier J. Chartrou published his valuable study, *L'Anjou de 1109 à 1151* (Paris, 1928).

CHAPTER I

THE ANGEVIN EMPIRE

I

In this book I wish to study the Norman state during the crisis which led to its union with France. This is not primarily a political, nor economic, nor military study, but rather a picture of the most advanced and self-sufficient country in Europe during the early years of the thirteenth century, in the period of its conquest by Philip Augustus. After three centuries of independence Normandy fell at the very time when the civilisation of Western Europe was asserting its supremacy. The papacy was at the height of its power. The foundations of the kingdoms of France and Castile were laid. In 1204 the Republic of Venice led the warriors of the west in the capture of Constantinople. In 1212 the Moors were driven beyond the Sierra Morena. The next generation combined the wisdom of east and west in metaphysical speculation and the practical arts. Its learning was expressed by the corporations of the universities; its treasures were housed in cathedrals and abbeys of new and surprising beauty. The trade of the east helped to create new political forms in the cities of Flanders and Italy. Normandy had contributed to the preparation for this life, but shared in it only as the demesne of the French king. Although the Norman dukes had elaborated political institutions which were fitted to control a complicated society, and Richard of the Lion Heart had taken the lead in the practice of the arts of fortification and attack as they were developed in the Latin States of Syria, Normandy found no protection in its institutions or its fortresses.

The history of the loss of Normandy, therefore, is of special interest to the student of mediæval society. Normandy had great resources, a tradition of unity, and an elaborate system of government. Its records, though far from complete, are numerous for the reign of King John. It is possible to study a mediæval state in action, in its strength and weakness, to understand its military organisation, and to estimate the influence of personal and impersonal forces. Moreover, Normandy was opposed by a State of very similar nature and capacity, controlled by a king who is possibly the best example of self-conscious feudalism. At the end of the twelfth century there was in most states no single principle of cohesion; the several principles of co-operation, military, religious, economic, were not consistent, and often fought against each other. The dreadful evils of the time were due to the fact that violence was no longer restrained by the reverence for tribal and family bonds, nor tempered by new relations. They were the evils of a sophisticated barbarism. Now among the French States which had sought to combine and restrain the various forces of society, Normandy and the domains of the French king had been most successful. The one, though nominally dependent upon its rival, had been knit together by strong rulers who had availed themselves of the traditions of racial unity; the other had become the ordered base of a lord whose claims and traditions dated from the monarchy of the Carolingian kings. They fought, and a combination of permanent and temporary advantages gave victory to the latter. The Normans found themselves in the position of the Athenians during the Syracusan campaign: the Sicilian were the only cities, says Thucydides, which the Athenians had ever encountered similar in character to their own.

When Rouen surrendered to Philip Augustus in 1204, and the valley of the lower Seine passed into the possession of a single lord, nature seemed to gain one more inevitable victory. Yet truth, even geographical truth, is not often simple. Normandy had for fifty years been in close political alliance with a group of States upon which she had claims to geographical affinity and long social intercourse. Men were unwilling to forget this connection, and fifty years more passed before it was altogether broken. In 1144 Count Geoffrey of Anjou had united Normandy to Anjou and Touraine; in 1152 Poitou and Aquitaine were added by his son Duke Henry upon the occasion of Henry's marriage with Eleanor of Aquitaine; in 1154 Henry became king of England. The great roads which linked Rouen and Caen to Bordeaux thus came under an authority as single and as firm, if not so natural, as that which in later years united Rouen and Caen to Paris. The fall of Rouen in 1204 was echoed by the fall of Chinon, the chief fortress of Touraine, in 1205; Anjou, Touraine, and the greater part of Poitou fell under French control; but it was not until 1259 that Henry III, in whose veins the blood of southern nobles mingled with the blood of Rollo and Fulk Nerra, surrendered his claim to unite Aquitaine, Normandy and Anjou.[1]

Even in the twelfth century an intercourse of fifty years could leave an enduring mark. In spite of many differences in custom, a single administration controlled the continental empire of Henry II;

[1] For Henry III's descent from the houses of Courtenay, Turenne, Angoulême, and his connection, through his great aunt Adelmodis of Angoulême with the houses of Albret and Armagnac, see Jaurgain, *La Vasconie* (Pau, 1898–1902), vol. ii, p. 592. Henry refers to his Gascon kindred in a letter of June 28, 1243, to Amadieu VII of Albret (*Rôles gascons*, No. 1030).

in time of war the various countries of which it was composed were, for military and financial purposes, regarded as one. It is impossible to write of Normandy without reference to the political system in which it shared.

In the second half of the twelfth century Paris was still but one among the great cities of France. Even in the limited Francia of that period, Paris, Etampes, and Orleans could be mentioned in the same breath,[2] and beyond its borders Rouen, Tours, Bordeaux, Toulouse were the centres of districts which were independent in a social and economic as well as in a political sense. It is true that intense influences were already at work to make Paris the capital of a larger France, influences which, as modern geographers remind us, were geographical as well as political; the royal revenues from Paris, though they do not point to an overwhelming superiority in size and wealth, were much greater than those from other places;[3] but the process was slow, and was not ended until in the eighteenth century the road system of France was perfected, and, radiating from Paris, proclaimed her supremacy over all provincial rivals. In the days of Henry II and his sons, the geographical conditions of the west and north of France could still be defined by the great roads laid down by the Romans.[4]

The salient facts in this definition were the connection between the north-west and west of France by way of Angers or Tours, and the comparative isolation of Paris. The old cities of Angers and Tours held the lower valley of the Loire and the roads from the north to Poitiers; indeed the strip of road which passes, through a geological gap, from Tours through Poitiers commanded, throughout the middle ages, the whole of north-western France, and was the key to the north and south. Around its northern end were clustered, in Angevin times, the fortresses of Angers, Loudun, Chinon, Loches. Communications were easy, not only between it and the great cities of north and south, but also between it and the towns lying along the ridges, which climb from the sea to the mountains of central France. On the heels of Goths and Vandals the Franks had passed along this road, and, as the place names show, had stamped a northern civilisation upon Poitou; it is possible that their outposts would have been pushed still further had the forest not turned them back. The races of east and

[2] Arnold of Lübeck, in the story of Otto of Brunswick's ride through France, lib. vii, c. 15 (*Monumenta Germaniae, Scriptores*, xxi, 246).
[3] Brussel, *Usage des fiefs*, ii, Appendix, p. cxlvi. For Paris at this period see Halphen, *Paris sous les premiers Capétiens* (Paris, 1909).
[4] I am indebted here, as elsewhere, to the description of France written by M. Vidal de la Blache for the *Histoire de France*, edited by Lavisse (vol. I, i). And see now the first part of Boussard's book, especially Chapter iii, on the geography of the Angevin Empire.

west had met there: for there Charles Martel had routed the Saracens. In later times the counts of Anjou and Poitou fought for the possession of the road, and the house of Plantagenet, after losing it, tried in vain to recover a footing in Anjou and Normandy. And just as this district had been the stronghold of the Angevin Empire, so it became in the fifteenth century the last defence of the kings of France; through it the empire of Henry II had been possible; when it separated Rouen from Bordeaux, the empire of Henry V was impossible. The 'king of Bourges' was able to maintain himself against the 'king of Paris', because he held Tours and Poitiers and Chinon. Charles VII received Joan of Arc at Chinon; she was examined by the doctors of the church at Poitiers; the sword which she carried to the border city of Orleans was found at Sainte-Catherine-de-Fierbois in the way between Poitiers and Tours.

A combination of causes, some temporary, others permanent in their nature, had contributed to the importance of this district in the twelfth century. By a happy accident the Normans of the Seine had acquired the country between the valley of the Seine and the borders of Brittany, and thus were enabled to avail themselves of the traditional connection between what became Western Normandy and the lands to the south, Maine, Anjou, Touraine, Poitou. The main routes from Rouen and the Seine to Tours, by way of Dreux and Chartres, could be easily closed to the Normans, and when Dreux became an appanage of the French house under Robert the son of Louis VI, they fell definitely under hostile control. On the other hand, the roads from Caen and other towns of Normandy by Le Mans fell under Norman control, first by the conquest of Maine, afterwards through the union of Anjou and Normandy. It is worthy of note that, when linguistic differences become clear in the tenth century, western Normandy is found to have peculiar affinities with the counties of the Loire, distinct from its peculiar affinities with the rest of Normandy and north-eastern France.[5] Social intercourse was now strengthened by political union.

The succession of Henry of Anjou to Normandy would, however, have been precarious if his Angevin predecessors had not secured possession of Touraine, and especially of Tours. The absence of mountains in this part of France tends to obscure the fact that, in the middle ages, Tours dominated the passage from north to south. From this great city roads radiated towards Blois and Orleans, Dreux and Rouen, Le Mans and Caen, Angers and Nantes, Poitiers and Bordeaux, Bourges and central France. It was undoubtedly the greatest religious and commercial centre west of the Rhine, and it attracted to itself from Berri, Poitou, Brittany and the north the

[5] See Gaston Paris in *Romania* (1885), xiv, 598–9.

wealth and energy which were later to be diverted to Paris. The union of Anjou and Touraine will be referred to later in this chapter; here it is sufficient to note that the possession of Tours had placed the house of Anjou in a position of strategic advantage. A ring of fortresses protected the eastern approaches to Anjou, and from them it was as easy to direct affairs in the heart of Aquitaine as in the heart of Normandy. The only way by which the king of France could control the west was closed to him, and the Plantagenets shared in the benefit which the merchants from Flanders and Navarre who passed each other in the great south road, or the pilgrims bound for Compostella who crowded the streets by the noble abbey of St. Martin, brought to the citizens of Tours.[6]

The possession of Tours by the counts of Anjou blocked, we have said, the only way by which the kings of France could hope to control the west. The frequent references in this narrative to the attacks made by Philip Augustus upon the city are sufficient proof of its importance as the key to the Angevin Empire, and as the gate between Paris and Poitou. The reasons for this were based upon a simple geographical fact; Paris was separated on the south-west from Berri and Poitou by a stretch of difficult baffling country, the district known as Sologne.[7] Free though they were to penetrate into the valley of the Rhone, the French kings found it very difficult to master the barren lands which stretched between the mountains of Auvergne and the valley of the Loire. In consequence of this barrier the turbulent landholders of Berri and Auvergne had fallen, by natural causes, within the boundary of the old duchy or kingdom of Aquitaine. They looked across from their strongholds upon the rich countries along the Atlantic, or along the chalk ridges to the castles and cities of Poitou, or down the tributary valleys of the Loire into Touraine. This confederation, loose and troubled though it was, had given a unity to Aquitaine; and in consequence Henry of Anjou, on his marriage with Eleanor, entered upon a vast dominion which comprised nearly ten of the modern departments of France.[8] It is true that Bourges, in

[6] The dean of St. Paul's makes a special note of a voluntary gift of 2000 marks which the citizens gave to Richard I in 1194 (Rad. Diceto, ii, 117). See the pæan on the land of 'Martinopolis' in the *Narratio de commendatione Turonicae Provinciae*, edited by Salmon, *Recueil de Chroniques de Touraine* (Tours, 1854), p. 292.

[7] Vidal de la Blache in Lavisse I, i, 154-5. See also Arthur Young's remarks on this 'wretched country' in his *Travels in France* (edited Betham Edwards, 1905, p. 19).

[8] For the extent of Aquitaine, see Longnon, *Atlas historique de la France*, Texte, p. 226. F. Lot, in his *Fideles ou Vassaux?* (Paris, 1904), p. 49, has described the contests of the counts of Auvergne, Poitou, and Toulouse for the dukedom. See now J. Dhondt, *Etudes sur la naissance des principautés territoriales en France* (Bruges 1948) especially chapter iv.

the extreme north-east, which had for some time been the capital of the Frankish duchy,[9] had been bought by Philip I of France, from its crusading viscount, in 1100;[10] but the successors of Philip had done little to profit by the bargain. Louis VII and Philip Augustus made it part of their policy to force a way into Aquitaine by way of Bourges, but their progress was slow and uncertain. Even when Philip Augustus had succeeded, after his father and he had made several compromises with Henry II and his two successors, in allying himself with the barons of Poitevin or western Berri, the relations between the latter and Paris continued to be very precarious for nearly half a century and were firmly established only after the destruction of Henry's empire. The footing which Louis VIII secured in Languedoc, to the rear of Auvergne, and the strong rule of his son Alfonse in Poitou really made success in this direction possible; and in the meanwhile, through the possession of Touraine, the French kings had been able to keep in touch with the south, and to separate Henry III's well-wishers in Normandy from his Aquitanian vassals. In this case also lordship over the northern half of Aquitaine was made possible through lordship over Anjou and Touraine.

Such were the geographical conditions which had secured a cohesion for the Angevin Empire which has often been underestimated. It is clear that the Angevin conquest of Touraine made the empire possible. This conquest was part of a steady advance in all directions over an area which possessed natural unity, including parts of several Frankish divisions, Poitou, Saintonge, Touraine, Vendôme, Maine and Nantes; and the gradual advance was accompanied by a progressive system of government and defence. There was no sudden victory, no hard and fast distinction between the methods of conquest and the methods of occupation. In this respect the rise of Anjou to power in western France was similar to the steady extension of the French domain in the Vexin (1076) and in the district between Paris and Orleans.

II

Anjou [11] first appears as a semi-independent country in the first half of the tenth century. Fulk the Red, who is known to have been

---

[9] Lasteyrie, *Etude sur les comtes et vicomtes de Limoges* (Paris, 1874), p. 34.   [10] Longnon, p. 226.

[11] Halphen, *Le Comté d'Anjou* (Paris, 1906); Kate Norgate, *England under the Angevins*, vol. i, pp. 97–260. Halphen has also contributed a valuable study on the early expansion of Anjou in his *Essai sur l'authenticité du fragment d'histoire attribué au comte d'Anjou, Foulque le Réchin*, in the *Bibliothèque de la Faculté des Lettres* of the University of Paris, xiii (1901), pp. 7–48. His work has been continued in the studies by Chartrou and Boussand, noted above, p. 5.

viscount of Anjou and abbot of Saint-Aubin in 898, was in all probability the deputy of the dukes of France. In later years, when the
counts of Anjou had quarrelled with the house of Paris, they liked
to maintain that their title was derived from a Carolingian grant, but
there seems to be no doubt that in the ninth and tenth centuries the
whole borderland between the Seine and the Loire was in the hands
of the dukes of France, and that the viscounts of Anjou, of Touraine,
and of each of the three counties of la Beauce were their deputies.[12]

In the district of la Beauce, Theobald, viscount of Tours, absorbed
the jurisdiction of his two neighbours Chartres and Blois, and
assumed the title of Count of Chartres (943) and similarly, from
929 onwards Fulk the Red seems to have called himself count of
Anjou.[13] Although he and his successors took up the traditional
position of Frankish counts in a Frankish *pagus*, they remained faithful to the duke of France and supported him after his elevation to
the French throne in 987. This fact is of importance in comparing the
status of Anjou with the status of Aquitaine or Normandy. In the
controversy which has been fought over this question in recent years,
the truth seems to lie with those who insist that there was no 'legal'
distinction between Anjou and the greater provinces of France so far
as their feudal relations to the king of France were concerned.
Francia, in its geographical sense, was the limited area over which
the kings of France had direct dominion; the counties between the
Seine and the mouth of the Loire did not form an ethnic group bound
together by closer ties than those which bound the duke of Normandy
or the count of Flanders to his lawful suzerain.[14] Yet, though this was
the case, the whole history of the lands between the Seine and the
Loire forced the counts of Anjou and Chartres into closer feudal
dependence upon the king of France than the dukes of Normandy
and Aquitaine allowed for themselves. They could not, like the duke
of Normandy, point to rights of conquest, nor, like the dukes of
Aquitaine, to the great traditions of a duchy which had, for a time,
been a kingdom. When, in the twelfth century, actual power sought

---

[12] It must be remembered that the *ducatus Franciae* which was delegated
by the later Carolingians to the counts of Paris, was not a geographical title.
It involved the subjection of princes far beyond the narrow limits of Francia.
Lot, *Fidèles ou Vassaux?* p. 188 and note. On the meaning of Franciae cf. also
J. Kurth, *Etudes Franques* (Paris, 1919), i, 67 ff.

[13] See Guilhiermoz (p. 162, note 66) for examples of the ease with which
the title could be assumed in late Carolingian times.

[14] M. Flach follows Pardessus in regarding 'Francia' in this sense, as a group
of counties immediately subject to Paris, bound together in some special
manner. For the contrary view see Halphen's review in the *Revue historique*
(1904), vol. 85, p. 276: 'aux yeux d'un Angevin, d'un Manceau ou d'un
Vendômois, la *Francia* est une province étrangère à la sienne.' Halphen's
evidence is quite conclusive for the eleventh century.

legal right by means of fictitious claims, the dukes boldly acted as independent princes, but the counts of Anjou only insisted upon a more dignified dependence. Richard of Aquitaine was crowned as duke at Limoges;[15] Anglo-Norman writers sought proofs in the story of Rollo of the equality of kings of France and dukes of Normandy;[16] but the partisans of Anjou claimed for their lord the title, 'seneschal of France'.[17] The continuous dependence of Anjou upon the kings of France was not unimportant in the history of the Angevin empire as a whole.[18]

Within the county and its neighbourhood the successors of Fulk the Red gradually built up a strong and independent state. In earlier days the main function of the viscounts of Anjou had been the defence of the lower Loire against the northmen; and in consequence their energy had been chiefly spent in the district west of the Mayenne; but in this direction the long wars of the later counts with the counts of Rennes and Nantes had small result. To the west they gained permanently only a strip of forest land on the bank of the Mayenne. In the north, Maine was for some time subject to Fulk Nerra and Geoffrey Martel, but after some experience of the intolerable *dominatio* of the Angevin, its count Herbert II did homage to William the Conqueror duke of Normandy. In this way Anjou and Normandy were brought into collision; and the long struggle lasted until the marriage of the Empress Matilda to Count Geoffrey of Anjou in 1128. By this marriage Henry I of England and Normandy, finding that it was impossible to keep the Angevins out of Maine, united the two families and prepared the way for the union of Anjou, Maine and Normandy under Matilda's son, Henry II.[19] Towards the south, the counts of

[15] M. Lot, while insisting upon the close feudal ties between Richard and Louis VII, to whom he did homage in 1169, remarks that this coronation of 1167 shows that he was regarded as almost absolute (p. 82). The 'ordo ad benedicendum ducem Aquitaniae', in a manuscript of the chapter of Saint Etienne at Limoges, was written after Richard's coronation, in order to claim fictitious precedence for Limoges as the seat of quasi-royal prerogatives. Lasteyrie, *Etude sur les comtes et vicomtes de Limoges*, pp. 36–7. [For further details see M. Bloch, *Les rois thaumaturges*, Strasbourg, 1924, p. 194, note.]

[16] Lot, pp. 227–33; and below, p. 292.

[17] For the famous tract, *De senescalcia Franciae*, composed in the reign of Henry II, see Baluze, *Miscellanea*, iv, 486; Viollet, *Hist. des institutions politiques*, ii, 110–1, and the authorities there mentioned. Lot, p. 234.

[18] Perhaps special circumstances account for the charter in which Philip I of France, at the request of Fulk of Anjou, freed a serf belonging to Fulk, at Orleans in 1069 (Prou, *Actes de Philippe I*, no. 41, p. 118). If not, it is significant.

[19] For Maine, see especially Halphen, *Essai sur l'authenticité du fragment d'histoire*, pp. 20–1; Latouche, *Histoire du Comté du Maine pendant le xe et le xie siècle* (Paris, 1910), pp. 31–56; and Flach, *Origines de l'ancienne France*, iii, 555. Latouche (p. 55) points out that William the Conqueror and his son Robert recognised the suzerainty of Anjou over Maine.

Anjou secured useful but less brilliant successes. For some years they were lords of Saintonge and its capital, Saintes; but the geographical separation of this district from Anjou prevented the endurance of the union, and Saintonge was lost, probably in 1061. Anjou, on the other hand, never relaxed hold on the great fortress of Loudun, a place of great strategic importance on the way to Poitiers, which Geoffrey Greygown (960–87) had wrested from William II of Poitou, the enemy of his suzerain Hugh Capet. The possession of Loudun and northern Poitou also exposed the southern frontier of Touraine to attack, and when Touraine had been annexed helped to knit the Angevin territories together.

The union of Anjou and Touraine was, as has been explained earlier in this chapter, the essential fact in the history of the Angevin empire. The eastern neighbour of Anjou was the count of Chartres, or, as he was generally called, of Blois. By his rule over the three Frankish *pagi* of Tours, Chartres and Blois, he held the valley of the Loire and the approaches to Tours from the north-west and from Paris. Conflict was inevitable between the counts of Blois and their ambitious rivals of Angers, and was so prolonged that even the struggle between Stephen of Blois, brother of Theobald the Great, and Geoffrey of Anjou, the husband of Matilda, in which England and Normandy were at stake, was only an episode in its course. The history of this rivalry falls into two periods. In the first period the counts of Anjou could rely, as a rule, upon the support of the French king, for Blois was near the royal domain, and its union with Champagne between 1022 and 1027 made the counts of Blois dangerous neighbours to the king. The value to Anjou of royal friendship was most apparent in the first half of the eleventh century. In 996 Fulk Nerra of Anjou had actually captured Tours, but the city was retaken during his absence on pilgrimage to Jerusalem, owing to an alliance between King Robert II and the count of Blois. In a few years the situation completely changed, and the kings of France lent their approval to the steady advance of Angevin influence in Touraine. Henry I definitely granted the county to Geoffrey Martel in 1044,[20] but the great successes of this year were but the last steps in a long penetration of the country. The first count of Anjou, Fulk the Red, had, by his marriage with the daughter of a rich landholder of Touraine, added Loches and other places in Touraine to the Angevin domain. These fiefs, which were of course held of the counts of Blois, became the nucleus of the Angevin settlement in the country between Loches and the Angevin possessions in northern Poitou. Gradually, with the exception of Saumur, which held out in the extreme west of Touraine under an intractable and courageous lord, the borders

[20] Lot, pp. 166–7.

between the two counties became for all practical purposes indistinguishable; Saumur also fell in 1026, and it was only a matter of time before Tours and the rest of Touraine fell away from the counts of Blois altogether. The end came, as we have said, in 1044. At first the counts of Anjou did homage for Tours to the counts of Blois—for example, Fulk le Réchin did homage in 1068—but later the county was held immediately of the king of France.

Still another bulwark of Anjou against aggression was found in Vendôme, to the north-east. A count of Vendôme married the daughter of Fulk Nerra, and with the consent of Henry I of France, their young son did homage to his uncle Geoffrey Martel, who administered his lands. Henceforward the lords of Vendôme were vassals of Anjou. Geoffrey left a lasting memorial of his period of government in the famous abbey of La Trinité.

The second period in the history of the relations between Anjou and Blois may be said to begin in the years in which occurred the deaths of Theobald the Great and Geoffrey of Anjou, the union of Anjou and Normandy and the marriage of Henry Plantagenet with Eleanor of Aquitaine. Louis VII of France finally turned his back upon the Angevin alliance, and joined himself to Theobald's children in Blois and Champagne. It is true that signs of rivalry between the counts of Anjou and their suzerains may be traced in the eleventh century in the original chronicle of St. Maurice of Angers,[21] and in the claims put forward by Fulk Réchin to a Carolingian origin for his title.[22] The capture of Tours in 1044 was, in a large sense, the origin of these assertions; it had caused a widespread sensation not only in Touraine itself, where the practical supremacy of the count of Anjou was asserted with masterful effect,[23] but also abroad; and, as M. Halphen has said, but for the death of Geoffrey Martel without children in 1060, the power which the counts had won within seventy years might have been strengthened by still greater triumphs.[24] But the succeeding century, though very important in the inner history of Anjou and Touraine, brought no increase of prestige beyond their borders, until the startling successes of Geoffrey the Fair and his son Henry spread Angevin rule from sea to sea,[25] and divided France into

[21] *Recueil d'annales angevines et vendômoises,* ed. Louis Halphen (Paris, 1903), p. 57.
[22] Halphen, *Essai sur l'authenticité,* p. 17.
[23] A charter of Marmoutier, quoted by Halphen in *Le Comté d'Anjou,* p. 59, contains the phrase 'in illa rerum conversione et mutabilium mutatione quae facta est cum comes Gaufredus Turonorum civitatem cepisset'.
[24] *Le Comté,* p. 12.
[25] The annals of Saint Aubin, containing the annals of Saint Maurice, describe Henry II, 'famosus et potentissimus a mare usque ad mare' (MS. B. a. 1189, *Recueil d'Annales Angevines,* p. 19).

two halves independent of each other in all but name. Then Paris and Troyes drew together to resist the combination of Caen, Tours and Poitiers; and from this time onwards historical minds on both sides invented claims and counterclaims in support of their masters. The assertion that the counts of Anjou were entitled to be seneschals of France dates from the early years of Henry II; the solemn coronation of the boy Richard at Limoges came soon after; on the other side, the young Philip Augustus was trained in a circle where the poetical renascence of Carolingian legend especially flourished. The third crusade first disclosed in their full strength the rival schools of patriotism. Men from all the provinces of France were crowded together, and soon lost sight of their holy purpose amidst the daily temptations to conflict. Thoughtful men reflected on the contrast between the troubled and divided age in which they lived, and the days of Charles the Great, when all Franks lived together in unity.[26] The death of Richard, however, revealed what may also be traced in the history of the crusade [27]—the essential lack of union in the Angevin Empire, and the tendency to the formation of local groups. The young duke of Brittany became the rallying point of one of these groups, the count of La Marche of another. Philip Augustus seized his opportunity, and summoning legist and antiquary to his aid, cut asunder the ties which bound Poitevin, Breton and Norman. And so, in his person, on a wider field, the old counts of Blois avenged themselves upon their adversary.

[26] Ambroise, *L'Estoire de la Guerre Sainte* (ed. G. Paris), ll. 8479 onwards.
[27] According to Ambroise, Angevins, Manceaux, Poitevins, and Bretons marched together during the third crusade. At a tournament in 1174 they fought together against French, Normans, and English (*Hist. de Guillaume le Marèchal*, iii, 20).

CHAPTER II

THE COMMON ELEMENTS IN THE
ADMINISTRATION OF THE ANGEVIN EMPIRE

I

THE constitutional, no less than the political, history of Normandy after 1150 is closely connected with the constitutional history of Anjou and Poitou.[1] Politically almost every crisis in the history of Normandy, the war of 1173, the quarrels between Henry and Richard, and between John and his nephew Arthur, the results of John's marriage with Isabella of Angoulême, had an external origin. In the same way, although it is no longer possible to speak of an Angevin invasion or of an Angevin reconstruction of English and Norman society, it is true to say that most of the administrative changes made by Henry II and his sons originated in their desire to keep the peace throughout a large empire. It was necessary to subordinate each part to the whole in this varied group of states, if all were to be governed effectively. Moreover, it is possible to trace here and there the influence of Anjou in Henry's autocratic rule. Henry would have made tradition his servant wherever he had ruled, but it would be rash to assert that, if his sway had been confined to England or Normandy, the impulse and shape which his genius gave to English or Norman institutions would have been the same as they were when these countries formed part of a wider whole with Anjou and Touraine as its centre.

It is said that Count Geoffrey of Anjou, when he lay dying, urged

---

[1] AUTHORITIES. Besides the better known chronicles, the chronicles of Anjou, etc., in the *Recueil d'annales angevines et vendômoises*, edited by Halphen (Picard's Collection de textes, Paris, 1903); Beautemps-Beaupré, *Coutumes et Institutions de l'Anjou et du Maine*, especially pt. ii, vol. i, 'Recherches sur les jurisdictions de l'Anjou et du Maine pendant la période féodal' (Paris, 1890); the *Coutumes de Touraine-Anjou*, edited by M. Viollet in the third volume of his *Etablissements de Saint Louis* (Paris, 1883); also Guilhiermoz, *Essai sur l'origine de la nobless* (Paris, 1902), the works of Halphen referred to in the previous chapter, together with his paper on Angevin judicial institutions in the eleventh century (*Revue historique*, 1901, lxxvii, pp. 279–307), etc. For Poitou, A. Richard, *Histoire des Comtes de Poitou* (778–1204), Paris, 1903. [In addition to the later edition of texts and studies published since 1913 and noted in the previous pages, the first volume, 'Institutions Seigneuriales', of the *Histoire des institutions françaises au moyen age*, edited by F. Lot and R. Fawtier (Paris, 1957), is especially relevant to the theme of this present chapter.]

his son to respect the customs of his various territories without seeking to impose the traditions of one country upon the rest. These doctrines of a sane imperialism, which Geoffrey regarded as the secret of successful rule, were interpreted in a limited sense by Henry. It is clear that local customs were generally left to develop undisturbed. Just as the law of Wessex and of Mercia survived for many years after the Norman Conquest of England, and customs continued to differ in different shires or even in different townships, so the variations of local law in Normandy were observed by the courts in the thirteenth century.[2] One result, indeed, of the frequent inquests and recognitions was to record and perpetuate these variations. If this was the case within an area so indivisible politically as England or Normandy, it was much more the case within the empire as a whole, where all traditions of Carolingian unity had long faded away. Thus King Richard refused to enforce a treaty which his Norman officials had made with Philip of France, on the ground that it set aside Poitevin custom;[3] and in circumstances less favourable to himself King John was forced to observe the law of Poitou with regard to the forfeiture of sub-vassals.[4] Under the shadow of Henry II's government, in all parts of the empire, from England to Gascony, legal principles and customs were reduced to writing in response to the pressure of local forces.[5] This process was fraught with much danger to the political stability of the empire. One natural consequence of it was that vassals who felt that their privileges were invaded were encouraged to appeal from their lord to the king of France. John lost the greater part of the empire as a result of an appeal. But in this chapter it is rather my task, after a brief analysis of this diversity, to trace the extent to which Henry II imposed a common administration upon and developed the common elements in his continental states.

Let us go back to the early history of Anjou and compare it with

[2] See below, p. 36.

[3] Howden, iii, p. 255, 'quia videlicet rex Angliae violare nolebat consuetudines et leges Pictaviae vel aliarum terrarum suarum in quibus consuetum erat ab antiquo, ut magnates causas proprias invicem gladiis allegarent'.

[4] When John received the homage of Chalon de Rochefort after his treason (May 23, 1214) he secured him this right: 'si vero aliqui hominum suorum *ad servicium nostrum* redire noluerint, vel in aliquo nobis foris fecerint, unde de terris suis disseisiri debeant, idem Chalo habebit *in manu sua* terras eorundem et proventus earum *secundum consuetudinem Pictavie* donec redierint ad servicium *nostrum*' (*Rot. Chart.*, 198b).

[5] M. Rogé has recently shown that the renovation of the *For général de Béarn* goes back to 1188, and not to 1288. See a review of his *Anciens fors de Béarn* in *Revue historique* (1910), civ, 107–8. The early custumal of Anjou and Touraine, printed by Viollet in the *Etablissements de Saint Louis*, though of later date, probably describes the customs of the twelfth century. For the *Très ancien Coutumier* of Normandy, see above, p. 3.

that of Poitou and Gascony. Fulk Nerra (987–1040) and Geoffrey
Martel (1040–60) had bound their territories together, as in chains of
iron, by their fortresses, many of which became the homes of new
families dependent on the favour of the count. In the reigns of
their successors the rough and ready feudalism of Fulk's day was
elaborated and refined. It must be remembered that the counts of
feudal times were for the most part the successors of the Frankish
counts. These latter had been local administrators appointed by the
Frankish kings, and their jurisdiction did not extend—or at most
extended very partially—over the greater royal vassals or churches
and religious houses on the royal demesne. In some parts of France
these greater vassals succeeded in maintaining their direct relations
with the kings down to the twelfth century, and in this respect Poitou
was in contrast with Anjou and Touraine. John of Salisbury, for
example, refers in his letters to Poitevin abbots who denied the jurisdiction of the count, and regarded themselves as immediate vassals
of Louis VII,[6] and the constant appeals of the barons of Berri and
Auvergne to the French king were a permanent source of weakness
to the duke of Aquitaine. In Anjou, on the other hand, the counts
succeeded in securing the control over the royal vassals, as did many
other counts in the tenth century.[7] It is true that the process was very
slow; the distinction remained between greater and lesser vassals, and
the former gradually became identified with the fortunate people who
held castles. This fact, conversely, gave a distinctive and independent
character to the successors of Fulk Nerra's castellans, who had
occasionally contributed to the expense of erecting the strongholds
entrusted to them.[8] These greater vassals naturally recognised few,
if any, rights of jurisdiction in the count. In the eleventh century, all
disputes between them were decided, however many formalities may
have been observed, by reference to a judge selected for the occasion
by both parties; or, in cases of oppression, by resort to the strength
of a powerful neighbour.[9] The officials of the count, the *vicarii*, or,
as they were called later, the *prepositi*, administered the demesne;
they received the dues, demanded customary labour, directed the
levy, did justice on the peasants; but they did not interfere in other
matters.[10] The power of the count grew because he was stronger than

[6] *Memorials of Thomas Becket*, ed Robertson (Rolls Ser.), vi, p. 456. The
abbot of Charroux said at La Ferté Bernard that his monastery belonged to
the king of France and had done so since its foundation by Charles the Great.
[7] Guilhiermoz, *Essai sur l'origine de la noblesse*, p. 139.
[8] Château-Gontier is the best example. Below, p. 181.
[9] Halphen, in *Revue historique* (1901), vol. lxxvii, p. 305.
[10] Halphen, *Le Comté d'Anjou*, pp. 107 *seq*. The title of vicarius lingered
on. *Vicarii* appear frequently in Angevin charters of Henry II (Delisle, *Intro·
duction*, p. 220).

his neighbours: strength rather than law gave him predominance. If he had no legal machinery at his disposal, he had tremendous powers of enforcing his will, and no one questioned his absolutism if he could secure it. A family may be prosperous in one generation; it comes against the power of the count; there is a struggle and it disappears. The rough remedy of extermination is always in reserve, and Fulk Nerra did not hesitate to use it. In time his successors, under its sanction, worked out forms of government.

Aquitaine, on the other hand, never lost its composite character. At their court in Poitiers the dukes had, it is true, encouraged learning, and elaborated a chancery.[11] But even in Poitou the distinction between the ducal domain and the feudal estates seems to have been more marked in the twelfth century than it was in Anjou; the vassals were necessarily influenced by the independent leanings of such important persons as the viscount of Thouars or the lord of Issoudun.[12] Outside Poitou, Aquitaine was a medley. Saintonge and, so far as its inhabitants allowed, Gascony were governed by the duke. The rest of the duchy consisted of separate states in which the duke had no powers other than those of overlord. The Carolingian kingdom of Aquitaine, which came to an end in 877, had extended from the Loire to the Pyrenees. Its centre had been Berri and Auvergne, and its capital seems for some time to have been Bourges. Its ancient dependence upon the king of the Franks is attested by the numerous charters of the tenth century which include the phrase, 'rex Francorum et Aquitanorum'.[13] After 877, the duchy—as it now became—was a cause of strife between the great counts of the south and west, the counts of Poitou and Auvergne within the borders of Aquitaine, the count of Toulouse without. The counts of Auvergne held the title between 885 and 927; it then came to Raymond of Toulouse; finally, sometime after 950, it was attached to the count of Poitou. From this time Auvergne ceased to be the centre of the duchy, and the titles of Poitou and Aquitaine, though they are distinguished in the charters at the end of the twelfth century, became almost synonymous. The effect of these changes was to shake the allegiance of the states on the border. Gascony broke away, and was only restored between 1037 and 1060, partly by conquest, partly by rights of inheritance

---

[11] For the Poitevin chancery compare Giry, *Manuel de diplomatique*, p. 809, and the charters in the *Recueil des actes de Philippe I* (pp. 216, 219), with Prou's notes. [12] Cf. below, p. 151.

[13] Modern historians have enlarged upon the folly of Louis VII in adding the title 'dux Aquitanorum' to his name after his marriage with Eleanor, as though he were not overlord of Aquitaine already. See Lot, *Fideles ou Vassaux?* pp. 49–50. Louis surrendered the title in 1154. Delisle, *Introduction*, p. 131. [On Aquitaine and its early history see, in addition to Boussard, *Le gouvernement*, pp. 113–55, F. J. Dhondt, *Etudes*, p. 14, note 3.]

in the counts of Poitou. The greater part of Berri, including the viscounty of Bourges and the county of Bourbon, attached itself to the king; the rest, divided into the lordships of Déols, Châteauroux and Issoudun, recognised the count of Poitou as suzerain.[14] Auvergne also recognised the new dukes (955) and was administered by viscounts who, like the viscounts of Chartres and Anjou, assumed the title of Count.[15] Similarly the Limousin which had possibly held of Toulouse in the ninth century, came to Aquitaine in the tenth; its lords, like those of Turenne, Thouars, and Châtellerault, who were also dependent upon the counts of Poitou, retained the old title of viscount. Périgord, and those counties of Gévaudan, Brioude and Velay, which gave access from the west to the Rhone, were also in Aquitaine. Querci was definitely attached, on the other hand, to the great county of Toulouse. These states on the borders were the stakes in the long game which the Capetians and Plantagenets played against each other. To defend them or subdue them needed men and money ; and in getting men and money Henry II made changes which affected the future history of England and Normandy. The meaning of the 'scutage of Toulouse', with which he paid his way in his first campaign, is still far from clear, but at the least it reminds us of this.

This bald summary is sufficient to suggest the extent to which the duchy of Aquitaine was divided as compared with Normandy or Anjou; and the shifting politics of the several states in their relations to their suzerain or to each other simply reflected on a larger scale their internal chaos. The congenial spirit of this distraction was voiced by the songs of Bertrand of Born; its nature is revealed for us in the passionate struggle between the counts of Auvergne and the bishop of Clermont, in the lamentations of harassed and weary travellers, in the awful ravages of the *cotteraux* of Berri or Gascony, with the equally terrible punishments which they suffered.[16] It was in the heart of this country, at le Puy-en-Velay, that, in 1182, the country folk, worn out by evil, gathered round the carpenter, Durand Dujardin, and vainly sought to restore peace by organised association against the mercenaries. Faced by such a disordered society Henry II and his sons could enforce their feudal claims only by an appeal to self-interest or by means of the sword; and Richard especially, who was half a Poitevin, was a master in the art of both weapons. He was never so much at home as when he was pitting one Aquitanian baron against another. Henry was less patient of these

---

[14] Longnon, *Atlas*, Texte, p. 218.   [15] Lot, pp. 78-9.
[16] In his posthumous work, *La Société française au temps de Philippe Auguste* (Paris, 1909; English translation by E. B. Krehbiel, London, 1912), the late M. Achille Luchaire illustrates many of his conclusions by reference to these and other incidents in the history of central France.

methods; he would gladly have come to terms with the French king, had the latter's ambition and his own masterful sense of legality permitted it. There is something curiously ironical in his contention, sound enough in its way, that Berri should belong to him because the archbishopric of Bourges once belonged to Aquitaine.[17] The king of France possibly reflected that throughout central France there was not a single dignitary of the Church who could live at peace with his lay neighbours for more than a few months.

The relation of Gascony to the dukes of Aquitaine seemed still more precarious than the relations of Auvergne or the Limousin, since the racial exclusiveness of the Gascons, afterwards so advantageous to the rule of the English kings, made unity with the rest of the duchy almost impossible. Just as Normandy took its name from the Northmen, Gascony took its name from the Vascones, who had settled in the district known in Roman times as Novempopulania, ecclesiastically the archbishopric of Auch. They formed a state apart, a people with idiosyncrasies famous in history, and still more famous in literature. Abbo of Fleury, who was afterwards killed (1004) in a scuffle between the Gascon and alien monks of the same religious order, said of his Gascon home : 'In the possession of such a dwelling I am more powerful within these lands than our lord, the king of the Franks, himself; for here no one has reverence for his lord.'[18] After the disappearance of the kingdom of Aquitaine, the Gascons had called back their native line of dukes from its exile in Spain, and continued in their independence for two centuries. Unlike most of their neighbours in the south of France, they continued to express recognition in their charters of the kings of the Franks after the accession of Hugh Capet, whose father, Hugh the Great, even seems to have become a mythical hero in Gascony; but within their borders the dukes possessed all the powers of royalty. This was especially the case after their acquisition of the county of Bordeaux in the middle of the tenth century. They referred to their lordship as a 'regnum', called ecclesiastical councils and appointed bishops. They founded abbeys, including the magnificent house of Saint-Sever. But at the

[17] Ben. Pet., i, 10. The contention was not irrelevant, since there had been a close connection between political and ecclesiastical divisions. For Normandy and the archbishopric of Rouen see below, p. 37. The conquests of the counts of Anjou in the eleventh century added the 'pagus Medalgicus' (des Mauges), south of the Layon, to the diocese of Angers (Longnon, *Pouillés de la province de Tours* (1903), p. 45).

[18] *Vita Sancti Abbonis*, in Migne, *Patrologia Latina*, cxxxix, 410. For Gascony, see Jaurgain, *La Vasconie* (Pau, 1898–1902); Degert, in *Revue des questions historiques* (1902), lxxii, 424; Barrau-Dihigo, *La Gascogne* (Paris, 1903), in the series 'Les Régions de la France'. [Add, on the extent of ducal authority, Boussard, pp. 27–31.]

same time the independence of the nobility increased. The heritability of fiefs was firmly established. The subdivision of the ducal family created the families of the counts of Fézensac and Astarac; the counts of Armagnac and of Bigorre, the viscounts of Béarn, Lomagne, Oloron, Dax, and Marsan maintained themselves independent of control; the viscount of Béarn even cast off the yoke altogether. In consequence these upland baronies, lying along the banks of the countless streams which run steeply down the northern slope of the Pyrenees, lost any common centre they might have had and were exposed, indifferently, to influences from north, south, east and west. There is little geographical distinction between the eastern states of Gascony and the great county of Toulouse, along the upper Garonne; the passes of the Pyrenees, again, gave access to the kingdoms of the south, which crossed the mountains in the east and west. After the reunion of Gascony and Aquitaine in 1039, Duke Guy Geoffrey had to fight for many years against his rival, the count of Armagnac, before, in 1060, Gascony gave in its allegiance, and he could have the satisfaction of leading Gascons against William of Normandy, whose successors were also to be his successors. From this time the Gascons remained loyal, after their own treacherous and rebellious fashion, to their overlords, Poitevin, Angevin, English. Bordeaux became the centre of government. Originally this city, an alien settlement of the Brigantes, had no connection with Gascony, to which it was not added until the middle of the tenth century. It was always a colony, a sea-city; although a great market with profound influence upon the valleys of the Garonne and Dordogne, it was not, even in the thirteenth century, so great a centralising force as Paris or Tours.[19] But, by its situation, Bordeaux, with its ring of towns stretching as far as Saint-Macaire and Castillon, was the natural base of a foreign domination. For three centuries, as the link between Gascony and England, the city attracted trade, dictated the nature of agriculture for the sake of export, and set up a standard of life in rivalry with the feudalism of the hills.

In virtue of its racial coherence Gascony took a position midway between Poitou and Saintonge, on the one side, and the remaining states of Aquitaine on the other. The principle of contract, in all its naked simplicity, was frankly regarded by the barons of Aquitaine as the beginning and end of the motives upon which their relations to the duke were based.[20] As is well known, this was the ruling principle

[19] Vidal de la Blache, in Lavisse, *Histoire de France*, I, i, p. 373.

[20] See Gervase of Canterbury, Rolls Ser., i, p. 211. After the conference at Soissons had been broken off (1168) Louis VII retired to Bourges and received the oaths and hostages of the 'proceres Pictavorum'. See John of Salisbury's letter in the *Memorials of Thomas Becket* (vi, 408, cf. p. 411).

in feudalism of every degree, but it was interpreted more and more in favour of the overlord in those communities where the idea of the state was most developed. In Gascony the tradition of unity was still sufficient to cause response to the strong hand of the duke; and in later years Henry III and Edward I were able to apply many of the principles of government which had been applied by Henry II in Normandy or Anjou. But in the reigns of Richard and John, Gascony was on the fringe of the empire; its organisation was only developed after the loss of those lands which were the centre of imperial strength. It was in these that feudalism first became the basis of a real state.

I have laid stress upon the diversity in the political condition and in the history of the various lands which were brought together under the rule of Henry II. Is it possible to point to any common element, any institutions by means of which these territories could acquire some sort of constitutional unity?

There is abundant evidence that Henry II regarded his continental dominions as a whole, in contrast with England. Our chief authority upon this point is [Roger Howden in the chronicle] known under the name of Benedict of Peterborough. In September, 1177, Henry, after he made peace with Louis VII and had decided to go with him on a crusade, held a court at Verneuil. Here, in the presence of his barons, he promulgated a statute dealing with the debts of feudal lords and limiting the responsibility of their vassals for them. The king, adds the chronicler, ordered the statute to be observed in all his estates (*villae*) and everywhere in his dominions (*potestas*), namely, in Normandy and Aquitaine, Anjou and Brittany.[21] In the same year Henry made changes in the personnel of his administration in Normandy 'and his other lands across the sea'.[22] Again, in 1180, he kept Christmas at Le Mans; it is expressly stated that the archbishop of Bordeaux was present; and after the feast Henry issued an assize of arms, which he ordered to be published and observed ' throughout his lands across the sea'.[23] The model of this assize was followed, we are told, by Philip of France and Philip of Flanders, and by Henry himself in England. Traces of its operation may be found in the middle of the following century, in the inquests ordered to be made by Alfonse of Poitiers in his Poitevin domain.[24]

[21] Ben Pet., i, 194. [On the authenticity of the document abstracted by Howden, see the references discussed in Boussard, p. 527, note.]

[22] *Ibid.*, i, 198. 'justitias suas et rectores, de quorum fidelitate et prudentia confidebat, in Normannia et in caeteris terris suis transmarinis constituit.'

[23] *Ibid.*, i, 270.

[24] See the *Etat du domaine du comte de Poitou à Chizé*, edited by A. Bardonnet in *Archives historiques du Poitou*, vii, 73. On pp. 113–4 is a section 'de armis apud Faiam Monjant', with the following entries: 'Hii sunt qui debent habere loricas et capella ferrea et enses et lanceas vel arcus cum

These measures, though they imply the existence of similar judicial and ministerial systems in all these continental states, do not carry us very far. The scanty details which may be gathered from the local chroniclers and the numerous charters are more suggestive. As a starting point the difference between the administrative unit in England and on the Continent must be noticed. In England the unit was the shire, throughout the continental domains it was the city, castle or royal vill. Even the Norman bailiwick, based though it was on Frankish territorial divisions, was an administrative rather than a geographical area, and in the old Frankish counties, such as Anjou and Touraine, the Frankish divisions, or *vicariæ*, had disappeared. Hence there was no method of comprehending efficiently as one whole the demesnes of the duke or count in a given area. In England the sheriff was responsible for the royal dues and for the administration of royal justice within the borders of his shire; even if a borough had contracted for separate treatment, he was brought into direct relations with it in half a dozen ways. It is true that, at the end of the twelfth century, the English shire was regarded, so to speak, as appurtenant to the royal castle at its centre, where a castle existed; and that a somewhat similar relation between the castle and bailiwick is frequently observable on the Continent about the same time. As will be shown in the next chapter, the conditions in Normandy were somewhat peculiar. The general truth holds, however, for all the continental lands, that the geographical divisions were secondary and subject to change, and that the power of the overlord had grown through the development of the demesne, combined with the activities of a central civil service. In this development the castle played the chief part.[25] I will endeavour first to trace it in Anjou, and afterwards in the continental empire.

II

The crude feudalism which regulated Angevin society in the first part of the eleventh century had been gradually displaced by organ-

sagittis'; also 'qui debent habere loriculas', etc.; and 'qui debent habere perpunctos cum aliis armis'. Compare the requirement from persons possessing 100 l. Angevin, in 1180: 'equum et arma militaria scilicet loricam, scutum, gladium et lanceam', etc. (Ben. Pet., i, pp. 269, 270.)

[25] The distinction between England and the continental lands is well expressed, officially, in the charter to the Templars, of August 31, 1199, confirming a charter of Henry II (*Rot. Chart.*, p. 13b). The king grants one silver mark a year from every English shire (vicecomitatus) which brings in 100 l. or more to the exchequer, 'et de unaquaque civitate et castello et villa aliarum terrarum nostrarum, videlicet, Normanniae, Cenomaniae, Andegaviae, Turoniae, Pictaviae, et Gasconiae, quae annuatim nobis c. li. vel plures reddit, unum cipphum argenteum'

ised government during the century previous to Henry II's accession. Fulk Nerra and Geoffrey Martel had imposed unity upon Anjou and Touraine, and it is worth while to observe the process which made these districts such a perfect example of the feudal state. From the outset Fulk placed his reliance in the great stone keeps with which Touraine is still crested. He built Langeais and established a new family there, in 984, with the expressed purpose of securing easier access to the earlier acquisitions of his family, especially Amboise and Loches.[26] At Montrésor he established a *fidelis* who bore the expressive name of Roger the Devil. In Anjou he built Baugé, Château-Gontier, and probably commenced to build Durtal; in the north of Poitou, now attached to Anjou, he built Mirebeau (where Arthur of Brittany two centuries later attacked his grandmother Eleanor of Aquitaine), Montreuil-Bellay, where he established a recreant vassal of the count of Blois, and Passavant.[27] Many of these fortresses passed into the hands of new feudal families, but whether they remained with the count or not, they altered the social aspect of the compact territories which they bound together. Some of them, like Baugé, became the centres of new towns; monasteries were founded in the neighbourhood of others; and gradually the borders between the old counties became practically indistinguishable. A common custumal served, in the thirteenth century, for Anjou and Touraine. In the reign of John one seneschal administered Maine, Anjou and Touraine.[28] The greater abbeys, such as Saint-Aubin, Saint-Florent near Saumur, and Marmoutier, sent out colonies which further helped to bind the two counties together.[29] From early times the counts of Anjou had been apt in law and letters; their example was copied in these new foundations, so that in the days of Fulk Réchin a historical school, in which the count himself took the lead, flourished in most of the chief monasteries in his territories.[30] The

[26] *Hist. S. Florent*, in Marchegay, *Eglises d'Anjou*, p. 274. For Fulk's castles, see Halphen, *Essai sur l'authenticité du fragment d'histoire*, pp. 22 seq. In Anjou and Touraine, as in Normandy and England, the stone castles were sometimes preceded by mounds crowned by structures of wood; see a charter of Geoffrey the Bearded (1061) edited by Marchegay in *Bibl. de l'école des chartes*, xxxvi (1875), 396–'avus meus et avunculus castellum, terraeque cumulo ac lignis magnae altitudinis asylum, circa monasterium Beati Florantii quod Vetus dicitur construxerunt'.

[27] The same process is seen in Maine. See Latouche, *Histoire du Comté du Maine*, pp. 57–69. In other respects the history of Maine is parallel to that of Anjou.

[28] *e.g.*, William des Roches. *Andegavia* seems occasionally to be used to include a wider district, in the royal letters.

[29] Halphen, *Le Comté*, pp. 91–3. For the extensive penetration of the abbey of Saint Florent into Poitou, see *Archives hist. du Poitou* (1873), ii, pp. 2, 3.

[30] Halphen, in works mentioned, and *Etudes sur les chroniques des comtes d'Anjou et des seigneurs d'Amboise* (Paris, 1906).

great families, in their turn, contributed to the co-operation of Church and State by supplying bishops. It is true that the archbishopric of Tours was beyond the count's influence, and the abbey of Saint-Martin possessed a cosmopolitan rather than a local importance, but otherwise the count seems to have kept a firm control over the clergy, and, however independent the ecclesiastical life of Tours might be, it brought him prestige and indirectly added to his wealth.

In course of time the demesne was administered systematically by *prepositi* who formed part of the count's civil service; the court developed ritual and ceremony and the great feudal officers, the seneschal and constable, the chaplain who acts as chancellor, appeared. For a time the greater barons often served in the great offices, and so were worked into the administration; while the ceremonial gatherings or courts, at which all kinds of business could be formally transacted, were held more regularly at fixed places. The count, in virtue of his strength, was able to provide speedy justice. After all, a Frankish county was not very large; traditions of Frankish procedure still lingered; [31] and it was not difficult for the count to take cognisance of what went on throughout his dominions.

All the attributes of a feudal state are visible in the reign of the learned Fulk le Réchin.[32] The element of fixity alone was wanting: it was necessary that the castles should be, to a great extent, in the count's hands, that no other person should be allowed to build without permission, that the chancery should use writs for drawing cases before the count, that the seneschal, controlling the use of the seal, should be able to exercise authority in the count's absence. If we examine the state of Anjou just before the accession of Henry II, we find that, despite the civil wars of the previous hundred years, it had developed along these lines. The count or his seneschal is seen issuing summonses to litigants to appear before him on a particular day; [33] the inquest by twelve men is what Glanvil would call an engine of the count,[34] and Count Geoffrey on at least one occasion sent a special commission empowered to hear a case upon the spot. The seneschal is clearly capable of exercising the powers of the count.

[31] As in the use of Frankish phrases: boni homines, rachimburdi, etc. For all this see the passages in Beautemps-Beaupré, pt. ii, vol. 1, which I have summarised in the *English Historical Review*, xxi, pp. 648–9.

[32] Halphen, *Le Comté*, pp. 192 ff.

[33] Professor Haskins, who is sceptical about the existence of Angevin influence in Normandy, has pointed out to me that we have no Angevin writs, and that Count Geoffrey adopted the Norman forms in Normandy. [This page should now be read in the light of later investigation; cf. Boussard, *Le Gouvernement de Henri II*, pp. 285 ff., 357 ff., on changes during Henry's time.]

[34] Beautemps-Beaupré, pp. 117–18, 204. For the inquest see also *Coutume de Touraine-Anjou*, c, lxxii (Viollet, *Etablissements*, iii, p. 47).

He holds the castles in trust.[35] He is supreme over seneschals and bailiffs, who, in the next half century, will form a sort of hierarchy.[36] Yet the seneschal is a servant, subject to the count's will and forced to proceed in judicial cases even against his own will. The custumal of the thirteenth century, moreover, shows how precise the legal relations between the count and his subjects were to become. The country is regarded as divided into castellanies, whose lords possess rights of high and low justice; [37] and his vavassors also have their courts. Not only is the law of persons and property carefully defined, but the law regulating appeals from one court to another is also clearly laid down.[38] The right to rebel in default of justice, a right latent in feudalism at all times, is recognised but so as to be almost valueless. If a man summons his tenant to fight against the count, the tenant must go to inquire whether justice has been denied or not, and if justice is promised and the lord still insists upon his service, he need not obey and cannot lawfully lose his fief.[39] A great deal of all this had been known for a long time in England and Normandy; it is possible that the Angevins may have borrowed from their Norman neighbours; but, on the other hand, the close grip and the administrative habit of mind which are found in Henry II must have owed much to the Angevin example. The principles of his administration which he saw most clearly, and which stand out so simply in his reign, such as the importance of the castle, the value of system and centralisation in judicial affairs, the responsibility of the seneschal, are Angevin, just as financial organisation was peculiarly Norman.

Both Norman and Angevin practice seems to have influenced Henry II and his sons as dukes of Aquitaine. As a general rule the administration of the demesne and the supervision of feudal relations between the duke and his Aquitanian vassals were entrusted to a single seneschal. There were exceptional periods; it is probable, for

[35] Early in Henry's reign Chinon appears definitely as the royal treasure-house, in the charge of a special official. This is clear from the annals of Vendôme, for the year 1163 (*Recueil des annales angevines et vendômoises*, p. 73), when the special official was Stephen of Tours, who was afterwards seneschal (Delisle, *Actes de Henry II, Introduction*, p. 460).

[36] See the list of Angevin officials in Henry II's charters, in Delisle, *Introduction*, pp. 210, 220. In 1201 John orders the knights, burgesses, and others of the honour of Mirebeau to obey his official in all things, 'salvis placitis et finibus que pertinent ad capitalem senescallum nostrum Andegavie' (*Rot. Pat.*, p. 6).

[37] Besides many other passages, compare chapter xxiv in the custumal (*Etablissements*, iii, p. 15). 'Nuns vavassors ne puet faire forsban, ne ne peut faire à home fors jurer la chastelerie sanz l'asentement dou baron en qui chastelerie il sera.' Cf. Guilhiermoz, p. 167 and note.   [38] *Ibid.*, cc. 24, 74, etc.

[39] *Ibid.*, c. 43. For the *défaute de droit*, see Viollet, *Hist. des institutions politiques*, ii, 219.

example, that in the early part of Henry's reign, Saintonge had a separate seneschal,[40] and that Poitou was distinguished from Aquitaine in a similar way; in Richard's reign, Gascony and Poitou were separate administrations.[41] Again, for some time John divided Gascony and Périgord from Aquitaine.[42] But as a rule the duchy was regarded as a whole—it is noteworthy that Henry II never used the title count of Poitou, but only styled himself duke of Aquitaine [43]— and King John insisted emphatically upon the vice-regal powers of the seneschal.[44] The importance of this command is obvious. The seneschal had not merely to direct the ducal officials in those districts, such as Saintonge,[45] which were peculiarly subject to the duke; he had, in his master's absence, to calm the rivalry and enforce the allegiance of semi-independent princes. The war in Angoulême during Richard's captivity is a case in point.[46]

The royal letters to some extent prove the contention which the Poitevin barons constantly urged against their Angevin suzerains, that their customs and privileges were not observed. Important vassals like the viscount of Thouars could only be expected to provide service in case of need,[47] but less powerful persons, at any rate in the last years of the century, had to contend against demands for the fines or contributions of their sub-tenants.[48] To what extent these

[40] 'Hoc anno (1163) Radulfus, senescallus tunc temporis in Sanctonia' (Annals of Vendôme in *Recueil des Annales angevines*, p. 82). Delisle identifies this person with Ralph de Faye (or Faie) (Introduction to *Actes de Henri II*, p. 416); cf. Boussard, p. 354.

[41] Delisle, p. 220. For Richard's reign see Richard, *Les Comtes de Poitou*, ii, 301. The name Aquitaine, except in the royal style, was not officially used in the later twelfth century.   It only occurs once in the Patent Rolls of John (*Rot. Pat.*, 154).

[42] *Rot. Pat.*, p. 21, December 4, 1202, a letter to Robert Turnham, seneschal of Poitou, 'sciatis quod constituimus . . . Martinus Algeis senescallum nostrum Gwasconiae et Petragor. Unde vobis mandamus quod illi integre balliam illam habere faciatis'. Gascony and Poitou were joined again in 1215 (*ibid.*, 152b).

[43] Delisle, *Introduction*, p. 124. Similarly Henry is never styled Count of Maine (*ibid.*, 206).

[44] *Rot. Chart.*, 102b, 'manifestum est quod qui senescallum non obedient mandatum domini contempnunt'.

[45] Saintonge is specially picked out for notice in several of Henry's charters (Delisle, p. 210).   [46] Rog. Howden, ii, 216–18.

[47] *e.g.*, *Rot. Chart.*, 102b, 103. Letter of viscount to John after his reconciliation: 'terram meam et totum posse meum et amicos meos voluntati vestrae et vestro servicio expono'. These words express the humility of a vassal who was independent in his own lands.

[48] See charter of exemption to the men of Humbert of Forz. *Rot. Chart.*, 8, August 1, 1199. They are to be quit 'a tallagio et ab omnibus illis consuetudinibus quae dominus Pictavie de illis accipere solet pro terris suis', in certain fiefs. Hallam has noticed instances of interference with Poitevin custom (*Middle Ages*, 8th edition, i, p. 128, note).

demands were justified by custom it is difficult to say. It is possible that Poitou proper and Saintonge had developed on the same lines as Anjou and Touraine, but that the difficulties in which their rulers found themselves made it possible for the barons to secure better bargains. When Richard gave Poitou as a fief to his nephew, Otto of Brunswick, who made himself very unpopular during his brief residence, he showed an indifference to the exploitation of his subjects which would explain a great deal of resistance.

It is, at any rate, clear that the distinction between the actual demesne of the counts of Poitou and Saintonge, and the lands of their vassals was very marked. The old sub-divisions, or *vicariæ*, lost their importance in Poitou as they did in Anjou and were absorbed by the new feudal areas whose lords had acquired all the privileges of jurisdiction.[49] The demesne, on the contrary, was carefully farmed. The accounts of Alfonse of Poitiers, which carry us back to the administration of Poitou before the final conquest in 1242,[50] reveal a financial system exactly parallel to the familiar methods of the Norman or English exchequer. The exchequers of Poitou and Anjou are implied in royal letters,[51] and the treasurer of Poitou was a well-known official; and it is interesting to find that, where accounts have survived from a later period, they should wear the same appearance as those presented in the twelfth century at Westminster and Caen. The demesne included the *preposituræ* of Poitiers, Niort, Benon, la Rochelle, Saint-Jean-d'Angeli, Fontenay-le-Comte, and the forest of Moulière, with other property. Most of this was farmed; the three citizens, for example, who farmed la Rochelle and the 'great fief' of Aunis, took over in their bargain all rents and the proceeds of small fines and forfeitures, and accounted separately for the reliefs, sale of woods, and smaller additional items.[52] These official bailiwicks, some of which are mentioned in Henry II's charters,[53] were evidently administered from the castles of the same names,[54] and some of the inquests of Count Alfonse give valuable pictures of their inner economy. One of these inquests, the survey of the honour of Chizé,

[49] Redet, *Cartulaire de l'abbage de Saint Cyprien de Poitiers*, p. 21 (*Archives historiques du Poitou*, vol. iii (1874)).

[50] Edited by A. Bardonnet in *Archives historiques du Poitou*, vol. iv (1875).

[51] *Rot. Norm.*, p. 28. Cf. the reference to the king's money changers at Tours and Le Mans (*Rot. Scacc.*, i, 38).

[52] *Archives historiques du Poitou*, iv, 8, and passim.

[53] *e.g.*, 'prepositis de Pictavi et de Chiseis et de Rochella et ceteris prepositis et servientibus suis de Aquitania' (Delisle, *Introduction*, 210). A claim in John's charter to Ralph of Mauléon, September 30, 1199, implies this financial system—'decem millia solidos monete Pictavie annuatum sibi percipiendis in prepositura de Rupella' (*Rot. Chart.*, 24b). Cf. for Saintes, 197b.

[54] Bailiff's accounts for payment of garrisons, *Archives historiques du Poitou*, iv, p. 13.

will be found useful on a later occasion. It gives life to the dry and meagre summaries of the count's rights which sometimes appear in the earlier charters.[55]

The records of one or two episodes are available to give precision to the difference between the power of the counts in the well-farmed demesne of Poitou and in the independent lordships on its borders. The county of Angoulême [56] lay across the route between Poitiers and Bordeaux, and seriously hampered the authority of Richard, as count of Poitou and duke of Aquitaine. Its four hundred parishes were divided among about thirty-one *castellaniæ* with Angoulême at their head. These castles, some of which claimed Charles the Great as their founder, guarded especially the valley of the Charente and the approaches from Poitou; and after the quarrel between Henry II and Louis VII broke out, proved most valuable allies to the French king. It seems to have been Richard's policy to pit the house of Lusignan against the counts of Angoulême, in a constant endeavour to wear away this obstacle set in the very heart of his dominions. He was so far successful that, as a result of almost unceasing warfare, a large part of the lower county, in the valley of the Charente, became dependent upon him. The lord of Cognac and Merpins deserted early and did homage to Henry II [57]—Richard married the heiress of Cognac to his bastard son—and from his fief the whole county could be, and more than once was, overrun. Still the counts succeeded in asserting their independence, and paid direct homage to the king of France.[58] Then came the diplomatic revolution of the year 1200. John suddenly deserted his allies of Lusignan, and bound himself by marriage to Ademar of Angoulême. Ademar died at Limoges in the summer of 1202, while he was trying to get together an alliance in John's favour, and John entered upon the inheritance of his ' very

---

[55] These rights are well described in a charter of Richard I's in favour of Pierre Bertin, to whom he confirmed land at Andilly 'ita quod homines de villa et ad dominium vel baillias ville pertinentes, cuiuscunque officii sint de consuetudinibus et serviciis que nobis reddere solebant, nemini de cetero reddere, etc.' Peter is to follow 'in expeditionibus et exercitibus' (*Archives historiques du Poitou*, vii, pp. 154–5.)

[56] Boissonade, *Quomodo comites Engolismenses erga reges Angliae et Franciae se gesserint* (Engolismae, 1893). [Add now Boissonade's long study on La Marche and Angoulême between 1137 and 1314, noted by Boussard (p. xli from *Bulletins et mémoires de la société archéologique et historique de la Charente* for the years 1935 and 1943.]

[57] After the conquest of Poitou by Alfonse of Poitiers, the question arose whether Cognac belonged to Poitiers or to Angoulôme. The story, as it was known in 1242, is told in the manuscript of accounts (*Archives historiques du Poitou*, iv, pp. 21, 22).

[58] Boissonade, pp. 8, 9. Ademar did homage to Philip in 1194, and also after Richard's death.

dear father'. Then we see the familiar machinery at work: the men of the county are placed under the direction of the seneschal of Poitou,[59] and in due course a special seneschal is appointed;[60] the castles are handed over, Philip the bastard being bought out in Cognac, Merpins and Jarnac;[61] the royal writs direct the payments of money of Angoulême as of Norman or English money;[62] the seneschal performs the usual duties, leads the royal servants, provisions the castles, pays the soldiers, guards captives, treats for peace, puts fiefs under the ban. In return royal privileges are showered upon the county, and especially upon the citizens of Angoulême, for Philip of France was also bidding for their favour, and the bribe had to be large—the right to a mayor and commune on the model of Rouen, then, a few months later, on the model of Rochelle.[63]

The later administration of Gascony [64] corresponds, in a still more striking manner, to the system which was common to the various territories of King John and his father, Henry II. The regulation of appeals to the French parliament, with its careful distinction between lands administered by written law (*ius scriptum*) and lands administered by customary law, presupposes a definite system of courts and of law.[65] The comprehensive duties of the 'constable of Bordeaux', an official who appears first in 1253, corresponded to the duties of the Norman barons of the exchequer. The functions of the seneschal, as defined, for example, in 1313, probably went back to Angevin times. He was entrusted with the duchy for the honour and profit of the king of England; and he possessed full powers of appointment and dismissal of his subordinates, of expenditure, and subject to the advice of the barons and communities, of levying taxation. Finally, the great inquiry made by Edward I in 1273—itself

[59] *Rot. Pat.*, 13, June 23, 1202.

[60] Bartholomew 'de Podio' first appears as seneschal on the Patent Rolls in 1214 (116b) though he was in John's service from the outset. After the city of Angoulême received its commune, Bartholomew became mayor. La Marche apparently had been for a time in Ademar's possession; he had claims through his mother. Brandin was made seneschal of La Marche in July, 1202 (*Rot. Pat.*, 14b).

[61] Boissonade, p. 15. Cognac was entrusted later to Robert of Turnham, and Merpins to William le Queu.

[62] *Rot. Norm.*, p. 54, June (July?) 14, 1202: 'preceptum est Barth. de Podio quod reddat magistro P. Rosinnoil x. li. Engol. monete que expendit in servicio domini Regis ibi'.

[63] *Rot. Pat.*, 29, 48.

[64] [See Powicke, *The Thirteenth Century* (1953), chapter vii, but much has been written since; cf. the bibliography in Boussard and, in particular, the papers of E. Chaplais, *e.g.* on the status of Gascony, in *Le Moyen Age*, lxi (1955), 121–37, and in *Annales du Midi*, lxix (1957), 5–38.]

[65] Langlois, *Textes relatifs à l'histoire du Parlement* (Paris, 1888), pp. 130–5.

D

contemporary with the English inquests recorded upon the Hundred rolls—recalls the famous measures of Henry II in 1166 and 1172 and the still earlier inquest made by the Norman King Roger of Sicily.[66]

The forms and practices common to all Angevin administration did not differ materially from those which were produced in other feudal states with Frankish traditions. The facts that Anjou had been a mere border *pagus*, and that it was so easy to adapt its government to Angoulême or Gascony combine to prove that Henry II employed no very novel methods. His empire was in some ways like the recent empire of India, where native states and the imperial government met similar problems; King John's administration in Angoulême probably made as little change in the actual state of affairs as would the intervention of the Indian government in Mysore during a minority. But this criticism is in itself eulogy. For the first time since the days of Charles the Great, a common system of government had been imposed upon a great part of Western Europe. Henry II, using the methods to which he was accustomed, trained a civil service to use them also. His writs and letters controlled the payment of money or the course of business in all parts of his dominions whether he directed them from a hunting lodge in Northamptonshire or an Aquitanian fortress. The instruments were simple and reproduced on an imperial scale the economy of a manor—seneschal and bailiff, writ and inquest, castle and mercenary.[67] They added little to statecraft and nothing to the theory of the state; they were powerless to resist for any length of time the racial or economic tendencies of the age. Yet under their direction local custom became articulate and the many-sided activities of society were protected; while, at the same time stress was laid upon the intellectual element in law and government, upon the power of a strong ruler to change law and adapt the means of government to ends. For example, in spite of his general observance of local customs and tradition, it is clear that Henry II revised the rules of succession throughout his domains, partly on Angevin, partly on Norman lines.[68] This mingling of bold thinking

[66] On Edward I's inquiries and ordinances, see Powicke, *The Thirteenth Century*, pp. 295–304. For the South Italian *Catalogus Baronum*, see E. Jamison, *The Norman administration of Apulia and Capua*, in Papers of the British School at Rome, vi (1913), especially pp. 338–42, which modifies C. H. Haskins in *English Historical Review*, xxvi (1911), 657–61.

[67] The habit of multiplying copies of charters provides instances of the relation between local and imperial government. Thus the seneschal of Anjou in 1201 certifies a copy of a charter granted by John to Marmoutier when the monks found it necessary to send the original to England. (Quoted by Delisle, *Introduction*, p. 181, note.)

[68] For spread of Angevin tenure by parage and of the apparently Norman rule of wardship, see Guilhiermoz, *Essai sur l'origine de la noblesse*, pp.

with reverence for custom is, as one would expect, most marked in England, where the writings of the great lawyers and chroniclers who were in close touch with Henry, reproduce the terseness and precision of the king's official correspondence.[69] But the administration of Normandy is almost as good an example of this quality, and was based, moreover, to an extent impossible in England, upon the general lines of government which have been brought into relief in this chapter.

To Normandy, then, we may now turn.

203–5; and Hallam, *Middle Ages* (8th edition, 1841), i, 128, note. See also next chapter for these and other instances of legislation.

[69] The similarity has been noticed by M. Delisle. It is sufficient to recall the *Tractatus de Legibus Angliae*, parts of the *Dialogus de Scaccario*, Roger of Howden, Ralph dean of St. Paul's, and, in a somewhat different way, Gerald of Wales. For the close connection between the custumal and administration in Normandy, see Coville, *Les états de Normandie* (Paris, 1894), p. 22; and the next chapter.

CHAPTER III

THE ADMINISTRATION OF NORMANDY

I

THE duchy of Normandy consisted of several distinct counties or *pagi*, and was not a single political area in Frankish times as the counties of Anjou and Poitou had been. The Norman divisions had been occupied by the Northmen at various times [1] and continued to develop local peculiarities of custom; [2] moreover, they retained and developed a Frankish civilisation. The view of some older scholars that the land to which the Northmen gave their name became in any real sense a Scandinavian country, is no longer tenable. The language of the Frankish inhabitants prevailed in the court as well as in the fields, and Scandinavian place names are found especially along the coast of Caux, where little pirate towns grew beneath the cliffs, and in the bold promontory of the Côtentin. [3] It is hard to say whether the men who settled in the valley of the Seine were Danes or came from Norway or Sweden, so quickly did the memory of law and speech and kindred fade.

The obscurity in which the history of the Norman settlements is

[1] Prentout in *Revue de synthèse historique*, xx, 42. [See now D. C. Douglas, 'The Rise of Normandy' in *Proc. of British Academy*, 1947; and his paper on Rollo of Normandy in *English Historical Review*, lvii (1942), 417–36; also F. M. Stenton, on the 'Scandinavian Colonies in England and Normandy' in *Trans. of Royal Hist. Soc.*, 4th sec., xxvii (1945), 1–12.]

[2] The most striking example is the difference between the rules of succession in Caux and those which prevailed in the rest of Normandy; see Génestal, *Le Parage Normand*, p. 32. The custumal and the judgments of the exchequer, in the thirteenth century, frequently refer to local varieties of custom. See also Viollet, in the *Histoire littéraire de la France* (xxxiii, 78–9), where it is pointed out that the grand custumal and later reformed custom were only in full force in the Côtentin. Note also the local additions in the Vatican MS. of the earliest custumal (*ibid.*, p. 56). The fact that fouage or *focagium*, a tax on the hearth to compensate for the depreciation of the unchanged coinage, which was levied every third year (Stapleton, I, xvi, cxxxvi), was not paid in Mortain, Breteuil, Alençon and other places tells in the same direction (Brussel, *Usage des fiefs*, i, p. 212: the *scriptum de foagio*. Cf. Viollet, p. 78, note).

[3] *Revue de synthèse historique*, xix, 55, 57. [The statement in the text needs revision, as the articles by Douglas and Stenton (above, note 1) show. Jean Adigard began the publication of a collection of Norman place-names between 911 and 1066 in 1947 (for Orne) and 1951 (for La Marche); see his work, *Les noms des persones Scandinaves dans les noms de lieux Normands de 911 à 1066* (Upsala, 1955).]

hidden, has not revealed its secrets to modern inquiry. It is still impossible to measure the extent of Scandinavian influence upon the development of Frankish institutions, just as it is impossible to guess to what extent, if any, Frankish institutions had to fight for their continued existence. It is certain that the tradition of the north must have done something to produce the peculiarities of Norman society and Norman administration, such as the simple and effective financial system, or the subtle combination of ducal authority with feudal privilege. It is abundantly clear that the Norman baronage retained a strong sense of racial unity, which took the form of a self-conscious mastery of alien institutions. Their wonderful energy and certainty of purpose are stamped upon the history of Europe as they were stamped in stone from Ireland to Sicily. But it is wiser to be content with this obvious truth, and to leave on one side inquiries into Scandinavian origins.[4]

The old Frankish counties can be discerned as the obvious base of Norman divisions even at the end of the twelfth century. To some extent, as, for example, in the case of the district between the rivers Seine and Risle, new districts had been formed in accordance with natural barriers. Here and there, especially along the border between Normandy and the more southern provinces, new fortresses had become the centres of new divisions, as Verneuil, Nonancourt and, near the coast, in the Bessin, Amanville (Osmanville). One or two of the ancient boundaries, as that between the *pagus Lexoviensis* and the *pagus Oximiensis,* had become confused, a fact which was reflected in the confusion of ecclesiastical boundaries. Yet, for the most part, the older *pagi* continued to exist for one purpose or another. The areas of the dioceses and archdeaconries had of course helped to maintain the secular areas. In the diocese of Rouen, which comprised several *pagi,* the archdeaconries seem to have corresponded to the Frankish *pagi* and to the later Norman bailiwicks.[5]

[4] The chief authority for the administration of Normandy in the twelfth century, and to some extent for earlier centuries also, is the exchequer rolls. They show the administrative areas and give a wealth of detail which can be elucidated by means of the ducal and other charters, the earliest custumal, the later judgments of the exchequer, and the other Norman rolls. For these see the introduction, above pp. 1–5. [In addition to the works of Stapleton, Delisle, Prentout, L. Valin's *Le Duc de Normandie et sa Cour* (Paris, 1910), and Haskins' *Norman Institutions*, with its bibliography, see Boussard's bibliography.]

[5] This results from a comparison of the districts in the exchequer rolls with the archdeaconries. See, for the latter, Longnon, *Pouillés de la province de Rouen* (1903), pp. xi, xii. For the *pagi*, see *Revue de synthèse historique*, xix, 221, and, among the authorities there mentioned, Le Prévost, *Anciennes divisions territoriales de la Normandie*, in *Mém. de la Soc. des Antiquaires de Normandie*, xi. [Cf. D. C. Douglas in *Cambridge Hist. Journal*, xiii (1957), 109–10.]

The archdeaconries of the dioceses of Bayeux, Avranches, and Coutances correspond on the whole to the Norman viscounties into which the earlier counties of the Bessin, Avranchin, and Côtentin were divided.[6] The evidence is sufficient, therefore, to permit a direct connection to be made between the Carolingian and the Norman counties and viscounties; in fact the counts of Evreux (*pagus Ebroicensis*) and of Eu (*Talogiensis pagus*), and, for a brief period, a count of Avranches,[7] had as much independence of the.duke of Normandy as was compatible with Norman feudalism.

Some of the greatest franchises, however—the honours of the counts of Mortain and Alençon, for example—were of more artificial origin. The unity of Normandy and the nature of the duke's authority, which was that of a count,[8] put the older divisions at the mercy of the central power. As a result of these facts the older divisions never tended to become hard and fast units of local government like the English shires. It is true that the Norman bailiwicks of the later twelfth century might have become similar to the English shires, governed as they were by an almost identical system of law and judicial procedure; indeed, it is possible to observe a tendency of this kind in the second half of Henry II's reign.[9] But the interference of the great franchises, the needs of defence, and, it may be added, the course of trade, prevented such a result. The ducal borough, the ducal castle and the ducal demesne were the real units of Norman administration, and though in their origin and grouping these units show the influence of Frankish divisions, Normandy was a land of cities and châtellenies, like Anjou and Poitou—not a land of shires, like England.[10]

This quality of Norman administration was connected with the chief principle of Norman society. All historians have observed the superior position of the duke in Norman feudalism when compared

[6] The chief fact is the division into the city and the county proper: Bayeux and the Bessin, Coutances and the Côtentin, etc.

[7] Henry II's charter to Earl of Chester, quoted in Stapleton, I, p. xcii. [But see Douglas on the earliest Norman counts, in *English Historical Review*, lxi (1946), 129–56.]

[8] The duke is so called as late as 1092 in Philip I's charter to the archbishop of Rouen (Prou, *Recueil des actes de Philippe I*, p. 323). See, for its significance, Haskins, *Norman Institutions*, p. 26 and note 96.   [9] Below, p. 54.

[10] Above, p. 26; and below, c. vii. The Norman charters collected by Delisle in his *Cartulaire Normand* provide many instances of the word *castellania*, e.g., no. 39, p. 278, 'Castellum Paciaci cum tota castellania' (1195). The royal demesne was the centre and origin, in like manner, of some of the English shires; e.g., the *Wiltunensis paga* and the *Summurtunensis paga* of Asser (*De rebus gestis Aelfredi*. c. 55, ed. Stevenson, p. 45) take their names from the royal vills of Wilton and Somerton. Cf. Chadwick, *Studies on Anglo-Saxon Institutions*, pp. 236, 255.

with the position of other feudal lords who held extensive lordships;
but, owing to a curious perversion of the facts, most of the older
writers have seized upon the monopoly of justice as the distinctive
mark of this superiority. While recognising, of course, that every
feudal lord exercised purely feudal jurisdiction, these writers have
contended that the duke of the Normans succeeded in keeping to
himself all higher jurisdiction comprised in the 'pleas of the sword'.[11]
Now it is certainly difficult to say whether the pleas of the sword had
been held by any Norman magnate apart from a grant from his lord;
the name seems to imply that originally, as later, they could not have
been held otherwise. But it is certain that from the outset the early
companions of the dukes and the great monasteries founded by the
dukes exercised what later lawyers call *haute justice*. The superior
position of the duke of Normandy did not lie in a monopoly of this
jurisdiction, but in the fact that in Normandy the right to feudal
service was insisted upon and gradually interpreted in logical fashion
in favour of the lord. The Northmen regarded Frankish feudalism
with fresh and curious gaze. They seem to have fastened upon the
idea of the *beneficium*, or, to use its later name, the fief (*feodum*)
with pertinacity and without fear; and, in spite of the evidence that
the companions of Rollo claimed to be equal with their leader, there
is no real doubt that the military relations of the pirate host were
translated into terms of feudalism without any period of delay. It is
true that in the lands which became western Normandy, and which
are geographically so different from the uplands and valleys on either
side of the Seine, the presence of fresh arrivals and settlements, the
wars with the Bretons, and the civil strife of the Normans themselves,
may have permitted independent communities to be formed which
did not at once acknowledge ducal authority; although it is curious
that the demesne of the duke was most extensive in this part of
Normandy. But, however this may have been, the leader of the
Northmen seems to have had the lands granted in 911 by King
Charles the Simple at his disposal, and to have divided them out as
benefices, with a very large share for himself. We are told that the
forms of written conveyance were regarded very lightly by Rollo
and William Longsword,[12] but his successors adopted more systematic relations with their tenants. Within one hundred and fifty

[11] *Norman Institutions*, pp. 27–8, for criticism of Brussel and Luchaire; a
less guarded criticism in L. Valin, pp. 182 ff., and cf. below, pp. 59–62. The
early custumal gives every lord his court: *Statuta et Consuetudines*, c. (Tardif,
Coutumiers, I, i, 50). See now Douglas, *Rise of Normandy*, noted above, p. 1.
[12] See the doubtful charter of Richard II for Saint Ouen, quoted by L. Valin
(p. 145), from the *Archives de Seine-Inferieure*. 'Quae omnia noster atavus
Rolphus, praenominato loco, partim restituit, partim et dedit, sed propiis
cartulis ad noticiam futurorum minime descripsit. Huic subnectimus cessioni,

years they had worked the somewhat crude material provided by
the Frankish benefice into a systematic form. This feudalism was
not first elaborated by the Normans upon English soil, but was taken
from Normandy into England, where congenial feudal institutions
were ready for adaptation. And, to repeat, whether this feudalism
had or had not assumed the duke to be the origin of all judicial
immunities, it was not based upon the monopoly of the duke in more
important jurisdiction, but rather upon the close control which the
dukes had secured, in virtue of their feudal lordship, over vassals
who possessed very great immunities indeed. The interference of
these immunities with the older areas of jurisdiction caused the unit
of administration to be the demesne rather than the county.

The evidence for this description commences with the authentic
records of the chief monastic houses, more particularly of Fécamp.[13]
These take us back to grants made by Rollo and his successors. The
narrative of Dudo of Saint Quentin, though now regarded as almost
entirely worthless, has some significance as evidence of the relations
between the dukes and their followers. On the one side, there was the
claim to be the equals of the lord; on the other, there was the fact of
the benefice with its implications of dependence and service. He
describes how the Norman chieftains, plotting against the duke,
decided to beg lands from him in return for service. If he agreed they
would have a crowd of warriors at their command, and he would
be reduced to naught.[14] The intention to deny obedience does not
deprive the scheme of its meaning for the historian. These lands are
evidently lands stocked, or to be stocked, with warriors (*milites*) and
were to be granted in return for service. Before 1066 the Norman
dukes were able to regard their country as divided for the most part
into a certain number of knights' fees, the source for military purposes of a host of so many knights or fully-armed warriors. The
grouping of warriors was symmetrical and was evidently imposed
from above.[15] In some respects it may have found an origin in the

quae etiam avi nostri Willelmi industria simili modo absque cartarum
notamine concessit.' The charter has a suspicious appearance, but is suggestive.

[13] Haskins, *Norman Institutions*, pp. 7–10, 254–60, and *passim*.

[14] Dudo, ed. Lair, p. 187. The phrase is, 'si voluerit nos promptos habere
sibi *ad serviendum*, largiatur nobis terram usque ad flumen Rislam. Nos
frequentia *militum*, si dederit, ditabimur.' On the unreliability of Dudo,
see Prentout, *Etude critique sur Dudo de Saint-Quentin* (Paris, 1916), and
Douglas, p. 105 and notes.

[15] The symmetrical basis has always been clear for the twelfth century in
the list of knights holding of the church of Bayeux (c. 1133, *Red Book of the
Exchequer*, ii, 645) and in the larger list for Normandy of 1172 (*ibid.*, p. 624).
As in England, the body of ten knights was the original unit (Round, *Feudal
England*, 259, 261). Haskins collected the evidence and proved the existence

similar system of Picardy and the lands of the lower Rhine; but the Norman system possessed one characteristic of great importance, which was typical of Norman genius. In Picardy the fief of the tenant-in-chief was the unit and paid the same service whether it comprised few or many warriors; in Normandy the fee of the warrior became the unit and the fief was regarded as containing this or that number of fees for which it was responsible.[16] At first, as we have seen, the number of knights' fees for which a lord had to account in the field was estimated in round numbers, that is, imposed from above; indeed, it is this fact which shows most clearly how centralised and dependent Norman feudalism was; but the fact that the fee was the unit of calculation was of great service to the later dukes, when they desired to give a fiscal value to the number of fees at which the lands of a tenant-in-chief were assessed.

The list of ducal privileges and Norman customs which was drawn up in 1091 for the sons of William the Conqueror [17] indicates that precedents had been asserted for ducal control of the baronage before the conquest of England. Castles, we are told, could only be built by the licence of the lord; the right of private war was subject to rigid limitation; and in case of invasion the duke could call out the national levy. These customs or claims were enforced later to the duke's profit. Thus, at the commencement of his reign, Henry II took many of the Norman castles into his custody; [18] the Norman custumal forbids private warfare; [19] and King John summoned the national levy.[20] But perhaps the most striking illustration of rights of the lord, and consequently of the feudal supremacy of the duke, is afforded by the Norman law of wardship. That the lord had the right to take the lands and heir of his vassal into custody until the heir was of age is a fact so familiar to English students that its exceptional nature is forgotten. It could only have survived in a land where the logical

---

of knight service and the symmetrical group in Normandy in the eleventh century. A considerable amount of land must have been held otherwise than by military service, for the *Statuta et consuetudines*, c. viii (Tardif, pp. 8, 9) refers to the case of inherited *eschaetae* or divisible lands being of more value than the knight's fee, as though it were common.

[16] Guilhiermoz, *Essai sur l'origine de la noblesse*, p. 183.

[17] Haskins has given a critical text and commentary of the *Consuetudines et Justiciae* of 1091 in *Norman Institutions*, pp. 277–84.

[18] Below, p. 181.

[19] *Statuta et consuetudines*, c. 31 (Tardif, I, i, p. 27).

[20] For the arrière-ban, in Normandy and elsewhere, see Guilhiermoz, p. 293, and especially his important note on p. 292, when he amends the reading of the Bayeux inquest of 1133. For John and the arrière-ban, see *Rot. Norm.*, ed. Hardy, 36, John's letter of June 5, 1201, to William of Caïeux: 'vobis mandamus quatinus ad nos cum retrovvarda accedatis desicut retrobannum nostrum mandavimus'. Cf. below, p. 210.

interpretation of the benefice as a precarious or temporary grant had
been understood; and its survival in Normandy is a clear sign that
Norman society was not merely feudal but essentially and logically
feudal.[21] Logic of this kind, which was very probably only possible
for a people whose tribal or ethnic traditions survived after the ties of
family had become weakened,[22] was all in favour of the overlord.
The leader of a band of alien pirates, whose northern origin was their
chief bond of union, was transformed into the model of a feudal
monarch. It is significant that the Angevin dukes of Normandy found
the right of wardship so precious that they seem to have tried to
introduce it in their lands south of the Loire.[23]

Consistent with the strictly feudal relations of the duke with his
chief vassals, was the comparatively slow progress of the rights of
interference with his sub-vassals. The complete mastery over all
subjects was probably not attained, even in law, until Angevin times,
and shows traces of English and Angevin experience. But there is
evidence to show that Normandy was ready for a clear statement of
ducal prerogatives with regard to sub-vassals before the middle of
the twelfth century. As a monarch and judge, the duke was of course
brought into direct contact with all his subjects; the judicial activity
of the viscounts and the right to call out the levy show this; and
feudal usage allowed sub-vassals to do homage to the duke, and
therefore to be bound to direct service. This act, however, seems to
have required the consent of the lord even in the reign of Henry I.[24]
The custom of Normandy in later times put the duke in a preferential
position which recalls the prerogative rights of English royalty; thus
he had the custody of all the lands of a wardship if the ward held
anything of him directly by military service or by serjeanty.[25] There
are early suggestions of the right of a lord to restrain alienations of
land—a right which would work in favour of the duke.[26] But it is
dangerous to argue back from evidence of this kind. The duke's lordship over all Normans could hardly have become effective until the
judicial reforms of Henry II had helped to stamp out private war
and to supplement the truce of God.[27]

[21] See the *Statuta et consuetudines*, c. xi (Tardif, I, i, pp. 10–12), with the
'elegant and delusive embroidery' of its reasoning (*Hist. litt.*, xxiii, 56):
Pollock and Maitland, *History of English Law* (2nd edition), i, 71, 326–8.
[22] To this extent the thesis maintained by M. Flach in his *Origines de
l'ancienne France*, iii, 89, seems to me to be fruitful and suggestive.
[23] Above, p. 34, note 68.
[24] Valin, pp. 62, 63; from *Orderic Vitalis*, ed. Prévost, iv, 459 and *seq.*
[25] *Statuta et consuetudines*, c. xi (Tardif, I, i, pp. 6, 12).
[26] Pollock and Maitland, i, 70, note; 340–3.
[27] The note, which was added to this chapter in the first edition of this
book, on the truce of God in Normandy and the right of private warfare (pp.
93–8) has been omitted. Reference should now be made to J. Yver, *l'Inter-*

The most difficult problem of early Norman law is the problem of succession. The duchy was never divided, nor were the great fiefs which had their origin in hereditary offices of count or viscount. In these cases the precarious origin of the grant would naturally be insisted upon, and would combine with the indivisibility of the office to prevent the division of the fief.[28] The practice of the Norman kings of England suggests that they used their influence to oppose the division of baronies; at any rate the Norman barons do not seem to have applied invariably the principle of division beyond the separation of English from Norman fiefs. Although there were numerous cases of large families of sons, the greater holdings of Normandy remained, on the whole, intact. The story of Tancred of Hauteville, who urged his sons to seek their fortunes elsewhere, explains this to a great extent.[29] The epic poets of the twelfth century reveal a similar view that it is good form for younger sons not to stay at home.[30] Again, a good marriage, a sudden death, or the cloister brought relief as often as not. It is probable that, so far as baronies were concerned, the statutory doctrine of the *Statuta et consuetudines*, which forbade the division of the *single* fief, legalised general practice. The necessity of maintaining entire the service of the barony operated in favour of primogeniture. Moreover, Normandy is not likely to have been uninfluenced by the early appearance of primogeniture in England.

Apart from the barony, equal division among males was the rule. It is possible that, at the other end of the social scale, local custom may have maintained peasant holdings entire in some parts of Normandy. So far as it goes, the existence of a class of 'cottars' might be urged as evidence of this.[31] But, if we take the great majority of Norman holdings, we see them subjected to division among the male heirs. The emphatic assertion of the equality of brothers in a thirteenth century custumal may have been influenced by the custom of parage which was defined in the second half of the twelfth century; but in the early *Statuta et consuetudines* it is stated that any brother who felt himself unfairly treated by a paternal division of the

diction de la guerre privée dans le très ancien droit Normand (Caen, 1928, 45 pages).

[28] Pollock and Maitland, ii, 264–7.

[29] On this see v. Amira in *Historische Zeitschrift* (1878), Neue Folge, iii, 248–50.

[30] *e.g.*, the address of Aymeri of Narbonne to his sons, in *Les Narbonnais*, quoted by Bédier, *Les Légendes Epiques*, i, 35.

[31] Local custom might override the rule of division in Normandy, as in England (cf. Glanvill, Bk. vii, c. 3, § 3). For 'cottars' in Normandy, see Delisle, *Etudes sur la condition de la classe agricole*, p. 15. The class of cottars is now supposed to be the younger men of the family who are landless and settle in crofts round the main holdings. (Vinogradoff, *English Society in the Eleventh Century*, p. 460.)

property could claim a formal revision on the death of his father.[32] Henry II encouraged primogeniture in order to prevent the constant division of knights' fees or of portions of a knight's fee. He also tried to maintain the integrity of holdings, even where primogeniture was not enforced.[33]

The combination of feudal with social principles of other kinds due to a sense of national unity or family justice, was characteristic of the Norman State as a whole, and enabled the dukes to introduce changes of great importance in public law. Throughout the history of the duchy until the conquest of Philip Augustus the dukes transacted important public business in assemblies of the magnates. Nearly thirty councils of *principes, optimates, proceres* or *majores*, to give some of the titles by which the magnates are named, have been counted in the chroniclers for the period between 927 and 1066. At these assemblies the great questions of state, ducal succession, relations with France, war and peace, the maintenance of order, were discussed, and oaths of fealty were taken.[34]

It is not paradoxical to say that feudalism in Normandy was worked out in such a logical and systematic way because feudal relations were regarded as the material of the state rather than as the end of its being. In England this was still more the case, mainly on account of the maintenance of the old courts of public law and of the old areas of administration. From this point of view England and Normandy differ, for in Normandy, as I have explained, these local institutions took a secondary place, or disappeared. The state in Normandy was more distinctly feudal, and feudal law developed on more logical lines than it developed in England. For example, after the French conquest, when the native energy of Norman law had more freedom, a divergence between English and Norman law at once became apparent. Thus, while the English lawyers encouraged free alienation of land subject to the extensive power of the king to control it, the Norman lawyers, whose thinking had always shown more feudal precision, strengthened the rights of the lord.[35] Again, the English lawyers gave very wide extension to primogeniture, but took away the right of the eldest son to share by consent or by reversion in the grants made by his father. In Normandy feudal development was less arbitrary; primogeniture, in accordance with current sentiment, continued to be limited to certain forms of tenure and to the

[32] C, x (Tardif, I, i, p. 10).

[33] Guilhiermoz, pp. 214–19. On parage, on which a long note was included in the first edition of this book (pp. 98–102, omitted in this edition), see R. Génestal, *Le parage Normand* (Caen, 1911); cf. Haskins, *Norman Institutions*, pp. 22, 159.

[34] Coville, *Les états de Normandie* (Paris, 1894), pp. 10–20.

[35] Pollock and Maitland, i, 340–3 and notes.

single fief; but, on the other hand, the rights of reversion of the eldest son were secured.[36] The difference was not only due to the influence of purely feudal ideas in France: it goes back also to the difference between Normandy and England in the twelfth century, which a common administration obscured. But, in spite of this fact, the Norman kings and their advisers simply applied more thoroughly in England the principle which they had used in Normandy—that feudalism may form the basis of a state.[37]

II

Under the early dukes the Frankish *pagi* and *vicariæ* were still the names of local divisions in Normandy.[38] The former became counties; the latter died out. The counties were reserved for the relatives of the sovereign. They were distributed with an arbitrary hand, and although occasionally granted as late as the middle of the twelfth century,[39] the position of count was gradually confined to the borders or marches of Normandy, where the counts enjoyed the franchises of a great baron. Their official origin, however, may still be traced in the fact that viscounties and *prepositura* survived, in more or less feudalised form, upon their lands, as in Normandy as a whole. The county or honour of Mortain contained viscounties, and its vassals contributed the *auxilium vicecomitis*;[40] Evreux contained a viscounty and *prepositura*;[41] the counts of Meulan, a French title, who succeeded the counts of Brionne in Brionne, seem to have had a viscount of Brionne among their vassals.[42] There would have been nothing very remarkable in the growth of independent sovereigns, like the counts of Blois or of Anjou, on Norman soil. But the distribution of the office and title among their near relatives was evidently part of a general policy by which the dukes kept Normandy together; and with the exception of those who survived as great marcher barons the counts were succeeded by the administrators of the ducal demesne.

In the twelfth century, besides the counts of Eu, Aumâle, Evreux, Alençon, and Mortain, a number of rich families and corporations

[36] *Ibid.*, ii, p. 313.

[37] See in general J. R. Strayer, *The administration of Normandy under Saint Louis* (Mediæval Academy of America, 1932).

[38] Stapleton, *Observations*, I, lvii.

[39] Duke Robert sold the counties of Coutances and Avranches to his brother Henry; and Henry II, before he became king, gave the county of Avranches to the Earl of Chester. On the counts see above, pp. 37–8 with notes, and especially D. Douglas in *English Historical Review*, lxi (1946), 149 ff.

[40] *Rot. Scacc.*, i, p. 9. *Cart. Norm.*, p. 66, no. 412.

[41] *English Historical Review*, xxi, 647, note.

[42] *Cart. Norm.*, p. 7, no. 24.

had secured lands and franchises in east and central Normandy.
The west, especially the Avranchin, was, for the most part, occupied
by less important persons, and most of the castles were in the ducal
demesne.[43] English or French earls, Chester, Leicester, Giffard,
Meulan; wealthy monasteries like Fécamp, St. Ouen, Mont Saint-
Michel; bishops; and feudal families, such as those of Bertram, Montfort, Bohon, Vernon, Gournai, Saint-Saens, had built up vast lordships which imposed a serious limitation on the ducal authority.[44]
Like the counts, these feudatories reproduced upon their own estates
the financial and judicial administration which was characteristic
of Normandy. They had their feudal court and administrative
officers, and, as the escheats mentioned in the exchequer rolls show,
farmed their lands in a similar manner to that of the ducal officials.[45]
Many of them had the right to hold the pleas of the sword except
recognitions and other pleas of late origin. In the rest of Normandy
the duke was represented by the viscounts, and it is probable that
some ducal property was farmed separately by *prepositi* from an
early date,[46] subject to the general control of the viscounts. The
Frankish viscount was originally the representative of the count, and
took the place of his *missi* about the middle of the ninth century.[47]
Gradually these officials were localised and granted areas of jurisdiction, but they did not lose the plenitude of power which their original
position and their name imply that they possessed. This conclusion
is further established by the fact that when the Norman viscounts first
appear with territorial titles they take their names from the old counties, the Bessin, Côtentin, Avranchin, Lieuvin, the Oximin, Romeis,
and Caux or Grand Caux and the Vexin.[48] In addition to these were

[43] Gerville, *Mémoire sur les anciens Châteaux du département de la Manche*
in *Mém. de la Soc. des Antiquaires de la Normandie*, 1827, p. 65.

[44] For the geographical distribution of the great families, see Delisle,
Bibliothèque de l'Ecole des Chartes, xi, 400–3. The most convenient list is
in the *Red Book of the Exchequer*, ii, 624.

[45] The escheats, farmed or accounted for in the Exchequer Rolls, frequently
owed tithes and payments of old standing. See also the list of alms payable
from the honour of Evreux in *Cart. Norm.*, p. 21, no. 117; and cf. no. 120.

[46] Haskins, *Norman Institutions*, pp. 43–4.

[47] Lasteyrie, *Etude sur les comtes et vicomtes de Limoges antérieurs à l'an
1000* (Bibl. de l'école des hautes études, Paris, 1874), pp. 48–50, 61.

[48] All these appear, generally as survivals, in the roll of 1180. I imagine their
farms at this period to have consisted largely of the *auxilium vicecomitis*,
e.g., in the case of the old viscounty of the Oximin; cf. a charter of King
John to William of Briouze, releasing his men from payment of the aid of
the viscounty (*Rot. Norm.*, p. 20). M. Delisle thinks that the viscounts at
this early time performed the functions of the later bailiffs rather than financial
functions (*Bibliothèque*, x, 264); I incline to think this was true of the officials
who took their name from the county. For the curious survival of the viscounts
of the Vexin, see Stapleton, *Observations*, I, cxxii.

officials of smaller jurisdictions, such as the Vau de Vire and Conte-ville. On the analogy of the archdeaconries some other early viscoun-ties had their centres in the cities, Caen, Rouen, Exmes, Argentan, Coutances and others.[49] As time went on the dignity of the name was forgotten and the words *vicecomitatus, prepositura, baillia* were used indiscriminately in common speech. Indeed, from the outset the viscounts were officials who took rank after the bishops and counts; they were never at the head of the Norman Baronage.[50] But, at the same time, a chronological inquiry shows clearly that the later confusion in terminology concealed the results of a period of change during which the early viscounts lost their distinctive import-ance.

This change begins to be marked before the conquest of England, but the viscount was still a very important person in the reign of Henry I. The extent of his powers may be seen in the case of the notorious Robert of Bellême, who was viscount for the duke in Argentan, Exmes and Falaise, that is, in the viscounty of the Oximin with its subordinate ministries.[51] His predecessors of the house of Montgomery had erected a veritable despotism on the basis of their office. Robert's power extended into Maine, where Henry I had succeeded, in the days of his brother Duke Robert, in depriving him of Domfront.[52] In 1112 he was deprived of his office as viscount owing to his refusal to pay his accounts into the treasury. His career shows that the viscount had charge of the castles [53] in his viscounty and that he farmed the ducal estates.

With regard to the farming of the demesne, C. H. Haskins has shown, by means of an ingenious argument,[54] that not only were the viscounties and *preposituræ* well defined before the year 1066, but also that the fixed payments or farms of these areas were paid in money into a treasury and were distinct from the casual receipts of the ducal *camera* or privy purse. If this were so, a record must have been in existence. The viscount's aid (*auxilium vicecomitis*) which was included in the farm, was a tax upon the land which apparently

---

[49] See the list in Delisle's *Introduction* to the *Recueil des Actes de Henri II*, pp. 212, 213. See above, pp. 37–8.

[50] They were important people, as the early charters show, *e.g.*, those printed in the *preuves* to Delisle's *Histoire de Saint-Sauveur-le-Vicomte*, but H. Brunner seems to me to exaggerate their importance (*Enstehung der Schwurgerichte*, p. 148).

[51] Ord. Vit., iv, 305 (cf. *ibid.*, p. 236). Cf. Galguso in 1135 (*ibid.*, v. 56).

[52] Stapleton, I, lxxviii. Latouche, *Histoire du Comté du Maine*, pp. 46, 47, 49, 62.

[53] The viscount transacted judicial business, and held the castles 'quia vicecomes erat'. Haskins, *Norman Institutions*, pp. 46–7 and note 198. He was also at the head of the troops; Delisle, *Bibliothèque*, x, 264.

[54] Haskins, *op. cit.*, pp. 41–4, 105.

goes back to this early period.[55] The financial system, with its payments in money instead of in kind, was the most characteristic feature of Norman administration. It is not unconnected with the arithmetical nicety with which the dukes and their barons regulated military service, and throughout Norman history before 1204 it was the use of money which enabled the dukes to adapt feudal institutions to their needs, to develop their judicial prerogatives, to levy new taxes and so to hold their castles and to pay their mercenaries. To the old farm of the viscounty were added new sources of revenue, especially the farms of the towns and seaports, the rents of the holdings which clustered round the new castles, the fines and amercements paid for the sale of feudal privileges or the non-observance of feudal duties. But it should be noted that this familiarity with hard cash, this knowledge of bookkeeping, is found as soon as our Norman records become reliable, and stamps a character on Norman administration from the first. It may go back to the commercial precocity of the Scandinavian traders who dealt so early in the coinage of the East.[56] It probably was assisted by the trade for the pursuit of which the towns of Normandy were so conveniently situated. As always, it fed on itself and increased as its creatures increased. It accounts very largely for the early disappearance of serfdom in Normandy, of serfdom, that is, which means arbitrary labour service and dues in kind, for in Normandy, as in Kent, there must have been some connection between trade and a free peasantry.[57] In its turn, the free peasantry increased the population and wealth of the community.[58] If we except

[55] That the *graveria*, or viscount's aid, a universal tax payable by all but vassals of the greatest honours, was an early tax, is clear from the charter of the Empress Matilda to the abbey of St. André-en-Gouffern (Round, *Calendar*, no, 593), commented upon by Stapleton, I, lxxxviii. For other instances, see Haskins, *op. cit.*, p. 40, note 165.

[56] [The work of Montelius and others has now been replaced by S. Bolin, in the *Scandinavian Economic Hist. Review*, i (1953), 5–39. It has been urged, however, probably rightly, that the bulk of Arabic and other Eastern coins found in Scandinavia was due to loot rather than trade. See a suggestive, though exaggerated, article by F. J. Himly, 'Y-a-t-il emprise musulmane sur 'l'économie des états européens du viiie au xe siècle?' in *Revue suisse d'histoire*, v (1955), 31–81.]

[57] Delisle, *Etudes sur la condition de la classe agricole*, pp. 18–25; Pollock and Maitland, ii, 271–3 (for Kent). On the spread of the use of money from the non-agricultural communities, the *Dialogus de scaccario*, ed. C. Johnson (1950), pp. 40–1, though not historically exact (Round, *Commune of London*, p. 69) is suggestive. The substitution of money for services in Normandy was going on rapidly in the twelfth century.

[58] That the change in the condition of the peasantry was not due to racial reasons is clear from the facts that, as in Kent, it seems to have encouraged partibility which was not especially a Scandinavian custom—indeed the tendency in Scandinavia seems to have been towards primogeniture; and, secondly, that enfranchisement was preceded by peasant risings which ex-

part of the Côtentin which provided for the needs of the ducal house-hold, and some fishing villages, whose herrings were as useful as money, the revenues of Normandy were paid almost entirely in money.

I have said that a change in the position of the viscounts is to be traced even before the conquest of England. The system of farms was continuous, and even the amounts of the farms; some of the families of viscounts maintained their offices as hereditary fiefs down to the end of the duchy's independent existence; [59] but before 1066 Duke William seems to have insisted on their removable character.[60] In the reign of Henry I the term *ballia*, bailiwick, appears, and it is possible that his experience of Robert of Bellême hastened the process which merged the old viscounties into the general system of ducal administration. A new class of officials arose, people with obscure names like Trossebot,[61] and the line of distinction between the servants of the household and the local officials became faint. The castles were placed under the more direct supervision of the duke, the viscounts worked side by side with the servants (*ministri*) and justices: the word *ballia*, a vague general word, was employed indiscriminately for offices and jurisdictions of every kind.[62] At the centre, on the other hand, order and precision appeared. The body of justices was separated from the barons, and formed a court apart. This was the court of the exchequer, which was to combine in Normandy the functions of the courts of common pleas and exchequer.[63] The seneschal was not yet the president of the court, but he was an essential member of it.[64] A system of writs and recognitions, as we shall see,

tended all along the north of France, from Brittany to Flanders. These risings began in the first half of the ninth century, in Flanders. See the interesting facts collected by M. Sée in his book, *Les Classes rurales et le régime domanial en France au moyen age* (Paris, 1901), pp. 73–6. For the Norman rising in the reign of duke Richard II, see Delisle, *Etudes*, pp. 120–5. According to the chronicle of Nantes, Alain Barbetorte, count of Brittany, sought to increase the population of Brittany, about 950, by means of freed serfs who had come from France. M. de la Borderie thinks that he abolished serfdom on all his domain (*Histoire de Bretagne*, ii, 415; iii, 100).

[59] The earls of Chester were hereditary viscounts in the Bessin. An interesting figure in Henry II's reign was the viscountess of Rouen, who seems to have had hereditary office in Rouen, before the citizens farmed the viscounty. See Delisle, *Introduction* to the *Recueil des Actes de Henri II*, pp. 214–16.

[60] The Conqueror seems to have regarded the local officials as removable, and also to have created new centres of jurisdiction (Haskins, *Norman Institutions*, p. 47 and note 208; Valin, p. 98).

[61] Ord. Vit., iv, 164. For this 'ignoble' family, see *Early Yorkshire Charters*, x (ed. C. T. Clay, 1955), 5ff.

[62] See Haskins, *op cit.*, pp. 151–2, for the word 'bailia'.

[63] Below, p. 62.

[64] Haskins, *op. cit.*, p. 99. Bishop John of Lisieux was at the head of the

E

has also been developed. The main lines of Angevin administration had been laid down before the death of Henry I.

III

The next period includes the rule of Geoffrey of Anjou, who seems to have made several important changes in Normandy, and the first part of the reign of Henry II. For the previous period the only authority of real value, apart from a few pages in the chronicle of Orderic Vitalis, is the evidence of charters. For the next period charters can be confirmed and explained by the important chronicle of Robert of Torigni, abbot of Mont St. Michel, and by the earliest custumal, which, though compiled in the last years of the century, consists largely in the statutes and the results of inquiries made by Henry I and his successors, of whom Henry II was, of course, supreme. Of Henry II's inquest in 1171 there survives a detailed statement of ducal and other rights in the Avranchin.[65] The very valuable list of knights' fees, drawn up in 1172, gives some idea of the important bailiwicks.[66]

The energy of Henry II has become proverbial. It received tiresome recognition from the endless stream of suppliants who would not leave him at peace, says a contemporary, during the mass nor give him time to say a paternoster.[67] He took up the work of his grandfather Henry I, and ruled England, Normandy, Anjou, and Poitou as easily and confidently as Geoffrey Martel had managed Anjou alone. It is doubtful if he introduced any Angevin practices in his other states, unless he introduced the practice of succession by parage; but the influence of Anjou cannot be set on one side. Angevin law, while enforcing succession by parage, had early laid stress on the rights of the eldest son. During Henry II's reign parage seems to have been systematised and defined, or at least recommended as the ordinary rule of succession in Normandy, and even in Brittany, except in the cases of the single barony, knights' fee, and military

exchequer in Henry I's reign, probably as chief justiciar; with Robert de la Haie, the seneschal, as the principal member of the court.

[65] This document is in Delisle's *Introduction* to the *Recueil des Actes de Henri II*, pp. 345–7. Haskins has proved that it belongs to the inquest of 1171: *Norman Institutions*, pp. 338–9.

[66] I have shown that the headings in the list, as given in the *Red Book of the Exchequer* (ii, 624–45), have become confused in transmission from the original roll (*English Historical Review*, xxvi, 89–93) but the list is none the less valuable, as testimony to the bailiwicks.

[67] Peter of Blois puts these words into Henry's mouth in one of his writings, a dialogue between the king and the abbot of Bonneval (Migne, *Patrologia Latina*, ccvii, 975 *seq.*).

serjeanty: in these cases Henry insisted upon primogeniture.[68] By these measures—for they were definite enactments [69]—Henry shaped the law of property in Normandy. The habits of Angevin administration probably had as much influence upon the king as the principles of Angevin law. In a previous chapter I have singled out the castle, the inquest, and the seneschal as the main instruments, personal and impersonal, of Angevin government. All these instruments were used by Henry I in Normandy; but it is perhaps not fanciful to see the influence of Angevin traditions in the extension which Henry II gave to their importance throughout his empire. Central government rested upon the power of the seneschal. Local government was developed on the general principle that a bailiff, who might or might not exercise the other functions of the older viscount or prévôt, administered a large area from a royal castle, and was endowed with judicial rather than financial powers. Finally, by means of the writ of recognition, the judicial system was developed, and judicial authority was gradually controlled by, even when not actually vested in, the duke and his officials.

Henry II was served by a series of great seneschals, Robert of Neufbourg, Richard of Ilchester, and William Fitz Ralf. At one time during his short reign in Normandy Stephen had delegated his powers to two justiciars; but it is only under the Angevin dukes that we find the whole administrative machinery in the control of the seneschal. The seneschal was inspector-general and chief justice in one person.[70] More intimately connected in Normandy with the barons of the exchequer than were his counterparts elsewhere, he was the president of the exchequer at Caen. As chief justice, he presided over the full court of the duke in important cases throughout Normandy.[71]

[68] See above, p. 44 and note.

[69] The words in the *Statuta et Consuetudines*, show that the rules about primogeniture were of this kind; 'et si escaetas nunquam habuerint et solum feodum lorice vel dimidium quod partitum fuerit ante hanc constitutionem', etc. (c. 8, Tardif, I, i, p. 9). The *assisa comitis Gaufredi*, original copies of which, sealed with the seals of Constance and Geoffrey, were distributed among the great barons of Brittany, is best edited by Planiol, *La très ancienne coutume de Bretagne, avec les assises, constitutions de Parlement, etc.* (*Bibliothèque Bretonne Armoricaine*, ii), Rennes, 1896, pp. 321-3. It is dated, Redon 1185, and is issued at the request (*petitio*) of the bishops and barons of Brittany, in order to prevent the great loss to the land (*detrimentum terrae plurimum*) which arose from partibility. See especially Guilhiermoz, pp. 214-20.

[70] See Orderic, v, 91; Valin, pp. 155-63. Mr. Vernon Harcourt, whose views as expounded in his book, *His Grace the Steward* (1907), are effectively criticised by M. Valin, lays stress (p. 35) on the influence of the practice of Anjou; but see Haskins, *Norman Institutions*, p. 124.

[71] The case between Engelger of Bohon and Ralph of Arden (April 7, 1199) was settled before Fitz Ralf at Vaudreuil, in the presence of some of the chief

William Fitz Ralf, during King Richard's absence, was literally at the head of the State, a legislator,[72] as well as an official. Papal legates and Count John found to their cost that they had to deal with a man who was responsible to the duke alone.[73] It is clear that John, when he became king, was uneasy and suspicious of such a powerful servant. William Fitz Ralf was succeeded by others who rapidly followed each other out of office.[74] Indeed, the responsibility entrusted to the seneschal at a time of crisis was immense. It was his duty, as the rolls of John's reign testify, to go about from castle to castle on a tour of inspection, to fix the number of the garrisons, and to order repairs.[75] In the course of a single year more than 7,300 li., Angevin money, passed through the hands of Guérin of Glapion, in order to be expended upon the fortifications of royal castles and in wages.[76] William Crassus, the last baron to hold the office under John, was placed in charge of several strongholds at once, and was left by the king as guardian of the duchy with a special grant of 500 li. per annum.[77]

Before the year 1172, when the list of Norman knights' fees was compiled, the Norman bailiwicks had been formed. They were part of a grand reconstruction of local government, which Henry took in hand after the civil wars. The chief measures were the recovery of ducal rights and property which had been lost or granted away,[78] and the erection of new or the seizure of old castles.[79] Some of these acquisitions were farmed as escheats rather than as viscounties. The county of Mortain and the honour of Montfort are cases in point.[80]

---

barons of Normandy (Stapleton, II, p. xxxv). The news of Richard's wound at Chaluz reached them during the trial (*Hist. de Guillaume le Maréchal*, iii, 158).

[72] *English Historical Review*, xxii, 20. For Fitz Ralf as a legislator, see *Statuta et consuetudines*, cc. lx–lxv (Tardif, I, i, 61–7), and Tardif's remarks, p. lxxv.

[73] Howden, iii, 203, 204, 254. Below, p. 95.

[74] Valin, pp. 102–3.

[75] *Rot. Norm.*, ed. Hardy, pp. 120–1.

[76] Receipts, March 1201 to March 1202 (*Rot. Scacc.*, ii, 501).

[77] *Rot. Norm.*, 118.

[78] Robert of Torigni (ed. Delisle), i, 284. Important inquiries were held in 1163 (i, 344), in 1171 (ii, 28), 1176 (Diceto, i, 415). They correspond to similar actions in England. In my opinion, also, an *iter* of inquiry was made in Normandy in 1194 along with the inquiry of Hubert Walter in England (*Rot. Scacc.*, i, 146, 167, 271).

[79] Below, pp. 181 ff.

[80] The *Dialogus de Scaccario* explains the difference between the treatment of an escheat and of the royal domain, Bk. ii, cc. 24, 27 (ed. Johnson, pp. 121, 123–4). Roger fitz Landri had the farm of the honour of Montfort in 1180 (*Rot. Scacc.*, i, 82). Mortain was not farmed as a whole, but the subordinate farms were paid direct into the exchequer (*Rot. Scacc.*, 8, 9), and Nigel fitz

But the greater number were treated as part of the ducal demesne. Hence it was easier for Henry, continuing a policy perhaps already begun by his grandfather, to reorganise the administrative divisions of Normandy.[81] The duchy was divided into bailiwicks which, while corresponding for the most part to the old areas took account of the new condition of things. At the same time reasons of state and changes in the law combined to make it desirable to distinguish these areas of local jurisdiction from the fiscal centres: the viscounties and *preposituræ* of old and new demesne were regarded as the units of financial organisation. When it is remembered that, during the previous two centuries the primitive demesne of the dukes had steadily decreased, it is easy to see why the old viscounties appear, for the most part, as survivals of secondary value in the exchequer rolls of 1180 and of later years, while the new fortresses built or acquired by Henry I and his successors have become the centres of flourishing *preposituræ*.

This distinction between the administrative and financial systems is not clear at first sight for several reasons. In the first place, the bailiffs were, as local justices and administrators, financial officials also. They accounted for the proceeds of fines, proffers, amercements and special receipts which were not included in the fixed farms.[82] In the second place, several of the bailiwicks continued the old viscounties and preserved the old titles; for example, the old viscounty of the Roumois or Romeis, in the Seine valley, was merged into the new system.[83] Thirdly, in many cases the head of the bailiwick was also the farmer of the demesne, or part of it; also, it is confusing to find that he was sometimes castellan and sometimes not. All these cases, however, are capable of a simple explanation of one kind or another. When Verneuil, a new foundation, became the centre of a bailiwick, it was natural to entrust it altogether to one servant of the king;[84] on the other hand, the castle of Alençon was the centre of an old and established jurisdiction which had but recently been added to the

---

Robert, the seneschal of Mortain, accounted for the 'auxilium vicecomitis', the proceeds of St. Hilaire, and the fines, etc. (pp. 9, 10).

[81] As pointed out above, p. 50, Geoffrey of Anjou may also have played a part.

[82] Alvered of St. Martin, the bailiff of the district of Bray, in which lay the castle of Drincourt and the honour of St. Saens, rendered account 'de censis novarum domorum de Drincourt qui sunt *extra firmam prepositurae*' (*Rot. Scacc.*, i, 57).

[83] This district, which is called 'baillia Wilhelmi de Malepalet' in 1172 (*Red Book of the Exchequer*, ii, 636) is called the viscounty of the Romeis (Roumois) in 1180 (*Rot. Scacc.*, i, 77). There are other instances.

[84] That Verneuil was a bailiwick is clear from a comparison of the roll of 1180 (*Rot. Scacc.*, i, 84) with that of 1198, where the fines, etc., are accounted for (ii, 312).

demesne; here therefore it was thought to be safer that the farmers should act as bailiffs, and that the castle should be placed in the hands of a man of high rank, Fulk Paynel, who was paid handsomely for his services.[85] But, in spite of these varieties of policy, and in spite also of the confusion in terminology, it is clear that the farmers were theoretically distinguished from the chief officer of the bailiwick, and that the latter was generally in charge of the castle at its centre. As will be seen, the tendency was to concentrate these important commands, which, unlike many of the older farmed offices, were tenable absolutely at the will of the duke, in the hands of a few trusted servants and companions. King John came to rely upon a very limited number of persons in his last years in Normandy.[86]

The last years of Henry II brought the final changes in the fiscal system of Normandy.[87] The connection between England and Normandy was exceedingly close in Henry's reign; and in 1176 the arrival of Richard of Ilchester, bishop of Winchester, as seneschal in Normandy was followed by a thorough examination and revision of Norman finances.[88] The bishop, who might be described as an experienced 'permanent official in the Treasury', did his work in a year and a half. It has been suggested that the exchequer as a judicial department dates from Richard's period of office, and that he introduced the system of keeping accounts and the exchequer roll into Normandy.[89] This is, I believe, erroneous; but there is sufficient evidence of his activity in other directions. The exchequer rolls are a striking parallel to the great Rolls of the Pipe kept by the English Exchequer; for example, there is the same distinction between those fines and amercements for which the bailiff is responsible personally, and those for which the persons concerned are responsible;[90] and it is possible that Richard of Ilchester reformed the Norman method of bookkeeping on English lines. Again, in the end of the century the word *vicecomes* returns in legal usage as the name of the normal local

[85] *Rot. Scacc.*, i, pp. 18 and following.

[86] *English Historical Review*, xxii, 30, and note.

[87] A change in the chancery is expressed by the adoption of the formula 'Henricus Dei gratia rex Anglorum' in 1172–3. H. Prentout attempts to associate the change with the revolt of the young king in 1173: *De l'origine de la formule 'Dei gratia'* (Caen, 1920).

[88] See Haskins, *Norman Institutions*, pp. 174 ff.

[89] Valin, p. 134. On M. Valin's view with regard to the court of exchequer below, see also below, p. 62, note 130. I also think it is impossible to believe that no rolls of the exchequer existed before 1176. There are references in the roll of 1180 to debts which had been accumulating through seven years. (*Rot. Scacc.*, p. 94) and even through twenty years (p. 12). Since all the rolls after that of 1180 perished except four, it is not difficult to assume the existence of rolls long before 1180, as in England.

[90] *Dialogus de Scaccario*, Bk. ii, c. xii (ed. Johnson, p. 105).

official. This is significant; for there is no change in the system of bailiwicks just described; it looks very much as though a common system has given the Norman bailiff a common name, and that the *vicecomes* of the early custumal,[91] is not, in the writer's mind, a Frankish viscount but an ordinary English sheriff, and his sphere of jurisdiction an ordinary English shire. At any rate it is curious that the custumal should speak of the 'viscounty' where the roll of 1172 speaks of the 'ballia'.[92] But the English administrator did not come to introduce English methods or terminology, and it would be rash to ascribe these changes to him. His work was to restore financial order after the great rebellion of 1173. The war between Henry and his sons had upset the whole state. There had been much redistribution of land, and many changes in the official world. There had also been much bargaining in claims and rights. Opportunity was taken to revise the farms of the bailiffs, and possibly to renew the extensive inquiries, by means of local juries, into the lapsed rights of the Crown.[93] Hence the frequent references in the rolls to lands recovered by jury, and to the roll of 1176 as a standard of reference.[94] Hence probably the change of officials implied by the almost universal distinction between the old farm and the new farm.[95]

I will take the bailiwick of Falaise as a typical and concrete case of the administrative system here described. The noble castle of Falaise might be expected to be the centre of a bailiwick, and it would necessarily be a *prepositura*. The bailiwick is apparently not of old standing, for it is called simply the 'ballia of Richard Giffart'

[91] *Statuta et consuetudines*, cc. xliv, lv (Tardif, I, i, 37, 44).

[92] *English Historical Review*, xxii, 22, 23, where I think I have made too much of these variations. John generally addresses his letters to bailiffs. A viscounty might be spoken of as a 'prepositura' if it really meant a farm, *e.g.*, the viscounty of the Avranchin appears as a 'prepositura' in the exchequer rolls (I, 40; ττ, 537) probably because the castle, etc., was not farmed and did not form a 'prepositura' by itself, as Falaise, Vire, Alençon did. (See the interesting inquiry in Delisle's *Introduction* to the *Actes de Henri II*, p. 345.) Delisle has given a list of the various titles and addresses used by Henry II in referring to his ministers, pp. 209, 221. See also R. L. Poole, *The Exchequer in the Twelfth Century* (Oxford, 1912), pp. 57–69, on the Norman and English Exchequers.

[93] Diceto, i, 415.

[94] Geoffrey Trossebot 'habet in munitione castri de Bonnavilla, blada viva et bacones et caseos et moretum, sicut continetur in Rotulo anni mclxxvi' (p. 69). The entry is repeated in 1198 (p. 370). The accounts of Dieppe are settled in 1180 for the past five years (p. 66). See *English Historical Review*, xxii, 23, 24. I think M. Valin is in error in regarding the roll of 1176 as a starting point (Valin, p. 134). See above, p. 54.

[95] Benedict of Peterborough states that there was a change of officials in Normandy and elsewhere in 1178 (i, 198). For the meaning of the phrases 'vetus firma' and 'nova firma', see *Dialogus de Scaccario*, Bk. ii, c. 9 (ed. Johnson, p. 92).

in the roll of 1180, though it appears as the 'ballia Falesie' in the roll of knights' fees in 1172.[96] In 1180 Richard Giffart was the castellan, and Odo, the son of Vitalis, farmed the *prepositura*. About the time of the loss of Normandy King Philip Augustus ordered an inquiry into the value of the revenue from Falaise as it was on the day in which King Richard crossed the sea on crusade. The jurors testified that the *prepositura* was farmed for 540 li.; and they made a very neat summary of the receipts which were not included in this sum. These were the proceeds of the pleas of the sword, the escheats, the viscounty and the corn rents known as bernage.[97] The viscounty was the relic of the old jurisdiction of the Oximin, which had been so important in the time of the Montgomeries, but was now only represented by a farm of 100 li.[98] The bernage of the Oximin was also accounted for separately on the rolls,[99] and for the remaining exceptions to the farm of the *prepositura*, the proceeds of the pleas of the sword and the escheats, the bailiff was responsible. On the roll of 1198 the bailiwick and *prepositura* are distinguished from each other still more carefully, for after the death of Henry II the *prepositura* was granted to the old Queen Eleanor, with the exception of certain local payments, amounting to 90 li. 4s.[100] Consequently on the roll of 1198 we find the accounts of the *prepositura* separated from those of the bailiwick of Falaise, and added as a kind of postscript on the membrane of the roll.[101] The bailiff in this year, Robert Reinnard, was kept very busy by the levying of tallages, the management of escheats, the collection of bernage and of fines, proffers and amercements of various kinds.[102] The farm of the old viscounty was still accounted for by other officers, but was sadly in arrears, and evidently could only be collected with difficulty.[103]

[96] *Rot. Scacc.*, i, 41; *Red Book*, ii, 641.

[97] *Cart. Norm.*, p. 19, no. 111. An inquest of c. 1205 (*Cart. Norm.*, p. 22, no. 120) on Evreaux and Gaillon, gives the contents of a typical farm: 'molendina, terre arabiles, census, placita de quibus bellum non poterat evenire', etc.

[98] *Rot. Scacc.*, i, 106, where it is also stated that Robert 'de Capella' had paid 20 li. for the right to farm it. See Stapleton, *Observations*, I, lxxi *seq.*, lxxviii, cxxxiii.

[99] *Rot. Scacc.*, i, 49.

[100] *Cart. Norm.*, p. 19, no. 111. The exemptions to the grant are identical in this inquiry and in the account for 1198 (*Rot. Scacc.*, ii, 414). For Richard's charter, granting the reversion to Berengaria, May 12, 1191, see Stapleton, *Observations*, II, cix, note.

[101] *Rot. Scacc.*, ii, 414. This does not imply that Eleanor had the castle in her possession; that went with the bailiwick; she had the farmed revenues only. In January, 1203, King John granted the castle and bailiwick of Falaise to John Marshal (*Rot. Pat.*, 24).

[102] *Rot. Scacc.*, ii, 397.

[103] *Ibid.*, ii, 404.

The roll of 1198, when compared with that of 1180, brings out another point of interest. The old county of the Oximin had extended from the sea, in the diocese of Bayeux, to the southern borders of Normandy beyond Argentan. This unwieldy area, cut up as it was by lay and ecclesiastical franchises, had been divided; but most of it seems to have been farmed by Robert of Bellême and his predecessors before 1112. As has been said, the relic of this jurisdiction, the viscounty of the Oximin, was accounted for in the rolls under or near the account of the bailiwick of Falaise, which represented the chief centre of the old viscounty. The other jurisdictions split off from the Oximin were the bailiwicks of Exmes (Oximis), known generally as a viscounty, and of Argentan. In the year 1180, the northern part of the old county in the diocese of Bayeux had been attached with the exception of the upper portion to the bailiwick of the Auge; but in 1195 and 1198 it appears independently as a separate bailiwick, with the confusing title 'ballia de Oximino'. Hence in 1198 we have, in the old county of the Oximin, the new bailiwick of the Oximin in the north-east, the bailiwicks of Falaise and Argentan, the old viscounty of the Oximin (now unimportant), the bailiwick of Exmes, which is attached to the viscounty and prepositura of Exmes, the viscounty of Argentan with the prepositura; and the prepositura of Falaise, Queen Eleanor's dower. There could be no better example of the development of Norman administration, a development simple enough in its main principle, but most hopelessly confusing if attention is paid to its terminology alone.[104]

Our account of this subject would be incomplete without a reference to the Norman forests.[105] These great stretches of silence are still the chief glory of Normandy; and when we recollect that the hand of man has been more or less fitfully engaged upon their destruction since the establishment of the great abbeys of the eleventh and twelfth centuries, it is not difficult to realise how important a part they took in mediæval administration. No strict boundaries were needed when the huge forest of Gouffern separated Argentan from Falaise, or the vast woodlands of the Seine valley cut off the river from the uplands of Caux. Until the end of the fourteenth century no special department

---

[104] For the new bailiwick of the Oximin, see Stapleton, *Observations*, I, clxvii; II, cvii; and *Rot. Scacc.*, i, 240, 246, where the title is given, and ii, pp. 409–14. Stapleton makes his description needlessly confusing by referring to the bailiwick of Falaise as the bailiwick of the Oximin (I, clxxii). The new bailiwick excluded the district known as Cinglais, which was part of the bailiwick of Falaise (I, cxxviii, clxiii).

[105] Delisle, *Etudes sur la condition de la classe agricole et de l'état de l'agriculture en Normandie*, pp. 344–417. For later work on the jurisdiction of the forests, especially the writings of Petit-Duteillis., see Haskins, *Norman Institutions*, pp. 47–8, and note 216.

controlled the forests,[106] though at times, as in 1180, several of
them were entrusted to the charge of a single officer.[107] They were
farmed, and administered independently, sometimes by the local
bailiff, who also held inquiries into encroachments and accounted
for the proceeds of the 'reguard' or forest pleas. In this respect the
Norman forests were managed like the English forests, except that
the 'farm' was replaced in England by a more fluctuating 'census'.[108]
The value of the forests to the Norman dukes is evident on nearly
every page of the exchequer rolls. Some of them were in private
hands,[109] but for the most part they were in the demesne. Occasionally new settlements were established within them, which provided
new sources of revenue. Thus, in the forest which encircles Lillebonne
new vills had grown up in Henry II's time which brought in 292 li. in
one year to the exchequer. They are still traceable by their names.[110]

IV

The administration of justice alone remains to be considered.

In the middle of the twelfth century, and even later, the Frankish
county was still referred to in legal speech as the centre of 'public
justice'.[111] As a rule, however, the bailiwick, or as the custumal calls
it, the viscounty, was the unit in the reigns of Henry II and his
sons.[112] The bailiff or viscount of this period had lost the right to hold
pleas of the sword unless he sat with the itinerant justices of assize,
but his jurisdiction in petty cases linked him with the great officials

[106] Delisle, p. 336.
[107] See the accounts of William de Mara in 1180 (*Rot. Scacc.*, i, 99, 100).
[108] A detailed comparison of the English and Norman forests in the twelfth
century is worth making. For the 'census', see *Dialogus de Scaccario*, Bk. i,
c. 5, and Bk. ii, c. 11 (ed. Johnson, pp. 30–1, 103–4) and the Pipe Rolls.
[109] Compare this entry: 'Nigellus de Moubraio reddit compotum de xxv.
li. de m. quercubus quas Willhelmus filius Johannis *emit ad edificia Regis*
de Buro' (*Rot. Scacc.*, i, 30).
[101] *Rot. Scacc.*, i, 89, and Stapleton's *Observations* in same volume, p. cxxii.
[111] For the phrase *publica justitia*, see a charter of the abbot of Fécamp
(1028–78) quoted by Haskins, *Norman Institutions*, p. 29, note 109, where
the abbot retains it. Here it obviously refers to the ducal *consuetudines*, i.e.,
to the rights of ducal justice granted to the abbey. Compare the references
to the *fora patrie* in the custumal (Tardif, I, i, p. 32). In an assize at Caen,
early in Henry II's reign, 'diffinitum est in plenaria curia regis utpote in
assisa, ubi erant barones quatuor comitatum Baiocassini, Constantini,
Oximini, Abrincatini'. (See the 'Appendix ad Scaccarium Normanniae',
attached by M. Lechaudé d'Anisy to his edition of the Norman rolls, in *Mém.
de la Soc. des Antiquaires de Normandie*, xv, 197; Robert of Torigni, ii, 251.)
Rot. Chart., ed. Hardy, 59b. 'quamdiu fuerit justiciarius itinerans in ballia
de Costentino et Baiocassino.'
[112] *Statuta et consuetudines*, c. iv (Tardif, p. 44).

of the past, who, as we have seen, had often taken their titles from the county.[113] There was therefore an unbroken tradition in the administration of public justice. For example, although the earl of Chester, who inherited the right to farm the old viscounty of the Bessin, had no official duties in the Bessin, these were still sustained, in 1180, by the important bailiff, Hamo the Cupbearer.[114]

This continuity of public or ducal justice has been disputed by one recent writer in his reaction against the erroneous views of Brussel that the duke of the Normans preserved from the first the monopoly of all but strictly feudal justice. In the view of this writer the great franchises held their rights in virtue of the Norman settlement; Rollo and his immediate successors made no grant of jurisdiction. The dukes of Normandy only secured the control of important pleas—the pleas of the sword—very slowly and never universally.[115] In other words, the early dukes were not sovereigns within their *regnum*,[116] but only feudal lords. In the previous pages I have urged that the dukes secured their control by means of their peculiar insistence upon feudal rights, rather than upon their judicial authority, and to this extent I have expressed agreement with the view here described. We saw how by the regulation of services and the control of castles, and by the high farming of the demesne, the dukes built up a power which the great lay and ecclesiastical lords, in spite of their extensive franchises, were powerless to resist.[117] But, although I believe this to be the true interpretation of early Norman history, it seems to me impossible to believe that the dukes were able to achieve all this simply in virtue of their feudal lordship. Their position implied an element of sovereignty. Probably in no case is it possible to separate the popular from the feudal position of the lord in any early state which possessed stability; certainly it is impossible in the case of Normandy, where a band of alien warriors evolved order out of the chaos they had made. Now sovereignty implies that the sovereign is ultimately the source of justice; and the scanty evidence goes to

[113] Above, p. 37; cf. Boussard, p. 335.

[114] *Rot. Scacc.*, p. 1. Hamo styled himself 'Pincerna Regis Anglie et Senescallus Baiocarum' (Stapleton, *Observations*, I, lix). As Henry II's charters show, *senescallus* was frequently used in this general sense. In this case, it means that Hamo, as bailiff, had his seat at Bayeux. Stapleton identifies *senescallus* with *prepositus*, but whether this be right or not, Hamo did not farm the *prepositura*.

[115] Valin, *Le Duc de Normandie et sa Cour*, p. 182. For a similar view, see Pissard, *La Clameur de Haro* (Caen, 1911). See the criticism in Haskins, *Norman Institutions*, pp. 27–30.

[116] In a charter of Dreux, count of the Vexin, confirmed by Philip I of France, the words appear: Constat hec facta donatio tempore Roberti regis Francorum *Ricardo comite viriliter regnum gubernante Normannorum*. (Prou, *Recueil des Actes de Philippe I*, 406, no. 163.)   [117] Above, p. 39.

show that, in spite of the extensive exceptions to the judicial authority of the duke throughout Normandy, the duke was from the first the source of justice, and regarded these great exceptions or franchises as the result of ducal grant, whether explicit, or, as in the case of original settlements, implied.

The direct evidence that the duke was the source of justice and stood in the place of the Frankish rulers is, it must be confessed, scanty, until the middle of the eleventh century. But this conclusion seems to follow from the facts that the viscounts so often took the titles of the old counties, that they collected a tax from other lands than the ducal demesne,[118] and appear in the reign of the Conqueror not simply as the judges in the local courts, but also as the judicial official to whom appeals can be made in certain cases against the inaction of local lords.[119] The whole tenor of the early history of Normandy implies that the ducal officials were expected to keep the peace, and were not rigidly limited to judicial functions on the ducal estates. In the same way, when documents begin to be available, the duke's court appears as a compulsory court of justice in cases of disputes between tenants in chief.[120] On the other hand, the local courts lacked the continuity and popular character of the shire and hundred courts in England. The continuity of public justice in Normandy, if it really existed, must be sought in the maintenance by the duke of his authority in special cases, or pleas of the sword. In a country so full of franchises, the reservation of these pleas was necessary to the duke's judicial supremacy, and it is only by an examination of their history that we can discover whether they constituted 'public justice' from the outset, or were the result of other forces.

It is significant that the counts, who had a plenitude of justice if any vassals of the duke had, were for some time removable officials, and members of the ducal family. This would hardly have been the case if the chief Norman settlers had been regarded as judicially independent from the time of settlement. Again, many of the Norman monasteries were of Frankish origin, and we find that the Norman

[118] The *graveria*, or as it is called in the twelfth century, the *auxilium vicecomitis*, seems to have been a tax of this nature.

[119] *e.g.*, in the statutes of Lillebonne (1080) the judicial functions of the early viscounts are very important, see Haskins, *Norman Institutions*, pp. 46–7. An excellent instance later is the right to abjure a feudal court if an award of boundaries cannot be obtained (Tardif, I, i, 89; cf. Glanvill lib., 9, c. 14). In 1207 the Norman exchequer instituted an inquiry 'utrum comes Robertus (of Alençon) est vicecomes de terra sua, et utrum vicecomes unquam fecit divisam in curia nisi prius curia [comitis] fuerit fors jurata' (Delisle, *Jugements*, no. 25).

[120] Haskins, *op. cit.*, pp. 55–6. By agreement, reference could be made to the ducal court early in the dispute.

dukes, in re-establishing them, renewed their immunities. These immunities, whatever their effect in establishing private jurisdictions, did not create exemption from the authority of the count.[121] They are described in various ways: they are ducal *consuetudines*, rights of public justice, royal liberties, and so on. Later they appear as pleas of the sword. The first list of these pleas, confessedly incomplete, comes from the inquiry of 1091, but the charters of Bec and other monasteries show that they were regarded as 'prerogative' pleas of the duke long before this.[122] It is true that the monasteries who possessed them were on the ducal demesne, but the way in which they are described, the fact that even bishops had to prove a prescriptive right to them,[123] goes far to justify the view of later witnesses in the twelfth century that those barons who possessed them owed their privilege to ducal grant or acquiescence.[124]

In spite, then, of the poverty of direct evidence,[125] the conclusion seems to be justified that from the first the duke was sovereign. Normandy was composed of innumerable jurisdictions—every landholder, from the vavassor to the baron,[126] could hold his court for his

[121] Haskins, *op. cit.*, pp. 29–30.

[122] *Ibid.*

[123] For Bayeux, see the *Livre Noir* (Soc. de l'hist. de Normandie), i, 23; and for Lisieux, Martène, *Thesaurus*, i, 761; and *Rot. Chart.*, p. 19; also Valin, p. 228.

[124] The jurors who reported upon ducal rights in Henry II's time (*Statuta et consuetudines*, c. lxx: Tardif, p. 64) said that the plea of homicide, whether *murdrum* or not, belonged to the duke alone, 'aut quibus antecessores ejus, vel ipse, illud dederunt'. Note that, if Tardif's reading be accepted, the author definitely attributes 'murdrum' to a Danish origin—' "homicidium", sive clam factum fuerit, quod lingua Dacorum murdrum dicitur, sive palam'. This should be compared with the evidence of the Anglo-Norman lawyers (see the note in the Oxford edition of the *Dialogus*, 1902, pp. 193–4).

[125] M. Valin brushes this evidence on one side for reasons which seem to me to be too juristic. Of these, the chief are that peace was really maintained by the Truce of God rather than by the duke and that the pleas of the sword grew from crimes committed in protected places into crimes of a general nature, *e.g.*, assault in a house to homicide generally (*Le Duc de Normandie et sa Cour*, pp. 188–91). M. Valin thinks that, since assaults in protected places, when they resulted in death, were not punished more severely than murder generally, the former must have preceded the latter as a plea of the sword. This argument is too abstract. The point surely is that any assault in a protected place, whether it led to death or not was a plea of the sword, whereas in other places it might not have been. On the other hand, it is certainly probable that in Normandy, as apparently in England before the Conquest, crimes committed in the places protected by the duke's peace were very rarely granted away, whereas the jurisdiction over general crimes was (see Pollock and Maitland, *History of English Law*, second ed., ii, 455–6). On England, cf. Helen Cam, 'The evolution of the mediæval English Franchise', in *Speculum*, xxxii (1957), 427 ff.

[126] *Statuta et consuetudines*, c. xli (Tardif, I, i, p. 34).

tenants, where the duel could be fought, and where in later days trial
by jury might be made by agreement; [127] and of these courts, some,
perhaps many, had judicial rights more than feudal, extending to
cases of life and limb;—but from the first these extraordinary non-
feudal rights of justice were regarded as originally vested in the duke.
The duke or his officials dealt with them unless they belonged by
special grant or in virtue of long prescription to the lord. And
in consequence, just as the duke was sovereign as well as feudal
suzerain, the local officers were public magistrates as well as administrators of the ducal demesne.

On this basis judicial administration developed swiftly from the
time of the Conqueror onwards.

In the first place, the machinery became more elaborate. At an
early date the viscount shared the administration of justice with a
body of judges. It is not easy to fix a precise date for their appearance
since the viscount is frequently described as a justice himself in
early Norman documents, and references to the *justicia* may really
allude to him. [128] But their existence is clear in the first years of the
twelfth century. Some of these judges were local officials, others
served the duke throughout the duchy. [129] Before the death of Henry I
some of them formed a body apart from the rest, at the head of the
profession. These select persons could form a 'full court' under the
presidency first of a chief justiciar, afterwards, in Angevin times, of
the seneschal. This interesting parallel to the English 'curia regis',
in its narrower sense, became the Court of Exchequer, at which civil
suits of various kinds, but chiefly cases dealing with property, could
be tried in addition to pleas of a financial character. [130] Its business
comprised the work of the English chancery, [131] so far as this did not
follow the king, of the later English court of common pleas, and of
the English exchequer. It issued writs and was a court of record.
Its members, the barons of the exchequer, formed a limited body of
professional men, who heard appeals, registered settlements, and
before the end of our period had begun to affect the customs of
Normandy by their decisions, which became a kind of case-law, just

[127] *Statuta et consuetudines*, c. liv (Tardif, I, i, p. 44).

[128] Haskins, *Norman Institutions*, pp. 99–100, 103. For the *justicia* in
England, see Davis, *England under the Normans and Angevins*, p. 523.

[129] The chief evidence is afforded by the documents in the *Livre Noir
de Bayeux*, and the Montebourg charters, published by Haskins, *op. cit.*,
pp. 101–3.

[130] Cf. Haskins, *op. cit.*, pp. 88 ff. Valin's views, which I discussed in the
first edition of this book (p. 85, note 3), are here definitely refuted by Haskins;
see especially, note 18.

[131] Haskins, *op. cit.*, p. 97. Even at the end of the century the English
chancery issued writs very sparingly in the king's absence.

as the duke affected them by the addition of his statutes.[132] By this time there was no doubt of the competence of the seneschal and justices to decide matters of all kinds, even the procedure of baronial courts.[133] Moreover, in Normandy, as later in England, the formation of a fixed tribunal at Caen was followed by the development of new procedure of which the duke had a complete monopoly. Ducal control of civil and criminal jurisdiction grew rapidly as the jury of presentment and the well-known recognitions of novel disseisin, mort d'ancestor, etc., were created as instruments of inquiry. Henry I, as the records of Bayeux show, had ordered sworn inquests to be made in certain cases,[134] and had gone a step further than his father the Conqueror; but the close connection between the central and local courts, by means of the possessory assizes, with the consequent interference in the feudal courts, seems to have been due to the policy of the Angevin Duke Geoffrey, the father of Henry II.[135] At any rate, most of the great reforms associated with the name of Henry II can be traced in Normandy before they appear in England. A system of itinerary courts was necessary to put these reforms into practice; and before the end of the century the pleas of the sword, swollen, as a result of Henry's rigorous inquisitions, in importance as well as in number, were also tried by the itinerant justices. As the judges moved from bailiwick to bailiwick, all feudal courts ceased to sit, and the knights and barons of the district gathered at the place of session.[136] Quite apart from the juries of recognition, juries of knights, whose number varied with the size of the bailiwick, were appointed to assess the chattels of those who had fallen in the mercy

[132] The custumal, c. lvii, lxi (Tardif, I, i, p. 52), gives cases of pleadings or decisions which modified existing law. The seneschal and the justices on assize of course shared in this process. The judgments of the exchequer in the reign of Philip Augustus show it more clearly.

[133] *e.g.*, in an assize at Domfront before Arnulf of Lisieux and Robert of Neubourg it was decided that all tenants-in-chief in Normandy were able if they wished to summon all trials by battle to their *mansio capitalis* (Robert of Torigni, ed. Delisle, ii, 241). All pleas involving the duel were summoned from Gaillon to Evreux, accordingly (*Cart. Norm.*, no. 120, p. 22). Below, p. 198.

[134] For the reign of Henry I, see Haskins, *Norman Institutions*, chapter vi.

[135] For this and what follows, see, besides the chapter referred to in the last note, Valin, pp. 194–219; *English Historical Review*, xxii, 15–21; Delisle, *Introduction* to the *Recueil des Acts de Henri II*, pp. 137–8. Haskins is careful to insist that the jury, though used much by Geoffrey of Anjou, was 'obviously a Norman, not an Angevin institution'; see his *Norman Institutions*, pp. 149–50. The custumal explains the possessory assizes admirably. Bigelow, *History of Procedure in England*, pp. 4, 5, notes some differences in Norman procedure. On the criminal jury of presentment, see c. lv (Tardif, p. 44).

[136] *Statuta et consuetudines*, c. xliv (Tardif, I, i, p. 37).

of the duke.[137] Only special grant could exempt the local gentry from attendance; no privilege could exempt even a count or baron from the jurisdiction of the court.[138]

The exchequer rolls, our only witness to this busy life before the reign of John, testify to the energy with which the judicial work was done. The variety of the fines and amercements show that it was not done easily, and the custumal reveals another difficulty which was due to the complexity of the system itself. (The rapid increase in the number of officials provoked some remonstrance in the twelfth century.[139]) Henry II, Richard and John in turn ordered inquiries to be made into the debts or exactions of their bailiffs,[140] and, according to the custumal, one of the chief functions of the itinerant justices was to supervise the conduct of the viscounts or bailiffs and to see that they had done justice to the poor.[141] The bailiffs had to prepare the business of the assizes, to seek out pleas of the sword in those lordships which did not possess the right to hold them,[142] and to account for the proceeds, unless a special official had been appointed to keep the pleas.[143]

The farmers of the demesne also, who often paid large sums for

[137] *Statuta et consuetudines*, c. lvi (Tardif, I, i, 45). A charter of John for William of Briouze (*Rot. Norm.*, p. 20) shows that the bailiff, like the English sheriff, had right of entrance into those fiefs—some of which were very important—which did not possess the pleas of the crown (cf. Maitland, *Select Pleas in Manorial Courts*, vol. i, p. xxv). The charter also proves that pleas of the crown were tried by the itinerant justices in John's reign. I have quoted it in *English Historical Review*, xxii, 19. I think it very probable that Henry II experimented in Normandy as in England, and that for some time the assizes dealt with the statutory possessory actions only, while the bailiffs continued to hold pleas of the sword. According to a writ quoted by M. Valin (p. 227 n.) sent from Henry II to the viscount of the Oximin (not, I suggest, of Exmes) the land of Robert Marmion is to remain quit of the pleas which belong to the viscount, 'salvis placitis meis de gladio que spectant ad baillivos meos de Falesia'. The pleas of the viscount would at this time (after 1173) be trivial. See above, p. 62.

[138] *Statuta et consuetudines*, c. lvi (Tardif, I, i, 45).

[139] Peter of Blois, *Epistolae*, ed. Giles, i, 297–8.

[140] For Richard, see exchequer roll of 1195 (*Rot. Scacc.*, i, 146. 'Johannes de Pratellis reddit compotum de dc. li. xviii li. xii. d. de jurea facta super eum per omnes Ballias Normannie'). For John, the letters against the 'tolta et molestias' of the bailiffs (November 23, 1201. *Rot. Pat.*, p. 3).

[141] *Statuta et consuetudines*, c. lv (Tardif, I, i, 44).

[142] Above, note 138.

[143] In 1171 a local official kept the pleas of the sword in the Avranchin 'Galfridus Peile vilain feodum suum, qui est inde dominicus serviens regis ad custodienda placita regis'. Delisle, *Introduction* to *Actes de Henri II*, p. 346. See *English Historical Review*, xxv, 710; for the date see Haskins, *ibid.*, xxvi (1911), 326–8. This is apparently like a serjeanty like those of Sewale fitz Henry and Philip of Ulcot in Northumberland (*Red Book*, ii, 466, 564).

the privilege of office,[144] did not escape frequent inquiry. Moreover, the seneschal, upon whom the responsibility of inspection mainly fell, could not always rely upon the judicial officers themselves. William Fitz Ralf, the great seneschal who governed Normandy from 1180 on to the death of Richard, became especially well known as a disciplinarian. A man of the same stamp as that active English judge, Martin Pateshull, he swept away many abuses. The author of the custumal refers particularly to the manner in which technicalities in pleading could be used to entrap simple or ignorant people;[145] one of which illustrates remarkably well the cruel and pedantic buffoonery of a half-civilised man of law. The pleaders,[146] he says, used to declare simple folk in mercy because when they came to take the oath, they used to kneel down without the consent of the judge; and then, when as they knelt they heard themselves accused of kneeling, they would rise, whereupon the pleaders would accuse them of rising without the consent of the judge; and so the clerk would write them down as in mercy on his parchment. Norman d'Orgierville referred to this when he said that he had lived long enough to see 'Silly Bernard' played in the court of the lord king; as the boys play, who say 'rise, Bernard', and then, if he does not rise, prick his face. Indeed this is exactly what the clerk does when he writes on his parchment: he unjustly pricks in the names of these simple people as being in mercy. The seneschal, to put an end to this, ordered the pleaders who gave such unjust judgment to be kept in prison until they had handed over their chattels to the very last farthing, that henceforward they might be of no credit (*infideles*) with their neighbours.

The statutory recognitions, to which the extension of judicial machinery was largely owing, illustrate the formative character of Norman law. As presented by the earliest law book, the *Statuta et consuetudines*, Norman law was a body of custom modified and enlarged by statute. The instance just given shows that in order to check the rapacity of officials further interpretation was sometimes necessary in the interests of equity. The circumstances of war or accident might also make changes desirable: for example, in King

---

[144] In 1203 King John made a characteristic bargain. The king owed money to William des Preaux. He gave him the viscounty of the Lieuvin at a farm twice the sum of the old farm, and this was to go to William until the debt was paid. The unfortunate people whose lands were subject to the rents and pleas of the viscounty had to pay double in order to get rid of John's debts, and the creditor was also the collector (*Rot. Norm.*, pp. 89, 116). It is also worth noticing that the farmer of the viscounty was also generally the bailiff of the Lieuvin.

[145] *Statuta et consuetudines*, cc. lxii, lxiii, lxv (Tardif, I, i, pp. 53–7).

[146] *Ibid.*, lxv (Tardif, I, i, pp. 56, 57). The 'placitatores' here seem to be legal assessors.

F

Richard's reign, the rights of daughters were set aside, owing to the war, in favour of the sons of a brother.[147] Again, the justices had occasion to adapt the law to meet new problems.[148] The result of these changes was that stress was laid upon the idea of the state rather than upon the principles of feudalism. Although, as we have seen, Norman society was essentially feudal, and in many respects Norman law was more logical than English in its interpretation of feudalism, the general result must have seemed very much the same in both countries before they separated. In spite of the great advantages which the Norman and Angevin rulers had in England, where the system of local courts hindered the formation of hard and fast franchises from the outset, Normandy was ahead of England in judicial reform. From a very early date, for example, the Norman dukes had refused to respect persons in their management of the ducal forests. All men, clerk and lay, were equally liable to incur the penalty of breaking the forest law;[149] moreover, the necessity of attending the 'reguard' must have prepared all men, however great they might be, for attendance at the assizes.[150] Another incentive to the rapid development of state law in Normandy may be found in the influence of the Church. It is clear that the relation between Church and State, and the problems arising out of conflicting jurisdictions, had caused much thought. The necessity of dealing with such matters encouraged a self-conscious attitude towards the customs of the country. The clergy were on the whole well educated and far from provincial in their outlook; and the early study of canon law in Normandy is reflected in the pages of the custumal, not merely in its treatment of the recognitions but also in its logical and comprehensive structure and in its phraseology.[151]

Apart, therefore, from the solidarity of the people, circumstances

[147] *Statuta et consuetudines*, c. xii (Tardif, I, i, p. 13).

[148] The following is a case in point. In 1195 certain persons paid 'xx li. pro habendo judicio utrum avunculus eorum potuit totam hereditatem suam dare in religionem' (*Rot. Scacc.*, i, 183, a. 1195). This question is decided generally in the custumal, c. lxxxix (Tardif, I, i, p. 99) *de donationibus elemosine*; cf. the next chapter 'quod homo potest vendere totum tenementum'.

[149] Haskins, *Norman Institutions*, p. 48, for the reign of the Conqueror. G. J. Turner has shown (*Select Pleas of the Forest*, p. lxxxviii) that less success attended Henry II's attempt to make the clergy liable in England.

[150] Cf. this entry on the exchequer roll for 1180 (*Rot. Scacc.*, i, 59). 'Hugo de Gornaio debet c. li. quia non venit ad summonitionem Justicie ad reguardam foreste.'

[151] See Tardif's introduction to the *Statuta et consuetudines* (*Coutumiers de Normandie*, I, i, p. lxxxiv). The last chapters of this custumal, forming the second part, were compiled in the early thirteenth century. They show traces of the direct influence of the civil law (pp. lxxii, lxxxv). Viollet added some important suggestions upon the date and method of redaction of the two parts in the *Histoire littéraire de la France*, xxxiii, 47, 58–64.

in Normandy were favourable to the extension of ducal power in the interests of the state. The Angevin dukes brought new energy and experience. As though to compensate for the loss of so much of the ducal demesne, they guarded jealously and increased their judicial prerogatives. Henry and his bureaucrats were willing to sell ducal rights at a high price,[152] for by doing so they forced the confession that these were theirs to sell. They maintained the undoubted rights of others, because they realised that these kept the state together.[153] The early dukes had protected life, the home, the plough, the army, the Church. Then the roads and merchandise came under their care. Henry II protected possession. Wreckage and treasure trove, which belonged to no one, and the great fish of the sea, which no humble fisherman could claim, came under the duke's control.[154] As possession was protected, private war gradually ceased. The wager by battle fell into disrepute, with laymen as with clerks, when they had learned to put themselves upon the duke's assize,[155] just as scholars began to contrast the barbarian idea of wreckage with the superior doctrines of the code.[156] The dukes had restrained the baronage by taking away their castles; they sapped their judicial independence by taking away their business. Many men, it is true, had castles, and many held pleas of the sword, but both were held by licence, and availed little; for there were some pleas, and these the most seductive, which no man was allowed to have, just as no man was long allowed to hold so great a fortress as Alençon.

[152] The lord had the right of wardship. Here is a case of selling the right to a mother. 'Clementia quae fuit uxor Roberti Monteforti reddit compotum de d. li. de *remanente* finis sui pro custodia terre puerorum suorum' (*Rot. Scacc.*, i, 40).

[153] Cf. an English example of August 23, 1199, from *Rot. Chart.*, 11b. 'Memorandum quod Robertus Mauclericus debet impetrare assensum abbatis Sancti Albani de custodia terre Rogeri de Crokelay antequam utatur litteris domini Regis.'

[154] The history and growth of the pleas of the sword from the early part of the eleventh century may be traced in the following documents: (a) The early charters granting ducal pleas and customs, which are discussed by Haskins, *Norman Institutions*, pp. 25–30; (b) The *Consuetudines et Justicie*, in inquest of 1091, edited with a commentary, *op. cit.*, pp. 277–84; (c) The charters of Henry I in the *Black Book of Bayeux*, and in Haskins, *op. cit.*, p. 90; (d) The inquest into royal customs made by Henry II, preserved in the second part of the custumal, cc. lxvi–lxx (Tardif, I, i, pp. 59–65); (e) The custumal generally, especially the first part, for the state of things at the end of the twelfth century.

[155] The duel, which was about this time condemned by the ecclesiastical councils in favour of the jury, occurs less frequently in the exchequer rolls after 1180. See Canel on the judicial duel in *Mém. de la Soc. des Antiq.*, xxvii, 575, 616 seq. The use of the voluntary jury in feudal courts would work in the same direction. All duels had to be recorded in the duke's court (*Statuta et consuetudines*, c. xxix, Tardif, p. 26).

[156] Giraldus Cambrensis, *Opera* (Rolls Series), viii, 118.

NOTE TO CHAPTER III

THE NORMAN BAILIWICKS

In his early essay in the *Bibliothèque de l'Ecole des Chartes* (x, 260–2), M. Delisle gave a list of the Norman bailiwicks, but unfortunately it does not distinguish between new, old and temporary bailiwicks. In his later introduction to his *Recueil des Actes de Henri II* (pp. 212–13) he gave a valuable list of the viscounties only. M. Valin's list in his *Le Duc de Normandie et sa Cour* (p. 289) is also misleading and rather defective. I give here, with a few explanatory notes, the various bailiwicks, viscounties and farmed 'prepositurae' for 1180, so arranged as to elucidate the description in the text of the last chapter. In each bailiwick the list gives the castle and states whether the bailiff who was responsible for the proceeds of jurisdiction and administration generally was castellan, as the usual practice was, or not. The names in italics are the viscounties or 'prepositurae', most of which were of great age, within the bailiwick. Most of the great viscounties of the eleventh century are to be found in italics, since they had lost their judicial and administrative powers; but some, as in the Roumois and the Lieuvin, were definitely merged in the new system as bailiwicks. The arrangement is geographical, from east to west, and the references are to the *Rotuli Scaccarii*, vol. i. A list of *bailliages*, etc., in the mid-thirteenth century, given by J. R. Strayer, *The Administration of Normandy under Saint Louis* (1932) pp. 7–9, illustrates later development under the French kings.

CAUX. The name of the bailiwick in *Red Book*, ii, 632. Also known as ARQUES, unless Arques was, for a time, a separate bailiwick; *Actes de Henry II*, no. 623, vol. ii, pp. 233–4. The bailiff, Geoffrey de Blainville, farms many escheats, including the honour of Count Giffard, *i.e.*, Walter Giffard, earl of the county of Buckingham (59–65). The bailiff also accounted for the bernage for Richard Courtenay.

   Castle, Arques. Robert of Stuteville, paid castellan (90–1).
   Magnus vicecomitatus de Kaleto (Caux). Farm, 120 li. (90).
   Bernage of the great viscounty (67).
   Viscounty of Arques. Farm 1100 li. The farmer, Richard the chaplain, also accounts for the forest and its pleas, bernage, etc. (90–1).
   Prepositura of Dieppe. Farm 1100 li. The farmers are four citizens (68–9).
   Viscounty of Fécamp. Farm 100 li. (90).[157]
   Lillebonne. Farm 700 li. Farmer, Robert of Estouteville (68).
   Montivilliers, a viscounty granted to Ida of Boulogne, with the revenues of Harfleur, Etretat and Bénouville (90. See Stapleton,

[157] Cf. *Rot. Norm.*, 95 (at foot); *Rot. Pat.*, 30 (top).

p. cxxiii). Hence these are not accounted for. The bernage of Monti-villiers was accounted for (67).

Blossville. This fief formed a bailiwick apart. Geoffrey Ridel and Geoffrey of St. Denis held it 'pro duabis capis ad pluviam,' for which they paid 40s. They levied tallages etc. for the duke, and accounted for fines and amercements (84, 167). It is a curious case, since they did not hold the pleas of the sword, yet were exempt from the bailiff's interference, and so accounted on the rolls (cf. Stapleton, p. cxix).

BRAY. The names DRINCOURT and St. SAENS (*Sanctus Sidonius*) also appear; see *Actes de Henri II*, no. 623 (as above) and Stapleton, I, cii. The bailiff, Alvered of St. Martin (57–8).

Castle, Drincourt, *i.e.*, Neufchatel-en-Bray. No castellan named, but probably the bailiff, since in 1184 he was castellan and also farmed the 'prepositura' (116).

Drincourt, 'prepositura'. Farm 600 li. Farmer, Robert the Bur-gundian (92).

Saint-Saens, an escheated honour. Farm 142 li. 11s. 10d. In 1180 called a 'prepositura' (59).

Ministerium of Bray. See under Vexin.

[VEXIN]. The bailiff, Martin de Hosa (71–3).

Castle, Gisors. Castellan, Martin de Hosa, paid from farm of Rouen (70). Similarly, in 1184, William earl of Arundel was bailiff and castellan (109–12). Note that Gisors was evidently a fortress only, not self-supporting. No 'prepositura' is mentioned, but special funds were applied for the upkeep of the castle (72, 110). The two other fortresses along the Epte in this border province, Neaufle and Neuf-chateau-sur-Epte were also maintained from the revenues of Rouen, under the direction of Martin de Hosa. Joscelin Rossel was castellan of Neuf-chateau (70); in 1184 the Norman Vexin was a great military command.

Viscounty of Vexin, survived as 'barra de Neelfa'. Farm 40 li. (90). The viscounty was hereditary in the family of Crispin (Stapleton, p. cxxii).

Lions, 'prepositura'. Farm 300 li. Farmer, Robert of Stuteville (73–4). The forest included.

Ministerium de Braio de foresta de Leons. Farm 45 li. Farmer, Enguerrand the Porter (74–5). Enguerrand was castellan of Beauvoir-en-Lions, and was paid from the farm of his 'ministerium'.

ROUMOIS. The bailiff, William of Maupalet or Malpalu (*de Malapalude*, a district in Rouen; cf. *Cart. Norm.*, no. 688, note). See *Red Book*, ii, 636. The bailiff in this case also farmed the *viscounty of the Roumois*, or Romeis (77–81). Farm 40 li. So in 1203 (*Rot. Scacc.*, II, 549–53; *Rot. Pat.*, 26b). Forest of Roumare farmed separately (75).

Castle, Rouen. Castellan, Hugh de Cressi (70). The stories about Arthur's murder seem to show that in 1203 the bailiff, Robert of

Vieuxpont, was castellan (cf. R. Coggeshall, ed. Stevenson, p. 143). He certainly had charge of prisoners (*Rot. Pat.*, 15). Later in the same year Richard of Beauchamp was castellan (*Rot. Norm.*, 107).

Rouen, viscounty or 'prepositura'.[158] Farm, 3000 li. Farmers, the citizens (69–71), one of whom generally farmed for himself and colleagues (*e.g.*, p. 153, in 1195). Hence, in the rolls of 1203, Laurence of the Donjon, who was a citizen of Rouen (*Rot. Pat.*, 86) appears as viscount of Rouen as representative of his colleagues (*Rot. Norm.*, 107, cf. *Rot. Pat.*, 25). The citizens of Rouen had but a very limited independence in judicial matters (Giry, *Les Etablissements de Rouen*, i, 19, 27; ii, 38, § 31, 40, § 34). Hence the bailiff of the Roumois is also styled bailiff of Rouen (*Rot. Pat.*, 26b).

VICECOMITATUS INTER RISLAM ET SEQUANAM. Bailiff, Ralf of Frellencourt. Called the *Ballia* of Ralf in *Red Book*, ii, 641; later the *Ballia Lundae*, after the name of the bailiff of 1195 (Stapleton, p. cxlvi). The bailiff also farmed the *viscounty*. Farm 30 li. (100–2).

The viscounty was of small value, since most of the land between the rivers Seine and Risle was either forest or in private hands, especially of the count of Meulan. Hence the most substantial revenue came from the escheated *honour of Montfort-sur-Risle*, farmed for 650 li. by Roger Fitz Landri (82–3). In 1198 the bailiwick was more valuable as a source of judicial revenue, apart from the farm (*Rot. Scacc.*, II, 488, 491–3).

VAUDREUIL. Bailiff, Ralf of Wanneville, chancellor of Henry II, afterwards bishop of Lisieux (92–4). He also farmed the castle and domains, but had made no account for seven years (94). He still owed an account for six years in 1195 (261). For the form of the name, see Delisle, *Introduction*, pp. 99, 100.

Castles, Vaudreuil, Pont de l'Arche. Pont de l'Arche, except the castle, belonged to the abbey of Jumièges, and was therefore not farmed (Stapleton, II, clxi).

Vaudreuil, 'prepositura'. Farm, 700 li. (111).

Beaumont-le-Roger, a castle of the count of Meulan, was also in this bailiwick, which extended across the north of the diocese of Evreux (*Rot. Scacc.*, II, 484). Beaumont was in 1180, as frequently, in ducal hands; its castellan was paid out of the revenue of Ste-Mère-Eglise (98).

---

[158] The viscounty of Rouen had by 1180 been farmed along with the excise on wine ('modiatio'), the shipping and the mills (*Rot. Scacc.*, i, 70). It also included the 'aquagium' (*ibid.*, 71). Under French rule the viscounty was known as the 'viccomitatus aquae' or vicomté de l'eau. (See Delisle, *Introduction*, pp. 3, 213.) The continuity may be clearly traced from William the Conqueror's charter granting to the nuns of Saint-Amand the tithe of the 'modiatio' (*Monasticon*, vii, 1101) to the charter of Philip III in 1278, confirming same, 'levanda per manum vicecomitis nostri aque Rothomagensis' (*Cart. Norm.*, p. 224, no. 917).

NONANCOURT. Bailiff, Saer de Quinci (76–7).
Castle, Nonancourt. Castellan, Saer de Quinci (76).
Prepositura of Nonancourt. Farm 250 li. 'de xx modis frumenti'.
Farmers, apparently the burgesses (75–6).

VERNEUIL. A bailiwick clearly in 1198 (*Rot. Scacc.*, II, 312).
Castles, Verneuil, castellan, Thomas Bardolf (84), and Tillières, taken from the family of Crispin (Stapleton, cxx), castellan, Ralf of Verdun (84).
Prepositura of Verneuil. Farm, 700 li. Farmers, the burgesses? (84).

BONNEVILLE-SUR-TOUQUES. Bailiff, Geoffrey Trossebot, who farmed the *viscounty* in 1180 (68–9). That Bonneville was a bailiwick is clear from the roll of 1195 (*Rot. Scacc.*, II, 142, 233–5; cf. *Cart. Normnd.*, no. 111, p. 19). Farm of the viscounty, 160 li.
Castle, Bonneville-sur-Touques. Castellan, Geoffrey Trossebot (69).

[AUGE], or, as afterwards, PONT AUDEMER. In 1180 Pont Audemer was still in the possession of the count of Meulan. During the wars between France and Richard I, the count took the side of Philip, and Pont Audemer fell into royal hands. The change may be seen taking place in 1195 (*Rot. Scacc.*, I, 199, 208, Stapleton, p. cliii). In that year the bailiff of Auge, William de Mara, took charge of the honour. In 1198 the bailiwick definitely appears as *Ballia de Ponte Audemeri* (*Rot. Scacc.*, II, 450).
In 1180, bailiff, William de Mara (94–100). William's jurisdiction included several of the forests of Normandy, mostly outside his bailiwick. He also had the following farms in Auge:
Viscounty of Conteville. Farm 170 li. (98). In 1198, the farm sank to 27 li. 3s., because the manor of Conteville had been granted to the abbot of Jumièges in exchange for Pont de l'Arche. The abbot paid a rent of 20 li. (*Rot. Scacc.*, II, 450, Stapleton, II, clxi). King John granted the manor, after restoring Pont de l'Arche to Jumièges, to Gerard de Forneval (*Rot. Norm.*, 19; *Rot. Scacc.*, II, 553).
Viscounty of Ste-Mère-Eglise, not to be confused with the place of the same name in the Côtentin. Farm 140 li. (97).
The bailiwick of William de Mara included, in 1180, part of the diocese of Bayeux, west of the Dive, which had originally formed part of the country of Exmes, *i.e.*, Argences and other places. This was afterwards formed into a separate bailiwick lying between the bailiwick of Falaise and Caen, under the title BALLIA DE OXIMINO. See above, p. 57.
The bailiwick of Auge also comprised the *viscounty of Auge.* Farm 20 li. Farmer, Robert Bertram (40).

LIEUVIN.[159] Bailiff, Richard Beverel, 85–9.
Viscounty of Lieuvin. Farm, 25 li. Farmers, Richard Beverel and Joscelin Rossel (85).

FALAISE. Bailiff, Richard Giffart (41–9).
Castles, Falaise, castellan, Richard Giffart (50); Pommeraye, castellan, Robert of Pierrefitte—a place near Pommeraye (50).
Viscounty of the Oximin. Farm, 100 li. Farmer, Robert de Capella (106).
Prepositura of Falaise. Farm, 480 li. Farmer, Odo, son of Vitalis (50).

EXMES. Bailiff, Gilbert Pipart (103–4), who also farms *viscounty*, etc. Farm, 110 li. (103).
Castle, Exmes. Castellan, Gilbert Pipart (104), partly paid in kind, partly out of farm of Falaise (50).
Prepositura of Moulins and Monmoulins. Farm, 300 li. Farmer, Robert Pipart (105). The entries among the fines show that these castles were within the jurisdiction of Exmes (104). The farmer was castellan of Bonmoulins in 1180 and 1195 (245); but in 1180, William de Soliis was castellan of Moulins (57). After 1195 the 'prepositura' disappears from the rolls.

ARGENTAN. Bailiff, Richard of Cardiff (20–3).
Castle, Argentan. Castellan, Richard of Cardiff (39).
Viscounty and prepositura of Argentan. Farm, 700 li. Farmer, Adam de Gravella (39).

CAEN. Bailiff, Richard Fitz Henry (53–6).
Castle, Caen. Castellan, William Fitz Ralf, the seneschal (56).
Prepositura of Caen. Farm, 1000 li. Farmer, Roger, son of Thierri (56–7).

BESSIN. *Red Book*, ii, 638. Bailiff, Hamo Pincerna (1–7).
Castle, Bayeux. Castellan, probably Hamo, since he is styled in a Savigny charter, *Senescallus Baiocarum* (Stapleton, p. lix). In 1195, Robert de Groceio, who had apparently shared in the labours of the bailiwick, was castellan (265, 272).

[159] The bailiwick was extensive, since it included most of the district called Ouche, which had been attached, through the action of its chief inhabitants, to the diocese of Lisieux in the twelfth century. This high forest land, along the upper courses of the Charente and the Touques, cut into the diocese of Séez. Hence the bailiff of Exmes was deprived of much of what would have been his natural jurisdiction. The archdeaconry of Ouche, on the other hand, was in the diocese of Evreux. (Ord. Vit., iii, 2; Longnon, *Pouillés de la Province de Rouen*, xl, lv; Stapleton, I, xxxvii.) The bailiwick was, except at the death of a bishop, deprived of most jurisdiction in the banlieu and viscounty of Lisieux (see *Rot. Scacc.*, I, 261, 262, where the banlieu is accounted for separately during a vacancy. Stapleton, p. clxix).

Viscounty of Bessin. Farm, 140 li. Hereditary farmer, earl of Chester (40).
Prepositura of Bayeux. Farm, 300 li. Farmer, John Bernard (7), *prepositus de Baiocis* (8).
Prepositura of Osmanville, a castle built by Henry II (cf. p. 28). Farm, 170 li. Three farmers (8).

BALLIA DE ULTRA MONTEM LINCHE, later called CONDE. This bailiwick included the southern Bessin beyond Monte de l'Encre except the bailiwick of Vau de Vire, and Tenchebrai (Stapleton, p. lxix). It appears as the ballia of Condé in 1195 and 1198 (*Rot. Scacc.,* I. 171; II, 409). Bailiff in 1180, Jordan de Landa (16–17).
Castle, Condé.
Prepositura of Condé. Farm 300 li. Farmer, Geoffrey Duredent (17). It disappears in the later rolls, when John became count of Mortain, since the châtellenie belonged to the honour of Mortain *Cart. Norm,* no. 412, p. 66).

[TENCHEBRAI]. Called a 'ballia' in 1172 (*Red Book*, ii, 640), and in 1180, as 'ballia' of the farmer and castellan Erchenbold of Briquebec (*cum mitra*), but there is no evidence that it was more than a 'prepositura'. Farm, 100 li. (52–3). As a fief of Mortain, it disappears from the rolls till 1203, when it is farmed by the bailiff of Mortain (*Rot. Scacc.,* II, 540).

ALENÇON. Bailiffs, Robert Waleis, Ralph Labbe, Durand the prevôt (18–20).
Castles, Alençon, castellan, Fulk Paynel (18). Roche Mabille; castellan, Fulk Paynel.
Viscounty and prepositura of Alençon. Farm 500 li. Farmers act as bailiffs. In 1198, Ralph Labbe was bailiff and castellan, and farmed the viscounty and 'prepositura' (*Rot. Scacc.,* II, 386).

PASSEIS. This bailiwick included the march of Normandy, which, geographically, lay in Maine, and may be said to date from the occupation of Domfront, the castle of Robert of Bellême, by Henry, afterwards Henry I. After the recovery by Henry II of the castles of Gorron, Ambriéres and Coumont, 'novum castrum super fluvium Colmiae', in 1162 (Stapleton, p. lxxv), these three castles, south of Domfront, were gradually added to the bailiwick of Passeis. In 1180, Gorron and probably Ambriéres were separate bailiwicks, and they, like Domfront, are later referred to as 'bailiwicks', in a general sense (*Rot. Scacc.,* I, 28; II, 353, 355). Passeis was a comprehensive bailiwick in 1172 (*Red Book*, ii, 639).
Bailiff in 1180, Reiner the Tallager (27–8).
Castles, Domfront, Gorron, Ambriéres, Coumont.
Prepositura of Domfront. Farm, 240 li. Farmers, apparently burgesses in 1180 (28). In 1198 the bailiff was 'prepositus' (II, 352).
GORRON. Bailiff and castellan in 1180, William de Bennenges

(23–4). In 1195 farmed separately, but in bailiwick of Passeis (222).
So in 1198 (II, 354). Farm, 120 or 130 li., probably 130 li. (24, 222).
Farmer in 1180, William de Bennenges. In 1180 the *metairie* of
Fosse-Lovain was added to Gorron, also in 1195 (223) and 1198
(355).

AMBRIERES? Only a 'prepositura' on the rolls of 1195 and 1198,
not distinct from Domfront, but may have been a separate bailiwick
in 1180, when omitted on the roll. Farm in 1195, 50 li. (220).

Novum Castrum super Coumont. Farm, 21s. 10d. (II, 356; called
censi in 1195, I, 220). Accounted for by William Gere in 1195 and
1198.

In May, 1199, Arthur, duke of Brittany, and count of Anjou,
restored these three castles with the forest of Fosse-Lovain to Juhel
of Mayenne (*Cart. Norm.*, no. 48, p. 280).

VAU DE VIRE. In 1172, the 'baillia de Castro de Vira' (*Red Book*, ii,
638). Bailiffs, Alban of Vire and Reinald of Doit (29–30).

Castle, Vire. Castellan, William du Hommet, the constable (29).
Viscounty of Vau de Vire. Farm, 20 li. Farmed by the bailiffs.
Prepositura of the castle of Vire. Farm, 180 li. Farmed by the
bailiffs.

The viscounty and 'prepositura' were in the honour of Mortain,
and so, like Tenchebrai, did not appear on the rolls again till the
reign of John, when the earl of Chester farmed them (II, 537).

[MORTAIN]. In the reign of John a full bailiwick, including Tenchebrai and Cerences (*Rot. Scacc.*, II, 538–48). In 1180 treated as a
bailiwick, but presents some curious features, which are repeated
in the reign of John, and show that it had been independent of
ducal control. Disappears as a royal bailiwick in the reign of Richard
except for escheats in 1195 (215).

In 1180, bailiff, Nigel fitz Robert, described in charters as the
Seneschal of Mortain (Stapleton, p. lxv). He collected *auxilium
vicecomitis* (9–11).

Castles, Mortain, Le Tilleul (Teolium).
[*Viscounty of Vale of Mortain.*] Appears in the accounts of the
auxilium vicecomitis (9). Cf. *Cart. Norm.*, no. 412, p. 66.

[*Prepositura of Mortain.*] The name in *Rot. Norm.*, 15, 'prepositus' (cf. *Rot. Scacc.*, 9). Farm of toll, ovens, mills, 160 li.
Farmer, Ralph Ros (8).

Le Tilleul. Farm 60 li. (p. 9). Farmers, apparently inhabitants.
CERENCES, a bailiwick in 1180, and styled a ballia in 1172 (*Red
Book*, ii, 640), but apparently only for convenience, since Cerences
was a *viscounty* in the honour of Mortain. It disappears in the time
of Richard, and reappears in the rolls of John as a viscounty in the
bailiwick of Mortain (*Rot. Scacc.*, II, 540).

Bailiff in 1180, Stephen of Saukeville (14–5).
Viscounty of Cerences, 150 li. Farmer, Stephen of Saukeville.
This ancient farm seems to include a 'prepositura', since fixed pay-

ments out of the farm of Montmartin went to the viscount and 'prepositus' of Cerences respectively (30).

Ferio de Monte Martini. Farm, 300 li. (30). This valuable property, the proceeds of the great fair at Montmartin, a place on the coast of the Côtentin near Cerences, deserves special notice. It belonged to the counts of Mortain (*Cart. Norm.*, no. 412, p. 66) and therefore only reappears on the rolls in the reign of King John.

COTENTIN. Bailiff, Osbert de la Houze (*de Hosa*) (30–38). See *Red Book*, ii, 643. Castles, Cherbourg, Valognes. Castellan, Osbert de la Houze (30).

The bailiff succeeded the earlier viscounts of the Côtentin, and farmed a great deal of the extensive domain separately.

Cherbourg. Farm 150 li. 10s.	These, with other property and es-
Valognes. Farm 153 li. 10s.	cheats, farmed by the bailiff (30–2).
Brix. Farm 200 li.	Much was kept in demesne, and not farmed out (32).

Viscounty of Côtentin. Farm 70 li. Farmer, Robert the Angevin (38).

Barfleur. Farm 60 li. Farmer, Robert the Angevin (37).

St. Marcouf. Farm 200 li. (38).

Poupeville. Farm 220 li. (38).

Varreville. Farm 200 li. (38).

Ste-Mère-Eglise. Farm 140 li. (39).

COUTANCES. Called bailiwick in 1172 (*Red Book*, ii, 634), and treated as such on rolls.

Bailiff, in 1180, William de Ponte, the agent of the hereditary viscount (51–2).

Viscounty of Coutances. Farm, 50 li. Farmer, hereditary, William of St. John (50, cf. 12). The farm is a small one, considering the size of the city, because Coutances was divided very largely between the count of Mortain and the bishop (Stapleton, p. xcviii,; cf. *Cart. Norm.*, no. 412, p. 66).

GAVRAI. Bailiwick in 1172 (*Red Book*, ii, 634); in 1195 (*Rot. Scacc.*, I, 197), and in 1198 (II, 292–4) and 1203 (II, 512–14). Omitted in 1180.

Castle, Gavrai.

The bailiff accounted for the proceeds of the honour 'de exitu honoris de Wabreio cum villa de Torneor'.

AVRANCHIN. Bailiff, Geoffrey Duredent (11–13).

Castles, Avranches, Pontorson, St. James-de-Beuvron. The castle and city of Avranches were not farmed, and the castle had a special castellan placed there by the king. Consequently the only proceeds of the bailiwick, except the pleas of the sword, came from outside Avranches. (Inquest in Delisle, *Introduction* to the *Recueil des Actes de Henri II*, pp. 345–7; *Rot. Norm.*, p. 87).

Viscounty of the Avranchin, or as it is sometimes called, the 'prepositura' (*Rot. Scacc.*, I, 40, 215; II, 537). Farm, 60 li. Farmer, hereditary, earl of Chester (40). The farm was really 80 li., but 20 li. were allowed by the exchequer because of the manor of Vains, near Avranches, which William the Conqueror had given in free alms to St. Stephen of Caen (Delisle, *op. cit.*, p. 345; Round, *Calendar of Documents preserved in France*, p. 158).

Prepositura of St. James-de-Beuvron. Farm, 100 li. Farmer, hereditary, earl of Chester (40, also II, 537).

Prepositura of Pontorson. Farm 220 li. Farmer, Michael of Tessey. Castellan in 1180, William du Hommet, the constable (40). Pontorson was given outright to the earl of Salisbury in 1203 (*Rot Norm.*, 97).

CHANNEL ISLES. The islands were regarded as a whole (*Rot. Scacc.*, I, 28). William de Courcy, who died in 1177, had farmed them as a unit (44), and it is probable that they were judicially administered by a viscount, for in 1179 the 'curia domini regis' in Guernsey was held by Gilbert de la Hougue, 'tunc vicecomite' (Haskins, *Norman Institutions*, p. 185, and note 170). Although Earl John was nominally lord of the islands and, from at least 1198 received the net surplus of their revenues (*Rot. Scacc.*, II, 390), he did not farm them: (cf. II, 225 with 390). In 1200, after his succession as king, he entrusted them as a whole to a *custos* or warden, Peter of Préaux, who held them as lord by a reversible grant (*Rot. Pat.*, 15; *Rot. Chart.*, 33b). Hence, in spite of their unity, the islands were not styled a bailiwick on the exchequer rolls. Financially, they consisted of four *ministeria*. In general see Haskins, *op. cit.*, pp. 129, 185, 189, and note 194; J. Havet, in *Bibliothéque de l'école des chartes*, 1876, 1877; J. H. le Patourel, *The Medieval Administration of the Channel Islands, 1199–1399* (Oxford, 1937), pp., 26–9.

In 1180 the various farms were as follows. For the names see Stapleton, I, lxxvi.

Ministerium de Groceio, in Jersey. Farm 140 li. Farmer, Roger Godel (25).

Ministerium de Crapout Doit, in Jersey. Farm 160 li. Farmer, Richard Burnulf (25).

Ministerium de Gorroic, in Jersey. Farm 160 li. Farmer, Gilbert de la Hougue (26).

Guernsey. Farm 240 li. Farmer, Gilbert de la Hougue (26. See also 225; ii, 390).

It would be rash in spite of the statements in the custumal to conclude that the ducal courts and assizes were held in each self-contained bailiwick. Early in Henry II's reign the bailiwicks seem to have had their local judges (*e.g.*, Mortain, Stapleton, I, p. lxv), and the bailiffs may have been able to hold pleas of the sword (see the writ of Henry II quoted above, p. 64 n.). Moreover, as John's charter for William of Briouze shows (*Rot. Norm.*, 20), the itinerant justices, when trying the pleas of the sword, might sit specially in baronial courts. The scattered escheat of the honour of Peveril, which was not only farmed as a whole in 1180, but treated as a bailiwick for the return of the proceeds of ducal justice (105–6), must have taken its pleas for trial to some neighbouring place of assize, unless the constable, who acted as bailiff, dealt with them himself. But now see Haskins, *Norman Institutions*, chapters V and VI, and the appendices, pp. 321–43.

It is clear from the roll of 1195 that there had been a great inquiry into the escheats of Normandy. Many bailiffs make special returns of their escheats. The measure would be necessary because of the changes wrought by the crusade, the attempt at rebellion engineered by John, and, above all, the war with Philip of France. But the inquiry had an administrative value, and is an additional proof that the Norman bureaucracy undertook in the duchy a great investigation parallel to that ordered by Hubert Walter in England. The justices of this English itinerary of 1194 were especially instructed to deal with escheats. One result of these inquiries was that special officials could be appointed to collect special revenues throughout a very large area, thus relieving the bailiffs. Thus in Richard's reign tallages were levied by particular persons and accounted for from many bailiwicks. John, in the following letter, made the experienced official Richard of Villequier his escheator through-out Normandy (*Rot. Pat.*, 37, November 30, 1203):

> Rex etc senescallo et omnibus ballivis etc. Sciatis quod liberavimus Ricardo de Wilek custodiam escaetarum Normannie et Judeorum praeter Judeos Rothomagi et Cadomi quamdiu nobis placuerit. Et ideo vobis precipimus quod ei sitis intendentes tanquam custodi escaetarum et Judeorum et ei escaetas per ballias vestras custodiendas habere faciatis.

A similar tendency was the concentration of bailiwicks in a few hands, and the separate distribution of the castles. This is very marked in the roll of 1203, but is also noticeable in the rolls of King Richard's reign.

The list given above shows that a viscounty survived in every ancient province, Caux, Bray, Vexin, Roumois, the district between the rivers Seine and Risle, Auge, Lieuvin, Oximin, Bessin, Vau de Vire, the Côten-tin and Avranchin; also in the counties of Alençon and Mortain, with its dependent viscounty Cerences; in the cities or castles of Rouen, Lisieux (where the bishop successfully disputed its rights, Stapleton, I, clxix), Exmes, Argentan, and Coutances. Viscounties of this kind were some-times, as in Alençon, Argentan and Exmes, so merged in the 'prepositura' as to be almost indistinguishable, but they were of distinct origin. Thus the joint farm of the viscounty and rents of Exmes was 110 li., but as the tithe of the viscounty was 7 li., the latter must have been worth 70 li. out of the 110 li. (*Rot. Scacc.*, 103). In this instance, as at Mortain, the rents are described separately (censis et teloneis et feriis et molendinis et campartis dominicarum terrarum), so that we may see of what items a prepositura might be composed. The viscounty, on the other hand, partly consisted of pleas, like the farms of the English shires (*Dialogus de Scaccario*, bk. I, c, xvii, ed. Johnson, pp. 64–5 'tota non exurgit ex fundorum redditibus, set ex magna parte de placitis provenit'). Thus the farms of the viscounty of the Oximin and of the Avranchin included the proceeds of pleas reserved to the viscount, presumably upon the lands which produced in rents or aids the rest of his farm. In the Avranchin the earl of Chester had in farm 'census et theloneum et omnia placita ad vicecomitem pertinentia'; and he held his court three times a year in Ardevon and Genest (*Recueil des Actes de Henri II. Introduction*, 345, 346). Similarly, the farm of the castle of Gaillon, when the castle was dependent upon Evreux, included 'placita de quibus bellum non poterat evenire' (*Cart. Norm.*, p. 22, no. 120). The creation of a single farm for both viscounty and 'prepositura' in towns and castles was hastened by the formation of new farms in which the double tradition did not exist. Thus the lands of Robert of Rhuddlan in the Côtentin probably produced the ducal farms at St. Marcouf, Poupeville, and Varreville (Stapleton, I, lxxxvij), and the new viscounty of Houlme (*Rot. Scacc.*, I, 262), which is found on the roll of 1195, seems to have been formed after 1180 from escheats in the Bessin. But, of course, new castles provide the best instances of new farms. In the new bailiwicks of Osmanville and Verneuil, the farm is styled 'firma prepositurae' only; in Nonancourt and in the castles of the Passeis it is the same or 'firma' simply. Hence, after the new arrangements made by Henry II it was easy for the terminology to get confused, so that, while in some cases the terms 'viscounty' and 'bailiwick' were interchangeable, in others we find 'viscounty' and 'prepositura' merged into one.

CHAPTER IV

KING RICHARD AND HIS ALLIES

AT the end of the twelfth century the sovereignty of the Norman
state became an important legal question. If we look at Normandy
alone, the supremacy of the duke seems to have overshadowed the
system of contracts upon which a state like Aquitaine was based. But
when we turn to the attitude of the legal-minded Philip, Normandy
shrinks to a dependency. It is true that the barons and clergy of
Normandy did not appeal from the ducal court to the king of France,
and did not, as Normans, occupy the equivocal position of owing
service both to the duke and to the king.[1] But the king of France
did not acknowledge any distinction between the dependence of
Normandy and the dependence of the other great fiefs of the Crown.
After the conquest of England the dukes of Normandy had acquired
the dignity of independent princes, and during the eleventh and
early twelfth centuries Normandy alone had been more powerful
than France proper. The only sign of dependence was the homage
paid by the dukes to the kings of France, and this act was usually
performed on the frontier between the two countries. The Englishman, Henry of Huntingdon, followed by his friend the Norman
chronicler, Robert of Torigni, sought to reconcile the theory of
Norman-French relations with practice, by an interpretation of early
Norman history which denied that the formal act of homage had
anything to do with the Norman fief. Similarly, at the end of the
tenth century Dudo of St. Quentin had argued that the Carolingian
king had given Normandy to Rollo outright as a kingdom free of all
service.[2] King John definitely put forward the claim that he was not
obliged to have any dealings with his suzerain, even in answer to a
summons to appear before his court, except on the marches of
Normandy.[3] Philip rejected, of course, all these arguments. Unfortunately, his success was so rapid that it never became necessary for

[1] The text of the Bayeux Inquest of 1133, as given in the *Red Book*, ii, 646,
is misleading. The bishop owed to the duke, not to the king, the service
rendered in support of the king. See, for this important document, J. H.
Round, *Family Origins* (edit. Page, 1930), pp. 201–16, especially p. 211, and
Stenton, *English Feudalism*, pp. 12–13, with references to texts and criticism.

[2] For the texts, see Valin, 29–31; and Lot, *Fidèles ou Vassaux?* 230–3.
M. Lot regards the later chroniclers as the victims of Dudo. He brings together
all the evidence for homage, and other relations, in his sixth chapter.

[3] Lot, pp. 228–30. See now J. F. Lemarignier, *Recherches sur l'hommage
au marche et les frontières féodales* (Lille, 1945).

him to press his claims as overlord upon the Normans themselves. His legal action was based upon the appeals of Poitevin, not of Norman barons. Nor was Arthur, whose captivity and death caused the prolongation of war, a Norman baron. Hence it is impossible to say whether Philip recognised the practical sovereignty of the duke of Normandy within his duchy, or was prepared to extend the right of appeal as Philip the Fair and his successors afterwards pressed it in Gascony.

Mediæval theory did not draw a very clear line between the feudal contract and what we should call a treaty. In both cases the confirmation by means of the sworn oath played a large part. Again, the normal feudal relations between a lord and his man were often supplemented by other relations, created by the grant of a castle, the sale of an important feudal right, the formal act of reconciliation after a quarrel, and the like.[4] Relations of this kind were often strengthened by the delivery of hostages or the oaths of sureties; and these precautions were also an almost essential safeguard of a treaty. Of course, in the case of a treaty sureties were reciprocal, whereas in the former cases they were only found by the vassal; but the unreality of this distinction when the relations between great feudatories was concerned may be seen from the fact that Philip Augustus, even in an agreement which pledged the king of England to do homage for his continental lands, did not hesitate to find sureties for the operation of his own promises.[5] In fact, the contractual nature of the vassal relation made it easy for a vassal to treat with his lord, as the dukes of Normandy or the counts of Flanders treated with their suzerain, the king of France. The services owed by the vassals were reduced to a minimum; indeed, by a curious but quite natural argument, the performance of service was regarded as putting an end to the fact of dependence, so that the vassal was afterwards justified in acting as he liked. Hence arose the distinction between liege-homage and simple homage. Originally all homage was liege-homage; for no person could be the man of more than one lord: he owed homage to him alone, and was free so far as others were concerned.[6] But when homage

[4] The Norman rolls and the Exchequer rolls abound in instances. One of the most interesting is the explanation of some hasty words of disloyalty by the Earl of Chester, *Rot. Norm.*, pp. 96, 97. The vagueness of the distinction between the feudal contract and every other agreement may be seen from the use of homage in some countries to establish a merely private obligation, *e.g.*, in Catalonia (Lot, p. 248). See the section on homage in Guilhiermoz, *Essai sur l'origine de la noblesse*, pp. 78–85.   [5] *e.g.*, at Messina in 1191.

[6] See Lot, pp. 237–41. M. Pirenne, the historian of Flanders, has published a study of liege-homage, in which he adopts a similar line of argument, in the *Bulletin de la classe des lettres de l'Académie royale de Belgique* (1909): see *Revue historique*, ciii, 442. In the text I have used the word homage in the sense of the entire act of submission by a vassal. As M. Lot points out,

became the sign, not of servitude, but of service, the receipt, so to speak, for so much land or other property, it became necessary to distinguish the lord proper from the casual or secondary lords. The man was not, like the serf, free in regard to all but his lord, but free to enter into as many obligations as he liked, saving the irksome rights of his lord. It is for this reason that feudalism, as a social bond, required the guidance of a strong lord who could prevent the formation of these illicit unions. Lordship, in those states which were most properly feudal, was tempered by sovereignty.

The extent of the obligations which liege-homage secured, and the kind of action which might accompany their performance may best be seen from a treaty between Count Robert of Flanders and Henry I of England almost a century earlier. This treaty (1101) seems to have served as a model for later agreements. The king of England, in return for a money fief, had received the homage of the count of Flanders. The count promised his support even to his life, 'saving his faith to Philip, king of the Franks'. If the king of France planned an invasion of England, the count would dissuade him in every way that he could; and if the king persisted, would join in the expedition with the minimum force necessary to prevent his forfeiture of his French fief. Should Henry require his help in Maine or Normandy, he would come unless the French king forbade him by the judgment of his peers; and should the French king invade Normandy, the count would join him with only ten knights, leaving all the rest of his following in the Norman host to fight against their companions.[7]

It is clear from this account that there was no hard and fast division between those feudal states, which like England and Normandy, insisted on full obedience, and the loose confederation of feudatories, in which a variety of relations crossed each other. All kinds of modifications were possible, and even for England and Normandy it would be impossible to lay down a fixed rule. Alliance and allegiance were

---

this act included the oath of fealty. Homage in the narrow sense did not constitute the vassal relation. Louis VI strictly owed homage, though as king he refused to pay it to the abbot of St. Denis for the French Vexin (Viollet, *Hist. des instit. politiques*, ii, 183). Homage was originally a Frankish custom only.

[7] P.R.O. Exch. T. R., Diplomatic Doc. 2, best edited in F. Vercauteren, *Actes des comtes de Flandre, 1071–1128* (Brussels, 1938), no. 30; cf. Lot, pp. 23–5. For the date, Dover, March 10, 1101, *not* 1103, see *Regesta regum Anglo-Normannorum*, ii (1956) 7, no. 515. For the significance of this treaty in the development of the money fief, see Bryce D. Lyon, in *E.H.R.*, lxvi (1951), 179, with the references to other comments. Sometimes a party to a treaty saved his rights to more than one lord. Thus, in August, 1205, Thomas of Saint-Valéry made a pact to help his brother William, count of Ponthieu and Montreuil, in the most emphatic manner, against all men 'excepto domino meo rege Francie regeque Anglie' (Teulet, *Layettes du Trésor des Chartes*, i, 295, no. 779). (See note at end of this chapter.)

G

never far apart in the mediæval world. After the loss of Normandy, though some lords begged to be allowed to serve John in their hearts because they felt compelled to serve the king of France with their bodies, the English kings began, as we shall see, to draw a strict line between aliens and Englishmen.[8] It has been suggested that the events of 1204 were the real cause of the English law of aliens;[9] if so the loss of Normandy, by turning vassals into subjects, helped lawyers to work out a most important chapter in the legal theory of the modern state. But in the meantime it was, as we have said, not easy to draw a hard and fast line. Doctrines of citizenship were opposed not merely to facts, but were opposed to the contractual element in feudalism. We saw in the last chapter how strong this was in Norman history. Again, the idea that citizenship was confined to one part of the earth's surface, to the exclusion of other parts, was opposed also to the whole teaching of the Church. All Christians were citizens of the world, protected by natural laws as well as by the law of their own countries. And here we are brought to another problem which was of great interest during the struggle for Normandy. This was the problem created by Papal interference. So long as the dukes of Normandy were strong enough, the French kings were content to treat with them as with equals, in spite of their positions as suzerains. Philip Augustus had very cleverly succeeded in maintaining the distinction between Normandy and the rest of the Angevin empire, but he had never got a legal footing in Normandy itself. Owing to the quarrels between the sons of Henry II, who would not do homage to each other, he had stopped Henry's plan of uniting Normandy, Anjou, and Aquitaine under one head. Richard did homage to him for Aquitaine,[10] and Philip acted as arbitrator, if not as a court of appeal between him and his father.[11] He received the homage and listened to the appeals of the barons of Poitou. But with Normandy, with Henry or Richard as dukes of Normandy, he acted as an equal.[12] When, however, in the reign of John, the balance of power was seriously threatened,

[8] *Histoire des ducs de Normandie* (ed. Michel, 1840), p. 99. And below, p. 296.

[9] Pollock and Maitland, *History of English Law* (2nd edition, 1923), i, 460–2. A problem which prevents such great legal difficulties in our own days was, of course, never solved completely by mediæval lawyers, and the account in the text merely states the tendency in theory and practice.

[10] Rigord, ed. Delaborde, i, 93; *Gesta Henrici*, ii, 50.

[11] According to Rigord (i, 79) the papal legates bound Henry and Richard to abide in 1187 by the judgment of the French court. See Lot, *op. cit.*, 81–3, 230.

[12] Later chroniclers affirmed that Henry was condemned by Louis of France to lose all his fiefs after the marriage with Eleanor of Aquitaine (1152) but it is doubtful whether this is correct (Lot, *op. cit.*, 205–11). Rigord speaks of a summons before the French court when Henry refused to surrender Gisors in 1186. If he is correct, this is the first time that the legal claim was made by Philip: Rigord, pp. 77–8; Lot, *op. cit.*, 230, note 1.

Philip made claims which John refused to admit; and then it became necessary to appeal to a higher than feudal law, the law of right and wrong, to which all nations are subject. Innocent III, therefore, entered upon the scene, as the spiritual suzerain of Philip and the administrator of what philosophers term the law of nature. Innocent declared expressly that he was no judge of local or temporal law; he made no claim to set aside the feudal rights of the king of France; but all kings are bound by a higher law, which if they disobey, they may rightly be displaced. Hence he directed his legates to inquire into the rights of the case.[13] Here, also, it is not easy to distinguish the threats of a spiritual ally from the injunctions of a suzerain.

With such considerations in mind it will be easier to interpret aright the treaties, negotiations, claims of suzerainty, threats of forfeiture and so on, in the reigns of Richard and John.

The treaty which Richard made with Philip at Messina, on their way to the Holy Land, is the most convenient text with which to commence an inquiry into the state of political affairs after the death of Henry II. The treaty was made in March, 1191. It is of additional interest to us because from the outset its tenor was disputed. Immediately after his hurried return to France King Philip presented himself on the Norman border, and, showing at a meeting with the Norman magnates what seemed to be Richard's charter containing the treaty, demanded the surrender of his sister, Alice, and the great castle of Gisors. The seneschal, William Fitz Ralf, refused to surrender Gisors without definite instructions, and was justified in refusing.[14] He had received no letters from Richard directing the surrender of one of the great strongholds of the Norman Vexin, upon which Henry II had lavished such wealth and labour.[15] As the French barons refused to join Philip in an attack upon the lands of a Crusader, the king of France was forced to retire.[16] Now, while Philip displayed what purported to be Richard's charter, the English Exchequer preserved the treaty in the charter of the French king. The original has not come down to us,[17] but the evidence is certainly in favour of

[13] See especially Innocent's letter of October 31, 1203, to Philip of France (Migne, *Patrologia Latina*, ccxv, 176; Potthast, *Regesta Pontificum Romanorum*, vol. i, no. 2009). He urges Philip to let his legate decide 'non ratione feudi, cuius ad te spectat judicium, sed occasione peccati, cuius ad nos pertinet sine dubitatione censura'. [14] *Gesta*, ii, 236.
[15] See the fragmentary Exchequer roll of 1184 (*Rot. Scacc.*, i, 110).
[16] *Gesta*, ii, 236–7; Will. Newb., p. 367. Richard's change of seal, though mainly due to fiscal reasons, implied the danger from false seals. See the charter in Delisle's *Introduction* to *Recueil des Actes de Henri II*, p. 192. For false seals, cf. Walter Map, *De nugis curialium*, ed. Wright, p. 235.
[17] The treaty was printed by Rymer (ed. Record Comm., 1816), i, 54, and in a better form by H-F. Delaborde in *Recueil des Actes de Philippe-Auguste*, i (Paris, 1916), 464–6, no. 376, from a document now in the Record Office

the official text under Philip's seal preserved in England. Philip agreed to surrender all claims to the Norman Vexin and Gisors, which, though they had long been subject to the Norman duke, had always been regarded since the marriage of the young King Henry to Margaret of France as the dowry of a French princess. After the death of Margaret they became the dowry of Philip's sister Alice. Richard had refused to marry Alice, and Philip claimed the dower. At Messina he consented to give up his claim.[18]

The fate of Normandy turned upon the surrender of the French claim to the Norman Vexin. When the chroniclers of the period summarised the treaty of Messina, they excluded everything but that. When Richard's envoys were urging the grievances of their master at the Court of Rome in 1198, they made the surrender at Messina the basis of their case against Philip.[19] So long as this district between Epte and Andelle threatened with its fortresses the French domain, the valley of the Seine was safe. If it were lost, the king of France could control, from its uplands, the rich pastures of the land of Bray, and pass along the right bank of the Seine as far as Rouen. It is certain that such a strategist as Richard would be ready to make sacrifices in order to secure the unchallenged right to the Norman Vexin. It is incredible that he thought of surrendering, in return for the meagre benefits which came to him from the rest of the settlement, a land

---

(Exch. T. R. Diplomatic Doc. 6) which is a fragment of a roll of the second half of the fourteenth century. This roll contains also the treaties of 1195 and 1200. The original with Philip's seal was noted in the *Gascon Calendar* compiled in 1322 by direction of the treasurer Stapledon (edited by G. P. Cuttino for the Royal Historical Society, 1949, p. 10, no. 28). Both this original and that under King Richard's seal have disappeared.

[18] On the whole matter see L. Landon, *The Itinerary of King Richard I*, (Pipe Roll Soc., 1935), pp. 219–34, an appendix on the Vexin with texts; and especially D. M. Stenton on Roger of Howden in *E.H.R.*, lxviii (1953), 574–82. Richard of Devizes (Howlett, *Chronicles of Stephen*, etc., iii, 403) and the dean of St. Paul's (Rad. Dic., ii, 86) who were of course contemporaries, give the version in favour of Richard. The *Gesta Henrici* (ii, 161, 236), agree with Philip. In fact the most important witness to Philip's claim that Gisors according to the settlement at Messina, was to be restored to him when his sister Alice was, is Roger of Howden, who is now known to have compiled the *Gesta Henrici*, gone to Syria with King Richard, and to have returned with King Philip; but there is no evidence that Roger had seen the actual text of the treaty. Moreover he was back in England before Philip appeared on the Norman border.

[19] Innocent III thus summarises the English view of the treaty, bearing out the text in Rymer; 'in qua pro decem millibus marchis argenti quas ei reddere promisisti praedictus Rex a contrahendo cum sorore sua matrimonio te absolvit, et Gisortium cum Vulcassino tibi quietum in perpetuam omnino dimisit' (Migne, *Patrologia Latina*, ccxiv, 196–9; Potthast, no. 235; *Histor. de France*, xix, 359–61).

already in his possession, which, save for a period of sixteen years (1144 to 1160), had been an integral part of Normandy during three centuries.[20]

By the treaty of Messina, then, Richard was released from his promise to marry Alice of France, and retained the Norman Vexin in return for 10,000 silver marks of Troyes. The fortresses on the Epte were only to return to France if Richard should die without direct male heirs. The English king could not foresee that he would die without legitimate children, and would live to see the Norman Vexin wrested from him. His marriage with Berengaria opened a new chapter in Angevin policy. The French alliance had not brought peace, nor prevented the steady advance of French influence in Aquitaine. Once the main object of the unnatural series of agreements had been secured by the recognition of his rights in the Norman Vexin, Richard preferred to establish his base in the south. He was a southerner, and had spent the greater part of his life amid the stormy politics of Aquitaine. Thanks to him, this magnificent dowry had been a source of weakness to his father. Richard determined to make it a source of strength.

Henry II, in the closing years of his life, had found that he could not hold the heart of his ancestral possessions, because the gradual advance of French authority in Berri and Poitou had opened a way into Touraine from the rear. If the key to the empire could be threatened in this way, it was useless to expect Normandy and Aquitaine to remain united. Richard was not likely to forget those memorable days in the summer of 1189, when the old king, deserted by his sons, forced from Le Mans, driven to bay at Chinon, heard

[20] The Vexin, both Norman and French, remained a whole ecclesiastically as an archdeaconry, attached to the diocese of Rouen (Prou, *Recueil des Actes de Philippe I*, p. 323, no. 127) though it seems to have been divided in the twelfth century (Longnon, *Pouillés de la Province de Rouen*, p. xi). The county of the Vexin after the Norman settlement of 911 was the French Vexin, between the Epte and the Oise. It was held of the abbot of St. Denis, since the Vexin, both Norman and French, had been a fief of the abbey. The duke of Normandy held the Norman Vexin originally as advocate of the abbey. (See Flach, *Les Origines de l'ancienne France*, iii, 525.) For a time after 1032 the county also came to the duke of Normandy, and the archbishop of Rouen always had considerable land within it (*Cartulaire Normand*, p. 31, no. 202) some of which seems to have been held of the duke of Normandy ('si vero est de archiepiscopatu, de comite Normannorum teneat, cuius est archiepiscopus': Philip I's charter of 1092, in Prou, p. 323). The county came to the French king in 1076. In 1144 Geoffrey of Anjou bought off the French king by the grant of the Norman Vexin. It came back as a marriage portion in 1160. For details and texts see Landon, *op. cit.*, pp. 219 ff., who, however, fails to note the cession of 1144 confirmed by Henry, Geoffrey's son, in 1151; see A. L. Poole, *From Domesday Book to Magna Carta* (1951), p. 162, note 3. For the bailiwick of the Norman Vexin, see above, p. 69.

the news that Philip Augustus had taken Tours.[21] Hence, with his mother's help, he began to find allies in the south. The marriage with Berengaria of Navarre was the first step; it not only led to quicker trade between the Angevin provinces and the kingdoms of Spain; it also brought about a political alliance which was of great value to John in later days. The next step was the treaty with Raymond VI of Toulouse in 1196. Ever since, in the last years of the eleventh century, Raymond of Saint-Gilles (1088–1105) had usurped the lordship of Toulouse, the dukes of Aquitaine had claimed the county.[22] Henry II had taken up the quarrel, and forced Raymond's successors to do homage for Toulouse. The king of France had acknowledged the rights of the dukes of Aquitaine, but made the continual quarrels between Raymond V and Richard an excuse for asserting his own authority. In 1168 Richard agreed to submit his contentions to the court of Louis VII, and at Messina twenty-three years later Philip Augustus formally acknowledged his rights to Querci, with the exception of the royal abbeys of Figeac and Souillac. This advantage, however, could only be another source of trouble so long as the count of Toulouse refused to acknowledge the rights of the duke of Aquitaine to Querci, which Richard had seized so lately as 1188. Richard therefore decided to get rid of annoyance, and made the agreement of 1196 with the young Raymond VI.[23] Querci was restored to Toulouse; Raymond married Richard's sister, Joan, the widow of William II of Sicily; and the Agenais was ceded to him as her dower. On his side Raymond consented to hold the Agenais as a fief of Aquitaine, and to contribute a force of 500 knights for one month in case of war in Gascony.[24] From this time Toulouse gave little more trouble. When their own trial came to the count and his men, these heretics of the south were glad to seek the alliance of Henry III, and that orthodox monarch was not unwilling to grant it.[25]

This southern policy was continued by John. Within the borders of the duchy he turned from the house of Lusignan to Angoulême and the Limousin. By this means he was able to command the entire length of the road from Tours to Bordeaux. Beyond the Pyrenees he made terms with the king of Castile.

[21] *Histoire de Guillaume le Maréchal*, iii, 106–11.
[22] Lot, p. 127. The claim rested on the fact that the heiress Philippa was married to duke William IX of Aquitaine.
[23] Philip tried in vain to bind the count of Toulouse to his interests by giving him his rights over the abbey of Figeac (1195): *Recueil des Actes de Philippe August*, ii (1943), 8–9, no. 485.
[24] Richard, *Les Comtes de Poitou* (Paris, 1903), ii, 298; Lot, pp. 127–32.
[25] See the letter of December, 1226, from the consuls of Toulouse to Henry III, P.R.O. Ancient Correspondence, vol. v. no. 61, quoted in *Revue historique*, lxxxvii (1905), 58–9.

The treaty of Messina dealt with wider questions than that of the Norman Vexin. The Angevin empire was destined to be broken up by the barons of Poitou, and especially by the barons of Poitevin Berri. Henry II had claimed Berri as part of Aquitaine,[26] but since the year 1100 when the viscount of Bourges gave up his lands, the kings of France had made more active claims. The viscounties of Déols, with its enormous wealth,[27] of Issoudun and of Châteauroux remained in dependence upon the counts of Poitou; the rest of Berri, except the barony of Graçay, was secured by the king of France. At Messina Richard accepted the terms which Philip Augustus had forced upon Henry II in the last conflict for the marches of Aquitaine. He surrendered all his rights over the Auvergne, and all claim over the baronies of Issoudun and Graçay. But the settlement was not lasting. To Richard the mountain fortresses on the bounds of Aquitaine were always an attraction, and to the end he bandied songs of defiance with their lords, for whom, as for him, war and politics were not a serious dogged business, but were rather like one vast tournament, in which men were friends one day and foes the next.[28]

Lastly, Richard acknowledged Philip as his liege lord for all his continental provinces and consented to make the succession to them a matter of public treaty. As duke of Aquitaine he had refused to do homage to his elder brother, and consistent in this, he arranged as king that if he should leave more than one son, the eldest should hold in chief of Philip all that he ought to hold of him south of the Channel, but the second should hold his share, whether Normandy, or Anjou and Maine, or Poitou and Aquitaine, directly of the French king.[29] The law of parage was thus extended to the succession. Although there is no reference to Brittany in the treaty of Messina, Philip is said to have acknowledged its dependence upon the duke of Normandy;[30] and it should be remembered that, in case Richard should die childless, the young Arthur of Brittany was at this time recognised as his heir.[31]

[26] Above, p. 23.
[27] The heritage of Denise, daughter of Ralf of Déols (d. 1176) was said by some 'tantum valere quantum valet redditus totius Normanniae'. (Robert of Torigni, ed. Delisle, ii, 69, or ed. Howlett, *Chronicles of Stephen, Henry II and Richard I* (Rolls Series), iv, 274.) [28] Cf. Cartellieri, iii, 146.
[29] 'Et, si rex Anglorum haberet duos heredes masculos aut plures, voluit et concessit ut major natu teneat in capite a nobis (*i.e.*, Philippo) totum id quod debet tenere a nobis citra mare Anglie, et alius unam ex baroniis tribus tenebit a nobis in capite, videlicet dominium Normannie, aut dominium Andegavie et Cenomannie, aut dominium Aquithanie et Pictavie.' *Recueil des Actes de Philippe Auguste*, i, 464–5. See Guilhiermoz, p. 204; Rad. Dic., ii, 18; *Gesta*, i, 291, for Richard's earlier action. [30] *Gesta*, ii, 161.
[31] Treaty with Tancred of Sicily at Messina, Cartellieri, ii, 144–6, and the authorities given.

Within a few months the agreement at Messina was torn up by the sudden return of Philip from the Holy Land, and by the captivity of Richard in Germany. The centre of interest was transferred from the borders of Aquitaine to the Rhine.

The death of Philip of Alsace, count of Flanders, during the Crusade (June 1, 1191) was probably more connected with King Philip's return than the Normans and English were willing to admit. In the disappearance of this great statesman and warrior, the king of France saw an opportunity of resuming his earlier success in the north-east of France; and as he reflected upon his policy the chance of including within its scope the conquest of the Norman Vexin must have intensified his desire to return. For centuries the fortunes of the lands between the Seine and the Scheldt had been connected, and Philip could not hope to unravel the innumerable ties and conflicting interests of Flanders and its neighbours before securing himself from Norman attacks upon the French Vexin. Moreover, some near neighbours of Normandy were at this time his friends.[32] On the other hand, Richard was able to save Normandy by his commanding influence among the princes of the Rhine valley. Philip reached beyond them to the emperor and to Denmark. For a few years the politics of Northern Europe were involved in a common system.

The history of the Low Countries during the life of Philip of Alsace was complicated to an unusual degree. It had its centre in the relations between the three most important princes in that part of Europe, the count of Flanders and the dukes of Brabant and Hainault. Of these princes Philip of Flanders was a vassal of the French king—his imperial fiefs were unimportant—and the dukes of Hainault and Brabant were vassals of the empire. Each ruled a land of important towns, and each had ambitions natural to wealthy monarchs who had seen the new greatness of the kings of France and England. Any one of them might well have succeeded, as the dukes of Burgundy succeeded in the fifteenth century, if the others had not stood in his way. Philip of Alsace had sought to become great in two ways. Putting aside old rivalries, he became the friend of Louis VII of France and the relative of Baldwin of Hainault, a most astute politician. Baldwin married Philip's sister, and their child, Philip's niece, was married to the young Philip Augustus. The count of Flanders himself had acquired the counties of Valois and Vermandois as the dowry of his wife, Isabella of Vermandois. But the very complexity of these connections defeated the aims of Philip of Alsace, and the young king of France turned them to his own advantage. He

[32] Besides the bishop of Beauvais and Baldwin of Hainault, he could probably rely upon Bernard of Saint Valéry and John of Ponthieu who had been his pledges at Messina in the treaty with Richard. For the connection

began by taking a leaf from the book of Flemish policy and made peace with Henry II of England. The supremacy of Flanders in the politics of northern France depended upon the hostility of France and Normandy; and in the past the counts of Flanders had successfully played one State off against the other. Now, with the aid of the Normans, Philip Augustus broke up the coalition which Philip of Alsace had formed in order to secure control over him.[33] In the second place, by fair means and foul, Philip Augustus set enmity between the count of Flanders and his brother-in-law of Hainault, and as the latter's son-in-law, bound him to his own interests. His first great success came in 1185 after the death of Isabella of Vermandois (1182). He claimed the inheritance of Vermandois and added to his domain Amiens and Montdidier; a wedge was thus driven between Normandy and the Flemish fiefs, and the gap between the royal domains in the Ile-de-France and at Montreuil-sur-mer was partially filled. Philip of Alsace turned to the east and formed a coalition with the duke of Brabant against his brother of Hainault; but the Crusade and his death in the Holy Land terminated this alliance. Philip Augustus had scored his second point. The late count of Flanders had made an elaborate agreement with him with regard to the dowry of his niece Isabella of Hainault. The count had granted as a dowry in 1180 all the western part of Flanders beyond what was known as the new Foss: the district known as Artois, including Arras, Bapaume, Saint-Omer, Aire, Hesdin, the *avouerie* of Béthune, Lens, Ardres, Saint-Pol, Guines, Richebourg. In possession of this valuable territory, Philip Augustus might well hope to control the whole north of France. By the treaty of Mons, however (1185), Philip of Alsace had secured the right to rule Artois during his own lifetime; and Artois was to remain with France only if Philip Augustus died leaving a direct heir, who also had direct descendants. This provision was fulfilled, and Artois technically became part of France in 1226, on the accession of St. Louis. But long before that Philip Augustus, hurrying home after the death of Philip of Alsace, had entered upon his wife's dowry, while Baldwin of Hainault secured the succession to the rest of Flanders in right of his wife, the count's sister. Thus the new count of Flanders, by scrupulously respecting the rights of his daughter and her husband to Artois, added Flanders to Hainault under the protection of the king of France.[34] Moreover, he had shortly before been

between the death of Philip of Alsace and Philip Augustus's return, see William of Newburgh, p. 357; Coggeshall, p. 34; Cartellieri, ii, 238–46.

[33] Lavisse, *Histoire de France*, III, i, 86. Even in this severely diplomatic summary, the affection which the young king felt for Henry II's sons, Henry and Geoffrey, should not be forgotten, as a factor in the alliance.

[34] For the above, see Pirenne, *Histoire de Belgique* (1902), i, 197–204; Borelli de Serres, *La réunion des provinces septentrionales à la couronne par*

recognised as a new prince of the empire, in spite of the protests of
Brabant.[35] In 1191 the alliance between France and Flanders seemed
secure: Baldwin was indisputably the greatest man in the valley of
the lower Rhine, and Philip had gained a large tract of rich country
on the flank of Normandy. Richard of England was absent, his brother
was willing to betray him, the emperor was friendly; Gisors and the
Vexin, if not Normandy, might be won.

Such was the situation when events in Germany altered the whole
aspect of affairs, isolated Baldwin and Philip, and induced the former
to resume the traditional alliance between Flanders and Normandy.

The rivalry of Richard and the emperor Henry VI had been very
welcome to Philip. Both men caught the fancy of the age, and figured
in the apocalyptic visions of Joachim of Flora. The aspirations of
Henry were well known. He desired, says the Greek princess Anna
Comnena, to be king of kings. In the west this aim was interpreted
as being especially directed against France.[36] A man of his type, who
combined with an alert and practical energy the fertile imagination
of an eastern conqueror, could not fail to be impressed by the exploits
of Richard. Richard had not only made a name for himself in the
Mediterranean which was to linger long after Henry was forgotten;
he had also thwarted the emperor's chief hopes. By his alliance with
Tancred he had checked the advance of the Hohenstaufen in Sicily;
he had overthrown Henry's relative in Cyprus, and had quarrelled
with Henry's subjects in Syria. Moreover, nearer home Richard was
the mainstay of his brother-in-law Henry the Lion and of the Saxon
house. No wonder that Philip Augustus found it an easy task to pit
the emperor against this magnificent rival.

The king of England was taken prisoner in December 1192, and
was surrendered to the emperor in the following February. Before

---

Philippe Auguste (Paris, 1899); Count Maxime de Germiny in the *Revue
des questions historiques,* lxvii (1900), 245. Cartellieri, iii, 3–13, gives very
full details of the various treaties of 1191 and 1192. The chief text is Gilbert
of Mons in *Mon. Germ. Scriptores,* xxi, 574–6; cf. Cartellieri, ii, 281–2.

Isabella of = Philip of Alsace,	Margaret = Baldwin of Hainault.
Vermandois. Count of Flanders.	Count of Flanders *jure uxoris* (1191–Nov., 1194).
Baldwin IX. of Flanders (1194) and VI. of Hainault (1195), abdicated 1202, Emperor of Constantinople (1204–5).	Isabella = Philip Augustus.

[35] Smets, *Henri I, duc de Brabant* (Brussels, 1908), pp. 41–4.

[36] Scheffer-Boichorst in *Forschungen zur deutschen Geschichte,* viii (1868),
498.

the end of June three agreements had been made between the two men,[37] in the last of which the terms of Richard's release were decided. Philip had done much in these few months; Gisors had fallen, the Vexin had been occupied and Rouen besieged; but the news that Richard and the emperor had come to terms forced on a treaty with the former which was effected on July 9. Philip and Count John had done their utmost to prevent the agreement between the emperor and his captive, and this arrangement of July 9 was only a safeguard in case of Richard's release.[38] As a matter of fact, the king was not released for some time, and Philip continued to use active measures against him. They took the form of preparations for an invasion of England, and direct negotiations with the emperor.

In spite of his negotiations with Richard, Philip did not cease to offer bribes to Henry VI in order to prevent Richard's release at the stated time. Envoys offered 50,000 marks of silver on Philip's behalf, and 30,000 on behalf of Count John, on condition that the king of England were kept a prisoner until the following Michaelmas (1194); or if the emperor preferred, they offered to pay 1,000 pounds of silver at the end of each month of Richard's captivity; or, if still another plan was preferred, the king of France would give 100,000 marks of silver (equal to the ransom) and Count John would give 50,000 marks, on condition that the emperor either surrendered Richard or kept him in captivity for a year from that date.[39] This was the last of several attempts to bribe Henry VI which were made during the year 1193. But more direct action against Richard's possessions were preparing during the same year. Early in the year Philip Augustus had collected a fleet at Witsand, which was to convey to England a host of his Flemish allies.[40] And his alliance with the king of Denmark was in great part due to his desire to carry out the favourite scheme of an invasion of England. Denmark was at this period feeling the full influence of French manners, art and scholarship. Indeed the hatred with which the ordinary Anglo-Norman viewed the growth of French fashions is some measure of their influence in those lands where political and religious forces combined to welcome them. Hence, when Philip Augustus offered himself as the husband of Ingeborg,[41] the

---

[37] See Cartellieri, iii, 40, 51, 54.

[38] Howden, iii, 217, gives the text of the engagements made at Mantes by Richard's agents. They recognised Philip's position in Normandy, and as the emperor had made peace with Philip one of his conditions of Richard's liberation, were a necessary concession to the king of France; cf. the note in *Recueil des Actes de Philippe Auguste*, i, 550, no. 454.

[39] Howden, iii, 229

[40] Gervase of Canterbury, i, 514–5; and see below, p. 95.

[41] A small literature has been dedicated to Ingeborg. For the chief authorities, see Lavisse, *Histoire de France*, III, i, 144; and Cartellieri, iii *passim*.

daughter of King Cnut VI, the prospect of a closer alliance was found too attractive at the Danish court to be resisted. At first, however, there was considerable hesitation. Philip asked for the transference to himself of Cnut's claims to the English throne and for the use of the Danish fleet and army for one year. The genealogies of Danish kings became an object of political excitement at the French court, and Philip aspired to invade England as the successor of the great Cnut. But the Danish nobles wished to have an ally against their German neighbours, not an ally who would rob them of what defence they actually possessed. Philip therefore consented to receive a large dowry of 10,000 marks of silver, and King Cnut hesitatingly agreed. William, abbot of St. Thomas of the Paraclete, was the chief agent in overcoming his scruples. 'My lord king,' he wrote, 'no small honour is offered to your grace. A word in your ear: if you are bound by friendship to the king of France, you need fear German greed no more.'[42] Philip took the money in August and repudiated the wife in November, and Saint William—for the abbot was afterwards canonised—had to turn his energy to the task of vindicating the rights of the poor princess.

As is well known, the repudiation of Ingeborg involved Philip in the inconveniences and expense of a long quarrel with Rome. The illconsidered marriage brought another evil upon him. He had overestimated his influence at the imperial court, and his meddling in the intricacies of German and Danish politics strengthened in all probability the alliance between the emperor and King Richard.[43] At first apparently he tried to cover his mistake by planning a marriage with the emperor's cousin, Agnes, the daughter of the Count Palatine.[44] But the lady's mother, naturally anxious for her daughter's happiness, and influenced by political views which did not harmonise with those of the king of France, married her in haste and secrecy to Henry of Brunswick.[45] Philip had to surrender. He was able to delay the release of his enemy until February 4, 1194. After that date he had to look to his own.

Richard, on the other hand, had attained a position of great influence in Germany. From the first he had been supported by the malcontent nobility of the empire. Resistance to Henry VI had come to a head after the murder of Bishop Albert of Liège (November 24,

[42] *Historiens de France*, xix, 310–11. The other chief authority is William of Newburgh, who, though he confuses the dates, seems to have special information: pp. 368–70.

[43] Cf. Scheffer-Boichorst in *Forschungen zur deutschen Geschichte*, viii, 493.

[44] William of Newburgh, 384–6; *Mon. Germ. Scriptores*, xvi, 227 (Annales Stederburgenses).

[45] Henry of Brunswick was son of Henry the Lion, and nephew of Richard.

1192), in which the emperor was suspected by many persons to have been an accomplice.[46] The anxieties and uncertainties which, up to the very last, preceded Richard's release and which were renewed during his homeward journey;[47] the continuous stream of ecclesiastics and barons, astonishing the Germans by their multitude,[48] who passed from England and Normandy to visit the captive; the traditional share which his family had taken in imperial politics; all these things invested him with the prestige of an imperial statesman engaged in a great contest rather than with the forlorn dignity of a suppliant. This position was evident to the world after the emperor had been dissuaded from breaking the early arrangements with Richard and from meeting the king of France in June, 1193.[49] Richard began to play the part of a peacemaker, and great nobles of all shades of opinion co-operated to procure his release in the following February.[50] In the treaty of June 29 he had arranged to marry the sister of Arthur of Brittany to the son of his captor, the duke of Austria.[51] It seems probable that in the general settlement Richard even consented to desert the old Henry the Lion.[52] Peace was as welcome to the emperor as to Richard. He was now free for a time to pursue his Italian policy. Moreover, it was essential that the commercial route through Brabant should be kept open, and that the powerful duke of Brabant, the brother of the murdered bishop, and the soul of the recent opposition, should be placated.[53] Hence the duke, in exchange for his hopes of the imperial throne, was allowed to follow up his ambition in the valley of the lower Rhine.

Thus instead of seeing themselves at the head of a German party, Philip Augustus and the new count of Flanders were faced by a great confederation of the princes in north Germany. On his way back to

[46] For Richard in Germany, see Howden, iii, 195-9, 208-20 *passim*. On the whole there is no reason to doubt the suggestion of Howden (p. 214) borne out by the disappointment of Baldwin of Hainault and Flanders (see Gilbert of Mons, who reflects Flemish feeling, *Mon. Germ. Scriptores*, xxi, 583-5) that the emperor thought of coming to terms with Philip of France, but was not unwilling to be forced to treat with the German rebels upon whom Richard relied. For the bishop of Liège, see Smets, pp. 59-63; Cartellieri, iii, 49.

[47] Howden, iii, 232; William of Newburgh, pp. 404-5.

[48] Rad. Dic., ii, 110. cf. Pipe Roll 5 Ric. I, pp. xx, xxii and references.

[49] Howden, iii, 209-12, 214. Henry and Philip had arranged to meet on June 25. The final treaty for Richard's release was made June 29.

[50] Howden, iii, 232; William of Newburgh, p. 403.

[51] *Infra septem menses* (Howden, iii, 216). See below, p. 110.

[52] The arrangement about Henry the Lion is obscure. Howden, iii, 215 *seqq.*; Cartellieri, iii, 53-4. I have not thought it relevant to refer to the arrangement between Henry VI and Richard by which Richard did homage for his lands, and was promised Arles. See the discussion of this problem by A. L. Poole, 'England and Burgundy in the last decade of the twelfth century', in *Essays in History presented to Reginald Lane Poole* (Oxford, 1927) pp. 261-73.   [53] Gilbert of Mons (*Mon. Germ. Scriptores*, xxi, 585).

England, Richard knit together that system of alliances which was not finally broken till Philip Augustus won his great victory at Bouvines in 1214. The duke of Brabant, the count of Holland, and several of their neighbours did homage to the king of England in return for annual pensions, and promised their aid against Philip. The archbishops of Mainz and Köln and the new bishop of Liège, the Elector Palatine, Conrad of Swabia the late emperor's brother, even the duke of Austria and Boniface of Montferrat were among Richard's pensioners.[54] The merchants of Köln, that centre of unrest, were his political and commercial allies.[55]

Between this powerful group and Philip, Baldwin of Flanders had to make a choice, and he decided that the dukes of Normandy and Brabant were more dangerous enemies than the king of France. The desire to resume the interrupted trade between England and Flanders, and the chance of recovering his daughter's dowry doubtless weighed with him. He allowed his young son, the future emperor of Constantinople, who was one of Richard's admirers, to become also one of his vassals and pensioners.[56] Richard lingered for some time on the Flemish coast, and was not molested. Before the middle of 1195 Flanders and Brabant had made peace with each other, and the way was open for a renewal of the old relations between Flanders and Normandy.

It is true that Richard's Rhenish allies gave him little help. 'He, as usual, did not keep his promises,' says Gilbert of Mons drily, 'and they were not in the habit of keeping theirs.'[57] But the king of England had gained his end, just as Edward III did nearly one hundred and fifty years later. He had destroyed Philip's plans in the north-east of France, and had prevented an alliance, to his own hurt, between Philip and the emperor.

[54] Howden, iii, 234. Conrad of Montferrat was receiving his pension ('de feudo suo') in 1198 (*Rot. Scacc. Norm.*, ii, 301).

[55] Stubbs' note in Howden, iii, 235.   [56] Howden, iii, 234; Smets, pp. 67–70.

[57] *Mon. Germ. Scriptores*, xxi, 583. [W. Kienast, *Die deutschen Fürsten im Dienste der Westmächte*, i (1924), 135 ff., gives the most detailed account of these arrangements, but, following Gilbert of Mons, is less than just to King Richard's observance of them. See an important paper on 'Richard the First's alliances with the German princes in 1194', by A. L. Poole, in *Studies in Medieval History presented to Frederick Maurice Powicke* (Oxford, 1948), pp. 90–9.]

ADDITIONAL NOTE ON LIEGE-HOMAGE (above, pp. 80–83): The nature of liege-homage and its wider implications has been studied intensively since 1913, when this book appeared: see Stenton, *English Feudalism*, pp. 29–31; H. Mitteis, *Lehnrecht und Staatsgewalt* (Weimar, 1933), pp. 556–90; Marc Bloch, *La Société féodale: la formation des liens de dépendance* (Paris, 1939), pp. 330–2; and W. Kienast, *Untertaneneid und Treuvorbehalt im England und Frankreich* (Weimar, 1952), on which cf. A. L. Poole in *E.H.R.*, lxix (1954), 473–4.

CHAPTER V

RICHARD I AND NORMANDY

I

WHEN Philip Augustus heard that Richard was a prisoner, he prepared forthwith to attack England and Normandy.[1] The seneschal of Normandy had called a conference at Alençon, where the barons might discuss measures for their lord's release. Count John crossed the Channel to join Philip. The seneschal sought to divert him and begged him to come to Alençon; John demanded an oath of fealty; but the seneschal and the barons refused to take such an oath. Hence John passed by to Paris and did homage to Philip for Normandy and for Richard's other lands. Philip promised to give him that part of Flanders to which he had recently succeeded, as the dowry of his sister Alice, whom John was to marry. In return John promised to surrender Gisors and the Norman Vexin. Moreover, it was said in English official circles[2] that John had also done homage for England, and it was at this time that Philip planned the invasion of England. He collected ships and men at his Flemish port at Witsand, and tried, as we have seen, to win over the king of Denmark, and to keep King Richard in captivity.

Count John with a band of mercenaries made civil war in England, but with small result. His chief stronghold at Windsor was besieged by the archbishop of Rouen[3] and the royal justices.[4] King Henry's strong government lived after him and forced John to make peace till the feast of All Saints of this year 1193.[5] Moreover, a general levy guarded the coasts and put an end to thoughts of invasion.[6] In July, John, hearing from Philip that his brother was to be set free, fled to France.

---

[1] For what follows, see Howden, iii, 203; Coggeshall, p. 61; Gervase of Canterbury, i, 515; William of Newburgh, p. 384. During 1192 Philip and John remained quiet. Richard's later protests against Philip's attacks upon his lands, while he was in the Holy Land, are not to be taken too seriously. See Innocent III's letter to Richard of May 31, 1198, as edited and translated in *Selected Letters of Pope Innocent III concerning England*, edited by C. R. Cheney and W. H. Semple (1953), pp. 3–8.   [2] Howden, iii, 204, 207.

[3] For Walter of Coutances, archbishop of Rouen, and his rôle in England from 1191 to 1194, see A. L. Poole, *From Domesday Book to Magna Carta*, pp. 355–8, 364, 369.   [4] See Pipe Roll 5 Ric. I, introduction, pp. xviii–xix.

[5] Howden, iii, 206–7. The truce was made after the arrival of bishop Hubert of Salisbury who came from Richard. See Gervase, i, 516.

[6] Cf. Pipe Roll, 5 Ric. I., pp. xv–xvii.

The real strain was felt in Normandy. The Normans, says William
of Newburgh, were like sheep not having a shepherd; the fate of their
king sapped their loyalty.[7] The monks of Canterbury were by no
means certain of the fidelity of the archbishop of Rouen, and their
chronicler breathes a curious slander against the aged seneschal,
William Fitz Ralf.[8] The surrender of Gisors, the key to the Norman
defences, in April, 1193, was more than sufficient to justify suspicion,
for it was lost through the treachery of the castellan, Gilbert of
Vascoeuil. King Richard, when he made his last arrangements for the
safety of his lands, had sent this man home from Messina. He had been
specially entrusted with the most important fortress on the frontier.
His treachery became a byword. He lost his lands in Normandy and
failed to gain the confidence of the French.[9] But he was to have
many successors in treachery during the leaderless rule of John.

With Gisors, Neaufle had also fallen, and Philip occupied the
Vexin. The French king, save during one short period, never again
gave up his claim upon the Vexin. He immediately restored Château-
neuf-saint-Denis[10] to the monks of Saint Denis, and began that
process of settlement whereby he bound Normandy bit by bit to the
French throne. By the fall of Gisors the way to Rouen was also
opened. The men of Rouen feared a siege above all things, for they
depended upon their industry and trade. They would relax their
chartered right to refuse hospitality, in favour of a great baron who
would protect them. He was sure of good entertainment, of special
wines, and fruits and nuts for his table.[11] In this crisis Rouen was
defended by Robert earl of Leicester, one of the heroes of the Crusade.

---

[7] William of Newburgh, p. 390. In this period any man might be suspected:
cf. the story of the attempt to implicate the Marshal as a traitor in 1192 in
Histoire de Guillaume le Maréchal, iii, 128–9 and notes.

[8] This seems to be the meaning of the phrase in Gervase of Canterbury (i,
515) describing the earl of Leicester's action at Rouen before the siege of
1193: 'procuratorem, immo proditorem, Normanniae, ut ferebatur, vinculis
coartavit.' Gervase and William of Newburgh describe the justiciar of England
as 'procurator'. The seneschal held the corresponding office in Normandy.
Gervase refers to the archbishop of Rouen as *malefidus* (i, 515).

[9] Howden, iii, 206: 'sed vilis habitus est inter illos [Francos] propter pro-
ditionem.' For Gilbert, see Tardif in the *Coutumiers*, I, i, 108. The author
of the custumal (c. lxiv) refers to him as a means of dating: 'in tempore
Gisleberti de Vascuil.' Cf. also Coggeshall, p. 61; William of Newburgh, p.
389; *L'Estoire de la Guerre Sainte*, ll. 1166–7; and *Itinerarium Ricardi* (ed.
Stubbs), p. 176. In 1195 Gilbert's lands in Normandy were farmed for 260 li.
by William of Ely, the chancellor (*Rot. Scacc.*, i, 155).

[10] Rigord, p. 123; Delaborde, *Recueil*, ii, no. 551 (March, 1197: confirmation
of an exchange made by the monks of St. Denis).

[11] See the story of the manner in which the Marshal and his companions
get a good meal in 1202 (*Guillaume le Maréchal*, ll. 12321–12404). The point
of the story seems to lie partly in the privilege of the citizens, first granted

The lord of extensive lands in England and Normandy, having more than 120 knights in his service from his Norman honours alone,[12] this great baron had every inducement to preserve the connection between the two countries. His prestige and his exhortations nerved the men of Rouen to such unexpected resistance that after a short demonstration of force, Philip burned his engines and wrathfully withdrew.[13] The success of the campaign, however, was by no means small. Besides the Vexin, Aumâle and Eu had probably fallen in the north-east, and the fortresses of Ivry and Paci surrendered to Philip on his return.[14] He had broken the Norman frontier at three important points by these acquisitions on the uplands of Caux and the Vexin and in the valley of the Eure. From all three directions he hoped to advance in the spring of 1194. In January John surrendered any claims he might have to the whole of Normandy east of the Seine, with the exception of the city, and restricted *banlieu* of Rouen. On the west bank of the river he gave up Vaudreuil and all the territory south of the river Itun, east of a line drawn from the Itun southwards to Chennebrun on the Avre. This meant the surrender of Verneuil and Evreux. In other words, John made over to Philip the whole frontier of Normandy, with its castles, from the country east of the central forests, where so many of the smaller Norman streams have their source, to the shore of the English Channel.[15] To fulfil the bargain Philip suddenly invaded Normandy by way of the valley of the Eure in February, 1194, and approached Rouen for the second time.[16] Evreux, Neubourg, even Vaudreuil fell to him after little or

---

in 1150: 'Item, quod nemo infra Rothomagum aliquem hospitetur ex precepto nostro nisi per proprium marescalum civitatis.' The privilege was modified by Philip in 1207. See Giry, *Les Etablissements de Rouen*, ii, 63.

[12] *Red Book*, ii, 627.

[13] The date of the siege in the composite chronicle of Rouen, *Kalendis Maii* (*Histor. de France*, xviii, 358). Interesting details in Howden, iii, 207; Gervase, i, 515–6. Cf. Gilbert of Mons in *Mon. Germ. Scriptores*, xxi, 583; Coggeshall, p. 62.

[14] Coggeshall says that Philip prevailed 'usque ad Diepe' (p. 61). Howden's reference to the invasion (iii, 205) seems to be an anticipation of what follows, as often in his chronicle. Miss Norgate regards it as an allusion to a previous attack (*Angevin Kings*, ii, 363).

[15] The treaty, sealed as proclaimed by John, still exists. The best editions in *Cart. Norm.*, no. 1055, p. 275; Teulet, *Layettes du trésor des chartes*, i, 175, no. 412; see also Rymer, *Foedera*, i, 57. It is dated 'Actum Parisiis anno . . . mcxciii mense januarii'. Although the form of dating used in France at this period is doubtful (Giry, *Manuel de diplomatique*, p. 113) and Delisle attributed the treaty to 1193, internal evidence proves that 1194 is the correct date; *e.g.*, the reference to the four castles pledged by Richard in July, 1193, below, p. 99. Cf. Delaborde in his edition of Rigord, i, 126.

[16] Rigord, i, 125–6; William of Newburgh, p. 403. It is clear from a phrase in the *Histoire des ducs de Normandie* (ed. Michel), p. 88, and from the Annals

no resistance. The citizens of Evreux had prepared to meet the danger. Their count and bishop had recently died; the new bishop had gone to King Richard in Germany; the county was farmed by a Norman bailiff. The seneschal advised the citizens to form themselves into a commune and to defend themselves. Accordingly they formed a commune under Adam the Englishman, as mayor. They dug a ditch through the episcopal lands on the Lord's Day, and the archdeacon absolved them. Four men guarded each earthwork and fenced it with a hurdle.[17] What resistance they made when Philip approached we do not know. The new government of the city was disregarded, and John, who had already been entrusted with the great castles of Arques and Drincourt in eastern Normandy,[18] was now put in charge of Evreux.[19]

King Philip passed on to Rouen, but rumours of the great preparations which Richard was making in England must have caused his withdrawal once more. He made a truce and retired to France.[20] The brief quiet was disturbed, according to a chronicler who wrote in the diocese of Arras, by the arrival of men from England, forerunners of the king.[21] On the 10th of May, Philip, again marching north-west, laid siege to Verneuil. At Portsmouth a hundred great ships were waiting storm-bound, but at last, on the 12th, Richard landed at Barfleur.[22]

In the last two years the king of France had shaken the Angevin power in Aquitaine and in Touraine as well as in Normandy. At the end of 1192 Sancho of Navarre, the brother of Queen Berengaria, had to come to the aid of Richard's government against a revolt of the Gascon barons, who were headed by the count of Périgord.[23] The seneschal of Poitou, Peter Bertin, had shown great vigour. The troops of Poitou and Navarre had in one campaign invaded Toulouse, and, in another, defeated and captured the count of Angoulême. But Philip Augustus was none the less able to turn the restlessness of the western vassals of Richard to account. Ademar of Angoulême had insisted that he owed allegiance to Philip alone, and Philip insisted upon his liberation from captivity in the treaty which he concluded

---

of St. Aubin (in Halphen, *Recueil des annales angevines*, p. 26) that Rouen was besieged twice.

[17] From a later inquest; see Stapleton, *Observations*, II, clxxiv–v.

[18] William the Breton (ed. Delaborde, i, 196); Howden, iii, 228.

[19] Wendover, i, 230 (and cf. *E.H.R.*, xxi, 289).

[20] William of Newburgh, p. 403. Philip's charters show that he was in Paris in May, so that he could not have marched from Rouen to Verneuil, as Miss Norgate thinks (ii, 364).

[21] *Historiens de France*, xviii, 547.

[22] Howden, iii, 251.

[23] Howden, iii, 194; Richard, *Les Comtes de Poitou*, ii, 279–80.

with Richard's legates at Mantes on July 9, 1193. In the following January, as part of the agreement between himself and John, Philip got recognition of the homage of Ademar for all his lands except certain places which were recognised as part of Aquitaine.[24] French claims upon Touraine were still more dangerous; for in the same treaty John surrendered the keys to the west, Tours and its dependencies as far as Azai, Amboise, Montbason, Montrichard, Loches: the chief passages of the Loire, the Cher and the Indre. Moulins and Bonmoulins were to have gone once more to the count of Perche, so that Touraine might be cut off from Normandy; and with a similar purpose Vendôme had been allotted to Louis of Blois.

King Richard had peculiar reason for his anger at the news of this suggested division of his inheritance; for, if Philip succeeded in realising his share of the bargain Richard had, in part, himself to blame. In the previous July, when the end of the captivity seemed near at hand, and John had left England in terror, the king of France had met William of Ely and other agents of Richard at Mantes. The treaty which followed was ineffective. Philip found more hope of profit in the continued imprisonment of his enemy. But by its terms four great fortresses, Arques and Drincourt in Normandy, Loches and Châtillon-sur-Indre in Touraine, were entrusted to the French king; they were to be garrisoned by French troops at the expense of the Norman and Angevin exchequers, as sureties for the payment, in four instalments, of 20,000 marks of silver.[25] By his later treaty with John, Philip kept control of these castles,[26] and they were in his possession when Richard reached Normandy in 1194.

II

The squire of William the Marshal retained in his memory a vivid picture of Richard's return to Normandy, and of his reconciliation with his brother John.[27] It was the middle of May, and the king was followed by a great crowd of joyful people from Barfleur to Caen. They joined in dances and rounds; old and young came in long procession, singing 'God has come again in his strength'; and the bells rang everywhere. The rejoicing of the north was echoed in the fierce

[24] *Cart. Norm.*, p. 275; the distinction between the fiefs which Ademar held of Philip and those which he held of John by this treaty is explained by Boissonade, *Quomodo comites Engolismenses*, p. 8.

[25] See the treaty of July in Howden, iii, 217–20. For points of interest in the agreement, see below, p. 291.

[26] *Cart. Norm.*, p. 275. 'Castellum vero de Lochis cum pertinentiis suis, et castellum de Castellione cum pertinentiis suis, et castellum de Driencourt cum pertinentiis suis et castellum de Archis cum pertinentiis suis regi Franciae remanebunt in perpetuum.'

[27] *Histoire de Guillaume le Maréchal*, ll. 10432–52.

exultation of Bertrand of Born in the south.[28] The lion had come, and the wolf would now be caught in the net of his own contriving.

John came to Richard at Lisieux in May and found him in the house of John of Alençon, the archdeacon. The king was trying to sleep, but could not, owing to his anxiety for Verneuil. The archdeacon entered the room with the news that John had come. His air was distressed, and Richard at once guessed the reason. 'Why do you look like that? You have seen my brother—don't lie. I will not reproach him. Those who have driven him on will soon have their reward.' The archdeacon went to John and brought him in. Still fearful, he fell at Richard's feet. The king raised him and kissed him, and said: 'John, don't be afraid. You are a child.[29] You have had bad companions, and your counsellors shall pay.' Turning to John of Alençon, he inquired what there was to eat. Just then a salmon was brought to him as a gift, and he had it cooked for his brother.[30] Richard had never feared John. He was ten years older and had seen him grow to manhood. During his captivity he had soon thrown off his depression at the news of John's treachery. 'My brother John,' he had said, 'is not the kind of man to subject lands to himself, if anyone meets his strength with a little strength.'[31] A few months before the reconciliation he had been willing to receive John's homage and to restore him his castles in England and Normandy, but the royal officials had feared treachery, and refused to hand them over.[32] In 1195 and 1196 Richard, while assigning to his brother more than a competency, retained his castles in his own hands.[33]

From Lisieux Richard took the road to Verneuil. Verneuil was one of the strongest castles built by Henry I in that effective style of architecture which in 1194 was only beginning to go out of fashion. It lay in a stretch of flat upland country on the very edge of

[28] See the references in Cartellieri, iii, 85.

[29] John was 27 years of age.

[30] *Histoire de Guillaume le Maréchal*, ll. 10363–10419. Cf. iii, 137, notes.

[31] Howden, iii, 198.

[32] Howden, iii, 225. A writ was not enough; compare above, p. 83. At Lisieux neither lands nor castles were restored; see Landon, *Itinerary* (Pipe Roll Society, n.s., xiii, 93).

[33] Howden, iii, 286. In 1195 Richard allowed John the possession of his honours of Mortain, Eye and Gloucester 'exceptis castellis, et pro omnibus aliis comitatibus et terris suis dedit ei rex per annum octo millia librarum Andegavensis monetae'. For the restoration of the third penny of the county of Gloucester and of the issues of the honour of Eye, see Pipe Rolls, 7 Ric. I, p. 171, and 8 Ric. I, p. 121. Mortain does not appear on the Exchequer rolls of 1195 and 1198 (see above, p. 74) and in 1198 the revenues of Argentan, the forest of Gouffern and Guernsey are allotted to John (*Rot. Scacc.*, ii, 390–1). For John as 'dominus Insularum', see above, p. 76; for his English lands and revenues before 1194, see A. L. Poole, *Domesday Book to Magna Carta*, p. 348.

Normandy; and was so prosperous, or had been so well endowed with 'appurtenances', that it was farmed for 700 li. a year.[34] In 1194 its castellan was one of the ablest among the younger officials of the empire, William of Mortemer. Indefatigable as well as able, the castellan defended Verneuil against King Philip for nearly three weeks. He was assisted by a body of knights and arbalasters whom Richard managed to throw into the fortress, and he was encouraged by the success with which the English king cut off French provisions. Philip raised the siege on May 29; and when Richard entered the town men recognised that Normandy was saved.[35]

Philip had not waited for Richard's approach, probably on account of the foul news from Evreux. For after his reconciliation with Richard, John had hurried off to Evreux with one of the bodies of picked knights which the king was sending to the frontier. Philip, it will be remembered, had entrusted the city and castle to John earlier in the year. The count secured the good will of the citizens and after a day's siege captured and slew the garrison.[36] According to the story told some years later by Philip's chaplain, John made merry with the Frenchmen, and slew them by guile. Their heads were stuck on long poles.[37] Some time later Philip took his revenge. He burned the city, slaughtered the citizens, destroyed the churches and carried off the sacred relics.[38] When we wonder why Normandy was afterwards lost so easily, we must remember that the strongest king could not protect the frontier from this sort of treatment.

Thirty-seven days after Philip raised the siege of Verneuil, says the careful dean of St. Paul's,[39] the king 'broke in terror into Châteaudun'. The occasion of this second flight was the rout of the French at Fréteval, a place on the road between Châteaudun and Vendôme. The fight came about as follows. After the success at Verneuil, King Richard had only waited to capture the count of Meulan's castle on the Risle, Beaumont-le-Roger, and to order the

<hr/>

[34] See Stapleton, *Observations*, I, cxx. The privileges of Verneuil, confirmed by Henry II, probably date from Henry I's foundation, though, as Giry points out, Verneuil was not a commune in Angevin times. *Ordonnances*, iv, 634; Giry, *Les Etablissements de Rouen*, i, 52.

[35] *Histoire de Guillaume le Maréchal*, iii, 136–9.

[36] Rigord, i, 127; Annales Aquicinctenses, in *Historiens de France*, xviii, 547; *Histoire de Guillaume le Maréchal*, iii, 139.

[37] Will. Bret. (ed. Delaborde, i, 196); also in the *Phillippid*, iv, 445 (*ibid.*, ii, 115). Norgate, ii, 365, note. *English Historical Review*, xxi, 290.

[38] Rigord, i, 127; Robert of Auxerre, in *Historiens de France*, xviii, 261. Howden gives the order of events, iii, 255.

[39] Rad. Dic., ii, 117–18. For what follows, see Landon, *Itinerary*, pp. 95–6, where a more detailed chronology (June 28–July 22, 1194) is attempted. Landon follows William le Breton in giving Belfou as the scene of King Philip's discomfiture.

destruction of its keep,[40] before hastening to establish his authority
in Touraine and Poitou. An Angevin contingent which had come to
the relief of Verneuil, preceded him on its way homeward, and took
Montmirail in its march.[41] Richard's own campaign was especially
directed against the count of Angoulême and Geoffrey of Rançon;[42]
but he had injuries to avenge on the clergy of Tours and he could not
leave the great fortress of Loches in French hands. Sancho of Navarre,
who had also brought help to his brother-in-law, had besieged Loches
in vain. Richard was more successful. Loches fell, and the way to
Poitou lay open. Just at this time King Philip, fresh from a successful raid in Normandy, invaded Touraine in Richard's rear, and
approached Vendôme. He had reached Lisle,[43] six or seven miles
from Vendôme, when Richard arrived on the scene. The French king
fell back on Fréteval, where he encamped. Richard encamped outside Vendôme, since the place had no walls.[44] After some boastful
parleying, Philip retreated before Richard's sudden approach, and
the retreat became a flight. While William the Marshal kept together
the rearguard,[45] Richard pursued the French king. He had not yet
seen Philip since they had parted from each other in the Holy Land; his
mind must have been full of angry memories—the seduction of John,
the loss of Gisors and Loches, the unendurable inaction of his captivity.

'During the flight', says Roger of Howden,[46] 'the king of France
drew apart from the crowd and entered a church at some distance
from the straight road in order to hear mass. The king of England
did not know that he had hid himself; he came up breathing out
threats and slaughter against the men of the king of France, and
sought for him that he might slay him or take him alive. A Fleming
told him that the king was far ahead, and so the king of England was
deceived and advanced on a swift horse beyond the border, and when
his horse failed him, Mercadier, the leader of the Brabançons, brought
him another horse. So the king of England returned to Vendôme,

---

[40] The count of Meulan had joined Philip; for the fall of Beaumont, see Will.
Bret., i, 196; *Guillaume le Maréchal*, iii, 139; *Rot. Scacc.*, i, 253, refers to the
destruction of the keep, 'pro turre de Bello Monte prosternenda, xl so'. A
garrison was placed in the rest of the castle. *Rot. Scacc.*, i, 260.

[41] Annals of St. Aubin (MS. E) in Halphen, 27; Rad. Dic., i, 116–17.

[42] For the relations between Geoffrey and King Philip, see Teulet, *Layettes*,
i, 175, no. 415; Cartellieri, iii, 75–6.

[43] Howden (iii, 253, 255) should be interpreted by Rad. Dic. (ii, 117) at
this point. Lisle is mentioned by the Annals of St. Aubin (Halphen, p. 26—
Insula Jeremie). The identification of Insula Jeremie with Lisle is made by
R. de Saint-Venant, *Nouveaux aperçus sur le combat de Fréteval* (Vendôme,
1905). Compare Diceto's *prope Vindocinum*.

[44] Richard had destroyed Vendôme six years before. See *Annals of Vendôme*,
in Halphen, p. 74.

[45] *Guillaume le Maréchal*, iii, 140–1.   [46] Howden, iii, 255.

not having found the king of France, with great booty of men and horses, and much money.'

The royal treasury and chapel—the machinery of state—as well as the engines of war, and the rich stuffs and vessels of the tents were captured. Richard gained a large addition to his fortune and the means of acquiring more; for Philip had carried about with him the bonds of those subjects of Richard who had joined or had promised to join Count John and himself.[47]

Within three weeks Richard subdued Poitou and reduced the count of Angoulême and Geoffrey of Rançon.[48] He then returned to Normandy.

Even during these two months of triumphant war, a strong peace party had asserted itself in Normandy. The Normans under Count John,. the earl of Arundel and Earl David of Huntingdon, had not been very successful during Richard's absence. In June, while Richard was in Touraine, Philip had made another raid in the direction of Rouen, and the earl of Leicester had been captured during a counter raid in the district of Gournai. The archbishop of Rouen, on his return from Germany, found the estates of the church in confusion owing to the war, and was eager for a truce. After two attempts he succeeded, with the seneschal and constable, in arranging the terms of a year's truce.[49] Richard, however, refused to regard the truce as binding upon the barons of Poitou—Normans, he said, could not bind Poitevins—and the arrangement broke down; moreover after the capture of Loches he was in no mood to cease operations.[50] During his absence in Aquitaine, negotiations began once more. Count John and his colleagues had failed in an attempt to besiege Vaudreuil;[51] and a truce, to last until All Saints' Day in 1195 was made on July 23, 1194. The truce was unwelcome to Richard. He had just concluded his castigation of the Poitevin and Aquitanian barons, and was now free to attack Philip in force. Outside official circles, the Normans themselves were not ready for peace, so that

[47] Howden, iii, 255; *Guillaume le Maréchal*, iii, 141. It is possibly through the accident of this capture that Richard was able to reap such a harvest in fines and forfeitures, and that the escheats and *terrae traditae* of the next exchequer roll (1195) are so numerous.

[48] See Richard's letter of July 22 in Howden, iii, 256. For details, see Richard, *Les Comtes de Poitou*, ii, 292–3; Cartellieri, iii, 96.

[49] June 17, 1194 (Howden, iii, 254–5). The terms included the surrender of church property captured during the war. The archbishop had been in Normandy for about a fortnight (Diceto, ii, 115).   [50] Howden, iii, 253, 255.

[51] The *exercitus de Tuebuef et de Walle Rodolii* is mentioned in the Exchequer roll of 1195 (*Rot. Scacc.*, i, 171). Tuboeuf is on the Itun, and the fact that troops met there seems to show that the roads from Verneuil, Chennebrun and L'Aigle here crossed the road along the Itun from Breteuil to Bonmoulins.

hostilities of an informal kind continued.[52] But the truce was observed officially, with one brief interval in the summer of 1195, and was succeeded by a definite peace in January, 1196. The treaty then made at Louviers was designed to mark the end of the war; in reality the conclusion of the long negotiations seems to have exhausted the desire for rest. King Richard gathered allies in Flanders and the Rhineland, built his famous castle at Andeli, and began a systematic attack upon his enemy, which continued until his death in 1199.

We have now, therefore, to consider the character of the negotiations which ended in January, 1196, and to follow the course of the subsequent war.

III

An influence was asserted during the summer of 1194 which grew more intense in the following years. This was the influence of the Church. From the point of view of the pope, the contest for Normandy was a wicked and tiresome obstacle to his wider plans; it harassed the local clergy, stood in the way of the relief required by the Spaniards and Portuguese in their struggle with the Saracens[53] and prevented a new crusade. Moreover, the rivalry of Richard and Philip Augustus indirectly increased the difficulties which the pope had to face in Italy. The projects of the emperor Henry VI were becoming clear in Sicily and Naples; and just when the Pope required allies in the north of Europe, King Richard not only absorbed the attention of the king of France, the natural ally of the papacy, but also maintained a friendly understanding with the emperor himself. Such was the situation, at all events, before the election of Innocent III to the papal chair, and the election of Otto of Brunswick as king of the Romans.

The truce arranged on July 23, 1194, between Verneuil and Tillières was largely due to the persuasions of the Papal legate, Melior, cardinal priest of SS. John and Paul.[54] Richard did not like the truce, and liked it still less as the work of ecclesiastics. Richard was in some ways a religious man. He loved the daily offices and order of the

[52] Howden, iii, 276, 278. Cf. Round, *Feudal England*, 548-9. It was on account of this truce that Richard deprived Longchamp of the great seal and entrusted it to Eustace, dean of Salisbury, who became chancellor and bishop on Longchamp's death in 1197 (*Ann. Mon.*, i, 23). Eustace appears as vice-chancellor in a charter of March 24, 1195 (*Cart. Norm.*, no. 556, note), and is mentioned as such by Howden, iv, 12, 21. See *English Historical Review*, xxiii, 226 and notes.

[53] Howden gives the Moorish invasion as a reason for the renewal of negotiations in July, 1195 (iii, 302).

[54] In a letter of the French commissioners, Philip is said to have granted a truce 'ad preces cardinalis et abbatis Cisterciensis' (Howden, iii, 257). See below, p. 107 and notes, for the terms of the truce.

Church. During the months of inaction which followed the energy
of June and July he spent much of his time in the direction of religious
endowments and in religious exercises. An attack of sickness and a
warning hermit recalled him from a lapse into immorality; he restored
the holy vessels which had been taken from the Church for his ransom,
did acts of penance, and reconciled himself to Queen Berengaria.[55]
But the king had no place for the Church in politics; his was the piety
of the new chivalry to which he belonged; and he pursued a political
enemy with greater zeal if, like the bishop of Beauvais, he were an
ecclesiastic. He was an Angevin, well used to the grim jest about his
Satanic origin; in the confidence of his great strength he liked to terrify
the weak and unarmed if they dared to oppose his physical might with
authority of another kind. He never mocked, like John, at the services of the Church; he never tortured the clergy; but he would never
have surrendered his kingdom to the pope. He suspected that Philip
—physically timid, equally attracted by the supernatural, but cleverer
than himself—was in league with the powers of the Church against
him; and the suspicion maddened him. Hence, in the last years of his
life, in spite of the energy of his attack and the subtlety of his com-
binations, Richard is an isolated figure. He becomes more and more
Titanic, always vigorous and hopeful, but increasingly impulsive,
increasingly a victim of chance. He, the greatest of the Crusaders,
was struck down in the hot warfare of Aquitaine, and his allies went
forward to conquer the eastern empire. Not he, but a count of Flanders
was destined to realise the dream of Bohemond and of Henry VI.
The thought of Richard before Constantinople makes the heart leap.

The interval between July, 1194, and January, 1196, was filled to
a great extent by military preparations, and the history of the
negotiations is sufficient to show that the conclusion of peace was
likely to lead to an outbreak of war. Indeed, those who lived through
this time felt that the occupation of Vaudreuil in July, 1195, was the
real beginning of the great war.[56] Soon after midsummer in this year
the emperor had urged Richard to proceed. In the midst of his
successes, peace in the north of France would have been most dis-
tasteful to him. Apart from his own feelings, Richard was bound to
the emperor; for one cause or another he was Henry's man; the ransom
was not paid up; some of the hostages were still in Germany.[57]
Desiring to be assured of the emperor's sincerity, Richard sent the
bishop of Ely to him. Philip felt the danger, and having tried, without
success, to detain the bishop as he passed through French territory,
declared that the truce had been broken and resumed the war.[58] Both
kings naturally resorted to Vaudreuil, of whose safety Philip seems

[55] Howden, iii, 288–90 (April, 1195).   [56] *Guillaume le Maréchal*, iii, 139–40.
[57] Cf. Howden, iii, 300.   [58] Howden, iii, 301. Rigord, i, 131.

to have entertained grave doubts. He decided to destroy the castle, and the mines were hurriedly dug beneath its walls, while a conference between the two kings was actually taking place not far away. King Richard heard the crash of the walls, and swore by the legs of God that saddles should be emptied that day; his knights rushed upon the French, and Philip leaving Vaudreuil fled across the Seine, and broke down the bridge behind him.[59] From this time Vaudreuil and the valley of the Eure were never again out of Richard's power. The great castle was renewed at great expense,[60] and the bridge over the Seine at Portjoie was afterwards built as a link between Vaudreuil and Chateau-Gaillard.[61]

Still the negotiations went on. Early in August Philip's unfortunate sister Alice, who had been carried from place to place in Normandy for so many years,[62] was at last handed back to her brother, and was immediately betrothed to William III of Ponthieu.[63] The sister of Arthur of Brittany, previously destined for the heir of Austria, was, according to a new treaty, to marry Philip's son Louis.[64] Negotiations had been hurried by the news of a disaster in Spain. But the proposed marriage and the other terms of the treaty were postponed for full ratification until November 8, when the will of the emperor might be known. The emperor objected to the treaty. It was a shameful thing, he thought, to quitclaim anything that was not under one's control. He would remit 17,000 marks of the ransom to help Richard to recover all that he had lost.[65] Consequently the meeting of November 8, which took place near Verneuil, was a failure.[66] War was resumed in the north-east, where Philip had recently allotted the county of Eu and Arques as the dowry of his sister Alice. Perhaps it was now that Richard laid siege to Arques, while the French, on November 10, burned Dieppe and destroyed its shipping by means of Greek fire.[67] This act was the renewal of the desperate policy of destruction begun at Vaudreuil. Philip meant the real brunt of the war to be borne by Richard at the weakest spot in his empire; and he laid siege to Issoudun in Poitevin Berri. When the news came that Philip had taken the town and was besieging the castle, Richard was

---

[59] *Guillaume le Maréchal*, iii, 139. Howden, iii, 301. For the chronology, see Meyer's note to *Guillaume le Maréchal*, and Cartellieri, iii, 108-9.

[60] The exchequer rolls show with what expense. Cf. *Rot. Scacc.*, i, 137, etc.

[61] *Guillaume le Maréchal*, iii, 140.

[62] Howden, iii, 303. For Alice in Normandy, compare the entry in *Rot. Scacc.*, i, 233. 'pro hernesio sororis Regis Francie deportando de Bonnavilla usque Cadomum v. so. per breve Regis.'

[63] Delaborde, *Recueil*, ii, no. 108. Cf. Cartellieri, iii, 114.

[64] Howden, iii, 302; see Landon, *Itinerary*, pp. 103-4.

[65] Howden, iii, 303-4; Gervase of Canterbury, i, 530.   [66] Howden, iii, 304.

[67] *Ibid.* Cf. Rigord, i, 131. Rigord's chronology is somewhat confused.

at Vaudreuil. In three days he had covered the distance between Vaudreuil and Issoudun.[68] A large force had gathered round him on the way, and Philip, taken by surprise, tried in vain to obtain leave to retire. Richard seized the opportunity and treated for a favourable peace. On December 5 terms were arranged:[69] a strict truce was to be maintained until their ratification in full assembly on the feast of St. Hilary (January 13). Richard spent Christmas at Poitiers, and met Philip at Louviers between Vaudreuil and Gaillon. After long consultations peace was made on January 15.[70]

A comparison of Philip's position in the truce of 1194 with that which he accepted early in 1196 is some measure of the effect produced by Richard's vigorous government after his return. In 1194 the line drawn from the Eure to the Seine showed that Philip held Vaudreuil with the neighbouring fiefs of Louviers, Acquigny and Léry,[71] as a self-contained outwork on the Norman frontier.[72] Behind this line Philip included in the truce Vernon, Gaillon, Paci, Illiers l'Eveque, Louye, Nonancourt and Tillières: in other words the Evrecin and the old frontier of Normandy to the west were either in his own hands, or had been distributed among his friends and servants.[73] To the east of the Seine the French king retained most

[68] An entry in *Rot. Scacc.*, i, 136, seems to refer to the speedy relief of Issoudun: 'baronibus et militibus euntibus ad Regem apud Isoldun tempore guerre, m. li. cccc. li. xl. li. de dono'; but in this case the exchequer roll would belong to 1196, not to 1195. Richard had been at Issoudun on July 3, 1195 (cf. Cartellieri, iii, 221, no. 236).

[69] Howden says December 9 (iii, 305), but the later treaty refers to the terms arranged, 'in vigilia Sancti Nicholai, inter Exoldunum et Charrocium'.

[70] Richard's ratification of the treaty is in Teulet, *Layettes*, i, 182–4, no. 431; Delisle, *Cart. Norm.*, pp. 276–7, no. 1057. For Philip's ratification see Delaborde, *Recueil*, ii, no. 517, printed from the late fourteenth century copy, P.R.O. E. 36; also, with errors, in Rymer, i, 66. An English summary is given in Landon, *Itinerary*, pp. 106–9. For the place, see Howden, iv, 3. The date in Rigord, i, 133–4. The letter from the archbishop of Rouen to Ralph de Diceto shows that the conference began before the 13th January (*infra octavas Epiphaniae*, Rad. Dic., ii, 135). The archbishop left on Saturday, the third day of the conference. In 1196 the 13th was a Saturday. This gives Thursday for the opening of the conference and Monday for the conclusion of peace. Cf. Cartellieri, iii, 119. Landon construes this letter differently (p. 109).

[71] The line ran from Pont de l'Arche along the wooded slope above the Eure to La Haye Malherbe. Louviers and Léry were dependent on Vaudreuil (*Rot. Scacc.*, i, 111). See the interesting text in Delaborde, *Recueil*, ii, no. 824 = *Cart. Norm.*, no. 1076.

[72] For the truce, see Howden, iii, 257–60; summary in Landon, *Itinerary*, pp. 96–7.

[73] Of the places named in the text, Richard of Vernon afterwards exchanged Vernon for other lands (*Recueil*, ii, no. 519, and *Layettes*, no. 441) and Robert of Leicester ceded Paci (*Cart. Norm.*, nos. 36–41; cf. Howden, iii, 278). For Illiers l'Eveque, see Stapleton, I, cxv.

of the centres of military and civil administration: Arques, Drincourt, Eu, Gisors and the Vexin. Hugh of Gournai seems to have absorbed, as Philip's vassal, the honour of Aumâle and the neighbouring district (*officium*) of Beauvoir; the count of Boulogne had submitted his Norman fiefs to France; the wealthy William of Caïeux had been secured by the grant of Mortemer;[74] and a Frenchman, William Garland, held the castle of Neufmarché.[75] In 1196 Philip retained the Vexin (except Beauvoir) and the southern half of the Evrecin; Gisors, Vernon, Gaillon, Paci, Ivry and Nonancourt protected France in the later war;[76] but Evreux and Vaudreuil to the west, and all the French conquests east of the Seine, with the exception of the Vexin, were recovered by Richard. The archiepiscopal manor of Andeli was given an elaborately safeguarded neutrality.[77]

A great assembly of clergy, barons and officials met at Louviers to discuss the affairs of Normandy. The position of some among the great barons and landholders of the duchy was defined in the treaty, and the restoration of north-eastern Normandy necessitated a precise understanding with regard to many more. Ralph of Exoudun was able to resume possession of his county of Eu; Richard of Vernon decided to throw in his lot with Richard and to receive back his lands in the Côtentin;[78] but the position of others was more equivocal; it may be of interest to dwell at greater length upon the relations of some of these with King Richard.

Like Richard of Vernon, Hugh of Gournai came back to the side of King Richard. By the terms of the treaty, his future allegiance had been left to his own choice.[79] In the reign of King John this important

---

[74] Below, p. 109.   [75] *Recueil*, ii, no. 501.

[76] In his later wars against the duke of Normandy it is worthy of notice that Philip seems to have made Vernon his usual headquarters. Here, as generally, he was careful to maintain the identity of its administration and the interests of its inhabitants. Cf. *Recueil*, ii, nos. 498, 510.

[77] See below, p. 114.

[78] Richard of Vernon had originally received lands in France in exchange for Vernon (*Recueil*, ii, no. 519). Later, apparently, these lands were commuted for 800 li. of Paris (*Layettes*, no. 441). This sum was guaranteed in the treaty to Richard of Vernon: the lands of Hugh of Gournai outside the Vexin were set apart for the purpose. My own reading of the treaty suggests, in opposition to Stapleton's (I, cxliv), that Richard of Vernon was anxious to join King Richard. He was certainly with King Richard in 1198: Round, *Calendar*, p. 537.

[79] 'De Hugoni de Gornai ita erit: hominagium ejus remanet regi Francie ad vitam dicti Hugonis, nisi voluerit redire ad nos et post mortem ejusdem Hugonis debet totum feodum suum de Normannia ad nos et heredes nostros redire . . . Terre vero militum de terra Hugonis de Gornai qui venerunt ad nos, reddentur illis ita quod de terris illis facient hominagium et servicium Hugoni de Gornai, salva fidelitate quam ipsi nobis debebant.' Hugh was with Richard in 1198. See Round, *Calendar*, p. 119. Cf. *Rot. Scacc.*, ii, 386.

baron was to acquire an evil reputation as a man of both sides:[80] the position of his lands, which stretched along the rivers Epte and Bresle and included scattered manors in the French dioceses of Amiens and Beauvais,[81] almost forced upon their possessor the policy of the trimmer. Lying between the two countries, Gournai was frequently selected as a suitable spot for tournaments;[82] and its local law suggested a habit of detachment from the customs of Normandy and France.[83] Naturally it was always one of the first places to be attacked, and after the loss of Gisors was in still more dangerous proximity to the French. King Richard was fortunate in being able to reckon upon the services of the lord of Gournai.

William of Caïeux (*Kaeu*)[84] also returned to his allegiance, and figures impressively in the exchequer roll of 1198.[85] The defection of this baron had stirred King Richard to vehement reproaches during his captivity. Although primarily a vassal of the count of Flanders, William's extensive lands in Normandy made him a striking figure in Norman society; and his tastes must have made him congenial to the king. He was fond of legends and *chansons de geste*: at his request a poet of Beauvais had translated into verse the story of Charlemagne's journey to Constantinople. At Messina he had been in the closest relations with Richard; but during the recent war he had accepted favours from Philip, who included him in the truce of 1194. In later years he rose high in John's service, and he fought against the French at Bouvines.

William of Caïeux, like the lords of Gournai and Vernon, had deserted his suzerain. Baldwin of Béthune was a companion whose fidelity to King Richard was beyond dispute. This younger son of the advocate of Béthune is a consistently attractive person. His loyalty was proverbial; he was a man who would suffer no one to slander his friend.[86] As the younger son he had few prospects in the small though distinguished Flemish court of his father; he became devoted to Richard, joined him in the Crusade, was one of his few companions on his homeward journey, and was captured with him. He was released and for a time came back to England, but soon rejoined Richard in Germany. When the king was set at liberty, Baldwin remained as a hostage. We are told that when Richard met some of his most faithful men at Huntingdon and had thanked them for their efforts on his behalf, he remarked that he owed more to

---

[80] *Histoire des ducs de Normandie et des rois d'Angleterre* (ed. Michel), p. 92.
[81] Stapleton, I, clxxix *seqq*. Tardif, *Coutumiers de Normandie*, I, ii, p. 52, note.   [82] Cf. *Guillaume le Maréchal*, ii. 2473, 5492, 5506, 5976.
[83] *e.g.*, in the fief of Gournai the archbishop of Rouen could only hold three pleas (Round, *Calendar*, p. 477).
[84] See Gaston Paris in *L'Estoire de la Guerre Sainte*, p. 543.
[85] Stapleton, *Observations*, II, Index, s.v.
[86] See *Guillaume le Maréchal*, iii, 54, note, 72, 134.

Baldwin than to any other man. 'Sire,' the Marshal agreed, 'Baldwin is loyal; I would pledge my head that he will serve you always and never waver.' Then William of L'Etang, who had also been a companion to the young King Henry and remembered the Marshal's troubles, joined in: 'Well may you pledge your head, Marshal, for often has he used his in your service against your slanderers.'[87] Baldwin was at the court of the duke of Austria at that time, in real peril. The money did not come, nor, as the treaty of Richard's release required, did the king send the young princesses of Brittany and Cyprus; the duke threatened the hostages and sent Baldwin to inform Richard of their danger. The king immediately sent the ladies on their way under Baldwin's charge, but as they drew near to their journey's end, the news of the archduke's death reached them;[88] whereupon Baldwin brought them home again.[89] Shortly afterwards he got his reward; the count of Aumâle died, leaving a widow. This lady, a granddaughter of King Stephen, had already been married twice, and was to be married twice more. Baldwin became her third husband, and received from Richard the county of Aumâle.[90] The new count and his wife celebrated their marriage at Séez at the king's charge,[91] and stayed in Normandy until the treaty of 1196 restored Aumâle.

Baldwin's enjoyment of Aumâle was brief. The town commands easy access to several of the valleys which run down to the Channel from the plateau of north-eastern Normandy, and its exposed position on the frontier provoked frequent assault. King Philip had possibly intended the honour of which it was the head as part of his sister's dowry upon her marriage with the count of Ponthieu. A dowry was found elsewhere, but Philip did not lose sight of Aumâle. Within six months of the conclusion of peace Philip laid siege to it: the town was lost after a spirited fight between the Norman and French forces, in which King Richard suffered one of his few rebuffs.[92] In August the castle surrendered and was destroyed. Aumâle does not appear again to have been surrendered by the king of France.[93]

[87] See *Guillaume le Maréchal*, iii, 133–4.

[88] The archduke died on Christmas Day, 1194. His attitude towards the hostages evidently made a great impression, which was deepened by his death. See Howden, iii, 275–8; Gervase, i, 528–9; Coggeshall, p. 66; Diceto, ii, 124; and a letter from Pope Celestine to the duke (Diceto, ii, 119).

[89] For expenses entailed by the princesses later, see *Rot. Scacc.*, i, 154.

[90] Howden, iii, 306, and Stubbs's note; *Histoire des ducs de Normandie*, p. 88

[91] *Rot. Scacc.*, i, 210; Stapleton, I, clvii.

[92] William the Breton, *Philippid*, v, 180–257 (Delaborde, ii, 131–4). Richard had Poitevins with him and Guy of Thouars was captured. Richard gave 3,000 silver marks as ransom for the knights and sergeants captured by Philip in Aumâle (Howden, iv, 5). Philip gave a charter of protection to the monks of Foucarmont in July, at Aumâle (*Recueil*, ii, no. 541).

[93] In 1204 the count of Boulogne got the castle (*Recueil*, ii, no. 862).

IV

The war in which the siege of Aumâle was one of the first incidents, was attributed by contemporaries to various causes. One alleges Richard's action in Brittany,[94] another his lack of faith in attacking Vierzon in Berri,[95] a third his obvious intention of fortifying Andeli.[96] All these reasons doubtless helped to strengthen Philip's feeling that peace was more dangerous than war; they all illustrated the strength, pride and ability of his enemy, and were the first steps in the policy of consolidation by which Richard attempted to restore the empire and to equal the influence of his father. The invasion of Brittany was followed before long by an alliance between the Bretons and the Normans:[97] the attempt of Constance to assert her son's independence was checked.[98] The attack on Vierzon[99] was designed to show that the sub-vassals of Poitevin Berri were no longer to turn to the king of France as a court of appeal. In the course of the same year Richard, as we have seen, secured an important ally in the count of Toulouse, who had hitherto fought as an ally of Philip. Richard was enabled to direct more attention to Norman affairs, and to leave Poitou under the more or less nominal direction of his nephew, Otto of Brunswick.[100] Indeed this interest in the fortunes of Otto prepared the world for the elaborate diplomacy of the next two years which marshalled the counts of Flanders, Boulogne, and Saint-Pôl against Philip, and secured Otto's election as king of the Romans.

As early as the middle of April, 1196, King Philip had become so restless in the face of Richard's activity as to satisfy the latter that he meant war rather than peace.[101] Military preparations were hurried on. In the letter to the archbishop of Canterbury, in which Richard

[94] *Historiens de France*, xviii, 332 (Chronicle of Penpont, in Brittany). Cf. Richard's letter to the archbishop of Canterbury, April 15, 1196, from 'Minehi Sancti Cari' (Minehy-Trequier), printed by Stubbs in Diceto, ii, lxxix, in which he says 'magis putamus imminere nobis guerram a regi Franciae quam pacem'.

[95] Rigord, i, 135; *Philippid*, v, 86. See below, note 99.

[96] *Philippid*, v, 70. Richard's itinerary shows (pp. 111–13) that he was at Andeli at various times in March, April, May and June.

[97] In 1197. Howden, iv, 19. For Constance's imprisonment by Randle of Chester and the subsequent war which provoked Richard's attack, see Howden, iv, 7; *Philippid*, v. 147.

[98] A. de la Borderie, *Histoire de Bretagne*, iii, 287.

[99] The order of the narrative in Rigord (i, 135) would give the date as the end of June, 1196. Cf. Meyer in *Guillaume le Maréchal*, iii, 141. Charter evidence, however, confirms the Vierzon chronicle that Richard's attack took place in 1197, almost certainly in July. See Landon, pp. 119–21 *passim*.

[100] Richard, *Comtes de Poitou*, ii, 298–315.

[101] See above, note 94, and below, p. 212.

expressed his suspicions of Philip, he ordered a military levy in England; and still greater demands were made in the following years.[102] Vast sums were spent upon fortifications, mercenaries and alliances. Before the peace, Verneuil, Pont de l'Arche, Vaudreuil, Moulins and Bonmoulins had been repaired or partially reconstructed.[103] After the outbreak of fresh hostilities many more castles, great and small, were strengthened; the walls of Eu were rebuilt at a cost of over 5,000 li.;[104] above all, the rock of Les Andelys was crowned by Chateau-Gaillard. Well might the anonymous poet of Béthune say that the king of France suffered from the power and wealth of Richard. Then there was Richard's pride. 'The king of England was proud above all men, and did not deign to be obedient to his lord.'[105] And, on the other hand, Richard's hatred of Philip was such that during many years he is said to have refused to receive the sacrament, because he did not wish to forgive his enemy.[106]

Philip's success at Aumâle was followed by another at Nonancourt. This important fortress on the Eure had been surrendered to Richard by Nicholas of Orphin, but was soon recovered by Philip and entrusted to Count Robert of Dreux. Nicholas, like Gilbert of Vascoeuil a few years earlier, was disgraced; but, unlike Gilbert, he later sought to recover himself in public opinion. He assumed the habit of a Templar and joined a holier warfare in the east.[107]

The loss of Aumâle and Nonancourt was to some degree met by the successful attack made by Count John upon the Vexin. John captured Gamaches, a castle lying between Gisors and Les Andelys:[108] the attack had doubtless been intended to cover the building operations which were now beginning to attract general attention at Rouen, Paris and Rome. The desultory conflict of this year was merged in

[102] See below, chapter viii, pp. 212 ff.

[103] *Rot. Scacc.*, i, 156, 245, etc.

[104] *Ibid.*, ii, 386.

[105] *Chronique française des rois de France par un anonyme de Béthune*, ed. Delisle (*Historiens de France*, xxiv, part ii, 758), an interesting account of Richard's resources in feudal levies and mercenaries. Compare Coggeshall's description of Richard's power, p. 34.

[106] Coggeshall, p. 96. Miss Norgate (ii, 386, note) observes that Richard took the sacrament at his coronation in 1194, and that therefore Coggeshall's story is not literally correct.

[107] For Nonancourt and Nicholas, see *Philippid*, v, 112–19 (Delaborde, ii, 129). Cf. Howden, iv, 5; Rigord, i, 136.

[108] Howden, iv, 5. The exchequer roll of 1198 shows that Richard paid a good deal of attention to the fortification of Gamaches. Cf. ii, 300. 'Elye de Elemosina cccc li. ad operationes de Gamasches per breve Regis.' It is significant that Richard about this time attempted to recapture Gaillon, on the other side of the Seine. He was wounded during the siege (*Philippid*, v, 258–75: Delaborde, ii, 135).

a diplomatic struggle for the rock of Andeli. In this struggle Richard for the first and last time had to face serious opposition from the Church.

The quarrel between the kings of England and France was a very serious matter for the Norman clergy. On the whole the reign of Henry II had been peaceful, and what warfare had broken out was confined to certain persons or places; but now the resources of two great States were engaged in a life and death struggle. Moreover, success had hitherto been for the most part on the side of Philip; Normandy had suffered several invasions; the loss of property, and especially of ecclesiastical property, had been great. During the war the Church assumed a neutral position and fought for peace and compensation against both combatants. As the head of the Norman clergy the archbishop of Rouen, Walter of Coutances, was involved in one dispute after another; and, in spite of his many services to King Richard, found himself forced into a triangular conflict. He returned from Germany, where he had been confined as one of Richard's hostages, to find his church in disorder, and it is significant that, within a few days of his arrival in Normandy (1194), a year's truce was arranged.[109] He next devoted himself to the restoration of ecclesiastical property. King Richard had avenged a grudge which he bore St. Martin's of Tours,[110] and King Philip had afflicted the province of Rouen. On November 11, the day dedicated to the patron saint of Tours, Richard restored the goods which he had confiscated;[111] while Archbishop Walter tried to persuade Philip to do the same.[112] But his independent action and the use of ecclesiastical weapons annoyed the kings and led them to form a curious alliance against him. They hit upon the plan of using the clergy for sureties for their public treaties, and thus of binding them to the maintenance of secular agreements which might or might not be in the interests of the Church. King Philip brought forward the archbishop of Tours and four of the chief abbots of the country; King Richard offered the

[109] Diceto, ii, 115, 'transitus in Normanniam tertio Kalendas Junii'. See above, p. 103. For the effect of the war, see the archbishop's letter to the dean of St. Paul's (Diceto, ii, 144). Cf. Richard's charter of compensation, Round, *Calendar*, p. 18, no. 67; Stapleton, *Observations*, II, xxi.

[110] According to the *Chronicon Turonense magnum* (Salmon, *Chroniques de Touraine*, i, 144) Richard, on his return from Loches, June 11, 1194 ('in festo Beati Barnabae apostoli') expelled and dispersed the canons of St. Martin. Previously, according to Diceto (ii, 117), he had received a free gift of 2000 marks from the burgesses of Tours. We do not know whether Richard's attack extended further. It must be noticed that the archbishop of Tours, in spite of some earlier precedents, was emphatically a French prelate. Cf. Delaborde, *Recueil*, i, no. 148.

[111] Diceto, ii, 122.
[112] See the letters in Diceto, ii, 122.

I

archbishop of Rouen.[113] Moreover, in order to bind the archbishop of Rouen, the treaty of Louviers (January, 1196) comprised an elaborate arrangement with regard to the archiepiscopal manor of Andeli. Both kings desired to possess Andeli, which was now on the frontier of Normandy;[114] neither would give way to the other; hence it was agreed that the place should be put outside the *dominium* of either. Just as the eleven parishes which formed the deanery of Andeli were regarded as an *ecclesia extravagans*,[115] so now the manor was to be neutral ground, subject to the archbishop or, during a vacancy in the archbishopric, to the chapter of Rouen; and it was to remain unfortified.[116] Yet, at the same time, the future conduct of the archbishop was to be the measure of his control of this demesne. Andeli was the main source of archiepiscopal wealth.[117] If, in the future, he laid an interdict on, or excommunicated persons in the lands of Philip[118] or of Richard in his diocese, either king was to be at liberty to confiscate the revenues of Andeli, until a special tribunal of four deacons or priests, two to be elected by each king, had decided whether or not the interdict or excommunication were just. Archbishop Walter very properly refused to become surety for an arrangement which placed his ecclesiastical authority under the control of a semi-secular court.[119] Refusing to take part in the conference, he retired to Cambrai;[120] further, he took up again the wrongs of the inferior clergy and laid an interdict upon the lands of King Philip. Philip, in his turn, apparently seized Andeli.[121]

The quarrel was not ended till the middle of the year, after prolonged negotiations. The king of France seems to have thought that a reconciliation with the archbishop might be a useful move in the game against Richard; hence the archbishop was invited to France

[113] Diceto, ii, 136; *Cart. Norm.*, p. 278, no. 1058 = *Layettes*, no. 432. That the archbishop of Tours was Philip's surety is proved by a letter from Richard to the bishop of Evreux (Diceto, ii, 139).

[114] Besides the terms of the treaty, which represent a compromise, see Howden, iv, 3, 4. 'Praeterea (at Louviers) rex Franciae petiit ad opus suum Andeli, manerium Rothomagensis archiepiscopi. Quod cum nulla ratione fieri posset,' etc.

[115] Longnon, *Pouillés de la province de Rouen* (1903), p. xiv.

[116] *Cart. Norm.*, p. 277; *Recueil*, ii, p. 56.

[117] 'patrimonium ecclesiae solum et unicum' (the archbishop of Rouen to the dean of St. Paul's, Diceto, ii, 148). See Miss Norgate, ii, 376.

[118] *i.e.*, the French Vexin; see Longnon, *Pouillés de la province de Rouen*, pp. xi, xii; *English Historical Review*, xxvii, 107. Howden says that at this time Philip sought to secure the fealty of Walter for archiepiscopal property in the French Vexin (iv, 4).

[119] See his letters in Diceto, ii, 135–50 *passim*.

[120] Diceto, ii, 137. A *societas* for mutual shelter was formed in this year between the chapters of Rouen and Cambrai. (Martène, *Thesaurus*, i, 663–4.)

[121] See his letter to the archbishop; Diceto, ii, 139.

and was kindly received. The king of England found it expedient to make terms: the sureties on both sides were released from all obligations; the clergy were compensated; and the archbishop returned to his church triumphant. One of his last acts was to insist upon the restoration of their possessions to the four abbots of Marmoutier, Cluny, St. Denis and La Charité which had been seized by Richard after the revival of hostilities between the two kings.[122] The abbots had been the sureties of the French king; and by his action the archbishop maintained the independence of the clergy as a whole, and established the unity of the church of Rouen with the other churches of the west.

The incident had important effects upon the future of Andeli. The curious arrangement made in the treaty had obviously failed; yet the archbishop must have felt that his tenure could never be secure so long as the existing boundary between France and Normandy remained; and King Richard especially realised that if he did not seize the rock above the town, Philip would. Although it is not likely that he laid hands upon the manor before the war recommenced, he did not hesitate long.[123] He first seized and fortified the 'isle of Andeli' in the river, then began fortifications on the mainland, with the purpose of protecting the town. In great alarm the archbishop expostulated, but finding Richard obdurate, laid Normandy under an interdict, and on the 7th of November set out for Rome. As was usual in such quarrels, King Richard found ecclesiastics to support him, of whom the most prominent was the bishop of Lisieux, William de Rupierre. He and Philip, the bishop elect of Durham,[124] acted as the royal advocates at Rome. The main argument which weighed with the Pope Celestine III and, indeed, with the archbishop of Rouen himself, was that the rock was a natural fortress, and that the fortification of the island had become necessary in the face of French attack.[125]

[122] I gather this from a comparison of Howden, iv, 4; and Walter's letter in Diceto, ii, 145. For the whole episode, see my paper, *King Philip Augustus and the archbishop of Rouen* in the *English Historical Review* (1912), xxvii, 106–16.

[123] The narrative of Miss Norgate (ii, 377–81) is full and careful on the acquisition of Andeli. Howden gives a good summary (iv, 14, 16–19). The contemporary letters are in Diceto, ii, 148–58. Richard's charter of exchange is given from the original by Deville, *Histoire du Château-Gaillard* (Rouen, 1829), 112–18. Its date is October 16 1197, and it was confirmed by John on the same day (see Landon, *Itinerary*, pp. 124, 208 with facsimile). John's confirmation as king is in *Rot. Norm.*, 1, 2. Pope Innocent III's confirmation (April 26, 1198) is printed in Migne, ccxiv, 93.

[124] Howden, iv, 17, 19. The chancellor, who was to have made a third, died on the way at Poitiers, January 31, 1197 (Diceto, ii, 150).

[125] Rog. Howden, iv, 18; cf. the archbishop in Diceto, ii, 154: 'omnes enim intelligentes situm Andeleii paci ineptum et guerrae vicinum et expositum.' Matthew Paris later inserted in Howden's narrative of the quarrel that the

The Pope and cardinals were accepted as mediators, and finally, on October 16, 1197, the archbishop quitclaimed nearly the whole of his manor to the king,[126] and received in exchange the flourishing seaport of Dieppe, the manor of Bouteilles near Arques, the forest of Alihermont, and the manor of Louviers with the *ministerium* of the forest of Bort. The normal annual value of these valuable properties amounted to about 1,400 li. Angevin,[127] a very fair provision for the archbishop.

Richard had begun to build his castle on the rock before the final agreement was reached; and the greatest fortress in the west of Europe was finished in the course of the following year.[128]

In an interesting letter written about this time Bishop Stephen of Tournai remarked that he doubted the wisdom of risking the inconvenience caused by sentences of excommunication, on the ground that so little respect was paid to them.[129] The success achieved by the archbishop of Rouen proved that this could not be said to be the

---

archbishop laid the interdict and appealed to Rome, 'stimulante Francorum rege' (*Chron. Maj.*, ii, 420), but there is no proof of this very likely suggestion.

[126] 'Excepto manerio de Fraxinis cum pertinenciis suis . . . ita quod tam milites quam clerici et omnes homines tam de feodis militum quam de prebendis sequentur molendina de Andeliaco sicut consueverunt et debuerunt, et moltura erit nostra.' From the text as given in the facsimile of Richard's charter (Landon, frontispiece).

[127] This was a net revenue, made up as follows (*Rot. Scacc.*, i, 68; ii, 421, 481):

	£	s.	d.	£	s.	d.
Annual farm of Dieppe . .	1100	0	0			
Less stated alms, tithes, etc., according to Richard's charter	372	0	0			
				728	0	0
Annual value of Bouteilles . . .				100	0	0
,, ,, forest of Alihermont . .				177	0	0
,, ,, Louviers, etc. . .				400	0	0
				£1405	0	0

In addition, it should be noted that the forest of Alihermont produced corn rents of wheat and oats in the forest, which seem to have been paid into the Exchequer first (cf. *Rot. Scacc.*, i, 91, with ii, 421). On the other hand, the war had lessened the value of Dieppe (*Rot. Scacc.*, i, 235), and it appears from Richard's estimate of the stated tithes, alms, etc., in Dieppe, 372 li., that these had been lately increased, since they only amounted to £211 6s. 8d. in 1195 (*ibid.*).

[128] In his charter of October, 1197, Richard refers to his 'new castle of the Rock'. He was constantly at the 'Bellum Castrum de Rupe' between February, 1198, and January, 1199 (see the *Itinerary*, pp. 125–42 passim). Building was proceeding in May, 1198 (Diceto, ii, 162).

[129] *Lettres*, ed. Desilve (1893), p. 31. A letter of 1197 referring to Baldwin of Flanders.

effects of an interdict; the recent interdicts had caused distress to king and people.[130] Yet the troubles of the archbishop remind us that those secular movements which were to be so characteristic of the thirteenth century had begun. Those movements were peculiar, not through the conflict of physical strength with spiritual force, nor even by reason of the conflict of great principles of law, as in the tragedy of Thomas of Canterbury. They expressed the steady and precise formulation of secular life, partly as the result of social organic growth, partly in opposition to the assertion of papal claims and of ecclesiastical rights generally. The change was not confined to the centres of government. The archbishop of Rouen had to face the same independent attitude among the shopkeepers of his cathedral city;[131] no less than in the arguments about the interest of the state put forward by King Richard at Andeli. War merely precipitated and embittered a struggle which was bound to come. For the moment the Church was, on the whole, victorious, mainly because she was united and able to play off her rivals against each other: the Norman clergy helped to change the ruling dynasty in Normandy, as Innocent III controlled the downfall of the Emperor Otto and of King John. But the sense of unity did not last, and later writers are able to see in the events of this time the faint prophecy of Gallican liberties, and to trace in the policy of Richard and Philip the expression of imperial claims which sought no papal sanction.[132]

While the towers of Chateau Gaillard were rising, Richard was engaged in projects which were truly imperial. He was in a large measure responsible for the struggle in Germany which lasted until the battle of Bouvines. The Emperor Henry VI died in September, 1197, and Richard used his popularity in Germany to secure the election of his nephew Otto of Brunswick as emperor in opposition to Henry's brother, Philip of Suabia, who had been elected at Mühlhausen in March 1198.[133] A friendly emperor was of obvious

[130] Howden (iv, 16) says that Richard was *confusus* because the archbishop refused to relax the interdict. 'Corpora enim defunctorum insepulta jacebant per vicos et plateas civitatum Normanniae.'
[131] For this quarrel between the merchants and canons of Rouen, see Chéruel, *Histoire de Rouen*, i, 40–54; and compare the archbishop's letter in Diceto, ii, 144. King Richard's letters on the subject, commencing with a letter from Worms in 1194, in Round, *Calendar*, nos. 64, 65, 67. Celestine III's letters in Martène, *Thesaurus*, i, 659–61. The dispute was not really ended until the fourteenth century.
[132] The spread of Carolingian forms and names is remarkable in France during the reign of Philip Augustus. See the interesting remarks of Alfred Leroux in his article 'La Royauté française et le saint empire romain' (*Rev. Hist.*, 1892, xlix, 255–9).
[133] The chief text for the Germany policy of King Richard is Howden, iv, 37–9. For the latest treatment of the evidence and for the literature on the

advantage to the king of England, and he could expect devoted support from the young man who had been trained at his court and had received so many benefits at his hands.[134] The new pope, Innocent III, was also friendly; he admired Richard's exploits in the Holy Land; he appreciated his hostility to the Hohenstaufen; and he realised his value in the tussle with Philip of France.[135] For, so long as the latter refused to recognise Ingeborg of Denmark as his wife, there seemed little chance of peace between France and the papacy. The king of England stood out for a few months as the head of the secular princes of Europe, the patron of an emperor, the friend of the pope. His position was, it is true, an unstable one; and if he had lived he could hardly have prevented the series of compromises which bound Innocent and Philip Augustus together and caused the downfall of the north German princes; but for the time Philip Augustus was isolated.[136]

Some months before the election of Otto in June, 1198, Richard had gathered round him a small band of powerful allies. The two kings had been busy bidding against each other since 1196. In June of that year Philip evidently felt in a strong position; he had given his sister Alice in marriage to William of Ponthieu; the counts of Flanders and Boulogne pledged themselves to support him against his enemies, and powerful ecclesiastic sanctions were invoked to secure their fidelity.[137] These diplomatic successes were closely followed by the military triumph at Aumâle. King Richard was, however, the wealthier and more impressive man; he had checked the Bretons, rallied the Poitevins, and made friends with the dangerous count of Toulouse. He understood the art of giving; and the counts of Flanders and Boulogne did not long withstand a generosity which was so like the easy expression of magnanimous nature.[138] William

matter, see Cartellieri, iii, 165 seqq., and the writings of W. Kienast and A. L. Poole mentioned above, p. 94 notes.

[134] Cartellieri, iii, 172. Cartellieri somewhat exaggerates the importance of Otto's position as count of Poitou and in Anglo-Norman society.

[135] Cf. Innocent's letters of May 29 and 31, and Richard's letter to the Pope, August 19, 1198, for Richard's relations with the Pope; Cheney and Semple, Selected letters of Pope Innocent III, pp. 1–8; and, for Richard's letter, Patrologia Latina, ccxvi, 1001.

[136] Cf. Luchaire, Innocent III: Les Royautés vassales, pp. 252–60. Philip allied himself in the meanwhile with Philip of Suabia, at the end of June, 1198: see Cartellieri, iii, 176.

[137] Actes, nos. 497–500, pp. 117–19; Rigord, i, 135; Pope Innocent's letter in Migne, ccxiv, 117; Potthast, no. 153—a later confirmation by the papal chancery. For the career of Renaud de Boulogne, see Henri Malo, Un grand feudataire, Renaud de Dammartin (1898).

[138] Howden, iv, 19–20. Howden states that Richard gave 5000 marks of silver. There are frequent references in the exchequer roll of 1198 to Richard's gifts, e.g., to the count of Boulogne, 500 marks of silver (Rot. Scacc., ii, 301); to the count of St. Pol the same (p. 302); to William of Hainault, the uncle of

the Marshal, who was one of the most persuasive barons at Richard's court, was sent to win over the counts, and an agreement was reached. This was finally ratified at Les Andelys with special formality, probably early in July, 1197.[139] With his brother's consent Count John also bound himself in an alliance with the counts of Flanders and Boulogne.[140] The young Otto took part in the solemn ratification of both treaties, and within a few months shared in their benefit; for we are told that, in his desire to please the king of England, Baldwin of Flanders actively supported Otto's candidature for the empire.[141]

All these events caused much anger and annoyance in Philip Augustus. The spring of 1197 had brought misfortunes in the field; in April Richard had swooped down on the seaport of Saint-Valery, part of the dowry of the princess Alice, and after burning the town carried away the relics of the saint.[142] In May he made demonstrations from Gournai in the neighbourhood of Beauvais; while he took the castle of Milli,[143] a band of mercenaries under the notorious Mercadier met and captured Philip of Dreux, bishop of Beauvais, whom the king hated.[144] It is probable that during this summer Philip, while Richard was engaged in his Berri campaign and the capture of Vierzon,succeeded in capturing the important castle of Dangu, which guarded a ford over the Epte, and which Richard had recently taken into his own hands.[145] In August he proceeded to chastise the count

the count of Flanders, 160 li. (p. 369); to the count of Boulogne again, 108 li. (p. 432).

[139] Rymer (ed. 1816), i, 67; Stapleton, *Observations*, II, lxxiii; *Guillaume le Maréchal*, iii, 141; Cartellieri, iii, 164. Landon, *Itinerarium*, pp. 118–19, gives the lists of sureties. A letter of King Philip, written early in August, speaks of Baldwin's formal defiance of the French king and of his alliance with Richard (*Recueil*, ii, no. 566). War had begun in July.

[140] Martène, Thesaurus, i, 1158. Richard's regnal year began on September 3, but John's letters of September 8 are dated in the eighth instead of the ninth year of the reign; so also were Richard's and John's charters of October 16. See Stapleton, II, lxxiii–iv, Landon, pp. 121–4, 207–8.

[141] Gervase of Canterbury, i, 545. Cartellieri, iii, 176. Like Ralph de Diceto (ii, 152–3) Gervase attributes the diplomatic successes of King Richard to the ability of archbishop Hubert.

[142] Howden, iv, 19; Diceto, ii, 152.   [143] *Guillaume le Maréchal*, iii, 147–9.

[144] May 19, 1197 (Diceto, ii, 152). For the other authorities and the conflicting evidence on this incident, see Meyer's note, *Guillaume le Maréchal*, iii, 148, to which add *Rot. Scacc.*, ii, 301. 'Hugoni de Noefvill ad expensam episcopi de Belvais c. li iiij. li.' William of Mello, who was captured with the bishop, accounted for a ransom of 1000 silver marks (*ibid.*).

[145] Howden, iv, 20. For Dangu, see below, p. 121. On the other hand, William the Breton (*Philippid*, v, 105, ed. Delaborde, ii, 129) gives the date 1195. See Landon for the date of the capture of Vierzon (pp. 119–21 *passim*). The chronology of the years 1197–8 is hopelessly involved and can only occasionally be tested by official documents. Howden, still the safest guide, occasionally goes astray at this period, and often repeats himself.

of Flanders for his desertion. The consequences justified all Richard's hopes. Baldwin had laid siege to Arras, the main acquisition of Philip in the north-east; the king began to lay waste Flanders, and was cut off in the neighbourhood of Ypres.[146] He had to surrender, and come to terms. Within a week or two the alliance of Normandy and Flanders was consummated, and Philip had to suffer the mortification of seeing his vassals of Flanders and Boulogne in the company of Richard at Andeli. A conference had been arranged between the two kings, but in his anger Philip broke it up. But he saw that he was no longer a match for his enemy; a truce was arranged with a view to peace; and Philip sought the help of Rome.[147]

The moment was a favourable one for a settlement. The emperor had just died; a new and vigorous pope was elected in January, 1198. The king of England hoped to secure Innocent's approval of Otto as a candidate for the empire; the king of France would wish to turn aside the inevitable interference with his matrimonial affairs. The kings accordingly sent proctors to Rome, and the papal chancery was busy throughout 1198 with the affairs of France and Normandy. As Innocent's letters show, the whole field of controversy was covered: the pope listened patiently while the royal proctors argued about the precise meaning of the treaty of Messina, interested himself in disputes about Richard's ransom, advised the archbishop of Rouen upon the problems of canonical privileges raised in 1196 by the treaty of Louviers, and reviewed in detail the history of the last eight years. On May 31, in a long letter to Richard, he announced his intention of making peace in person; but later in the year he sent his legate, Peter of Capua, with powers over France and the western provinces of the empire, to preach the Crusade, secure peace and bring about the restoration of Ingeborg as queen of France.[148]

The legate arrived in Paris between Christmas and the new year. The truce had meanwhile come to an end in the autumn of 1198,[149] when Philip suffered the last serious disaster of his reign at the hands of an English king. The fighting occurred, as in the previous year,

[146] See Cartellieri, iii, 159–60.
[147] Gervase says on the occasion of the conference, and gives the date September 8 (i, 544). See also *Guillaume le Maréchal*, iii, 142, in the course of a spirited narrative whose chronology is very confused; *Howden*, iv, 21, 24; Landon, p. 122. The truce was to last until Christmas, 1198, or, according to Howden (iv, 24), till St. Hilary's day (January 13, 1199). In the event it lasted till the autumn of 1198 (iv, 54).
[148] In addition to the long letter from the pope of May 31, edited and translated in Cheney and Semple, *Select letters of Pope Innocent III concerning England*, pp. 3–9, see the letters in Migne, *Patrologia Latina*, ccxiv, nos. 236, 241, 260, 345–8, 355.
[149] Howden, iv, 54: 'finitis trengis quas rex Franciae et rex Angliae statuerant inter se, donec segetes hinc et inde colligerentur.'

on the borders of the Vexin and in the valley of the Epte, for Richard had revived the dispute about the possession of Gisors. In spite of the explicit arrangements made in 1196, he felt able to attempt the recapture of what Philip still retained in the Norman Vexin: the Flemish alliance protected him in the north, and new allies, in the centre of France as well as in the Rhinelands, had been attracted to his side.[150] The king of France had, therefore, to limit his operations, and to rally the barons of Champagne and the east.[151]

The French force crossed the Epte by the ford at Dangu and invaded the Norman Vexin in September, after the harvest.[152] Although Richard was unprepared, having scattered his army, he was speedily in a position to resist attack, for in the spring he had ordered in England the special taxation and the special levy so familiar to students of constitutional history.[153] He was apparently at this time in the neighbourhood of his new castle at Andeli. With two hundred knights, and the aid of Mercadier's troop, he cut off the French. Philip fled on his old war horse to Vernon.[154] The king of England now turned aside with his whole army to the ford at Dangu[155] and invaded the French Vexin. On Sunday, September 27, he took the castle of Courcelles-lès-Gisors by assault, and captured the fort at Boury.[156] In the evening he returned to Dangu. King Philip was at Mantes, and hearing that Courcelles was in danger set out to the relief with three hundred knights and a local levy.[157] Richard, for reasons which he does not state in his letter to the bishop of Durham —our main authority for what occurred—imagined that Philip would cross the Epte below Dangu and attack the Anglo-Norman forces on the left or Norman bank of the river; he accordingly left his main army at Dangu and reconnoitred with only a small following on the right bank. The king of France preferred to march directly from Mantes towards Gisors.[158] Mercadier and Hugh of Corni, a knight

[150] See the list in Howden, iv, 54. It includes Geoffrey count of Perche, and Arthur of Brittany; and, most significant, Louis of Blois. Cf. the chronicle of William the Breton (Delaborde, i, 202).
[151] See *Layettes*, nos. 474, 482, for definite agreements of Odo of Burgundy and Theobald of Champagne, in this year. Philip compelled the count of Flanders to temporary submission in April (*Recueil*, ii, no. 580; Malo, pp. 58, 59, 256, 259; Cartellieri, iii, 182) but the success was only temporary (*Actes*, nos. 529–32).
[152] Howden, iv, 59.   [153] *Ibid.*, 40, 46.   [154] *Ibid.*, 59.
[155] According to Rigord he had 1500 knights (i, 141). See Richard's letter to the bishop of Durham in Howden, iv, 58. Apparently Dangu was taken, though no reference is made to it.
[156] Richard's letter (Howden, iv, 58).
[157] 'Cum ccc militibus et servientibus et communis suis.'
[158] Rather more than 30 kilometres, not allowing for the slight detour to Courcelles.

familiar with the district, who had been sent on by Richard, reported upon the strength of the French army, and, in spite of its superiority in numbers, advised an immediate attack. The king sent them back for reinforcements, and hastened himself to examine the enemy from a neighbouring height. His trained eye satisfied him that the risk could be run,[159] and without waiting for his full strength, he called those within reach, and burst upon the French 'like a hungry lion upon its prey'.[160] It was a second Jaffa. Philip was routed; Richard's army gathered in pursuit: 'We had them so pressed in the gate of Gisors that the bridge broke under them, and the king of France, it is said, drank of the river, and twenty of his knights were drowned. And in that place we unhorsed Matthew of Montmorenci, and Alan of Ronci, and Fulk of Gilerval with a single lance and kept them captive; and of the French force there were captured well upon one hundred knights; we send you the names of the more important, and you shall have the names of others when we know them, for Mercadier took about thirty whom we have not seen.'[161] A contemporary adds the information that the clouds of dust and the caprice of Dame Fortune contrived to save from capture many more.[162]

Such was the fit ending of Richard's war with Philip Augustus. Mercadier went off to plunder in the direction of Flanders, and spoiled the French merchants at the fair of Abbeville;[163] in October, William le Queu (*Cocus*), castellan of Lions-la-Fôret, captured a French force on the way to garrison Neuf-marché.[164] But King Richard occupied himself with the fortification of the Seine; above the isle of Andeli another island was strengthened by the fortress of Boutavant; on his part Philip built a new French castle, Le Goulet.[165] In November the usual truce was made, to last till the fast of St. Hilary on January 13, when, with the assistance of the papal legate, a durable peace might once more be attempted.[166]

The biographer of the Marshal preserves memories of the negotiations in January, 1199, which, unjust and prejudiced though they are, reveal the mind of Richard and the point of view shared by his secular companions. The king felt in 1199 about the papal legate as

[159] A good narrative in *Guillaume le Maréchal*, iii, 145. That the risk was great is clear from Richard's letter: 'sed nos idem non fecimus immo Deus et jus nostrum per nos; et in hoc facto posuimus in causa caput nostrum et regnum etiam, supra consilium omnium nostrorum.'
[160] *Guillaume le Maréchal*, iii, 145.
[161] Richard to the bishop of Durham, in Howden, iv, 58.
[162] *Guillaume le Maréchal*, loc. cit.   [163] Howden, iv, 60.
[164] *Ibid.*, 78. For William le Queu, see below, p. 200.
[165] *Ibid.*, 78. For Boutavant, see the note in Cartellieri, iii, 140. There is some dispute about its position.
[166] *Ibid.*, iv, 68.

he had felt in 1194, when a truce had been made in his absence;[167] but on the later occasion annoyance was intensified by a sense of degradation. On both sides men sympathised with Richard in having to meet an ecclesiastic whom they regarded as a secret ally of the king of France: the French were touched by the ridicule in which Philip was involved; the Normans felt contempt and chose to represent the cardinal as a sly creature, mean in person and despicable in character, who had been bought from Rome by French gold.[168] That the legate was a learned and able man, whose main object was the restoration of Philip's lawful wife, that the majestic influence of Rome was threatening France with the horrors of an interdict, did not occur to the courtiers of King Richard, and would hardly have interested them if it had.

Richard evidently shared this attitude, and went to meet the cardinal in January between Vernon and Le Goulet in no gracious mood.[169] According to the Marshal's biographer, Richard, after hotly repudiating all responsibility for the war, was prevailed upon to agree to a five years' truce in the interests of the future Crusade, on the condition that, while keeping in pledge the Norman castles in his possession, the French king should surrender all claims to the possession of the surrounding lands. Nothing remained to be done but to shake hands in ratification, when the legate turned to an ecclesiastical subject, and demanded the release of the bishop of Beauvais.[170]

'The court of Rome requires of you the release of her man whom you hold in prison against all law and with great wrong.'

'I hold him?' replied the king, 'not I.'

'Sire, make no denial. I refer to the bishop of Beauvais; he is under the protection of Rome. It is unlawful to detain in this way a man who has been anointed and consecrated.'

'By my head! he is rather the reverse, and a false Christian,' said the king. 'He was not taken as bishop, but as knight, fully armed, with laced helmet. Is this your man? Sir hypocrite, you play the game ill; if you were not here on a mission, the court of Rome would not save you from a thrashing to show the Pope as a souvenir from me. So the Pope thinks I am a fool? I know how he mocked at me, when

---

[167] Above, p. 103.

[168] See *Guillaume le Maréchal*, ll. 11355–72, and iii, 151, note, for this view of Philip's relations with Rome.

> Quer toz diz convient que l'om oingue
> A la cort de Rome les paumes;
> N' i estuet chanter autres psaumes (11362–4).

[169] See *Guillaume le Maréchal*, iii, pp. 153–7, for what follows.

[170] It is clear from other authorities that the bishop was kept in strict confinement.

I begged him to come to my aid in prison, servant of God as I was. He paid no heed; and now he demands of me a bullying brigand and incendiary who spoiled my lands day and night! Out of this, sir traitor, sir liar, trickster, simoniac, and see that you never cross my path again.'

The legate fled in terror, we are told, and the five years' truce was finally arranged by the archbishop of Reims, on the terms settled between Richard and the cardinal.[171] The kings met on the Seine between Andeli and Vernon, Richard in a boat, Philip on horseback on the bank.[172] It is curious to reflect that within the five years proposed, Normandy was lost.

Richard set off for Aquitaine; but peace was still insecure, for Philip at once began to build a new fortress near the Seine.[173] Richard returned and declared through his chancellor that he would denounce the truce if reparation were not made. By the legate's advice Philip promised to destroy the castle, but Richard demanded a definite settlement. The legate accordingly produced a grandiose scheme, by which Richard might be satisfied, and the peace of the whole west established at the same time. Whether Gisors had or had not been granted to Philip at Messina, why should not Richard definitely cede it now? It might form the dowry in the marriage settlement of Philip's son Louis; let Louis marry Richard's niece, Blanche of Castile, and receive Gisors and a handsome sum of money, say 20,000 marks of silver. In return Philip might quitclaim to Richard all the other Norman lands which he had seized, and in addition settle an old quarrel by surrendering his lordship over the archbishopric of Tours. Finally, if Philip would give up his foolish opposition to Otto of Brunswick and join his party, the peace of Normandy would lead to the peace of Europe: England, France, Spain and Germany would be united and free to attack the enemies of Christendom.[174]

Full consideration of the plan was postponed until Richard's return from Aquitaine. It is not in the least likely that Philip Augustus would have agreed to it.[175] He still held firmly some of the chief border castles of Normandy;[176] through the archbishop of Tours he was still hoping to bind together ecclesiastical interests in the west of France, and to subordinate the Breton to the French Church;[177]

---

[171] *Guillaume le Maréchal*, iii, 156.
[172] Howden, iv, 79–80. The date was January 13.   [173] *Ibid.*, 80.
[174] I have amplified this from Howden, iv, 81.
[175] Cartellieri (iii, 202) remarks that only 'das naive Selbstbewusstsein eines päpstlichere Politikers' could have expected success. Compare the remarks of M. Delaborde in the *Journal des Savants* for 1910, p. 559.
[176] The southern castles of the Norman Vexin, including Gisors and Baudemont; also Vernon, Gaillon, Paci, Ivry, Nonancourt. The earl of Leicester made two futile attempts in 1198 to recover Paci (Howden, iv, 60).
[177] It was in this year, 1199, that Innocent III abolished the metropolitan

his friendship with Philip of Suabia was his main weapon against the Pope on the one side, and against the house of Anjou on the other; if he acquiesced in the cause of Otto, the family interest of the Angevins would bind together the north of Europe from the Elbe to the Pyrenees, and he could not hope to arrange his domestic contest with the Pope. Yet it may be doubted whether the work of Henry II ever showed a result so magnificent as when a papal legate ventured to suggest such terms to a king of France.

King Richard set off to the scenes of his earliest warfare fresh from these military and diplomatic triumphs. He had few followers;[178] the great men of Normandy were engaged upon a lawsuit at Vaudreuil when, on the 7th of April, a messenger arrived with the news of his wound at Chalus.[179] Death alone could release him from his own fitful passions and from the persistence of his enemy. A few significant charters show that, even during the period of truce, Philip was receiving the allegiance of the discontented lords of Angoulême and the Limousin.[180] It was not, however, in chastising them, but in a subsidiary quarrel, that Richard met his death. Someone came upon a relic of Gallo-Roman paganism in the territory of the lord of Chalus; and rumour magnified the discovery into a find of great wealth.[181] The king claimed the treasure and marched to enforce his claim.

It is sad to reflect that Richard died in such a sordid quarrel. Yet he was fighting for his *regalia*, and the incident is symbolic of his whole career; his mind had burned with the same enthusiasm to rescue

---

dignity of the bishop of Dol, and submitted the dioceses of Brittany to Tours, after a long controversy. Howden, iv, 100–2; Innocent's letters in Migne, ccxiv, 635–6; Potthast, nos. 721–4; and see Borderie, *Histoire de Bretagne*, iii, 205. Philip had taken the side of Tours in 1184; *Recueil*, i, nos. 148, 149. In 1200 Arthur of Brittany showed his fidelity to Philip by trying to enforce the judgment of the Pope; Innocent, on May 12, 1200, placed Brittany under an interdict (*Bibliothèque de l'Ecole des Chartes*, 1872, xxxiii, 595). On the early history of the dispute see Duine in *Annales de Bretagne*, 1915; cf. Halphen, *Revue Historique*, 1917, cxxv, 104–5.

[178] William of Briouze, Thomas Basset, Peter of Stoke, Gerard of Fornival, Geoffrey de la Celle, and two chaplains attest Richard's last charter of April 5, the day before his death—a confirmation of charter of April 25, 1194, to Noel, the king's servant (*Calendar of Charter Rolls*, ii, 101).

[179] *Guillaume le Maréchal*, iii, 158 and notes. For the final concord between the parties on April 7, see *Curia Regis Rolls*, vi (11–14 John), 398–9.

[180] *Recueil*, ii, nos. 598–600. The death of Richard hastened negotiations, but Ademar of Angoulême and Ademar of Limoges must have commenced them earlier. See Richard, *Comtes de Poitou*, ii, 322–3.

[181] See the ingenious theory of Richard, *Comtes de Poitou*, ii, 322, note, in explanation of Rigord's description of the treasure (i, 145). For Richard's death, see Arbellot, *La vérité sur la mort de Richard Cœur de Lion* (1878), and Norgate, *England under the Angevin Kings*, ii, 382–7.

the Holy Sepulchre. In this case his imagination was kindled by a useless relic of antiquity; in other cases it was kindled by traditions which are still potent in the world.[182] Richard's deeds attain the dignity of history because his matchless energy was always at the service of his imagination. A like significance invests the theme of this chapter. From one point of view we have been concerned with the border forays of half-tamed barbarians; from another we have been watching the slow action of imperial influences, and the beginnings of the modern state.

[182] Two years later, in 1201, John's cupidity led him to make excavations at Corbridge, which have been resumed with such extraordinary success in our own day: 'Cum venisset ad Extoldesham et audisset quod apud Chores-brige esset thesaurus absconditus, fecit ibi fodere, sed nihil inventum est praeter lapides signatos aere et ferro et plumbo' (Howden, iv, 157).

CHAPTER VI

THE LOSS OF NORMANDY

THE unexpected death of Richard Cœur-de-Lion before the castle of Chalus was, says M. Delaborde, not only the signal of the downfall of the continental empire of the Plantagenets; it was at the same time prophetic of the certain, if distant, triumph of the Hohenstaufen.[1] It may be doubted whether king Richard could have prevented the victory of the Hohenstaufen over his nephew Otto of Brunswick; but it is certain that his death hurried on the loss of Normandy. The figure of the great soldier had stood as a screen between the Normans and the operation of those forces which were working in favour of Philip Augustus. The house of Capet had successfully asserted its right to maintain the authority of the Carolingians: Philip Augustus was a Carolid.[2] For half a century the princes of larger France had been learning to recognise the claims of the kings of Francia.[3] The church, always conscious of the Frankish origin of its privileges, was, even in Normandy, losing the sense of provincial duty. Moreover, the tendency of the new chivalry, fed upon Carolingian romance, was towards personal rather than national loyalty. The Norman had no love for England and could lose respect for England's king. Provided that his local privileges were maintained, his conception of the power to which he owed service might embrace a larger France as easily as the duchy; moreover the ecclesiastical writers who chose to speak of politics were not tempted to dogmatise, as we are, upon the relation between the state and such facts as nationality and race.[4] Hence the Normans, speaking the same tongue, living along the same roads, benefiting by the same trade and belonging to the same Church as their French neighbours, could oppose few sentimental barriers to the claims of France.[5]

---

[1] *Journal des Savants*, 1910, p. 559.

[2] Cf. William the Breton, *Philippidos Nuncupatio*, l. 28 (ed. Delaborde), ii, 3.

[3] The geographical distinction between France and Normandy or Poitou was very clear even in this period. Cf. Walter of Coutances to the Dean of St. Paul's in 1196: *in partibus Galliae jurisdictioni nostrae subjectae* (Diceto, ii, 142). On the general question, see Halphen in *Revue Hist.*, lxxxv (1904), p. 276.

[4] Cf. Helinand, *De Bono Regimine Principis*, on the place of the knight in the state (Migne, *Pat. Lat.*, ccxii, 745). Luchaire has brought together some interesting criticisms passed upon the nobility by Peter of Blois and others in *La Société Française sous Philippe Auguste* (1909), pp. 291–4.

[5] For some of these points, see chapter x, and above, pp. 16, 17.

The death of Richard tore away the veil which had concealed these facts. He was succeeded by a man who, in spite of certain useful qualities, was unable to command respect. It is strange to the modern mind, accustomed to think of John's enormities, to find that he was at first despised on account of his lack of vigour and his love of peace.[6] His cruelty and lasciviousness could not have been more marked than the cruelty and lasciviousness of his elder brother; it was only in course of time that the callousness of John gave to his crimes a peculiar significance. There was nothing large or attractive in his nature; he could be a boon companion, but never a leader. 'The Normans', says the biographer of the Marshal, 'were not asleep in the days of the young king.[7] Then they were grain, but now they are chaff; for since the death of King Richard they have had no leadership.' Men lost heart and forsook John; many left their homes for the Holy Land or to go on pilgrimage.[8]

Free from the glamour cast upon them by Richard, the Normans could not long be inattentive to the havoc which war, pestilence and famine had made in their country during the last five years. The constant warfare and castle building had cost large sums; the appeals to Rome and the search for allies had also swallowed up a great deal of money. Moreover, as the war went on, bitterness increased; not only had the methods of actual warfare become more cruel,[9] but the wanton destruction of towns and villages had been resorted to by both sides,[10] nor had the incendiaries always been careful to distinguish between friends and foes.[11] These attributes of war had been intensified by the use of mercenaries, whose employment by John was to

[6] Gervase of Canterbury, ii, 92–3. 'Johannem molle gladium' eum . . . detractores . . . vocabant. Cf. Robert of Auxerre (*Historiens de France*, xviii, 263): the factious Richard succeeded by John, 'juvenis quidem remissioris animi, amansque quietis'.

[7] *Guillaume le Maréchal*, iii, 58. The young king is Henry, son of Henry II.

[8] Cf. William the Breton's chronicle (ed. Delaborde, i, 211): 'Interea Flandrensis, Blesensis, Perticensis comites, et alii proceres qui Philippo regi domino suo defecerant videntes se per mortem Richardi regis auxilio et consilio destitutos, cruce assumpta,' etc.

[9] See particularly Howden, iv, 54.

[10] Besides Howden, see Rigord, i, 142.

[11] Howden has a curious story (iv. 60) which may serve as an illustration: 'Postea rex Franciae congregato exercitu intravit Normanniam et combussit Ebroicas et septem alias villas. Comes autem Johannes, frater Ricardi regis, combussit Novum Burgum; quod rex Franciae sperans a suis fieri, milites misit ad prohibendum suis ne procederent; ex quibus capti sunt xviii milites et servientes multi.' It is, of course, possible that John burnt Neubourg in defence, but destruction was congenial to him. Cf. the entry in *Rot. Scacc.*, ii, 292. 'In defectu molendinorum vastatorum per guerram per Comitem Johannem' (at Gavrai). Allowance was of course made at the exchequer for waste (cf. *Rot. Scacc.*, i, 156).

become the main source of his strength and, in turn, one of the chief reasons of his failure to secure the support of his subjects.[12]

We possess a valuable description of the condition of the country during the last months of Richard's reign, in the life of Saint Hugh of Lincoln. The bishop was on his way to argue in person with the king about his recent exactions. At Angers, in the abbey of St. Nicholas, he was entertained with such stories of Richard's threats against those who withstood him, that the listening clerks were struck with very natural terror.[13] The clergy of three dioceses, both those of Angers and those who were present from Lincoln and Hereford, urged the saint to surrender. The attendant dangers were sufficient to have daunted him. 'Nothing was safe, neither the city to dwell in, nor the highway for travel.'[14] The king died before Saint Hugh could reach him, but, though his companions had not to face the living lion, they endured fresh anxiety from the violence and lawlessness, which increased on the news of his death. The men who were bringing money from England for the bishop's use were robbed; and his horses were stolen at La Flêche.[15]

The last few years had been generally years of dearth, and we need not wonder if, when the horrors of famine were added to those of war, men lent an ear to preachers and prophets. As the century drew to a close, these foretold the end of the thousand years of the Apocalypse, after which Satan was to be unloosed.[16] During the great storms of 1197, a rumour spread in France that Antichrist had been born in Egypt and that the end of the world was at hand.[17] Such fancies, like the effect produced by the contemporary preachers Fulk of Neuilly and abbot Eustace of Flay,[18] may be directly connected with the gloomy records of war and bad harvests.[19]

There was little hesitation as to Richard's successor. Even if the principles of primogeniture had been established more exactly than they were, the case of succession to the duchy would naturally have been regarded as unique. The earliest custumal notices that King Richard had set aside the ordinary rules of female succession in

[12] Cf. *Guillaume le Maréchal*, iii, 171, and below, pp. 227–32. The use of mercenaries, which should not be confused with the development of quotas of knight service and of money-fiefs, had been familiar since the Norman Conquest: see J. O. Prestwich in *Trans. R. Hist. Soc.*, 5th ser., iv (1954), 19–43, and cf. J. Boussard, in *Bibliothèque de l'Ecole des chartes*, cvi (1945–6).

[13] *Vita S. Hug.* (Rolls series), p. 281.   [14] *Ibid.*, 282.

[15] *Ibid.*, 284, 295.   [16] Howden, iv, 161–3.   [17] Rigord, i, 141.

[18] Howden, iv, 76, 123, 167–9, 172. Some saw in Fulk the forerunner of Anti-Christ: annals of Winchester in *Ann. Mon.*, ii, 67–8. For Fulk of Neuilly, see the passages referred to by Cartellieri, iii, 183, note.

[19] See especially the annals of Anchin in *Historiens de France*, xviii, 549–50. The Norman facts are brought together by Delisle, *Etudes sur la condition de la classe agricole*, pp. 624–5.

K

Normandy on account of the war;[20] in a critical turn of public affairs
the great men of Normandy would have had no duty to be too
scrupulous in their acknowledgment of Richard's successor. It has
been suggested that in 1197 the archbishop of Canterbury and other
great men who attested John's covenant with the count of Flanders
in September and his confirmation in October of Richard's agreement
with the archbishop of Rouen about Les Andelys, implicitly associated
themselves with Richard in tacit recognition of John as his brother's
heir. At this time Arthur of Brittany was in the wardship of the king
of France.[21] But, as a matter of fact, English law was in a transitional
stage,[22] and Norman law was inclined to favour the uncle at the
expense of the nephew. Indeed, Arthur as a stranger to Normandy
had claims inferior to those of a count of Mortain.[23] An interesting
conversation between the archbishop of Canterbury and William the
Marshal reveals a very exact picture of the difficult situation. Before
his death King Richard had instructed the Marshal to take custody
of the keep at Rouen and the royal treasure. The messenger arrived
on May 7, and was followed by another, three days later, with the
news of Richard's death. It was late at night, and the Marshal was
going to bed. He dressed immediately, and went to the priory of
Notre Dame-du-Pré, on the other side of the river, where the archbishop was staying. The archbishop, seeing the late hour of the visit,
guessed its cause.

'The king is dead,' he cried. 'What hope remains to us now? There is
none, for, after him, I can see no successor able to defend the kingdom.
The French will overrun us, and there will be no one to resist them.'

[20] Tardif, I, i, 13.

[21] Landon, *Itinerary of Richard I*, pp. 122, 124, 207, 208.

[22] See especially *Hist. Eng. Law*, ii, 284-5. The *casus regius*, as the succession of the younger brother instead of the nephew was called, caused hesitation
among lawyers until the reign of Edward I. To the English mind, the weak
point about John's succession seems to have been the judgment against him
after Richard's return from captivity. Cf. Annals of Margam in *Ann. Mon.*,
i, 24. The legal argument is used later (Wykes in *Ann. Mon.*, iv, 51) and was
of course influenced by the civil war at the end of John's reign. It should be
remembered, however, that Arthur seems to have been regarded by many as
Richard's heir from the first. See Howden, iii, 63, 65; Diceto, ii, 85, 86. For
Longchamp's view of the succession, see Round, *Commune of London*, p. 216.

[23] 'Si voro contingerit patrem vel matrem filios vel filias habere quorum
primus vel secundus uxorem duxerit et filios habeat et nullam terre habuerit
portionem vivente patre et matre, et ita maritus obeirit filii ejus non habebunt
herditatem avi; sed avunculi eam habebunt quamvis postgeniti; propinquiores
enim sunt filii hereditatis patris quam nepotis.' This is the Vatican MS. of the
earliest custumal (chapter xxxii, § 2; see Viollet, in *Hist. Litt. de la France*,
xxxiii, 62). The rights of the son of the elder were admitted in an exchequer
judgment of 1224, but the *Grand Coutumier* still speaks of contrary customs
which pervert the sound law (*ibid.*, p. 130).

'We must choose his successor at once,' said the Marshal.

'In my opinion we should choose Arthur.'

'Ah, sire, that would be a bad thing,' replied the Marshal; 'Arthur has bad councillors, and he is proud and passionate. If we put him at our head he will cause trouble, for he has no love for the English. There is Count John; he is the next heir to the lands of his father and brother.'

'Marshal,' replied the archbishop, 'do you really mean this?'

'Yes, sire. It is right; the son is nearer the land of his father than the nephew is.' [24]

'Marshal, it shall be as you wish. But I warn you that you will never repent of anything as you will repent of this.'

'So be it; it is my view all the same.' [25]

John had not waited for the support of the Normans. Richard had declared him his heir, and the count, who was staying, curiously enough, with Arthur in Brittany, hastened to secure the Angevin treasure[26] at Chinon. He was invested as duke of Normandy at Rouen on April 25 after a characteristic display of vigour, cruelty and frivolity, in which the machinery of government had been seized, Le Mans burnt, and the Church flouted.[27]

The key to the situation, as John had seen, was the control of the Loire. The barons of the Angevin counties, Anjou and Touraine, and also of Maine, which bordered on Brittany, seem to have welcomed the opportunity of asserting their independence; while John secured Normandy they accepted Arthur as their lord.[28] It was fortunate for John that Robert of Turnham had surrendered Chinon, Saumur and the other castles in his custody,[29] and that Mercadier had put his troop of mercenaries at the count's disposal.[30] As it was, Arthur

---

[24] See preceding note. It has not been observed that the Marshal is quoting a Norman law book.

[25] *Guillaume le Maréchal*, iii, 159–60.

[26] Howden, iv, 86; Coggeshall, 99. Richard, according to Howden (p. 83), left three-fourths of his treasure to John; according to the Stanley continuator of William of Newburgh, to Otto (Howlett, *Chronicles of Stephen*, etc., ii, 503; see also Howden, iv, 116. Cf. annals of Winchester in *Ann. Mon.*, ii, 73).

[27] See the *Life of St. Hugh*, pp. 287–94, for a vivid description of John. Cf. Howden, iv, 87, for his movements. It is possible, as has been suggested, that Le Mans was not burnt at this time, but later in the year (Richard, *Comtes de Poitou*, ii, 363, note).

[28] The various sections of the empire fell apart. Aquitaine was held by Eleanor, who wisely did homage for the duchy to Philip (Rigord, i, 146), and later transferred it to John (*Rot. Chart.*, 30b; Richard, ii, 353). The Angevins, on the other hand, accepted Arthur on legal grounds, just as the Normans accepted John (Howden, iv, 86).

[29] Wendover, i, 285–6; Coggeshall, 99; Howden, iv, 86.

[30] Howden, iv, 88, refers to Mercadier's ravages in Anjou 'eo quod Arturum receperunt'.

received the support of Le Mans, Angers, Tours and most of the country.[31] King Philip concentrated his efforts in the same quarter. Although, as soon as he heard of Richard's death, he occupied the city and county of Evreux,[32] and later in the year took Conches,[33] the Norman border was hardly affected. Constance of Brittany used the opportunity of a French alliance without hesitation. For three years she had been powerless to resist Richard's influence in Brittany; now at Tours she gave her son into Philip's keeping, and allowed French garrisons to be placed in the towns and fortresses which had declared against John.[34]

During this time the new duke of Normandy was in England, where he was received as king. The contest in western France resolved itself into a duel between Constance and the old queen Eleanor. On the one hand, the cause of Arthur was maintained by the judicious purchase of the great men of Maine and Touraine: Juhel of Mayenne was established as a marcher baron in Gorron and Ambrières to watch the Norman frontier;[35] William des Roches was made seneschal of Anjou and Maine.[36] On the other hand, Eleanor, as duchess, made a grand tour through Poitou and the Bordelais. All interests, of barons, clergy and towns, were secured. The great barons of Poitou, Aimeri of Thouars, Hugh of La Marche, Geoffrey of Lusignan, rallied round her.[37] On May 23 they attacked Tours where Arthur was still staying, and succeeded in capturing that part of the city, the Châteauneuf, in which lay the abbey of St. Martin.[38] They retreated on the approach of French reinforcements; but the prompt action of Eleanor had shown that the supporters of Arthur, if they wished to avoid invasion from both north and south, would be forced to choose between the support of Philip and submission to John.

About the same time, Eleanor, on her way to Normandy, did homage for the duchy of Aquitaine at Tours.[39] Relations between the king of France and the various sections of the Angevin empire outside Normandy had thus been established, and Philip could hope to force

---

[31] Howden, iv, 86–7.

[32] Rigord, i, 145, who says that he ravaged the country as far as Le Mans; Howden, iv, 85.   [33] Howden, iv, 96.

[34] Philip 'saisivit in manu sua civitates, castella et munitiones quae Arturi erant, et custodibus suis tradidit custodienda' (Howden, iv, 87. Arthur was taken to Paris (Rigord, i, 146; Howden, iv, 87).

[35] Confirmation by Philip, in May, at Montlandon (Recueil, ii, no. 607).

[36] Confirmation by Philip (Recueil, ii, no. 608).

[37] Eleanor's actions and itinerary have been worked out from the Charter Rolls and other sources by Richard, Comtes de Poitou, ii, 332 seqq. See also above.

[38] Salmon, Chron. de Touraine, p. 145.

[39] Rigord, i, 146. Richard, Comtes de Poitou, ii, 353, note, fixes the date July 15–20.

John to a compromise. A truce was arranged after John's return from England, to last until August 16, and on that day a conference was opened in the usual meeting place between Boutavant and Le Goulet. After the royal agents had conferred for two days, the kings talked face to face for an hour on August 18. There seemed to be no reason why the war should commence again after the death of Richard, so long as John was prepared to treat. Philip had been the aggressor; from the Seine to the Loire he had seized the advantage given to him by the disaster at Chalus. He now insisted upon his rights as overlord, and began the long feudal lawsuit, whose various pleadings lasted as long as John lived. He knew his man of old. John, unlike his father and brother, was not a sensible man, and was fond of legal quibbling. He had received the duchy of Normandy and had made no effort to secure the approval of his lord to a somewhat doubtful succession.[40] Philip made the most of this fact. He demanded the Angevin counties and Maine for Arthur,[41] and secure possession of the whole Norman Vexin for himself. The recent fighting in the valley of the Epte, followed by the unsatisfactory treaty of the previous January had seriously weakened Philip's hold of the Vexin. If he could make sure of his authority along the Norman march, from the forest of Lions to the borders of Maine, and also establish Arthur's rights to the old centres of Angevin power, the empire of Henry II would cease to be a danger. Anxious though John was for peace, such a solution was impossible. Negotiations were broken off and the war went on.

Within a few weeks fresh preparations for peace were arranged by the indefatigable papal legate. Circumstances had forced Philip to moderate his tone; his hopes had been centred in Anjou and William des Roches, but either he grasped too quickly at power, or the seneschal thought a safer game could be played with King John than

[40] Philip complained that John had acted without his licence. 'Ipse sine licentia illius occupaverat Normanniam, et alias terras. Debuerat enim in primis ad eum venisse, et eum requissise *de jure suo*, et inde homagium ei fecisse' (Howden, iv, 95).

[41] According to Howden, he had previously knighted Arthur and invested him with Normandy and Poitou in addition to Anjou, etc. (iv, 94). The same chronicler also states that he claimed Poitou for Arthur from John at the conference (p. 95). Both statements are probably false. Arthur was knighted in 1202, when he was sixteen years old (Coggeshall, 137; Rigord, i, 152). Although knighthood at any early age was frequent in the case of royalty, as indeed the ceremony of 1202 proves, it is not likely that Philip would knight a boy of thirteen. The young King Henry was knighted at the age of eighteen. (See Meyer's remarks in his edition of *Guillaume le Maréchal*, iii, p. 26.) As Stubbs has shown in his introduction to Howden (iv, xxix–xxx) the chronology of this chronicler is very shaky for the years 1200 onwards. The last part of the chronicle was hastily compiled. As for the claim to Poitou on Arthur's behalf, it is not likely that, after receiving the homage of Eleanor, Philip would attempt to divide the duchy of Aquitaine.

with King Philip; certainly, during September the way was prepared for a reconciliation between John and his nephew. A formal treaty, of the familiar feudal type, was arranged on the 18th, and shortly afterwards John was at Le Mans.[42] Apparently Philip was unaware that he had been betrayed and made no efforts to secure the person of Arthur. He pursued the war in Maine, took the fortress of Ballon, and destroyed it. William des Roches made this act of violence the occasion of a quarrel; John and the Poitevins had in the meantime repulsed Philip at Lavardin; and all the parties in the late disturbances, Arthur and his mother, William des Roches and his army, the viscount of Thouars and the Poitevins, met round the king of England at Le Mans early in October.[43]

These events forced Philip to make terms which, if John had acted with ordinary prudence, might have been lasting. The legate arranged a truce which was to lead to a peace, as in the autumns of 1195 and 1198. Once again there was to be a solemn colloquy on St. Hilary's day (January 13).[44]

The treaty of Le Goulet, which brought peace to Normandy, was arranged on May 22, 1200, in accordance with terms settled at this earlier conference when the two kings had met face to face, and talked alone in the centre of a circle of their followers.[45] It is worthy of some attention.[46]

John was recognised by Philip as Richard's lawful heir.[47] After

[42] *Rot. Chart.*, 23b, 30b. M. Alfred Richard (*Comtes de Poitou*, ii, 359) suggests acutely that Constance of Beaumont, the wife of Roger of Tosny (Toeni), who was connected with some of the Angevin families, had arranged the treaty. Shortly before Philip Augustus had taken Conches, her husband's castle (Howden, iv, 96), and now and afterwards she received benefits from John (*Rot. Chart.*, 20b; *Rot. Norm.*, 52—the latter a writ of June, 1202, for Constance, *domina de Conchis*). If this surmise is correct, it illustrates the cross currents in the family histories of Normandy and Anjou.

[43] The chronology is doubtful. I have combined Howden with the facts of John's itinerary. John was in Le Mans again in October (8–11) and Howden ascribes the surrender of the city, as also the destruction of Ballon, to this month (iv, 96). In an act dated Anet, October, by which Andrew of Chauvigni promises to hold his Angevin fiefs of Arthur or of the heir to the county, Philip Augustus seems still to pose as Arthur's ally (*Layettes*, no. 504).

[44] Howden, iv, 97. Rigord, i, 147, who says the truce was to last till December 27. The annals of Winchester incorrectly date the truce in September (*Ann. Mon.*, ii, 73).   [45] Gervase of Canterbury, ii, 92.

[46] John's ratification, printed from the original, is in Teulet, *Layettes*, i, 217, no. 578; *Cartulaire Normand*, p. 280, no. 1063. Philip's ratification, printed from his Register, is in *Recueil*, ii, no. 623; also in Howden, iv, 148 (cf. Stubbs' note thereto). The text of the French ratification in the *Foedera*, i, 79, is from a transcript on the fourteenth-century roll, Exchequer, Diplomatic Documents, E. 30, no. 6. On the topics of this treaty, their variants and falsifications, see Ch. Petit-Dutaillis in *Bibliothèque de l'Ecole des Chartes*, cii (1941), 35–50.   [47] 'Sicut rectus heres regis Ricardi.'

inquiry, Philip's court adjudged Anjou and Brittany to him. There was in the case of Normandy no judicial enquiry. Arthur was to hold Brittany as John's man; and his rights, though legally protected, were safeguarded only by the interposition of John's court: John promised that he would in no way diminish Arthur's position without a judgment of his court.[48] As Philip's man, John was to be responsible lord over his father's continental fiefs, including Brittany.[49] Events were to show that the king of France was able to give a new reality to this relationship between John and himself; but to all appearance the unity of the Angevin empire was preserved.

In return for the recognition of his claims to be Richard's heir, John went back to the settlement made at Issoudun in 1195, and confirmed at Louviers in January, 1196.[50] By taking this treaty as a basis of agreement, the disputes which had arisen during the later war and which had not been settled by the abortive truce of 1199, were set on one side. Again, Philip was able in this way to break up the coalition which had been formed against him after the death of the Emperor Henry VI. John promised to refuse aid in the future to his nephew Otto[51]—a promise which he fulfilled so long as he could do without him. The equivocal relations between Philip and his important feudatories, the counts of Flanders and Boulogne, of which Richard had availed himself with such skill, were deprived of their sting by John's admission that, as they were vassals of France rather than of England, he would countenance them in no attack upon their proper lord.[52]

[48] 'Nos vero recipiemus Arturum in hominem, ita quod Arturus Britanniam tenebit de nobis, et nos sicut rectus heres tenebimus de domino rege Francie omnia feoda, sicut pater noster et frater noster rex Ricardus ea tenuerunt a (sic) domino rege Francie et sicut feoda debent. . . . De Arturo sic erit, quod nos non minuemus eum, nec de feodo, nec de dominio Britannie citra mare, nisi per rectum juditium curie nostre.' Coggeshall asserts that Philip received John's homage for Brittany et hoc secundum judicium curiae suae—this remark, if not due to a misunderstanding of the treaty, gives us fresh information, and explains the procedure by which Philip, in the words of the treaty, surrendered Brittany to John (feoda Britannie que rex Francie nobis dimisit). Howden says that John became Philip's man (iv, 115).

[49] See previous note and below, p. 138, note.

[50] 'Nos tenebimus . . . pacem quam frater noster rex Ricardus fecit illi inter Exoldunum et Charrotium, exceptis hiis que per presentem cartam excipiuntur vel mutantur, propter interceptiones quas idem frater noster illi fecit de pace illa.' Cf. Rot. Chart., 58b: 'carte de pace facta inter regem Ricardum et regem Franc' apud Exsoldun' liberate eidem Gaufrido apud Cadom' eodem die et eodem anno' (i.e., January 26, 1200).

[51] 'Nos nepoti nostro Othoni nullum auxilium faciemus, nec per pecuniam, nec per milites, nec per gentem, nec per nos, nec per alium, nisi per consilium et assensum domini regis Francie.' The annals of Winchester (Ann. Mon., ii, 73) and Howden (iv, 116) show that John acted on this promise.

[52] 'Qui melius sint aut debeant esse homines ipsius regis Francie quam nostri.' On January 2 the counts had made the important treaty of Peronne

Thus, although comprehended in the treaty, the counts lost the advantage which had been theirs, or at least that of the count of Flanders,
in the past; and, by which, owing to their alliances with the dukes
of Normandy, they had been able to limit their feudal service to the
king of France to its legal minimum.[53] John's agreement with Philip
was a concession to the theory of the French state, which interpreted
feudal duties in a less pedantic fashion than did the count of Flanders;
and, besides involving the loss of his allies, it strengthened a policy
soon to be directed against himself.

Two or three important modifications were made in the treaty of
1195–6, with regard to the frontier. The manor of Andeli, which had
belonged to the archbishop of Rouen and which now contained the
castle of the Rock and the forts of the isle and of Boutavant on the
Seine, was cut off from the Norman Vexin and retained by John as
part of Normandy: it will be remembered that in the previous treaty
it had been regarded as neutral ground. In the rest of the Norman
Vexin, which was recognised as Philip's territory, a strip of land
between Gamaches, and the forests of Vernon and Andeli was to
remain unfortified. On the other side of the river Seine a more elaborate arrangement was necessary. In spite of the care bestowed by
Richard upon the fortifications of Evreux,[54] that unhappy city had
again been overcome by Philip. John agreed to the surrender of the
place together with a great part of the county. The treaty of 1195–6
had fixed the boundary half-way between Gaillon and Vaudreuil from
the Seine to the Eure, then—as of old—along the Eure and Avre. It
had also given to France Paci, Ivry and Nonancourt—important
fortresses on these rivers.[55] The new boundary was apparently to
follow the Itun from its junction with the Eure, instead of the latter
river, but was also to take in a stretch of country to the north, defined
by a point midway between Evreux and Neubourg.[56] Damville on the
Itun was to remain Norman, also Tillières on the Avre ; hence we may
suppose that a line drawn between the two rivers, east of these places,
was to mark the connection between the new boundary and the old.

A marriage and a dowry were to guarantee the permanence of the

with Philip (*Recueil*, ii, no. 621; see Longnon, *Atlas historique, Texte*, pp.
230–1). In 1199, as a remark in the autobiography of Gerald of Wales shows,
the war between Philip and Baldwin of Flanders, 'qui regi Angliae Johanni
tunc adhaes erat', made travelling from Flanders to France very dangerous
(Gir. Camb., *Opera*, i, 118).

[53] See Lot, *Fideles ou Vassales?* p. 24, and above, p. 81. The treaty did
not put an end immediately to relations between John and his Flemish neighbours. See arrangement with Boulogne on May 9 (*Rot. Chart.*, 57b) and entry
in *Rotuli de Liberate* (p. 3) of October 20, in favour of the count of Flanders.

[54] *Rot. Scacc.*, ii, 463–4.
[55] See above, p. 107, note 70.   [56] See note A at end of this chapter.

treaty. They were old expedients, and usually very vain. Yet on this occasion the project is interesting, for it shows the desire of the negotiators to secure peace in the west of Europe. Blanche, the niece of John, and the daughter of Alphonso of Castile, was to marry Louis, the son of Philip. Between January and May John was busy with the arrangements for this marriage.[57] As a dowry, besides certain hypothetical gifts,[58] he surrendered in Berri the fiefs of Issoudun and Graçay and the fiefs of Andrew of Chauvigni.[59] Philip was to hold these lands until the marriage of Blanche and Louis, who were as yet but children, should be consummated. They were married on the day after the treaty was made, at Portmort near Le Goulet, by the archbishop of Bordeaux.[60]

Finally, and in some ways this is the most significant fact in the treaty, John gave Philip 20,000 marks sterling, as a relief for his lands (*rechatum*) and as payment for the recognition of his overlordship in Brittany.[61] This large payment not only involved a heavy carucage in England;[62] it must have impressed the more warlike element among John's subjects as an unfavourable sign of change. On the king's mind it probably impressed still more forcibly the one-sided theory of feudal duty which worked his ruin in the future. It is not fanciful to connect his feudal extortions of the following year with the novel exaction to which he himself submitted.[63] From Philip's point of view the payment was a fresh acknowledgment of the judicial supremacy of the French court; it must be connected with John's acquiescence in the stricter relations between Philip and the great feudatories of the north, Flanders and Boulogne. Philip, by the

[57] See *Rot. Chart.*, 58b. The charter rolls show considerable activity at this time in the reorganisation and settlement of Poitou and Gascony. Queen Eleanor went for Blanche (Howden, iv, 114; Richard, *Les Comtes de Poitou*, ii, 366–73).

[58] The lands ('citra mare Anglie') of Hugh of Gournai, the count of Aumâle and the count of Perche were to be added to the dowry, if John died without heirs. Coggeshall (p. 101) and especially Rigord (i, 148) write carelessly of this part of the treaty.

[59] See *Rot. Chart.*, p. 96; *Layettes*, no. 579; *Cart. Norm.*, p. 281.

[60] Howden, iv, 115. Portmort was the last church before the border. As France was under an interdict, the marriage could not take place on French soil. St. Louis was the child of Blanche and Louis.

[61] Both versions of the treaty give this sum. Most of the chroniclers say 30,000 marks. The annals of Margam state the sum as £20,000 (*Ann. Mon.*, i, 25).

[62] The connection between the carucage and the payment to Philip is emphasised by the annals of Dunstable (*Ann. Mon.*, iii, 27) and Coggeshall, p. 101.

[63] Howden, iv, 157. Compare the remark of M. Luchaire (Lavisse, *Histoire de France*, III, i, 126): 'jamais les Plantagenêts n'avient fait aux Capétiens de pareilles concessions.'

recognition of John's rights in Anjou and Brittany,[64] got more than he gave, for John had received them by an award of his court. In the meantime, Arthur, deserted though he was by the Angevins, was still a weapon held in reserve; for after he had done homage to his uncle at Vernon, on May 23—the day of his cousin's wedding with Louis of France—the boy had been handed again into Philip's keeping.[65] Whether the legal net would suffice to hold John in the future would depend upon the way in which he availed himself of the peaceful opportunity which Philip's embarrassments now offered him.

Such was the last of the four attempts which were made to secure the future of the Angevin empire after Henry II's death. The next treaty between a king of England and a king of France was made under very different conditions nearly sixty years later, when, in 1259, the barons of England forced Henry III to acquiesce in the annexation of Normandy to the French crown.

II

During the period of these negotiations, from October, 1199, to May, 1200, and for some months afterwards, John's position was by no means unfavourable. William des Roches had surrendered Le Mans to him, and the way was open for a settlement between the uncle and nephew. The position was one of some delicacy, for the temptation to play upon the suspicion which the action of William must have created was obvious. In reality John could not afford to divide the party of Arthur. If he had seized William des Roches, he would have alienated by his treachery the baronage of Maine and Anjou; if he tried to get rid of Arthur, he would immediately unite the Bretons and Angevins against him. There is no evidence that the seneschal wished to desert the cause of Arthur altogether; he seems rather to have hoped for an arrangement. Certainly, as later events were to prove, the personal safety of Arthur was the condition of his support. In addition to the difficulties raised within the Arthurian party by the precipitate action of the seneschal, there was the problem created by the alternative administration which the king had established in

[64] According to Coggeshall (p. 101, cf. above, p. 135, note 48), Philip's court judged Brittany to John; according to the chronicle of St. Martin of Tours, John on his later visit to Paris 'de comitatu Andegavensi fuit per curiae regalis judicium investitus' (*Historiens de France*, xviii, 295).

[65] Arthur, in his tenth year, had first been entrusted to King Philip during Richard's invasion of Brittany (1196: see Landon, *Itinerary*, pp. 111, 112 under date April 7, 1196). In 1198 he seems to have been with Richard. In 1199 (the exact date is uncertain) his mother again entrusted him to Philip (above, p. 132) and he seems to have returned to the French court after the reconciliations of May, 1200; but it is hard to be sure where he was at definite dates between 1199 and 1202.

Anjou. His position had been maintained by the Poitevin allies whom Queen Eleanor had rallied. To one of them, the viscount of Thouars, John had entrusted the castle of Chinon and the seneschalship of Anjou and Touraine. It would now be necessary to make some new arrangement. John was apparently so delighted by the adhesion of William des Roches and the surrender of Le Mans, that he felt safe enough to disregard the susceptibilities both of Arthur and of the Poitevins. The viscount of Thouars, who had come to Le Mans on the day of its surrender, was forced to give up Chinon and the seneschalship. The rumour spread that Arthur was to be imprisoned. In consequence the parties were brought together. Constance and the viscount combined to hurry Arthur off to Angers; regardless of her marriage with the earl of Chester, Constance married Guy of Thouars, the viscount's brother; and so a dangerous alliance of Breton and Poitevin interests was formed, which was, through its hostility to the king of England, bound in the end to turn again to Philip of France.[66] The incident is an admirable illustration of the checks and balances which composed the feudal state.

For the present, however, the adherents of Arthur were isolated. In other quarters the old allies of Richard had rallied to John in the hope of war; and the king could rely upon the support of his other nephew, the emperor.[67] The quiet of the next two years may well seem to justify the claims to statesmanship which have been made on John's behalf. The Norman border was preserved almost intact, and Arthur was forced to remain satisfied with Brittany. By his marriage with Isabella of Angoulême John secured the alliance of a power whose hostility was very dangerous. Throughout the Angevin dominions, as the spread of communal rights might be said to show, there was a revival of prosperity and common interests. On the other hand, we must remember that, during this very period, French politics were disordered by the quarrel between Philip and Innocent III.[68]

[66] The authority is Howden, iv, 96, 97. See Dubois, in *Bibliothèque de l'Ecole des Chartes* (1869), xxx, 416 *seqq.*

[67] Baldwin of Flanders, in August, 1199, at Rouen, *devenit homo Johannis regis Anglie* (Howden, iv, 93). The treaty is in *Rot. Chart.*, 31a. A similar convention against Philip was made with the counts of Flanders and Boulogne at Roche Andeli on August 18, immediately after the failure of the negotiations (*Rot. Chart.*, 30; Malo, *Renaud de Dammartin*, pp. 61, 62). At the same time, according to Howden, conventions were made between John and the French allies of Richard (Howden, iv, 95). The emperor also urged John to hold out (*ibid.*, 96). Cf. also annals of Winchester (*Ann. Mon.*, ii, 72): on the morrow after John's coronation in England, *i.e.*, May 28, the duke of Louvain, and the counts of Boulogne and Guines demanded *jura sua quae tenentur habere in Anglia.*

[68] The legate, Peter of Capua, had already laid an interdict on Normandy and France on account of the captivity of the bishop of Beauvais and the

Moreover, by the very terms of peace, John had broken up the system of alliances which his brother had arranged; no preparations were made for a future struggle, and when war broke out, there were none to help.

Throughout the summer of 1200 John devoted himself with extraordinary energy and success to the consolidation and government of his vast possessions. The records of his chancery bear out the statements of the chroniclers that he established his authority to the Pyrenees,[69] and by peaceful means or by force secured the submission of those who had joined Philip against him.[70] It is significant that in the spring or summer of this year the seneschals of Normandy, Poitou and Anjou were either changed or re-established. In Normandy the aged Fitz Ralf was succeeded by Guérin of Glapion; Geoffrey de la Celle combined the governorships of Gascony and Poitou; William des Roches was granted hereditary powers in Maine, Touraine and Anjou.[71]

The royal wanderings in Aquitaine ended in a dramatic change of policy, none the less important in the future history of the province because it was the result of passion. According to one of the clauses of the recent treaty with France, Ademar of Angoulême and his half brother, the viscount of Limoges, were included in the peace with restitution of their rights, and were to pay homage to John.[72] A year before they had joined Philip on somewhat the same conditions. Now

bishop elect of Cambrai by the kings of England and France respectively, and had brought about their release. The great interdict on France, on account of Ingeborg, was laid on January 15 (Howden, iv, 94, 112; Diceto, ii, 167; Rigord, i, 146, 147 and notes).

[69] *Chron. S. Albini*, MS. B. 1200. 'Octava autem die ante festum beati Johannis-Baptistae cepit Rex Johannes Andegavim et acquisivit totum regnum quod erat patris sui usque ad Crucem-Caroli Regis' (Halphen, *Recueil des annales angevines*, pp. 19, 20. The reference is to the cross at Chateau-Pignon near Roncevaux). For John at Angers, where he took 150 hostages, see Howden, iv, 125. Relations with Raymond of Toulouse were also established (*ibid.*, iv, 124–5; *Rot Chart.*, 97b).

[70] Gervase of Canterbury, ii, 92. For John's expedition in Aquitaine in July and August, see Howden, iv, 119; Annales Sancti Edmundi (Liebermann, *Ungedrückte Anglo-Normannische Geschichtsquellen*, p. 139; *Mem. of St. Edmund's Abbey*, ii, 8); *Guillaume le Maréchal*, iii, 161–2 and notes, and the *Rotuli Chartarum, passim*. For a connected narrative based on these authorities, see Richard, *Les Comtes de Poitou*, ii, 374–82.

[71] Guérin of Glapion succeeded William Fitz Ralph on the latter's death, in the first part of 1200 (cf. *Rot. Norm.*, p. 25; Stapleton, II, ccxix); Geoffrey de la Celle was appointed seneschal of Poitou on February 22, 1200 (*Rot. Chart.*, 59b). He had been sent *ad pacificandam Wasconiam*, on January 29 with his predecessor Ralph of Mauleon, who died in the interval (*ibid.*, 58a). William des Roches received his appointment on June 24 (*ibid.*, 72a).

[72] 'De comite Engolismi et vicecomite Lemovicensi sic erit, quod nos recipiemus eos in homines, ita quod eis jura eorum dimittemus' (*Cart. Norm.*,

between the house of Angoulême and the great house of Lusignan in Poitou, there was rivalry for the county of La Marche.[73] The short-lived alliance between Count Ademar and King Philip after Richard's death had as its object the judicial recognition in Philip's court of Ademar's right to La Marche. But, during the troubles of 1199–1200, in which the county of Angoulême seems to have suffered severely,[74] the county of La Marche had been allowed by Eleanor and John to belong to Hugh IX of Lusignan,[75] the brother of Ralph of Exoudun, the count of Eu. In this time, also, Hugh IX had become betrothed to Isabella, Count Ademar's daughter, and it might have been expected that the conclusion of peace would have restored complete harmony. The result was, however, very different. John met the count of Angoulême and the viscount of Limoges at Lusignan itself on the 5th of July, and the treaty of Le Goulet was executed by their reconciliation.[76] Not long afterwards John was attracted by Isabella of Angoulême.[77] He had recently been lawfully separated from another Isabella, the daughter of the late earl of Gloucester,[78] and was engaged in negotiations with the king of Portugal with a view to a marriage with one of his daughters.[79] The sight of Isabella of Angoulême changed all his plans. He married her at the end of August,

p. 281, and the texts noted above, p. 134, note 46). Cf. Philip's letter to Guy of Limoges (*Recueil*, ii, no. 634).

[73] Boissonade in *Annales du Midi*, 1895, vii, 280–3; the claim of the counts of Angoulême to La Marche came through Margaret of Turenne, the mother of Vulgrin III (d. 1181) and his brother Ademar (d. 1202).

[74] Innocent III's letters in *Historiens de France*, xix, 450.

[75] *Rot. Chart.*, 58b; cf. S. Painter, in *Speculum*, xxx (1955), 378.

[76] See the safe conducts, etc., in *Rot. Chart.*, 97a.

[77] Richard, *op. cit.*, ii, 376. Richard follows Delisle in identifying the proposed husband of Isabella with the count of La Marche, as is stated by many contemporaries. [In spite of Boissonade's argument, accepted in the first edition of this book, that Isabella must have been betrothed to the count's son, the later Hugh X, it has now been shown that she was betrothed to the father, not the son, and that his marriage to Matilda, daughter of Ademar's brother and predecessor, Vulgrin III (d. 1181) took place after her cousin Isabella had married King John. Hugh X was the son of Hugh IX (d. 1219) by an unknown first wife. Matilda was still alive in 1233. Ademar, count of Angoulême, died in June, 1202. See H. S. Snellgrove, *The Lusignans in England* (1950), p. 13, note 17, and the discussion by H. G. Richardson, S. Painter and Fred. A. Cazel, Jr., in *English Historical Review*, lxi (1946), 289–314; lxiii (1948), 83–9; lxv (1950), 363–71; lxvii (1952), 233–5; also, S. Painter on the house of Lusignan in *Speculum*, xxx (1955), 374–9.]

[78] On this see especially *English Historical Review*, lxi, 290–94 and lxiii, 89. The marriage was always 'voidable' and was dissolved apparently in Aquitaine (Howden, iv, 119; *Guillaume le Maréchal*, iii, 161).

[79] Envoys came from Portugal in January (*Rot. Chart.*, 58b). For John's embassy, probably sent in July, see Diceto, ii, 170; and *English Historical Review*, lxiii, 84–5.

1200.[80] Soon after the king brought his bride to England; and on October 8 she was crowned at Westminster.[81]

The excitement which was created by this hasty wedding is familiar to every student of English history. The general view, held at any rate in England, was that John had followed the crafty suggestion of the king of France. So suicidal a deed seemed to demand a stronger motive than passion.[82] In the light of John's character such an explanation is superfluous, nor were the consequences necessarily so serious as they have been represented. The politics of Aquitaine were essentially unstable; it is doubtful whether under the strongest ruler concord between its various elements would have been maintained for many months, and, although it is true that the defection of the house of Lusignan was the proximate cause of John's downfall on the continent, it should be noted on the other side that he secured a turbulent independent vassal as a strong ally. In right of his wife John was heir to Angoulême. The county, which lay in the heart of Aquitaine, across the roads between Poitou and Gascony, had been a source of weakness throughout the life of Richard. The count had claimed to hold directly of the king of France. If it were necessary to choose between the party of Lusignan and the party of Angoulême, later events proved that John acted wisely in preferring the latter. The loyalty of Angoulême during the end of his reign, and during the early years of Henry III, protected the more southern provinces, and enabled the king of England to establish himself in Bordeaux.[83] Only if it was possible to guide at once the destinies of Lusignan and Angoulême—both disciplined in rebellion—can we be confident that John's sudden frenzy was altogether a misfortune.

At all events, an excitable and powerful woman was added to the little group, whose conflicting wills were henceforth to influence the course of affairs. The aged Eleanor, who at this time seemed to be ending her days at Fontevrault,[84] but was still to have three or four active years of life, Constance of Brittany, Berengaria, Blanche of

[80] Annals of St. Edmund (Liebermann, p. 139); Richard, op. cit., ii, 378 seqq. Boisonnade (Quomodo comites, p. 12) regards the ceremony at Angoulême as the sponsalia, and the marriage as taking place at Chinon, where John endowed his wife (Rot. Chart., 74b), but the evidence is not explicit.

[81] Howden, iv, 139. A legendary account of the marriage between John and Isabella is found in sixteenth century writers; cf. Richard, ii, 379; Lecointre Dupont in Soc. de Antiq. de l'Ouest, 1845, xii, 125–7.

[82] Howden, iv, 119. Lecointre Dupont (p. 123) suggests that Isabella may have been present at the marriage of Blanche of Castile, when Philip and John were together. There is no evidence for this.

[83] Above, p. 32. Boissonade passim.

[84] Howden, iv, 114 (April, 1200). She was still very ill in February, 1201, when the viscount of Thouars came to see her (Rot. Chart., 102b; Richard, ii, 386, note).

Castile, and the slighted Ingeborg move in the forefront of events. They had fit contemporaries in less famous women, such as the wife of William of Briouze and Nicolaa of La Haye. Of the two young queens who were to grow old together in trouble, Blanche of Castile had need of and revealed a greater power of endurance, and a surer statesmanship; but in the varied fortunes of Isabella of Angoulême lies the story of an experience more dramatic than the energy or sufferings of all her contemporaries.

The consequences of John's marriage did not bring the king back from England, where, unlike his predecessor, he spent a great part of his time, until the spring. A vendetta, in which the count of Eu took the lead, was commenced by the house of Lusignan, and, according to the information received by John, was to begin after Easter in 1201.[85] Preparations to meet the danger were made in Normandy and Poitou. In the south John was able to rely upon his father-in-law, the count of Angoulême, who was anxious to add La Marche to his territory, and upon his mother, who was at Fontevrault. Eleanor was responsible for an important success in February and March, 1201, when she reconciled the viscount of Thouars to her son. The viscount's brother, Guy of Thouars, was already recognised as count of Brittany, in spite of Constance's former marriage with the earl of Chester; indeed, it appears that negotiations had taken place between him and Philip Augustus in the previous year.[86] But for the prompt action of Eleanor, therefore, the house of Thouars might have become a most dangerous ally of the house of Lusignan.[87] Moreover, in March, John, through his officials, took over the direct administration of La Marche.[88]

[85] Hugh of Bailleul and Thomas of St. Valèry, on March 6, 1201, were given a free hand to harm Ralph, count of Eu, 'in werra incipienti ad clausum Pasche anno secundo regni nostri'. (*Rot. Chart.*, 102a.) [For the brothers of Lusignan, Hugh and Ralph, and the relations between the family and La Marche and Angoulême, see P. Boissonade's study, published in the Bulletins et Memoirs of the *Soc. archaeologique et historique de la Charente* (1934-5). This study, entitled 'L'Ascension, le déclin, et la chute d'un grand état féodal', etc., covers the period, 1137-1314. See also S. Painter on the lords of Lusignan in *Speculum*, xxx (1955), 374 *seq.*, and xxxii (1957), 27 *seq.*, especially, for Ralph of Eu, pp. 42-4.]

[86] According to an act dated Paris, November, 1200, Peter, son of Robert, count of Dreux, bound himself to hold to an agreement between Philip and Guy of Thouars, count of Brittany, 'et alii barones et homines *ipsius regis* de Britannia' (Teulet, *Layettes*, i, 223, no. 601). On August 29, 1202, Guy is styled *quondam comitem Britannie* (*Rot. Pat.*, 17b).

[87] See the letters in *Rot. Chart.*, 102b-103a. Cf. above, p. 30.

[88] March 8, 1201. *Rot. Chart.*, 102a. Boissonade, who thinks that La Marche had been promised on John's marriage to Ademar of Angoulême, brings together the records of John's relations with his *pater carissimus*. (*Quomodo comites*, etc., p. 12).

In Normandy, it was important to anticipate rebellion and to confiscate the possessions of the count of Eu, which lay along the
north-east border. In addition to Eu, they included the castle of
Drincourt, which had been granted to the count by King Richard.
As early as March 6 John took measures to secure the control of
Drincourt and to crush the power of the count.[89] The seneschal of
Normandy was instructed, apparently later, to lay siege to the place,
when it was found that more warlike measures were necessary.[90] In
the meantime the king made preparations in England for another
expedition across the Channel. These preparations, owing in part to
the opposition of the earls, mark another step forward in the direction
of a paid mercenary army.[91]

John landed in Normandy at the end of May, to find that the immediate danger was over. The facts are not very clear, but it seems that
the king of France had after some hesitation used his influence to
maintain peace. According to Roger of Howden, he broke up the sieges
by which the rebellious barons south of the Loire were beginning to
harass the government of Poitou,[92] and he met John alone near
Andeli. There were several reasons why Philip should prefer a quiet
settlement. For one thing, the Rhenish allies of Richard were making
preparations for their departure to the East; John's letters show that
he was trying to maintain good relations with Baldwin of Flanders
and his officials,[93] and Philip would realise that he would be more at
liberty to pursue an anti-Norman policy after the crusaders were well
on their way. Again, the energy of John's government in Aquitaine
must have impressed Philip; until French influence could create more
disunion among the Poitevin barons, or eat its way once more into
Touraine, it was useless to renew the war. Finally, Philip had learned
that John was a more pliable rival than Richard. John had already
surrendered the Evrecin, where Philip was steadily making his
government felt;[94] a little pressure might end in further concessions.
So Philip kept the peace, met John and invited him to Paris.[95]

John left Normandy in the last days of June; he had made peace
with the count of Eu,[96] and had nothing to fear. In Paris he was

---

[89] *Rot. Chart.*, 102a.   [90] Howden, iv, 161.

[91] Howden, iv, 161, 163. Below, pp. 213–15.

[92] Howden, iv, 161.

[93] John orders payment of stated pensions, arrears, etc., to Baldwin, his
uncle, his chancellor, to the counts of Ponthieu, Nevers, Namur, Hainault.
See *Rot. de Liberate*, pp. 15–21 *passim*, June to September, 1201.

[94] See the *Recueil* for 1200–2, *e.g.*, nos. 637, 646, 653, 655, 674. Some of
these are in favour of Norman abbeys still in John's dominion.

[95] John was at Paris on July 1 (*Rot. de Lib.*, 18). Rigord and Howden are
confused in their chronology.

[96] This follows from a letter to Geoffrey fitz Peter of June 15, from Jumièges:
'Sciatis quod dederamus Waloni de Fruges c. solidos terre in terra comitis

royally entertained, although, according to one malicious story, his companions preferred bad wine to the good.[97] The treaty was secured by a special agreement with regard to the sureties on both sides;[98] and John went on to Chinon. There he settled a handsome dower on Richard's widow, Berengaria[99]—a necessary preliminary to the negotiations with Sancho of Navarre, which were commenced in the autumn, and ended in a close alliance at Angoulême on February 4, 1202.[100]

About the same time, strengthened by the friendship of the family of Thouars, the king secured the peaceful execution of the last acts made by Constance of Brittany.[101] Constance had died in the previous August, to all appearance reconciled. With her death a last page of painful memories could be turned, and John might well think that he had come through his dangers.

III

Yet even in the autumn of 1201 the insecurity of John was manifest. The Lusignans broke away from him again in October, and appealed to Philip of France. Philip and his court had set John up, and they were now ready to pull him down. In the war which followed their judgment John was left almost alone. The terms of the treaty with Sancho of Navarre show that hostility might be expected from the kings of Castile and Aragon. The viscount of Limoges and the count of Toulouse, the latter of whom held important fiefs of Aquitaine by definite service, deserted.

The appeal made by the Poitevin enemies of King John to the court of Philip must be connected with the somewhat curious method by which John tried to enforce justice. He had acted with a high hand in taking control of their lands,[102] and in October, 1201, he attempted

---

Augi et quia *reddidimus eidem comiti terras et feoda sua*, vobis mandamus quod predicto Waloni c. solidos terre alibi assignetis.' (*Rot. de Lib.*, 16.)

[97] French chronicle printed by Delisle in *Historiens de France*, xxiv, part ii, p. 760. It was upon this occasion that John and Philip granted one-fortieth part of their revenues for one year for the relief of the Holy Land. (See Delaborde, in *Bibliothèque de l'Ecole des Chartes*, lxiv, 306–13; Delisle, *Actes*, no. 619, p. 144, where the grant is wrongly attributed to May 1200; cf. Delaborde, *Recueil*, ii, no. 680; Howden, iv, 187.)

[98] Howden, iv, 175, gives a confirmation of this year which probably belongs to this time. For the sureties, see *Cart. Norm.*, p. 281, and the texts noted above, p. 134, note 46. [99] Howden, iv, 164, 172.

[100] For authorities, see Boissonade, *op. cit.*, p. 13. *Rot. Pat.*, 3, 5b.

[101] *Rot. Pat.*, 5.

[102] It is clear that the Lusignans complained, not of John's marriage, but of his treatment of them after their rebellion. Cf. Coggeshall, p. 135. The Patent Rolls show how, in Anjou, Normandy, and Aquitaine John adminis-

L

to put their cause to the test of a trial by battle. According to Roger of Howden he had brought with him picked champions for this purpose.[103] The rebels refused to come, saying that they would acknowledge no judge but their peers;[104] the first sound of that famous cry which was to be dinned into John's ears by his English vassals.

It is easy to study in the rolls the way in which—in a time of disturbance—John, as feudal lord, dealt with his vassals and officials. As we have already seen, he relied upon comparatively few servants, frequently changed his castellans and officers, and bound his barons by elaborate guarantees. In the autumn of 1201 he made Robert of Turnham the seneschal of Poitou,[105] and in Normandy displaced Guérin of Glapion, after a very short period of service, by Ralph Tesson.[106] During the spring of 1202, when so many were suspect, Guérin seems to have been trusted in delicate negotiations in Normandy and Maine; but he deserted John in 1203.[107] An arrangement which John made with the greatest baron in Maine, Juhel of Mayenne, illustrates the precautions which he found it desirable to take. Juhel had been granted the castles of Ambrières and Coumont by Arthur during the latter's brief tenure of Maine in 1199.[108] On October 14, 1201, at Chinon John received Juhel's fealty and arranged that, while the fortresses should be retained, a son of each of their castellans should be given as hostage by the lord of Mayenne. If a hostage should die, his father was to be replaced by another castellan, who was in his turn to give up a son as hostage. Moreover, Juhel's knights and sureties gave charters, and the men of his towns swore that, if Juhel failed to keep the terms of the agreement or to stand by the judgment of the king's court, they would fight against him and do him all the harm in their power.[109] The convention is characteristic of the way

tered their lands. The passage in Howden apparently refers to this: 'Pictavi enim praevaluerunt adversus *custodes terrarum suarum*, et castella sua obsederunt' (iv, 160).

[103] Howden, iv, 176. John 'volens appellare barones Pictaviae de sua et fratris sui proditione, multos conduxit et secum duxit viros arte bellandi in duello doctos, etc.' Cf. a reference to the king's *campiones*, brought to Isle of Andeli in 1198 (*Rot. Scacc.*, ii, 481, 'contra regem Francie'). John collected his forces at Argentan, as a letter from Verneuil of September 27 proves (*Rot. Pat.*, 1). He was at Mirebeau on October 9. [104] Howden, iv, 176.

[105] Robert appears as seneschal of Poitou and Gascony, September 23 (*Rot. Pat.*, 1).

[106] An exchequer account remains dated 'Recepte Garini de Glapion . . . a die Martis post clausam Pentecostim anno secundo regni Regis Johannis, usque ad diem Martis in festo Sancti Leonardi anno tercio regni ejusdem' (*Rot. Scacc.*, ii, 501). These dates, June 6, 1200–November 6, 1201, apparently mark the limits of the seneschalship. Ralph Tesson was seneschal before November 23, 1201. See Stapleton, II, ccxviii–ccxxi.

[107] See note B at the end of this chapter. [108] Above, p. 132.

[109] *Rot. Pat.*, 3 Joh. m. 8, printed in Rymer, O, i, 125–6.

in which, in small affairs and in great, John went behind the immediate relations between himself and his tenants-in-chief. Philip was about to treat him in the same way.

On a Sunday in October, very probably the same Sunday as that on which Juhel of Mayenne was reconciled with John, Ralph of Exoudun, the count of Eu, denounced his feudal obligations.[110] Ralph was lord of Eu in right of his wife, and the king immediately wrote to the burgesses reminding them of their duty to himself, and ordering them to obey whomever he should send to harm their lord.[111] In the following spring, believing that the count's wife had died, he definitely deprived him of the county and established John of Eu in his place.[112] But these measures were unavailing, for Eu and Drincourt fell at the beginning of hostilities, and even before war broke out, the citizens had made arrangements for the removal of their chattels and themselves to ducal territory.[113]

It is clear from an authoritative account inserted in the chronicle of Coggeshall, and from later papal letters that, while John was securing himself against treachery and preparing for war, the king of France was urging the cause of the brothers of Lusignan. He relied upon the facts that John was his man and that justice was denied the rebels, who were relentlessly afflicted by John's displeasure.[114] A colloquy was arranged, and the agents of the kings met at the usual place between Boutavant and Le Goulet upon March 25.[115] Philip

[110] John, in an undated letter to the burgesses of Eu, says 'vobis mandamus quod Radulphus Exoldinus comes Augi nos defidavit Dominica proxima preterita non ob culpam nostram et (sic sed?) ob culpam suam et superbiam' (*Rot. Pat.*, 2a).

[111] *Rot. Pat.*, 2a.

[112] Ralph of Exoudun had his barony in Poitou, and ruled Exoudun, Chizé, and other places. (See Delisle, *Bibl. de l'Ecole des Chartes*, 1856, xvii, 546; who shows that Ralph of Issoudun was a different person altogether.) John of Eu was throughout supported by John as possessor of the count's Norman fiefs. *Rot. Pat.*, 8b (April 1, 1202); *Rot. Norm.*, 59 (August 7).

[113] See the facts collected by Delisle (*op. cit.*, 547–8), and Stapleton, II, ccxxi–ccxxii.

[114] *Chronica Anglicanum*, especially pp. 136–6; for Innocent's letters see Cheney and Semple, *Selected letters*, pp. 56–68. The pope speaks as though Philip had delayed for a year before taking action. If this was the case, the Poitevins must have appealed in the spring of 1201. This is not likely; but it does seem probable from the words of Arthur's act of homage to Philip (below, p. 326) that hostilities had been begun by John which brought matters to a crisis. I am unable to accept Miss Norgate's view that there was no judgment. (*Trans. Royal Hist. Soc.*, new series, 1900, xiv, 53; cf. the criticism in *Revue Hist.* (1901), lxxvi, 213; and Holtzmann in *Hist. Zeitschrift* (1905), xcv, 39; and see the important review of the whole matter by Ch. Petit-Dutaillis in his study *Le déshéritement de Jean sans terre* (1925), pp. 4–18.)

[115] John's letters support the statement of the annals of St. Edmund that

demanded the surrender of Andeli, Arques and even Falaise,[116] and ordered John to appear at Paris a fortnight after Easter to reply to the charges of injustice which would be brought against him.[117] A long interchange of arguments commenced, in which it is significant to note, the archbishop of Canterbury, who had been called across the Channel, took a leading part on John's behalf.[118] The main argument upon which John relied was that, as duke of Normandy, he was not obliged to treat with his suzerain anywhere else than on the borders. The obvious reply was made that he was summoned as lord of Aquitaine and Anjou.[119] The crisis came with the failure of a conference arranged for the week after Easter, that is, after the 21st of April. Philip gladly availed himself of the judgment of his court that, as a contumacious vassal, the king of England should be deprived of all the lands hitherto held of the French crown.[120] With no further delay, he dashed forward, took Boutavant and levelled it to the ground.[121] This was the first blow.

King John immediately prepared for the defence and reinforcement of Normandy. The archbishop of Canterbury, whom Philip had dismissed from his territory when negotiations were broken off,[122] was sent to England to lay before John's subjects the story of Philip's high-handed and insolent behaviour.

'We send,' the king wrote to his officials in England on May 11, 'our venerable fathers in Christ, the lord archbishop of Canterbury and the bishop of Ely who were our spokesmen in the conversations between us and the king of France. They will relate to you with what

---

the kings acted through agents (Liebermann, p. 140). The date is in Diceto, ii, 174.

[116] So states Gervase of Canterbury, ii, 93; as the archbishop of Canterbury had come to Normandy to act with the king, the chronicler's testimony may well be true. The continuator of Robert of Torigni says that war was resumed because John would not surrender Vaudreuil and Roche Andeli (*Historiens de France*, xviii, 341). The French chronicles of Béthune both state that at Paris John had granted lands to Blanche of Castile (*Histor. de France*, xxiv, ii, 760; *Hist. des ducs de Normandie, etc.*, p. 91) and this may be referred to in these later negotiations.

[117] Annales of St. Edmund, Liebermann, p. 140.

[118] Gervase of Canterbury, ii, 93; Rad. Dic., ii, 173; below, note 123. Geoffrey Fitz Peter, the justiciar, also came to Normandy, so seriously was the situation regarded. He attests a royal letter May 2 (*Rot. Pat.*, 10). Cf. a reference to his visit in a later letter, p. 12.   [119] Coggeshall, p. 136.

[120] *Ibid.* The account in Roger of Wendover is not trustworthy (i, 313). M. Bémont, in his well-known article in *Rev. Hist.* (1886) has shown that Normandy was confiscated as well as Poitou and the other lands across the sea.

[121] According to William the Breton (Delaborde, i, 207) Boutavant and Tillières had been promised by John as sureties for his appearance.

[122] Gervase, ii, 93-4.

humility and moderation we bore ourselves before him, and what insolence (*superbia*) they always found in him, and how he openly acted against the terms of the peace which had been made and confirmed between us.'[123]

And in a later letter of July 7, in which he asked for a loan from the Cistercian abbots in England, he said:

'You are sufficiently aware of what is common knowledge: how the king of France contrary to the peace which was made between us, and which was confirmed by oaths and charters, unjustly attacks us and strives by all the means in his power to deprive us of our inheritance (*ad exheredationem nostram omnibus modis aspirat*).'[124]

Taking his stand upon the breach of the treaty of 1200,[125] John resumed relations with Otto, sent agents to the Papal court,[126] and under penalty of confiscation called on the men of the Low Countries who held Norman fiefs to come to his aid.[127] At the same time, he raised loans and tallages, and sent round his recruiting officers.[128] Rouen was strengthened against another possible siege, several towns were urged to form communes for defensive purposes, and the officials of the Channel Isles were set to watch the seas.[129]

Except for an excursion in June into Maine, John stayed in the valley of the Seine and made his headquarters at Pont de l'Arche, and the neighbouring abbey of Bonport. From this point he could watch the valleys of the Eure and the Andelle. The king of France without difficulty overran the north-eastern frontier, from Eu to the forest of Lions, and after securing Eu, Aumâle, Drincourt, Mortemer, Lions and other places,[130] turned to besiege Gournai. Both sides

[123] *Rot. Pat.*, 10b (May 11, 1202).
[124] *Rot. Pat.*, 14 (July 7). This letter affords additional proof of the judgment in Philip's court, which has not, I think, been noticed.
[125] The count of Boulogne, who joined Philip at that time, significantly alleged as his reason that John had made peace in 1200 (Coggeshall, 136). A treaty of marriage between Renaud's daughter and Philip Hurepel, son of the French king, had been arranged in August, 1201 (*Layettes*, no. 613; cf. *Philippid*, vi, 74). After the outbreak of war the count was entrusted with Aumâle (Coggeshall, 136).
[126] *Rot. Pat.*, 11b (to citizens of Köln). For relations with the pope, see below, p. 163.
[127] Letters of May 25 (*Rot. Pat.*, 11b). The lands of the count of Boulogne in Lillebonne and elsewhere had been seized earlier (*ibid.*, 9b).
[128] *e.g.*, William de Cresec (*Rot. Pat.*, 10) and Simon de Haveret (*ibid.*, 12).
[129] *Rot. Pat.*, 10b, May 11: the citizens of Rouen to have as much wood as they like; 13b–14: communes for Fécamp, Harfleur, Montivilliers, with orders to prepare *ad terram nostram defendendam*; 15: to men of Jersey, etc.
[130] Rigord, i, 152; Wendover, i, 313; Gervase of Canterbury, ii, 94. At Lions-la-Forêt, Philip confirmed the property and privileges of the abbey of Mortemer-en-Lions (*Recueil*, ii, no. 719). For the fiscal value of these districts, see above, p. 68 ff.

attached great importance to this place.[131] After the fall of the castles in the forest of Lions, which separated Gournai from the rest of Normandy, John could hardly expect to retain it. On the other hand, its site rendered it capable of defence, and Hugh of Gournai was in favour with the king. The garrison had been placed under the charge of Brandin, a trusted soldier of the last two kings; he and his companions were urged by John to maintain his honour and theirs at Gournai: he appealed to their sense of duty and offered large rewards.[132] But Gournai fell early in July; the garrison was outwitted by that ruthless ingenuity which made Philip a dangerous opponent everywhere but in the open field. Seeing that the fortress was unapproachable by reason of the skilful use to which the engineers had put the waters of the Epte—for Gournai lay in a marsh surrounded by deep moats—Philip turned its defences against it by breaking the dam of a large weir which lay higher up the river. In the flood everything was carried away and the walls were broken. From this time Gournai became part of the royal demesne.[133] Its lord, Hugh of Gournai, on July 28, received a grant of £500 from John,[134] and Brandin was sent off to his native Poitou to act as seneschal of the county of La Marche, now definitely part of the Poitevin administration.[135]

From Gournai King Philip moved on to Arques, a still more formidable fortress. Arques was the seat of government in Caux, and protected Dieppe. Philip reached the place before July 21, for on that day John ordered the barons of the Cinque Ports to cut off the French ships which were bringing provisions to the army.[136] He stated that he would on his side cut off supplies by land. John was thus occupied with the defence of the marches when the news came that Arthur of Brittany had again stirred up rebellion in Touraine, and was besieging his grandmother, Eleanor, in the fortress of Mirebeau, on the way from Angers to Poitiers.

Both kings had from the first realised the value of Arthur. At the end of March John had summoned him to appear at Argentan during the coming Easter;[137] but Philip had kept the boy by his side. In

---

[131] Above, p. 109.

[132] Hugh of Gournai was with John in March (*Pat.*, 7). Brandin and his son, Henry Bec, Simon de Houes and others, were the leaders of the garrison (*Rot. Pat.*, 13b). Henry Bec was with John in Ireland, in 1210 (*Rot. de Lib.*, 198). Later, in July, Simon de Houes was granted a mill (*Rot. Norm.*, 56).

[133] The siege was over before July 13, for on that day Brandin was made seneschal of La Marche (*Rot. Pat.*, 14b). For the siege of Gournai, see Rigord, i, 152; William the Breton, i, 210, and *Phil.*, vi, 210–61 (ii, 160); Wendover, i, 313; Robert of Auxerre in *Histor. de France*, xviii, 265.

[134] *Rot. Norm.*, 58. For Hugh, see below, p. 161.

[135] See note 133. Brandin also received the castle of Torigni in Normandy (*Rot. Pat.*, 14b).   [136] *Rot. Pat.*, 15.   [137] *Ibid.*, 7b.

April Philip promised to give him his daughter Mary to wife;[138] in July, after the capture of Gournai, he knighted him and received his homage for Brittany, Poitou, Anjou, Maine and Touraine.[139] It is significant that Arthur styled himself duke of Brittany and Aquitaine, count of Anjou and Maine. With two hundred knights and a large sum of money the young duke was sent off to win his possessions.[140] At Tours he was joined by the Lusignans, Andrew of Chauvigni, Raymond of Thouars, Savari of Mauléon and many other great men of Poitou. His sister Eleanor was also with him. The old queen was still living, in bad health, at Fontevrault: apparently she was on her way to Poitiers, when she was caught by Arthur's forces, a thousand or so in number, at Mirebeau.[141] This was in the last days of July, just when John, perhaps suspicious of Arthur's movements, was moving from place to place on the southern frontier of Normandy, and then, on receiving a definite warning from William des Roches had come to Le Mans. It was there, on July 30, that he heard of the siege of Mirebeau; and, rushing to the rescue with amazing speed, he and the seneschal reached the spot on the night of the 31st. Eleanor had been driven from every part of the castle but the keep, and her persecutors had secured themselves by blocking up all the gates save one.[142] They were surprised early in the morning, and after a fierce fight all were captured. One of John's companions, William of Briouze, secured Arthur and handed him over to the king.[143] The anonymous poet of Béthune describes the scene with much vigour. We can see William des Roches attacking the gate at dawn, the fierce assault of John and his mercenaries on the unprepared knights in the narrow street. Geoffrey of Lusignan, he tells us, was at breakfast when the attack came; but refused to move from his lodgings until he had finished a dish of pigeons. The prisoners were manacled and sent off in carts, some to England, some to the chief places in Normandy. Elaborate precautions were taken to prevent their escape.[144]

[138] *Actes*, no. 726. Cf. Coggeshall, p. 137.

[139] *Recueil*, ii, no. 723; and *Layettes*, no. 647; see below, p. 326.

[140] Rigord, i, 152.   [141] See Richard, *Comtes de Poitou*, ii, 405.

[142] Coggeshall, 137; Wendover, i, 314.

[143] The chief authority is John's own letter in Coggeshall, 137–8. All the chroniclers refer to the siege of Mirebeau and Arthur's disaster. The best account is in the *Histoire des ducs de Normandie et rois d'Angleterre* (ed. Michel), pp. 94–6.

[144] For the treatment of the prisoners, over 200 knights and barons, see Hardy's introduction to the Patent Rolls p. x, and the Pipe Roll for 4 John (Pipe Roll Soc., 1937), pp. xv, xvi; cf. Coggeshall, pp. 137–8; Wendover, i, 315; *Guillaume le Maréchal*, iii, 169 (for the prisoners at Chinon). Richard, *Comtes de Poitou*, ii, 407 *seqq. passim*, gives from the rolls all the information about the Poitevin prisoners. For Geoffrey de Lusignan, uncle of Hugh IX and Ralph of Eu, and his great distinction in feudal history, see S. Painter in *Speculum*, xxx (1955), 375–7, and the genealogical table, *ibid.*, p. 376.

The news of this disaster forced Philip to retire from Arques; he had surrounded the castle with his engines and was trying to wear down the resistance of the castellan, William of Mortemer.[145] He had with him Ralph, count of Eu, the brother of Hugh IX of Lusignan, and the biographer of the Marshal relates how the count received the news of the capture of Hugh and Geoffrey. The Marshal was at Anglesqueville,[146] a place between Arques and Rouen, where, with the earl of Salisbury and the new earl Warenne,[147] he was evidently watching King Philip's movements. A monk, travelling night and day, brought the news from Mirebeau to the earls:

'The monk,' says the Marshal's biographer, gave his message courteously, and reported the capture of Arthur, Geoffrey of Lusignan, his nephew, Hugh of Lusignan, the count of La Marche, Savari of Mauléon and the other great men who had joined Arthur. The Marshal rejoiced greatly, and said to the monk, 'Take this news to the count of Eu, in the French army at Arques; it will please him.'

'Sire,' replied the monk, 'I beg you to excuse me. If I go there he will be so enraged that he may kill me. Send some one else.'

'Make no excuses; you shall go, master monk. It is not the custom of this country to kill messengers. Off with you; you will find him in the army.'

The monk made haste to Arques and gave the news from Poitou to the count of Eu. The count had expected very different tidings. He changed colour and kept silence. He went to bed very perplexed, for he did not wish to tell anyone what he had heard.[148]

While the count of Eu was plunged in these painful reflections, letters reached the king of France containing the bad news, and the siege was at once raised. The French army retired up the valley in good order. The Marshal and his companions, who were informed by spies of the retreat, came up with the rear of the host, but withdrew before a detachment which the king sent up a side valley with the object of cutting them off.[149] Philip continued his march un-

[145] *Guillaume le Maréchal*, iii, 164. There is no other evidence that William of Mortemer was castellan during the siege. The castle and bailiwick were entrusted to him and to William Martel on December 28 (*Rot. Pat.*, 22). William of Mortemer was to be bailiff of Caux, and Martel to have the prepositura (cf. Stapleton, II, cclx). At this time the Marshal's bailiffs were in charge of Arques.

[146] Meyer suggests Anglesqueville-sur-Saanes, near the Marshal's property at Longueville.

[147] William, earl Warenne, succeeded his father before May 12 of this year (*Rot. Pat.*, 10b). He was a cousin of Alice, the countess of Eu, according to Stapleton (II, ccxxxii). The king had ordered the Marshal to put him in possession of the count of Boulogne's lands at Lillebonne (*Rot. Norm.*, 47; June 4).

[148] *Guillaume le Maréchal*, iii, 165–6.   [149] *Ibid.*, iii, 166, 167.

molested, and, infuriated by the failure of his plans, ravaged the Norman borders.[150] As in the reign of Richard, disaster was the signal for a conflict of unsparing ferocity.

For the next few years the natural theatre of war was Anjou and Touraine. Richard had always been able to control this region, which, as we have seen more than once, was the key to the empire. John's successful negotiations in 1200 were made possible by his triumph here and in Poitou. It might have been expected that his great victory at Mirebeau would have secured his rule throughout Normandy and Aquitaine for the next few years. Arthur was a prisoner; the capture of the Lusignans and their allies had wiped out a source of disaffection in Poitou; William des Roches and the viscount of Thouars, the one the most influential baron in Anjou, the other in north-western Poitou, were on John's side. Yet now, as in 1199, the submission of Arthur was the beginning of new difficulties. William des Roches was almost at once set on one side. The seneschal had planned and carried out the attack upon Arthur and the Poitevins at Mirebeau. At the time of his defection from Arthur in 1199 he had extorted a promise from the king that his counsel in Angevin affairs should be supreme.[151] Moreover, the attack upon Arthur had been made on the understanding that the fate of the young duke should be decided in accordance with William's advice.[152] First at Chinon, then at Le Mans, the king disregarded the seneschal's claims and paid no heed to his remonstrances against the cruelty with which the prisoners were treated. In consequence of this return for his services the seneschal, with the viscount of Thouars, deserted.[153] Aimeri of Thouars, great man though he was, played an unimportant part in the later struggle; his numerous changes of side show him to have been the weathercock of fortune.[154] The actions of William des Roches, on the other hand, were the result of intelligent ambition. He had secured the counties of the Loire for

[150] The biographer of the Marshal remarked on the good order maintained by the French troops. Wendover (i, 315) and Gervase of Canterbury (ii, 94) refer to the burning of churches and villages.

[151] See the account of the dramatic interview between the king and the seneschal, in *Guillaume le Maréchal*, iii, 167-70.

[152] This is stated explicitly to a continuator of the annals of St. Aubin (MS. G). William said 'quod rex Johannes ei promiserat se de Arturo liberando suam facere voluntatem et consilium, et quia rex noluit, guerram movit contra eum' (Halphen, *Recueil des annales angevines et vendômoises*, p. 29). This continuator, of the years 1199-1206 (see Halphen, p. x), is an important authority for Angevin history during John's reign.

[153] Cf. the *Chronicon Turonense magnum* (Salmon, *Chroniques de Touraine*, i, 147).

[154] He was doubtless influenced by the Johannine policy of his brother Guy. For his tergiversations, see *Actes de Philippe-Auguste*, no. 742; *Rot. Pat.*, 21; and Imbert, in *Mém. de la Soc. des Antiquaires de l'Ouest*, xxix (1864), 372-5.

John, and, if he had been trusted, might well have averted the down-fall of the Angevin empire for several years; the strategic importance of the district would have made it, if well administered, the most important guarantee against the loss of Normandy. But the defection of the seneschal altered the whole situation. In spite of his efforts to build up an independent administration, John was gradually deserted by his vassals. As early as January, 1203, the roads between Le Mans and Chinon were almost impassable by his agents.[155] The officials of Aquitaine were left to raise money as best they could.[156] Before the summer was over, Angers and Tours were completely in French hands, nor is it a coincidence that at the same time, while the whole valley of the lower Loire was given over to ruin and anarchy,[157] Philip Augustus was able to lay hands on Normandy with a new, almost a serene confidence. It is important, therefore, to fix our attention in the first place upon the southern conflict.

For some months after the capture of Arthur and Philip's retreat from Arques, John's vigorous rally met with some success.[158] Tours was occupied by mercenaries, and its temporary surrender to Philip only provoked a new attack. In the course of the siege which followed Philip's departure for France the Châteauneuf was destroyed, and the French garrison in the city was forced to surrender.[159] Le Mans and Angers, as well as the chief castles of Touraine and northern Poitou had been secured without any difficulty,[160] by the aid of Guy of Thouars, William de l'Etang, the seneschal of Poitou and others. The great administration of William des Roches was divided: Girard d'Athée becoming seneschal of Touraine, and Brice the Chamberlain the seneschal of Anjou.[161] Yet John's position was by no means secure. The leader of an important band of mercenaries, Martin Algais, was defeated and captured, and in spite of his release the band

[155] *Guillaume le Maréchal*, iii, 172. As I point out below, M. Meyer erroneously refers this passage to October, 1202.

[156] *Rot. Pat.*, 25b, 31; Richard, *Comtes de Poitou*, ii, 421. A Gascon loan was, however, raised in Normandy this year. (Cf. *Rot. Scacc.*, ii, 545; *Rot. Norm.*, 92).

[157] Annals of St. Aubin (Halphen, p. 21), 'Deinde de die in diem multiplicata est miseria in regionibus Cenomannie, Pictavie, et Andegavie et Britannie, ita ut, villis et castris et oppidis depredatis et combustis, nulli etati aut conditione parceretur'.

[158] The modern authorities are, beside Richard and Lecointre-Dupont, the article by Gaston Dubois on *Guillaume des Roches* in the *Bibliothèque de l'Ecole des Chartes*, xxx, xxxii, and especially xxxiv, 502 *seqq.*; and Beau-temps-Beaupré's note in his *Coutumes de l'Anjou*, etc., part ii, vol. iii, p. 241.

[159] *Chroniques de Touraine*, i, 147–9.

[160] See the letters in *Rot. Pat.*, 17.

[161] *Rot. Pat.*, 17a, b. In consequence of Brice's promotion, the castle of Tillières in Normandy was entrusted to Roger de Montbegun (*ibid.*, 18).

seems to have been put *hors de combat*.[162] Much more serious were the occupation of Angers by William des Roches on October 30,[163] and a simultaneous movement upon Tours by the lord of Amboise, which resulted in the confinement of the garrison to the castle.[164]

These disasters must have strengthened John's desire to come to an understanding with the house of Lusignan. From the outset a distinction had been made between the company of Hugh le Brun and the rest of the prisoners, and after long negotiations, in which the count of Eu seems to have taken part,[165] Hugh was allowed to buy his freedom early in 1203. Unfortunately the king did not buy his loyalty; and more than one contemporary writer speaks in severe terms of his misplaced leniency.[166] That John hoped to establish himself on the basis of an alliance with the Poitevins seems very likely when we consider that the old rival of the Lusignans, the viscount of Limoges, was kept in strict captivity at Chinon,[167] and that John so readily dispensed with the inconvenient services of William des Roches. Moreover, since the king had now succeeded peacefully to the inheritance of Angoulême, and could rely upon a loyal administration in the rest of Aquitaine, he had every inducement to renew good relations with the house of Lusignan, and less reason to fear it.[168] It is, finally, of significance that he was beginning to look still farther afield. In a begging letter written on September 8 to the clergy of the province of Canterbury, he refers joyfully to the renewal of an alliance between himself and the Emperor Otto, and anticipates much good to his fortunes from the friendship of pope and emperor.[169] Throughout the year his envoys had been busy at the Roman Court.[170] Also during the following months, negotiations began for the restoration of an alliance with Castile.[171]

[162] See Richard's ingenious deductions from the entries in the Patent Rolls, *Comtes de Poitou*, ii, 414-15. Martin Algais was made seneschal of Gascony and Périgord on December 4th, these provinces being cut off from the administration of Robert of Turnham (*Rot. Pat.*, 21). Cf. above, p. 30.

[163] Annals of Saint-Aubin (Halphen, 20, 21). Cf. Coggeshall, p. 139.

[164] *Chron. de Touraine*, i, 140. These events kept John in Saumur or Chinon from the last part of October until the beginning of December.

[165] The count apparently came from France to negotiate safe conduct; in *Rot. Pat.*, 20. Richard (ii, 417) erroneously states that he was a prisoner. See above, p. 152.   [166] e.g., *Guillaume le Maréchal*, iii, 170; Coggeshall, p. 138.

[167] For his capture, see letters in *Rot. Pat.*, 18; Richard, ii, 412.

[168] For the administration of Angoulême, see above, p. 33. It is not probable that La Marche was restored to Hugh le Brun. Richard summarises the letters which describe the negotiations with the Lusignans. I refer to them as prisoners in another connection, see below, p. 244.   [169] *Rot. Pat.*, 18.

[170] *Rot. Pat.*, 5a, 10b, 26; letters of credit of January 21 and May 16, 1202, February, 1203.

[171] John had received favourable news of these negotiations before April 5, 1203 (*ibid.*, 28).

In the absence of any consecutive evidence, it is not possible to follow the changes in John's mind; but even if he had been a more resolute man than he was, the time was not opportune for far-reaching schemes. Outside Anjou and Touraine, the defences of Normandy called for attention—they were especially weak in the Evrecin[172]— and the Bretons, having failed to come to an arrangement for the release of Arthur,[173] were preparing for war.[174] The letters enrolled upon the Patent Rolls reveal the fact that, in spite of his hopes of support from pope and emperor, John tried at the end of December, while holding his court at Caen, and doubtless on the advice of his counsellors, to arrange for a conference with Philip.[175] Contrary to custom the autumn campaign had ended without a truce.[176] But the king of France saw his way clear; he must already have begun to intrigue with the Norman barons who deserted John early in 1203, and to have realised the advantage which he could gain from the anxiety felt in Brittany and the neighbouring counties about the fate of Arthur. He, therefore, refused terms, and both kings began to prepare for the decisive campaign.

The Christmas court at Caen was the last great feast held by a duke of the line of Rollo in a united Normandy. Already the unrest caused by Arthur's imprisonment had spread from Anjou and Brittany. On August 24 the king had issued a sinister warning to the barons of Brittany that Arthur was the pledge of their good behaviour;[177] and it was probably early in December that the untrue story of Arthur's mutilation and death began to spread abroad.[178] The Bretons

[172] The statements in *Guillaume le Maréchal*, iii, 171, about John's fear of traitors in the marches east of Verneuil, and his detour in travelling from Verneuil to Rouen must be placed over against the reference to the well defended marches in the annals of Winchester (*Ann. Monast.*, ii, 78, 79).

[173] An attempt was made in the end of August. Letter to Alan Fitzcount, etc., of August 24 (*Rot. Pat.*, 17a–b).

[174] The Bretons were allied with the Angevins (*Guillaume le Maréchal*, iii, 171). Deserters from Normandy were in Brittany in December, *e.g.*, Guy of Laval in *Britannia contra nos* (*Rot. Pat.*, 21b).

[175] On December 26, John sent William du Hommet the constable and others to Philip, as persons in whom Philip may have faith 'de treuga . . . et de colloquio inter vos et nos capiendo' (*Rot. Pat.*, 22).

[176] Rigord, i, 153. Cf. below, p. 311. A note in *Rot. Norm.*, 65, shows that earlier in December there had been talk of a truce. 'Mandatum est constabulariis de Marchia Normannie quod de treuga inter dominum Regem et Regem Francie tenenda faciant quod Rogerus de Thoni et Petrus de Rupibus Thesaurarius Pictavie eis simul mandabunt.'

[177] *Rot. Pat.*, 17b. The letter of safe conduct concludes 'mandamus autem vobis quod nihil faciatis unde malum eveniat nobis *vel Arturo nepoti nostro*'.

[178] Below, p. 312. Hubert de Burgh, so far as the scanty references to him in the records testify, was employed elsewhere in October, but was at Falaise later. John's movements prove nothing, since he was not in Falaise between the first half of August, when he took Arthur there, and the end of January, 1203.

demanded justice of King Philip. In spite of the assertion in the chronicle of Coggeshall,[179] it is probable that the defections which began at this time were due to the example of Bretons and Angevins, and the revelations of John's cruelty and lack of purpose rather than to special interest in the future of Arthur.[180] The biographer of William the Marshal speaks of treachery as of a kind of epidemic which afflicted Normandy, and especially the districts bordering on Maine, at this time.[181] The reaction had begun against the rule of Henry II. Yet the interest created by Arthur certainly formed the nucleus of disaffection, and John found it expedient to remove him from Falaise to Rouen at the end of January.[182] He was too late to divert the suspicions of the Bretons.

In the meanwhile John had made preparations with a view to a southern campaign. Stores and troops were collected at Argentan, one of the most suitable centres in Normandy from which to start on a southern expedition, and a general levy was called out to meet at the same place.[183] But disasters began before his preparations were completed. News came from Chinon that Queen Isabella, who had been left in Touraine, was cut off from her husband and in danger of falling into the hands of the rebels.[184] John immediately set off with a band of mercenaries, and after waiting for a few days in Alençon, where he was entertained by the count,[185] reached Le Mans on January 21. Here the news awaited him that, owing to the numbers

[179] Coggeshall, p. 141.

[180] It must be remembered that the vast majority of our authorities are uncertain whether Arthur was murdered or not. There seems to be no doubt that he had legally forfeited his territory. He had done homage to John in May, 1200 (Howden, iv, 115).

[181] *Guillaume le Maréchal*, iii, 170, on the *tournés*; Gervase of Canterbury, ii, 95.

[182] Coggeshall, p. 143. John was at Falaise on January 30, and stayed till February 1, 1203. It is significant that this step immediately followed the treachery of the count of Séez.

[183] The advantages of Argentan, as a meeting place, will be obvious to anyone who, like the writer, has followed the road from Falaise and noted its relation to the other Norman roads. The evidence for the statements in the text is contained in the following passages of the records. On December 9, 1202, the king authorised his marshal to make arrangements for the service of the military classes (*Rot. Pat.*, 21b: letter addressed to all knights, etc.). On January 7, he issued another general letter as follows: 'Mandamus vobis quod fidem habeatis hiis que dilectus noster Ricardus de Wilekier vobis dicet vel mandabit per litteras suas de veniendo ad nos apud Argentan' (*ibid.*, 22b). Cf. *Rot. Norm.*, 73: A man is excused his debts to the Jews on condition that he is at Argentan in the king's service on February 3. On April 1 the king issued an order of payment, on behalf of William Poignard, for stores taken from Caen to Argentan (*ibid.*, 85). The stores include wine and great quantities of rope, apparently for tents.   [184] *Guillaume le Maréchal*, iii, 171.

[185] *Ibid.*, and the Itinerary, which corrects the poem.

158   THE LOSS OF NORMANDY

of the enemy, the roads to Chinon were impassable; and these bad tidings were soon followed by worse. Count Robert of Alençon, or, as he is more often styled, of Séez, had become Philip's man and handed Alençon over to the French as soon as John's back was turned.[186] The records of the next few days are full of acts of confiscation, by which the lands of the count and his men were distributed to the king's followers.[187] In a day or two Peter of Préaux, one of the most faithful of the latter, managed to bring the queen in safety to Le Mans,[188] and John returned to Argentan. In order to avoid Alençon, the company made a detour to the east through Mamers and the neighbourhood of Bellême.[189]

This was the beginning of the end. John's fury gradually gave way to fits of lethargy, interrupted by moods of suspicion, by which the fidelity of none, from the earl of Chester downwards, was untouched.[190] An English chronicler ascribes this incompetence to the presence of his wife, for John was the most uxorious of men.[191] The great expedition never took place, the last attempt to combine the forces of north and south failing when, a few days after John's retirement from Le Mans, the seneschal of Poitou made a destructive but not very effective attack on Angers.[192] In March King Philip

[186] *Guillaume le Maréchal*. The editor, M. Meyer, ascribes these events to October, 1202, when John also reached Le Mans from Alençon. Several facts are conclusive against this view. The roads were not infested in October, nor was Chinon in danger, for the king went on from Le Mans and stayed for some weeks in Touraine. Count Robert was in John's confidence as late as December 27 (see *Rot. Norm.*, 66), when he received money 'ad opus R. vicecomitis Bellimontis'. The confiscation of his lands begins dramatically on January 22. Lastly, the itinerary proves that the king returned to Séez and Argentan from Le Mans. It states erroneously that he passed through Alençon, January 25 being a mistake for 15th (cf. *Rot. Pat.*, 23b *ad fin*).

[187] *Rot. Pat.*, 23b; *Rot. Norm.*, 79 *seqq.*, 75, 78, etc.

[188] *Guillaume le Maréchal*, iii, 172.

[189] *Guillaume le Maréchal*, iii, 172. John reached Séez on the 25th, having apparently taken two days for this difficult cross-country journey. He went on to Argentan on the 28th, and to Falaise on the 30th of January.

[190] Below, p. 167.

[191] R. Wendover (Rolls ed.), i, 316, 317. John put off the time of war: 'cum regina epulabatur quotidie splendide, somnosque matutinales usque ad prandiandi horam protraxit.' Compare the lines in *Guillaume le Maréchal*, 12648–56, on John's mental attitude after the arrival of the queen at Le Mans.

[192] According to the annals of Saint-Aubin, the attack took place on January 25, 'die autem mercurii ante Purificationem beate Marie accessit Robertus de Turneham ad eandem civitatem et, ea miserabiliter depredata et in parte combusta, secessit' (Halphen, p. 21; who prints the best text). Dubois (*Bibliothèque*, xxxiv, 522), as Halphen and Richard point out, is misled by an inferior text and supposes that the seneschal of Poitou attacked Mirebeau. It is significant that the attack should have been made at this time, when John was expected from Le Mans. A combination between Robert and John seems to have been planned prior to the advance of the main army. On

organised the resistance of Maine, Anjou, Touraine and parts of Poitou by a series of agreements with the chief barons of the disaffected party. The terms of these agreements, which were identical, show that by this time the Bretons were co-operating with the king of France, and that the negotiations fastened on the uncertain future of Arthur and of his equally unfortunate sister. The conventions made between Philip and Arthur were before all else to be observed; if Arthur should be released on conditions which forbade their observance these barons of Maine and Anjou swore to repudiate him; if he were to die, they would only acknowledge his sister if she were married through the agency of Philip and the Bretons.[193] In any case therefore Philip maintained his hold upon the centre of the Angevin dominions.

It is possible that the king of France had planned an invasion of Poitou, and there is evidence that he could rely on the co-operation of the count of Toulouse in the south, in spite of the domestic alliance between the latter and the Angevin house.[194] This project, if it was ever seriously entertained, was not carried out. King Philip, shortly after Easter, journeyed along the Loire by boat as far as Saumur,[195] the most important place between Tours and Angers, and having received its submission, turned against the Norman frontiers. The support of the barons of Maine and Brittany, and the successes of William des Roches in his rear made it desirable to resume the attack on the familiar lines. His decision was justified. Within a few weeks Normandy was isolated, Le Mans probably surrendered before the end of April,[196] and John was thus cut off from the faithful government of Poitou by the triple barrier of Alençon, Le Mans, Angers. The administration which the king had set up after the battle of

the 12th of January John wrote from Argentan that on account of urgent business he was unable to attend a great council at Rouen (*Rot. Pat.*, 23).

[193] Delisle, *Actes de Philippe-Auguste*, no. 752, p. 506.

[194] At Le Mans, in January, John wrote letters to the clergy, knights, burgesses, etc., of the bishopric of Agen, which show that he had heard of the count's hostility about this time—January 22 (*Rot. Pat.*, 23a, b).

[195] Rigord, i, 157, 158, says that Philip invaded Aquitaine, but is probably using the name in a loose sense. For Philip at Saumur, see the annals of Saint-Aubin (Halphen, p. 21). At the same time William des Roches was rapidly extending his authority in Anjou. On the Monday before Good Friday, April 7, he took Beaufort (arr. Beaugé) and later forced Chateauneuf-sur-Sarthe to surrender (Halphen, *Annales*, p. 21; Dubois, *Bibliothèque de l'Ecole des Chartes*, xxxiv, 525, 526). He was thus free to march on to Le Mans. See below, note 196.

[196] On April 19 John addressed from Bec an urgent letter to the citizens of Le Mans, begging them to withstand the King of France (*Rot. Pat.*, 28). It does not seem to be known in what manner Le Mans actually fell. Dubois, *Bibliothèque*, xxxiv, 529; Richard, ii, 425, are based on conjecture.

Mirebeau collapsed. In the official correspondence Brice the chamber-lain appears as seneschal of Anjou for the last time on April 16.[197] He was afterwards transferred to Normandy.[198] In Touraine Girard d'Athée, though he also ceased to bear the title of seneschal,[199] kept his ground until 1205. Early in the spring of 1203 he was reinforced by Hubert de Burgh, who took up his headquarters at Chinon,[200] while Girard held out in Loches.[201] But from the first the outlook was hopeless; in August we find the King ordering the demolition of Montrésor and all castles not immediately under Girard's jurisdiction, lest they should fall into hostile hands;[202] in the course of 1204 the garrison in the citadel of Tours, which still withstood the French and their allies, at last surrendered.[203] Loches and Chinon were left for a last terrible onslaught in the following year.

King John never approached Anjou again from Normandy. His next visit in 1206 was paid during his invasion from the south. By that time his enemy had laid hold on every foot of Norman soil with the exception of the Channel Isles.

We have seen that the Norman preparations for the campaign of 1203 had been made with a view to a southern expedition from Argentan. After the loss of Maine and the defection of Count Robert of Alençon, no advance was made in this direction until August, when a fruitless siege of Alençon was followed by an equally fruitless invasion of Brittany. In the meanwhile King Philip had dealt several crushing blows along the middle frontier, and the defection of Count Robert had been followed by that of many more, among whom the great baron Hugh of Gournai attracted universal opprobrium.

Some attempt had been made to meet possible attack before hostilities began. The urgent needs of the war became 'the main pre-occupation of John's representatives in England'. The royal writs entered on the *Liberate* roll 'show that between 17 October 1202 and 8 October 1203 as much as £14,733 6s. 8d. was received from the English exchequer in sums which vary between 300 and 4050

---

[197] *Rot. Pat.*, 28b.

[198] The king entrusted the castles of Mortain and Tenchebrai to him in September (*Rot. Pat.*, 34b, 35) and at the same time he was given some of the English lands of Guy of Thousars (*Rot. de Lib.*, 65). For a time he deserted John; his manor of Wildmundcot is included in the roll of lands of the Normans in 1204 (*Rot. Norm.*, 138), and he needed a safe conduct in England (*Rot. Pat.*, 39). On the other hand, Philip Augustus, in September, 1203, gave away Brice's lands at Fleuri: see *Recueil*, ii, no. 761.

[199] He is styled seneschal on April 7, 1203 (*Rot. Norm.*, p. 86).

[200] That Hubert was at Chinon in February may be proved by a comparison of a letter in *Rot. Pat.*, 25b (dated by a slip of the copyist from Chinon), with another in *Rot. Norm.*, 86, of April 5.

[201] Salmon, *Chroniques de Touraine*, i, 150.   [202] *Rot. Pat.*, 38.

[203] Salmon, *op. cit.*, i, 149, 150.

marks'.[204] This treasure from England helped to pay the garrisons
of the march at Arques, Radepont, Pont de l'Arche, Vaudreuil,
Verneuil, etc.[205] Provision was made for the safety of the burgesses
of Dieppe, in case the fortune of war should force them to leave the
town.[206] All due service was demanded, though without very much
success, from the foreigners who held Norman lands.[207] Loans and
aids were exacted in England and Normandy; privileges were
scattered broadcast among the Norman towns,[208] and bribes among
the king's personal followers. But leadership was lacking. The
defences upon which so much care had been lavished were undermined by treachery. In the last week of April or the early days of May,
two of the most important men among the Norman barons, Hugh of
Gournai and Peter of Meulan, deserted John.[209] They surrendered to
the French the two fortresses which controlled the valley of the Risle
—the river which was a second line of defence to central Normandy.
Of these, the more northern castle at Montfort-sur-Risle was immediately re-occupied by the king; it lay beyond the reach of Philip;[210]
but Beaumont-le-Roger, the other fortress, was lost for ever.[211] By
this time the French king had reached the Evrecin from the west and
prepared to advance beyond the boundary marked out by the treaty
of 1200. Neubourg stood out, and was still in John's possession in

---

[204] Pipe Roll for 5 John (Pipe Roll Soc., 1938), p. xi. See below, pp. 235 and
passim.
[205] See letters of January 19 (*Rot. Norm.*, 69), February 10 (*ibid.*, 75).
[206] February 26, 1203 (*Rot. Pat.*, 26).
[207] An interesting letter to the provost of Bruges (*loco comitis Flandrensis*)
of March 5 (*Rot. Pat.*, 26b). The date fixed for those who hold fees is *infra
clausum Pasche.* From *Rot. de Liberate*, 41, it appears that the constable of
Boulogne and the *advocatus* of Béthune had not responded to the call for
service.
[208] *e.g.*, in February communes for Falaise, Auffai, Domfront (*Rot. Pat.*,
24b, 25b, 26).
[209] Important entries in the Jumièges continuation of Robert of Torigni
(*Histor. de France*, xviii, 342). Cf. Wendover, i, 317. The dates are established
by the rolls. Hugh of Gournai deserted John between April 21, when he was
with the king at Verneuil (*Rot. Norm.*, 89), and May 4, when the confiscation
of his property begins (*ibid.*, 92). The confiscation of Peter of Meulan's lands
begins on May 8 (*ibid.*, 93).
[210] *Histor. de France*, xviii, 342: a source unnoticed by Miss Norgate (ii,
411). The itinerary shows that John went from Verneuil to Montfort on April
23 or 24 and was not again in Montfort before July 18.
[211] Philip gave it in October to Guy de la Roche (*Recueil*, ii, no. 766).
In January and March Peter of Meulan had received money, corn, and
ammunition, the former 'ad emendam warnisionem ad castrum nostrum
de Bello Monte' (*Rot. Norm.*, 72, 82). Peter died before Philip's gift of
October, 1203, was made, according to the *querimonia* of Ralph de Meulan in
1247, noted below, p. 345, note 20. Cf. the evidence collected by Stapleton, II,
cc; for his livings, for he was in orders, see Stapleton, II, cxcvii–viii and note.

M

the autumn.[212] Conches, however, was taken,[213] and probably all the smaller forts between the Risle and the Eure. In June Philip advanced along the tongue of land which lies north of Gaillon between the Eure and the Seine, and set up his engines around the great castle of Vaudreuil. We have already seen[214] how this fortress, greatly strengthened by King Richard, was the key to the Seine valley upon the left bank of the river. If it fell only Pont de l'Arche and Roche Orival lay between Philip and Rouen. In the summer of 1203 the garrison, which included some knights of the bishop of Norwich, was under the command of Robert Fitz Walter and Saer de Quinci. The men had been paid in February, and provisions had been brought up the river. John himself moved in the direction of Vaudreuil as far as Roche Orival and Pont de l'Arche, and seemed intent upon energetic measures; urgent messages were sent down stream to hasten the boats laden with food and war-material.[215] Everything pointed to a desperate resistance, when the garrison suddenly surrendered before a stone had been cast.[216]

The indignation aroused by the loss of Vaudreuil was widespread and intense: the disaster was attributed to the treachery of the castellans, whose conduct became a subject of satirical doggerel.[217] In Normandy the surrender was regarded as a proof of English indifference to the fate of the duchy:[218] the commanders were barons of English interests, and English knights had formed part of the garrison. The king cannot have improved matters by a letter of July 5 in which he declared to all and sundry that the castle had been surrendered at his command.[219] The diplomatic or strategic reasons for the command were as mysterious to contemporaries as they are to us; and, with the exception of Count Robert's desertion, the surrender of Vaudreuil did more to demoralise the cause of John than any event of the year.

It is, indeed, difficult to understand the king's mind during this summer. The curious lethargy of which the chroniclers speak undoubtedly accounts for much of his conduct. It is evident that he was

---

[212] *Rot. Pat.*, 35. Caen, October 10, 1203: 'militibus et servientibus commorantibus apud Novum Burgum, etc. Sciatis quod ex quo feceritis negocium quod fidelis noster R. de Plesseto vobis ex parte nostra dicet, vos statim de liberacionibus vestris pacari faciemus.' For Robert of Pleshey, see below, p. 248.   [213] Rigord, i, 157.

[214] Above, p. 105.

[215] *Rot. Norm.*, 69, 75, 80–2; *Rot. Pat.*, 30a, b. Fulk de Cantilupe was in charge of the stores. For the knights of the bishop of Norwich, *Rot. Pat.*, 31b.

[216] Wendover, i, 317, 318.

[217] Coggeshall, p. 144.

[218] *Hist. de ducs de Normandie*, ed. Francisque-Michel, p. 97.

[219] *Rot. Pat.*, 31. See my remarks on this incident in *English Historical Review*, xxi (1906), 296.

mentally diseased: he refused to be disturbed by the news of continued disaster. His reply to the messenger who told him how Philip led off the castellans of the conquered fortresses bound to their horses' tails was merely, 'Let him alone: I will win back all his booty some day.' Those who witnessed his levity could attribute it to nothing but sorcery.[220] Yet, to this cause of John's inaction we should probably add the fact that he was awaiting papal, if not imperial, interference. In February he had despatched the new prior of Dunstable to Pope Innocent,[221] and towards the end of July the messenger returned with a legate, the abbot of S. Giovanni di Casamario.[222] The king of France, on his part, had begun to express indignant alarm in June, when he got Renaud of Dammartin, the count of Boulogne, to declare at Evreux that he had advised the king on no account to be forced by the pope to conclude any peace or truce with the king of England.[223] This declaration was followed by others in July and August, in which the greatest persons of France, of either sex, gave the same counsel.[224] John seems to have been looking forward to a truce of at least two or three years;[225] but Philip was inexorable. In any case he was opposed to the policy and actions of Innocent, and he was prepared to face an interdict rather than to lose such an opportunity of securing Normandy.

The pope's letters to his legate and to the two kings were very persuasive and reveal a sincere anxiety to see the end of the war. In the letters in which he announced the mission of the legate, he dwelt upon the horrible effects of the war: the rich made poor, the poor oppressed, churches destroyed, monks forced to wander and beg, women prostituted.[226] Philip deferred a reply until the assembly of clergy and nobles at Mantes which he summoned for August 22. Then his answer was decisive: all matters of feudal law and vassalage such as had arisen between the two kings were beyond the competence

[220] Wendover, i, 317.

[221] Annals of Dunstable (*Ann. Monast.*, iii, 28). Letters of credit in *Rot. Pat.*, 26: Master R. Peccator went with the prior.

[222] *Ann. Monast.*, iii, 28. The Pope announced the mission of the legate in May. Cheney and Semple, *Selected letters of Pope Innocent III*, pp. 56–9, edit the letter to King Philip; probably written on May 21, 1203.

[223] *Layettes*, no. 678.

[224] *Ibid.*, nos. 683–92, and, for Blanche, Countess of Champagne, see *Recueil*, ii, no. 759. Most of these declarations were issued on the occasion of the great assembly at Mantes on August 22 (Rigord, i, 158).

[225] See a phrase in an interesting letter about Master Ivo the Engineer (*Rot. Pat.*, 31b), dated Rouen, July 29: 'quousque cum rege Francorum habeamus pacem vel treugam duorum vel trium annorum.' A few weeks earlier John had sent the Marshal to negotiate with Philip (*Guillaume le Maréchal*, iii, 172). This was early in May, during the siege of Conches, since the Marshal returned to Falaise, where John was from May 4–9.   [226] *Selected letters*, p. 58.

of the Apostolic See.[227] Supported by the assembly, Philip hastened to resume the campaign. On the last day of August he laid siege to Radepont, the outlying fortress above the deep furrow of the Andelle, which had been strengthened by John as the last protection of Rouen to the south. The old road from Rouen to Paris over the upland country here crossed the first stream in its path, and the capture of Radepont, after a three weeks' siege, brought Philip within easy distance of the Norman city.[228] It did more than this. Before the siege of Radepont was concluded, Philip had begun the investment of Château-Gaillard, and had captured the Isle of Andeli with its fortification.[229] The fall of Radepont cut off all hope of relief from the east bank of the Seine, just as the loss of Vaudreuil and the isle made it impossible to bring help up the other side of the river.

We may leave Philip to the heroic encounter which alone adds dignity to this miserable war, and turn to follow the movements of King John. Before the meeting of the French assembly at Mantes, he had thrown off his lethargy, and turning westwards tried to recover Alençon. The itinerary shows that he lay before the town from the 11th to the 15th of August, and then moved hurriedly in a north-easterly direction across the wooded heights behind Moulins and Bonmoulins and along the valley which runs down to the Charenton

[227] See the pope's letter to Philip of October 31, 1203 (*Patrologia Latina*, ccxv, 176). Innocent refers to Philip's contention, 'quod de jure feudi et hominis tuo (*sic*) stare mandato sedis apostolicae vel judicio non teneris et quod nihil ad nos pertinet de negotio quod vertitur inter reges'. This letter, in which the pope sums up the history of the legation, is one of a series written on October 31, 1203, which are of great interest. We learn that Philip had made capital out of John's treatment of the clergy at Tours; and, as M. Petit-Dutaillis has shown, the letters offer conclusive proof that Philip had tried John on the appeal of the Poitevins, and had confiscated Normandy (above, p. 147, note 114). Finally, we have the distinction between public morals and feudal law; above, p. 83.

[228] See Stapleton, I, cxxvi. The exchequer and Norman rolls show that large payments had been made for the strengthening and garrison of the castle. After the loss of the Norman Vexin Radepont became very important, and was unsuccessfully attacked by Philip after the outbreak of war in 1202 (Roger of Wendover, i, 313). John's sense of the importance of the place is seen in the fortification of Douville, a manor belonging to Stephen Longchamp on the other side of the Andelle. The king paid for the fortification and the garrison (*Rot. Norm.*, 75, 87; cf. Stapleton, II, cxiv). King Philip gave Radepont to P. de Moret by a deed which, though dated c. 1210 in the *Cartulaire Normand*, p. 29, no. 184 (printed on p. 297), should be dated September, 1203: see text and note in *Recueil*, ii, no. 761. The charter illustrates the value attached to the stronghold. The grantee and his heirs 'facient jurare omnes illos qui in fortelicia Radepontis manebunt, quod quicquid de illis contingat, sive de morte, sive de prisonia corporum suorum, sive de alia re, nulli reddent forteliciam Radepontis, nisi nobis vel certo nuncio nostro bene cognito qui nostras litteras patentes de hoc portaret' (*Cart. Norm.*, p. 297). [229] William the Breton, i, 213-16.

at Chambrais, the modern Broglie.[230] At this castle, which was a
favourite stopping place on the road from Lisieux to Verneuil[231], the
king probably found reinforcements, for he immediately set off to
Verneuil, which he reached on August 20. It was presumably on this
occasion that the king made his last demonstration on French soil,
for, according to William the Breton, about the same time as his fruitless attempt at Alençon, he appeared in force before Brézolles, a
fortress on the little stream of the Meuvette, a few miles to the south
of the Norman frontier.[232] Here again the French, moving on interior
lines, approached in sufficient numbers to force a retreat. On the
21st John was back again at Chambrais.

A month later the king undertook another rapid journey. It is
obvious that he feared or was unable to come to close quarters with
the French army; for, while Philip Augustus was planting his siege
engines round Radepont, he withdrew from Rouen to the west. On
September 18 he left Mortain for the Breton frontier. The strategic
motive of the new plan, as of his demonstration against Alençon,
was probably the same as that which had succeeded in the previous
year; he desired to withdraw Philip from his attack on the Seine
valley just as by his success at Mirebeau he had forced him to raise
the siege of Arques. But John's resources in the autumn of 1203 were
not those of May, 1202: he could not now rely upon local aid. Indeed,
one reason why he chose this particular moment for his rush into
Brittany may well have been that he had heard of the new count's
defection. Guy of Thouars had been a supporter of John so long as
the latter seemed strong enough to procure him the succession to
Brittany, but from the beginning of September he was in opposition
along with the Bretons.[233] However this may be, the invasion of

[230] See the itinerary prefixed to the Patent Rolls. According to the entry
for August 18, the king was at Cambay on this day, and at Chambrais on the
following day (Rot. Pat., 33b). Although the name is subpuncted in the roll,
it is possible that the king really did pass Cambaium (Cambois), which was
a royal residence near Exmes, not far from the line between Alençon and
Chambrais (Rot. Scacc., ii, 386; Rot. Chart., 96; Stapleton, Observations,
I, clxii).

[231] For Chambrais, which belonged to Henry of Ferrières, see Stapleton, II,
lxix. John stayed here on three or four occasions, and it is mentioned as a
stopping place by the biographer of the Marshal (ll. 10453, 12775). The road
from Lisieux continued through Lire, where it crossed the Risle, and the forest
of Breteuil to Verneuil.

[232] William the Breton (ed. Delaborde, i, 212). On the other hand, the king
was at Verneuil again in November (1–3) for a longer period and may have
attacked Brézolles then. From a clause in the treaty of 1200, it appears that
the lordships of Tillières and Brézolles were conterminous (Cart. Norm., p.
280). For the position of Brézolles in the defences of the French frontier, see
Bonnard, La Frontière franco-normande entre Seine et Perche (1907), p. 28.

[233] The confiscations begin at Trianon on September 11 (Rot. de Lib., 63).

Brittany was a failure; the cruelty and destructiveness of the king and his mercenaries simply added fuel to the hatred of the Bretons and provoked reprisals in the following year. The cathedral of Dol was sacked and burnt, and the territory of the lords of Fougères was ravaged;[234] the precious relics of St. Samson and St. Magloire, which one of John's barons, Philip of Colombiéres, had rescued from the hands of the soldiers, were carried off to Rouen;[235] but on September 22, five days after he had set out, John was back again at Mortain. He returned to Rouen[236] slowly by way of Falaise, Lisieux and Montfort-sur-Risle. This was the end of his last campaign in Normandy.

John remained for two more months, but excitement and suspicion preyed upon him. For some mysterious reason he left Rouen on October 7 almost alone. After crossing the river by boat to Notre-Dame-du-Pré, he appears to have ridden in the day to Bonneville-sur-Touque, an enormous distance even for him.[237] Two days later he celebrated the feast of Saint Denis at Caen, with much drinking of wine.[238] The king next spent some days in the Côtentin at Valognes,

---

On the 19th, at Dol, the earl of Leicester was granted the honour of Richmond except the castles of Richmond and Bowes (*ibid.*). In October we have a charter of Philip for Guy of Thouars (*Recueil*, ii, no. 764). Guy had been with John at Easter (*Rot. Pat.*, 27).

[234] William the Breton (i, 212) with Delaborde's note for other authorities. William of Fougères, who had the wardship of the young heir to the lordship (Stapleton, II, ccxlviii), had negotiated on Arthur's behalf with the Breton lords in August, 1202 (*Rot. Pat.*, 16, 17), joined count Robert of Alençon in January (*Rot. Norm.*, 71), and by February 7 (*ibid.*, 74, 77) had definitely thrown in his lot with the Bretons.

[235] The chief authority for what happened at Dol is a charter of January, 1223, in which the archbishop of Rouen declares that he restored the relics. It is quoted in A. de la Borderie, *Hist. de Bretagne*, iii, 293, note. Philip of Colombiéres was fermor of the forest of Roumare (*Rot. Scacc.*, ii, 552). He was faithful to John: in June, 1204, King Philip gave away his Norman lands (*Recueil*, ii, no. 808). He accompanied John to Ireland in 1210 (*Rot. de Lib.*, 210, 217). His chief holding, owing service of ten knights, was in Somerset (*Red Book of the Exchequer*, i, 231, ii, 544; Pipe Roll, 3 John, p. 37).

[236] I am inclined to regard this as the visit to Rouen mentioned in *Guillaume le Maréchal*, iii, 173, although the editor, relying on the order of the narrative, ascribes it to February, 1203. These leaps in the narrative are frequent in the poem. According to the writer, Stephen Longchamp was in prison at Rouen when John arrived: now the confiscation of Stephen's lands is implied on September 22 (*Rot. de Liberate*, 64). On August 3 he was in favour (*ibid.*, 56). He was released in October, since his son, a hostage, was sent to Wallingford on or before October 22 (*ibid.*, 69). On November 23 he received back some of his lands (*Rot. Norm.*, 113). It is possible that he was imprisoned on account of the loss of Douville (above, p. 164, note 228), which must have fallen when Radepont fell in September.   [237] *Guillaume le Maréchal*, iii, 174.

[238] 'Computate dilecto nostro R. de Veteri Ponte iiii tunellos vini quos

then dashing back to the Touque, he set off on a last inspection of Verneuil, the solitary outpost on the frontier. Not daring to make his way across to Rouen by Neubourg, he came all the way back to Lisieux and Hebertot, and so to Rouen. 'It was not the straight way, but the other seemed dangerous to him, for he would have come upon his enemies.'[239] John had now decided to leave Normandy. It is possible that he merely desired to rally his English vassals, whose money he had been spending at a ruinous rate;[240] certainly he tried to make people in Normandy believe that he would soon be among them again;[241] but the ordinary view was that he really intended flight,[242] and we are bound to admit that his movements go far to justify this view. He had much cause for alarm, most of all in the defections in the Norman baronage. Since the days when he had confiscated the estates of the Poitevins and denied them ordinary justice in his court, he had fallen back more and more into the mood of nature. He had treated the prisoners captured at Mirebeau with indignity and cruelty; in many cases he had probably put them to death; the chief prisoner, the heir to John's throne, had disappeared, and since Easter the idle talk of the Bretons must have been repeated in Normandy with a sharper sense of conviction. It is significant that, with the exception of Count Robert, the more important deserters, the count of Evreux, Hugh of Gournai, Peter of Meulan, Guy of Thouars and many more had changed sides soon after the date upon which Arthur was most probably murdered.[243] For a short time the great earl of Chester himself had been suspected, and had been forced to find sureties and to surrender the castle of Similli in the week after Easter.[244] We may be reasonably sure that sympathy with Arthur was not the ruling motive for the conduct of these great barons. Deep questions of law and equity were being mooted as the result of John's

---

ipse nobis promisit apud . . . potavimus apud festum Sancti Dionisii apud Cadomum.' To the seneschal and barons of the Norman exchequer, October 28 (*Rot. Norm.*, 109). On the Saturday following the feast (October 11) the king received the regalia from the bishop of Norwich (*Rot. Pat.*, 35). The itinerary must contain an error for October 9.

[239] *Guillaume le Maréchal*, iii, 175.

[240] On the export of English treasure, especially in 1203, see above, p. 160, and below, p. 235.

[241] At Caen, November 15, he forbade the impleading of Ralph of Cailly 'de aliquo libero tenemento suo quod teneat nisi coram nobis *quousque nos Deus reduxerit de Anglia in Normanniam*' (*Rot. Pat.*, 36). Also December 5, at Barfleur (*Rot. Norm.*, 119).

[242] Cf. *Hist. des ducs de Normandie et des rois d'Angleterre*, p. 97; the chronicle of Andres: 'tanquam ad asylum confugiens' (*Histor. de France*, xviii, 573); Chronicle of Mortemer (*ibid.*, 354).

[243] See note C at the end of this chapter for the chief deserters in 1203.

[244] *Rot. Norm.*, 96.

appeal to force: the state of nature was soon to end with the social contract of 1215. In the meanwhile Philip had absolved John's vassals from all duty of obedience.[245] John might well fear violence as well as treachery.[246]

This was not all. John's last military venture had failed: the *exercitus de Alencon* had been disbanded,[247] and outside a few castles Normandy was defended by mercenaries. The irresponsible depredations of these social outcasts had alienated both clergy and people to such an extent that in Aquitaine, even more than in Normandy, popular indignation was a serious menace to John's authority.[248] Finally, the distractions of war had not preserved the king from several quarrels with the clergy, especially in the diocese of Séez, and in the autumn of 1203 the misery of Normandy was increased by the horrors of an interdict.[249] England must indeed have seemed an asylum to John and Isabella.

The biographer of the Marshal, who is a safe guide to feudal opinion, has described John's last journey in Normandy; and the passage will be a fit conclusion to this chapter:

'The king stayed but a short time at Rouen, and announced his intention of going to England in order to ask aid and counsel from his barons; then, he said, he would return without delay. But he took the queen with him, which made many fear that he would stay in England until it was too late. Preparations were soon made, for the king had sent his baggage train on privately in advance. On the first night he slept at Bonneville, not in the town, but in the castle, for he suspected treason: in fact he had been warned

---

[245] This is stated in the papal letters to John: Cheney and Semple, *Selected letters*, p. 62, (October, 1203).

[246] *Guillaume le Maréchal*, iii, 175; chronicle of Mortemer (*Histor. de France,* xviii, 354). The remarks of Wendover (i, 318) imply the same view of John's fears.

[247] A special tallage had been raised for the expedition against Alençon. See the references to the *talliata exercitus de Alencon* in *Rot. Norm.*, 115.

[248] See below, p. 230.

[249] The ecclesiastical disputes which occurred during the early years of John's reign lie beyond the scope of this volume. So far as they concerned Norman churches, they must have embarrassed his political position. For a summary, see Gütschow, *Innocenz III und England* (1904), pp. 105–26; Luchaire, *Innocent III: Les Royautés vassales*, pp. 182–90. The interdict, conditionally ordered by Innocent on May 25, 1203, if John should not receive the new bishop of Séez (*Patrologia Latina*, ccxv, 69; Potthast, no. 1919) was at least partially enforced, in spite of John's letters of October 9 (*Rot. de Lib.*, 72) ordering a courteous reception of the bishop. The interdict is referred to on October 26 in a letter addressed to the seneschal and bailiffs of Normandy; 'mandamus vobis quod non permittatis impedimentum fieri Abbati de Blanchelanda quo minus ipse possit redditus suos juste perquirere *quamdiu interdictum duraverit*' (*Rot. Pat.*, 35).

that the greater number of his barons had sworn to hand him over to the king of France, and although he pretended to be ignorant of their intention, he kept at a safe distance from them. He commanded the Marshal and those in whom he felt most confidence to be ready in the morning before daybreak; and so the king left without taking leave while he was supposed to be still asleep; and when his departure was discovered he was seven leagues away. He made for Bayeux, by way of Caen, riding more than twenty leagues on that day[250]—leagues of the Bessin, too, which are longer than French leagues. From these he went on towards Barfleur where many of his companions took their leave of him:[251] it was quite clear that they could not look for a speedy return.'[252]

NOTES TO CHAPTER VI

Note A. The Division of the Evrecin according to the Treaty of May, 1200

A twelfth-century treaty was a very literal affair, even though it were not observed, and we are able, thanks to a fortunate enrolment on a charter roll, to observe how boundaries were mapped out in accordance with the treaty of 1200, as easily as we can follow the work of boundary commissioners in the nineteenth century. According to the treaty a boundary was to be fixed midway between Evreux and Neubourg, and the distance between it and Conches was to be regarded as a fixed unit of measurement: boundaries at the same distance from Evreux were to be set up between Conches and Evreux on the one hand, and Acquigny

[250] Unless the itinerary is faulty, the poet is slightly in error here; but it is more probable that his memory of such a fateful journey is correct, and that John halted, but did not stay at Caen. On the other hand, the poet omits to state that, from Bayeux, John turned southward and visited Domfront (November 20–1) and Vire (November 21–3) before making for Barfleur (December 5).

[251] The following list of John's companions during this journey may be compiled from the rolls and from a charter tested at Gonneville, November 29 (in Round, *Calendar*, p. 304, no. 45). Those whose names are in italics accompanied the king to England: *William the Marshal, earl of Pembroke;* the *earl of Arundel*; the seneschal, William Crassus; the constable, William du Hommet; *Robert of Vieuxpont, William of Briouze*; Ralph Tesson, Richard of Fontenay, *Peter Stokes, Thomas Basset, Warin Fitzgerald* (?). The earls of Chester and Salisbury joined the king at Morfarville but stayed to defend the western frontier. According to the *Histoire des ducs*, p. 97, *Baldwin of Béthune, count of Aumale*, also accompanied John to England, and there were probably others, *e.g., the bishop of Norwich*. Peter of Verneuil, who was important in the Gascon administration, took letters from Barfleur to Gascony, and had probably accompanied John during November (cf. *Rot. Pat.*, 36b).

[252] *Guillaume le Maréchal*, iii, 175.

and Evreux on the other. In these instances, however, the surveyors
were to follow the winding valley of the Itun,[253] in which Evreux lies.
The report of the jury under whose direction the measurements were
made states that by means of a rope, twenty toises[254] in length, boundaries were found (a) between Bacquepuits and Bernienville on the road
to Neubourg; (b) between Glisolles and Angerville-la-Rivière (now united
with Glisolles) in the direction of Conches; (c) near a place which is
probably La Vacherie in the direction of Acquigny.

An exception was made to this division in the case of Quitteboeuf,
which, although it might lie beyond the boundary (as it did) was to go
to the king of France; it was, however, not to be fortified. Existing forts
within the respective areas might be retained with the exception of
Portes and Londes, which were to be destroyed.

The boundary of Normandy to east and south of these limits had
partly been fixed in 1195, and we must assume that in 1200 as then, the
area between the Eure and the Seine was divided by a line midway
between Gaillon and Vaudreuil.[255] Damville on the Itun, and Tillières
on the Avre were to remain Norman; the boundary therefore to the
south would lie along the Itun as far as Damville, and thence along a
line drawn to the Avre between Tillières and Nonancourt.

I add the text of the survey preceded by relevant extracts from the
treaty.

I. EXTRACT FROM TREATY OF MAY, 1200

[John's original leters in Tr. des Chartes, *Angleterre*, II, No. 1, Carton
J. 628, ed. Delisle, *Cartulaire Normand.*, p. 280, No. 1063; Teulet,
Layettes du Trésor des Chartes, I, 217–19, No. 578.

Copies of Philip's letters in the Record Office, Exch. T. R. Diplomatic Doc. 6, 13th cent., ed. Rymer (Rec. Comm. 1816), i, 79–80;
and in Howden, ed. Stubbs, iv. 148–51; also, in Delaborde, *Recueil*,
ii, no. 633.]

[253] After visiting the ground I interpret the words of the treaty in this way.
The long winding slopes on either side of the Itun valley would make measurement across country very difficult. Another possible version of the words 'ex
ea parte ubi abbatia de Noa sita est sicut aqua Ytonie currit' would be that
from the site of the abbey the Itun should form the boundary (*i.e.*, southwards). The phrase *sicut fluvius currit* is used in this sense of the same river
in John's earlier treaty with Philip, January 1194, before Richard's return
from captivity (*Cartulaire Normand*, p. 275; see above, p. 97 and note).
[254] The *tesia* (between two and three feet) is mentioned occasionally in
contemporary documents, *e.g.*, *Cart. Norm.*, p. 33, no. 213; *Rot. Norm.*, 85;
Rot. Scacc., ii, 303.
[255] *Cart. Norm.*, p. 276, no. 1057. 'Et sciendum quod mete ponentur inter
foreliciam Gallionis et forteliciam Vallis Rodolii in media via; et ex illa meta,
sicut se portabit usque in Secanam et ex alia parte usque in Euriam, id quod
erit ex parte Gallionis, erit regis Francie et id quod erit ex parte Vallis Rodolii
erit nostrum.' The words in italics appear to mean according to the natural
declivity, or at right angles. The text is useful as evidence upon the way in
which the boundary marks were connected.

Johannes, Dei gratia, rex Anglie, dominus Hibernie, dux Normannie, Aquitanie, comes Andegavie, omnibus ad quos presens carta pervenerit, salutem. Noveritis quod hec est forma pacis facte inter dominum nostrum Philippum, illustrem regem Francie, et nos, scilicet quod nos tenebimus illi et heredibus suis pacem quam frater noster rex Ricardus, fecit illi inter Exoldunum et Charrotium, exceptis hiis que per presentem cartam excipiuntur vel mutantur, propter interceptiones²⁵⁶ quas idem frater noster illi fecit de pace illa, scilicet quod nos donavimus illi et heredibus suis, sicut rectus heres regis Ricardi, fratris nostri, civitatem Ebroicarum et Ebroicinum cum omnibus feodis et dominiis, sicut subsequentes mete determinant. Mete autem sunt posite in media vie inter Ebroicas et Novum burgum, et totum id quod erit inter has metas ex parte Francie erit domini regis Francie; id autem quod erit ex altera parte versus Novum burgum erit nostrum; et quantum terre habebit dominus rex Francie versus Novum burgum, tantum terre habebit versus Conches, et versus Akenny ad eandem mensuram,²⁵⁷ ex ea parte ubi abbatia de Noa²⁵⁸ sita est sicut aqua Ytonie currit. Guitebo,²⁵⁹ ubicumque sit, donavimus domino regi Francie. Tillerie cum pertinentiis suis et Danvilla remanent nobis, ita tamen quod dominus de Bruerolis habebit id quod debet habere in dominatu de Tilleriis, et dominus de Tilleriis habebit id quod habere debet in dominatu de Bruerolis. Concessimus etiam de episcopatu Ebroicensi domino regi Francie id quod est intra has metas, unde episcopus Ebroicensis domino regi Francie et heredibus ejus respondebit; idem autem Episcopus nobis et heredibus nostris respondebit de hoc quod erit extra has metas. Et sciendum quod neque dominus rex Francie neque nos poterimus firmare intra metas constitutas intra Novum burgum et Ebroicas, neque apud Guitebo, neque nos ex parte nostra neque dominus rex Francie ex parte sua, nisi ubi firmatum est infra metas predictas. Praeterea fortelicie de Portes²⁶⁰ et de Landes²⁶¹ in

²⁵⁶ *Exceptiones*, Howden. For a similar use of *interceptio*, see Arthur's letters of adherence to Philip, July, 1202, printed below, p. 326.

²⁵⁷ I follow Stubbs's punctuation.

²⁵⁸ For this well known abbey, evidently a landmark, see *Gallia Christiana*, xi, 665; Charpillon, *Dict. hist. de toutes les communes du département de l'Eure*, i (1868), p. 415. The site of the abbey, just north-east of La Bonneville, by the Itun, is now occupied by a farm.

²⁵⁹ Quitteboeuf, just beyond the boundary between Evreux and Neubourg in the direction of the latter. It was farmed as part of the honour of Evreux in 1198 (*Rot. Scacc.*, ii, 462). In 1204–5 Philip Augustus surrendered Quitteboeuf, with the neighbouring fiefs of Ecrosville and Feuguerolles to Roger of Meulan, who ceded all claims to the viscounty of Evreux (*Actes*, p. 183, no. 806).

²⁶⁰ Portes lies west of Evreux, just east of the main road between Le Neubourg and Conches, and about 7 kilometres north of the latter. Its lord, Roger de Portes, a benefactor of La Noe, was compensated by John after the loss of Portes in May, 1203 (the passages from the Norman rolls are collected by Delisle, *Cart. Norm.*, p. 14). Portes was granted in 1203 by Philip to Bernard du Plessis, *Cart. Norm.*, p. 13, no. 70.

²⁶¹ This fort was probably near Les Londes, on the west side of the road between Le Neubourg and Conches, about 9 kilometres south of the former. The name is very common (cf. *Rot. Norm.*, 4), and this place must not be

continenti diruentur, neque ibi alie fortelicie poterunt reedificari. Hcc autem omnia, que comes Ebroicensis infra has metas tenebat, fecimus domino regi Francie quietari a recto herede Ebroicarum. . . .

Actum apud Guletonem, anno ab Incarnatione Domini millesimo ducentesimo, mense maio.

II. SURVEY MADE BY JURY OF FRENCH AND NORMANS

(*Rotuli Chartarum*, ed. Hardy, p. 97; translated by Stapleton, *Observations on the Rolls of the Norman Exchequer*, II, clxxii–iii.)

Hii interfuerunt metis ponendis inter Ebroycas et Novum burbum: ex parte Regis Anglie Willelmus de Humet constabularius Normannie, Robertus de Harecurt, Robertus de Tresgoz, Henricus de Gray, Ricardus de Argentiis, Ricardus Silvanus, Revellus clericus;[262] Ex parte regis Francie Johannes de Rous, Hugo de Maudester, Hugo et Willelmus de Capella, Hugo Brancharcht, Cadoc, Hugo de Melleto.[263]

Predicti acceperunt cordam unam que continet viginti teysas et mensuraverunt totam terram que est a muro civitatis Ebroycarum usque ad murum Castelli de Novo burgo et posuerunt metas in medio vie. Meta vero posita est in [loco] qui dicitur vallis de Karlon, scilicet in divisione feodi de Bakepuid[264] et de Bernoinvilla[265] inter campum Rogeri Laval[266] de feodo de Bernoinvilla et campum Willelmi Boudrot de feodo de Bakepuid. Ab Ebroycis[267] usque ad medium vie Novi burgi ubi meta posita est sunt cccix cordae, que corda continet xx teysas.

Ad eandem vero mensuram posita est meta inter Ebroycas et Conches, scilicet inter Glisores et Angervillam[268] in loco qui dicitur haya de Talcund, scilicet ad parvam pirum quod est in feodo Mathei Foliot in campis de Angervilla in divisione campi Londr' Le Caron et campi Petri Billard'. Ad eandem similiter mensuram que est inter Ebroycas et Novum burgum posita est meta inter Ebroycas et Aquinem et est meta apud vacariam ad Nucerium qui appellatur Nucerium de Valle in valle,[269]

confused with *Londa*, between the Seine and the Risle, a centre of Norman administration.

[262] Of these Norman jurors, all except Robert of Harcourt were engaged in local administration. Robert of Tresgoz was bailiff of the Côtentin, Henry Gray of Verneuil, Richard of Argences had been bailiff of the honour of Evreux, Richard Silvain of the Avranchin and other parts. Master Revel was apparently a clerk of Henry Gray's (*Rot. Scacc.*, ii, 314).

[263] Guillaume de la Chapelle, and Hugh Brauchart, the king's squire, appear in the Acts of Philip-Augustus. Cadoc is the famous mercenary of that name.

[264] Bacquepuits, 12 kilometres from Evreux.

[265] Bernienville, 13·1 kilometres from Evreux.

[266] For this person, see Charpillon, *Dict. hist. de l'Eure*, i, 337–9.

[267] *Ad Ebroycum* (*Rot. Chart.*).

[268] Angerville-la-Rivière, a commune now joined to Glisolles, 13 kilometres from Evreux. The bridge of Angerville crosses the Itun at Glisolles. (Blosseville, *Dict. Topographique du dép. de l'Eure*, 1877, p. 5; Charpillon, ii, 288.)

[269] Stapleton translates 'La Vacherie-au-noyer, which is called Le Noyer du Val'. No *Nucerium* seems to exist in this part of the Evrecin to-day, but La Vacherie lies between Evreux and Acquigny, in the valley. Unfortunately

scilicet subtus monasterium ejusdem ville ex parte Aquiney inter . . . .
Walteri Calet.

NOTE B. GUÉRIN OF GLAPION

The career of Guérin of Glapion is an interesting example of the way in which a man of comparatively humble origin could rise to great importance both as baron and official under the Angevin empire.[270] He held the small fief of Glapion of the honour of Sainte-Scolasse-sur-Sarthe, near the borders of Maine. In 1195 he is found in the ranks of Norman officials as farmer of the *prepositura* of Moulins and Bonmoulins.[271] Stapleton has suggested that he came under the notice of King John during the lifetime of Richard, when John held Sainte-Scolasse as part of the Gloucester inheritance, in right of his wife. However this may be, the records of the next few years show that Guérin had rapidly amassed estates throughout Normandy. In 1200 he succeeded William Fitz Ralph as seneschal of Normandy, but he only held this office from June 6, 1200 until November 6, 1201,[272] when he gave way to Ralph Tesson, who in his turn was superseded by William Crassus in August, 1203.[273] It is possible that the strain of the office was so heavy in John's troubled reign that its holders sought early relief from its labours, but more probably the king was pursuing the policy of frequent changes which he seems to have adopted in less important cases. Both Guérin of Glapion and Ralph Tesson continued to take a prominent place in Norman politics after their retirement from office. The former was especially useful in Maine, where, by reason of his origin, he had many acquaintances.[274] In the end of March 1202 he was sent by John to the earl of Chester and to important persons in Maine and Anjou to secure vital adhesion to certain unspecified guarantees of loyalty.[275] In 1203 he followed the barons of Maine in deserting John.[276]

For a short time Philip Augustus placed him again at the head of

---

it is 16 kilometres from Evreux, and we must suppose either that the surveyors saved space by cutting across corners of the valley, or that another *vacaria* is meant, nearer to Evreux. For La Vacherie, see Charpillon, ii, 945–6.

[270] For Guérin and his estates, see Stapleton, *Observations*, II, ccxix *seqq.*, supplemented by Delisle in *Cart. Norm.*, pp. 153–4, and now by L. C. Loyd, *The origins of some Anglo-Norman Families*, 1951, pp. 46–7.

[271] *Rot. Scacc.*, i, 244.

[272] *Ibid.*, ii, 501, 502. Ralph Tesson was seneschal on November 23, 1201 (*Rot. Pat.*, 3).   [273] *Rot. Pat.*, 33b.

[274] Cf. *Rot. Pat.*, 14, 20.

[275] See *Rot. Pat.*, 8, and cf. note on enrolment of charter of suretyship by the archbishop of Canterbury and two others for the earl of Chester, *ibid.*, 7b. The erroneous explanation of these letters in the first edition of this book, pp. 257–8 and notes, should be deleted.

[276] He turned before Michaelmas, 1203, since in the Pipe Roll of that year Robert of Vieuxpont accounts for his land at Belboeuf among the escheats of the Romeis (*Rot. Scacc.*, ii, 552). References in the other rolls begin in October (*Rot. de Lib.*, 67).

Norman administration. He appears as seneschal in two cancelled enrolments of charters issued by Philip in his favour.[277] Memories of his doings are recorded in the *Querimonæ Normannorum* of 1247, where like another *novus homo*, William Crassus, he appears as a notorious robber of other men's property.[278] According to one of these complaints he had joined John again but returned to Philip. He was, however, finally deprived of his lands on the charge of having relations with the Emperor Otto.[279] In 1208, according to Stapleton, he made a pilgrimage to the Holy Land, from which he never returned, and his scattered estates, which had not had time to form themselves into a single honour,[280] were divided once more.

Note C. Norman Deserters during 1203

The following list contains the names of those who are known to have deserted John during 1203, and whose lands are recorded among the confiscations entered on the rolls. The list is not exhaustive, for, apart from omissions due to oversight, the barons and knights whose lands were not granted away must have been numerous, and their names are not entered in the records of *terra data*.[281] Moreover, the inhabitants of those parts of Normandy which fell into Philip's hands were not mentioned by name except in a few cases of those who, like Roger of Portes,[282] remained with John and received compensation, or of those who, like the count of Evreux, possessed lands elsewhere which were confiscated.

The names given in the list fall for the most part into two divisions, the names of those who followed the barons of Maine and Count Robert of Séez, and of those who joined Philip after the total loss of the Evrecin in May.

The men whose names are printed in italics possessed lands in England which were given away to others.

Argences, Richard of, hardly belongs to the list. He joined Philip apparently in 1202, having been farmer of the honour of Evreux, and his lands were distributed in the summer (*Rot. Norm.*, 53, 59). King John offered to pardon him on 16 Feb. 1203 (*Rot. Pat.*, 25), but he

---

[277] *Recueil*, ii, nos. 793, 802.
[278] *Querimoniae Normannorum*, nos. 516, 522, 527, 530, 549 (*Recueil des historiens de France*, xxiv, part i, pp. 68–70, 72).
[279] *Ibid.*, no. 530. Guérin had spoken with Otto, Philip's adversary, 'sine Hugone de Surgeriis, milite'. The confiscation seems to have resulted from double dealing during negotiations between Otto and Philip in this critical year.
[280] Guérin's lands are treated as one in a privilege of February 28, 1202 (*Rot. Pat.*, 6b): no plea regarding any of his Norman lands was to be put forward except before the king himself.
[281] e.g., the Exchequer rolls show that the land of Guérin of Glapion in the Roméis was escheated during the summer of 1203, but there is no reference to his desertion on the rolls before October (above, p. 173).
[282] Above, p. 171, note 260.

does not appear to have availed himself of the offer. King Philip
made him grants of land (*Recueil*, ii, nos. 793, 802). He took part in
a judgment at Rouen in 1214 (*Cart. Norm.*, no. 230).

Argences, Calvados c. Troarn.

Argences, Ralph of; lands in Lieuvin given away about 27 August (*Rot.
Norm.*, no. 103).

'Berners', Herbert of, a follower of Count Robert; land at 'Anescy'
given away 28 Jan. (*Rot. Norm.*, 71).

'Buelles', Helyas of;[283] Carevilla, in Caux, given away 10 May (*Rot.
Norm.*, 94).

Boulogne, Baldwin, Constable of. On 12 June grace given till 24 June
(*Rot. de Lib.*, 41). Confiscation of English lands 20 July, on account
of defect of service (*ibid.*, 50).

Cambernon (?) (Campus Arnulfi, Champernol), Jordan of; land in bailiwick of Tenchebrai given away, 9 May (*Rot. Norm.*, 93).

Cambernon, near Coutances, was held by a Jordan in 1172 (*Red
Book of the Exchequer*, ii, 636; Stapleton, II, ccxxxvii). See Lewis C.
Loyd, *Anglo-Norman Families*, p. 26.

'Campens', William of,[284] a follower of Count Robert; land at 'Aibri'
given away 26 Jan. (*Rot. Norm.*, 71).

'Channey' [=Chenay, near Alençon?], William of. Lands in bailiwick
of Falaise at Mesnil Renard, given away 26 June (*Rot. Norm.*, 71).

Chaunont, Geoffrey of, a knight of William Talvas, brother of Count
Robert; his land in bailiwick of Argentan[285] confiscated, 28 Jan.
(*Rot. Norm.*, 72).

Chaunont, near Roche-Mabile, of which William Talvas was lord
(Stapleton, II, lxxxvi).

Doucelles, Philip de; lands in bailiwick of Richard of Fontenay (Mortain) given away 31 Jan. (*Rot. Norm.*, 73).

Doucelles, s. of Alençon, near Beaumont-sur-Sarthe.

'Ernenville', Matthew of. Matthew was in France in June, 1202 (*Rot.
Norm.*, 51), and held in part of St. Ouen. His lands in Robert of
Vieuxpont's bailiwick given away 26 July, 1203 (*ibid.*, 100).

Ernenville perhaps is Ernentruville, the old name for St. Sever,
a suburb of Rouen on the left bank of the Seine. (Cf. *Cart. Norm.*,
p. 222.) Robert of Vieuxpont was bailiff of the Roumois in 1203.

Etouteville, Henry of; his English land at Kirkby given away 8 May
(*Rot. Norm.*, 92).

Etouteville (Stuteville) in Caux, near Yvetot.

Evreux, Amaury, count of; English lands forfeited before 8 May (*Rot.

---

[283] 'Clearly Bouelles, from the lords of which Shellow Bowels derives its
name', J. H. Round, in *English Historical Review*, xxviii (1913), 770. There
is a Carville, in Caux, near to Caudebec. The unusual name Elias belonged to
an 'Elias of Carville', in England, in 1166 (*Red Book*, i, 231).

[284] There are many possible equivalents of this name. Aibri is probably one
of the Aubri's near Falaise.

[285] Richard de la Tour, to whom the order is addressed as bailiff, was bailiff
of the Argentan (cf. *Rot. Norm.*, 61, 105).

Norm., 92). Apparently back again in October (*ibid.*, 110). See Stapleton, II, clxxiii–iv.

Ferrand, William; lands granted by king in La Londe and Caux (*Rot. Norm.*, 76, 99: 11 Feb., 25 July). A very heavy forest fine may have something to do with his desertion (*Rot. Scacc.*, II, 559; cf. *Rot. Norm.*, 90). The name is found in Norman records of the 13th century (*Cart. Norm.*, 664, cap. xxi, 1143).

Fougères, William of. See above, p. 166, note 234. For English lands *Rot. de Lib.*, 44.

Gisors, John of, does not properly belong to this list, though Tôtes, which was part of his escheated lands, was given away by King John on 11 May, 1203 (*Rot. Norm.*, 94). He had joined Philip in Richard's reign. See Stapleton, II, xxvi–vii.

Glapion, Guérin of. See above, p. 173. For English lands, *Rot. de Lib.*, 66, 67.

Gournai, Hugh of. See above, p. 161, and below, pp. 340–1.

La Houlme (Holm, Ulmo), William of; lands given away 7 and 10 May (*Rot. Norm.*, 92, 94). William was pardoned with Pain of Montreuil on 11 Sept. (*Rot. Pat.*, 34).

> Houlme, Homme, etc., is common. I have assumed that William came from the district north-east of Alençon.

Lascelles, Ralph of, a follower of Juhel of Mayenne; lands in bailiwick of Falaise given away, 31 Jan. (*Rot. Norm.*, 72).

La Londe, Odo of; his lands at Rougemontier (between Rouen and Pont-Audemer, in the bailiwick of La Londe) granted 11 Feb. (*Rot. Norm.*, 77).

Merlai, William of, a companion of Count Robert; land granted 26 Jan. (*Rot. Norm.*, 71). He was probably a member of the family which held lands at Grandmesnil, in the bailiwick of Falaise (Stapleton, II, xc).

Meulan, Peter of, son of Count Robert, see above, p. 161, and note.

Ménil (?) (Manil), Payn of, a follower of the viscount of Beaumont (Maine); land at Bretteville, in bailiwick of Falaise, given away 31 Jan. (*Rot. Norm.*, 73).

> There are numerous places of this name round Falaise and Alençon.

Montigny, Enguerrand of; lands in neighbourhood of Arques given away 10 May (*Rot. Norm.*, 93, cf. 95).

> Montigny, probably the place of that name near Rouen in the forest of Roumare. There is, however, a Montigny near Alençon; and Stapleton's map identifies Montagny, a hamlet north of the forest of Lions, west of Gournai, with an earlier *Montigneium.*

Neuilly, Garan of, a follower of Count Robert; Norman lands given away, 25 Jan. (*Rot. Norm.*, 70).

> Probably Neuilly-le-Bisson, near Alençon.

'Orte', Richard of, a follower of Juhel of Mayenne; land in neighbourhood of Domfront given away, 18 Jan. (*Rot. Norm.*, 69).

> Identified by Round (*English Historical Review*, xxviii, 770) with L'Orti (*Urtiacum*). Cf. *Book of Fees*, Index, *s.v.* Lorty, iii, 383.

Le Pin, Henry of; lands in bailiwick of William of Mortemer (probably near Pont-Audemer, in the bailiwick of La Londe, cf. *Rot. Scacc.*, II, 559) given away 10 May (*Rot. Norm.*, 93–4).

[Poignard, William, viscount of Caen, an important official, suffered confiscation in the autumn of 1203 (*Rot. Norm.*, 105, 110), and on 4 Dec., at Cherbourg, bought back the royal favour for 2000 li. Angevin (*Rot. Pat.*, 37); but it does not appear that he was a deserter.]

Séez, Count Robert of. See above, p. 158.

'Super Ponte', Reginald de, probably of Montfort, where he had land which was given away 26 July (*Rot. Norm.*, 99).

Thouars, Guy of, see above, p. 165. Swaffham, in king's hands by 11 Sept. (*Rot. Lib.*, 63).

'Tieneri', Richard; land in Lieuvin granted 12 May (*Rot. Norm.*, 95).

Troarc, John of; land in Oximin given away 13 July (*Rot. Norm.*, 98).
Troarc = Troarn, in bailiwick of Oximin, east of Caen. For the identification cf. *Rot. Pat.*, 28b. 'Abbas Robertus de Troarc.'

La Val or Laval, Guy of (Maine); confiscations from 16 Dec., 1202 (*Rot. Pat.*, 21b). For English lands, *Rot. de Lib.*, 49–50.

La Vacherie, William of; lands granted to his nephew (*Rot. Norm.*, 76). The lands included land at Mousseaux (Muches, *ibid.*, 84).
La Vacherie, near Andeli; Mousseaux on the Seine, south of Andeli; for the order is given to the constable at Chester, at this time castellan of Château-Gaillard and bailiff of Andeli.

Vernon,[286] Richard of; his lands in the Roumois and Côtentin given away 4–15 Aug (*Rot. Norm.*, 101, 102). See Stapleton, I, cxlii; II, cclxxix.

'Vilers', Richard of, a companion of Count Robert; his land at Potigny, in the bailiwick of Falaise, given away 7 Feb. (*Rot. Norm.*, 75). See Stapleton, II, xc.
Probably Villers, west of Falaise.

---

[286] Richard of Vernon, who held extensive lands in France (*Actes*, p. 278, no. 33: p. 31, no. 200, note) after the exchange of Vernon in 1195–6, apparently decided for France in 1203. In the Exchequer rolls of 1198 (*Rot. Scacc.*, ii, 449) and 1203 (*ibid.*, 530) he still appears in Normandy, see above, p. 108. He must not be confused with his namesake in England, who was sheriff of Lancaster.

N

CHAPTER VII

THE NORMAN DEFENCES

I

The feudal State was essentially a military administration, controlled by men who could fight as well as collect dues or preside in a court. During the reigns of Richard and John, Normandy was put to the most severe military test in the history of the duchy, and the records reveal an organisation in which the financial and judicial arrangements which have been described in a previous chapter, fall into a secondary place. We see a strong ring fence of fortresses, supported in the interior by the magnificent castles of Falaise, Domfront, Caen, Montfort. The defences of this extended frontier were organised on definite lines: knights and serjeants took up their appointed tasks in the castles of the March, and were reinforced by mercenaries drawn in small bands from a motley reserve of Welsh, Brabançons, Gascons, even Saracens. Along the main roads between these fortresses and the chief centres of Norman government, Rouen, Lisieux, Caen, Argentan, passed stores, weapons, carpenters' material, military engines; the Seine, carefully policed by a service of bailiffs, joined Rouen to Vaudreuil or Château Gaillard; and behind all lay the ports, Barfleur the chief, and the constant ferry[1] across the Channel. Administrators, some of them full of memories of the crusade with King Richard, and great barons who had learned to fight in the school of the young Henry, joined with a crowd of rising self-seeking men, with leaders of mercenaries, and with the king's clerks, in the service of this vast machine. The machine itself was fed by loans, aids and tallages collected with increasing frequency on both sides of the Channel.

This was the stage upon which the dukes of Normandy waged war. They fought with mercenaries and a depleted feudal levy. Behind the feudal and mercenary troops the arrière-ban or host, including the communal forces of the self-governing towns, lay in reserve. The campaign generally came to an end at the time of harvest, when an autumn truce intervened, followed, after the solemn Christmas feast, by a colloquy in January on Saint Hilary's day. If the colloquy were

---

[1] See especially the accounts of the *prepositura* of Barfleur, *e.g.*, in 1203 (*Rot. Scacc.*, ii, 505). One of the numerous entries reads 'pro passagio clericorum et servientium Regis pluries euncium in Angliam xxvij li. iiij so. per breve Regis'.

futile, war began again. There was little method in the fighting; it was an affair of forays and quick tussles in the open field, of elaborate sieges and defence in the castles, of booty, prisoners, and hostages everywhere. We must seek in writs and chronicles for the clue to this 'ordered insanity, in which king takes queen, and ace takes king'.

The frontiers of Normandy were not natural frontiers; only at one point, where the forests of Perche and La Trappe rise in broad folds, and the boundary turns north-westwards from the Avre, could a prominent barrier be seen. In the more important districts the fortunes of war had fixed a line along a river or across a plain. Hence in times of peace there was constant intercourse between the inhabitants on either side of the frontier, and in times of war there was certain devastation. Feudal custom and local commerce paid small heed to political distinctions. Fiefs of Gournai carried Norman law into the Beauvaisis. Along the Avre the lord of Tillières in Normandy and the lord of Brézolles in the Chartrain possessed rights in each other's domains.[2] Important barons who lived across the border, such as the lord of Fougères and the count of Perche, held lands in England and Normandy. The Bretons came in large numbers to the famous fair of Montmartin in the Côtentin—their absence from it in time of war seriously diminished the receipts of the Norman exchequer.[3] In consequence of this close intercourse special arrangements were enforced when hostilities broke out; for example, the custom of Vernon forbade the prosecution of suits of inheritance during the period of actual warfare.[4] Some rules applied to the marches as a whole at all times, such as that which forbade the sale of woods without the consent of the duke or his representative.[5] The problem of the marches was, however, most serious in ecclesiastical cases. The ecclesiastical and secular frontiers did not altogether coincide. The diocese of Rouen included the French Vexin, the diocese of Séez ran into Perche. During war the churches suffered severely, and the attacks were not confined to the property of the church which lay within the political boundary. At one time, in the year 1196, the questions raised by this condition of things were so serious that the archbishop of Rouen, in his outraged

[2] See the treaty in 1200, as quoted above, p. 171.
[3] Stapleton, II, ccl, and I, lxxx.
[4] See Lebeurier, *Coutumes de Vernon du xiie siècle* (*Bibliothèque de l'Ecole des Chartes*, xvi, 1855, p. 527). This French translation (fourteenth century) of customs drawn up shortly after the cession of Vernon to France reveals other interesting traces of the connection between Vernon and the neighbouring parts of France and the Chartrain. For example, Lebeurier finds a similarity between the mayor of Vernon, who was not a communal officer, and the mayors of the villages and bourgs of the Chartrain (p. 523).
[5] *Très ancien Coutumier* (Tardif, i, 28), c. xxxiii. The original Latin version is preserved in the Vatican MS., not known to Tardif, and reads 'Nemora non

dignity, forced the two kings to combine against him as against a third power.[6]

The open nature of the march gives the Norman castles peculiar importance in history. In this chapter I will first deal briefly with the legal position of the castle, and afterwards examine the line of Norman defences and the place of the castle in war.

Reasons of state have their origin in reasons of defence; only gradually are they explained by general considerations of utility. The earliest cases of interference with the customary rights of the Norman vassal concern the power of the duke over the castle, even the castle of a vassal. The customs of the duchy, as stated in 1091, not only forbade the erection without leave of castles and elaborate earthworks; they also allowed the duke to take possession of such as existed whenever occasion made it desirable for him to do so.[7]

It was one thing to insist that a castle should be licensed; it was another to claim the right of entry; and we may suspect that the latter right was of recent growth and showed William's clear apprehension of the fact that, if Normandy was to be strong and united, reasons of state must override feudal privilege. As a rule the policy of the dukes lay rather in the safer plan of checking the growth of fortifications outside the ducal demesne. In England the number of private as compared with royal castles was highest in the north and west.[8] In Normandy many of those of which ruins still exist do not seem to contain remains of later than the eleventh century.[9]

I have referred in a previous chapter to the policy adopted by the

---

vendatur in meatibus marchie, nisi assensu ducis vel ejus justitie', (Viollet, *Hist. litt. de la France*, xxxiii, 62.)

[6] See my article, *King Philip Augustus and the Archbishop of Rouen*, in the *English Historical Review.*, xxvii, 111 seqq.

[7] *Consuetudines et justicie*, c. 4 (ed. Haskins, *Norman Institutions*, p. 282). 'Nulli licuit in Normannia fossatum facere in planam terram nisi tale quod de fundo potuisset terram jactare superius sine scabello, et ibi non licuit facere palicium nisi in una regula et illud sine propugnaculis et alatoriis. Et in rupe vel in insula nulli licuit facere fortitudinem, et nulli licuit in Normannia castellum facere, et nulli licuit in Normannia fortitudinem castelli sui vetare domino Normannie si ipse eam in manu sua voluit habere.'

[8] According to Stenton, *William the Conqueror* (1908), p. 453, fourteen castles east of Gloucester, or about half of those known when he wrote to have been built in William's reign, were in private hands. [This statement and also the remarks in the text above should be reviewed in the light of later investigation; see, for example, S. Painter's article on English castles in the early middle ages in *Speculum*, x (1935), 321–32; and R. A. Brown on Kenilworth and other twelfth-century castles in the *Archaeological Journal*, cx (1954), 120–4.]

[9] *e.g.*, Briquessart, Le Pin, Le Plessis Grimaut, La Pommeraye, Brionne. See the lists in Enlart, *Manuel d'archéologie française*, I, ii, (1904), pp. 635 ff. This is not very conclusive, since so many have entirely disappeared.

counts of Anjou. Fulk Nerra shared the expense of his numerous erections with his immediate followers, who often were able to found new families which rose to great importance.[10] Although this policy led to much disorder in later reigns, the share of the count in the creation of the castles was not forgotten. The story of Château-Gontier is particularly instructive.[11] About 1007 Fulk Nerra fortified the site and entrusted it to a vassal, who was merely a castellan in charge; after some time he began to build a large and expensive tower, but finding himself unable to complete it, he left the work to Renaud Ivon, who worked hard and finished it. We cannot suppose that Renaud had no share in the completed structure, but, adds the narrator, 'the count, wise man as he was, retained personal lordship of the tower'.

Hence Angevin custom as well as hard experience had trained the counts of Anjou to continue the work of William and Henry I in Normandy. During the years 1141–5 Count Geoffrey took castle after castle; he first secured Exmes, Falaise, Bayeux, and the district between the Risle and the Seine, then worked steadily east, south, west, until the fall of Arques in 1145 completed the conquest.[12] At this time several great barons, in return for the rest of their land, gave up fortresses which afterwards became the centres of local administration; William of Warenne, for example, surrendered Neufchâtel-en-Bray or, as it is usually named, Drincourt, and Hugh of Gournai surrendered Lions-la-Forêt.[13] The submission of the baronage was completed by the suppression of the rebellion of 1173, when lands were confiscated, castles destroyed, and several important fortresses, including those of the count of Meulan,[14] passed into ducal hands. In the meantime Henry II had gradually continued his father's work, building a castle here, confiscating another there. In 1161 Montfort-sur-Risle, one of the chief fiefs of the count of Meulan was secured and remained in the duke's hands, separately farmed. The family of Montfort continued to provide castellans, but lost all proprietary

---

[10] Above, p. 27. Halphen, *Essai sur l'authenticité du fragment d'histoire attribué au comte d'Anjou, Foulque le Réchin*, in *Bibl. de la Faculté des lettres* of the University of Paris, xiii (1901), p. 22. Halphen points out that the word *aedificare* may refer to castles built by vassals of the alleged builder. In a list of Fulk's castles, he mentions those whose first castellans founded new families.

[11] Cartulary of Saint-Aubin, quoted in Halphen, *Comte d'Anjou*, p. 158.

[12] Robert of Torigni, ed. Delisle, i, 225–37, with Delisle's notes. Also in Howlett's edition in the Rolls Series, *Chronicles . . . Stephen, Henry II and Richard I*, iv, 139–50. [13] *Ibid.*, 235; Rolls Series, pp. 148–9.

[14] *Guillaume le Maréchal*, iii, 33; Robert of Torigni, ii, 35–6; Rolls Series, p. 256. The counts of Meulan were unfortunate at least three times between 1160 and 1200, but got back their lands in Normandy except Montfort and Pont-Audemer.

rights in the castle.[15] In 1166 the count of Alençon and his heirs surrendered the castles of Alençon and Roche Mabille: in this case the
local family continued to hold its other lands, but, at any rate until
the death of Richard, the custody of the castle at Alençon, which
became the centre of an important bailiwick, was entrusted to ducal
officials.[16] Roche Mabille was, later in the century, in the hands
of the count's brother.[17] In 1168 the count of Perche gave back
to Normandy the castles of Moulins and Bonmoulins.[18] Finally,
Henry II held at various times the fortresses of the Eure, Ivry, Anet
and the castles of the honour of Evreux.[19]

Many of these arrangements were not lasting; but Henry's rule
established several important principles. The right of the duke to
enter upon the castles of a vassal was exercised; indeed Robert of
Torigni suggests that the occasion of the surrender by the count of
Alençon was the evil customs enforced in the honour,[20] not military
exigencies or the suspicion of infidelity. With this right of entry was
established the right or, as the case might be, the duty of sharing in
the defence of the castles both in men and money. Thus Tillières on
the Avre was practically a ducal castle, in spite of the existence of
a nominal lord;[21] and so to a less degree were Conches, Neubourg
and Neufmarché-en-Lions, all of which played so important a part
in the reigns of Richard and John.[22] Gournai in 1202 was entrusted
to ducal commissioners. During the preparations of 1203 Stephen of
Longchamp was given a licence for the fortification of his manor at
Douville and a grant-in-aid was made for the purpose.[23] But the

[15] On January 31, 1200, Hugh of Montfort quitclaimed all rights to the
castle, admitting that the honour of Montfort was in the demesne of Henry II
when the latter died. 'Et sciatis quod nullo alio jure vel alique alia ratione
nisi solius nomine custodie honorem illum recepi, vel in manu mea habui'
(*Rot. Chart.*, 59). See Robert of Torigni, i, 329–30; Rolls Series, p. 209; and
Stapleton, I, cxviii.

[16] Robert of Torigni, i, 360; Rolls Series, p. 227; Stapleton, I, lxxiv. Ralph
Labbe was castellan and farmer in 1198, but was at the exchequer in John's
reign. The ease with which Count Robert IV surrendered Alençon to Philip
Augustus in January, 1203, suggests that he was in charge of the castle then.

[17] Stapleton, II, lxxxvi.

[18] Stapleton, I, cxxxiv.

[19] Robert of Torigni, ii, 68, 179; Rolls Series, pp. 274, 326.

[20] i, 360; Rolls Series, p. 227.

[21] Tillières did not become an administrative centre, but was in all other
respects in the same position as Alençon. The castle appears frequently in
the Exchequer Rolls and had its royal castellan. Cf. Stapleton, I, cxx; II, xlv.
The rights of the lord in the honour of Brézolles were secured by the treaty
of 1200. Above, pp. 171, 179.

[22] I can find no evidence for Stapleton's statement (II, ccxv) that Neubourg
was a ducal residence.

[23] Above, p. 164, note 228. The wages of the garrison were paid by the king
(*Rot. Norm.*, 75).

most important result of Henry's firm handling of the castles was that a clear distinction was drawn between ownership of a castle and local administration. When Henry began to reign this distinction was not clear either in England or Normandy; traces of the old confusion may be found in the vested interests preserved by later records.[24] In the reigns of his sons the castellan is rarely a local magnate.[25] He is a member of the administrative service, removable at will, sometimes acting as bailiff, sometimes confined to military duties with a salary.[26] Only during the last months of John's rule in Normandy, when he had spent his treasure and was forced to make what arrangements he could, do we find a tendency to return to the old beneficiary system. The process may be followed at Torigni. On November 9, 1202, the *prepositus* and men of Torigni were instructed that John du Bois was to be castellan: they were to obey him as constable.[27] In March 1203 John was ordered to surrender the castle and bailiwick to the seneschal;[28] it appears that the king, before giving John fuller powers decided to destroy the fortifications, since on May 12 the seneschal is directed to hand over the town and its appurtenant lands to John du Bois, after the castle had been levelled (*cum castrum de Torengy prostratum fuerit*).[29] It is uncertain whether the order was carried out or was countermanded, since one of the last acts of the king before leaving Normandy was to confirm the position of John by granting him the castle of Torigni with the service of the knights who held of

[24] The rights of the earl of Chester in the castle of Lincoln are a case in point; Petit-Dutaillis in *Mélanges Julien Havet* (1895), p. 378. The contrast between the state of things in 1154 and 1200 is seen vividly in King John's grant of 20 li. of the third penny of the county of Hereford to Henry Bohun *unde eum fecimus comitem Herefordie*, compared with the vast privileges granted in the beginning of Henry II's reign to Earl Roger; besides lands, the mote of Hereford with the castle, the shrievalty of Gloucester with the custody of the castle, etc. See *Rotuli Chartarum*, p. 52, and *Fifth Report on the Dignity of the Peerage*, p. 4.

[25] There are a few instances. For example, Robert of Roos seems to have been constable of Bonneville-sur-Touque in Richard's reign partly in virtue of his relationship with the Trossebot family. See Stapleton, II, lxxvi.

[26] For the administrative side of this change, see above, chapter iii. The place of the castle is seen in the wording of John's letters of protection for the abbot of Fécamp, July 27, 1202, addressed 'omnibus castellanis et baillivis suis Normannie' (*Bibliothèque de l'Ecole des Chartes*, 1904, lxv, 396). For the castle as the centre of justice, cf. the inquiry of 1258 upon certain petitions of the bishops: 'secundum consuetudinem Normannie cause super hereditate mote tractentur in assisia castellanie in qua sita est res de qua agitur' (*Olim*, i, 59–63). Cf. J. R. Strayer, *The Administration of Normandy under Saint Louis* (Mediæval Acad. of America, 1932), p. 20, note 9.

[27] *Rot. Pat.*, 20. In 1154, Torigni was in the possession of Richard, son of Robert of Gloucester. It may have come to John after the death of Richard's son, Philip de Creully (see Robert of Torigni, ed. Delisle, i, 287, ii, 58; Rolls Series, pp. 180–1, 269; Stapleton, II, xlv).   [28] *Rot. Pat.*, 26b.   [29] *Rot. Norm.*, 95.

the *castellaria*.[30] In any case John was now established as a baron on the site of a ducal castle. He received the service of its dependents and retained its revenues, loans and aids.[31] We cannot tell whether this reversion to feudal type would have become common in Normandy if local resistance to King Philip had lasted for a few years instead of a few months; but the story of Torigni is very suggestive.[32]

II

The Norman march[33] was strengthened by those great builders Henry I and Henry II in the exercise of the authority which has just been described. At the end of the twelfth century, the March was regarded as a military whole, varying in its course as war expanded or restricted the political boundary, but stretching from Eu to the bay of Mont Saint-Michel.[34] At the close of Henry II's reign, the boundary may be defined by the course of certain rivers whose banks had provided suitable sites for works of defence. Starting from Eu and ending at Pontorson, it followed more or less closely the Bresle, Epte, Eure (between Ivry and the junction of Eure and Avre), Avre, Sarthe, Mayenne, Colmont and, after an interval marked by the limits of the diocese of Avranches, the Couesnon. This line was only in part coincident with the ecclesiastical boundary of the province: thus, the Epte cut across the diocese of Rouen and separated the French from the Norman Vexin; and the southern portion of the diocese of Séez, containing Mortagne and Bellême, no longer formed part of the duchy; while, on the other hand, Roche Mabille (attached to Alençon) and the forts which protected Domfront on the Colmont

---

[30] *Rot. Pat.*, 36b, November 23, 1203.

[31] In July the seneschal was ordered to hand over to John the loan which he had raised from the men of Torigni (*Rot. Norm.*, 98). It is significant that Brandin, who had received the *terra* of Torigni before John du Bois (*Rot. Pat.*, 14b), received it free of tallage.

[32] The grant of the Channel Isles to Peter of Préaux (above, p. 76) is still more suggestive. English analogies could be found in times of war.

[33] MODERN AUTHORITIES. Stapleton, *Observations*; Adolphe de Dion, *Exploration des Châteaux du Vexin*, in the *Bulletin Monumental*, 1867, xxxiii, 330–66; and the same writer's *Etude sur les Châteaux féodaux des frontières de la Normandie*, delivered at the *Congrès archéologique de France*, 1876, pp. 352–74; L. Bonnard, *Une Promenade Historique. La Frontière franco-normande entre Seine et Perche (ixᵉ au xiiiᵉ siècle)*, Chartres, 1907. Léon Coutil, 'Le Château-Gaillard' in *Recueil des travaux de la société libre d'agriculture, sciences, arts et belles-lettres de l'Eure*, 1906, VIᵉ série, iii, 49–108, is useful for the defences of the Seine.

[34] *e.g.*, in February, 1203, when the march was restricted to the Andelle, Bartholomew the clerk of the royal chamber was ordered to pay wages at Douville, 'sicut aliis de Marchia fieri precepimus' (*Rot. Norm.*, 75); so for the men of Neubourg and Pontorson (*ibid.*, 77).

had been originally part of Maine,[35] and were still in the diocese of Le Mans. Whether traditional or recent the line was artificial; at its weakest spot, in the open plain of the upper Avre, Henry II is stated to have strengthened it by elaborate earthworks,[36] and at every point a strong military administration was required for its defence. Where the rivers flow along parallel lines, as in Caux and the Evrecin, it was possible to fall back upon a second system of defences. Thus, after the loss of the valleys of the middle Eure and the lower Avre in 1196, the Normans fell back on the fortresses of the Itun, supported by Conches, Neubourg and Breteuil with its forest; similarly on the right bank of the Seine, the Andelle with Radepont took the place of the Epte, and after the fall of Eu and Aumâle on the Bresle, the eastern frontier was withdrawn to the valley of the Béthune[37] in which the great castle of Arques lay.

Until the reign of Henry I the dukes were mainly dependent upon their vassals for the defence of this extensive frontier. Richard II, in the beginning of the eleventh century, seems to have adopted the practice of Fulk Nerra, for Domfront and Alençon were built with his approval by Ivo, a military engineer (*balistarius*) from France, and both these strongholds, together with the family fortress at Bellême were within the jurisdiction of Ivo's successors.[38] Yet Richard himself built his first important castle on the Avre at Tillières,[39] and a change of policy is apparent by the time of the Conqueror, who insisted on his right to control the castles of his barons.[40] It was Henry I, however, who after the anarchic administration of Duke Robert, first organised the Norman defences upon a scientific plan. When he was count of the Côtentin he had acquired Domfront, then in Maine, whose inhabitants had revolted against Robert of Bellême (1092);[41] and as duke he built, added and repaired on a large scale. The age of *motte*

[35] The land between Domfront and the Colmont was known as the district of Le Passeis, and was farmed as a bailiwick.
[36] A remark made by Robert of Torigni under the year 1169, seems to be the authority for referring the earthworks to Henry II: 'Rex Henricus fecit fossata alta et lata inter Franciam et Normanniam ad praedones arcendos' (ed. Delisle, ii, 13; Rolls Series, p. 242).
[37] This river was known as the Dieppe (*Deppa*) in the twelfth century.
[38] Stapleton, I, lxxi.
[39] Tillières (*Tegularia*) was in the eleventh century the key to the valley. The honour afterwards came to the family of Crispin. See Bonnard, pp. 22–3; Stapleton, I, cxx, II, xlv; Stenton, *William the Conqueror*, p. 77.
[40] At the request of his son William II, Robert of Bellême built the great castle at Gisors (*Ordericus Vitalis*, iv, 21). According to Dion it was a tower on a central mound (*Bulletin Monumental*, xxxiii, 334).
[41] Stapleton, I, lxxviii. Juhel of Mayenne finally surrendered the castles of Le Passeis (Gorron, Ambrières, and Neufchâteau-sur-Colmont) in January, 1162. See Robert of Torigni, i, 334; Rolls Series, pp. 211–12.

and ditch had passed, and a company of strong keeps, high and broad, rose to reinforce the scanty towers of Duke Richard's time.[42] In Rouen he built a great wall round the keep, in Caen he built the keep itself. In Arques, in Gisors, Falaise, Argentan, Exmes, Dom-front, Ambrières, Vire, Gavrai, Vernon, Henry built a keep;[43] also at Coutances, Evreux and Alençon.[44] Along the March he built new castles altogether; Drincourt and Lions-la-Forêt in Caux and Bray, Châteauneuf on the Epte, Nonancourt and Verneuil on the Avre, Bonmoulins on the borders of Perche, the new castle on the Colmont in Le Passeis, Pontorson over against the Breton frontier near Mont Saint-Michel, and in the interior Vaudreuil, owed their origin, accord-ing to Robert of Torigni, to King Henry.[45] Most of them still stood firm, their white stone work but little worn, when King Philip came.

Robert of Torigni is also our chief authority on the means taken by his friend Henry II for the preservation and improvement of his grandfather's work.[46] 'He improved or renewed nearly all his castles, and especially Gisors, on the Norman frontier. He enclosed with a paling his park and dwelling-house at Quevilli, near Rouen.[47] He built a marvellous lazar house near Caen. He renewed the hall and rooms (*cameras*) in front of the keep at Rouen. And not in Normandy alone, but in England, Aquitaine, Anjou, Maine, Touraine he worked at his castles and houses, either building new ones or restoring the old. Moreover, he built the castle at Osmanville on the river Vire.'[48] The rolls of the exchequer for 1180 and 1184 confirm and enlarge this evidence. We can see the king's men at work on walls and towers, mills and causeways.[49] A thousand oaks were felled for the construc-tion of the palace at Bur;[50] the forests of Caux provided palisading for the royal dwellings in the Côtentin.[51] Some operations, great or small, were paid for in 1180 at nearly every castle on the March,[52] and

[42] *Congrès archéologique*, 1876, pp. 368-74.

[43] Robert of Torigni, i, 164-5; Rolls Series, pp. 106-7.

[44] *Ibid.*, 197; Rolls Series, p. 126. It is possible that, in the cases of Evreux and Alençon, the duke built keeps in order to watch the local families, since these places were not in the demesne.

[45] *Ibid.*, 196-7; Rolls Series, p. 126.

[46] Henry II does not appear to have built many new castles, at least in Normandy.

[47] This afterwards became a lazar house, well endowed. See Stapleton, I, cxlvi; Delisle, *Actes de Henri II*, no. 486.

[48] Robert of Torigni, i, 331-2; Rolls Series, pp. 209-10; Osmanville was farmed separately in 1180. *Rot. Scacc.*, i, 8.

[49] At Osmanville, Condé, Argentan, Gorron, Domfront, Vire, Pontorson, and especially at Tenchebrai, Verneuil, Arques. *Rot. Scacc.*, i, 8, 17, 24, 27, 28, 29, 52, 84, 90; also Sainte-Mère-Eglise, Exmes, Moulins, Bonmoulins; pp. 98, 104, 105.　　　　[50] *Ibid.*, i, 30.　　　　[51] *Ibid.*, 31, 82.

[52] 'In margine etiam ducatus Normanniae fere omnia sua castella, et maxime Gisorz, melioravit vel renovavit'; Robert of Torigni, *l.c.*

especially in the Norman Vexin and the cluster of castles in or about the forest of Lions. It is also clear from the rolls that local responsibility had been defined: the revenues of Rouen were applied especially to the constructions in Bray and the Vexin, for these were the main defence of the city, but in the rest of Normandy the *prepositurae* were for the most part self-supporting or depended upon grants made from neighbouring budgets by royal writ. The system was by no means rigid and expenses of considerable magnitude, such as those incurred by the construction of the mills at Gorron,[53] were met by liberal subventions drawn from a large area; but small precedent appears in Henry's reign for the special efforts required in the reigns of Richard and John.

I will take as an illustration of this financial system the expenditure on the castles east of the Seine. In 1180 the chief outlay was directed on the castle of Beauvoir (*Bellum Videre*) in the northern part of the forest of Lions. The castle was important enough to be an independent *ministerium* and was in the charge of Enguerrand the Porter. Over £450 had been spent on the operations; and of this sum the revenue of Rouen contributed in the year 1179–1180 £353 4s. 1d., the farm of Drincourt £50 and the local farm of the ministerium £48 17s. 11d.[54] A remark that the greater part of this expenditure was vouched for by three local witnesses reminds us of a fact upon which the later Norman and English rolls often insist, that sworn 'viewers' were appointed to testify to the accuracy of the expenditure reported by the accountants at the Exchequer.[55]

The works at Lions-la-Forêt and Neufmarché had cost £112 5s., which had been paid out of the farm.[56] They included the construction of rooms in the keep at Lions, which had been heightened. Repairs at Neufchâteau and Neufle on the Epte had cost £87 3s. 9d., of which £40 had come from Rouen.[57] At Gisors the repairs of 1180 were not very great—they included a frieze (*echina*), repaired ditches, and a rope which cost 40s. for hauling up timber[58]—but four years later the valley of the Epte must have been very busy. King Henry had realised that the Norman Vexin would be the first object of his young rival's attack. A great military command which included, besides the bailiwick of the Vexin, custody of all the castles on the lower Epte and of Vaudreuil on the other bank of the Seine, was entrusted to William Earl of Arundel; and among the earl's duties was the

---

[53] *Rot. Scacc.*, I, 9, 14, 28. Moneys from Mortain, Le Teilleul, Domfront.

[54] *Ibid.*, 75, and cf. 70, 74. A comparison of these passages proves that the castellan had received more from Rouen than is accounted for on the rolls.

[55] The wording of the writ generally runs 'per visum et testimonium legalium hominum de visneto'. On the practice generally see the *Dialogus de Scaccario*, edit. C. Johnson (1950), pp. 89, 90.

[56] *Rot. Scacc.*, i, 73.   [57] *Ibid.*, 70, 72.   [58] *Ibid.*, 72; Stapleton, I, cxii.

direction of repairs.[59] For this purpose he received no less than £4270, collected from the English and Norman treasuries and from Normandy.[60] This money was expended as follows—the record may serve as an illustration of many similar returns in this and succeeding reigns:

Moneys received *ad operationes castrorum de Marchia*:

	£ Angevin
From the treasury at Caen through Herbert of Argentan[61] and William of Calviz[62]	600
From the English treasury through the same, £100 sterling =	400
From the treasury at Rouen, *de focagio*,[63] through the bishop of Lisieux, treasurer, and Herbert of Argentan	1700[64]
From the *camera regis*,[65] £100 sterling =	400
From Walter of Chanteloup[66]	200
From John *de Botell* (Bouteilles?) *prepositus* of Dieppe	200
From Alvered of Saint-Martin[67]	100
From Ralph, son of Matthew of Loriol	100
From Richard Beuerel[68]	100
From Richard Silvain[69]	260
From Saer de Quinci[70]	50
From Ralph of Frellencourt[71]	40
From Robert *Pratarius* (?)[72]	120
Total	4270

[59] *Rot. Scacc.*, i, 110–11.   [60] *Ibid.*, 110, 116, 118 *passim*, 121.

[61] This treasury official had previously farmed the forest of Gouffern (*Rot. Scacc.*, i, 17, 18).

[62] This financier seems to have been a large money-lender, for according to the roll of 1195, after his death, the exchequer confiscated his wealth in various parts of Normandy, *e.g.*, *ibid.*, i, 170.

[63] On the *fouage*, see Stapleton, I, xvi; Delisle, in *Bibliothèque de l'Ecole des Chartes*, xiii, pp. 104–5. In 1207 King Philip exempted the citizens of Rouen from the payment of this tax, which was levied every three years and in origin corresponded to the English *monetagium*. See Giry, *Etablissements de Rouen*, ii, 63.   [64] The roll says 1700 li. *sterling*, by mistake.

[65] Separate payments from the *camera regis* began very early (Haskins, *Norman Institutions*, pp. 40–1). Extraordinary payments went into this ducal treasury, which became very active in John's reign. Below, p. 237.

[66] In 1180 he was castellan of Beaumont-le-Roger, then in the king's hands: this subscription may have come from the revenues of this honour of the counts of Meulan. (*Rot. Scacc.*, i, 97.)

[67] *i.e.*, from Drincourt (i, 116).   [68] *i.e.*, from the Lieuvin (i, 118, 120–1).

[69] In 1198 he was farmer in the Côtentin.

[70] *i.e.*, from Nonancourt (i, 76, 117).

[71] *i.e.*, from the district between the Seine and the Risle (i, 100).

[72] An Anselmus *Parcarius* appears on the Roll for 1180 (i, 92), and Round, *Calendar*, no. 1282, but the abbreviation here is probably a slip for *Portarius*. Robert the Porter in Round, *Calendar*, no. 734, p. 268.

Expenses, *per breve regis*:

	£	s.	d. Ang.
Works at Gisors: re-roofing the keep, and expenses on the wall round the *motte*, the kitchen, the ditch outside the verge (*virgultum*), bridges, gates, wooden house within the bailey, base of the wall round the market	2650	1	11
Works at Neauflé on the keep and buildings (*domorum*) and heightening the wall and making the base (*pes*)[73] of the wall	195	4	8
Works at Neufchâteau-sur-Epte: heightening the walls round the *motte*, building a little tower before the door of the keep, and a wall to shut off the bailey from the castle,[74] repairing the houses and chapel of the castle	301	0	0
Works at Dangu: building a keep, repairs on walls, bridge and gates	208	10	0
For 29 shields *ad munitiones predictorum castrorum* (*i.e.*, at 7s. each)	10	3	0
For bows and swords for the same	5	0	0
For two windows in the king's chamber at Gisors	1	5	0
Carriage from Rouen to Gisors of 6 tuns of Poitevin wine and 27 English cheeses	2	12	0
Carriage of lead from Rouen to Gisors for the roof of the king's chamber and of the keep	1	12	0
For a bolt (*sera*) for the door of the keep at Gisors	0	6	0
The balance towards the earl's salary of £1000 'per annum pro custodia castrorum de Gisorcio et Neelfa et Dangu et Novo Castro super Ettam et Valle Rodolii'	894	5	6
	4270	0	1[75]

Our next records deal with the measures taken by King Richard after his return from captivity. In the war of 1194–5 the Vexin was lost, Caux had been wasted[76] and much damage done in the Evrecin and at Rouen and Vaudreuil in the valleys of the Seine and lower

[73] Stapleton suggests 'string course' (I, cxxxvi).

[74] This illustrates an interesting development of the 'motte and bailey' type of castle. A comparison between the plans of Arques made by Deville and Viollet-le-Duc suggests that a similar wall was built there. Château-Gaillard was built with an outer bailey in 1197.

[75] The extra 1d. is obviously due to a slip in the enrolment of one of the two entries at the beginning, *e.g.*, xxiijd. instead of xxijd.

[76] Instead of 1100 li. the *prepositi* of Dieppe accounted for only 600 li. in 1195 *pro guerra* (*Rot. Scacc.*, i, 235). Since Pentecost the port had been relieved of the payments from duties on hides, wool, and salt (*ibid.*).

Eure. The king seems to have been impressed by the strategic value of Vaudreuil, which, until the fortification of Andeli, was now the chief fortress on the frontier.[77] He also realised, as John afterwards did not, its relation to Pont de l'Arche, where an important bridge crossed the Seine at its junction with the Eure. Hence, although Richard paid attention to the other fortresses,[78] and especially to Verneuil,[79] his main care was the strengthening of Pont de l'Arche and Vaudreuil. The engineers in charge of the works were Master Urri or Urric and William Tirel.[80] Another castle which, owing to the temporary loss of Arques and Drincourt, came into prominence during these years, was Bellencombre, a few miles to the west of Drincourt, on the river Varenne.[81]

All previous efforts, however, were cast into the shade by Richard's activity in 1197, when Château Gaillard rose on the rock above Andeli with the unhurried speed and confidence of some magical creation. Like many great strategists, Richard preferred a bold, clean stroke in the open day to caution and intrigue. After the bickering and failure which followed the treaty of 1195-6, the king decided to clear the way by removing the archbishop of Rouen from Andeli altogether;[82] if the manor were once part of his demesne, he could control the river at the critical point, and cover the lines of the Andelle and the lower Eure. Above all he would have the opportunity of building a castle whose construction would be all his own, an experiment in all the newest engineering devices, based upon the latest experience in war.

In every case the construction of a new castle involved the settlement of new claims and some social readjustment. For example, the opening of suitable quarries or worksheds might interfere with private rights of ownership;[83] or, again, the service of the new chapel might lead to friction with the patrons of neighbouring parishes.[84] The story of such petty difficulties is very rarely preserved, and we know nothing

---

[77] It will be remembered that Arques and Drincourt, on the eastern frontier, were until the treaty of 1195-6 in Philip's hands, in virtue of the treaty of July, 1193. The payment of the garrisons, in accordance with the terms arranged in 1193, is accounted for on the roll (i, 137). See above, p. 99.

[78] Moulineaux, Orival, Moulins, Bonmoulins, Lions, Radepont, Osmanville, Gorron (i, 137, 222, 245); smiths and carpenters at Falaise (p. 270); engines of war, *perreria et mangonella*, refixed at Caen (p. 185).

[79] 'Ad operationes ville et murorum Vernolii dirutorum per regem Francie tempore guerre' (p. 233); 'in operationibus murorum castri de Vernolio' (p. 239).   [80] i, 156, 236-7; Master Elias was also employed (p. 137).

[81] *e.g.*, i, 137, 237.   [82] Above, p. 116.

[83] There are instances in this in the *Querimoniae Normannorum* or inquests of St. Louis, *e.g.*, at Bonneville-sur-Touque (*Histor. de France*, xxiv, nos. 24, 31).

[84] Compare a case which arose at Durtal in Anjou in the eleventh century. The neighbouring parishes claimed that part of the castle pertained *ad jus suum*. It was decided before the bishop and count: 'Ex antiquo esse consuetu-

of the revolution in the life of the old archiepiscopal manor which must have been produced by Richard's operations. A new bailiwick was created, and although the old town paid its farm directly into the exchequer, a handsome domain had been retained to serve the castle: it comprised meadows and vineyards, stretches of arable, woods, clearings and fishponds.[85] Royal officials collected the dues from the shipping of the river.[86] A new town was laid out by the riverside to serve the needs of the elaborate system of defences which bound together rock and water.[87] We can only imagine the local effects of the change. Fortunately, however, the exchequer roll for 1198 throws light on the building operations, and an inquiry of the thirteenth century survives to show King Richard at work on a similar task in Poitou.

When a young man of twenty-five years or so, Richard, as count of Poitou, had been impressed by the weakness of one spot on the road between Tours and Poitiers. Loudun and Mirebeau guarded the interests of the count between Angers and Poitiers, but Châtellerault, with its semi-independent lord, lay across the road to Tours. Richard decided to fortify Saint-Remy de la Haye on the river Creuse, a tributary of the Vienne which, during part of its course, separated Poitou from Touraine to the north-east of Châtellerault. In order to carry out this plan, it was necessary to make terms with the lord of Saint-Remy, the abbot of Maillezais. In 1184 Richard effected an exchange of territory, and promised to provide for a couple of monks who would continue to serve the church and inhabit the monastic grange at Saint-Remy.[88] He began to build a castle and laid out a town. A thirteenth-century inquest, arising out of a dispute between Count Alphonse of Poitou, and the viscount of Châtellerault, enables us, in spite of the conflicting evidence, to follow the history of this change of ownership.[89] A centenarian from Les Roches remembered

---

dinem in Andecavensi regione ut, si comes Andecavensis fecerit castellum in medio quarumlibet parrochiarum terre sue, ecclesia ipsius castelli tantum de circumjacentibus parrochiis obtineat quantum palus vel fossatum aut alia firmitas illius castelli in circuitu occupaverit' (Cart. de Saint-Aubin, quoted by Halphen, *Bibl. de la Faculté des lettres* of University of Paris, xiii (1901), 33; also by Marchegay, *Bibliothèque de l'Ecole des Chartes*, 1875, xxxvi, 395).

[85] *Rot. Scacc.*, ii, 449. Revenues for eleven months before Michaelmas, 1198.

[86] *Rot. Norm.*, 81. Writ to the constable of Chester and Henry of Rolleston: 'sciatis quod quietavimus dilecto et fideli nostro W. de Braosa unam navem de mala tolta usque ad summam quinquaginta li. de tali moneta qualem capitis de mala tolta.' The constable of Chester was castellan of the rock.

[87] This, and Saint-Remy mentioned below are good instances of the creation of towns for the sake of the neighbouring castle.

[88] Richard, *Comtes de Poitou*, ii, 230.

[89] *Comptes et enquêtes d'Alphonse, Comte de Poitou, 1253–69*, edited by Bardonnet in *Archives historiques de Poitou* (1879), viii, 39.

the prior of Maillezais holding the pleas of Saint-Remy eighty years
before; another witness had been present in the *platea* before the
monastery when the agreement of exchange was read, and Richard
and the abbot 'each had his part of the cyrograph'; a third, William
the monk, who had perhaps been one of the two monks left at Saint-
Remy, recalled how the monks had received the various rents and
dues,[90] and how, later, Richard and John had successively levied
them through their officials.[91] This witness and another, who had been
janitor, told also how the castle was taken by Bartholomew Payen
on King Philip's behalf and how it was destroyed.[92] Several others,
many of them advocates of the viscount's claims, spoke of the castle
and the town: one had seen the workmen at work and heard say that
Richard had proclaimed a free town there at five shillings the bur-
gage;[93] another spoke of the rich burgesses whose safety Richard
guaranteed against the hostility of Châtellerault—the new town meant
some loss for old towns; another had seen Master Philip, Richard's
clerk, giving over 'plots for a rent (*ad censum*) to Renaud Gorron
and his five sons and their heirs, and to many more, so that they might
build houses'. It would be a hard task to reconcile all these memories,
their chronology in particular; monk, baron, Templar, soldiers, and
peasants tell very different stories; but we can see rents, dues, and
forest, the mill and pond on the Creuse passing into other hands, walls
and towers rising, and the busy officials laying out the town.

Another record, the roll of the Norman Exchequer for 1198, is of
more direct value for the history of Château Gaillard than is this story
of Saint-Remy. The roll confirms and adds detail to the description
of Richard's work which has come down in the writings of William
the Breton.[94] We know from this chronicler that the king first fortified
and built a noble house on the Isle of Andeli, the most prominent,
though by no means the largest, of the islands which interrupt the
river at this point. Here the archbishop of Rouen had levied toll on
the shipping. The town of Andeli lies on the little river Gambon a

[90] 'scilicet frumentagium, avenagium, molendinum et exclusam et forestam
et alias res' (pp. 46–7).

[91] Master Philip, Geoffrey or Hugh Achard, Girard of Athée, Geoffrey de
Cella, are mentioned.

[92] pp. 47, 48. For the loss of Saint-Remy, see Richard, ii, 449.

[93] 'et audivet quod ex parte regis fuit ibi libera villa criata ad quinque
solidos' (p. 43). This reminds us of the artificial Norman and English towns
on the one hand, and of the Aquitanian *bastides* on the other. Cf. Henry II's
creation of Beauvoir in Maine: 'rex Henricus fecit castrum munitissimum
et burgum pergrande juxta haiam de Malaffre, quod vocatum est Bealveer'
(Robert of Torigni, ed. Delisle, ii, 14; Rolls Series, p. 243). For the development of urban rents at this period, distinct from the old *census* or *gablum*,
see Legras, *Le Bourgage de Caen* (1911), *e.g.*, p. 149.

[94] *Chronicon*, ed. Delaborde, i, 207–9; *Philippid.*, vii, 29–85 (ii, 177–9).

mile away, beyond the cultivated land (*Cultura*) which breaks the line of lofty chalk cliffs on the right bank of the Seine.[95] Richard proceeded to strengthen this strip of ground: a new town was laid out on the river, immediately opposite the isle, and just under the projection of cliff known as the Rock of Andeli; the two small streams by which the Gambon enters the river were diverted to enclose this town, and were checked sufficiently to allow its walls and earthworks to act as a dam; hence the lowest part of the valley, between the old and the new town, was turned into a pool, while the rest of the *Cultura* was occupied by the new town and a number of scattered buildings, ditches and defences (*hericones*).[96] The pool was probably banked in or intersected by a causeway which connected the two towns. The island and the new town (the present Petit Andelys) must thus have been very impressive. The spectator on the Rock saw the road from Tosny on the far side of the Seine protected by ramparts; [97] it passed by a series of bridges over the arms of the river and the long island of Gardon to the Isle; and the Isle, with its wall, tower, and palace, was in turn bound by another bridge to the new town; beyond the town lay the valley with its wide deep pool; 'and from the pool two streams, each of which might be called a river, flowed into the Seine in front of either entrance of the *bourg*'; and over both streams the king had built bridges,[98] and at the entrances and round about were 'towers of stone and wood, and in the spaces between were battlements and loopholes for the shot of the crossbows'.[99]

The whole series of defences was further protected by a stockade built across the river on the south side—a work rightly regarded, if we consider the strength and depth of the current, as one of the most marvellous features of these operations. The stockade and the battlements of the town were connected with the outlying works on the Rock; and above these rose Château Gaillard.

By the end of 1198 the valley of the Seine from Pont de l'Arche to the forest of Andeli had become a hive of soldiers and workmen, with Château Gaillard, clearly visible to the French from their castle of Gaillon, in the centre. Richard had bought out the monks of Jumièges at Pont de l'Arche,[100] just as he had bought out the archbishop at Andeli. Between the two places the river had been bridged at Portjoie, where there was a royal residence.[101] An advance work, called in

---

[95] Stapleton, II, xli.　　　[96] *Rot. Scacc.*, ii, 309.　　　[97] *Ibid.*
[98] The bridge over the Gambon, and the bridge Makade.
[99] William the Breton, i, 208–9. I have adopted Stapleton's translation (II, xlii).
[100] Continuator of Robert of Torigni in *Histor. de France*, xviii, 340; Stapleton, II, clxii. The manor of Conteville was granted in exchange. King John revoked the exchange.
[101] *Rot. Scacc.*, ii, 483, 485.

O

consequence Boutavant[102]—had been erected upon an island above the Isle of Andeli, opposite Tosny. The lord of Tosny was lent £100 for the defence of his house,[103] and on the east bank of the river, south of Château Gaillard, Cléry and perhaps other places had been fortified.[104] Thus the Norman Vexin, so far as it was still retained by the Normans, found a new centre in Château Gaillard, and the outlying fortresses in the valley of the Epte were no longer isolated.

The works at Andeli had been in charge of three clerks, Sawale or Sewal son of Henry, Robert son of Hermer, and Matthew son of Enard. Little can be discovered of these men, whose names appear here and there in the records of John's reign. Sawale farmed the issues of the Vexin, and was probably chief of the three;[105] he also seems to have held a serjeanty in Northumberland.[106] Robert, son of Hermer, was afterwards in charge of works at Vaudreuil, and was one of John's bailiffs there.[107] Matthew, son of Enard, had charge in 1198 of the prise of ships taken in war,[108] and in 1202 was promised a prebend at Angers.[109] They had been entrusted during 1197–8 with the vast sum of £48,878 13s. 8d., of which £15,000 odd had come direct from the Norman bailiwicks, over £18,000 from the royal camera, and £5600 from the treasury at Caen. The remainder was made up of the profits of prises and booty, ransoms, and the advances of money changers.[110] The money had been partly spent in wages and in works at places so far afield in the Vexin as Longchamp, Dangu, Gamaches; also in local operations at Cléry and Boutavant; but by far the greater part had gone to defray the cost of labour and material at the Isle and Chéteau Gaillard.[111]

[102] On the position of Boutavant, see Coutil, p. 79; Cartellieri, iii, 140. A place of the same name, once dominated by a castle, exists in Ireland between Charleville and Mallow, on the road from Cork to Limerick. See Lewis, *Topographical Dictionary of Ireland*, s.v. Butteavant.

[103] *Rot. Norm.*, 74. Ducal soldiers occupied Tosny in 1198 (*Rot. Scacc.*, ii, 310).

[104] *Rot. Scacc.*, ii, 310, Coutil, p. 77.   [105] *Rot. Scacc.*, ii, 311.

[106] Inquisitions of John's reign in *Red Book*, ii, 564: 'Sewale filius Henrici, terram per serjanteriam custodiendi placita coronae.'

[107] *Rot. Norm.*, 55, 75, 82. References to Robert also in *Rot. de Lib.*, 100; *Rot. Pat.*, 35.   [108] *Rot. Scacc.*, ii, 311.

[109] *Rot. Pat.*, 7b; if the Matthew son of Everd, king's clerk, there mentioned, be the same.   [110] *Rot. Scacc.*, ii, 309.

[111] I add the relevant part of this most important statement of accounts in a note at the end of this chapter. English readers will find a good account of Château Gaillard, based upon Deville's *Histoire du Château-Gaillard* (Rouen, 1829), in the second volume of Miss Norgate's *Angevin Kings*. Besides Deville, see also Viollet-le-Duc's *Dictionnaire raisonné de l'architecture française*, and the essays mentioned in the next note. [For plans, illustrations and some description in recent English works, see also S. Toy, *A History of Fortification* (1955), and R. A. Brown, *English Medieval Castles* (1954).]

The Isle of Andeli was a favourite residence of Richard's during the last two years of his life. It is clear that he personally directed the building operations around and upon the Rock, and if contemporary evidence did not exist, the magnificent ruins of Château Gaillard would still afford sufficient proof that he concentrated all his energy, skill and experience upon the work. It would doubtless be rash to argue that all the characteristic details of the buildings on the Rock were first developed by Richard and were entirely due to his study of the Latin fortresses in Syria; [112] but it is quite obvious that Château Gaillard marks a turning point in the history of western fortification; and it is incredible that Richard did not profit by his experiences as a Crusader. Apart from the boldness of the work as a whole, the structure of the elliptical citadel with its series of curvilinear bosses, [113] and of the circular keep with its wedge-like machicolation, [114] reveals a profound practical knowledge of fortification. The scientific use of military engines and other methods of attack had been brought in this age to such perfection that the existence beneath the walls of a single 'dead angle', or spot which could not be reached by missiles, might be the cause of disaster. The structure of citadel and keep, and to a less degree of the triangular advance work was designed to remove this defect, inevitable in a rectilinear fortress; and it was combined with a long sloping base (*talus*) from which the projectiles hurled from above would ricochet with increased force. [115] It has been pointed out by M. Dieulafoy that Philip Augustus was finally successful in the siege of the castle because he availed himself of the single defect in its scheme of defences. This defect was the protection afforded to the besiegers by the stone bridge which connected the citadel or second court with the outer court.

No Syrian castle combined all the characteristics of Château Gaillard. Some of them may be found in other western fortresses of this date; for example, in Pons, Etampes, Provins, Issoudun, La

---

[112] M. Dieulafoy, *Le Château-Gaillard et l'architecture militaire au xiiie siècle* in the mémoires of the *Academie des inscriptions et belles-lettres*, 1898, vol. xxxvi, part i, pp. 325–86; and the remarks of Coutil, *op. cit.*, pp. 68, 72–5. See also R. Fedden, *Crusader Castles* (1950), pp. 22–6.

[113] This enclosing wall of the inner court is the distinctive feature of the castle. 'It is preceded', in the words of M. Dieulafoy, 'by a *fossé* cut almost vertically out of the rock, and it consists of a chaplet of towers, or segments of circles on a chord of about three metres, which are united by strips of wall nearly a metre in width. Its *tracé*, elliptical in form, and its carefully conceived *profils* show profound knowledge. No *angle mort*, nor *secteur privé de projectiles* is to be found; the approaches and the *fossé* are covered by the fire of the garrison right up to the foot of the wall, and no sapper could touch any point in towers or walls, provided that the fortress was under the direction of an experienced commander' (p. 330).

[114] *Ibid.*, 333–4.   [115] *Ibid.*, 334.

Roche Guyon, Ghent. Nor could anyone who has stood before his rival's work at Angers or Gisors claim for Richard a monopoly of knowledge; indeed by his patience and subtlety Philip was the better engineer of the two. Yet we must regard Richard's wars in Normandy as a continuation of his fights as a Crusader. He was the chief soldier of his age; we may be sure that during the few years of his reign the unity of the soldier's life was never broken, and that his best talk was heard in the company of Mercadier the Brabançon or Master Ivo the Balistarius. He brought back with him from the east men who had been trained in Syria. Franks born in Syria, one of them from Nazareth, were among his artillerymen;[116] indeed, there is good evidence that he had brought back a band of Saracens to fight for him.[117] We are told that Greek fire—that terrible explosive—was used during these wars,[118] and if information were forthcoming the history of siege engines in these years would probably throw some light on the military results of the Third Crusade. We may think, then, that as he supervised the workmen at Andeli, Richard's thoughts often went back five or six years to the siege of Acre or to his visit to the great Syrian fortress of Margat.

III

Although the story of warfare which it has been possible to compile in previous chapters is in the main a story of sieges, the evidence is much too scanty to enable any modern student to follow in detail the wars between Philip Augustus and the dukes of Normandy. Indeed, it is probable that only a handful of persons were kept aware of all the military operations: only now and then did definite facts become matter of common knowledge. We are able to see from the terms of treaties and from casual letters enrolled by officials that, all along the Norman frontier, there was constant building, attacking, and destruction of fortresses,[119] of whose existence in most cases a piece of disordered ground, or perhaps a popular tradition, is the only record.[120] Fortunately, however, we are better informed about the organisation of the castle and its importance in time of war.

In the first place, it should be noticed that a castle rarely stood in

[116] 'Petro de Tanentonne et Martino de Nazareth et sociis eorum Arbalistariis liiij li. per breve Regis' (*Rot. Scacc.*, ii, 302). Cf. the reference to a Baldoin of Jerusalem (*ibid.*, ii, 301).

[117] I have discussed the evidence in the *Scottish Historical Review* for October, 1910, p. 104. The references are to *Rot. Scacc.*, i, 221; ii, 301; compared with text D. of the *Histoire d'Héracles* in the *Recueil des Historiens des Croisades*, Historiens Occidentaux, ii, 196.

[118] In 1195, when the French destroyed Dieppe (Howden, iii, 304).

[119] See, for example, the treaty of 1200, quoted above, p. 171.

[120] Bonnard, *op. cit.*, *passim*.

isolation, but was generally a part of a definite system of fortifications. Sometimes these arrangements were of a temporary nature, as in 1184, when the earl of Arundel commanded all the frontier castles from Vaudreuil to Gisors,[121] but more permanent affiliations can be traced beneath these extraordinary commands. In a few cases, a fortress relied partly upon its own strength, partly upon its intimate relation to a general system of communications. Thus Verneuil, with its triple town, earthworks and artificial ponds, was not only strong in itself; it had become the centre or objective towards which the energies of central Normandy as a whole were directed for the defence of the Avre. Behind it lay L'Aigle and Breteuil, upon the latter of which converged the road from Rouen by Neubourg and Conches and the important strategic route from Lisieux by Chambrais (the present Broglie) and Lire,[122] on either side lay the less important defences of the Avre,—Nonancourt, Tillières and Courteilles to the east, Saint-Christophe and Chennebrun to the west. The accounts of the bailiff of Verneuil, who was also the farmer, in 1198, gave a picture of its importance: there was frequent intercouse between Verneuil and the fortresses in the valley of the Seine;[123] the bailiff's expenses show that he supervised the administration of Tillières, and the defences of Damville, Courteilles,[124] and Cintray (to the north-west). Verneuil itself was the barracks of a little host of artillerymen and other mercenaries, one or two of whom bear strange-sounding names, and of mounted men-at-arms and foot soldiers.

Such great centres as Arques, Gisors, Vaudreuil, Falaise, and Argentan were, like Verneuil, places of national importance, intimately dependent upon the administration as a whole. Where this was not the case, a system of local grouping can generally be traced, such as is familiar in feudal history and in feudal literature. This grouping is naturally more marked in private honours, which, being on the whole more compact in Normandy than they were in England, could be organised as military units: the fifteen castles of the Widow Lady in the romance of the Holy Graal, or the more historical nine held by Robert of Bellême in Maine, find their counterparts in the *castellariae* of the honours of Mortain[125] and in France of Montfort-l'Amaury.[126] On the ducal demesne, however, the administrative

[121] Above, p. 187 ff.

[122] King Richard went by this road in 1194, and King John in 1203. See above, pp. 100, 165.

[123] 'Pro prisonibus captis in Gerra de Rothomago apud Vernolium [ducendis] et hantis et picoisis et venatione Regis et hernesio balistariorum pluries ducendis a Vernolio et Aquila apud Vallem Rodolii et Insulam de Andele' (*Rot. Scacc.*, ii, 311-2).

[124] 'Pro claudendo bailio de Corteilles de petra, ccc. li.' (*ibid.*, p. 315).

[125] Mortain, Cerences, Tenchebrai, Condé-sur-Noireau.

[126] Gressey, Haye-de-Herce, Richebourg, Gambais, Houdan, formed part

system often comprised a similar organisation of strongholds. Some of the groups were originally held by vassals or neighbours; others were due to official action; some again were more of the nature of federations, such as that which comprised the four castles of Lions, Neufmarché, Longchamp, Beauvoir,[127] or the union of Moulins and Bonmoulins; others consisted of a castle with subsidiary forts, such as Falaise and Pommeraye,[128] Vaudreuil and Louviers.[129] The erection of Château Gaillard brought with it the creation of a similar group of subordinate forts, Tosny, Boutavant, and Cléry.

We get a glimpse of the relations which were customary between the various *castellariae* of an honour, in an inquiry instituted by Philip Augustus into the rights of Evreux and Gaillon.[130] Until the occupation of Gaillon by the French king in 1193 or 1194,[131] it was part of the honour of the count of Evreux. The chief evidence was given by Geoffrey Barket, who had been the count's castellan when Philip besieged the castle. He pointed out the fiefs and woods which did not owe service at Gaillon, distinguished between those pleas which could be tried at Gaillon, and those which, involving a possible resort to the duel, had to go to Evreux;[132] and, finally, he enumerated the items which composed the farm of the estate. All damages sustained by the woods of Gaillon during the period of tenure by the farmers were assessed at Evreux; and the count or his bailiff enforced judicially the payment of stated alms and grants.[133]

The next fact which becomes clear from a study of available evidence is that the castle, from a military no less than from a financial standpoint, was inseparable from the surrounding or dependent area.[134] The *castellaria* or *châtellenie* comprised castle, lands, feudal duties and fiscal arrangements; it was an artificial bundle of property and services,[135] designed for the maintenance of the fortress and the

---

of the *châtellenie* of Montfort l'Amaury south of the Avre; Dion, *Etude sur les châteaux féodaux des frontières de la Normandie*, pp. 363–5.

[127] Stapleton, I, cxiii.   [128] Above, p. 72.   [129] Above, p. 107.

[130] *Cartulaire Normand*, pp. 21–2; no. 120.

[131] More probably in February, 1194. See the account of Philip's movements above, p. 97. For Richard's attempt to retake Gaillon, see p. 112, note 108.

[132] This is in agreement with a general statement made by the justices of Normandy in 1155 in an assize held at Domfront (Delisle, Robert de Torigni, ii, 241; Rolls Series, p. 333).

[133] 'si firmarii de Gaillon non persolverent elemosinas suas assignatas et feoda, justiciabet eos comes ad persolvendum, vel baillivus suus.'

[134] *e.g.*, Robert of Torigni, ed. Delisle, ii, 134; Rolls Series, p. 313: 'Quidam enim constabularius domini regis Henrici, Osbernus de Hosa nomine, qui castrum Caesaris Burgi, *cum patria que ad illud pertinet*, custodiebat.'

[135] I have not seen this stated elsewhere so clearly as in the following letter from John to the constable of Rockingham, dated Reading, April 13, 1216. (*Rot. Pat.*, 176b.) 'Precipimus tibi quod retentis in manu nostra ad castel-

profit of the lord.[136] Indeed, it is hardly paradoxical to say that it was easier to maintain a *châtellenie* without a castle than a castle without its *châtellenie*.[137] In war, the castle had to be an effective base for active operations. In 1193 King Philip demanded as sureties for the payment of 20,000 marks of pure gold Troyes the four castles of Loches, Châtillon-sur-Indre, Drincourt and Arques.[138] When in 1196 he recovered Nonancourt, his panegyrist refers to the success as the 'restoration of the castle to fiscal control'.[139] In both these cases occupation of the *châtellenie* is meant, for the possession of a strong-hold without its sources of revenue was inconvenient and unprofitable. This fact is stated very vividly by the biographer of the Marshal. It will be remembered how, on the intervention of the papal legate, Richard and Philip agreed in January, 1199, to a five years' truce, on the condition that Philip, while retaining during this period the Norman castles already in his possession, should surrender all claims to the control of the surrounding lands.[140] The advantage which could be gained from this arrangement was pointed out to King Richard by the Marshal. Richard evidently felt that he had been first tricked into a truce by the legate, and then insulted by a demand for the release of the bishop of Beauvais. After his interview he shut himself up in his chamber 'choking with rage like a wounded boar'. Only the Marshal dared to approach him. He called to him loudly to open, and spoke to him thus: 'Why be annoyed at such a trifle; you should laugh rather, for you have gained all. The king of France wants peace. Leave him the castles until the next passage to the Holy Land, but keep the land which belongs to us. When he can get nothing from the land and has to keep up the castles at his own cost,[141] he will find that he is carrying a heavier burden than a war. That is what will happen: I wager they will come back to-morrow.'[142] The Marshal's

---

lariam Rokingham maneriis de Geytinton et de Clive et de Brikestok et de Corby et custodiis militum qui sunt de feodo Abbatis de Burgo et tenseriis pertinentibus ad predictam castellariam omnia alia spectancia ad Vicecomitem Norhantonie et unde Vicecomes se intromittere solebat ante adventum tuum apud Rokingham, plenarie habere permittas dilecto et fideli nostro Rogero de Nevill Vicecomiti nostro Norhantonie.'

[136] It has been maintained by some writers that manorial monopolies in mills, ovens, etc., were due to an artificial organisation of this kind: the erection of a fortress involved the creation of monopolies. See C. Koehne's 'Studien über die Entstehung Zwangs-und-Bannrechte' in Lorraine during the ninth and tenth centuries, in the *Zeitschrift der Savigny-Stiftung*, 1904, xxv, 172–91.   [137] Torigni in 1203 (above, p. 183) may possibly be a case in point.   [138] Above, p. 99.

[139] The king 'in fisci castellum jura reducit' (*Philippid.*, v. 119, ed. Delaborde, ii, 129).   [140] Above, p. 123.

[141] In 1193, it may be noticed, the Norman and Angevin exchequers were responsible for the payment of the garrisons in the four castles surrendered to Philip.   [142] *Guillaume le Maréchal*, iii, 156.

advice was taken. William le Queu, one of Richard's most trusted mercenaries, who was at this time castellan of Lions-la-Forêt,[143] was given the task of harrying the French garrisons on the Epte, so that they could take nothing in the area subject to his command.[144] His band did the work so well that the French in Baudemont did not dare even to carry water from the spring outside the castle. Meanwhile William le Queu, disregarding the garrison in Gisors, continued to collect the ordinary dues and rents from the Vexin.[145]

Sufficient evidence remains to permit us to form a picture of the *castellaria* and of its economy. There are numerous references to castleguard as a form of military service,[146] and in addition, among the numerous services which were required in the management of any large estate, may be found the duties of work on buildings and earthworks.[147] The economy of the Poitevin honour of Chizé, which as described in the middle of the thirteenth century clearly goes back to the reign of Richard, is an excellent illustration of this complex of social and military relations. I have already referred to this document as evidence that the obligations of Henry II's assize of arms were observed in Poitou.[148] It begins with a statement of the services owed by certain vassals of the honour. Peter Payen, for example, is a liegeman of the count, owes military and riding services (*exercitus et equitatio*) and is obliged to go to the defence of the count's castle in case of need.[149] It is significant that the privileges enjoyed by these vassals in the lord's woods are particularly mentioned. No privileges were so jealously guarded by their owners or so carefully watched by the lords;[150] and when the bailiffs of Philip Augustus began to

---

[143] *Rot. Scacc.*, ii, 494; Howden, iv, 78.

[144] Evidently, after the loss of Gisors and the other castles on the Epte, the bailiwick of the Vexin, so far as was possible, found a new centre at Lions. Gisors had never been a self-supporting centre; see above, p. 69.

[145] *Guillaume le Maréchal*, iii, 157.

[146] *Red Book of the Exchequer*, ii, 632: Roger of Pavilli owes four knights during a third part of the year *ad custodiam de Lions*; cf. pp. 634, 636, 637. In 1247 Alexander, called the Abbot, a knight of Tournai near Troarn, claimed to be quit of dues and other charges, *pro quibus debet et tenetur ad stipendia propria custodire castellum de Wismes, i.e.*, Exmes. The exemption was enjoyed by his ancestors. (*Querimoniae Normannorum*, no. 545, in *Historiens de France*, xxiv, part i, p. 72.) For the duty in time of war, cf. the statement of the knight service owing to and by the abbot of Mont-Saint-Michel, in 1172 (edited by Howlett, *Chronicles of Stephen*, etc., iv, 349 *seqq*). On the text of the inquiry of 1172 see *English Historical Review*, xxvi (1911), 89–93.

[147] Delisle, *Etudes sur la condition de la classe agricole*, p. 83.

[148] Above, p. 25, note 24.

[149] *Etat du domaine du comte de Poitou a Chizé*, edited by Bardonnet in the *Archives historiques du Poitou*, vii, 75.

[150] See the very precise statement of customs in the *châtellenies* of Vernon and Paci in the *Cartulaire Normand*, nos. 199, 200, p. 30.

press hardly upon the Normans after the French conquest, it is note-worthy that a large proportion of their encroachments are alleged to have been made upon customary rights enjoyed in the ducal forests.[151] After the statement of these services and rights our document gives a careful list of the furniture and armoury of the castle at Chizé, such as Philip Augustus ordered to be drawn up in his Norman castles.[152] This is followed by a description of the parishes in the domain, of which twenty-one are named.[153] Widows, we may note, are exempted from tallage.[154] The *servientes feodati* are of special interest for our purpose. Geoffrey Ribemont had the duties of finding wood for the hospice of the count in the castle, of serving the kitchen with water and of attending upon the knights of the count for the washing of hands. For each of his services he had definite payments in loaves and wine, and in the scraps from the kitchen, while in virtue of his service of water he was free of all the ordinary dues and obligations.[155] Two fishermen and a farrier are mentioned. Peter Ostenc, the janitor of the town, was responsible for the keys, was paid in fixed dues on merchandise, and had as his perquisite the broken gates which could not be mended.[156] There were also the man who found wood for utensils, the dog keeper, the huntsman and the man at the lazar house. The customary tenants in the bailiwick of Fosses owed cartage services, as they did in the reign of King Richard;[157] wherever bullocks could go and draw the catapults and other great siege engines, they owed these services; moreover, when they were summoned it was their duty to carry palisading to the castle; and all these services, with the more general duties of riding and of service in the host and payment of tallage, they owed at their own cost.[158]

Some such system as this must be imagined to have existed in the ducal castles of Normandy. In times of peace these great erections of wood and stone were busy with life. No piece of land was unused: up to the very walls everything that was not reserved for the duke's private disposal,[159] was carefully farmed,[160] if it was not actually in

---

[151] *Querimoniae Normannorum, passim.*

[152] For Philip's stocktaking, see *Cartulaire Normand*, nos. 214, 215, pp. 33, 34 and in Register A, ff. 6, 90v–91.   [153] *Archives historiques du Poitou*, vii, 79.

[154] *Ibid.*, p. 80. 'vidue, quam diu sint vidue, non talliabantur.'

[155] *Ibid.*, p. 85, cf. 81.

[156] In Normandy, as a rule, the porter of the castle was paid a wage.

[157] *Archives historiques du Poitou*, vii, p. 97, 'sicut fecerunt tempore regis Ricardi'. A charter of Richard is quoted in the course of the inquiry, p. 123. It is probable that in Poitou, as in Normandy, the charters of John were invalid.   [158] *Ibid.*

[159] *e.g.*, the *turris*, chestnut-grove, and various pieces of land at Avranches were not farmed. *Rot. Scacc.*, i, 11; ii, 289. Delisle, *Introduction* to the *Actes de Henri II*, p. 345.

[160] The bailiff of Argentan accounted for 65s. 'de terra mote in Argentomo'

private hands; a new tower or ditch might involve the payment of compensation to some customary tenant.[161] And when the castle was the centre of an administrative district, the area and intensity of its economy were greatly increased. A hundred points of law and custom depended upon the existence of a mighty keep, whose military purpose, though never forgotten, had been overgrown by a variety of new functions and duties. Its maintenance was largely due to the labours and bargains of men who had built up the little town under its protection. Distant monasteries and local hospitals and lazar houses were supported from its revenues. In the castle hall the justices and the bailiff did justice over the countryside and kept an eye on the Jews who were allowed to transact their dangerous and increasingly complicated business.[162] All kinds of men met in the streets of the town—clerks with royal writs, recognitors, claimants, knights and servants conveying the royal treasure, falconers and dog-keepers with their precious charges; men with wine, fish, building stone, paling, rope and bundles of shafts or pikes; merchants, pilgrims, monks on the business of their houses;—they can all be seen as one turns the pages of royal letters and accounts.

In time of war came new activities. Repairs were hurried on, the ditches were cleaned out, and perhaps buildings were removed which might provide shelter for the enemy.[163] Some high official might come on a tour of inspection, to direct the necessary increase in the garrison and make arrangements for its payment. A special castellan might be sent down, with a force of mercenaries and a royal clerk; and on their behalf letters and writs were issued from the ducal chancery directing the payment of treasure or the immediate despatch of victuals and ammunition, so that, stocked and garrisoned, the castle might be ready for the enemy.[164]

One of the most vivid pictures of war in the twelfth century was drawn by Jordan Fantosme in his chronicle of the war in England during the rebellion of 1173.[165] In these rough but stirring verses we

---

(*Rot. Scacc.*, i, 20). This may, however, have been the site of an earlier castle. Compare, however, the 'camera domus Ricardi de Bailloul que est in fossato Regis' (*ibid.*).

[161] In 1247 there were outstanding claims for compensation by a person whose property King Philip had taken when he built a new tower at Falaise: *Querimoniae Normanniae*, no. 419. King John's *fossé* at Falaise had involved similar interference with private interests, nos. 403, 457.

[162] See below, p. 240.

[163] In 1206 the viscount of Thouars razed and transferred elsewhere a hospital near the ditch of his castle. His charter is quoted from the Fonteneau MSS. in *Mém. de la Société des Antiquaires de l'Ouest* (1839), iv, 182.

[164] See note B at the end of this chapter.

[165] The metrical chronicle of Jordan Fantosme, in Howlett, *Chronicles of the reigns of Stephen, Henry II, and Richard I*, iii, 201. Fantosme was an

can see in action the simple mechanism of which the castle was the centre. The young king Henry is in rebellion against his father in Normandy, while the Earl of Leicester and others lead the rising in England. The old king is across the sea, but he knows how every stronghold lies and how it is held; he sees the north of England as though he were reading a plan. The messengers bring him news. It appears that forty days are ample time in which to ride from Wark or Alnwick to Southampton, to cross the Channel, find the king, and return. 'The messengers depart, they spur their horses, on the great paved roads they slacken their reins. The horses are very good, which gallop under them.'[166] Throughout the poem we feel how enormous was the value of the horse:[167] the loss of the war horse is as serious as the loss of many soldiers who do not wear armour. The young king, on his part, sends messengers to Scotland; he writes a letter in French (*en Romanz*) and seals it with a ring.[168] He has a friend in Count Philip of Flanders, who sends Flemings to help King William of Scotland; and hundreds more are with the earl of Leicester. How the English hate the Flemings! They come for wool; they are mostly weavers, not true knights; they are mercenaries in a strange land. They are a bold race, and good fighters, but they are destroyed; they will never again cry 'Arras'. At the battle of Fornham 'they gathered the wool of England very late. Upon their bodies crows and buzzards descend, who carry their souls to the fire which never burns . . . . There was not in the country a villein or clown who did not go to kill Flemings with fork and flail. The armed knights intermeddled with nothing except the knocking down, and the villeins did the killing. By fifteens, by forties, by hundreds and by thousands they made them by main force tumble into the ditches.'[169] While the earl of Leicester fails in the Midlands, the king of Scotland goes from castle to castle in the north country. We see how casual an ordinary siege is, how easily the besiegers are diverted if they meet with resistance, if the castle is well stocked with corn and wine and the commander is loyal. Council is taken, the marshals come and go among the tents, serjeants and esquires fold the tents and take down the pavilions, and the huts are burnt. At Appleby there is only an aged castellan,

---

eyewitness of some of the events which he describes. On his life, see Howlett's preface, vol. iii, pp. lx–lxvi.

[166] ll. 317–19, p. 230. Here, as elsewhere, I give Howlett's translation.

[167] Compare the reference to Odinel of Umfraville's horse, ll. 1669, 1671, p. 342; and Howden's remarks on the old horse of Philip Augustus: 'super Morellem senem, quem, inquiuut, decem annos habuit' (iv, 59). The value of the war horse as a prize won in war or the tourney might be illustrated from the Marshal's life and from the rolls.

[168] *Chronique de Fantosme*, l. 246, p. 224.

[169] ll. 1060–2, 1085–91, pp. 292–4.

Gospatric the Englishman, and the castle is not properly garrisoned; it is soon taken. At Brough there is a small number of knights. They are driven from the stockade into the keep, and are burnt out; they have to surrender; but a knight who has newly arrived, goes back, hangs two shields on the battlements, and until the fire destroys them, hurls javelins and sharp stakes at the Scots. As a result of the capture of Appleby and Brough Carlisle is cut off from Richmond; corn and wine cannot reach it, and it is in great danger. We see, too, how the open country fares. The plan everywhere is—'first destroy the land, then one's foe'.[170] At Prudhoe they do not lose inside as much as might amount to a silver penny; 'but their fields they have lost with all their corn, and their gardens were stripped by those bad people; and he who could do no more damage took it into his head to bark the apple-trees; it was a mean revenge'.[171] We see the desecration of churches, and women fleeing to the monastery, and peasants led by ropes. Then the army of relief is got together, four hundred knights and more; the archbishop of York sends sixty. King William is surprised at the siege of Alnwick. There is much good fighting; but the king and his knights have to surrender. The victors send a messenger, who rides hard for three days, 'by day and night he fatigues himself with journeying'. Meanwhile King Henry has crossed the Channel and has been met by the loyal Londoners. He is at Westminster, heavy of heart. All his knights have gone to rest when the news comes: 'the king was leaning on his elbow, and slept a little, a servant at his feet was gently rubbing them; there was neither noise nor cry, nor any who were speaking there, neither harp nor viols nor anything was sounding at that hour, when the messenger came to the door and gently called.'[172]

NOTES TO CHAPTER VII

NOTE A. EXPENDITURE AT CHÂTEAU GAILLARD, 1197–8
(*Magni Rotuli Scaccarii Normanniae*, ii, 309–10)

In operationibus Belli Castri de Roka[173] et Castri de Insula et domorum Regis de Insula et [in] operationibus domorum et hericonorum et fossatorum de Cultura et in operationibus domorum Ville de subtus Rokam et in operationibus de pontibus et breticis et hericonibus de versus Toenie, scilicet:

---

[170] 'Primes guaster la terre et e puis ses enemis', l. 451, p. 242.

[171] ll. 1682–5, pp. 342, 344.

[172] ll. 1960, 1962–6, p. 366.

[173] This gives us the first official name of the new castle. The name Castrum Gaillart appears in official acts of King Philip from 1203. See *English Historical Review* (1912), xxvii, 117.

	£	s.	d.	Angev.
In virga et palo	1700	3	0	per breve Regiis
Boskeroniis [174] qui prostrabant et escaplebant maremia ad predictas operationes . .	2320	0	0	per idem breve
Carpentariis qui operabantur predicta maremia postquam fuerunt in platea apportata ad faciendas predictas operationes . . .	3350	3	6	,,
Minutis operariis, scilicet, hotariis oisereorum, paleorum, mortereorum, chivereorum, baiardeorum, [175] portatoribus aque in barillis et custodibus predictorum operariorum . .	9730	0	0	,,
Portatoribus maremiorum et quarellorum taillatorum	1004	5	4	,,
Fabris et in carbone forgeriarum ad predictas operationes faciendas	250	0	0	,,
Vigilibus et portariis predictorum castrorum .	543	0	0	,,
Flechariis qui faciebant flechas [176] ad engueinnas, sagittas et quarellos	202	0	0	,,
Minatoribus qui fecerunt bovas et scinderunt fossata de Roka et cellaria [177] . . .	1780	19	0	,,
In quaretereia [178] et costamento asinorum et asinariorum et in hernesio equorum et asinorum	4040	0	0	,,
In maconnereia	5520	1	0	,,
Quariatoribus qui trahebant petram de quarelliis	2600	5	6	,,
Tailliatoribus petre ad muros faciendos . .	2600	0	0	,,
In navibus et batellis qui aportabant maremium et petram	1700	5	0	,,
Reatoribus qui faciebant et apportabant calcem [179]	4010	0	0	,,
Pro sablone trahendo et apportando . .	1500	0	0	,,
Pro ferro ct clavis et acero [180] et plumbo et estaimmo [181] et quarellis et ferris engainnarum et portis castrorum ferrandis, pro seris et toroillis [182] ad portas	455	0	0	,,
Pro plastro ad camina et areas camerarum plastrandas [183]	80	0	0	,,

[174] Woodmen.   [175] Hodmen with baskets, mortars, handbarrows, tubs.
[176] Bolts.
[177] Probably the cellars under the courtyard, opening on to the *fossé* between the court and the castle proper. Both this *fossé* and the great *fossés* before and behind the triangular advance work had to be cut in the rock.
[178] Cartage.   [179] Lime workers.
[180] Steel.
[181] Tin.
[182] Locks and bolts.
[183] Plastering chimney pieces and floors

	£	s.	d.	Angev.
Pro cordis et caablis	185	0	0	,,
Pro claudando castro de Insula de petra .	1250	0	0	,,
Pro iij puteis in castro de Roka faciendis[184] .	300	0	0	,,
Pro ponte super aquam de Gamboon faciendo[185]	30	0	0	,,
Pro ponte de inter duas insulas faciendo[186] .	120	0	0	,,
Pro ponte Makade faciendo[187] . . .	25	0	0	,,
Pro ponte qui vadit per mediam Insulam de Gardon	60	0	0	,,
Pro molinis et domibus molendinorum de Andele faciendis	100	0	0	,,
Pro vivario Regis de super Andele faciendo[188]	194	0	0	,,
Pro iij navibus emptis	53	0	0	,,

The rest of the money in the hands of the clerks was expended in pensions, the wages of soldiers, and at outlying places.

NOTE B. THE ACCOUNTS OF THE HONOUR OF EVREUX IN 1198, SHOWING THE PREPARATIONS FOR WAR (*Rotuli Scaccarii Normanniae*, ij, 462–4)

The following statement of accounts made by Richard of Argences in 1198 as farmer of the honour of Evreux, at this time in ducal hands, is an excellent illustration of the manner in which a castle and town were organised for defence. I have summarised and tabulated the entries.

A. The farm, £560 Angevin, was spent as follows:

	£	s.	d.
In customary alms and charges[189] . . .	235	15	10
To the forester	3	4	8

[184] For the three wells, cut through the rock, see Coutil, p. 66.

[185] The bridge at the south end of the new town over the main stream of the Gambon.

[186] According to Stapleton and Coutil, *not* the bridge between the Isle and the island of Gardon, but between the Isle and the new town.

[187] The bridge at the north end of the new town over the other stream of the Gambon: according to Stapleton, named after the mercenary Mercadier.

[188] Stapleton regards the pond as the same as the pool behind the new town. In this case the name Andeli was at once given to the new town, otherwise described as the 'villa de subtus Rokam'. This seems to me to be very unlikely: it would mean that the new town was separated financially from the Isle and the rock, since the *villa de Andele* accounted separately at the Exchequer for the year 1197–8 (*Rot. Scacc.*, ii, 449), whereas town and castle usually formed a single *prepositura* in Normandy. Again, it is unlikely that rents were collected at the new town as early as the autumn of 1197, although they would naturally be collected at the old town as soon as the agreement between the king and the archbishop of Rouen had been reached. I conclude, therefore, that the store pond in question was made above the old town.

[189] These charges on revenue show that the farmers were carrying on an established financial system (cf. above, p. 46). It should be noticed, however, that the payments to the religious houses and churches of Evreux do not

	£	s.	d.
In works at the castle and on the hedges (*haiae*) of the forest, and in the repair of tubs and casks .	189	2	4
In the carriage of stores for the castle, *i.e.*, of wine, bacon, cheeses, salt, from Rouen . . .	10	14	0
To Robert Rossell, out of the *prepositura* of Avrilli	50	0	0
For 30 *muids* of wine kept in store in the castle, out of the farm[190]	60	0	0
In the execution of justice	1	12	2
	550	9	0 [191]

B. The loan levied in the bailiwick of Evreux, £10 each from eight citizens, amounted to £80. It was spent as follows:

	£	s.	d.
In the wages of knights, men-at-arms (*servientes*) and *balistarii*, by the king's writ . . .	48	10	0
In the same, and in the wages of watchmen and porters	97	0	0
	145	10	0
Surplus owing to Richard of Argences . .	65	10	0

C. The tallage collected in the bailiwick for the maintenance of men-at-arms on the March, amounted to £183 10s.:

	£	s.	d.
In the wages of one hundred men-at-arms staying at Evreux	216	13	4
To surplus aforementioned (B) . . .	65	10	0
	282	3	4
Surplus owing to Richard of Argences . .	98	13	4

D. The tallage collected in the bailiwick (here styled the Honour) for repairing the ditches of Evreux and palisading the walls of the castle,[192] amounted to £190 2s. 6d. This sum was exactly expended for this purpose.

E. Receipts of Richard of Argences from the Norman government, which were intended for the equipment (*munitio*) of the castle. These

---

correspond to the charges contained in *Cart. Norm.*, no. 117, p. 21, which purports to be a list of *elemosinae* paid from Evreux and Paci.

[190] The vineyards are expressly mentioned as contained in the farm.

[191] The discrepancy between this total and the farm of £560 is not noticed. Possibly some entries were accidentally omitted or wrongly transcribed.

[192] See above, p. 202.

were delivered to Thomas the Breton, who was in charge of the castle.[193] The following stores are mentioned[194]:

(a) 90 carcases of hogs (*bacones*), of which Thomas the Breton received 52½. Richard of Argences owed £9 7s. 6d. for the remaining 37½ (*i.e.*, 5 shillings for each carcase).

(b) Grain: 4 measures (*modii*) of heavy grain, 15 of wheat, and, from Stephen Longchamp, 8 setiers (*sextarii*) and 1 *mina* of pease. Richard owed the sum of £17 15s. for the grain which Thomas the Breton did not use. The details are given, and show that a measure of heavy grain, a measure of wheat, and a measure of pease were each reckoned at £3.[195]

(c) Wine: 15 tuns and 1 butt were received of Poitevin wine. Thomas the Breton had 10 tuns; the rest was spoiled. For the latter Richard of Argences owed £4 8s. (*i.e.*, 16 shillings the tun).

(d) Cheeses: 63 cheeses from England.

(e) Salt: half a *peisa*, and 2 *summae*.[196]

(f) Engines and ammunition: 12 dozen cords; cords to bind the mangonells; 7 slings for the *petreriae*; 8 *balistae*; 6,200 bolts or quarells; 4,000 arrows *ad quarellos*; 1 grindstone; 8 iron darts (*esperduita*); 7 spikes; 8 ironbound tubs; 1 handmill.

	£	s.	d.
The debts under section E amounted to . . .	31	10	6
Aforementioned surplus owing to Richard of Argences	98	13	4
Surplus owing to Richard	67	2	10[197]

[193] Cf. ii, 457. 'In liberacione Thome Britonis se x milite missi apud Ebroicas xl. li.', from the proceeds of the loan raised in Pont-Audemer.

[194] It seems clear, from entries on p. 413, that Richard of Argences bought some of the stores as part payment of his fine.

[195] These prices were by no means normal. During this year the measure of wheat cost £9 12s. od. at Evreux (*Rot. Scacc.*, ii, 462, 463, where this sum is paid instead of the customary alms of a measure of wheat). Either Richard of Argences is charged a wholesale price paid by the government, or this money is a kind of fine to cover waste. In no part of Normandy was the price of wheat so low as this in 1198. For prices, see Delisle, *Etudes sur la condition de la classe agricole*, pp. 591, 592; for the measures of grain, see pp. 539 *seqq.*, especially p. 544. The measure (*muid*) contained 12 setiers, and 24 mines: these latter contained a varying number of bushels.

[196] The *poise* apparently contained 18 mines; and the *somme* about 4; Delisle, *op. cit.*, pp. 568, 543.

[197] This sum is credited to Richard of Argences in another part of the roll (p. 413) towards the payment of his enormous fine of 1000 silver marks sterling (see *Rot. Scacc.*, i, 245) of which he still owed 439 marks, and 7s. 10½d. in sterling money in 1198. The silver mark was worth £2 13s. 4d. in Angevin money. Stapleton remarks (II, cviii) that the size of the fine 'is indication of the vast profits which the officers employed in the collection of the revenue were enabled to appropriate to themselves, and which, when labouring under the royal displeasure, they were compelled in this manner partly to disgorge'.

CHAPTER VIII

WAR AND FINANCE

In this chapter I shall first discuss the information contained in the records upon the structure, organisation and maintenance of the army in Normandy; and in the second place turn to consider two or three matters of a more general nature arising out of this discussion. The material is meagre and scattered, but it seems desirable to make as much use as possible of the administrative diary which the Chancery rolls of King John's reign contain—the first diary of its kind in English or Norman history.

I

The old national system of the feudal host supported by a national levy still existed in Normandy in 1204 as the chief factor in time of war. The system was badly strained, and was ill-fitted to comprehend the increasing mercenary element, but it was by no means discarded.

Henry II had by his assize of arms reorganised the national levy on the basis of wealth, and casual references to a *visus armorum* suggest that his regulations were enforced in John's reign.[1] Moreover, the Angevin kings had laid additional stress upon the public character of the army in less direct ways. For example, drastic and savage punishments for default take the place in the ordinances of Henry II and John[2] of the fixed amercements which are found in the Anglo-Saxon laws and in ordinary French practice.[3] And, more important,

[1] *Rot. Norm.*, 83. The men of Guy de Diva are to be free 'de taillagio ct de visu armorum quamdiu ipse fuerit in servicio nostro'. Cf. *Rot. Pat.*, 1, on the host which was to meet at Argentan; John, September 27, 1201, sends three officials 'ad videndum qui vestrum venerint et qualiter quisque venerit'. On the public liability of freemen, see Prou, in *Revue historique*, 1890, xliv, 313; Haskins, *Norman Institutions*, pp. 22-3. The inquest at Chizé (above, p. 200) illustrates this duty of 'exercitus et equitatio'.

[2] Assize of Arms, c. 10 (*Select Charters*, 9th edition, p. 184) mutilation, not loss of lands or chattels, to be the punishment for non-observance of the assize. Cf. the elaborate regulations for the organised defence of England in 1205, with their penalty of perpetual servitude; Stubbs, *Constitutional History*, i, 634. Such regulations were, of course, unusual, and are really important as showing the intensity of the royal will. In ordinary cases of non-attendance at the host, amercements were exacted. See below.

[3] Vinogradoff, *English Society in the Eleventh Century*, p. 28; Prou, 'De La nature du service militaire du par les roturiers aux xie et xiie siècles', in *Revue Historique*, 1890, xliv, 321-3.

any tendency on the part of the greater vassals to feudalise and turn to their own profit the public obligations of the freeman was checked by royal insistance upon the judicial and financial rights of the sovereign.[4] Hence, although the *arrière-ban* or national levy was less important in practice, it was fixed more firmly than ever in the administrative system of the country.

Although the *arrière-ban* is mentioned on the rolls, it is not quite clear whether a distinction was maintained at the end of the twelfth century between the feudal force (*exercitus*) and the host of freemen. The references concern the conduct of knights,[5] and it is possible that the later dukes were satisfied to summon the better armed subtenants, in addition to the stated feudal levy. At any rate it is apparent that the army, comprising large numbers of soldiers (*servientes*) on horse and foot was called out nearly every year between 1198 and 1204.[6] Its usual rendezvous was Argentan.[7] Its administration or organisation was the duty of the Marshal, if a single reference to the functions of John the Marshal may be trusted. Those great military officials, the constable and marshal, together with the seneschal or highest officer of state, still retained the functions which they had exercised in days when the host was the normal instrument of warfare.[8]

A more important element than the *arrière-ban* in the military

---

[4] Cf. *Statuta et Consuetudines*, c. xlviii (Tardif, I, i, 39), 'Nullus vero hominum audeat talias vel exactiones ab hominibus suis exigere, nisi per scriptum Ducis et ejus indulgenciam, scilicet pro gravamine guerre', etc. The privilege enjoyed by the archbishop of Rouen with regard to the *arrière-ban*, illustrates the practice to which it is an exception: 'De retrobanno Normannie sic erit, quod cum oportuerit submoneri retrobannum, secundum consuetudinem terre Archiepiscopus per nos vel per litteras nostras vel per capitalem Senescallum nostrum vel per litteras ejus submoneri debet, et ipse Archiepiscopus summonebit retrobannum secundum consuetudinem terre, et ducet vel duci faciet, et si retrobannum plenarie non venerit justicia erit Archiepiscopi.' (John's charter in *Rot. Norm.*, 3.)

[5] Account in 1198 'de misericordiis militum Ballie de Danfront qui non venerunt ad rerebandum exercitus ex quo summoniti fuerunt' (*Rot. Scacc.*, ii, 495). John's letter to William of Caieux, Argentan, June 5, 1200: 'vobis mandamus quatinus ad nos cum retrouuarda accedatis desicut retrobannum nostrum mandavimus' (*Rot. Norm.*, 36).

[6] The evidence for 1198, 1200, 1201, 1202, and probably 1203 rests upon *Rot. Scacc.*, ii, 445, 495; *Rot. Norm.*, 36; *Rot. Pat.*, 1, 21b; *Rot. Norm.*, 83. Most of these passages are quoted in previous notes. For *Rot. Pat.*, 21b, see note at the end of this chapter. *Rot. Scacc.*, ii, 445, contains this entry: 'Henricus de Ponte Audemer reddit compotum de x li. pro 1 summario cum apparatu quem Burgenses Fiscanni debent Regi quando exercitus Normannie submonitus est.' It should also be noted that local forces were occasionally summoned for special purposes, such as Count John's attack on Vaudreuil in 1194: above, p. 103.   [7] Cf. above, p. 157.

[8] See the note at the end of this chapter.

system of a feudal state was the organised militia of the communes.[9] It is true that in Normandy, although the militia was regarded as a potential field force, it was used mainly for defensive purposes, whereas Philip Augustus frequently employed it in the open.[10] But its defensive value was very great, and King John was fully alive to the fact. The communes which he created, many of which were very short-lived,[11] were designed to have a military function, and are excellent examples of the feudal character of these organisations. The immediate consequence, as Luchaire observed, of the communal bond was that the commune, as a *seigneurie* and member of the feudal hierarchy, owed military service.[12] The Norman towns, like the Spanish, were chartered 'ad persecucionem inimicorum', if not 'ad persecucionem inimicorum crucis Christi'.[13] 'It is our good pleasure,' John wrote to the men of Fécamp on June 30, 1202, 'that you and others in your neighbourhood shall have a commune for so long as it may please us, and that you be ready to defend your land by arms and in other necessary ways.'[14] Failure to serve in the communal levy was met with communal punishment. For example, according to the *établissements* of Rouen, a citizen who was not present at the hour fixed for the start upon a communal expedition was punished by the destruction of his house, or if he had no house of his own, by the imposition of a fine of one hundred shillings.[15] During a siege the pressure of public opinion would, of course, be still greater: the action taken by Evreux during King Richard's captivity,[16] and the preparations at Rouen in 1204 illustrate the military importance of communal feeling.

[9] Borelli de Serres, *Recherches sur divers services publics du xiiie au xviie siècle*, i (1895), 467 ff.; Giry, *Etablissements de Rouen*, ii, 36–ch. 28, 29; Luchaire, *Les communes françaises* (ed. 1911), pp. 177–90; Jean Yanoski, in the *Mémoires presentés par divers savants à l'académie des inscriptions et belles-lettres*, 1860, 2e series, vol. iv, part ii, pp. 1 105.

[10] Cf. Howden, iv, 56, 58. On the other hand it should be noted that Philip Augustus demanded fixed quotas of men and carts from the towns, and organised these according to districts; also that he frequently took money instead of service. Borrelli de Serres, *op. cit.*, 476, 489; and below, pp. 220–1. There are signs that fixed quotas were demanded from some Norman towns, *e.g.*, from Rouen, *Rot. Scacc.*, ii, 306, 'servientes quos cives Rothomagi debuerunt invenire Regi in gerra'.

[11] Delisle, *Cartulaire Normand*, pp. xv–xviii. Auffai, Domfront, Evreux (formed in Richard's reign), Fécamp, Harfleur, Montivilliers were of short duration.   [12] Luchaire, *op. cit.*, p. 178; see also Giry, i, 440.

[13] *Fuero del Teluel*, c. 2, quoted by Davis in *English Historical Review*, xxiii, 768.

[14] *Rot. Pat.*, 13b. The date given in the enrolment is July 30, but the context points to June 30.

[15] Giry, *op. cit.*, ii, 36, c. 28. See Round, *Feudal England*, p. 556, for this communal house demolition; also Mary Bateson, *Borough Customs* (Selden Soc.), 1906), II, p. xxxvi–vii.   [16] Above, p. 98.

It has been stated that the dukes of Normandy do not appear to have often availed themselves of the communal militia in the open country. Two obvious reasons would account for this fact. In the first place the military obligations of the towns were limited in many cases by local privilege. Henry II exempted the men of Pontorson from service in the host when the duke did not command in person.[17] By Richard's charter, the burgesses of Andeli were bound to serve on no expedition which would not enable them to go and return on the same day.[18] In the second place, the short period of service required from feudal levies—forty days—made a force of this kind ineffective. These disadvantages were shared to a large extent by all branches of the feudal host, and we are led, therefore, to consider the expedients adopted by the Angevin kings, and especially by Richard and John, to remove or neutralise them.

In a letter which King Richard addressed to Archbishop Hubert on April 15, 1196, the king made a marked distinction between those barons whose *capita baroniarum* were in Normandy, and those whose chief interests were centred in England.[19] He ordered the archbishop to send the former into Normandy without delay. The latter were required to cross the Channel by the Sunday before Pentecost and the form of their service was regulated more precisely. They were not to cumber themselves with many knights: and no baron should bring more than seven; on the other hand, they were to come so prepared that they could remain in the king's service for a long time.[20] The king then referred to the English bishops and abbots who owed military service. The archbishop was ordered to admonish them to send such aid as would win royal approval.[21] This letter lays down two principles: Firstly, the Norman and English military tenants-in-chief are distinguished, but only for the king's convenience; all owe

[17] Henry's charter survives in a vidimus of 1366 (Ordonnances, iv, 638). Delisle ascribed it to 1171–3: see the list of charters at the end of his *Introduction*, no. 294.

[18] See John's confirmation in *Rot. Chart.*, 65b: 'quod non eant aliqua de causa in aliquam expeditionem sive chevalcheam quod (*sic*) non possint redire ad hospitia sua eadem die qua decesserunt.'

[19] Edited by Stubbs in his preface to Diceto, II, pp. lxxix–lxxx. See above, pp. 111–2. Sufficient stress has not, I think, been laid upon this letter by previous writers.

[20] 'Summoneatis etiam omnes illos qui debent nobis servitium militis *in Anglia*, praeter Willelmum de Braus et Willelmum de Aubenei et barones de marchia Wallarum, quod omnes sint ad nos citra mare in Normannia proxima Dominica ante Pentecostan cum equis et armis, parati ad servitium nostrum; et veniant ita parati quod possint diu morari in servitio nostro; quod scilicet non gravent se multitudine militum, nec aliquis plures adducat quam vii. ad plus.'

[21] 'quod ita serviant nobis in militibus quod eos inde laudare et gratias agere debeamus.'

service alike, but it is expedient to organise the service due by English tenants. Secondly, King Richard implies that the obligations of the ecclesiastical tenants to serve out of England were not so precise or binding as those of the laymen. This point was emphasised by Bishop Hugh of Lincoln in the following year. We cannot do better than discuss the matter on the lines laid down here by Richard.

Henry II in 1157 and Richard in 1194 demanded a third of the knight service of England to fight against the Welsh and French respectively, with the object, it may be presumed, of securing a three-fold term of service.[22] In 1197, the year following that in which he wrote the letter to the archbishop, Richard proposed another plan, whereby his English tenants should equip three hundred knights for service in Normandy and pay them for a whole year. Although it seems that this plan fell to the ground, the king was successful in maintaining or assuming a claim upon the continental service of his vassals. He met with little opposition from the laymen; and those who refused service were deprived of their lands.[23] Similarly no objection was raised on legal grounds to such service in the early years of John's reign. This is clear from a study of the events at Portsmouth in 1201 and 1205, of which the chroniclers give many particulars. It is true that the earls met at Leicester in 1201 and decided not to cross the Channel with the king unless he did them right (*nisi reddiderit eis jura sua*),[24] but their action was an attempt at a bargain, a significant but not exactly a legal appeal to the fundamental agreement between a lord and his vassals. It must be connected with the private arrangements which certain powerful barons were able to make with the king during the stress of war,[25] and with the lavish grants or numerous exemptions from debts by which John sought to retain the fidelity of his subjects.[26] Again, the refusal of the Marshal to follow the king in

[22] Stubbs, *Constitutional History*, i, 631.

[23] According to Jocelin of Brakelond (ed. H. E. Butler, p. 86), the abbot of St. Edmund's feared 'ne amitteret saisinam baronie sue pro defectu servicii regis, sicut contigerat . . . *multis baronibus Anglie*'.

[24] Howden, iv, 160, 161.

[25] For the alleged action of William of Briouze, see below, p. 321. A significant note is added by the clerk to the enrolment of a charter to Robert of Harcourt, September 4, 1199 (*Rot. Chart.*, 17b): 'memorandum quod terra ista assignata ei quousque assignaverit cuidam filio suo c. libras redditus in maritagio. Et propter warram talem extorsit cartam.'

[26] *Rot. de Liberate*, 44: 'sciatis quod Thomas de Arcy nobis serviet se tertio militum ad custum suum proprium, scilicet per unum annum . . . per sic quod nos eidem Thome perdonemus cc et xxv marcas quas debet Judeis et Judeabus super cartas suas et cirographa', etc. Towards the end of the struggle in Normandy, on October 15, 1203, the king exempted Richard of Ounebac of his debts, apparently in return for twenty days' service at Tillières (*Rot. Norm.*, 107). Other cases in *Rot. Norm.*, 47, 60, 61, 64, 73, 87; *Rot. Pat.*, 18b, 30; *Rot. de Lib.*, 37, 42, 45, 48.

1205 was based upon the peculiar ground of his feudal relation to Philip Augustus, not upon a legal right to refuse service.[27] Only in 1213, after John's failures abroad and at home, do we find the lay tenants in the north of England refusing to join him abroad for reasons of privilege.[28] The question was not settled in the thirteenth century,[29] although according to one suggested settlement in 1215, King John was willing to compromise by confining the duty of foreign service to service in Normandy and Brittany.[30]

In 1201 and 1205, however, the objections which were to be raised in 1213, were not heard. In the former year, the whole knight service of England was summoned to Portsmouth. A large host came together at Pentecost. It is not likely that the king had ever intended to take across the whole number; at any rate he adopted his brother's policy. According to Roger of Howden, Earl William the Marshal and Roger de Laci, the constable of Chester, were sent over in advance, each at the head of a hundred paid knights (soldarii).[31] They, and others, were the representatives of the Portsmouth host, which was sent home after composition with John. Some barons paid a scutage of two marks on the fee, but for the most part fines which varied in amount were exacted from them and the knights separately.[32] It is noteworthy that the knights of the bishop of Lincoln, although compounded for by the scutage, were afterwards forced instead to make personal arrangements with the king.[33] A special roll was kept containing the record of these fines.[34]

The same plan was adopted in 1205. Again, in 1205 as in 1201, the leading barons opposed the expedition, this time on grounds of policy;[35] again a great company assembled at Portsmouth. The

[27] Guillaume le Maréchal, iii, 180.
[28] Walt. Coventry, ii, 217, and Stubbs' introduction; Round, Feudal England, p. 534. [29] Stubbs, Constitutional History, ii, 292, 293.
[30] In the 'unknown' charter of liberties, c. 7: 'adhuc hominibus meis concedo ne eant in exercitu extra Angliam nisi in Normanniam et in Brittanniam, et hoc decenter, quod si aliquis debet inde servitium decem militum, consilio baronum meorum alleviabitur.' McKechnie, Magna Carta, p. 570, 2nd edition, p. 486; Teulet, Layettes, i, 423; Petit-Dutaillis, Studies Supplementary to Stubbs' Constitutional History (tr. Rhodes), i, 118, 125. [31] Howden, iv, 163.
[32] Wendover, i, 311: 'veniente autem die statuto, multi impetrata licentia remanserunt, dantes regi de quolibet scuto duas marcas argenti.' A study of the Pipe Roll, however, would show great variety; see Pipe Roll, 3 John, pp. 21–3, 33–7, 70–2, 82–3, 118–19, 263; Rotuli de Oblatis et Finibus, 143–56.
[33] Rot. de Oblatis, 145: 'Milites Episcopi Lincolniensis quorum numerus viixx et iiij milites dant pro eodem scilicet de scuto ij marcas—Cancellantur quia inferius fuerunt separati.' See ibid., p. 153.
[34] Pipe Roll, 3 John, p. 82: 'Idem vicecomes [of Wiltshire] reddit compotum de xii li. vj so. et viij. d. de scutagiis militum de honore Walteri de Dunstanvill quorum nomina et debita annotantur in Rotulo quem Magister Radulfus de Stoke liberavit in thesauro ex parte justicie de finibus militum ne transfretent.' [35] Coggeshall, pp. 152, 153.

knights were not only willing but eager to accompany John; and much indignation was aroused when the king unwillingly consented to employ only a picked few.[36] Those who were sent away were ordered to pay the money which they had brought with them for the benefit of the rest. Moreover, after a hesitating cruise in the Channel, John returned and is said to have levied large sums on laity and ecclesiastics who had, he declared, refused to accompany him.[37]

The records of these expeditions prove that, in John's reign, no distinction was made between ecclesiastical and lay tenants; in other words, King Richard's vague discrimination of 1196 was no longer necessary. The question had been raised formally by Hugh of Lincoln in 1197: he refused either to serve or to contribute towards an expedition in Normandy.[38] Four years later, in 1201, a few months after the bishop's death, the knights of the bishopric make fines with King John in order to be released from service across the Channel.[39] The transition from resistance to submission may be illustrated, as Mr. Round long ago pointed out, by the action of St. Edmund's.[40] The bishop of Lincoln refused both men and money; the abbot of St. Edmund's admitted a claim for scutage, but denied that his church had ever been obliged to provide knights for service across the sea.[41] However, the abbot submitted. Richard, it is stated, had demanded a tenth of the knight service due from the fiefs of English bishops and abbots; the abbot, therefore, equipped four knights and gave them sufficient money to maintain themselves during the usual forty days of service. But at this stage the connection made by the king between small numbers and long service was pointed out to the abbot by his friends. His knights might be kept for a whole year, and their maintenance would be very expensive; it would be cheaper to make an arrangement with the king. This the abbot did: his knights might return after forty days, and the king received a fine of £100.[42] The royal rights were completely acknowledged.[43]

[36] Coggeshall. According to Gervase of Canterbury (ii, 98) 1500 knights came to Portsmouth. Coggeshall states that several thousand sailors also collected with ships from all parts. The discomfort and expense involved in this journey and in the delay in the unsanitary conditions of a medieval port must have been considerable. [37] Wendover, ii, 10. [38] See Round, *Feudal England*, pp. 528–34.
[39] The bishopric was at this time in the king's hands. It is clear, however, that some bishops contributed knights and served in person, *e.g.*, the bishop of Norwich. See above, p. 162. [40] *Feudal England*, p. 531.
[41] Jocelin of Brakelond (ed. H. E. Butler), pp. 85–6.
[42] The principle of representation, adopted by the Angevin kings, was in vogue on some ecclesiastical estates, and was, therefore, not unfamiliar. Representatives were elected by the tenants to perform the *servitium debitum*. See *Select Pleas in Manorial Courts* (Selden Society), pp. 50, 61.
[43] It should be noticed that John expressly disclaimed any right to exact service for Normandy from Ireland: *Rot. Chart.*, 133b. See below, p. 327.

John's relations with the barons and their tenants at Portsmouth help to establish the nature of scutage at the end of the twelfth century.[44] Unless local privilege, such as Saint Hugh claimed in 1197, involved a prescriptive right to offer payment instead of service, the duty to serve was clear. King John insisted upon the connection between fees (*feoda*) on the one hand, and horses and men on the other, with no uncertain voice.[45] On the other hand, the primary object of levying a scutage was the collection of wages for a hired force,[46] and as a rule King John was content to lay the heavy burden of an annual scutage upon the English. Payment and service were not interchangeable:[47] if the king called for service, only a special arrangement could justify the payment of scutage instead. Thus in 1201, although the scutage of two marks was accepted in many cases in lieu of service, the scutage was carefully distinguished from the fine *pro transfretatione*.[48] In many cases, however, the alternative character of scutage was sufficiently established to secure the exemption from payment of those who served freely. We cannot be sure that this concession was general, because we do not know exactly who served and who did not, but we can safely assert that it was frequent.[49]

In Normandy the practice seems to have been simpler. The feudal tax which corresponded to the English scutage, the *auxilium exer-*

[44] On the whole subject, see Baldwin, *The Scutage and Knight Service in England* (Chicago, 1897); Pollock and Maitland, *History of English Law* (2nd edition), i, 253, 266 *seqq.*; Round, *Feudal England*; and for this period A. L. Poole, *Obligations of Society in the XII and XIII Centuries* (1946), pp. 40–52, 59–60; H. M. Chew, *English ecclesiastical tenants-in-chief and knight service* (1932); and cf. M. R. Powicke, in *Speculum*, xxv (1950), 457 ff. The confusion of practice and theory which these discussions of the evidence reveal is due to the fact that, on the one hand, the payment of scutage and the performance of service were not interchangeable, while, on the other, no cases seem to have been found in which both service and payment were clearly exacted. Note S. K. Mitchell, *Studies in taxation under John and Henry II* (Yale University Press, 1914), p. 24.

[45] See his letters to bailiffs of the count of Flanders and to the *prepositus* of Bruges, in Rot. Pat., 11b, 2nb.   [46] *Dialogus*, lib. 1, c. 9 (ed. C. Johnson, p. 52).

[47] Cf. Ramsay, *Angevin Empire*, p. 390.

[48] For example, Pipe Roll, 3 John, p. 21: 'Lambertus de Scoteigni reddit compotum de xx li. ne transfretet et pro habendo scutagio suo de x militibus'; *ibid.*, p. 118, etc.: 'de finibus et scutagiis.' On exceptional occasions, in 1172 and 1213, we find a scutage paid by those who 'nec milites nec denarios miserunt', or 'nec ierant nec miserunt'. See Baldwin, *The Scutage and Knight Service in England*, p. 6.

[49] *Rot. Pat.*, 14b, July 17, 1202: in favour of Thomas of St. Valery, who 'nobis libenter servit et nos de ejus servicio multum laudamus'. Cf. *Rot. de Lib.*, 15, June 10, 1201: in favour of Thomas de Burgh, the king's *valetus*. This is an interesting case, because Thomas was a sub-tenant who paid scutage, here excused him, to several lords. Finally, compare the lists of exemptions in the Pipe Rolls under the several counties.

citus, was only levied upon the knight service actually owing to the king, whereas in England scutage was levied upon the number of knights enfeoffed.[50] It was, thus, easier to regard the service of 40 days and the aid as interchangeable; and as a matter of fact, although the feudal host was frequently called out, the aid appears to have been levied and deduction made in favour of those who served.[51] Occasionally, the aid was granted to the lord himself to maintain him in the ducal service,[52] just as was sometimes done in the case of scutage. The comparative rarity of entries relating to the aid which can be traced on the Exchequer rolls may be interpreted to show that service was more common than payment. There are cases of amercement for non-appearance.[53] But the evidence is not sufficient to prove this view. In the first place, only the debtors are mentioned on the Exchequer rolls; there may have been separate collection of the aid as a whole. In the second place, other entries point to an opposite conclusion, and would justify the view, so far as they go, that payment was more common than service: for example, a man might pay the aid and at the same time receive wages for service.[54] We must be content to state and leave the facts, which may be summarised as follows: The feudal host seems to have been summoned frequently, at least in John's reign. It was organised in the ordinary feudal manner by the ducal officials. It would presumably include the knights and armed *servientes* of the ducal demesne, and references to the *arrière-ban* and view of arms show that it might be reinforced by the military subtenants, if not by the national host. On the other hand, the service

[50] The proof of this lies in a comparison of the inquest into knights' fees in the *Red Book*, with the payments or debts enrolled in the Exchequer Rolls; for example, compare *Rot. Scacc.*, i, 208 (Montfort, for Coquainvilliers); ii, 448 (knights of Caux), 479 (Bohon), 513 (Rollos), with *Red Book*, ii, 627, 632, 628, 634.

[51] *Rot. Scacc.*, ii, 444, 445: 'Helouis de Venneval . . . reddit compotum de xxx li. de feodo iij militum de duobus quadraginta (*i.e.*, for two periods). In thesauro xx li. Galfrido de Sauchosa Mara x. li. pro servicio i. militis quod fecit. Et quieta est.' Cf. i, 145; ii, 559.

[52] *Rot. Norm.*, 105: 'quietavimus Gillebertum de Aquila de auxilio exercitus quod ab eo exigitur de exercitu Wasconie.' At the time of this grant, September, 1203, Gilbert of L'Aigle was serving with John (*Rot. Pat.*, 34b). Another case of exemption in *Rot. Norm.*, 92.

[53] Generally, however, for non-appearance on some special service, *e.g.*, the payments 'pro servicio Regis non facto apud Nonancourt' in 1202 or 1203 (*Rot Scacc.*, ii, 554–9 *passim*), also 1198 (*ibid.*, 458). Such an entry as the following (*ibid.*, 330) points, on the other hand, to a general amercement: 'Gueroldus Lailier reddit compotum de xxiiij li. pro ii servientibus quos debuit mittere in exercitum et non misit.'

[54] *Ibid.*, i, 270 (1195). 'Fulco de Veteri ponte xvi li. de auxilio exercitus de feodo ij militum. Et x li. quas habuit pro servicio Regis faciendo et non fecit.' But this service may not have been military.

due from each tenant-in-chief was fixed, and seems to have been regarded as redeemable by payment of the aid. The aid was levied regularly in time of war and was generally £5 Angevin, that is about 25 shillings sterling, on the knight's fee;[55] but it is uncertain to what extent and under what conditions payment of the aid was substituted for service, or, to express the same thing in other words, to what extent the host was composed of men who were serving for forty days at their lord's expense. The Exchequer records show that the knights and *servientes* were paid as well as the mercenaries.[56] The duty to provide *servientes* did not necessarily involve the duty to pay them.[57] On the whole the tendency of the evidence is to show that the Norman army was a paid army, and was paid by aids of all kinds, tallages, and loans. The defence of the March was the chief task of Normandy, and this required permanent garrisons.

In one respect, it would seem, Norman and English tendencies differed. In England the exigencies of service across the Channel brought about a closer organisation of the feudal force on a representative basis. There is no trace in Normandy of any system of representative service.[58] There was not the same excuse in Normandy for lengthening the term of service in the open, and permanent garrisons were more suitably composed of paid men. Moreover, it is

[55] There was some variation, as the entry in the last note shows; and cf. ii, 557 (1202): 'Willelmus de Mara lxx. so. de feodo dimidii militis de exercitu Normannie anni preteriti.' It is just possible that these variations point to special arrangements with the duke like the varying scutage or fines of 1201 in England. Above, p. 214.

[56] *Rot. Scacc.*, i, 115 (1184). Payment of £100 to Hugh of Cressy 'ad faciendas liberationes militum, quos duxit ad ultimam guerram Pictavie'; i, 145—repayment of money granted 'de liberationibus servientum qui debuerunt facere servitium Regis et non fecerunt'; ii, 480, 'Robertus de Tresgoz debet xxv so. de servientibus qui redierunt de exercitu de Aube Merle.' A previous entry (p. 478) seems to refer to wages, but may be an instance of amercement. The bailiff, Robert of Tresgoz, accounts for £112 10s. od. 'de denariis captis de servientibus qui debuerunt ire apud Goislanfontem in exercitus (*sic*) et non ierunt'. Gaillefontaine is between Neufchâtel and Gournai, in Bray.

[57] See the expenditure of the tallage of Caux in 1198 (*ibid.*, ii, 448). Much of it was given to lords on the March, 'de hominibus feodi sui'.

[58] The knights and barons who were sent to Issoudun in 1194 (*Rot. Scacc.*, i, 136, above, p 107) are the nearest example, but there is no evidence that they were systematically selected. I am, of course, not referring to the provision of knight-service by the knights of a fief for war or castleguard. The returns from Bayeux in 1133 show that in this respect a representative system was developed in Normandy as in England. In some cases this doubtless resulted in a long service system, especially on the marches: 'idem episcopus debebat servicium viginti militum in marchis Normanniae per quadraginta dies, ubicunque rex vellet, *et istud servicium faciebant quinque milites per unum*' (*sic*, ?annum. *Histor. de France*, xxiii, 699). There are many instances, *e.g.*, in the *Feoda Normanniae* compiled after 1204 (*ibid.*, p. 705).

quite probable that the different methods of assessing the aid in the two countries helped to encourage a representative system in England and to hinder it in Normandy. In Normandy, as we have seen, the aid was not payable on every knight enfeoffed, but only upon the *servitium debitum*.[59] When Henry II extended the assessment in England, he was doubtless thinking of the superior advantages of financial to military aid in his continental wars: it would be tedious to ship the military service of England across the Channel, and if taxation were resorted to, it might be general—not confined, like the old scutage on ecclesiastical fiefs, to a tax on the service which was legally due. The next step was easy. If personal service were needed, a proportion of the knight service legally due, or, better still, a hundred knights or so picked from the whole of England, would be much more useful, since they would be available for a longer period. On the scene of warfare no such necessity was apparent; and, in any case, it would have been more difficult to disturb military obligations which had been fixed before the conquest of England. But several important results might have followed the extension of Henry's policy into Normandy. The towns might have escaped with lighter tallages; the English scutages need not have been so onerous; and more scope would have been offered for the development of a national representative system of military service.

In England, after the loss of Normandy, the growth of such a system was checked, and it gradually gave way before different methods of raising an army; but no student of John's reign can doubt that military organisation had great influence upon later experiments in political representation. Is it too fanciful to suggest that if such a system had taken root in Normandy, the whole history of the duchy might have been changed?

[59] The aid was of course collected from all the knights during an escheat, *e.g.*, the long list of payments by the knights of the honour of Montfort in 1198 and 1203 (*Rot. Scacc.*, ii, 364, 559). In 1198 Richard Silvain accounted in detail for the aids of 22 and seven-twenty-fourths. The number of knights' fees in the service of the lord in 1172 was 22 and seven-twelfths (*Red Book*, ii, 642). Stapleton incorrectly identified these knights with the 33 and seven-twelfths *ad servitium suum* of Hugh of Montfort in Coquainvilliers, and suggests an emendation accordingly (II, lxvii), but Coquainvilliers was never in ducal hands. The aid was also paid upon all the knights during a minority, as in 1198 in the honour of Moion (*Rot. Scacc.*, ii, 298, compared with *Red Book*, ii, 629). The relief also seems to have been paid on all the knights; see the entry relating to Peter of Sablé's payment for the knights of Gacé (*Rot. Scacc.*, ii, 317). It is an interesting question whether the lord who was given power to collect an aid on his estates was expected to maintain himself in the ducal service from the surplus, after the payment of the aid on the *servitium debitum*. A ducal writ permitted a lord to levy an aid upon his tenants *pro gravamine guerre* (*Statuta et Consuet.*, c. xlviii, in Tardif, I, i, 39).

On the other hand, we cannot be certain that no attempts were made in Normandy to establish a definite territorial army, more national than the feudal levy by knight service. At all events, it is necessary, in the face of contemporary developments in France, to consider the possibility of such attempts. In France from 1194 onwards, if not earlier,[60] the royal demesne and the towns were expected to provide a definite number of *servientes* and waggons, and for this military purpose the demesne was divided and the towns grouped. The obligation did not remove the possibility of a universal levy, but for the most part it took its place, and, like the *arrière-ban*, involved a recognition of the Carolingian idea of service. The king called upon sub-vassals as well as vassals, and made no distinction between the vassal and the liege-man. The communes might be required, and indeed generally were required, to give money instead of sending their quota, but the decision rested with the king. Finally, the men-at-arms, when they were summoned, were paid by the king. Now it is not necessary to exaggerate the military value of such a force as this, which was more often than not translated into money, but its constitutional importance was great. It points to the organisation of royal resources, and the development of feudal relations on principles which were other than feudal. It would be strange if no such expedient were tried in Normandy, where the exploitation of the demesne had been so great. In England the survival of popular institutions gave vitality to the fyrd and permitted such a systematic organisation of local forces as was ordered by John in 1205;[61] in Normandy we should expect a more definite and centralised plan, like that betrayed by the quota-lists (*prisia servientum*) of France. And if we scan the evidence, some parallels to French practice certainly do appear. There is the reference to the men-at-arms whom the citizens of Rouen are obliged to send in time of war.[62] There are the occasional allusions to the 'servientes qui debuerunt facere servitium Regis', and who were fined for non-appearance. The bailiffs are apparently responsible for the payment of these men, who may therefore be regarded as tenants of the ducal demesne. The Assize of Arms may have been intended to facilitate the operations of a system of this kind; we are told that Philip Augustus copied Henry's Assize of Arms, and it is tempting to connect

[60] Borrelli de Serres, *op. cit.*, i, 467 *seqq.*, especially pp. 489, 493, 519. The *prisia servientum*, or quota lists, date from 1194, for as Borrelli de Serres shows, this is the date of the well-known document edited in the *Recueil des Historiens de France*, xxiii, 722; and in Giry's *Documents sur les relations de la royauté avec les villes en France* (1885), p. 39. The date is significant, for Philip Augustus was preparing to meet Richard after the latter's captivity.

[61] Stubbs, *Constitutional History*, i, 634.

[62] *Rot. Scacc.*, ii, 306; above, p. 211 and notes. Note that the citizens pay money instead.

it with Philip's military organisation of *his* demesne. If, that is to say, an Assize of Arms lay behind the military organisation of France, we might with more confidence presume a similar development from the Norman Assize. But the evidence is vague and uncertain, and we must be content to regard a Norman organisation on these lines as possible rather than probable.

II

King John kept together his paid army by recruiting, by lavish grants of pensions and lands, and by the maintenance in his service of bands of artillerymen, crossbowmen and mercenaries.

The failure of negotiations in April, 1202, forced the king to face a serious crisis, and his efforts to attract troops are illustrated by the open letters which he entrusted to his 'recruiting sergeants' in May. On May 2, William of Cresec was commissioned to enroll recruits on liberal terms.[63] On May 27, Simon of Haveret was set to work among the knights of Flanders, Hainault and Brabant.[64]

Just as he made special efforts to gather men together, John made special efforts to retain them in his service by grants of lands and money. It would be tedious to enumerate those who received pensions in return for service.[65] It is sufficient to remark that this form of vassal relation was frequently adopted by John.[66] The grants of land, which were as numerous as grants of revenue, are of interest to the student in so far as they illustrate the effect of warfare upon existing social relations.[67] For example, a reversion to the beneficiary system is clearly seen in such grants as those of Léry and Conteville to Gerard of Fournival,[68] and of the Channel Islands to Peter of Préaux.[69] These were not ordinary cases of enfeoffment. For the service of one

[63] *Rot. Pat.*, 10: 'et scialis quod factum servicium vestrum ita bene remunerabimus quod nobis et eidem Willelmo grates scietis.' William had just previously gone surety for Baldwin the chamberlain of Flanders 'quod ad servicium nostrum fideliter nobis veniet in Normanniam' (*Rot. de Lib.*, 29). He held lands in Wiltshire (*Red Book*, ii, 483, 484) and received many favours from John (*ibid.*, p. 555; *Rot. Norm.*, 60; *Rot. de Lib.*, 44, 51). For a time he seems to have been suspected, but in 1207 he made a fine for his lands (*Rot. de Finibus*, i, 377).   [64] *Rot. Pat.*, 12.

[65] *e.g.*, *Rot. Norm.*, 32 (Herveus de Preez), *Rot. de Lib.*, 4; *Rot. Litt. Claus.*, i, 113. The grant is usually accompanied by the words, 'unde homo noster est'.

[66] See the remarks of Viollet on this form of the relation *de fide et servitio*, in *Hist. Litt. de la France*, xxxiii, 133; also the essay of Bryce D. Lyon in *English Historical Review*, lxvi (1951) referred to above, on p. 81, note.

[67] Cf. Baldwin, *Scutage and Knight Service*, p. 79.

[68] *Rot. Norm.*, 19.

[69] *Rot. Chart.*, 33b; Havet, in *Bibliothèque de l'Ecole des Chartes* (1876), xxxvij, 188.

knight Gerard of Fournival was granted lands which had brought into the exchequer £40 per annum, and had been regarded as a fair exchange for Pont de l'Arche.[70] The enfeoffment of the Channel Islands to Peter of Préaux for the service of three knights was a measure of military precaution. Peter was warden in virtue of his position, and it is possible that important institutions which still survive in the islands can be traced to the period of his lordship.[71] The strain upon Normandy was evidently too severe for the government, and John's recklessness hastened its disintegration. We reach the logical outcome of such a grant in the surrender of the important castle of Tenchebrai with its revenues to Fraeric or Frederick Malesmains 'ad sustentandum se in servicio nostro et ponendam uxorem suam'.[72] The castle was in private hands for nine months and the exchequer lost the revenues of Tenchebrai during the interval.[73]

Equally reminiscent of an earlier age were John's relations with his household. He relied very largely upon the young warriors in his train (bachelerii de familia nostra), and on one occasion definitely sought to pit their counsel against that of the barons.[74] In contemporary literature, and indeed in general fact, the bachelors were the landless unknighted youths of the court.[75] John's bachelors appear to have been unknighted, but the king departed from usual custom by endowing them, at least in Normandy and his other continental possessions, with lands which he definitely states to have been given to them in expectation of their service.[76]

---

[70] Rot. Scacc., i, 239; Stapleton, I, clxvii, II, clxi; above, p. 193.

[71] For the royal administration of the isles through Peter of Preaux, see Rot. Pat., 3: regulations for the collection of an aid for the defence of the isles; ibid., 15, the inhabitants are to aid 'servienti nostro custodienti insulas predictas ad jurandos malefactores et latrones manentes in insulis illis et ad evacuendos eas de eis'. An inquest of 1248 ascribed the creation of the jurés to King John; see Havet, Bibliothèque (1877), xxxviii, 275-7. See also J. le Patourel, The medieval administration of the Channel Islands (1937), passim.

[72] Rot. Pat., 10b, May 12, 1202.

[73] Fraeric was ordered to give up the castle to the local bailiff on February 26, 1203 (ibid., 26a). He received £65 during the financial year 1202-3 (Rot. Scacc., ii, 540). The bailiff had been instructed to leave an official to keep watch over the forest (Rot. Pat., 10b).

[74] The incident is narrated in the Marshal's biography (iii, 181). John of Bassingbourne was spokesman for the bachelors.

[75] Meyer, Guillaume le Maréchal, iii, 181, note.

[76] I have collected the passages in the English Historical Review, xxii, 42. The entries in Rot. de Lib., 212, suggest a distinction between the members of the familia and the knights in attendance upon John. If this be so, John of Bassingbourne had ceased to be a bachelor between 1205 and 1210 (Guillaume le Maréchal, iii, 181; Rot. Lib., 183, 212) though he was still in John's intimate service (Rot. Lib., 182, 185; M. Paris, Chron. Maj., ii, 533). He had lands in Cambridgeshire in 1212 (Red Book, ii, 526).

Indeed John did not *insist* upon any qualification except that of personal dependence. In 1216 he retained in his service Thomas Malesmains, a man with marriageable sons and daughters and some claims to property. 'And we will look upon him,' adds the king, 'as one of our bachelors.'[77]

The great majority, however, of the men in John's service were, apart from the mercenaries, knights and men-at-arms who fought for a fixed wage. The knight received six shillings a day in Angevin money, the mounted man-at-arms or *serviens* two shillings and six-pence, the unmounted from eightpence to a shilling.[78] The occasional reference to terms of service (*termini*) implies that soldiers were hired for fixed renewable periods.[79] In addition to their wages, they were often accommodated with loans, especially if they came from England. It must, indeed, have been very easy to run short of the means of subsistence among the hazards of war and distant service; and the king seems to have advanced money, when possible, as a matter of course.[80] The evidence goes to show that wages were regularly paid, and were regarded as a first charge upon the revenue.[81]

These lists of wages prove the well-known fact that the armies of this period comprised hundreds rather than thousands; and I think they also point to a distinction between the permanent nucleus of knights and men-at-arms, and a changing kaleidoscopic force by which they were accompanied. The former, drawn from England, Flanders and other lands as well as from Normandy, probably never numbered more than a few hundred. They were stationed in the castles and were moved about incessantly, or formed part of the royal retinue. The latter would be local and temporary, already armed in accordance with Henry II's assize, gathered together for a few weeks by the attraction of pay or possibly, as we have seen, in accordance with a definite local organisation.[82] Some such levy would perhaps

[77] *Rot. Pat.*, 190b.

[78] *Rot. Scacc.*, ii, 513, 514: 'in liberationibus iij militum, scilicet unicuique vj. so. in die. Et v. servientum equitum, scilicet unicuique ij. so. vjd. in die. Et xx servientum peditum, scilicet unicuique xij d. in die: morantium apud Waureium a festo Sancti Ilarii usque ad festum Sancti Michaelis (*i.e.*, January 13th to September 29th) dc li. liij li. xix so. vj d.' Eightpence was the more usual pay of a foot soldier (*e.g.*, *ibid.*, ii, 484, 502).

[79] 'de pluribus terminibus', *ibid.*, i, 136; ii, 485.

[80] 'de prestito super liberationes suas', *ibid.*, 502; 'de prestitis factis a Rege ultra mare', Pipe Roll 3 Joh., p. 160. The *Rotulus de Prestito* of 1210 gives a complete list of loans made during the expedition in Ireland (*Rot. de Liberate ac de misis et prestitis*, 172 *seqq.*).

[81] See, for example, the accounts of Geoffrey the Money-changer in 1195 (*Rot. Scacc.*, i, 136–8) and of Guérin of Glapion in 1200–1 (*ibid.*, ii, 501–2).

[82] *e.g.*, *Rot. Scacc.*, ii, 327: 'in liberationibus de cxl servientibus missis apud Vernolium de xx diebus.'

explain the appearance of 890 foot soldiers at Andeli in 1197 or 1198, an unusually large body which received wages for eight days.[83] It should be remembered that wages were high and that a permanent force even of this size would have cost more than £12,000 a year. In this year nearly £2000 was raised by a tallage in the Côtentin to maintain men-at-arms in the March—a sum of £2000, where a quarter of wheat only cost 4s. and where one could buy a cock for 1d. or a ram for 1s.[84]—and yet a sum less than one-sixth of that required for the wages of 890 men during a twelvemonth. Such a study of prices precludes the conclusion that armies of any size could be permanently retained at such wages. The interests of the agricultural classes from which many of the knights and the majority of the men-at-arms were drawn, were also opposed to service far away from home or for a long period.[85] The claims of the annual harvest were too pressing.

The foregoing analysis of the military strength of Normandy and of the operation of its feudal forces has necessarily been somewhat hypothetical. When we turn to the professional soldiers of the twelfth century we are on firmer ground, for, though the facts are few, they are not obscured by legal and economic issues.

In the first place must be distinguished the artificers, crossbowmen and archers in the royal service. These were the *élite* of the military profession. The artificers appear as a corps, the later Royal Engineers,[86] in John's expedition to Ireland in 1210, and had probably been formed during the previous reign. The most conspicuous of these engine makers was Master Urric, who was endowed with lands by Richard and John, and was of sufficient social importance to hold lands by knight service. He accompanied John to Normandy in 1201 'ad facienda ingenia'.[87] The name usually given to these artificers was that of *ingeniator* or *enginneor*,[88] but Master Urric is also styled *balistarius*,[89] a word which generally means a crossbowman who used a *balista*. The confusion arose from the fact that as well as the crossbow, the various large siege engines and stone throwers were generically described as *balistae*.[90] Hence it is probable that some of

[83] *Rot. Scacc.*, ii, 310.

[84] *Ibid.*, 471, 473, 478. Prices varied so much that it is only safe to compare those of the same district for the same year. Unless otherwise stated, references are to Angevin money, the chief currency of Normandy.

[85] The men who returned from the army at Aumâle (*Rot. Scacc.*, ii, 480) and neglected to serve at Gaillefontaine (*ibid.*, 478), were from the Côtentin.

[86] Round, *The King's Serjeants*, p. 16.

[87] *Rot. de Lib.*, 14; Round, *op. cit.*, p. 15.

[88] *e.g.*, William the Enginneor in *Rot. Scacc.*, ii, 480; and John's *ingenitor* (*Rot. Norm.*, 107).

[89] *Bracton's Note Book*, case 1275, quoted Round, *loc. cit.*

[90] The distinction, however, is apparent in the list of the furniture in the

the more important *balistarii* in the service of Richard and John, such as Master Ivo and Lupillin, were artillerymen who worked the great engines rather than crossbowmen.[91] Lupillin was even trusted with a Poitevin castle by King John.[92] However this may be, the *balistarii* played a large part in the military operations of the time. They were endowed with lands and pensions,[93] ranked immediately after the knights,[94] and received in Normandy the handsome wage of four shillings a day.[95] The crossbow was peculiarly an eastern and southern weapon and came into use slowly in France and Normandy,[96] hence we find that Richard and his brother retained foreign arbalisters in their service, and especially Genoese.[97] They were moved about, sometimes separately, but more often in companies, and were used for the most part in garrison duty.[98] They were of varying rank or social status; for example, in a band of eighty-four which is mentioned in the Liberate Roll of 1200, twenty-six travelled with three horses apiece, fifty-one with two, and seven with one horse.[99] The king was apparently responsible for the weapons: they are occasionally referred to as his, and he refunded money which was expended upon them;[100]

Norman castles, of about 1210 (*Cartulaire Normand*, nos. 214, 215, pp. 33, 34; these are best studied in Register A, printed in facsimile by L. Delisle as *Le Premier Registre de Philippe-Auguste* (Paris), 1883, ff. 5v.–6, 90v.–91.

[91] The reader will remember that another Ivo Balistarius, who was an engineer, founded the great house of Bellême (Stapleton, I, lxxi). He was master of the engines of Hugh the Great.

[92] See John's letter of February 18, 1203, to Lupillin the *balistarius*; 'Mandamus vobis quod liberetis castrum nostrum de Vouent cui dilectus et fidelis noster Robertus de Tornham senescallus Pictavie illud liberare preceperit' (*Rot. Pat.*, 25b).

[93] *e.g., Rot. Norm.*, 62; *Rot. Scacc.*, ii, 311, 481.

[94] *Rot. Pat.*, 12b: 'rex . . . omnibus militibus, balistariis, servientibus existentibus in Marchiis Normannie.'

[95] This was the daily allowance of William Painchon at Vaudreuil in 1198 (*Rot. Scacc.*, ii, 483, 484). For the wages of *balistarii* of different grades in England, rather later, corresponding to grades of *servientes* with three horses, two horses and one horse, see *Rot. Litt. Claus.*, i, 28, 250b. A maker of crossbows, *e.g.,* Roger of Genoa, was paid less: *Rot. de Lib.*, 100, 101; *Rot. Litt. Claus.*, i, 9b; Pipe Roll, 6 John, p. 248.

[96] Its use in war between Christians was condemned by the Lateran Council of 1139, and William the Breton pretends that it was unknown in France as late as 1185 (*Phil.*, lib. ii, v. 316), but this is an exaggeration; see Delaborde's note (ii, 52, 53). Mr. Round has pointed out the existence of crossbow serjeanties in England as early as 1086 (*The King's Serjeants*, pp. 13, 14).

[97] *Rot. Norm.*, 47, 59; Round, *op. cit.*, 16.

[98] *Rot. Norm.*, 77.

[99] *Rot. de Lib.*, 6; cf. *Rot. Norm.*, 47; *Rot. Scacc.*, ii, 314, gifts to balistarii for the purchase of horses.

[100] *Rot. Scacc.*, ii, 314. 'Ricardo Walensi qui faciebat balistas Regis'—wages 2s. 6d. a day. *Rot. de Lib.*, 100, order for repayment of expenditure 'in nervis et cordis et clavibus balistarum nostrarum'.

Q

moreover, the various kinds of crossbow were, if we may argue from French practice a few years later, kept in the armouries of the royal castles.[101]

A well-known passage in the *Philippid* describes the part played by the arbalisters in the operations of a siege, and emphasises the value which Philip Augustus placed upon their services.[102] Some of those in Philip's service, and in that of his rivals, are known by name, and we possess a few details about the lands with which they were endowed, but that is all. The only man who stands out with any prominence from the shadowy background is Richard's follower, Master Ivo, who was probably an engineer. Ivo was evidently very skilful and much trusted. He had apparently been on terms of sufficient intimacy with his great master to feel the change from Richard to John as a personal loss; and his interest in and fidelity to John were certainly weakened by the middle of 1203. His quarrel with the king was so violent that he fled for sanctuary to the cathedral at Rouen, and John seems to have had some difficulty in patching up an understanding. The archbishop restored Ivo to the royal service, and Ivo gave his sons as hostages in pledge of his fidelity; but on the other hand he was to remain under the protection of the Church and was free to go where he wished, with wife, sons and chattels, so soon as peace or a truce of two or three years was made between the king and Philip Augustus. John bound himself under ecclesiastical penalties to accept this arrangement, and only stipulated that Master Ivo should not take service with his enemies.[103]

. I have described the *balistarii* as the elect of the military profession. At the other extreme were the outcast Brabançons and Cottereaux. Midway stood the Welsh mercenaries. We have already seen a Welshman at work upon the royal crossbows, and it is possible that there were Welshmen among the crossbowmen, but, as is well known from the writings of Gerald of Wales, the favourite weapon of his fellow countrymen was the longbow.[104] It is impossible to say whether the bands of Welsh mercenaries who enlisted under our Angevin kings were all archers, for the presence of archers in the Norman wars is but casually mentioned by the chroniclers, and the rolls only refer

---

[101] See above, p. 224, note 90.

[102] *Philipp*, lib. vi, vv. 263 *seqq.*, 661 *seqq.* (Delaborde, ii, 186, 202). The latter passage begins:

'Hic Blondellus erat, Perigas, aliique viri quos
Regi reddiderat ars balistaria caros,
Ditatos ab eo villis, et rebus et ere.'

[103] This interesting charter, dated Rouen, July 29, 1203, is enrolled in *Rot. Pat.*, 31b.

[104] Cf. *Guill. le Maréchal*, l. 7416 (ed. Meyer, i, 267).

to a company of archers under William of Vernon.[105] The history, however, of the Anglo-Norman conquest of Ireland would suggest that the Welsh would use the bow in Normandy.[106] Indirect evidence points to the same conclusion. They were especially useful in ambush. In 1174 Henry II sent them to cut off the provisions of the French as they were brought through the woods to the army which was besieging Rouen;[107] and in Richard's reign the Welsh had a reputation for the success with which they harassed the French in the forests.[108] They were not enlisted separately; but the government made arrangements with some Anglo-Norman tenant of the Welsh march, or with a native Welshman who collected a band and was responsible for the distribution of the wages.[109] Some of these companies were large. In 1204 John refers to one which contained two hundred Welshmen.[110] In 1195 at least five shiploads of Welsh cavalry and foot crossed to Normandy under various leaders.[111]

We now come to the mercenaries proper, who were carefully distinguished from the various branches of the artillery and from the Welsh.[112] The English hated John's foreign *balistarii*, but never

[105] *Rot. de Lib.*, 78, where the archer is distinguished from the arbalister. Sometimes, however, the archer is clearly a crossbowman, *e.g.*, the Genoese in *Rot. Norm.*, 47: Rigord mentions 'equites sagittarii' (i, 162).

[106] *The Song of Dermot and the Earl*, p. 52; Orpen, *Ireland under the Normans*, i, 148.

[107] Robert of Torigni (ed. Delisle), ii, 52; Rolls Series, p. 265. 'Venieus itaque Rothomagum misit marchisos suos Walenses trans Secanam, ut victualia, quae veniebant ad exercitum Francorum, in nemoribus diriperent.'

[108] The French chronicle in *Historiens de France*, xxiv, part ii, p. 738. Delaborde points out that William the Breton's description of the Welsh is based on Gerald of Wales (*Phil.*, lib. v, ll. 276–99, ed. Delaborde, ii, 136).

[109] *e.g.*, William de Marisco or Marsh in 1195; *Rot. Scacc.*, i, 236: 'Willelmo de Marisco et Walensibus suis' £296 10s. William was a West country man (cf. *Rot. Pat.*, 52, where he is collecting workmen and sailors). For William de Marisco, elder brother of Geoffrey, the justiciar of Ireland, and the connection of his family with the Welsh March, see Eric St. John Brooks in the *Journal of the Royal Soc. of Antiquaries of Ireland*, lxi, pt. i (1931), 27–38 *passim*.

[110] *Rot. de Lib.*, 88. The sheriff of Gloucester is to give William of Briouze ten marks 'ad opus Leisani Walensis filii Morgan qui veniet in servicium nostrum cum cc Walensibus'.

[111] *Rot. Scacc.*, i, 185, 'in passagio Walensium apud Ostreham in tribus navibus, viij li. x so.'; *ibid.*, 275, 'in passagio Philippi de Estapedona et Walteri de Escudemore et Helye de Chigehan et sociorum eorum Walensium equitum et peditum in ij navibus [to Barfleur] viij li.'

[112] See H. Géraud, 'Les Routiers au douzième siècle', and 'Mercadier. Les Routiers au treizième siècle', in *Bibliothèque de l'Ecole des Chartes*, 1841, iii, 125–47; 417–47; Boutaric's paper in the same, 1860, xxii, 7–12, republished in his *Institutions militaires de la France avant les armées permanentes* (1863); Luchaire, *La Société française au temps de Philippe-Auguste*, pp. 10–20;

confounded them with the *stipendiarii*.[113] The French expressed their disgust of the Welsh, but never confounded them with the Brabançons. Indeed in 1194, while the royal forces were waiting for a favourable wind at Portsmouth, the Welsh and Brabançons came to blows, and the king had to hurry back from his hunting to restore peace.[114] The struggle for existence which encouraged the surplus population of Wales to seek military employment had not destroyed family and tribal ties; the Brabançons and Cottereaux, on the contrary, were pariahs, outcasts from society and under the ban of the Church. Their gipsy-like organisation,[115] their anti-social and anti-Christian devastations shocked the conscience of western Europe. They were worse than the most illicit of corporations, or the most heretical of sects.

A closer scrutiny of the mercenary forces in the service of Richard and John enables us, however, to make some qualifications. It shows that the clear line of division drawn by the anathema of the Church in 1179 and by current opinion between the mercenaries and other paid soldiers was easily blurred in actual life. The *routiers* (*rutharii* or *ruptarii*), to give them their generic name, comprised elements which were drawn from many countries, from Aragon, Gascony, Bigorre, as well as from the populous Rhineland,[116] and it is hard to distinguish between bands which may have been recruited on the spot and the professional vagabonds who offered their services to the highest bidder. Yet the former would obviously be regarded as more respectable. Again, men of ability who were found trustworthy enough for high administrative office, such as Martin Algais, a mercenary who became seneschal of Gascony, can hardly be dismissed as social outcasts. The origin of many of John's favourite servants was so obscure that the transition from Martin Algais to the great Hubert de Burgh himself is not very difficult. We might begin this transition with the mercenaries in John's service who were always his subjects and whose military gifts had emancipated them from the caste system of feudalism: such were Fawkes of Breauté, and that upstart

---

Cartellieri, iii, 110; Delisle on Cadoc in his preface to the inquests of Saint Louis, *Recueil des historiens de France,* xxiv, part i, pp. 130*–133*.

[113] Magna Carta, c. 51, 'et statim post reformacionem amovebimus de regno omnes alienigenas milites, balistarios, servientes, stipendiarios, qui venerunt cum equis et armis ad nocumentum regni'.

[114] Howden, iii, 251.

[115] Cf. the anonymous chronicler of Laon's description of Ebbe of Charenton's ruse in 1185 (*Chronicon Universale*, ed. Cartellieri, p. 40), 'set propter pactum quod cum eis pepigit, uxores immo pellicentes eorum cum pueris et alia familia et rebus aliis eis extra castrum remisit'.

[116] The chronicler of Laon, p. 37, gives a brief list: 'importuna lues Ruthariorum, Arragonensium, Basculorum, Brabanciorum et aliorum conducticiorum.' Wages to *Bigordenses*, in *Rot. Scacc.*, i, 237.

kindred of Touraine, Girard of Athée and his cousins of Cicogné and Chanceaux.[117] Next we should come to high officials like Guérin of Glapion and William Crassus (*le Gros*), both seneschals in Normandy under John, both apparently of humble origin, and both men whose reputation was unsavoury in the land of their exactions forty years later.[118] There is little difference in character between such men as William Crassus and the leading *routiers*, and probably little difference in origin, and when King Richard began, for military reasons, to entrust Norman bailiwicks to his mercenaries,[119] the difference of status was swept away. In John's reign the practice of opening the civil service to mercenaries became common. Quite apart from military considerations John trusted his mercenaries more than his barons, took a natural pleasure in ignoble vigour, and delighted to flout social and political conventions. Hence Martin Algais became seneschal of Gascony, Girard of Athée seneschal of Touraine, Brandin seneschal of La Marche, and Louvrecaire a Norman bailiff.[120] Algais and Louvrecaire left John's service, but Girard and his kindred came to England where sheriffdoms and castles awaited them; their enormities there have been revealed to all students of English history by the publication of the Gloucestershire Plea roll of 1221, and may give us some idea of the indignation and misery caused by their rule in Touraine. It cannot be denied that if they were outcasts they were successful, much officialised outcasts, efficient soldiers and vigorous administrators.

Yet, if we think of the companions of a mercenary chief, it is clear that a prudent king would have kept the *routiers* at a safe distance, well outside the official circle. The company or *ruta*[121] of warriors with their families, or, to use the offensive phrase of the great charter, their litters (*sequelae*), fastened upon a countryside like locusts. They spared neither churches nor monasteries; and even large towns were not safe from their attack.[122] Although they were more terrible when no strong king could bind them to his interests and exercise some sort of control over them, their licence was fortunately a frequent cause

[117] Maitland, *Pleas of the Crown for the county of Gloucester* (1884), pp. xiii–xv.

[118] For Guérin of Glapion, see above, p. 173. The misdeeds of William Crassus are described in the *Querimonae Normannorum*, nos. 382–462 *passim*, about eighteen cases.

[119] *e.g.*, William le Queuin the Vexin; above, p. 200.

[120] That *Lupescar* was a bailiff is clear from the writs addressed to him, *e.g.*, *Rot. Norm.*, 103, 105; *Rot. Pat.*, 24b, 25b, and especially 32b, but the nature and extent of his duties are not clearly defined.

[121] Or *rupta*, as *Rot. Pat.*, 20b. Cf. Ducange, *Glossarium*.

[122] For a strange and confused tradition of an attack by the *routiers* upon Poitiers, see Lecointre-Dupont in *Mémoires de la Société des Antiquaires de l'Ouest*, 1845, xii, 117–19, 209–16, and the authorities discussed there.

of their undoing. As each band was separately organised under rival chiefs who had no interest in common,[123] they did not form any coalition sufficiently durable to be dangerous. They roused against them, if all other restraints failed, the irresistible strength of popular desperation, such as inspired the sworn associations which were organised by the carpenter of Puy-en-Velay about 1182.[124] Even if they were in the service of a great king like Richard, they were none the less regarded as *ferae naturae*. For example, after the truce of 1199, when Mercadier and his troop were on their way southwards from Normandy, they were attacked by the vassals of Philip Augustus and suffered much loss.[125] It is significant that King John had to bind his Norman barons with an oath to defend and maintain the hated Louvrecaire while he was in the royal service, and to insist in return that the mercenary should refrain from acts of annoyance and damage to the men and lands of his own subjects.[126]

The *routiers* undoubtedly did much to deprive the Norman wars of any national character that they may have possessed. They were detested by barons, clergy, towns and peasants. 'Do you know', asks the Marshal's biographer, 'why King John was unable to keep the love of his people? It was because Louvrecaire maltreated them, and pillaged them as though he were in an enemy's country.'[127] One evil bred another, so that as the king lost the esteem of his subjects the mercenaries gradually became the mainstay of his strength. In 1204 they held the most important posts in the defence of his dominions. A chronicler of Limoges refers to their defeat at Noaillé in that year as a deed which first broke the power of the king of England in Aquitaine.[128] John spared no effort to retain their services, and the peculiar privileges of the bands must have caused much annoyance to the decent vassal who was limited at all points by duty to his lord. Their booty was specially protected[129]—and very precious booty it often was, of treasures which no good Christian would dare to take. They kept their own prisoners.[130] Castles and lands were given to

---

[123] Mercadier was murdered in the streets of Bordeaux by a follower of Brandin, April 10, 1200 (Howden, iv, 114; cf. Richard, *Comtes de Poitou*, ii, 370–1).

[124] Anonymous of Laon, ed. Cartellieri, pp. 37–40; Luchaire, *La Société française*, pp. 13 *seqq.*

[125] Howden, iv, 80. King Philip repudiated the act.

[126] See the letter of November 7, 1203—a critical period—in *Rot. Pat.*, 35b. John of Préaux seems to have been the special object of Louvrecaire's attentions.   [127] *Guill. le Maréchal*, iii, 171.

[128] Chronicle of Saint Martin of Limoges in *Historiens de France*, xviii, 239, 'et sic brachium Regis Angliae in Aquitania primo confractum'.

[129] *e.g.*, *Rot. Pat.*, 21b, 24a.

[130] *e.g.*, *ibid.*, 15. Robert of Vieuxpont to deliver to Hugh of Gournai all the French prisoners taken in war, except those taken by Algais.

their leaders. Both Mercadier and Louvrecaire became, so far as lands went, barons of Aquitaine: the former received from Richard the land of Ademar of Beynac in Périgord;[131] and Louvrecaire was put by John in the temporary possession of fiefs in Gascony.[132] It would be tedious to collect the records of grants in land and money which were showered upon Algais, Brandin, Girard of Athée and the rest. Some gloomy satisfaction may be derived from the thought that John found pleasure in their company. There is probably much truth in the tactful letter which he wrote to the troop of Martin Algais after their leader's capture; he had, he says, never been so grieved by anything; he thought more highly of Martin's service than of the service of any other man.[133]

Many questions about the mercenaries remain unanswered. We should like to know something about the size of their companies, whether they had fixed wages,[134] the nature of their life in common and of its rough rules. It would be interesting to learn the composition of that 'army' which Mercadier boasted that he had led for King Richard. But we have to be content with the generalisations of hostile chroniclers. Of the leaders themselves much more is known. Philip Augustus depended largely upon a certain Cadoc, the rival of Mercadier in popular estimation.[135] Cadoc first came into prominence in 1196, when he defended Gaillon successfully against Richard. He was afterwards constable of this fortress, which was ultimately granted to him in full ownership together with the neighbouring Norman fief of Tosny. He joined in the siege of Château Gaillard in 1203, and helped to take Chinon in 1205. Under the French administration of the duchy he became bailiff of Pont-Audemer, and was an imposing and much hated figure in Norman politics for many years.[136] On the Angevin side the most striking adventurers were Mercadier and, in John's reign, Louvrecaire. Louvrecaire, who was in every way detestable, fought for many masters. He deserted John after surrendering

---

[131] Géraud in *Bibliothèque*, iii, 424, 444; Richard, *Comtes de Poitou*, ii, 321.
[132] *Rot. Pat.*, 30, May 27, 1203: 'delecto et fideli nostro Lupescar commisimus Riberiac et Albeterram ad sustentandum se in servicio nostro quousque ei ceteram gwarisionem assignaverimus.' [133] *Ibid.*, 20b.
[134] According to William the Breton, *Phil.*, lib. ll. 396–8 (Delaborde, ii, 192), Cadoc's band received £1000 a day—
'numerosaque rupta Cadoci,
Cui rex quotidie soli pro seque suisque
Libras mille dabat,'
but it is impossible to believe this. It is true, however, that very large grants to Cadoc, one for £4400 in Angevin money, are recorded in the accounts of Philip Augustus.
[135] Cf. the anonymous French chronicle in *Historiens de France*, xxiv, part ii, p. 738.
[136] Delisle, *ibid.*, pp. 130*–133*; and the authorities there given.

Falaise in 1204. Mercadier was of a nobler type, a fit companion for the king with whose history his life is bound up. Towards the end of his life he described his relations with Richard in a charter which he issued on behalf of some monks in Périgord. He refers to himself as the *famulus* of the king: 'I fought for him with loyalty and strenuously, never opposed to his will, prompt in obedience to his commands; and in consequence of this service I gained his esteem and was placed in command of his army.'[137] He had been with Richard in the Holy Land,[138] and was at this time about to enter upon the strenuous conflicts which filled the last three years of the king's reign. During this period he captured the bishop of Beauvais, invaded Brittany, shared in the victory at the bridge of Gisors, plundered Abbeville. His cooperation in the plans of Richard's new town at Andeli was commemorated by the name of the bridge Makade; his physician attended Richard at Chalus, and he is said to have shown his grief at Richard's death by the torture of the man who killed him. After a year's active service with the old Queen Eleanor he was murdered at Bordeaux on Easter Monday in the year 1200.

In the course of his faithful service, Mercadier caused great suffering and destruction. Indeed nothing shows how precarious and artificial was the unity of the Angevin empire more than the fact that such men as he was were required to hold it together, and were entrusted with important posts in the civil and military administration of its various parts. The history of these years enables us to understand still more clearly why in the century which followed, the struggle for constitutional reforms in England was bound up at every point with a hatred of all alien influences.

III

Contemporaries were astonished that Henry II and his sons were able to bear the financial strain of their numerous wars.[139] The increase in enfeoffments was not accompanied by a proportionate increase in fighting power, yet with a restricted demesne the kings

---

[137] Géraud, in *Bibliothèque de l'Ecole des Chartes*, iii, 444. For Mercadier's domain in Périgord, see above, p. 231.

[138] This follows from Richard's letters of credit, dated Acre, August 3, 1191, addressed on behalf of Mercadier and others to a Pisan merchant. The letter was edited by Géraud in his article upon Philip of Dreux, the bishop of Beauvais, *Bibliothèque*, v. 36.

[139] Giraldus Cambrensis, *De principis instructione* in *Opera*, viii, 316: 'quaeri ergo potest ab aliquo . . . qualiter rex Henricus secundus et ejus filii tot inter werras tantis thesauris abundant. Ad quae ratio reddi poterit, quia quod minus habebant in redditibus, totum in accidentabus, plus in accessoriis quam principalibus confidentes, supplere curabant.'

had to support an expensive army and an elaborate system of defences. To some extent the call was met by Henry's careful inquisitions into his *regalia*, and by Richard's high farming of the public offices,[140] but these methods of raising the revenue were in the nature of the case limited, and were neutralised or abused by the extravagance and recklessness of Richard and John.[141] The true answer to the problem is, as Gerald of Wales points out, that the extraordinary revenue (*accidentia*) was vastly increased during the second half of the twelfth century. The growth of a settled and industrious population, protected by the law in town and country, had multiplied these indirect proceeds of the land which were accessible to the government; if rents were inelastic, loans, tallages, and fines[142] were capable of vast extension.

Yet, as the struggle with Philip Augustus went on, it became clear that Normandy was unable to maintain the defence of her frontiers without English aid. The hardest fighting began in 1194, and in 1194 the duchy was already in debt. The money which had been drawn off for the Crusade did not come back,[143] but the returned Crusaders had to redeem from neighbour, monastery or Jew the lands which they had pledged before their departure. Moreover, the king's ransom saddled Normandy with her share in a great public debt: in the year 1194–5 the German envoys received £16,000 from the financiers of the duchy.[144] The redemption of this debt went on slowly; even in 1203 some Norman barons owed instalments of their contribution.[145] Then in 1194 the war expenditure began, including vast outlays upon men and fortresses. According to one account which survives from this period, the seneschal alone expended over £7000 in less than

[140] Richard's policy was systematic and extended to all his dominions; cf. Howden, iii, 267.

[141] John's unscrupulousness may be illustrated by the grant to William of Préaux of the Lieuvin, April 22, 1202. William had lent money to the king, who in order to pay his debt gave him the bailiwick at double the usual farm (*duplicando solitam firmam*) and ordered the barons of the exchequer to compute the farm to him until the debt was paid (*Rot. Norm.*, 89, 90).

[142] The fine was in the majority of cases a payment for a *licence*, and the opportunity for selling licences increased as the complexity and interdependence of social relations increased. In itself a legitimate tax upon the growing activities of feudal society, the fine was subject to easy yet almost incredible abuse by John. See Delisle, in *Bibliothèque*, xiii, 112; McKechnie, *Magna Carta*, p. 532; 2nd edition, p. 455.

[143] Compare Richard's letter from Acre, in *Bibliothèque*, v. 46: 'sciatis quod, cum quosdam fideles nostros pro negotiorum nostrorum opportunitate ad transmarinos partes remittendos duximus, nichil autem de proprio in hoc casu, secundum peregrinationis votum alienare possimus, dilecto nostro Jacobo de Jhota curam potestatemque commisimus.' [144] *Rot. Scacc.*, i, 136.

[145] *e.g.*, *Rot. Norm.*, p. 74. A 'rotulus Redemptionis' contained records of the payments made by the barons (*Rot. Scacc.*, i, 128).

eighteen months, in wages, repairs and incidental expenses,[146] and the seneschal's financial disbursements, though comprehensive, met only a small part of the annual call upon Normandy. Before 1198 was over, nearly £50,000 were spent upon the fortifications at Andeli[147] and its neighbourhood. It should be remembered, at the same time, that in 1193 King Philip had, as a result of his annexations, wrested the eastern bailiwicks from the control of the Norman exchequer,[148] and although the loss was, with the exception of Gisors and a few other places, temporary, the Norman Vexin and Bray were henceforward rarely at peace. Owing to the loss of Gisors they cost more for their defence than they could contribute. As Philip advanced, seizing a little here and a little there, he restricted the revenue-yielding area while he forced an increase in Norman expenditure.

The fixed farms of the Norman bailiwicks and *praepositurae* amounted to £20,000 a year in Angevin money. Now, if we take the usual military season about the year 1200, from Saint Hilary's day (January 13) to Michaelmas, and place a fairly small garrison of two knights, five men-at-arms of the cavalry class, and twenty other men-at-arms in a second-class fortress, we find that a cost of £650 is incurred.[149] Thirty such garrisons would consume the fixed revenue of Normandy, and the Norman government was responsible for the defence of about forty-five castles, many of which would need a much larger garrison than the one described.[150] It is of course true that the majority of these places were maintained by local effort, and would only be specially garrisoned during a critical period, but when we reflect upon the other expenses of the year, both military and civil, it is clear that the additional revenue required must have been great. As I have said, English aid was necessary, to supplement the proceeds of aids, tallages and loans.

If the series of exchequer rolls were complete, it would doubtless be possible to compile the financial history of Normandy between 1194 and 1203. But from the three rolls which survive only general conclusions can be drawn. Aids were imposed for special as well as for general objects, for a siege, a fortification or the wages of soldiers on the Norman march. Some of these were levied instead of service, some were probably taxes levied on the ducal demesne.[151] Casual

[146] Guérin of Glapion's statement of accounts for 1200–1 (*Rot. Scacc.*, ii, 500).   [147] Above, p. 194.

[148] Above, p. 97. Moreover the Norman exchequer, by the treaty of 1193, was responsible for the maintenance of the garrisons placed by Philip in Arques and Drincourt.

[149] *Rot. Scacc.*, ii, 513, 514. This was the garrison at Gavrai in 1203.

[150] Above, pp. 68 *seqq.*

[151] See Delisle, *Bibliothèque*, xiii, 120–6. As Delisle points out in a note on pp. 119, 120, the terms *auxilium* and *tallagium* were frequently used alternatively in Normandy.

references upon the exchequer rolls show that in 1202 a tallage was laid upon the lands of Normandy held in free alms, or in other words upon the Church,[152] and that in 1203 a general aid of two shillings was levied throughout the Norman bailiwicks.[153] This last evidently corresponds to the English carucage, and shows that under the stress of war the Norman and English financial systems were being assimilated. The greatest pressure, however, was felt by the towns. The richer burgesses or property holders were taxed at £10 and upwards, and their contributions reached a total, varying with the size of the towns, from £100 or so up to the £600 of Bayeux and the £650 of Falaise.[154] By these means enormous sums were raised for the defence of the March.

These exactions were supplemented by loans from towns, bailiwicks, Jews and private persons, by the proceeds of amercements, fines and sureties and the chattels of deceased usurers.[155] But as time went on John relied more and more upon his treasure from England. In 1203 the king was unable to pay the wages of his servants on the March; early in February, at the commencement of the most critical year of warfare, numerous orders were issued to meet the deficit by means of English treasure; half the arrears up to February 9 were to be paid, and full pay for fifteen or twenty days beyond that date.[156] Delisle calculated that during this year 18,120 marks of silver were sent from England into Normandy.[157] In Angevin money this sum would amount to £48,320, or more than double the fixed Norman revenue.

Two facts, which are closely connected, are revealed very clearly by a study of Angevin finance during the reign of King John. In the first place, although the various exchequers had in concert with the royal chamber developed a careful system of bookkeeping, they did not make any attempt at a financial policy. Enormous sums were gathered, distributed and spent; and every official concerned in their collection or expenditure rendered account of his service, but it was

[152] *Rot. Norm.*, 65: 'occasione tallagii positi super elemosinas Normannie.'

[153] *Ibid.*, 90: 'auxilium duorum solidorum quod positum fuit generaliter in Normannia.'

[154] Delisle, *op. cit.*, p. 130. For the method of assessment, see the exchequer rolls, *passim*. The numerous *emprumenta* or loans were collected in the same way. They are, of course, distinct from the loans made by individuals which are mentioned below.

[155] The chattels and lands of William of Calviz, a usurer, brought in large sums in 1195.

[156] *Rot. Norm.*, 75, 76. The statement in the text are deductions from the entries on these pages.

[157] Delisle, in *Bibliothèque*, x, 289. The calculation is made from the Liberate roll for 1203. The sum as calculated by the editor of the Pipe Roll for 5 John is greater: £14,733 or about 22,100 marks; see above, p. 160. For the export of treasure from Southampton and other ports, see Pipe Rolls, 4 John, pp. 79, 284 and 5 John, pp. 7, 145, 193.

nobody's business to inquire whether the money was exacted wisely or expended prudently. It was particularly desirable that the Angevin government should know how it stood because—and here I come to the second point—finance was becoming a cosmopolitan power. Credit, with its subtle operations and reactions, was growing. Untouched by the annual stocktaking at the exchequer, new forms of accommodation, fresh sources of wealth were opened to Richard and John by Jew, money-changer and Italian merchant. Centuries were to pass before the European states learned the elementary canon of sound finance, that the need for a careful examination of accounts grows in proportion to the ease with which money can be obtained; but a habit of financial criticism would have been sufficient to check the recklessness of the Angevin kings. Unfortunately, this habit could only be formed in a state which felt the unity given by national sentiment. It was possible in the England of Henry III; it was not possible in the Angevin empire, for the empire was only kept together by those very ties of a common financial administration which it is the function of national sentiment to control.

It is worth while to dwell upon and illustrate these aspects of Angevin administration.

The exchequers of the various states which formed the empire, England, Normandy, Anjou, Poitou, seem to have been regarded as parts of a single system.[158] The treasure which they collected and preserved was circulated freely from one part of the empire to the other.[159] It is true that a considerable proportion of the royal income was earmarked for special purposes, such as the payment of tithes. But most of these appropriations were of ancient date; though protected by reverence or custom, they did not affect the general principle of feudal finance, the confusion of 'public' with private revenue; they resulted from no development in public action, still less of public opinion. Hence the course of time, while it necessarily brought with it an addition to these obligations, brought no theory of the distinction between the national exchequer and the privy purse. The king issued the same form of writ for the passage of his dogs as he did for the

[158] The co-operation between the exchequers of Caen and Westminster may be illustrated by the arrangements for the payment of Queen Berengaria's dower (*Rot. Pat.*, 2b). Payments into one exchequer were deducted from payments due at the other (*e.g.*, *Rot. Scacc.*, ii, 496: the debts of the chamberlain of Tancarville). The Poitevin exchequer is mentioned in *Rot. Norm.*, 28.

[159] Above, p. 31. Compare *Rot. Scacc.*, i, 56, 57, 'pro thesauris portandis de Cadomo in Andegaviam et in plura loca per Normanniam'; *Rot. Norm.*, 31: to the seneschal and barons of the *Norman* exchequer 'computate R. Abbati 6375 marcas argenti quas liberavit in camera nostra *ante exercitum Gasconie* de thesauro nostro *Anglie* anno regni nostri secundo'. The Norman treasuries were at Caen, Falaise (*e.g.*, *Rot. Scacc.*, i, 39), and apparently Vaudreuil (*Rot. Chart.*, 17). See also Haskins, *Norman Institutions*, pp. 176—8 and notes.

payment of his mercenaries. With the proceeds of fines and dues he might march to relieve a city, rebuild a church, buy a new coat of mail or pay his gambling debts.

The royal power over the proceeds of the feudal state extended also to the sources of revenue. Here, again, no distinction was made between the public and the private position of the king. All tenures were equally public or equally private; and as they were equally protected by law and custom, so, beyond the scope of law, they were equally subject to royal policy or royal whim. The wisdom or folly of the king decided whether public policy or private caprice should dispose of demesne, escheats, wardships or forfeitures. By careful management Henry II had doubled his income; by mismanagement John brought chaos. In the latter's reign the royal chamber (*camera*) was a centre of intrigue and recklessness.[160] Treasure poured in and was poured out in heedless confusion. Writ after writ was issued at the dictation of the spasmodic policy or favour of the king, for the disposal of lands and rents. John was, it is true, a hard man at a bargain. The Bertram and a few other wardships sold well.[161] Those escheats which he kept in his hands were highly farmed. An elaborate system of pledges enabled him, with no expense to himself, to insure the fidelity of his vassals by making them go warranty for each other. But his astuteness went no further. Lands and wealth which might have been absorbed in the royal demesne and given strength to local administration were scattered. As Philip ate his way into Normandy and occupied more and more territory, this disregard for economy reacted with fatal effect upon the sound parts of the financial system. The bailiffs could not collect their farms, or availed themselves of the confusion to fill their own pockets. The men who had lost their lands either deserted or clamoured for compensation elsewhere. The rapid calls upon the exchequers of England and Normandy exhausted the treasure. John was thrown back increasingly upon men who were willing to profit by disorder and upon mercenaries whose depredations increased the general disaffection.[162]

[160] Although I am not convinced that this judgment is wrong, I should point out that, from some recent investigation, notably by J. E. A. Jolliffe, John emerges as a more business-like king: cf. Jolliffe on *Angevin Kingship*, chapter xi and in *Studies presented to . . . Powicke*, pp. 117–42.

[161] *Rot. Pat.*, 19, October 18, 1202: 'sciatis quod concessimus Roberto de Tebovilla custodiam terre et filii et filie Roberti Bertram pro sex milia li. And., ita quod habebit predictos filium et filiam in custodia donec ad legitmam etatem pervenerint.' The terms of the agreement which follows are detailed and interesting. See Stapleton, II, ccxi, note. The wardship was of the Norman honour of the Bertram house, which included property in Norfolk and Essex. It shoud be distinguished from the Northumbrian house (*Red Book*, ii, 698; *Rotuli de Oblatis et finibus*, 478).

[162] This paragraph is based upon conclusions drawn from the Norman and

In England the effect of these practices would have been apparent at once. They could not have been continued without open exactions which would have led to resistance. Such was the course of events which produced the charter of Henry I and was later to produce the Great Charter. In Normandy the poison worked with more subtlety. The reason for the difference between the two countries is closely connected with the more cosmopolitan nature of Norman finance. Wider opportunities for credit were open to the kings on the continent than in England. Money was drawn from all quarters, and through the alien influences of trade and exchange public opinion in Normandy was diverted from politics. This tendency is, indeed, but one illustration of the fact that the central position of Normandy weakened the expression in the duchy of political and racial feeling. It is significant that we hear of no constitutional opposition in Normandy. Except at the Christmas feast few great councils were summoned during this period.[163] No government was more consistently personal than John's; and the fact that he resorted so capriciously and unintelligently to credit, though it hastened bankruptcy, helped to silence criticism

---

Echequer rolls. As an illustration I may take the fine owed by Robert of Thibouville for the Bertram wardship (see previous note). According to the original arrangement (*Rot. Pat.*, 19) this sum, £6000 Angevin, was to be paid as follows: £1000 on November 30, 1202; the same sum at Easter and at Michaelmas, 1203; and £500 at each succeeding Easter and Michaelmas until the whole was paid. Robert actually paid £1000 on December 22, 1202 (*Rot. Norm.*, 66); £1000 about the following Easter (*ibid.*, 90); and £500 on the Monday after the feast of Saint Denis, *i.e.*, after October 9, 1203 (*ibid.*, 106). Before the next payment was due Robert of Thibouville had joined Philip (cf. *Cart. Norm.*, no. 204) and the English part of the Bertram inheritance came into John's hands (*Rot. Norm.*, 129; *Red Book*, ii, 805; *Excerpta e rotulis finium*, i, 288). But King John had only enjoyed the first paid instalment. All the rest he had at first assigned to Hugh of Gournai in recompense for his lost lands (*Rot. Pat.*, 26b) and one of Hugh's last acts, before his desertion in May, 1203, was to give a receipt for the second instalment of £1000 (*Rot. Norm.*, 90). If Hugh had remained faithful, part of the fine would have gone to pay his debts to William Crassus (*Rot. Pat.*, 28b). After his desertion John promised the next instalment to two of his Rouen creditors, Matthew the Fat and William the Miller: who had accommodated him with £400 and £100 respectively (*Rot. Pat.*, 30). The fourth instalment which, owing to Robert of Thibouville's desertion, was never paid, had been promised to Master Peter of Verneuil (*Rot. Pat.*, 43b). Hence, practically the whole of this vast fine for the wardship of a great Norman honour would have been frittered away, for it is clear that John borrowed in anticipation of the instalments.

[163] John announces his inability to be present on the day fixed for what seems to be a great council at Rouen (*Rot. Pat.*, 23). It was perhaps to have met on Saint Hilary's day, since the king writes on January 12, 1203. Of course there was frequent consultation between the king and his followers during the various negotiations with the king of France, but his self-reliance is shown at the interviews in 1200 and in June, 1201, when he met Philip alone (Gervase of Canterbury, ii, 92; Howden, iv, 164).

and to maintain the supremacy of the administration which had been unchallenged since 1174. Moreover, it should be remembered that Normandy was the seat of war and that the money drawn from England and from the king's creditors was spent there. Though famine and disorder destroyed individuals, though the general discomfort resulted in a general acquiescence in the change to a French master, Normandy as a whole was probably not impoverished and did not feel the strain which was put upon England by the constant exportation of men and treasure.

It would lead us too far from our course to analyse at any length John's relations with his creditors. He was able to use a system which extended from Piacenza and Genoa to Cologne and Rouen. It is suggestive of the position which Normandy occupied in the commercial world that nearly every kind of coinage circulated freely except her own;[164] indeed a daring attempt might be made to measure changes in the political situation of the duchy from year to year by the changes which were produced in the relative values of the currency by high prices and the importation of bullion.[165] The real danger to John's solvency did not, of course, lie in the fact that the accumulated wealth of Normandy or Touraine was at his service, but, as I have suggested, in the absence of any official restraint or audit of his operations. So long as the money-changers in the cities of Lombardy or the valley of the Loire[166] were employed to facilitate public business or to advance money to diplomatic agents, they performed a real service. King Richard found in Geoffrey of Val Richer, the important money-changer of Rouen, a most useful agent for the payment of his ransom;[167] and, later, when the building of Château Gaillard made it necessary to have recourse to a more centralised machinery than the local services, Geoffrey was again employed.[168] But Richard and John were unable to resist the temptation to borrow and to go on borrowing. John borrowed from everybody, so that the records of the last months of his rule in Normandy give the impression that the

[164] Delisle, in *Bibliothèque*, x, 185 *seqq.*

[165] The material is collected by Delisle, *op. cit.*, pp. 195 *seqq.*

[166] *Rot. Scacc.*, i, 38 (1180): 'in passagio episcopi Wintoniensis et Cambiatorum Regis de Turonis et Cenomannis.' For the merchants of Piacenza, see especially *Rot. Chart.*, 31, where it appears that certain men of Piacenza had lent a large sum to Richard's envoys 'ad negocium karissimi nepotis nostri illustris Regis Othonis in curia Romana faciendum'. John promised repayment in four instalments (cf. 96b). There are many other instances. Reference should also be made to John's dealings with the Templars; see Delisle's article in the *Mémoires de l'Académie des Inscriptions*, xxxiii, pt. 2, pp. 10 *seqq.*

[167] *Rot. Scacc.*, i, 136.

[168] *Rot. Scacc.*, ii, 300, 309. He was used permanently (cf. i, 236) as a financial agent, but the ransom and the building of Château Gaillard seem to have given him especial prominence.

revenue must have been far exceeded by his anticipations. The money which he received, for example, from Laurence of the Donjon, a wealthy citizen of Rouen, was almost entirely repaid by the officials of the English, not of the Norman, exchequer.[169]

How far John interfered with the actual operations of trade and the private obligations of his subjects is uncertain. The exigencies of warfare caused an occasional diversion of shipping,[170] or prohibition of the export of corn.[171] But, as a restriction of supplies would speedily have followed any tyrannical interference, the king seems to have been careful, on the whole, to respect commercial interests.[172] A more dangerous tendency was shown by the practice of rewarding public service by the remission of debts which his vassals owed to private creditors. That King John had recourse to such action as this is sufficient proof that he was getting to the end of his resources. But, in the majority of cases, the creditors who suffered were Jews,[173] and it is well known that the financial operations of the Jewish community were undertaken in face of the risks which were incident to their privileged position. Their elaborate system of agency and credit,[174] which has been explored by modern scholars, may well

[169] See especially *Rot. de Liberate*, 40, 57. Laurence was one of the viscounts, or royal farmers at Rouen (*Rot. Norm.*, 107), and apparently in this capacity received certain orders from John (*ibid.*, 48, 49, 50, 59, 100). He received £1000 in 1203 from the English officials which had been granted to the citizens of Rouen for the fortification of their city (*Rot. Pat.*, 25), and at the same time sterling money to the value of £2536 10s. 10d. Angevin, which he had lent to John (*ibid.*).

[170] See the case of Roger Wascelin of Barfleur and the merchants of Aquitaine (*Rot. Chart.*, 60).

[171] General inquisition into unlicensed export on February 11, 1203 (*Rot. Pat.*, 25).

[172] Cf. *Rot. Pat.*, 13b, July 6, 1202: a general order that victuals coming to Rouen by way of the Seine shall be allowed to pass, and not be bought 'nisi per bonam voluntatem mercatorum qui illud adduxerint antequam pervenerint apud Rothomagum'. On the subject generally, see *English Historical Review*, xxi, 642.

[173] See *Rot. Norm.*, 47, 60, 61, 73, 100. The release of debts was accompanied by restoration of charter and chirograph, which points to a royal control of Jewish bonds in Normandy and Aquitaine, as in England (*Select Charters*, 9th edition, p. 256). For the kind of service rendered in return, see *Rot. Norm.*, 107, where twenty days' service at Tillières is promised, and *Rot. Pat.*, 32b, 'sciatis quod quietavimus Radulfo de Ruperia de plegiagio Willelmi Lexoviensis Episcopi versus Deodanum (*sic*) Judeum de Vernolio de debito quod ipse Episcopus debuit eidem Judeo, et pro ista quietacione tenebit predictus Radulfus tres milites in servicio nostro cum equis et armis a Dominica proxima ante festum Beati Petri ad vincula anno regni quinto usque ad Natale Domini sequens'. Cf. *Rot. Norm.*, 100.

[174] Jacobs, 'Aaron of Lincoln', in *Jewish Quarterly Review*, 1898, x, 629; and the same writer's *Jews in Angevin England*.

have included means of mutual insurance. Moreover both Richard and John found by experience that it was wise to give definite protection to the Jews and to their bonds.[175] In Normandy, as in England, they were an integral part of the demesne, attached to the chief castles or grouped in the larger towns,[176] and placed under the supervision of special wardens.[177]

IV

I have dealt with the Norman army and tried to analyse the financial administration in time of war. It now remains to bring together some evidence which illustrates the general aspects of warfare in the end of the twelfth century and the policy pursued by the combatants with regard to booty, prisoners of war and the like.

It is impossible to estimate the waste products of these wars, the hardships which it was no one's business to redress, the vast domain of suffering where no principle save that of cruelty was observed. To some extent equity and charity were more active in time of war. The payment of dues was officially remitted on lands wasted in war,[178] preparations were made for the reception of fugitives from threatened towns,[179] compensation was sometimes secured for the destruction of ecclesiastical property,[180] and alms were more freely given to the poor.[181] But such measures as these offered no relief to the man who was forced, by the hardness of the times, to sell his lands or to leave

---

[175] Above, note 173. John's charter to the Jews of England and Normandy, 1201, in *Rot. Chart.*, 93. Pollock and Maitland, *History of English Law*, i, 468; McKechnie, *Magna Carta*, p. 266; 2nd edition, p. 225.

[176] Cf. *Cart Norm.*, nos. 207, 208; and in Register A, ff. lv, 84v. In February, 1203, John took £200 from the Jews at Domfront, for the payment of the garrison and for the building operations (*Rot. Norm.*, 79). There were also Jews at Verneuil, Rouen, Montivilliers, Lillebonne (*Rot. Norm.*, 61), L'Aigle, Bernay (*Rot. Scacc.*, ii, 315), Caen, Pont-Audemer (*Rot. Norm.*, 116, 118). In 1200 Deodatus of Verneuil found pledges up to a sum of £900 'quod non recedat a terra' (*Rot. de Oblatis*, 73).

[177] *Rot. Norm.*, 116: 'custodia escaetarum Normannie et Judeorum preter Judeos Rothomagi et Cadomi.' Richard Silvain collected a tallage of £1000 imposed by John on the Jews of Normandy (*Rot. Scacc.*, ii, 543).

[178] *e.g.*, *Rot. Scacc.*, i, 155, 156, 235, 237.

[179] *e.g.*, Dieppe *Rot. Pat.*, 2b.

[180] Round, *Calendar of Documents preserved in France*, p. 18, no. 67; Archbishop Walter's letter in Diceto, ii, 145. Cf. *English Historical Review*, xxvii, 114.

[181] *e.g.*, *Rot. de Liberate*, 57: 'Liberate de thesauro nostro sine dilatione Laurentio de Dunning (*i.e.*, of the Donjon) £510 9s. 10½d. sterling, pro pacatione quam faciet pro nobis pauperibus gentibus per preceptum nostrum pro cibo nostro.' The date is Alençon, August 11, 1203: when John was besieging Alençon during his last brief campaign.

R

the country.[182] They could not cope with the widespread effects of famine or with the passions of mercenary troops. We can only guess at the amount of beggary, prostitution and starvation produced by feudal warfare. All we can know with certainty is that those who suffered must have been very numerous.[183]

On the other hand feudal warfare was probably, by its very nature, less horrible than the warfare of later centuries, when society had lost its military character and was as yet unprotected by international conventions. It is impossible to believe that Normandy or Touraine suffered in John's reign as France suffered during the Hundred Years' War, or Germany before the peace of Westphalia. In spite of many changes feudal society at the end of the twelfth century was regulated by principles which applied to war no less than to peace. Law in a feudal society was inseparable from force, but was not obscured by it: they were combined in the theory of contract which informed all feudal relations and which was historically connected with the Germanic principle that every limb had its value, and almost every blow its price. Force was never absent, yet was never uncontrolled. In civil procedure we find the elements of war, such as the duel, and the hue and cry; and in war we find constant applications of legal theory. War was a great lawsuit. The truce was very like an essoin, a treaty was drawn up on the lines of a final concord, the hostage was a surety, service in the field was the counterpart of suit of court. The closeness of the analogy between the field of battle and the law court is seen in the judicial combat. Trial by battle was a possible incident in all negotiations.[184] In 1188 Henry II and Philip agreed to submit their differences to the test of a combat of champions chosen by each side, and the preliminary arrangements were actually made.[185] Philip made a similar suggestion to Richard some years later.[186] The obvious impossibility of securing guarantees that the issue would be regarded as a verdict no doubt prevented the pursuit of these proposals; the Marshal is said to have pointed out to King Henry in 1188 that, in order to secure fair play, the combat would have to be waged in the

---

[182] Cf. the charter of Geoffrey of la Bretêche (1200) quoted by Delisle from the records of Lire in his *Etudes sur la condition de la classe agricole*, p. 197; and the case of the person who lost his serjeanty by going into France in time of war 'propter inopiam' (*Querimoniae Normannorum*, nos. 460, 467).

[183] See especially Luchaire, *La Société française au temps de Philippe Auguste* (1909). Cf. *English Historical Review*, xxi, 636–7.

[184] See the interesting discussion in Lea, *Superstition and Force* (ed. 1870), pp. 155 seqq.; also Holdsworth, *History of English Law*, i, 140.

[185] *Guillaume le Maréchal*, iii, 87–90.

[186] Diceto, ii, 121 (1194). On the exchequer roll for 1198 (*Rot. Scacc.*, ii, 481) there is a reference to the 'campiones Regis, qui fuerunt ducti in insulam de Andele contra regem Francie'.

court of the emperor or of some other neutral power, such as the king of Aragon or of Navarre. But it seems to have been regarded as a natural and possible form of solution.[187]

The practices of war and peace touched each other too closely to prevent the extension of common principles even in details. The disposition of prisoners and booty was exactly parallel to the disposition of wreckage. From a wreck the king took gold and silver, silk, chargers and hawks and other precious things;[188] similarly knights and other captives of war and booty belonged to him, unless he surrendered his claim,[189] yet in both cases the captor was recognised to have an equitable right to a share.

Another point of contact between the courts and war was the curiously strict observance of the *lex talionis* which prevailed between combatants. A grim letter sent by John to Hubert de Burgh in February, 1203, illustrates the extent to which this strange passion for law could be felt. Hubert is ordered to exchange a prisoner in his keeping for Ferrand the engineer: 'If Ferrand be whole, let Peter be delivered whole also; but if Ferrand be lacking in any limb, Peter must first be deprived of the same limb (*eodem modo demenbratus*) and then delivered in exchange.'[190]

In such a case as this the *lex talionis* was compatible with an appreciation of the market value of the prisoner. Much evidence might be adduced to show how by means of booty and the exchange or ransom of prisoners, war was to a certain extent made to pay for itself.[191] But the desire for an exact revenge might easily become merely destructive. William the Breton, in a passage of his *Philippid*, relates that Richard, angered by the news that a body of Welsh mercenaries had been

---

[187] There is a Biblical precedent (2 Samuel, ii, 12–16) and several later instances. It should be remembered that questions of right between the king of France and the Angevin kings were settled by legal process, *e.g.*, the inquisition into the rights of Saint Martin of Tours and the count of Anjou in 1190 (Teulet, *Layettes*, i, 158–62, no. 371).

[188] *Statuta et Consuetudines*, c. lxvii (Tardif, I, i, 62).

[189] Cf. John's letter of February 7, 1203, to the constable of Radepont, *Rot. Pat.*, 24b: 'concessimus Radulpho Archer quicquid ipse lucrari poterit in Marchia super inimicos nostros et quod idem habeat, salvis nobis militibus et illis qua ad nos pertinent.' See also *Guillaume le Maréchal*, iii, 149, where the Marshal surrenders and receives again as a gift a noble prisoner.

[190] *Rot. Pat.*, 25. On the other hand some small compensation was occasionally granted for the loss of a limb in the king's service; *e.g.*, *Rot. de Liberate*, 32: 'mandatum est G. filio Petri quod faciat habere Alano Walensi qui pugnum suum perdidit in servicio domini Regis jd. de redditu primum qui liberabitur, et interim eum perhendinare faciat in aliqua abbatia', and the following entry.

[191] *e.g.*, *Rot. Scacc.*, ii, 309. The war horse was especially valuable, as the life of the Marshal shows. The chroniclers refer (*e.g.*, *Ann. Monastici*, ii, 70) to the 200 destriers captured in the fight at the bridge of Gisors in 1198, 'de quibus septies viginti cooperti erant ferro'.

244 THE LOSS OF NORMANDY

destroyed by the French,[192] threw three prisoners from the rock of
Andeli and blinded fifteen others whom he sent under the guidance of
a one-eyed companion, to the French king; whereupon Philip, in
reply to this rough jest, inflicted the same punishment upon exactly
the same number of *his* prisoners: three were cast from a high cliff,
and fifteen were deprived of their sight, and, accompanied by the
wife of one of their number, were sent to Richard. The reader may
justly feel that, with this story, we have reached a *reductio ad
absurdum* of the parallel between the principles of law and warfare.

Further examination, however, of the relations between captor and
prisoner, is of some interest and importance. A wealthy or powerful
prisoner was much more than a soldier out of action, or a source of
wealth to the captor. He represented political dignity and power; his
capture interfered with a body of relations between his kinsmen and
vassals and himself which were public in their nature. When King
John captured Arthur's company at Mirebeau he wiped out the
political influence of half a province. Hence much importance was
attached to the safe custody of prisoners, and elaborate precautions
were taken against their escape, and even against their communication
with their friends outside. For example, Hugh of Lusignan, after
being captured at Mirebeau, was confined at Caen under the strictest
regulations. The keep (*turris*) was cleared of all other prisoners, and
Hugh, heavily ironed, was placed under the guardianship of Hugh
Nevill,[193] who superseded the castellan for this purpose. Hugh's
uncle, Geoffrey of Lusignan, was treated in the same way at Falaise.
Their communications with friends were regulated with the most
minute care.[194] The less important prisoners taken at Mirebeau were,
on the contrary, massed together in England at Corfe, where they
were sufficiently free and sufficiently numerous to conspire and for
a short time to capture the keep.[195] But if the Margam annalist is
correct in saying that twenty-two of them were starved to death, they
paid dearly for their adventure.[196]

The responsibility of the gaoler was a heavy one. In spite of all

---

[192] *Philippid*, lib. v, ll. 300–28 (ed. Delaborde, ii, 136, 137). A comparison of
this passage with Diceto, ii, 163; Howden, iv, 53; *Annales Cambriae*, p. 61;
and the *Brut y Tywysogion*, p. 252, shows that William is really thinking
of the great Welsh disaster at Pain's castle in Radnor in the same year. (See,
on this massacre, Lloyd, *History of Wales*, ii, 586). He was not, in 1198, with
Philip, and probably confused one story with another.

[193] Hugh Nevill, a friend of Richard's (Matthew Paris, *Chron. Majora*, iii,
71) had been responsible for the custody of the bishop of Beauvais at Rouen
(*Rot. Scacc.*, ii, 301; Howden, iv, 40, 41) and, along with Thomas, a clerk
of the royal chamber, was entrusted with most of the business connected with
the prisoners of Mirebeau. [194] *Rot. Pat.*, 16 *seqq.*

[195] *Rot. Pat.*, 24, 33b. [196] *Annales Monastici*, i, 26.

precautions, prisoners sometimes escaped, and their keepers had to meet the loss of their ransoms by the payment of large fines.[197] Connivance at escape was punished with death. When Hugh of Chaumont, an intimate follower of Philip Augustus, escaped in 1196 from Bonneville-sur-Touques, his keeper was hanged, and Robert of Roos, the bailiff, who was immediately responsible to the king for Hugh's safe keeping, had to pay the enormous fine of 1200 marks.[198]

A fair amount of evidence goes to prove that on his release a prisoner was often compelled to undertake that he would retire from the fighting line. In addition to the payment of a ransom he made a promise similar to that made by a knight on parole.[199] In important cases homage was exacted; William of Scotland did homage to Henry II and Richard I to the emperor.[200] More generally, however, the prisoner was simply expected to retire from the scene of warfare. The bishop of Beauvais, for example, was compelled to forswear secular warfare against fellow Christians;[201] Martin Algais, after his release, was transferred by John from Touraine to Gascony;[202] less important people sometimes celebrated their release or sought to forget their sufferings by going on pilgrimage or taking the vows of a crusader. Thus Patrick of Chaworth (*Chaources*)[203] a few months after his release in February, 1203, started for Compostella.[204]

The career of Gerard of Furnival illustrates the practices to which I have referred in the preceding pages. Gerard had been with Richard in the Holy Land, and was afterwards a trusted companion of John. He was one of John's tenants in the English honour of Tickhill,[205] and received from him valuable grants in Normandy.[206] In the fight at Mirebeau he had the good fortune to take as his prisoner Conan, the son of Guiomarc'h, viscount of Leon, one of the most important

[197] e.g., *Rot. Scacc.*, i, 190. 'Thomas Portarius reddit compotum de £394 9s. 6d. pro prisonibus evasis.'

[198] Howden, iv, 14, 15. For Robert of Roos, see *Rot. Scacc.*, i, 233, and Stapleton, II, lxxvi, lxxvii.

[199] For the parole, see Jordan Fantosme (ed. Howlett, *Chronicles of Stephen*, etc., iii, 358, l. 1870) and Meyer, *Guillaume le Maréchal*, iii, p. xxxix, who points out that the parole was sometimes supplemented by the finding of sureties.

[200] A legal parallel to this is the 'homagium de pace servanda' or 'hominium pro emenda'.

[201] *Howden*, iv, 94.

[202] Richard, *Comtes de Poitou*, ii, 414, 415.

[203] A branch of the family of Chaources, now Sourches, in Maine, had long been anglicised; see Round, *The King's Serjeants and Officers of State* (1911), pp. 291, 292.

[204] *Rot. Pat.*, 23, 24, 25.

[205] For Gerard's English lands as held by his son in 1212 see *Red Book*, ii, 491, 504, 592.

[206] Of these, Conteville was the most important (Stapleton, II, clxii).

and intractable barons of Brittany.[207] In accordance with the usual practice, the prisoner was handed over to the king. Soon afterwards Gerard felt a desire to revisit the scene of his adventures in the east, and decided to make a pilgrimage to Jerusalem. He had more to remember than most men, for he had spoken face to face with Saladin himself.[208] But the pilgrimage would cost money, and Gerard was already in debt to the king; he had recently bought the marriage of the heiress to a manor in Caux, in order to settle his son, Gerard the younger. This had cost 400 marks which had not been paid.[209] The king came to the rescue. He gave back the prisoner whom Gerard had captured at Mirebeau and then bought him again for the amount of the debt.[210] After all John allowed Gerard but a small share in the value of his prisoner, for when the ransom was arranged a year later the king demanded no less than £4000 Angevin from Conan's Breton relatives.[211]

I have said that this episode illustrates the traffic in prisoners during these wars. It illustrates also the attraction of the crusade which was especially characteristic of this period, and cut across political obligations in the west. John had lost in this way his Flemish allies and his relatives, Geoffrey and Stephen of Perche.[212] In other words the alliance built up by Richard had been interrupted at its most important points. Moreover, the rumour of great intentions, and the magnetic energy of Innocent III decided men of all stations and from all parts of the Angevin empire to leave for the Holy Land or at least to satisy their restlessness by a journey to Rome or Compostella.[213] No feeling of solidarity bound the Englishman to the

[207] This was Guiomarc'h V. His father, Guiomarc'h IV, had been very energetic in his resistance to Henry II and Geoffrey. See Robert of Torigni, ed. Delisle, ii, 81, and Rolls Series edition, p. 281; Howden, ii, 192, and especially A. de La Borderie, *Histoire de Bretagne*, iii, 276, 279, 280.

[208] *Estoire de la Guerre Sainte* (ed. G. Paris), ll. 11425, 11899. Paris speaks of Gerard as a French knight, taking his name from Fournival (Oise); and, according to Round, he had only settled in England in Richard's reign (*English Historical Review*, xviii, 476).

[209] *Rot. Pat.*, 15b. This manor, of Louvetot, was afterwards given by Philip Augustus to Odo Troussel (*Cart. Norm.*, no. 106, p. 18).

[210] *Rot. Pat.*, 15b, Chinon, August 4, 1202.

[211] *Ibid.*, 33b.

[212] Geoffrey count of Perche had married Matilda sister of Otto of Brunswick, and niece of John. He pledged his lands in March, 1202, and borrowed money from the Marshal, but died before he could set out (*Rot. Pat.*, 7, 9b). He and his brother Stephen were at the head of a little group of crusaders from Perche. See Stapleton, II, lxxxiv.

[213] On the strength of feeling caused by the crusade between 1197 and 1204, see Bréhier, *L'église et l'Orient au moyen âge* (3rd edition, 1911), pp. 148–52; and the songs collected by Bédier and Aubry, in *Les Chansons de Croisade* (1909). Cf. also Bateson, *Mediæval England*, pp. 276, 277.

Norman, or the Norman to the Poitevin. John inspired his followers with no certainty of victory; so that the interest and imagination of men were easily diverted by wider issues than the struggle between him and Philip. The thousands who did not go waited eagerly for news of those who went, and their minds were still fed by memories of the exhortations of the preachers. Hence, although we cannot estimate the material effects of such an intangible movement of the human spirit, we may be certain that it increased the isolation of John. The tendency towards a reliance on paid troops and upon a handful of advisers was increased.

His own acts were partly responsible for the difficulty in which John found himself. In March, 1202, Pope Innocent commended his penitential mood and approved an earlier undertaking, recently charged upon him by the archbishop of Canterbury, to build a Cistercian monastery and to provide one hundred knights to defend the Holy Land for a year.[214] John founded the abbey of Beaulieu in Hampshire, but it was throughout a harder matter to part with his knights. We do not hear of any attempt to obey Innocent, and although many men pledged their lands and got licence to depart on crusade or pilgrimage,[215] John succeeded in dissuading some of his most useful officials from the immediate fulfilment of their vows. A papal letter of inquiry refers to the justiciar and six of John's intimates by name,[216] who thus delayed. They were, John stated, so essential to him in the defence of his kingdom and the administration of justice that the loss of their services would be most serious. They also agreed that in such a stormy time it was their duty to remain, although the Bassets were eager to go if they could find the means, and the justiciar with Hugh Bardolf and William Brewer only desired to postpone the passage.[217]

<hr>

[214] The letter of March 27, 1202, has been edited by Cheney and Semple. *Selected letters of Pope Innocent III* (1953), no. 13, pp. 37–9.

[215] The following crusaders and pilgrims are mentioned, among others, on the rolls. Reginald of Pavilli, of the Wiltshire branch of the house, who died on pilgrimage to Jerusalem (*Rotuli Chartarum*, 37b); Warin Fitz Gerold (*ibid.*, 100); Henry de Puteac (*Rot. Pat.*, 3b); Hugh, count of Saint-Pol (*ibid.*, 4); Robert of Leaveland, warden of the Fleet (*Rot. de Liberate*, 25, 26); Henry of Longchamp, lord of Wilton in Herefordshire (*Rot. Pat.*, 11b; *Rot. de Liberate*, 84); Gilbert of Minières (*Rot. Pat.*, 30b, 33b). Philip, bishop of Durham, like the last-named, made a pilgrimage to Compostella. He followed the Bordeaux route: see Howden, iv, 157, 161, 174; *Rot. Chart.*, 100b.

[216] The letter is dated by Potthast, no. 1733, September 28, 1202. It is printed in *Patrologia Latina*, ccxiv, 1088.

[217] The others mentioned are William of Estouteville and Robert of Berkeley, who had got dispensations from the archbishop of Canterbury which the pope evidently regards with some suspicion.

These men were, for the most part, employed in England; but a study of the Norman exchequer roll for 1203 suggests that in Normandy also John was tending to rely upon fewer men for the more important posts. I have described how the seneschalships of the empire were entrusted to mercenaries and upstarts.[218] Within the duchy the numerous bailiwicks of Henry II's day were, at the same time, gradually formed into larger units. Richard of Fontenai, for example, was bailiff of Coutances, Vire and Mortain. It is interesting to note that the large bailiwicks created after 1204 point to a systematic adoption of this process by Philip. Another sign of the times was John's reliance upon Anglo-Normans rather than Normans. Robert Fitz-Walter and Saer de Quinci, who had held and surrendered Vaudreuil, were English barons. The constable of Chester defended Château Gaillard, the earls of Salisbury and Chester Pontorson and Avranches. The castle of Neubourg, upon the border of Philip's conquests in the Evrecin, was guarded by a royal clerk, Robert of Pleshey, and his English band.[219] These were the men who with such well-tried Normans as Peter of Préaux, Richard of Villequier, Richard of Fontenai and William of Mortemer, with the seneschal William Crassus, and the mercenary Louvrecaire, were left by John to resist the king of France.

V

If now we seek to define the results of these various inquiries into the army and finances of the Norman State, a growing separation appears between the society of the duchy, with its feudal traditions, and its ruler, both in the organisation of the host, in the methods of collecting money and in the *personnel* of government. It is true that the forms and appearance of feudal warfare had not been changed; we may see them in the gathering of barons, knights and men-at-arms, in the charters of towns and grants of land for the promise of service, in the military aids and tallages, in the quasi-legal spirit of conflict and the settlement of prisoner and booty. But on the other hand, the king withdrew more and more behind the shelter of his mercenaries, became increasingly dependent upon and involved in the non-feudal operations of finance, and, in the administration of his estates, ceased to rely upon the energies of Norman society. Yet, if we go on to inquire whether these tendencies are sufficient to explain the collapse of Angevin rule, we must hesitate and grope for an answer. Some of these tendencies were not new or peculiar to

[218] Above, pp. 228-9.
[219] This seems to follow from a comparison of *Rot. Norm.*, 101, with Pipe Roll 3 John, pp. 205, 215.

Normandy; some were to be characteristic of the later state, they anticipate the centralised rule of Edward I and Philip the Fair. Indeed we may find a parallel to some in the contemporary France of Philip Augustus. Philip also relied upon mercenaries and Jews,[220] and preferred money payments for fixed services to the general feudal levy, and the feudal levy to the *levée en masse*. In so far as his financial system was less developed he suffered by contrast with John.[221] In Richard's hands the military and financial forces which have been described were potent weapons for checking Philip and sufficient agencies for the transitory direction of opinion against him. The causes of Angevin failure were less material than these. They lie partly, of course, in John's character, but they are to be found even more in the fact that, while in France the growing separation between feudalism and government was a symptom of national strength and purpose, in Normandy it was typical of a general disintegration. In crushing the power of resistance to themselves Henry II and his sons destroyed the desire to unite against an invader. The loss of the duchy has in consequence the inexplicable character which attaches to some men's moral downfall. With no apparent failure, maintaining to the end the exercise of their peculiar virtues, they lose their hold on life.

It will be necessary in the last chapter to deal at more length with one aspect of this problem.

NOTE TO CHAPTER VIII

SENESCHAL, CONSTABLE AND MARSHAL IN NORMANDY

There is clear evidence that the seneschal directed the distribution of the Norman garrisons. The castellans were, of course, appointed by the king. The statement of accounts for June, 1200, to November, 1201, presented by Guérin of Glapion as seneschal, shows that large sums were entrusted to the seneschal's care—in this case £7365—and that they

---

[220] For the recall of the Jews in 1198, which was due to Philip's difficulties in the face of Richard, see Cartellieri, *Philipp II August.*, iii, 184.

[221] Borrelli de Serres, *op. cit.*, 169–71; Viollet, *Histoire des institutions politiques*, iii, 364; R. Holtzmann, *Französische Verfassungsgeschichte* (1910), p. 260. Although the *taille* is mentioned in 1190, direct taxation really dates from a century later. It is the return to the idea of universal military obligation which is really important in Philip's reign, for this underlay the definition of services, even though money might be preferred in their stead (Borrelli de Serres, p. 519). For later work on this subject see *Cambridge Medieval History*, vi (1929), 327—9; E. Audouin, *Essai sur l'armée royale au temps de Philippe Auguste* (1913), F. Lot and R. Fawtier, *Le premier budget de la monarchie* (1932); cf. R. Fawtier, *Les Capétiens et la France* (1942), especially chapter x.

were very largely expended upon garrisons.[222] Moreover, a Norman roll for the fifth year of John's reign is endorsed with memoranda of the seneschal's actions in the enormous bailiwick of Richard of Fontenai. Richard had set a garrison in Mont-Saint-Michel, and afterwards 'posuit v. servientes armatos per preceptum Radulfi Taxonis tunc Senescalli Normannie.'[223] Richard also garrisoned Vire and Tenchebrai 'per preceptum Senescalli.'[224] The seneschal was sometimes accompanied by the constable on these important tours of inspection. On June 3 both these officers came to Mortain 'et ibi statuerunt remanere xv milites et x servientes et x pedites qui ibidem interfuerunt usque ad diem Martis in festo Apostolorum Simonis et Jude in Octobris, videlicet per C. et xl. dies'.[225]

The duty of the marshal is exemplified by letters patent of December 9, 1202, sent from Séez:[226]

> Rex etc. omnibus militibus et servientibus ad quos etc. Mandamus vobis quod sitis intendentes fideli nostro Johanni marescallo nostro, et servicium vestrum faciatis sicut vobis ipse dicet. Teste me ipso apud Sagium ix die Decembris.

John the Marshal is not merely entrusted with the arrangements for a levy. He is *marescallus noster*, our marshal. He was a nephew of John the Master Marshal, and of William the Marshal, being the son of a younger brother. John II, the elder brother of William the Marshal, acted as Marshal at King Richard's coronation, when he carried the spurs.[227] He died in 1194.[228] His brother William succeeded him as Marshal and was confirmed in his office by royal charter in 1200.[229] It is therefore interesting to find another John, William's nephew, acting as Marshal in Normandy in 1202, and performing those military duties which were especially attached to the marshal's office.[230]

In 1207 John was made marshal of Ireland.[231]

---

[222] *Rot. Scacc.*, ii, 501, 502. For other references to the duties of the seneschal see *Rot. Scacc.*, i, 137, 138: William Fitz Ralf in 1195 received £1196 10s. od. for the wages of knights and men-at-arms in time of war, and 'ad faciendas operationes Regis in pluribus locis per Normanniam'. Cf. *ibid.*, p. 236: wages for the knights who accompanied the seneschal and others along the March.

[223] *Rot. Norm.*, 120.

[224] *Ibid.*, 121.

[225] *Ibid.*

[226] *Rot. Pat.*, 21b.

[227] Howden, iii, 9, 10. Round, *The King's Serjeants and Officers of State*, pp. 349, 356.

[228] *Guillaume le Maréchal*, iii, 8, 132, and notes.

[229] *Rot. Chart.*, i, 46. See Round, *The Commune of London*, p. 306.

[230] This account of John corrects the statement in the 1st edition of this book, that John was the son of William's elder brother; see Meyer in his edition of *Guillaume le Maréchal*, iii, p. clviii, correcting his statement on p. 143, note 4; and S. Painter, *William Marshal* (Baltimore, 1933), p. 116.

[231] Round, *The King's Serjeants and Officers of State*, pp. 367-9.

CHAPTER IX

PHILIP AUGUSTUS AND NORMANDY

At the end of 1203, when King John left Normandy, Philip of France had mastered all the weak spots of the duchy. From the valleys of the Eure and the Itun he had pushed forward into the district between the Seine and the Risle, and had thus driven a wedge between eastern and western Normandy. In eastern Normandy—that is, in the lands on the right bank of the Seine—he had annexed the Vexin, the country of Bray, and the counties of Eu and Aumâle.[1] Western Normandy, on the contrary, he had hardly touched. In order to understand the campaign of 1204, it is desirable to define the extent of his influence in the east, centre and west somewhat more closely.

On the east of the Seine the Normans still administered the Roumois, or the valley of the river below Pont de l'Arche, and also the greater part of the triangular *pays de Caux*—that is, the district between Rouen and Dieppe which is bounded on two sides by the river and the sea. King Philip's charters show that, in addition to Arques, the Normans held, in October, 1203, the lower valleys of the Bethune and Varenne.[2] Meulers and Longueville were not surrendered till June of the following year.[3] The eastern boundary of Caux, therefore, was at this time represented by a line drawn from Dieppe through Arques and Bellencombre to Rouen. Beyond this line, except in the valley of the Seine, Philip was supreme. Drincourt, the great castle of Bray, otherwise Neufchatel-en-Bray, was his, also Radepont and the Andelle valley and the whole of the manor of Andeli outside the walls of Château Gaillard. Just before or during the siege of Château

---

[1] By 1204 the long contest on the frontiers had taught men to distinguish between Normandy and the southern districts of Normandy. Thus, in a letter to the king of Aragon, Philip Augustus announced the conquest of Gisois, Lions and the whole of Normandy except Rouen (*Actes*, no. 826, p. 188). Again, in their capitulation, the citizens of Rouen secured their privileges in Normandy, the Evrecin, Paci, the Vexin, and the land of Hugh of Gournai; below, p. 263.

[2] In October, 1203, Philip granted Bellencombre, Meulers and the forest of Eawi to the count of Boulogne, to be enjoyed when they had been conquered: *Recueil*, ii, no. 770, from Register A, where the document is cancelled.

[3] *Cart. Norm.*, no. 74, p. 14 = Register A, f. 10v. (cancelled). These places balonged to William the Marshal, and were dealt with in his agreement with King Philip at Lisieux in May, 1204. The Marshal promised to hand them over immediately to Osbert of Rouvrai, who in turn would undertake to hand them over to Philip on June 24.

Gaillard the king distributed his favours in these districts. Nicholas of Montigny, a Norman, received lands near Drincourt.[4] Peter of Moret, a Frenchman, was entrusted with Radepont.[5]

It is more difficult to draw the line of division between the French and Norman governments in the district lying between the Seine and the Risle. This bailiwick was farmed in 1203, and its accounts were presented at the exchequer at Michaelmas. The fortified ducal manor at Moulineaux on the Seine, and Montfort and Pont Audemer on the Risle, were certainly under John's control; but there is some evidence that Philip had begun to push forward from Vaudreuil and to drive a wedge between Neubourg and Pont de l'Arche into this important country.[6] All the lands south of a line drawn from Montfort to Pont de l'Arche were, with the exception of Neubourg, lost to the duchy. Beaumont and Conches had fallen in the previous spring. After the fall of Château Gaillard, if not before, Neubourg also must have surrendered. A brief study of the map will show the reader that when Philip advanced in May, 1204, east and west Normandy were practically cut off from each other.

West of the Risle, however, the valleys and highlands of western Normandy were as yet hardly touched by the French. It is true that in the south the continuity of the March from Alençon to Verneuil must have been broken, for nothing is heard of Moulins and Bonmoulins, of l'Aigle or Breteuil after John's departure for England. The reason is obvious. By means of his conquest in the Evrecin and the valley of the Risle, Philip could attack the fortresses on the Itun and in the forest country from two sides.[7] Only Verneuil stood out, self-supported and for the time impregnable. Beyond the March, on the other hand, Philip was able to do little until he could advance in full force from the Seine. Before he left John had, according to the Marshal's biographer, strengthened the fortifications of the Touque valley in the north-east at Bonneville and Trianon.[8] To the south were Lisieux and Falaise. Argentan and Domfront were sufficient to keep back the barons of Maine.

In the west a little group of strongholds, Avranches, Mont-Saint-Michel, Pontorson, Saint-James, Vire and Mortain protected the

---

[4] *Cart. Norm.*, no. 68, p. 283 = *Recueil*, ii, no. 778; at Anet, November, 1203. Later gifts in 1206–7, *Recueil*, ii, no. 937.

[5] *Recueil*, ii, no. 761, (September, 1203: see note).

[6] The value of this evidence turns on the identification of Landa, granted by Philip in October, 1203, to Raoul de Louvain, with La Londe, north of Pont de l'Arche: see Index to *Actes*, p. 609: *Actes*, no. 786 = *Recueil*, ii, no. 768. Le Prévost identifies it with lands at Canappeville (*Cart. Norm.*, no. 232, p. 301).

[7] *i.e.*, on the north from Conches and Breteuil; on the south from Dreux and through Maine.   [8] *Guillaume le Maréchal*, iii, 174.

Breton frontier. Within this strong cordon stretching from Bonneville to Pontorson, the administration may reasonably have been expected to hold out, even if Rouen and the Seine were lost. It still would control Caen, the centre of government, Barfleur and Cherbourg, its links with England, and the wealthy domains of the Côtentin and the Vau de Vire, as yet hardly touched by war.

John and his advisers in fact seem to have anticipated that concentration in the centre and west might be necessary. His fortification of the valley of the Touque was criticised in military circles on the ground that it was unwise to prefer the Touque to the Risle as a line of defence. Although this criticism, as it has come down to us, is faulty and ill-informed [9]—John seems, for example, to have paid special attention to Pont-Audemer on the Risle [10]—it would seem to be a survival of some discussion upon the most suitable system of defences in the case of defeat in the east. This view is strengthened by the statement of William the Breton, that, after the fall of Château Gaillard, Pont de l'Arche and Moulineaux on the Seine, and Montfort on the Risle were destroyed by the Normans.[11] In the west the year 1203 had been spent in careful inspection, restoration and garrisoning of the fortresses.[12] The bailiff Richard of Fontenai had expended large sums, largely consisting of escheats and the proceeds of a tallage on the Jews, in the payment of knights and men-at-arms, and especially in elaborate additions to the fortifications of Mortain.[13] One of John's last acts, before he sailed, was to give to this great official the control of Mont-Saint-Michel.[14]

All hopes of a prolonged defence proved to be vain. When King Philip advanced after his triumph at Château Gaillard, Normandy crumbled away before him. Perhaps the seneschal and his colleagues had not believed that the great castle could ever fall. They may not have anticipated the irrepressible rush of Bretons, or the treachery of Louvrecaire at Falaise, or the lack of English aid. They were surrounded on all sides, and those who did not go over to the enemy took refuge in Rouen, or escaped to England.

The famous siege of Château Gaillard lasted for six months—from the end of September, 1203, until the surrender of Roger de Laci on March 6, 1204.[15] The detailed narrative devoted to the siege by

[9] *Ibid.* It is faulty because the writer thinks that John should have fortified Montfort, Beaumont and Brionne, whereas the two last-named places were already in Philip's hand. Above, p. 161.

[10] *Rot. Norm.*, 116.

[11] *Philippid.*, l. vii, vv. 826–829 (ed. Delaborde, ii, 208).

[12] *Rot. Norm.*, 120—1; *Rot. Scacc.*, ii, 547–8.

[13] *Rot. Scacc.*, ii, 548.   [14] *Rot. Norm.*, 117.

[15] William the Breton's chronicle and *Philippid*, (ed. Delaborde, i, 212–20; ii, 176–209); also Delaborde's notes of dating in *Recueil*, ii, nos. 761–3; and

THE LOSS OF NORMANDY

William the Breton has given it an importance in history which has been denied to other incidents of the war. The preference of history is, perhaps, not quite just; it is possible that the investment of Rouen or the defence of Loches might have taken as permanent a place in our annals if the chaplain of Philip Augustus had had an equal interest in describing them.[16] Yet it cannot be denied that the operations against Château Gaillard were conducted on a scale which was especially elaborate and required all the resource of Philip's ingenuity. Antiquaries profess their ability to this day to trace the course of his lines.[17]

Except from the *Philippid* and the prose additions made by William the Breton to Rigord's chronicle, we know nothing of the inner history of the defence. The English records contain a few references to the captives;[18] but, so far as is known, the constable of Chester had with him no literary companion, and no stories of the siege have strayed into the English and Norman chronicles of the time. The garrison was, like the garrison of Vaudreuil, controlled by an Anglo-Norman baron, and was largely composed of Englishmen.[19] It would be interesting to know how they behaved in a stronghold so much more complicated in its structure than any castle of Kent or Yorkshire; only a description by one who had seen from within the fall of the outwork, of the outer bailey, and, finally, of the 'citadel' could solve the problems which are still unsolved. Was the castle too restricted in its dimensions? Were its elaborate arrangements mutually injurious?[20] Or did the defence of the apparently impregnable citadel, with its embossed curtain wall and the scientific angles of its keep, require a knowledge which was not possessed by the constable and his followers?[21]

Cartellieri, IV, i, 167. See also Viollet-le-Duc, *An Essay on the Military Architecture of the Middle Ages*, Eng. tr. (1860), pp. 90–4; Dieulafoy, in *Mém. de l'Institut: Academie des Inscriptions et belles lettres*, xxxvi, part i, pp. 373–8; Coutil, *op. cit.*, pp. 84–93.

[16] William the Breton hints as much in his reference to Loches and Chinon (Delaborde, ii, 225, 226).

[17] See the plan in Viollet-le-Duc and Coutil. On the other hand, it must be remembered that Charles VII also invested the castle in 1449 and drew lines of circumvallation.

[18] *e.g.*, *Rot. de Lib.*, 103, loan by the king for the ransom of the constable of Chester. There is also a notice of privileges granted to a Jew who had lent money to the constable at Château Gaillard; *Rot. Pat.*, 47.

[19] The archbishop of Canterbury was granted one of the prisoners captured at Mirebeau towards the redemption of his knights who had been captured at Château Gaillard; *Rot. Pat.*, 40b; *April* 12, 1204.   [20] Viollet-le-Duc, p. 9.

[21] Dieulafoy, p. 376. Dieulafoy points out that the castle contained at least one defect in the stone bridge which crossed the ditch between the outer bailey and the citadel. This bridge was fixed, and offered some protection to the engineers during the attack.

King Philip's attack on Andeli had begun in August, when he occupied the peninsula formed by the great bend of the Seine. The defenders of the new town and of the isle withdrew from their outworks in this plain[22] and broke down the bridge between them and it. It is supposed by modern scholars that Philip, not satisfied with the protection afforded to his operations by the possession of Vaudreuil and Gaillon, ordered a ditch and rampart to be made across the peninsula from Bernières to Tosny.[23] The palisade which King Richard had built across the stream above the Isle was broken down by strong swimmers, and a bridge of boats, which was protected by lofty wooden towers erected upon a platform of four broad ships, was constructed below the town. Andeli and Château Gaillard were thus cut off from the north. The Normans made one attempt to break down Philip's barrier. It was made by night. A troop of mercenaries attacked the camp at Bernières, while a fleet of boats was brought up stream. But the plan miscarried. The mercenaries destroyed the camp, but were unable to penetrate further. The French were roused on both sides of the river and repelled from the bridge the boats which the coming of dawn revealed. Soon afterwards the Isle and town surrendered. The investment of the Rock was commenced, and the fall of Radepont at the end of September cut off all hope of speedy relief.

For three months Philip was content to draw double lines of circumvallation and to await results. His headquarters were probably at Gaillon,[24] while his troops lay within the lines. In January the construction of great siege engines and towers began, and after a series of fierce assaults, in the course of which Philip resorted to every contrivance of which he was master, the castle surrendered on March 8. One record of these anxious weeks is an undated letter written by King John to the constable of Chester and the garrison in the castle of Andeli, a letter which fell into King Philip's hands and is preserved in his earliest register, now in the Vatican, with the caption 'Littere quas misit Rex Angliae obsessis in Gaillard'. After praising the defenders and urging them to further effort, John orders them to follow the orders which Peter of Préaux, William of Mortemer and

---

[22] Above, p. 193.

[23] This is Viollet-le-Duc's view, based on existing earthworks. But there is no reference to the ditch and rampart in William the Breton's description of the siege, and as the night attack by John's mercenaries was only stopped by the walls of the camp, their existence cannot be regarded as proved. Cf. above, p. 254, note.

[24] Cf. *Philippid*, l. vii, v. 576:
    'Temporis id circa rex e Gaillone profectus
    Venerat Andelii castrum visurus.'
But of course he did not stay in the neighbourhood all the time. See the itinerary in the *Actes*, p. cvi.

the king's clerk Hugh of Wells, would give them, if they should find themselves so straitened that they could hold out no longer.[25]

Rigord states that the garrison of Radepont had consisted of twenty knights, one hundred men-at-arms and thirty *balistarii*, and that at Château Gaillard thirty-six knights were captured and four slain.[26] Radepont was an important stronghold, and it is probably not far from the truth to conclude, as these figures suggest, that a garrison of double the size would be sufficient to defend the Rock. On this computation we may assume that besides the forty knights about two hundred *servientes*, and about sixty engineers and crossbowmen, or three hundred in all, had co-operated with the constable of Chester. At the beginning of the siege the place had also contained several hundred refugees, but Roger de Laci gradually dismissed all non-combatants. The last batch, over four hundred in number, were refused a passage by the French in the expectation that the constable would be forced to feed them and so to reduce his supplies. William the Breton suggests that many of them were friends and relations of those within the walls. But the constable and garrison were obdurate, and the story is known to all how the unfortunates lived through the winter in the caves and hollows of the Rock, victims of stray darts and stones, starved by cold and hunger.[27] When Philip at length took pity upon them and gave them food, nearly all died.

The way was now cleared, and the king entered Normandy on May 2, the Sunday after Easter.[28] He struck straight at the castles which protected Caen. After the fall of Château Gaillard the Normans had withdrawn from the Seine valley above Rouen and from the Risle.[29] Pont de l'Arche, Roche Orival,[30] Neubourg, Moulineaux and Montfort were either destroyed or surrendered about this time. Philip decided to follow up the Normans as they retired and to capture Falaise and Caen. It is probable, also, that he knew from deserters how disaffected Falaise was,[31] and that he suspected the treacherous leanings of Louvrecaire. Arques and Verneuil, on the contrary, were both strong and steadfast; and Philip had already experienced more than once the difficulties which accompanied an attack upon Rouen. A still more urgent reason for an invasion of central Normandy was that he could rely upon the co-operation of his Breton allies. There-

---

[25] Register A, f. 38v. The mention of Hugh of Wells suggests that his letter was sent with this intimate clerk in January, 1204; see below, p. 259, note 47.

[26] Delaborde, i, 159.

[27] William the Breton's Chronicle, *ibid.*, i, 217.

[28] *Ibid.*, i, 220, and Rigord (i, 160).   [29] *Ibid.*, ii, 208.

[30] Château Fouet according to Round, in *English Historical Review* (xix, 148); but the identification is not certain; cf. *Rot. Scacc.*, ii, 315.

[31] For such a deserter and the feeling at Falaise, see the *Querimoniae Normannorum*, nos. 431, 460, 462, etc.

fore, leaving Arques, Rouen and Verneuil for the present upon either hand, he marched westwards.

It is probable that the king took a road north of Verneuil through Lire, where he could cross the Risle. On May 7 he was at Argentan.[32] This place had been entrusted to Roger of Gouy, a Flemish knight, who in his youth had joined the following of the young King Henry and had been a close companion of William the Marshal. He was known to be a brave warrior, but somewhat too fond of gain.[33] Nothing is known of the fate of Argentan, but as Roger was afterwards for a time in Philip's service, we may presume that the place had surrendered voluntarily. The king passed on to Falaise. The seneschal had left Louvrecaire in charge, but the famous mercenary made no defence. The townsmen were afraid of the damage and inconveniences which a siege entailed, and after seven days the town and its noble fortress were surrendered. The Bessin was at Philip's feet. The citizens of Caen had already offered to surrender, and William the Breton raises a note of exultation over the addition of the Norman capital, second only to Paris, set by fair streams among fruitful fields, adorned with churches and rich in merchandise, to the domain of his master.[34] Bayeux and the other cities of central Normandy surrendered in their turn. William Crassus, whose unpopularity must help to explain Philip's rapid success, took refuge in Rouen,[35] and thither the king followed him, by way of Saint-Pierre-sur-Dive and Lisieux.[36] The investment of the city began before the end of the month.[37]

Before he left Caen Philip had been joined by Guy of Thouars, the count of Brittany, and a large force of Bretons. They were fresh from the capture of Mont-Saint-Michel and Avranches. The situation upon the Breton frontier at the beginning of May was a curious one. The great abbey of the Mount, which for centuries had been a reconciling power between Bretons and Normans, and through whose territories the Bretons had passed in their journeys to and from the fair of

---

[32] *Actes*, no. 813, ed. p. 507 = *Recueil*, ii, no. 788. Here Geoffrey of Martel offered his services and undertook to bring over to Philip as many as he could of the barons of the land.

[33] Roger of Gouy received Argentan on October 1, 1203 (*Rot. Norm.*, 105–6). He gave up his nephew to John as a hostage (*Rot. de Lib.*, 69). Although he was afterwards well known in England, he was forced for a time to abjure the realm (June, 1204, *Rot. Pat.*, 43b). On his character, see *Guillaume le Maréchal*, iii, 43.

[34] Delaborde, ii, 211–12. There may have been some resistance for Philip took some persons prisoner here (*Rot. Pat.*, 45b).

[35] He was one of the few persons excepted from the terms of the capitulation at Rouen (Teulet, *Layettes*, i, 250, no. 716).

[36] *Actes*, nos. 816–18, pp. 185–6.

[37] *Ibid*, no. 821, p. 187: 'in castris ante Rothomagum, anno 1204, mense maio.'

s

Montmartin, had been turned by John into a royal fortress. It was wrapped in new defences of wood and stone, and owed obedience to the bailiff of the Côtentin.[38] As late as the first of May its tenants were summoned by the king of England to provide an aid for its defence.[39] The whole district was organised to resist invasion. In the islands, out in the bay, the men of Peter of Préaux were on their guard against hostile ships. In Pontorson the earl of Salisbury barred the passage of the Couesnon. Behind him, in Avranches and Saint-James-de-Beuvron, the earl of Chester probably had his place as viscount of the Avranchin.[40] The latter's feelings at this time cannot have been pleasant. He had much to lose in Normandy, lands in the Bessin and the Avranchin, and the rich honour of Saint-Sever above the Vau de Vire. A few years earlier he had, as the husband of Constance of Brittany, been able to call himself the duke of Brittany. He had imprisoned his troublesome and unwilling wife in this very castle of Saint-James. Now he was waiting for the man who had robbed him, and this man had all Brittany at his back. Only one consoling hope may have sustained the earl. Far away in Yorkshire there stretched the great honour of Richmond. It was almost an integral part of the duchy of Brittany. There was no man who had such a claim on Richmond as he had, for Guy of Thouars was a rebel, Arthur was out of the way, and his sister Eleanor was shut up at Corfe. We may hope that such thoughts as these encouraged Earl Randle. In any case Richmond was to be his reward.[41]

Guy of Thouars also must have had anxious thoughts. John had recognised him as count of Brittany, and he ran some risk in joining Philip. If Arthur were alive or if Eleanor escaped, his own daughter had no claim to succeed to Constance. As he led the Bretons, mad with desire to avenge the murder of their count, Guy must have been a better man than we think if he did not hope that Arthur was really dead.

The Bretons had no doubtful thoughts. They had a long list of injuries to avenge, and their minds were full of recent memories of

[38] *Rot. Scacc.*, ii, 547; *Rot. Norm.*, 117, 120. On the social importance of Mont-Saint-Michel, compare the remarks of Courson, *Cartulaire de l'abbaye de Redon* (Coll. des doc. ined), p. liii.

[39] *Rot. Pat.*, 41b.

[40] The earl of Salisbury had received Pontorson in exchange for other lands, according to *Rot. Norm.*, 97. On May 31, 1203, the earl of Chester had been entrusted with the castle of Avranches (*Rot. Pat.*, 30) but it is uncertain whether he still held it. Brice the chamberlain had been placed in Mortain and Tenchebrai (*ibid.*, 34b, 35).

[41] *Rot. Pat.*, 51. Randle styles himself duke of Brittany in a charter for the canons of Montmorel, issued at Saint-James (Round, *Calendar* no. 786, p. 284). The date is uncertain, but must be between 1188 and 1214. The style 'duke of Brittany' was unusual at this period.

John's brutal mercenaries and the loss of the relics of Saint Samson. They moved quickly when they heard of Philip's advance. Those who knew the bay of Saint-Michael and the nature of the tides, told them that they had only four days in which safely to attack the Mount.[42] The gate was forced, and the whole place was destroyed by fire, in order that no time might be lost. Then apparently they left Pontorson on their right, seized Avranches, and, joining the French forces, which were securing the Bessin and Côtentin, they came to Philip at Caen.

Philip divided his army. Guy of Thouars was sent back together with the count of Boulogne, William des Barres and the mercenaries who had surrendered Falaise, to attack the castles upon the western frontier between Pontorson and Mortain.[43] How these castles fell is unknown. But, during the next few months they were all lost, Pontorson, Saint-James, Vire, Tenchebrai, Mortain, Domfront and the whole country as far as Cherbourg and Barfleur.[44] In the meanwhile Philip Augustus laid siege to Rouen.

By this time King John's half-hearted and irresolute preparations were useless. Whether he had seriously intended to return to Normandy or not, it is impossible to say, for the royal letters show quite clearly that, until Château Gaillard fell, he had not thought it necessary to move quickly. In January he received the consent of a council to a scutage,[45] and, according to the annalist of Saint Edmund's, the earls and the barons promised to join him in a Norman campaign.[46] Hugh of Wells, a cleric high in the royal confidence, was sent to Normandy at the end of the month,[47] and towards the end of February stores, treasure, and a few men were despatched.[48] The Master of the Temple in England also crossed on the financial business of the king.[49] But there was no alarm. On the very day that Château Gaillard fell orders were issued for the transport of beasts of chase, dogs, horses and falcons in preparation for the king's hunting when he should cross.[50] Then the disastrous news must have come. The papal legate, still intent on peace, was in England, and a great council was held,

[42] William the Breton, ed. Delaborde, i, 220–1; A. de la Borderie, *Histoire de Bretagne*, iii, 293.
[43] William the Breton, i, 221.
[44] Rigord, i, 160; Coggeshall, p. 145.
[45] Wendover, i, 320; ed. Coxe, iii, 175.
[46] Memorials of St. Edmund, ii, 12.
[47] *Rot. Pat.*, 38; *Rot. de Lib.*, 77, 81; he may well have brought the letter to the constable of Chester and his garrison of Andeli (above, p. 256, and note). On the career of Hugh of Wells, future bishop of Lincoln, cf. S. Painter, *The Reign of King John* (Baltimore, 1945), pp. 79–80.
[48] *Rot. de Lib.*, 84–5.
[49] *Ibid.*, 81; *Rot. Pat.*, 38b; he is to attend to the instructions of Hugh of Wells. [50] *Rot. de Lib.*, 82.

probably at the end of March,[51] at London. It was decided to send a strong embassy to Philip. The archbishop of Canterbury, the bishops of Norwich and Ely, Earl William the Marshal and the earl of Leicester were chosen; and they crossed with the legate on the 11th or 12th of April.[52] Shortly before, and no doubt as a result of the same council, the bishop of London was sent to the Emperor,[53] and steps were taken to secure the fidelity of those Rhenish barons who received pensions from the English exchequer.[54] Little was done to avert the coming catastrophe. The seneschal was instructed to further, as far as possible, the concentration of stores at Rouen,[55] and to assist the constable and barons in the victualling of their castles. Shortly before Easter two thousand marks were sent to him at Caen;[56] and we read of a few Welsh mercenaries who were sent across.[57] But still the king waited.

The negotiations, as might have been expected, came to nothing. Philip was sure of victory. He demanded either Arthur (of whose death he was now becoming certain)[58] or his sister Eleanor and all John's lands across the sea.[59] The bishops retired to Rouen, where they parted from the papal legate, and came back to England with the news of their failure.[60] Philip proceeded to invade Normandy. Later, when after the fall of Caen the king was on his way to the Seine, the Marshal met him again at Lisieux and made an arrangement with him which is a sufficient commentary upon the prospects of John at the end of May. The Marshal surrendered his chief lands to Philip, and paid a large sum of money in return for a respite of twelve months; if Normandy were lost during that time he would do homage to Philip for his Norman lands.[61]

The symbol of defeat had been sent from Caen a few days before this meeting at Lisieux. Sometime during the third week in May the Norman records arrived at Shoreham.[62] The Norman exchequer had ceased its work as the agent of an English king.

[51] Gervase of Canterbury, ii, 95. Coggeshall (p. 144) refers to a council as though it were held after mid-Lent (April 4) but John was at Westminster for several days at the end of March.

[52] For the dates, see *Rot. Pat.*, 40b. For the embassy, Gervase ii, 95; Coggeshall, p. 144; *Guillaume le Maréchal*, iii, 176.

[53] *Rot. Pat.*, 39b; Coggeshall, p. 147.

[54] *Rot. de Lib.*, 87.   [55] *Rot. Pat.*, 39b.   [56] *Rot. de Lib.*, 96.

[57] *Ibid.*, 85. Baldwin of Béthune, the count of Aumâle, also seems to have gone over for a time (*Rot. Pat.*, 41b).

[58] Below, p. 313.   [59] Coggeshall, p. 145.

[60] Gervase, ii, 96. According to the life of the Marshal (iii, 176), the envoys met Philip at Bec.

[61] *Cart Norm.*, no. 74, p. 14; Register A, f. 10v. (cancelled).

[62] *Rot. de Lib.*, 102–3, a letter from the king, who was at Worldham, May 21, 1204, to the Sheriff of Sussex: 'Mandavimus ballivis de Soreham quod

It is not difficult to imagine the state of men's minds in Rouen at the end of May. They had prepared for a great siege.[63] Peter of Préaux, acting in concert with the archbishop and the mayor, was in military command. He had with him the old official, Richard of Villequier, and other great barons of the neighbourhood, Henry of Etouteville, the young Robert of Esneval,[64] Thomas of Pavilli, Geoffrey du Bois and Peter of Hotot. Within the strong walls and triple fosse[65] of the city a host of refugees were gathered from Eu, Aumâle and Drincourt. Even those burgesses and vassals of Alençon who had refused to follow their count in his desertion, had found a home there. Provisions had been brought from England and from all parts of Normandy. The city had entered into a defensive alliance with Arques and Verneuil.[66] But as news came of treachery at Falaise and Caen the mood of Rouen changed. A story of stubborn resistance only broken down by superior force, would doubtless have had a different effect; but the advance of Philip had been so easy; his relations with the men of other places had been so pleasant and cordial. He had confirmed the privileges of Falaise, and had granted a fair of seven days at the Feast of the Exaltation of the Cross for the benefit of its lepers.[67] The mayor of Falaise, happy man, had received lands at Lassi and Campeaux.[68] The rights and privileges of Rouen were at stake; they extended through the whole Angevin empire, from Gournai to Bordeaux; they were worth saving; and King Philip was well disposed. If the men of Rouen were not careful they might find upstarts in their path. The men of Pont-Audemer, for example, so well placed near the mouth of the Risle, were already bargaining for a commune.[69] Decision was necessary, for some persons in the crowded city were already out of hand; it was said that they had seized and beheaded a number of King Philip's men, and the king would be sure to insist upon punishment.[70]

---

inveniant Petro de Leon clerico nostro carriagium et salvum conductum ad ducendos usque Londoniis rotulos et cartas nostras quas ipse nobis adduxit de Cadomo, unde tibi precipimus quod si ipsi non fecerint, tu id sine dilatione facias, et computabitur tibi ad scaccarium.'

[63] Chéruel, *Histoire de Rouen pendant l'époque communale* (1843), i, 86 *seqq.* The chief authority for the siege is the agreement of June 1, in *Recueil*, ii, no. 803 (from Register A, etc.) and in Teulet, *Layettes*, i, 250–2, no. 716 (the counterpart now in the *Trésor des Chartes*).

[64] Stapleton, II, cxlvii.   [65] *Philippid.*, l. viii, v. 159 (Delaborde, ii, 216).

[66] Rigord, i, 160: 'castra scilicet que cum Rothomagensibus fuerant conjurata.'

[67] *Cart. Norm.*, nos. 75, 1070, p. 283 = *Recueil*, ii, nos. 790, 791.

[68] *Ibid.*, no. 76, p. 15 = *Recueil*, ii, no. 77.

[69] *Ibid.*, no. 77, p. 284 = *Recueil*, ii, no. 809.

[70] See the additional clause in the arrangement of June I (*Layettes*, i, 252): 'Ego Robertus, major Rothomagensis, me vicesimo, jurabo quod capita

While Robert the mayor and his colleagues were considering these facts the canons of Rouen would hear of Philip's relations with the western dioceses. They would learn that many of the clergy had declared for Philip, even Abbot Samson, of St. Stephen's, who had sat for so many years at the board of exchequer;[71] and they would remember that the church of Rouen had more to lose in Normandy than in England. Moreover the king of France would doubtless assist them in the rebuilding of the cathedral.[72] The barons, also, must have been shaken. King Philip was losing no time in the disposal of Norman property. Confiscations and rewards were issuing fast from his chancery. There was Guérin of Glapion, for example: he had already secured Moyon and Montpinçon and lands at Cambois.[73] The constable had gone over,[74] the great earl Marshal had compromised,[75] and the earl of Meulan, weary and disillusioned, had retired from the contest on the first of May.[76] Some of these things had happened near to Rouen, or were transacted in King Philip's camp across the river. They were, therefore, not likely to be hidden from Peter of Préaux and his comrades.

For a time Peter hesitated. He sent urgent messages to King John, and on June 1 concluded with Philip a temporary armistice of a type familiar in feudal warfare. The barons and citizens would surrender the city if help did not come within thirty days; Philip, in the meanwhile, was to retain the barbican on the west side of the river. This outwork defended the bridge across the Seine, and had been besieged by the king. He stipulated that he should be allowed to strengthen it, and, if necessary, to demand that the citizens should destroy the four arches of the bridge next adjoining it. But these precautions were not needed. It is clear, from the terms of the armistice, that

hominum domini regis non fuerant amputata per nos in civitate Rotho-magensi, sed plus de hoc doluimus quam gavisi fuerimus, et si eos capere potuerimus qui hoc fecerunt eos ipsi regi trademus ad faciendam voluntatem suam.'

[71] John refers to his 'malevolentia' against the abbey of Saint Stephen 'occasione Samsonis abbatis illius loci' (*Rot. Pat.*, 70b).

[72] Burnt on Easter Day, 1200 (Howden, iv, 116). John had promised a large sum 'ad fabricam ecclesie' of which £460 were still owing in April, 1203 (*Rot. Norm.*, 86).

[73] *Recueil*, ii, nos. 793, 802.

[74] The Annalist of Winchester (*Ann. Monast.*, ii, 255-6) ascribes excessive importance to the constable. He states that King Philip subdued Normandy and Anjou 'seditione Willelmi de Humat, qui sub rege Johanne totius Norman-niae gubernaculum obtinuit, Johanne rege in Anglia moram faciente'. The annalist probably confused him with the other Williams, William Crassus and William des Roches, seneschals of Normandy and Anjou.

[75] Above, p. 260.

[76] At Préaux, near Rouen, where he gave over his English and Norman lands to his heirs. See Stapleton, II, cci.

Rouen was regarded as lost. They constituted a treaty of surrender. The knights and burgesses of Rouen, Eu, Aumâle, Drincourt and the tenants of Alençon, were to be secured in their holdings, if, after the expiration of the appointed time, they should do homage to the French king and their lords.[77] Those who did homage in the interval might depart at once to their holdings; and safe conducts were promised to recalcitrants who might prefer to retire from Normandy, provided that they made up their minds before the time had passed. On payment of the usual dues merchants who did not carry corn or bread were to be allowed to conduct their business; and, if the city surrendered, all its trading facilities and liberties within the old limits of Normandy and in Poitou, Anjou, Maine, Brittany and Gascony were to be retained. The men of Verneuil and Arques were to be granted the same terms if they should ask for them before the Wednesday after Ascension Day (June 9).

Hostages were given by the barons and citizens as security for the observance of the truce.[78]

Rouen did not wait for thirty days before the surrender. The end came on June 24, the Feast of St. John the Baptist. Verneuil and Arques surrendered also. It is probable that King Philip had spent the interval well, for the story went that Peter of Préaux had sold his defection.[79] Certainly his nephews were endowed by Philip,[80] and the mayor of Verneuil received a reward like that of the mayor of Falaise.[81] But Peter was a brave and had proved himself a faithful man; it is likely that circumstances were too strong for him.

The fall of Rouen, *urbs invicta*, brought the war in Normandy to an end. Resistance doubtless continued in certain places, but no record of it has survived. Normandy was rapidly forced by Cadoc and the other French bailiffs into Philip's administrative system. Only at Dieppe do we hear of any serious trouble. This great port was closely connected with England and seems to have enjoyed peculiar freedom on account of the uncertain relations which existed between the authority of the archbishop, its new lord, and the local bailiff of Caux, or, as he was styled sometimes, of Arques. Some of the problems raised by King Richard's exchange of Dieppe for Andeli had been settled in the year 1200; for example, the right to the prisage of wine and the regulations concerning the passage of the king's men to England.[82] But disputes necessarily continued over such matters

[77] *i.e.*, the counts of Eu and Alençon.

[78] *Layettes*, i, 251; *Recueil*, ii, 381. The forty hostages of the citizens were to be chosen by King Philip from the children or relatives (de parentela nostra) of the defenders. Cf. Rigord, i, 151 (who gives sixty as the number).

[79] *Histoire des ducs de Normandie*, ed. Michel, p. 98. Cf. Delisle's remarks, *Actes de Philippe Auguste*, p. cxiij.   [80] *Recueil*, ii, nos. 813-16.

[81] *Ibid.*, ii, no. 848.   [82] *Rot. Norm.*, 3.

as the *regalia*, and the royal monopoly of fishing rights in the river.
In 1204 Philip Augustus placed one of his followers, John of Rouvrai,
who had already received grants of Norman lands, in charge of the
castle and bailiwick of Arques.[83] Dieppe was disaffected, and apparently not yet occupied by Philip's troops. John of Rouvrai heard that
Roger of Mortemer had landed with the purpose of maintaining King
John's cause, and immediately set men-at-arms in the town. Roger
was taken.[84] The men of Dieppe offended King Philip in other ways,
both at home and abroad. Some of them joined the fleet which in 1206
sailed with King John to Poitou; and the archbishop of Rouen, as
their lord, only succeeded in making their peace with Philip in March,
1207.[85] The anxieties and disturbances of war had of course affected
the finances of the archbishop; and it is with an obvious sigh of relief
that a chronicler of Rouen refers to the happy restoration of order.
His words may form an epilogue:

'At Michaelmas, in the year 1206, archbishop Walter granted to
the chapter of Rouen, the tithe of Dieppe. He had promised it for
some time, but in the tempest of war he had not been able to collect
in full the revenues of that town, and the canons in consequence
could not receive their tithe. Now they were established again in
their rights, and on the same day the tithe was paid, a sum amounting to £13 14s., of which the canons, thirty-six in number, each
received sixteen shillings in money of Tours.'[86]

I do not intend to follow the course of the war in Touraine and
Poitou. It is true that, as the claim to Normandy was not given up till
1259, later hostilities always had the recovery of the duchy as one of
their objectives. But in reality the fall of Chinon and Loches in the
year 1205 opened a fresh chapter in the history of the Angevin empire,
a chapter which was not closed until the middle of the fifteenth century
with the defeat of the earl of Shrewsbury at Castillon. During the
greater part of this period Normandy was firmly annexed to the royal
demesne of France, and was by no means a continuous scene of strife.

[83] *Cart. Norm.*, no. 167, p. 27. At Rouen John of Rouvrai had received the
lands of earl Bigod in Normandy up to the value of £240 (*Recueil*, ii, no. 797).
See also Delisle's preface to the inquests of Saint Louis, *Recueil des historiens
de France*, xxiv, part i, p. 109*.

[84] *Cart. Norm.*, no. 167, p. 27. See also Stapleton, II, cxxii–iii.

[85] *Ibid.*, no. 132, p. 23, from the original; also copied into Register A, f. 45.

[86] *Normanniae nova chronica*, in *Mém. de la Société des Antiquaires de
Normandie* (1850), xviii, 15–16. It would appear from this division that the
£13 14s. was sterling money, which was worth about four times as much as
money of Tours, and that the canons were paid twice a year, at Easter and
Michaelmas. Both sterling money and money of Tours had legal currency in
Normandy according to the ordinance of Philip Augustus. See Delisle in
Bibliothèque de l'Ecole des Chartes, x, 204–5.

During the siege of Rouen King Philip, by receiving the homage of the count of Périgord,[87] had signified that the war would be resumed in Aquitaine, and John decided to meet him there. Normandy went the way of the Vexin and Evreux, and was added to Philip's demesne. The king of France was able from the first, in fact, to play off the northern against the southern duchy by making Normandy the centre of preparations for an attack on England. This project had been in Philip's thoughts in 1193, and occupied his mind continually after the occupation of Rouen. In 1204-5 circumstances were not unfavourable to the enterprise, and there is evidence that arrangements were made. The quarrels which had divided the princes of the low countries between Normandy and the Rhine were partially settled, and Philip could hope to combine some of them against England. The natural ally of John in such a crisis was the count of Flanders, but the count was engaged in a greater warfare. He had been elected emperor of the Byzantine east at midnight on May 9, 1204, when Philip Augustus was intriguing with the men of Falaise; he had been led to the church of Saint Sophia, clad in the imperial robes, about the same day as that on which Philip had met the victorious Bretons at Caen. The western emperor was nearer to John, but was not more able to help; he appears to have kept in touch with his uncle, but done nothing more.[88] In February, 1205, the probability of an invasion of England was explicitly announced at Vernon, where Philip met Renaud of Dammartin, the count of Boulogne, and the duke of Brabant. Renaud had been Philip's right hand during the invasion of Normandy, and was marked out in virtue of his command of the coast and his English possessions, as the leader of any attack upon England. The duke of Brabant and he had married sisters. Renaud had married the heiress of Boulogne, and, with Philip's sanction, had secured the county; but Henry of Louvain, the duke, had financial claims upon the county also. Hence the brothers-in-law had quarrelled.[89] Early in 1205 they were reconciled, and clauses in the deed of reconciliation which was drawn up at Vernon, provided for a joint attack upon England for

---

[87] *Actes*, nos. 821-4, in Register A, f. 31v. Nos. 822, 824 are edited in *Recueil*, ii, nos. 799, 800; nos. 821, 823 in *Layettes*, nos. 713, 714.

[88] See especially Coggeshall, pp. 147-8, for the mission of the bishop of London (above, p. 260), the wretched state of Otto, and the desertion of Henry of Brabant. The chief German authorities are referred to by J. Lehmann, *Johann ohne Land* (1904), pp. 254-5. John's letter to the men of Köln (*Rot. Pat.* 40b) illustrates Otto's difficulties; and compare this entry of December 5, 1204 (*ibid.*, 48), to the barons of the exchequer: 'Mandamus vobis quod cum dominus Cantuariensis Archiepiscopus reddiderit nobis tria milia marcarum quas recepit ad opus nepotis nostri Regis Othonis tunc inde quietus sit.'

[89] The important fact was Henry of Louvain's change of policy at this time; first in joining Philip of Swabia against Otto, secondly in being reconciled to

the recovery of their English lands.[90] They might expect to be joined
by others who had been deprived of English revenues as a result of
the separation of England from Normandy.

John and his advisers passed the year which followed the fall of
Rouen in much perplexity. The contemporary writers describe a
period of jarring counsels, of suspicion and personal rivalries. It is
clear that the archbishop of Canterbury suspected those who, like the
Marshal, had most to gain from peace and feared lest they should
allow the king to acquiesce too readily in the loss of Normandy. The
Marshal's biographer states that the archbishop went so far as to warn
the king of France that the Marshal, who was again sent to France in
the spring of 1205, had not full powers to treat.[91] Colour was given
to the suspicion under which the Marshal fell at this time by his
homage to King Philip for his Norman lands—the year of waiting
being over.[92] John and the archbishop could not appreciate the Marshal's moral code; and painful interviews occurred between the king
and this prominent vassal after the latter's return. These interviews
took place at Portsmouth, where the king was gathering ships and
men with a view to the war in Poitou.

To this expedition both the Marshal and the archbishop were
opposed.[93] It was well known that the count of Boulogne intended to
invade England. He would naturally seize the opportunity given by
John's absence, when the country was depleted of a large army.
Moreover the Marshal had brought back from Normandy a lively
sense of Philip's power, of the size of his armies, and the thorough-
ness of his occupation. He and others pointed out all these things to
the king, and the archbishop, to whom John turned for advice, joined
in their view. After a brief voyage in the Channel, during which the
argument was continued, the king surrendered and the large fleet was
dispersed. This was in June, 1205, a month before the archbishop

Renaud of Boulogne. Malo, *Renaud de Dammartin*, pp. 81–3; Smets, *Henri I,
duc de Brabant*, pp. 109–15; Pirenne, *Histoire de Belgique*, i, 208.

[90] Edited by Malo, *op. cit.*, p. 273, and often elsewhere (Delisle, *Actes de
Philippe Auguste*, no. 910, p. 209). Its importance was realised by Coggeshall,
pp. 148–9.

[91] *Guillaume le Maréchal*, iii, 178 *et seqq*. This private mission must have
been undertaken between April and the end of May, 1205. The Marshal was
in England at the beginning of June, for he was with John in the neighbourhood of Portsmouth (Coggeshall, p. 152). The Patent Rolls for the years
1204–1206 are unfortunately meagre and badly arranged.

[92] *Guillaume le Maréchal*, iii, 178. See the discussion in S. Painter, *William
Marshal*, pp. 138–44.

[93] Coggeshall, pp. 152, 153; Wendover, ii, 9–10, ed. Coxe, iii, p. 182;
Guillaume le Maréchal, iii, 182, and notes. On preparations for the gathering
of the host at Portsmouth—both naval and military—see Sidney Smith's
introduction to the Pipe Roll 7 John (1941), pp. xii–xxv.

died. He was the greatest survivor of Henry II's reign and had been found watchful and cautious—perhaps over-suspicious—to the last.

It was doubtless wise to postpone the expedition. The error had been committed in 1204, when John's return in force to Normandy had been so unwarrantably delayed. But, although the king's policy had been weak abroad, there had been no hesitation at home, and during these years England made an imposing demonstration of unity and wealth. Across the Channel Angevin power was undermined by provincial jealousies, by the scandal of Arthur's disappearance, and by the tendency of all feudal interests to rally to a strong suzerain against an unsatisfactory lord. In England the mere threat of invasion thrilled all men to resistance. Ten years of John's rule were still required to break down for a time the sense of unity. In April of 1205 the country was organised for defence. Every group of nine knights was to equip a tenth. The population was formed into a vast sworn commune, in which every male of twelve years of age and upwards was to bear arms. Shires and hundreds, cities and boroughs were placed under a hierarchy of constables for the arranging of this host.[94] At the same time, the preparations which had gradually been made since the beginning of the year 1204 for an expedition over sea, could now be diverted, if necessary, to the defence of the kingdom. The traders and fishermen of the ports had been busy in providing their quotas of ships for the fleet which gathered at Portsmouth. Even distant Galloway had contributed.[95] And the Cinque Ports were, on account of their closer organisation, always at the call of the government.[96]

During John's reign the tension was so great that the defence of the kingdom was hardly distinguished from enterprises abroad. For the first time in English history since the Conquest, war with France involved the constant possibility of invasion. The king of England was set upon the recovery of his lost possessions, the king of France upon carrying his victories across the Channel. In 1205 the danger of invasion was sufficient to keep John at home. In 1206 he was able to leave for Poitou, and to introduce Englishmen (*Angligenae*) to new scenes of warfare.[97] The situation was emphasised in 1207, when a thirteenth was levied upon the property of clergy and laity for the

[94] *Rot. Pat.*, 55; Gervase of Canterbury, ii, 96–7; cf. A. L. Poole, *Obligations of Society*, p. 50.   [95] *Rot. Pat.*, 51, for the *galiae* of Thomas of Galloway.
[96] On January 30, 1204, John bade the barons of the Cinque Ports send twelve men from each port to confer with the archbishop and others on the business of the king (*Rot. Pat.*, 38b).
[97] Wendover speaks of their prowess (ii, 14; Coxe, iii, 187). Many men had gone from England in 1205 (Coggeshall, pp. 153–4). For instances of fines 'ut milites non transfretent in Pictaviam', see *Rot. de Fin.*, 366. For this expedition to Poitou in 1205 from Dartmouth, see evidence in introduction to the

double purpose of defending the kingdom and recovering the continental lands;[98] and a sum of nearly £60,000 was collected in a few months.[99] In spite of the disaffection which succeeded the chaotic tyranny of the next few years, John persisted in his attempt. The emperor Otto, with whom he had been on the closest terms since 1204, came to England in 1207. The two princes conferred together at Stapleford in Essex, and doubtless discussed the joint attack upon Philip which they finally made seven years later, in 1214.[100] The disasters of that year brought their inevitable punishment, the invasion of England and the downfall of Otto.

Hence during the ten years or so which followed 1204, the affairs of Normandy were overshadowed by the events of a wider contest. After the treaty of Lambeth, in September, 1217, the future of the duchy became again an object of prime interest. The treaty of Lambeth did not deal with the conquests of Philip Augustus, it was concerned with the conditions of Louis' departure from England; but, according to Wendover and a London chronicle, the parties to the treaty paid some attention to the young King Henry's claims upon the old Angevin empire. Louis is said to have promised that he would restore Henry's possessions when he should come to the throne of France;[101] and this promise, whatever its origin and character may have been, was the basis of Henry's later contention that in spite of the conquests of Philip and the judgments of his court, the succession to Normandy and the other continental lands still lay in himself.[102]

Pipe Roll 7 John (1941), pp. xviii–xxi. On the expedition of 1206, see Lady Stenton's introduction to the Pipe Roll 8 John (1942), pp. xii–xxii.

[98] Stubbs' *Constitutional History*, i, 620.

[99] *Rot. de Fin.*, 459: 'Recepta tocius tredecime tam de communi quam de finibus religiosorum et de donis episcoporum, quinquaginta et septem millia cccxxjli. xjs. vd.' This sum would equal nearly £230,000 in money of Tours or Angers.

[100] For Otto's visit, see Wendover, ii, 35 = Coxe, iii, 210: and especially the annals of Saint Edmund (*Memorials of St. Edmund*, ii, 16) which give the place, Stapleford 'in thalamo Samsonis abbatis Sancti Aedmundi'. There is a reference to the visit in *Rot. de Fin.*, 384. See A. L. Poole, *From Domesday Book to Magna Carta*, pp. 449–55.

[101] Wendover, ii, 271 = Coxe, iv, 86; annals of Dunstable in *Ann. Monastici*, iii, 82–3; cf. *Liber de Antiquis Legibus*, ed. Stapleton, Appendix, p. 204. No promise to this effect is to be found in the treaty, but some conversation would of course take place upon the future of the continental lands. M. Petit-Dutaillis suggests that Louis may have promised to approach his father upon the matter; see his *Etude sur la vie et le règne de Louis VIII* (1894), pp. 175–6.

[102] Matthew Paris, *Chron. Maj.*, v. 193: 'Rex Henricus bis, ut jura sua ultramarina, praecipue Normanniam, de qua pater ejus judicio duodecim parium Franciae abjudicabatur, tanquam de caede nepotis sui Arthuri cruentus, in manu forti reposceret, cum exercitu transfretavit, et bis rediit inglorius, pauper et confusus.'

The claim to Normandy was not waived till 1259. In the charters and letters of Henry III, as in those of his father, reference is frequently made to the future recovery of the duchy, and relations between England and the Normans were frequent. From the outset John had been careful to encourage trade between English and Norman ports,[103] and Henry III was equally anxious, notwithstanding the measures which the English government took against French merchants, to maintain the goodwill of the Norman traders. The ships of Dieppe, Rouen and Barfleur were especially favoured.[104] Before the failure of Henry's expedition to Brittany in 1230, negotiations were also frequent between the king and the Norman barons and clergy. The rule of Philip Augustus and his successors necessarily involved hardship to some persons and caused disappointment to more. Guérin of Glapion, for example, was accused—high though he was in Philip's favour—of intriguing with the emperor Otto.[105] Many Normans joined the allies against Philip in 1214, and for a long time every crisis in French politics, the death of a king, a baronial revolt or an English invasion, reacted upon Norman society. In 1223, when King Philip died, in 1226, when Louis VIII died, and in 1230, when Pierre Mauclerc, the count of Brittany, welcomed Henry III, English agents were sent to rouse the barons of the duchy.[106] According to Roger of Wendover, Henry would, in 1230, have turned aside to join the malcontents in Normandy if Hubert de Burgh had not dissuaded him.[107] The French government realised that special precautions were necessary against English intrigue. For example, when the dean and two canons of Rouen desired to cross the Channel upon the business of their church, permission was only granted after they had taken an oath that they would do nothing against the interests of the king of France or his kingdom.[108]

[103] See the long letter of June 4, 1204, in *Rot. Pat.*, 42–3, an elaborate regulation of trade with the possessions of the French king. Safe conduct for particular merchants of Rouen and Caen in December, 1204, and January, 1205 (*Rot. Pat.*, 49, 49b).

[104] Berger, in his valuable *Histoire de Blanche de Castille, Reine de France* (1895), has illustrated this, *e.g.*, p. 76.

[105] Above, p. 174. Compare the case of Guy de la Roche, below, p. 283.

[106] Roger of Wendover, ii, 271, 316; and iii, 5–6 = Coxe, iv, 86, 136, 210; Annals of Dunstable, in *Ann. Monastici*, iii, 81, 100; *Calendar of Patent Rolls*, 1216–25, p. 405–6; Petit-Dutaillis, *Louis VIII*, p. 232; Berger, *Blanche de Castille*, pp. 160 *seqq.*

[107] According to Wendover (iii, 33), Hubert's advice on this occasion was afterwards made one of the charges against him. It is not noticed by Master Laurence of Saint Albans in his refutation (Matthew Paris, *Chron. Maj.*, Additamenta, vi, 63).

[108] Quoted from the archives of Seine Inferieure by Berger, *op. cit.*, p. 76. Compare the fears of Norman treachery attributed by Matthew Paris to Saint Louis in 1242, *Chron. Maj.*, iv, 204.

At the same time, Henry III was quite alive to the possibility of playing off his claim to Normandy against his claim to Poitou. As early as 1229 he was willing to acquiesce in the loss of Normandy in return for the restoration of the other provinces.[109] On more than one occasion Saint Louis is asserted by Matthew Paris to have proposed a similar division, or to have offered to surrender Normandy itself.[110] In the end an agreement was reached on these lines, but on terms much less favourable to Henry III. By the treaty of Paris various actual and contingent rights were recognised as his in Gascony and in the neighbouring provinces, and his claims to Normandy, Anjou, and Poitou were formally given up.[111] The prophecy was fulfilled: *miro mutationis modo gladius a sceptro separabitur.*[112]

Matthew Paris is responsible for a curious story,[113] which he repeats more than once, that the conscience of Saint Louis was troubled by the retention of Normandy, and proof of this statement has erroneously been found in the words of two Norman charters issued by the great king.[114] It is very probable that during a reign which was by no means free from crises of grave anxiety, Saint Louis thought seriously of a compromise with Henry. And it was quite in accordance with his character if his sense of justice was disturbed by the thought of his father's oath in 1217 and the knowledge that the statesmen of King John had called in question the procedure of John's trial and condemnation.[115] Moreover, Henry III was his relative, and had his own troubles, and the cause of the crusade was harmed by the long, tiresome war between them. On the other hand, it seems certain that Saint Louis was fully satisfied of his right to Normandy.[116] Matthew Paris himself states that the Norman clergy and the French barons

---

[109] See the proposals in *Royal Letters*, ed. Shirley, i, 350, no. 288. At the most Henry asked for territory in western Normandy to link his southern possessions with the Channel: 'de Normannia retineatur ad opus regis unus episcopatus vel duo, ad transitum habendum ad terras predictas; scilicet episcopatus Albrincensis et Constanciensis.'   [110] *Chron. Maj.*, iv, 203, 506.

[111] Gavrilovitch, *Etude sur le traité de Paris de 1259* (1899).

[112] Annals of Burton, in *Ann. Monastici*, i, 487.

[113] *Chron. Maj.*, iv, 646; v, 280-1.

[114] *Cart. Norm.*, nos. 473, 1185, pp. 78, 325; June, 1248. In these charters Saint Louis confirms a grant by Philip Augustus of Picauville and Saint-Hilaire near Carentan to Bouchard de Mailli, and guarantees certain payments to Port Royal on the revenues of the same. Each contains a clause *mutatis mutandis*: 'hoc etiam semper salvum retinemus, quod si aliquando dictaret nobis conscientia quod de dictis villis restitutionem aliquibus facere vellemus, nobis liceret,' etc.

[115] Above, p. 148. It should be remembered that the learned jurist M. Guilhiermoz doubts whether the sentences passed on John by the French court in 1202 could be applied to Normandy. The point is not whether this view is correct, but that there was room for doubt.

[116] Gavrilovitch, *Etude sur le traité de Paris*, pp. 41-5.

testified emphatically in his favour.[117] We may see in this story of Saint Louis' conscience, as in other passages of Matthew Paris, not, it is true, the fabrication of facts which never occurred, but the misleading deductions of a patriotic historian.

Long before the treaty of Paris Normandy had been firmly united to the demesne of the French king.

The material for a picture of Norman administration in the thirteenth century is considerable.[118] It shows that the French kings, while making important changes in the government of the duchy, availed themselves of the older constitution. The exchequer remained as the chief court of Normandy for administrative and financial, as well as for judicial purposes. The machinery for the collection of revenue from viscounty and *prepositura* survived. But Philip Augustus and his successors, by means of a few simple alterations, reorganised these institutions in order to bring them into more accord with the system of government which existed in the Ile de France.

The office of seneschal disappeared in Normandy as it had disappeared in France.[119] This change did not take place immediately;

[117] *Chron. Maj.*, iv, 646; v. 280–1.

[118] The publications of the *Société d' histoire du droit normand*, which commenced recently under the title *Bibliothèque d' histoire du droit normand*, deserve special mention; also the earlier studies of MM. Génestal, Perrot, Lagouelle, and Legras, upon legal and economic history. These matters fall outside the scope of this study. In the following pages I have relied chiefly upon the *Cartulaire Normand*, which is still the most important collection of texts, upon E. J. Tardif's edition of the custumals, and Delisle's edition of the *Querimoniae Normannorum* of 1247 in the *Recueil des historiens de France*, xxiv, pt. i (1904), 2–73. [On this important text see Ch. Petit-Dutaillis, 'Querimoniae Normannorum', in *Essays in medieval history presented to Thomas Frederick Tout*, ed. A. G. Little and F. M. Powicke (Manchester, 1925), pp. 99 118. In general see J. R. Strayer, *The administration of Normandy under Saint Louis* (Medieval Academy of America, 1932), with the bibliography, pp. 123–7, to which Strayer's edition of the text of a survey (1260–1266) in his *The royal domain in the bailliage of Rouen* (Princeton, 1936) should be added.]

[119] Tardif, I, i, pp. lxxv, lxxvi. The last official reference to the seneschal is in the ordinance *de mutacione monete*, probably of date 1204 (*Cart. Norm.*, no. 112, p. 20, and in Register A, ff. 40v.–41; *Bibliothèque de l'Ecole des Chartes*, x, 199–204). In unofficial writings or casual deeds various persons are occasionally described as seneschals; for example, the author of *Eustace le Moine* styles Cadoc seneschal, and other great bailiffs, Renaud of Ville-Tierri, and Peter of Thillai are found with the title. The last named frequently presided at assizes held in various towns. But the office of seneschal of Normandy had disappeared, and these instances of the word must be compared with the title which Henry II's bailiff, Hamo Pincerna, gave himself 'Pincerna Regis Anglie et senescallus Baiocarum' (Stapleton, I, lix). A mandate of 1219, addressed to the seneschal and justices of Normandy, survives in a *vidimus* of 1255 (*Actes*, no. 1910). The form of address is quite exceptional.

for a short time Philip re-established Guérin of Glapion as seneschal;[120] but it was soon found desirable to distribute his functions
among a smaller number of powerful bailiffs. In consequence of this
step the court of exchequer was left without its usual president, and
from this time a special commission seems to have been appointed to
preside over the great sessions of the court at Easter and Michaelmas.[121] The commissioners were generally sent from France, and
thus helped to maintain the connection between the exchequer and
the superior Parlement of Paris. For, until the date of the great charter
to the Normans of 1315, the Parlement of Paris acted as a court of
appeal, verified the accounts of the Norman bailiffs, and sometimes
assumed the initiative in the affairs of the duchy as a court of first
instance.[122] The proceedings of the exchequer and of the Parlement
are a most important authority for the history of local administration
during the thirteenth century.[123]

The management of the demesne was entrusted to the bailiffs of
Rouen, Caux, Gisors, Pont-Audemer, Verneuil, Caen, Bayeux and
the Côtentin.[124] Thus the tendency towards the concentration of local
administration which may be observed in John's reign, was brought
to a logical issue by Philip Augustus. All the bailiffs appointed by
Philip after the annexation of Normandy were Frenchmen, and
several of them had already filled important posts on the Norman
frontier. The king's pantler, who had done service during the wars
in the Vexin, became castellan or bailiff of Rouen. Cadoc the mercenary, now lord of Gaillon, became bailiff of Pont-Audemer. Nicholas
Bocel, the new bailiff of Verneuil, had been previously entrusted
with the control of the March along the middle Eure, and had thus
supervised the administration of Nonancourt and other fortresses
which had passed some years before into French hands. One of the

[120] He is described by Philip as his seneschal of Normandy in May, 1204
(*Recueil*, ii, nos. 793, 802). The king's hesitations may be illustrated by the
way in which he revised more than once the position of Guillaume des Roches
in Anjou (Teulet, *Layettes*, no. 723, p. 267; *Recueil*, ii, no. 948). In Anjou
and Touraine an hereditary office was established which lasted until 1331
(Viollet, *Histoire des institutions politiques*, iii, 258).
[121] Viollet, *op. cit.*, iii, 344–5, for the chief authorities. These sessions were
held at Falaise. See the *Jugements de l'échiquier de Normandie*, ed. Delisle,
in *Notices et extraits des manuscrits* (1862), xx, part 2.
[122] Viollet, iii, 345.
[123] *Olim* (ed. Beugnot); the *Jugements*; and E. Perrot, *Arresta Communia
Scacarii*, the first volume of the *Bibliothèque d'histoire de droit normand*
(Caen, 1910).
[124] Delisle's introduction to the inquests of Saint Louis in the *Recueil des
historiens de France*, xxiv, part i, pp. 97*–146*. Delisle shows, however, that
the bailiwick of Pont-Audemer was probably merged in that of Rouen after
the deprivation of Cadoc in 1219, and that the Avranchin was, late in the
century, detached from Bayeux and joined to the Côtentin.

first bailiffs, whom Philip established in the Côtentin, had been *pre-positus* of Paris. Pierre of Thillai, once bailiff of Orleans, filled the most important position of all in Caen and Falaise. In virtue of his control over the two chief centres of Norman government, he took to a great extent the place of the seneschals of Angevin times.[125]

It was inevitable that men who were entrusted in a newly conquered country with such vast powers, should at times be guilty of tyranny and extortion. Cadoc especially proved himself a corrupt though an able administrator.[126] But the king was successful upon the whole in continuing the policy which, as is shown by his charters and by the statements of his accounts for 1202,[127] he had adopted after the acquisition of the Vexin and the fortresses on the Eure. This policy was a twofold one; on the one hand, he concentrated in his own demesne the castles and territory which occupied positions of peculiar strategic or commercial importance, and at the same time retained definite control over the castles which he gave away; on the other hand, he was careful to observe with a few modifications the customs of Normandy in Church and state and to maintain private rights. In this summary of Philip's work I will confine myself to a brief consideration of this twofold policy.

Philip began his reorganisation of the demesne by ordering elaborate inquiries to be made into the ducal rights and customary revenues, and into the financial and social organisation of those estates which, like Vernon and Paci and Evreux, now ceased to be private property. The important record of accounts for the year 1202 shows that these inquiries must have been made in the south of Normandy after the treaties of 1195 and 1200. As a result the administration of Vernon, which became Philip's headquarters in the Seine valley, and of the district to the west of Vernon, was so satisfactory that the king had been largely able to carry on the war, or at least to maintain the garrisons on this part of his new frontier, out of local funds.[128] Philip formed the county of Evreux, the Norman Vexin, Paci and Vernon into a compact demesne which, from an economic point of view, he seems to have regarded as part of France rather than of Normandy.[129] After the conquest the rest of Normandy

[125] Delisle, pp. 134*–136*.

[126] *Ibid.*, pp. 130*–133*. Among other charges he was accused of embezzling £14,200 in money in Paris. See *Cart. Norm.*, nos. 363–6 and notes.

[127] This statement of accounts is printed in Brussel, *Nouvel examen de l'usage général des fiefs en France*, vol. ii, p. cxxxix. On its value, see Brussel's remarks, vol. i, 436–7.

[128] Brussel, *loc. cit.* Inquests in the *Cart Norm.*, nos. 116, 117, pp. 20–1, nos. 199–201, pp. 30–1, and no. 1079, pp. 287–8, also in Register A, ff., 86–86v.

[129] Philip's charters illustrate this. In 1205 the burgesses of Breteuil were exempted from dues in Normandy, Poitou, Anjou, Maine, except in the county of Evreux, the Norman Vexin, Paci, Vernon and the land of Hugh of Gournai

was submitted to similar inquiry and organisation. The viscounties, *prepositurae* and other units of the farmed revenues were probably grouped in viscounties within the bailiwicks.[130] Private and hereditary rights, such as those of the bishop of Lisieux, were investigated; in some cases their precarious nature was emphasised,[131] others were bought up,[132] others were disputed.[133] The more irksome claims upon revenue, of which Queen Berengaria's dowry in Falaise, Domfront and Bonneville-sur-Touque was the chief,[134] were exchanged for grants of lands or money elsewhere.[135] Investigation was also made into the condition and equipment of the royal castles. Careful inventories of the armouries and reports upon repairs have survived.[136] And, while he was dealing with these matters, Philip ordered an inquiry into the distribution of the Jews.[137]

Although the official records of the duchy had been removed by John's orders to London, adequate materials for Philip's investigations remained. The documents inscribed upon his register include, for example, the summary statement of knight service, based upon the inquest of 1172, which is also found in the Red Book of the English exchequer.[138] Many of the original deeds and documents, which had lain in the Norman archives and contained important evidence upon Norman customs, found their way into the Trésor des Chartes.[139] Unfortunately the existing records of Philip's inquests

---

(*Actes*, no. 902). Compare above, p. 250. Roger of Meulan was induced to exchange his rights in the viscounty of Evreux for lands in the county.

[130] Delisle in *Historiens de France*, xxiv, part i, p. 97*; cf. also his early essay upon the bailiffs of the Côtentin (1851) in the *Mémoires de la Société des Antiquaires de Normandie*, vol. xix, 61–119.

[131] *e.g.*, the letter of Jordan, bishop of Lisieux, October, 1204, in *Cart. Norm.*, no. 92, p. 17: 'nos domino Regi Francorum Philippo concedimus ut sufferentia, quam ipse nobis fecit de libertatibus civitatis et banleuge nostre, in nulla re nobis auxilietur contra ipsum per teneaturam,' etc.

[132] *e.g.*, the rights of Roger of Meulan in Evreux. See note above.

[133] *e.g.*, the archbishop's claims to *fouage* in Andeli; cf. *Cart. Norm.*, no. 132, p. 23, where a settlement is reached.

[134] Inquiry into the revenue of these places in *Cart. Norm.*, no. 111, also in Register A, ff. 40v. Berengaria received Le Mans in exchange. For other references to her, see *Actes*, nos. 805, 857, 892, 895, 1777. No. 857 is edited in *Recueil*, ii, no. 840.

[135] The count of Boulogne received in exchange for Mortemer the castles of Aumale and Domfront, and the village of Saint-Riquier. At the same time he received Mortain (*Recueil*, ii, nos. 862–3; *Layettes*, no. 733).

[136] Above, p. 224, note 90.

[137] *Cart. Norm.*, nos. 207–8; also in Register A, f. iv., 84v.

[138] *Recueil des historiens de France*, xxiii, 693–9, Hall in *Red Book of the Exchequer*, II, pp. ccxxxi–iv, 624–47 = Register A, ff. 32v seqq.

[139] *Cart. Norm.*, p. iii. Cf. the charter for Falaise, 1204, no. 75, p. 283: 'preterea volumus et concedimus ut stabilimentum commune eorum, sicut

are too fragmentary to enable the historian to construct a complete description of Normandy in 1204. They are only sufficient to give some idea of the scope and variety of the king's instructions.

Soon after the conquest Philip announced that he had added to his demesne the lands of several great barons, including the earls of Warenne, Arundel, Leicester and Clare, and of all those knights who were at the time in England.[140] A document, which is inscribed upon one of the registers, contains a list of the cities and fortresses which had been incorporated in the demesne.[141] All the cities (that is, the seats of bishoprics) and nearly forty castles are contained in this list. The most important exceptions are Argentan, Drincourt, Radepont, Nonancourt, Domfront, Mortain, Saint-James-de-Beuvron and Pontorson; and inquiry shows that the tenure of the barons who held these was in several cases subject to restriction. Thus Robert of Courtenai, to whom Philip gave Conches and Nonancourt, pledged himself not to sell, give or mortgage them.[142] Radepont was held by Pierre of Moret under special conditions of service.[143] Domfront was part of the grant to Renaud, count of Boulogne, in exchange for Mortemer. His presence in the west, and that of his brother in Saint-James-de-Beuvron really acted as a check upon the barons of Brittany.[144]

It is indeed interesting to notice how judiciously Philip played off one interest against another, or by apparent concessions strengthened his position. He was not afraid to establish powerful vassals on the Breton frontier, if at the same time, he could recover places of more strategic importance on the Norman border or in Touraine. Just as he bought the count of Boulogne out of Mortemer so he bought André and his brother Robert of Vitré out of Langeais.[145] At the same time, he tried to break down the barrier between Normans and Frenchmen by the settlement of his barons and servants in the duchy,[146] and by encouraging intermarriage between the great barons of Normandy and the Ile de France. For example, the daughter of the chamberlain of Tancarville married the son of Walter the younger, one of the royal chamberlains;[147] and the son of Count Robert of Alençon

continetur in rotulo qui coram nobis lectus fuit et in registro nostro transcriptus, inviolabiter observetur.' Also in Register A, f. 31.
[140] Cart. Norm., no. 113, p. 20; Actes, no. 887.
[141] Cart. Norm., no. 209, p. 32; also in Register A, ff. 60–60v. Gaillon is included, though Cadoc had a life interest in it.
[142] Cart. Norm., no. 97, p. 1; Actes, no. 900.
[143] Cart. Norm., no. 184, p. 297; also in Register A, f. 58. Compare a somewhat similar provision with regard to Montbason in Touraine (Actes, no. 1009). [144] Recueil, ii, nos. 862–3, 939. [145] Recueil, ii, no. 949.
[146] Grants to balistarii, Recueil, ii, nos. 736, 913; to his falconer, ibid., no. 914. [147] Recueil, ii, no. 888.

married the daughter of Bartholomew of Roie, one of Philip's closest companions, who in 1208 became grand chamberlain of France.[148]

While, however, King Philip secured his position in Normandy, he was careful to make the transition from Angevin to French rule as easy as possible. As king of France he was in any event overlord of the Normans. His relations with them, especially with the clergy, had commenced long before 1204. In the affairs both of Church and of state he sought to observe the 'usages and customs of Normandy'.

Throughout the process of annexation Philip professed to act in accordance with the forms of law. He had, he said, conquered Normandy in pursuance of a judgment duly given in his court, and he called upon the bishops and lay barons to swear fealty to him.[149] With the former he had small difficulty. In reply to an appeal for advice they were told by Innocent III to decide for themselves upon the justice of Philip's action; whereupon they submitted. Their successors emphatically recognised the right of the French kings in Normandy.[150] On his side, Philip, according to William the Breton, recognised the canonical rights of election of the Norman clergy which had been disregarded by King John.[151]

With the memories of the dispute about Séez fresh in their minds,[152] the clergy doubtless expected Philip to restore this and other privileges. They had a peculiar advantage in their opposition to interference, for at this period the compromise between the law of Church and state was more precisely defined in Normandy than it was in England. The privileges of the clergy had been secured by King Richard's constitution *pro clericis et sacerdotibus*,[153] and by the articles drawn up in 1190 by the clergy themselves.[154] It appears that John had disregarded this compromise when he imposed a tallage upon ecclesiastical property,[155] and doubtless a closer scrutiny of the rolls would reveal other instances of his anti-ecclesiastical tendencies. Philip before the end of 1205 called for a clear statement of Norman

---

[148] *Cart. Norm.*, no. 122, p. 22.

[149] See the pope's reply to the Norman bishops, March 7, 1205, Potthast, no. 2434; Migne, *Patrologia Latina*, vol. ccxv, p. 564: 'justitia praeeunte, per sententiam curiae suae Normanniam acquisivit.'

[150] Matthew Paris, *Chronica Majora*, iv, 646.

[151] *Philippid*, lib. viii, 241–64 (ed. Delaborde, ii, 219–20). Cf. *Actes*, no. 1109: the bishop of Coutances declares that, during a vacancy in the see of Rouen, the chapter have the administration of the temporalities and spiritualities of the archbishopric.   [152] Above, p. 168.

[153] *Statuta et consuetudines*, c. lxxvii (Tardif, I. i, 68).

[154] Diceto, ii, 86–8.

[155] *Statuta et consuetudines*, c. lxxii, 6: 'ne tallagia fiant super ecclesias et possessiones earum; si vero persona vel vicarius ecclesie feodum laicale habuerit secundum quantitatem feodi respondeat, si feodum amat.' For John's taxation, see above, p. 235.

customs with regard to those matters which were most frequently
causes of dispute between lay and ecclesiastical authorities; and in
November of that year a jury of important barons, all of them
laymen, made a declaration on several points.[156] The facts that
the statement is based upon lay evidence and lays stress upon the
limitations which were placed by Norman practice upon the laws of
the Church, go to show that the clergy had availed themselves of the
change of government to increase their claims. Yet a comparison of
this document with those of Richard's reign, with the custumals,[157]
and with the judgments of the exchequer in the thirteenth century,
shows that the continuity of custom in the Norman Church was unbroken by Philip's conquests and had only been temporarily disturbed
by the policy of John. The statutory additions were few. When in
1206-7 the archbishop of Rouen and his suffragans suggested a special
form of procedure in disputes about patronage, the king issued a
constitution giving legal force to the request;[158] this act, the result
of ecclesiastical initiative, seems to be the only important addition
made by Philip to the law relating to the Church in Normandy. During
the thirteenth century Norman law, in accordance with its earlier
tendency, developed naturally along lines which were more favourable
to the Church than was the contemporary development of the common
law in England.[159]

A Jumièges annalist complains of the exactions with which Philip
visited religious houses after the conquest.[160] It is likely that here
and there communities suffered, but there is sufficient evidence to
prove that, after, as before, 1204, Philip continued to confirm the

---

[156] Edited by Teulet, *Layettes*, i, 296, no. 785; French versions in Tardif,
I, ii, 89; English translation in Round's *Calendar of documents preserved in
France*. See also *Actes*, no. 961; *Cart. Norm.*, no, 124, p. 22. The date is
November 15, 1205.

[157] As Viollet has pointed out, the author of the first part of the earliest
custumal, the *Statuta et consuetudines*, was preoccupied by the rights of the
church: *Histoire Littéraire de la France*, xxxiii, 54, 60.

[158] *Statuta et consuetudines*, c. lxxvii, 7 (Tardif, I, i, 77). The custumal
limits the application of Philip's constitution, but the constitution itself does
not impose any limitation. It survives in letters addressed to the bailiffs
(incorporated in the custumal) and more fully in letters addressed to the
bishops (see G. Bessin, *Concilia Rotomagensis provinciae*, Rouen, 1727,
part i, pp. 105-6). The best edition of the original letter from the archbishop of Rouen to his suffragans is in Perrot, *Arresta communia scacarii*, pp.
127-9.

[159] Cf. Pollock and Maitland, *History of English Law* (2nd edition), i, 189,
247. For an interesting judgment, on the other hand, by which the exchequer
extended to laymen a privilege which had been previously confined to the
clergy, see *Jugements*, no. 230. It belongs to the year 1218, and deals with
the process *de feodo et elemosina;* cf. Tardif, I, p. lxxiii.

[160] *Historiens de France*, xviii, 342.

possessions and rights of monasteries and clergy, and to remain on friendly terms with archbishop Walter.

Norman laws and custom in general were as little affected as the relations between Church and state by Philip's successes. In a well-known passage of his *Philippid* William the Breton enlarges upon the king's attitude to Norman law and institutions. He accepted them entirely 'so far as they were not inequitable or did not touch the liberty of the Church'.[161] William refers in detail to only one of the few changes in the legal system, by which Normans were 'made equal to Frenchmen'. Philip, he says, abolished the privileged position of the appellant in the duel, whereby the appellant was simply liable to fine in case of his defeat, while the defendant, if defeated, was put to death.[162] For the most part the changes in Norman law during the thirteenth century were due to the judgments of the exchequer and Parlement, and the intellectual influences of the time.[163]

In the secular more than in the ecclesiastical world the annexation of Normandy to the French crown involved hardships to individuals even in the ordinary course of law. Some of the peculiar difficulties which the exchequer and the other courts had to face will come before us in the next chapter. In other cases general rulings must have borne hardly upon litigants. For example, it was obviously necessary that the courts in deciding certain claims to property, should insist upon the production of documents; and these might easily have been lost or destroyed.[164] Again, the courts refused to acknowledge deeds which had issued from the chancery of John, the prince who had forfeited his duchy;[165] hence many vested interests of recent origin must

---

[161] *Philippid*, viii, 226–7 (ed. Delaborde, ii, 219).

[162] *Ibid.*, viii, 228–40. An important ordinance issued by Philip Augustus in 1209, upon the division of fiefs, has been shown by M. Génestal to have had no effect in Normandy: *Le Parage Normand*, p. 36, note.

[163] The development of Norman law in the thirteenth century would have to be studied (*a*) in the thirteenth century custumal, or *Summa de Legibus*, as compared with the *Statuta et consuetudines*, or Tré-ancien Coutumier: (*b*) in the collections of judgments of the Exchequer and Assizes belonging to the thirteenth century. At the end of the century or early in the fourteenth century an intelligent scribe wrote out in the margins of the custumal those judgments and royal ordinances which bore more directly upon the custumal. This work became popular. Perrot has given a table of these marginal texts in his *Arresta Communia Scacarii*, pp. 33–44. See generally, J. R. Strayer, *The Administration of Normandy under Saint Louis* (1932), especially chapter iii, and bibliography.

[164] A case in *Jugements*, no. 34. Robert the Angevin lost his suit against the Templars. His charter, he said, had been burnt in his house ten years before (1198).

[165] *Olim*, i, 492, no. ix (1260): 'nec consuevit dominus Rex tenere litteras ipsius regis Anglie.' No recognition or confirmation of John's charters is contained in the documents collected by Delisle in his *Cartulaire Normand*, though earlier charters are frequently confirmed.

have been swept on one side, a fact which probably accounts for the disappearance of several of the communes which had been granted by John to Norman towns. But upon the whole one cannot but be impressed by the care with which the new government maintained the social and economic life of the Normans uninterrupted. The authentic charters of early Norman dukes, of the Conqueror and his sons, of Henry II and Richard were respected. The exchequer accepted the letters of contemporary English statesmen, for example, of Earl William the Marshal, as evidence of occurrences before the annexation.[166] The coronation of King Richard was established as the point of departure, or limit of legal memory, for fiscal enquiries and for certain important recognitions and prescriptive rights.[167]

In the meantime the Normans adjusted themselves to the new order of things. One of Philip's earliest acts was the regulation of the currency and the establishment of the rates of exchange between the monetary systems of Normandy and central France.[168] By this decree sterling money, and the money of Tours and Le Mans were given legal currency in Normandy, and all other money was to be exchanged at a fixed rate. Philip also defined or enlarged the privileges of the towns. Communes of the type of Rouen or of Mantes and other French towns spread through the duchy.[169] The men of Rouen even came to an agreement with the men of Paris about the commerce of the Seine.[170] Rapidly and imperceptibly the burgesses and peasantry and the bulk of the lesser gentry lost any interest they had in the old English connection. The loss of Normandy worked a violent revolution in the society of the Anglo-Norman baronage, but in it alone.

[166] *Jugements*, no. 246, Easter, 1219: 'cum in isto scaccario cognitum sit per litteras patentes domini archiepiscopi Cantuarie et etiam litteras patentes comitis W. marescali Anglie, quod idem Radulphus [obierat?] jam elapsis xx annis et eo amplius,' etc.

[167] Viollet, in *Histoire Litteraire*, xxxiii, 63–4. This date was abolished in the Charter to the Normans (1315) and replaced by a prescription of forty years; *ibid.*, p. 72.

[168] *Cart. Norm.*, no. 112, p. 20, also in Register A, ff. 40v.–41; Delisle in *Bibliothèque de l'Ecole des Chartes*, x, 199.

[169] *Cart. Norm.*, pp. xv–xviii; *Recueil*, ii, nos. 782, 806, 809, 877, 879–80, etc. For Philip's policy with regard to the towns, see Giry, *Les Etablissements de Rouen*, i, 31, 32, 52, 358.

[170] In January, 1210; *Cart. Norm.*, nos. 171, 1097; p. 296.

CHAPTER X

ON SOME SOCIAL AND POLITICAL
CONSEQUENCES OF THE WARS IN NORMANDY

Sir William mentioned the old laird of Bernera, who, summoned by his chief to join him with all the men he could make, when the Chief was raising his men for Government, sent him a letter to this purpose: 'Dear Laird,—No man would like better to be at your back than I would; but on this occasion it cannot be. I send my men who are at your service; for myself higher duties carry me elsewhere.' He went off accordingly alone, and joined Raasay as a volunteer.

Sir Walter Scott's *Journal* (1890), ii, 129.

MORE than one Norman in the years which followed the success of Philip Augustus had to face perplexities similar to that of the Scottish laird of Bernera; but few were permitted to avail themselves of his honourable compromise. The Normans were, indeed, in positions of varying difficulty. For the most part those who had lands in England and in Normandy had sooner or later to make a choice or lose all. One fortunate or quick-witted person is recorded to have exchanged his Norman property for lands in England,[1] but the majority of landholders were compelled to surrender their holdings upon one side or the other of the English Channel.

The legal and political consequences of this cleavage between the English and Norman baronage were far reaching. We may best approach the subject by considering (1) the policy adopted by Philip Augustus with regard to the Normans who had deserted their country to follow John; (2) the effect of this policy upon England; and (3) its importance in the history of the French state.

I

Many persons whose interests lay entirely within the borders of Normandy suffered severely.[2] There was not, it is true, so much hard-

---

[1] *Rot. de Fin.*, 219 (1204). 'Elyas de Wimblevill dat domino Regi xxx m. pro habenda terra de Dene cum pertinenciis suis qui fuit Alani Martell, quam idem Alanus ei dedit in excambio pro terra quam prefatus Elyas habuit in Normannia, et pro habenda illa secundum convensionem inter eos factam per cartas suas.'

[2] See the *Querimoniae Normannorum* of 1247 in the *Recueil des Historiens de France*, vol. xxiv, and Delisle's *Recueil des jugements de l'échiquier de Normandie*.

ship as might have been expected as a mere result of the change of government. Here and there privileges of the forest were lost, or rents were raised.[3] One suggestive case was brought to light at Montpinçon by the commissioners of Saint Louis: certain dues, it was alleged, were still exacted as in Angevin times although the market, in return for which they had originally been paid, was no longer held.[4] Again, a few people complained that owing to the poverty or weakness of their predecessors at the time of the conquest, they were deprived of their rights.[5] But it is not cases of this kind which most frequently attract the attention as one reads the *Querimoniae Normannorum* or the judgments of the Exchequer. The greater suffering was caused by the flight or disappearance of Normans during the first decade or so of the thirteenth century. The break between Normandy and England was complete; except to the merchant and other licensed travellers England suddenly became a forbidden land; and even the merchant was easily suspected.[6] Hence the man who had claims against a refugee, the lord whose tenant or the tenant whose lord had deserted, and the relatives whom the deserter had left behind, often found themselves in a position of extreme discomfort. There were those who had been under an obligation to the deserter or had suffered injustice from him or had otherwise been brought into peculiar relations with him. For example, William Crassus the seneschal had seized a meadow which one winter had been flooded by his pond; and, after the conquest, the meadow had been confiscated with his other lands and had thus been lost to its original owner.[7] Guy of Dive had seized some rents which had belonged to the father of Henry of Bruecourt, and because Guy had afterwards lost his lands Henry and his father had permanently lost the rents.[8] On the other hand gifts, sales and dowries which had been alienated before 1204 were frequently confiscated with the lands of those who had alienated them.[9] A lady had farmed out her dowerlands to a man who had afterwards gone to England, and the royal officials had seized the lands.[10] There were wards who had lost their inheritance through the desertion of their guardians,[11] and widows whose husbands died in England

[3] *Querimoniae*, nos. 95, 363, 369, 474, 481, 490, 504, 551.
[4] *Ibid.*, no. 355.   [5] *Ibid.*, nos. 81, 445.   [6] *Ibid.*, no. 70.
[7] *Ibid.*, no. 379.   [8] *Ibid.*, no. 7; cf. no. 94.
[9] *Ibid.*, nos. 60, 415, 426. See also judgments in cases of dower, given in favour of the claimants, in *Recueil des jugements*, nos. 7, 18, 20.
[10] *Jugements*, no. 21. This judgment illustrates the continuity of records: 'judicatum est quod Milisent, uxor Roberti de Praeeris habeat, si voluerit, recordationem assisae in qua tradidit Rogero Tirel dotem suam ad firmam, quae capta est in manu Regis, quia idem Rogerus de dote sua erat saisitus quando perrexit in Angliam.'
[11] *Querimoniae*, no. 78.

holding their land *jure uxoris*.[12] Several persons who had given their lands in pledge, found themselves deprived.[13] Upon all such cases lawyers could raise perplexing questions of fact. A second group of cases might also give rise to perplexing questions of law. Suppose, for example, that a man who had owned a little property in Normandy had entered an English monastery, or died in England in possession of an English benefice or in the course of his studies.[14] During his lifetime no proper disposition of his Norman lands may have been made; the authorities may not have been informed of his intention to leave Normandy or he may not have returned within the stated time. Is his land forfeited or not? Again there is the case of doubtful succession, in which the royal bailiff insists that A, who has fled, and not the loyal B, is the legal heir to a piece of land.[15]

If we turn from genealogical difficulties to those which were created in feudal relations, we find similar problems. Sometimes the rights of sub-tenants were swept away with those of their lord.[16] A certain B, for example, alleged that he had been deprived of A's services, because some muddle-headed or unscrupulous persons had sworn that A did not hold of B, but of C; and C had fled.[17] More frequently the rights of the lord suffered through the defection of his tenant.[18] In such cases important points of law might have to be settled; for example, if the royal bailiff had seized the land which the runaway A had held of B, would B have to show before he could enter upon it that the relation between himself and A was of long standing, or, if this were not the case, to prove that he had alienated the land to A with the consent of the overlord?[19] And what would be the position of A's kinsmen holding of him in parage, who had not left Normandy?[20] It is likely that the cases of the refugees would necessitate more precise definitions in the Norman law relating to forfeitures.[21]

For our more general purpose the significance of these cases lies in the evidence which they afford of Philip's attitude towards John's

---

[12] *Querimoniae*, no. 466.

[13] *Ibid.*, nos. 75, 372, 452.

[14] *Ibid.*, nos. 41, 46, 365, 390, 396.

[15] *Ibid.*, no. 410.

[16] *Ibid.*, no. 380.

[17] *Ibid.*, no. 49.

[18] *Ibid.*, nos. 6, 40, 59, 404, 456.

[19] See the *Statuta et Consuetudines*, cc. 89–91 (Tardif, I, i, 99–101); Pollock and Maitland, *History of English Law*, 2nd edition, i, 342.

[20] *Statuta et Consuetudines*, c. 88 (Tardif, I, i, 98–9).

[21] It is to be hoped that some Norman jurist will work out the precise effects upon Norman law of the separation of the duchy from England and the rest of the Angevin Empire. For example had it any share in defining the distinction between the 'fief noble' and the 'fief roturier'? According to the thirteenth-century custumal, only the former was escheated in the event of the tenant's condemnation. (Viollet, *Hist. Litt.*, xxxiii, 132.) For the chief thirteenth-century judgments *de forisfacturis*, see the references in Perrot, *Arresta communia scacarii*, pp. 34–5.

vassals. Yet the vigorous action which they reveal covered some hesitation and perplexity. It is true that Philip took very prompt measures. By a decree of 1204–5 he confiscated the lands of all those knights who had their abode in England. A definite term was assigned within which those who had left Normandy were permitted to return and make submission;[22] and absence in England was construed as a sign of disloyalty.[23] In Normandy men, especially those of high standing, who had any dealings with 'traitors', or were even suspected of plotting, were immediately punished. If the story which became current in Normandy be true, Guérin of Glapion was deprived of his lands because he had a private conversation with the emperor Otto.[24] Guy de la Roche, who had spoken with Walter of Mondreville, was obliged to surrender the castle of Beaumont-le-Roger and to swear that he would never again cross the Epte or the Eure into Normandy.[25] On the other hand, Philip probably regarded most of these decisive actions as measures of precaution, not as irrevocable judgments. His attitude after the critical years were over and the victory of 1214 had been won, shows that he was anxious to come to an agreement with those who were not in his peace.[26]

And if we turn to England and compare the attitude of John with that of Philip, it appears still more unlikely that Philip was pursuing a deep policy. Both sides expected that a settlement would be reached; and all vexed questions of private ownership would then be solved. The English chancery rolls for 1204 and the next few years show, as we shall see later, that John by no means hardened his heart, and Philip certainly had not any more reason to harden his.

The truth is that Philip's position in Normandy was unprecedented. For the first time a great fief, which had been independent in everything but name, had been added to the royal demesne as the result of a judicial sentence passed in the French court. In previous years John had freely acknowledged the competence of the court to decide the

---

[22] *Actes de Philippe Auguste*, no. 933A. *Jugements*, no. 339: Thomas Pouchin 'ivit in Angliam cum rege Johanne, nec rediit in Normanniam ad pacem domini regis, cum aliis qui redierunt ad terminum sibi a domino rege assignatum'. See also *Querimoniae*, nos. 100, 521, from the former of which it appears that those who returned were expected to report themselves to the king's justice.

[23] For cases of various kinds see *Querimoniae*, nos. 62, 64, 65, 73, 422, 429. In one case (no. 84) a man had gone to England with the king's consent but had died within the time allowed for his return. His Norman property was seized on the plea that he had deserted Normandy.   [24] Above, p. 174.

[25] *Cart. Norm.*, p. 289, no. 1080; *Actes*, no. 968. The date is January, 1206.

[26] *e.g.*, *Jugements*, nos. 145, 171. The last reads 'judicatum est quod duo sorores Alienor de Barnevilla que sunt ad pacem domini regis, habeant escaetam ejusdem Alienor defuncte, salvo jure tercie sororis que est in Anglia, si ad pacem domini regis venerit'.

questions arising from his succession to the Angevin dominions, but he had protested loudly against this attempt to disinherit him. The Pope had throughout refused to express any opinion upon the justice of Philip's action, and it was with some difficulty that the king of France established its validity in the minds of men. The situation would have been easier if Normandy had not been attached by the history of two hundred and fifty years to·a country which had no traditional connection with France and the French crown. Philip might confiscate Norman lands and regard the followers of John as felons, but he could hardly treat the Normans who stayed in England either as foreigners or rebels. At this period not only were the words 'foreigner', 'alien', 'traitor' invested with the vaguest political meaning, but even the political unity of France was hardly capable of definition.

France in the wider sense of the word represented a bundle of Carolingian traditions which had been maintained by feudal rather than by national institutions, and in which the Normans had the slightest share. In 1204 the French monarchy had not yet interpreted the unity of France clearly in terms of history and geography and law. Although Philip Augustus took the first step towards this interpretation, it only began to find clear expression after another century of legal intrigues on the Aquitanian border and of wrangling about the rights of the empire on the German frontier.[27] Even the clear-cut theories of the publicists of the sixteenth century and of the statesmen of the seventeenth did not resolve all the vagueness in the definition of the French state. Precision only came with the Revolution. Even then the determination of the National Assembly to have no doubts about French rights in Alsace precipitated the revolutionary wars.

With these considerations in mind we cannot be surprised that Philip Augustus did not press forward his vigorous policy in Normandy to what would seem to be its logical consequences. He could not immediately insist, as the Germans insisted in the case of the inhabitants of Alsace-Lorraine after 1871, that every Norman should decide whether he would be a Norman or an Englishman. He did not attempt to give a precise name to the crime for which the fugitives lost their lands. They were simply treated as felons, whose lands, like those of any other felon, lapsed to their lords after the king had enjoyed them for a year and a day.[28] It is clear that the cases of injustice or

[27] The reader may refer to Kern, *Die Anfänge der französichen Ausdehnungspolitik* (1910), pp. 15–56, 87–92; and, for the condition of France in this respect at the end of the *ancien régime*, Brette, *Les limites et les divisions territoriales de la France en 1789* (1907).

[28] *Jugements*, no. 30 (a. 1208), 'judicatum est quod Fulco Paganelli habeat terram fratrum suorum fugitivorum . . . quia dominus rex habuit exitus ipsius terre de anno'. Fulk had endowed his brothers in return for service and

hardship to which I have called attention in the preceding pages were
the result of official tyranny or of the inequitable anomalies incidental
to every body of law, and not of any additions to the law. Only after
a war of fifty years did Saint Louis finally insist that those barons
who still held lands both of him and of Henry III, should make their
choice between them. It is very unlikely—indeed, if we believe the
stories of Louis VIII's oath in 1217 and of Saint Louis' conscientious
scruples, it is incredible—that Philip and his successors regarded the
Normans who had not sworn fealty to them as traitors. Treachery was
a sin against a man, not a political crime against a ruler. In the minds
of all men, French and Norman and English, Gilbert of Vascoeuil,
who betrayed Gisors to Philip, and Nicholas Orphin, who betrayed
Nonancourt to Richard, and the count of Alençon, who deserted John
in 1203, were traitors;[29] but it is unlikely that William des Roches, in
spite of his tergiversations, was regarded as a traitor. He had made
certain arrangements with Philip in 1199 and with John in 1202, and
they had failed to observe them. Nor was William the Marshal a
traitor when he did homage to Philip for his Norman lands. The Marshal, on the contrary, was an authority upon moral questions of this
kind. He is said to have remonstrated with Philip upon the unchival-
rous way in which the latter availed himself of such traitorous vermin
as the count of Alençon and his colleagues. Philip might have replied
with justice that after his condemnation John had no right to expect
the support of his followers; we know that it had been one of the
objects of the condemnation of 1202, to give John's vassals an excuse
for deserting him.[30] But Philip knew that he was speaking to a gentleman, and he answered as a gentleman, mildly apologetic for himself
and frankly contemptuous of his tools. They were, he said, merely a
temporary convenience, to be thrown aside as soon as used.[31]

We know the fate of one of these men. Hugh of Gournai, after his
peculiarly disgraceful treachery in the spring of 1203,[32] found no
welcome at Philip's court. He took refuge at Cambrai. The story goes
that Hugh one day was riding outside the town with the bishop and

homage. The practice in Normandy before 1204 is clear from a letter in *Rot.
Norm.*, 51: John wrote to the abbot of Saint Ouen saying that he had given
to Richard Comin 'exitus terre que fuit Mathaei de Ernenvilla qui est in
Francea *in instanti anno* qui nostri sit. Et vos rogamus quid permittatis predictum Ricardum terram illam *interim* de vobis tenere per servicium quod
terra debet'. For the law, see the *Statuta et Consuetudines*, c. lxxxviii, 1
(Tardif, I, i, 98). On the custom of Poitou, see *Rot. Chart.*, 198b, and above,
p. 20.   [29] Above, pp. 96, 112, 158.
   [30] This follows from the papal letters of October 31, 1203: Cheney and
Semple, *Selected Letters of Pope Innocent III*, no. 20, pp. 60–2; Potthast,
no. 2013. See Petit-Dutaillis, *Studies Supplementary to Stubbs' Constitutional
History*, i, 113.   [31] *Guillaume le Maréchal*, ll. 12687–700.
   [32] Above, p. 161. Hugh is styled 'proditor regis' in *Rot. de Lib.*, 74.

some of its chief inhabitants, and remarked upon the wealth and beauty of the place. A burgess who was present innocently remarked: 'True, sir, but it has one bad custom.' 'And what is that?' asked Hugh. 'Sir,' the burgess replied, 'there is not a traitor nor thief under heaven whom it does not shelter.' [33] Hugh of Gournai stayed for some time at Cambrai, for his lands in England and Normandy were confiscated, but through the intercession of Otto he succeeded in making his peace with John once more at the end of 1206. [34]

A long time was to elapse before the royal power in France was able to extend the charge of treason to acts of open disobedience as well as to acts against the person of the king. [35]

II

In England, on the contrary, the most distinct result of the separation from Normandy was the development of the idea of treason and of the law relating to aliens. [36] So long as the baronage of England was as much at home in Normandy as upon the other side of the Channel treason in its political sense was an unknown offence. The relations between king and barons were primarily the relations between lord and vassal. The lord himself was a vassal of the king of France. Many

[33] *Histoire des ducs de Normandie et des rois d'Angleterre*, ed. Michel, p. 92; a slightly different version in the anonymous French chronicle edited by Delisle in the *Recueil des Historiens de France*, xxiv, part ii, p. 760. In September, 1934, Dr. Richard Hunt sent me a story in a sermon, probably of Alexander de Essebi (Peterhouse MS. 255, ii, f. 49v. a), how Hugh of Gournai, having been asked by the king of France to adhere to him as his lord, replied, 'Domino adherebo, non quasi suus miles sed quasi suus seductor', and prostrated himself as such.

[34] *Rot. Pat.*, 57b. The Hugh of Gournai, who is described in October and November, 1203, as John's *talliator* and servant (*Rot. Norm.*, 110, 113) is obviously a different person.

[35] In the thirteenth century the right of the vassal to rebel under certain conditions was still acknowledged in France (Viollet, *Histoire des institutions politiques*, ii, 219). The history of treason in France is bound up with the growth of the belief in the divine right of the king and the extension of the idea of lèse-majesté. See, for example, the chancellor D'Aguesseau's *Mémoire sur la jurisdiction royale*, written in 1700, to prove that, from the very nature of the secular power, no ecclesiastic charged with lèse-majesté can be exempt from royal jurisdiction (*Oeuvres*, vol. v (1788), especially p. 337). Illustrations of treason in France in the middle ages are the trial of Arnulf of Reims at Verzy in 991 and the charges against the bishop of Pamiers in 1301. Gerbert in describing the crimes of Arnulf speaks of his 'scelus proditionis et rebellionis' (*Lettres de Gerbert*, ed. Havet, p. 205). For the libels and other offences of the bishop of Pamiers against Philip IV, see Lavisse, *Histoire de France*, III, ii, 143. These cases are very similar to the trials in Merovingian times described by Gregory of Tours, v, 19, 49.

[36] Pollock and Maitland, *The History of English Law*, 2nd edition, i, 303, 461–463; ii, 500–508.

of his vassals, as tenants of the French lord, owed allegiance to the king of France also, just as they owed it to a duke of Normandy or a king of England. Under these conditions, even the famous definition of treason in the statute of 1352—levying war against our lord the king in his realm—would have been impractical. At the end of the twelfth century this crime was still nothing more than the neglect of feudal obligations and was punished by forfeiture. It was, in other words, felony. The idea of treason was confined to treachery and a few specific crimes against the king. Perhaps the nearest approach to a more public conception of the crime is seen in the popular indignation against Robert fitz Walter and Saer de Quinci for their surrender of Vaudreuil in 1203.[37] During the thirteenth century the distinction between the ideas of felony and treason became clear; and the change was due very largely to the attitude which was assumed by the kings of France towards the Norman vassals of the kings of England.

When the lands of those Normans who had been faithful to John were confiscated and residents in England were not permitted to answer to pleas in Norman courts, the kings of England retaliated against those Normans, obedient to France, who held lands in England. As the war went on and peace was not made, this policy of retaliation hardened into a definite theory that those who refused to return to the king's peace were traitors. The way in which this conclusion was reached is interesting. The contest was sufficiently drawn out to establish a distinction between the lands of the Normans and other forfeited property. Normally these lands, as the fiefs of vassals guilty of felony, would after a year and a day have gone to the lord, but the king, expecting a settlement, kept them in his own hands and diverted their proceeds to the exchequer. This plan was, at least in some cases, the result of a conscious policy, as is shown by the disposition of the English lands belonging to the honour of Grandmesnil. In 1204 Petronilla, the dowager countess of Leicester, who had brought the honour to her husband in 1168, gave 3,000 marks for the royal permission to resume her rights in it, with the exception of the 'lands of the Normans'.[38]

In course of time some reason for this anomaly—so contrary to the thirty-second clause of the Great Charter—had to be found. 'If there was any crime which would give the offender's land not to his lord, but to the king, that crime could not be a mere *felonia*.'[39] The crime

---

[37] Above, p. 162.

[38] *Rot. de Fin.*, 226. Petronilla's son, the well-known Robert IV of Leicester, died in this year; his death gave John an opportunity to exact this enormous fine. These exactions are forbidden by c. 7 of the Great Charter.

[39] Pollock and Maitland, ii, 502. As the writers point out, 'most of the traitors of the twelfth century were tenants in chief or the vassals of rebellious tenants in chief, and the king could claim their lands either as king or lord.

was treason. The Normans were assisting the common enemy against our lord the king.

The steps in this agreement are made clear by a consideration of a parallel development in legal theory. By the end of the thirteenth century the law relating to aliens was being defined. The main cause was undoubtedly the growing hatred of foreign politicians, papal nominees, and alien money dealers, but it is probable that the precedents, which gave to the Englishman a legal advantage over the foreigner in England, were those cases in which the followers of the French king tried in vain to establish their claims to English lands and rights. Cases from the early years of Henry III show that persons resident in France, within the power of a king who refused to answer the pleas of Englishmen, could find no protection in English courts. At the end of the century the count of Eu failed to secure a hearing for his claims on the ground that the French king still retained the possession of English barons. 'It seems that the king's claims to seize the lands of aliens is an exaggerated generalisation of his claim to seize the lands of his French enemies.'[40]

The lands of the Normans were seized in accordance with a general precept issued by John,[41] and became henceforth an object of distinct inquiry and treatment. Several fragmentary lists of the *Terrae Normannorum* survive. The earliest of these is a valuation of 1204. It was apparently drawn up in or after October.[42] It was followed by a series of inquiries, mainly into the disposition of the lands, the most comprehensive of which was made in the twentieth year of Henry III's reign.[43] The drastic action of Saint Louis in 1244, when the English who were still suffered to hold lands in Normandy were forced to make a choice between England and France, probably made further

The defection of the *Normanni* raised a new question on a large scale'. I doubt, however, whether the suggestion in this sentence that the *terrae Normannorum* were all, or even mainly, held by sub-tenants, is justified.

[40] Pollock and Maitland, i, 462–3. For the count of Eu, see below, p. 338.

[41] See the references in *Rot. de Fin.*, 334–5.

[42] It is entitled 'Rotulus de valore terrarum Normannorum inceptus regni Regis Johannis sexto', *i.e.*, after June 3, 1204 (*Rot. Norm.*, 122). The date seems to follow from the fact that it includes a reference to Bilsington in Kent, the land of Robert of Courci, as in the custody of Henry of Sandwich (*ibid.*, 140). Henry of Sandwich received Bilsington upon September 30, and apparently held it until it was granted to the earl of Arundel on October 18, 1207. See Stapleton, *Liber de antiquis legibus*, p. xl, note.

[43] For the writs issued by Alexander of Swereford, baron of the exchequer, on December 15, 1236, and the surviving returns, see *Book of Fees*, pp. 611–19. The writ of inquisition is in the *Testa de Nevill*, 271b, and is reproduced in Hubert Hall, *Formula Book of Ministerial and Judicial Records* (1909), p. 159. See also, for this and other inquiries, *The Red Book of the Exchequer*, ii, 798–806, and Hunter's *Rotuli Selecti ad res Anglicas et Hibernicas Spectantes* (1834), pp. 259–65.

inquiries unnecessary.[44] There was clearly no more hope of a settlement, and the disposal of the lands doubtless became permanent. The Hundred Rolls contain some evidence of their distribution in the reign of Edward I.[45]

That John did not expect the confiscation of the *Terrae Normannorum* to be permanent, and that it was frequently inspired by motives of retaliation, is shown by the royal letters of 1204 and of the next few years. He was slow to exact the full penalty for the disaffection of the Normans. The evidence proves rather that he welcomed a new means of filling his coffers. Those who returned were able to recover the lands which they had lost 'occasione Normannorum', on payment of a fine.[46] One of these persons, a tenant of Hugh of Longchamp, whose lands had also been confiscated, paid a fine of a hundred marks; on the other hand, he was relieved by the king from the payment of an annual rent of five marks which he had been accustomed to pay to Hugh; but the significant clause is added that if Hugh should chance to return to the king's grace, and to recover his lands, he might buy back his customary rights to the rent for the sum of forty marks.[47] The arrangement shows that the door was not closed to Hugh, although in the meanwhile the king was quite ready to fleece his tenants at his expense. In a similar humour John exacted fines for the confirmation of grants made by deserters before their desertion,[48] and was even willing to allow the claims of a loyal heir to confiscated property.[49]

The idea of retaliation may be seen at work in John's treatment of the lands held in England by ecclesiastical lords. These lands, or many of them, were seized in virtue of the general precept issued by John.[50]

[44] Matthew Paris, *Chronica Majora*, iv, 288.

[45] For example, there is the historical account of Casewick (hundred of Nesse, Lincolnshire), part of the honour of Chokes (*Rotuli Hundredorum*, l. 344). This may be verified from Domesday Book, f. 366b, and the *Book of Fees*, pp. 182, etc. The history of the large honour of Chokes, which lay chiefly in Northamptonshire, can easily be traced from its foundation after the Conquest by the Picard knight, Gunfrid of Choques, through the period of confiscation in John's reign, to the reports contained in the Hundred Rolls. Cf. Farrer, *Honors and Knights' Fees*, i, 20 ff. Much information about the confiscations, not included in the lists of *Terrae Normannorum*, may be found in returns to the inquest of 1212, contained in the *Book of Fees* and the *Red Book of the Exchequer*.

[46] Cases in *Rot. de Fin.*, 204 [cf. *Actes de Philippe Auguste*, no. 832], 221, 259, 267, 334, 335. The first step towards return was a safe conduct, *e.g.*, *Rot. de Fin.*, 278: 'Willelmus de Martywas dat domino Regi centum marcas et unum palefredum pro habendis litteris domini Regis de conductu veniendi in Angliam ad loquendum cum domino Rege et pro habenda terra sua unde disseisitus fuit.' [47] *Ibid.*, 228. [48] *Ibid.*, 238, 249. [49] *Ibid.*, 476.

[50] *Ibid.*, 335, 'occasione generalis precepti terrarum Normannorum et canonicorum'.

U

Some of them are mentioned in the fragmentary valuation of 1204.[51] This action, however, does not appear to have had permanent effects: the Norman clergy as a whole did not lose their English rents nor cease to control their English property. A few cathedral chapters and monastic houses suffered, but official records and chartularies agree in showing that the relations between the majority of English tenants and their clerical lords were not changed by the separation between the two countries.[52] The increased difficulty of travel must have been the main check upon their intercourse. At the same time, the fear of confiscation was a very real one to the Norman clergy. Precautions against it were sometimes inserted in the deeds of this period which were drawn up between English and Norman parties.[53] After Philip had confiscated the lands of those Normans who lingered in England, John was careful to retaliate upon the English lands, not merely of laymen, but of ecclesiastics, if they had allowed themselves to benefit by the losses of their neighbours. Thus Hasculf Paynel, who asserted that Norman clerks were withholding his rents, received the rents and advowsons belonging to the Norman church in the Channel Islands.[54]

III

Begun as a counter-stroke to Philip's policy of expropriation, John's measures hardened, as we have seen, into a tradition of hos-

[51] Lands of the following are mentioned, the abbots of Préaux, Bec, Caen, Grestain; the abbesses of Préaux, Caen, and Montivilliers; the prior of Noyon, the monks of Montebourg and Mortain, the canons of Coutances. See *Rot. Norm.*, 122–37 *passim*.

[52] The safe conducts enrolled upon the Chancery rolls show that in most cases the king had not retained these lands any length of time. There is a case of redemption by the abbot of Saint Wandrille in *Rot. de Fin.*, 400, as late as 1207. On the continuity of relations between Norman ecclesiastics and their English tenants, see, for example, Porée, *Histoire de l'abbaye du Bec* (Evreux, 1901), i, 446–7; on the assertion of royal authority, cf. J. Tait, in *V.C.H. Lancashire*, ii, 169.

[53] An interesting case in *Rot. Chart.*, 151b; also in Round, *Calendar*, no. 105. On May 30, 1205, John confirmed an agreement between the bishop of London and the abbot of Saint Ouen, by which the latter farmed certain English lands to the bishop. The king promised that 'si predicte terre occasione aliqua in manum nostram devenerint predictus episcopus terras bene et in pace teneat respondendo nobis de eadem firma quam abbati et conventui reddere debebat'.

[54] *Rot. de Fin.*, 437; *Rot. Pat.*, 81. A somewhat similar case in *Rot. Pat.*, 67b: a letter of October 12, 1206, to Geoffrey fitz Peter—'mandamus vobis quod faciatis habere Willelmo de Witefeld terram Abbatisse Mutervileriensis, scilicet Waddon, qui est in manu nostra, tenendam quamdiu eadem Abbatissa tenuerit terram ipsius Willelmi in Normannia'. Waddon, in Dorset, had been seized in 1204 (*Rot. Norm.*, 124).

tility to France and Frenchmen. This tradition had momentous effects upon English politics and English law. It gave precision to the growing self-consciousness of the nation. From a continental standpoint, however, Philip's policy had a feudal rather than a national tendency. The conquest of Normandy caused no very important change in Norman law or custom, and had far less influence upon the political institutions of France than it had upon the political future of England. But none the less it established, at a critical period in the history of the French monarchy, two very important feudal principles.

In the first place, the legal supremacy of the king of France over the great vassals of the crown was shown to be a reality and not a mere form. The moral effect of the condemnation and successful eviction of John was felt throughout the succeeding centuries. This result is closely connected with the second principle established by Philip. During the wars against Henry II and his sons, he insisted more and more upon a strict application of the theory of liege homage in his relations with the great vassals of the crown. This theory as it was defined in the twelfth century comprehended two points; first, that a vassal owed primary and personal allegiance to his liege-lord; and, secondly, that he had the privilege of being tried (and, conversely, was required to appear for trial) in his liege-lord's court.[55] The numerous treaties made between Philip and his Angevin rivals are of great significance on account of their rulings upon these points. Together with the various charters and concords which carried out their provisions they form a group of documents which are very important in the history of feudal law. For example, the treaty of Messina defined the relations between the Angevin empire and the king of France, while those of Mantes in July, 1193, and of Louviers in January, 1196, illustrate the problems of homage upon the borders. It is curious to observe how, as time went on, Philip interpreted the doctrine in his own favour, until John was finally caught in its legal meshes. During the reigns of Henry II and Richard the houses of France and Anjou were so nearly equal that the principle of liege homage, if applied with precision, was as advantageous to the solidarity of one as to that of the other. To take the most important example: the triangular relations of the king of France, the duke of Normandy and the count of Flanders. As late as 1163 the counts of Flanders construed their obligations to the king of France, their liege lord, to mean that they were only obliged to serve him in person with ten knights, and that under certain circumstances they might attend upon his ally of Normandy, *unless this was forbidden by his peers in the royal court.*[56]

[55] See Lot, *Fidèles ou Vassaux?* pp. 250, 251, 255; and, on the subject in general, Holtzmann, *Französische Verfassungsgeschichte* (1910), pp. 25-7. See now the note at the end of chapter iv, above, p. 94.   [56] Lot, *op. cit.*, p. 24.

In other words, the privilege of trial in the king's court was used as a safeguard of the count's freedom to neglect his feudal duties. Again, the reader will remember how, in 1197, Richard insulted Philip by appearing at an interview supported by the presence of the counts of Flanders and Boulogne, with whom he had recently concluded treaties.[57] This conduct must have stung Philip the more, in that by the treaty of Louviers Richard and he had explicitly agreed to respect the rights of each other to the service of their liege vassals.[58] It was of vital consequence to him that the count of Flanders should be tied to his service. But in the reign of John, Philip, by his juristic ability, turned the tables upon his enemy, and secured the advantages of his previous policy. As the change is of some importance in the explanation of our subject, I will briefly analyse the ways in which it was manifested.

(1) Philip extended the principle of liege homage to John himself.[59] By the treaty of Le Goulet, and by subsidiary or later acts, John agreed to pay Philip a heavy relief (*rechatum*), and to allow his claims to Brittany and Anjou to be established by the judgment of the French court. The later condemnation of John was a natural consequence of this complaisance.[60] John's position was further weakened by his agreement to repudiate the alliance with the count of Flanders, on the ground that the count owed peculiar duty to the king of France.[61] The advantage which Philip's control over John gave him may be seen if we compare his attempts to break through the allegiance of the Normans in Richard's reign with his success after 1202.

(2) As opportunity arose Philip had tried to counteract the obligations of Richard's liege vassals, but with little result. For example, there was his suggestion (in which of course John concurred) to separate John's continental lands from direct allegiance to Richard in the event of the latter's return from captivity.[62] The complicated arrangements which deal in the treaties of this period with the counts

---

[57] Above, p. 120.

[58] *Cart. Norm.*, p. 277, 'Neque nos recipiemus amodo homines ligios regis Francie contra ipsum quamdiu vixerit, nec ipse nostros homines ligios contra nos quamdiu vixerimus.' Also *Recueil*, ii, no. 517, p. 57.

[59] On the legal relations between France and Normandy, see Lot, *op. cit.*, chapter vi, and especially Robert of Torigni's interpolation in the chronicle of William of Jumièges, which attempts to explain them away: *ibid.*, p. 261.

[60] Above, p. 135.

[61] This clause was a repetition of the clause in the treaty of 1156, but the specific insertion of the count of Flanders strengthened Philip's position; see *Cart. Norm.*, p. 281; and *Recueil*, ii, no. 633, p. 183.

[62] See the treaty of January, 1194, between John and Philip, in *Cart. Norm.*, p. 275. 'Et si rex Francie faceret pacem cum rege Anglie ipse faceret michi pacem erga regem Anglie, ita quod ego [Johannes] terram, quam haberem pro pace citra mare, tenerem a rege Francie, si posset.'

of Meulan, and especially with Hugh of Gournai,[63] are more pertinent illustrations of his method. Thus, by the treaty of Louviers Hugh of Gournai's homage was to remain to Philip during Hugh's lifetime, unless he should wish to return to his allegiance, although the knights of the fief were allowed to reserve their duty to Richard.[64] But, except in the case of this particularly important fief, such cumbrous arrangements were not found desirable. Philip preferred to secure his rights in the border fiefs and castles which he had seized, by means of a public treaty and, at the same time, to force terms upon their unlucky lords. After his conquest of Vernon and Paci, which was confirmed by Richard in 1195–6, Richard of Vernon received lands in exchange, and for a time became a French vassal,[65] and Robert of Leicester, who was a captive, was forced to cede Paci as a ransom.[66] Yet Philip's regard for the earl's duty to King Richard is shown by an arrangement which he made with the earl's nephew, Simon de Montfort. Simon, as a French vassal, went surety for his uncle's promise that, after his release, he would never again use force against the king of France, or plot any evil against him, *unless war should again break out between the two kings.*[67] After John's condemnation Philip was no longer hindered by the accepted doctrine; he was, on the contrary, able to urge it in his own favour. In Richard's reign he had waged public war, in John's he punished a recalcitrant vassal. Hence he was able to push the theory to its logical conclusion and to insist upon the entire allegiance of John's vassals. Their service was now due to him, and those who refused to join him were rightly deprived, just as their lord had been deprived.

(3) At the same time Philip's attitude to the Normans was untouched by indignation. He had, as I have shown, no love for traitors and did not regard the Normans who were faithful to John as morally guilty. They were political unfortunates. In the terms offered to the refugees in Rouen, for example, he permitted those who so desired to retire

[63] Howden, iii, 218; *Cart. Norm.*, pp. 276-7.

[64] *Cart. Norm.*, pp. 276, 277; *Recueil*, ii, pp. 53, 55. So long as Hugh of Gournai remained true to Philip, Gournai would be comprehended with the Vexin, in the lands ceded to Philip; and I have included it within the line separating France from Normandy in the map at the end of this volume. Yet, presumably, in case of war between Richard and Philip, those of Hugh's knights who had remained true to Richard, and whose rights were safeguarded by the treaty, could join Richard's forces, or would not be expected to fight against him. It should be noticed that, although by the treaty of 1200 (*ibid.*, 281, *Recueil*, ii, p. 181) Philip retained the Norman Vexin, Hugh of Gournai and his lands were not included. Hugh was one of John's sureties.

[65] *Cart. Norm.*, nos. 33, 34, p. 9. Above, p. 108.

[66] *Ibid.*, nos. 36–40, pp. 9, 10, 278. Howden, iii, 278; iv, 5. Cf. the charter of the count of Evreux after the treaty of 1200, *Cart. Norm.*, no. 53, p. 281.

[67] *Cart. Norm.*, no. 41, p. 278.

from Normandy either by land or sea.[68] Consistent with this attitude was his eagerness to welcome all who would take the oath of fealty to him and do him homage. He made only three or four exceptions, the seneschal, the count of Meulan and Roger of Tosny and his sons.[69] And it is especially interesting to note that he was willing to show favour to some of the barons who had large interests both in England and Normandy. His agreement with the Marshal in 1204, is a striking confirmation of the fact that his general policy of excluding John's followers was nothing more than a drastic application of strictly feudal ideas. At Lisieux in 1204, the Marshal and the earl of Leicester, who had formed a part of John's mission to Philip, paid a large fine for a year's delay before deciding whether or not they would do homage to Philip for their Norman lands.[70] The earl of Leicester had died before the time had elapsed, but the Marshal—who, according to his biographer, had John's permission—did homage in 1205.[71] His family retained their Norman property during the early reign of Henry III.

Both the Marshal and the earl of Leicester were beyond reproach as men of honour. When the former died, after strenuous service in England on behalf of John and his son, Philip, then growing old after a reign of nearly forty years, spoke of him as the most loyal man of his time.[72] The earl of Leicester, the hero of the siege of Rouen in 1193, had suffered imprisonment and the loss of the important honour of Paci, in the service of Richard. It is interesting, therefore, to find that these men did not regard their action in 1204 as inconsistent with their duty to John; and it is still more significant that the Marshal, in spite of his devotion to John's interests, braved the king's anger by refusing to fight against his lord Philip, and found support in his refusal.[73] His action was pedantic and unnecessary.[74] It pushed the doctrine of

[68] Teulet, *Layettes*, i, 251.

[69] *Ibid.*, p. 250. The count of Meulan's position, as a baron in France, Normandy, and England, as the father of a traitor to John, and as a recent deserter from Philip, was peculiarly difficult.

[70] *Cart. Norm.*, no. 74, p. 14; *Actes*, no. 818; *Guillaume le Maréchal*, iii, 177; above, p. 260.

[71] *Guillaume le Maréchal*, iii, 178.

[72] *Ibid.*, iii, 268.

[73] For the scene between John and the Marshal, one of the most striking passages in the poem, see *ibid.*, iii, 180–1. It appears from the charter of 1220 (*Cart. Norm.*, no. 285, p. 43), by which the Marshal's son gave the Norman lands to his brother, that father and son did liege homage to Philip: 'et ego facerem pro eo domino regi Francorum hominagium ligium citra mare et quicquid deberem eo modo et in tali puncto in quo predictus Guillelmus pater meus fecit ei hominagium,' etc.

[74] The situation was, however, difficult. John was undoubtedly the Marshal's liege lord, but from the last note it would appear that Philip had put him in the apparently impossible position of having two liege lords, one for his lands on each side of the Channel. The later solution of the difficulty is given by

feudal loyalty further than Philip could have expected; it was, for instance, quite contrary to the principle of duty to the liege lord which Philip had tried to impose upon the count of Flanders. Possibly the Marshal was more impressed than his fellows were by the condemnations passed upon John by the French court. Yet, however exceptional his conduct was, there could be no more striking evidence of the fact that a great warrior and statesman of the twelfth century, whose loyalty was undisputed, might pass through the world without the faintest conception of what we call patriotism, or nationality, or treason. The 'rector Angliae' had no country, was French rather than English in mind and habits, and learned his political duties from feudal law books.

It is helpful to remember that the Marshal was also a great land-holder in Ireland, where the only standard of duty possible for the Anglo-Norman mind was feudal. The state of Ireland during John's reign reminds one of the kingdom of Jerusalem rather than that of England or Normandy. The settlers had no duties to the king outside Ireland, unless they held lands elsewhere. Ireland was not a part of the Angevin empire in the sense that England was.[75] Again, the Marshal was a very important Lord Marcher of Wales, where the feudal jurist could always find scope for his reasoning. When, five years after the loss of Normandy, John's fury was aroused against his old favourite, William of Briouze,[76] the Marshal sheltered the fugitive on his estate at Wicklow. The justiciar, John Gray, demanded him as a traitor to the king. But William of Briouze was the Marshal's lord, probably for some land in Wales, and the Marshal replied that, although he was ignorant of the king's anger against his guest, he could not surrender one whom it had been his duty to entertain. He also would be guilty of treason if he were to deliver his lord to the justiciar.[77]

According to Bracton, the Marshal's double position was shared

Bracton, f. 427b (ed. Rolls Series, vi, 374, 376). In the event of war, those vassals who held land both in England and France were expected to serve in person with the lord whom they generally served, and to provide the service due to the other. In other words the technical existence of two liege lords was ignored. The Marshal's sons were permitted to travel with five knights in Normandy, on condition that they and the knights took an oath that they would do no harm to king or realm. They were also required to surrender any of their fortresses on demand. See *Cart. Norm.*, nos. 1120, 285, 286; pp. 304, 43–4. On the situation in Poitou in 1204, see below, p. 326.
[75] See John's letter to Ireland, printed below, p. 327. [76] Below, p. 320.
[77] *Guillaume le Maréchal*, ll. 14224–6:
'Li evesques me deit guerre
Chose dont requeste me vienge
Ne qu'a traison apartienge.'
On the incident, see Orpen, *Ireland under the Normans*, ii, 239.

by many others.[78] Indeed, Philip expressed a willingness to respect
the tenure of all those who did him homage for their Norman lands
before a certain date. 'Many tears were afterwards shed by those who
did not avail themselves of this opportunity in time.'[79] The Picard
chronicler who wrote the 'History of the Dukes of Normandy', while
confirming this statement to some extent, throws a very valuable
light upon the state of John's court during these perplexing days. He
makes it quite clear that the Marshal's position must have been
exceptional and forces us to suspect the statement of his biographer
that the king consented to his arrangement with Philip. John was
evidently very anxious as well as angry. He had been, so he thought,
unjustly and treacherously despoiled of his duchy and now he was
faced by a request from the earl Warenne and other barons that they
should be allowed to do homage to the man who had robbed him.
The barons, says the chronicler, assured the king that, although their
bodies might owe service to their lord of France, their hearts would
most certainly be his. 'The king said that he would confer on the
matter. Accordingly he one day assembled his council, and after
laying before them the barons' request, demanded their advice.
Baldwin of Béthune, count of Aumâle, spoke first. He was a very
valiant gentleman, and a loyal and good knight; but he was so ill with
the gout that he was unable to walk, and had to be carried. He had
much weight with King John, who had always found him loyal and
true. 'Is it true, sire,' he said, 'that they have asked leave to go to
the king of France to beg for the lands which they have lost in
Normandy, and that, while their bodies will be for the king of France
against you, their hearts are to be for you?' 'Yes,' said the king; 'that
is what they ask.' 'Well,' the count replied, 'I do not know what you
intend to do; but were I in your place, and were their bodies against
me and their hearts for me, if the hearts whose bodies were against
me came into my hands, I would throw them into the privy.' These
words caused much laughter and prevailed, so that what had been
asked came to nothing. But the king afterwards gave to the earl
Warenne, who was his cousin, the town of Stamford—a very fair
place—in exchange for the land which he had lost in Normandy.'[80]

---

[78] Bracton, *De Legibus*, f. 427b (ed. Rolls Series, vi, 374), 'sed tamen sunt
aliqui Francigenae in Francia, qui sunt ad fidem utriusque [regis], et semper
fuerunt ante Normanniam deperditam et post, et qui placitant hic et ibi ea
ratione qua sunt ad fidem utriusque,—sicut W. comes Marescallus et (*sic*)
manens in Anglia, et M. de Feynes manens in Francia, et alii plures'. On the
Fiennes lands see *Exc. e rotulis Finium*, i, 415.
[79] *Guillaume le Maréchal*, iii, 176.
[80] *Histoire des ducs de Normandie et des rois d'Angleterre*, ed. Michel, pp.
99–100. The grant to the earl Warenne is referred to in *Rot. Pat.*, 52b, in letters
of April 19, 1205: 'sciatis quod commisimus dilecto et fideli nostro W. comiti

Hence the number of those who served two masters was few. Philip proceeded with his policy of confiscation, and the society of the two countries was severed. In 1244 Saint Louis put an end to the slight connection which still survived.[81]

A few general considerations, suggested by the foregoing inquiry, may bring this study of Norman politics and society to a close.

Gerald of Wales, in his *De principis instructione*, describes an interesting conversation which he had with Henry II's great justiciar, Ranulf de Glanvill. Why, Gerald asked, does Normandy defend herself less strenuously than of old?[82] Glanvill gave an historical reason for the change, based upon his reading in the epic literature of the day. The Franks had suffered so much during the wars which had preceded the arrivals of the Normans that their youth had become exhausted. A life and death struggle, such as that between Raoul of Cambrai and the house of Vermandois[83] made many gaps in the ranks. Now, on the contrary—so Glanvill implied—the balance between Frank and Norman was redressed. Gerald of Wales, after repeating the conversation, adds two other reasons. In the first place, the Normans had suffered from the effects of the conquest of England, for the violent despotism which the dukes had practised as kings of England, had been extended to their Norman subjects,[84] and had been followed by the usual disastrous consequences. And, secondly, the kingdom of France from the time of King Pippin onwards had given a striking proof of the truth, also illustrated by the careers of Alexander and Cæsar, that success in war always accompanies a pursuit of the arts. The French love of learning was a cause of their political victories.[85]

Warenne Graham et Stanford cum pertinenciis habenda quousque recuperavit terram suam Normannie vel quousque ei alibi fecerimus competens excambium. Ita tamen quod non possit talliare homines de Stanford nisi per preceptum nostrum.' A note is added after the enrolment—'liberate non fuerunt littere iste'. The date, it will be noticed, was just before the time fixed by Philip for the Marshal's homage, and probably fixes the date of the decree in which Philip announced the addition of the lands of the earl and others to his demesne (*Cart. Norm.*, no. 113, p. 20. Cf. p. 283 above).

[81] See Appendix II for some of the families which survived in both England and Normandy after 1204.

[82] Giraldus Cambrensis, *De principis instructione*, distinctio iii, c. xii: 'Quare se nunc segnius quam olim Normannia defendit' (*Opera*, viii, 257-9).

[83] On the twelfth century poem, Raoul de Cambrai, which is evidently in Glanvill's mind, see Bedier, *Les Legendes Epiques*, ii, 320 *seqq.*

[84] 'Effecti violento dominatu et insulari tyrannide Normannos sicut et Anglos oppresserant' (*Opera*, viii, 258).

[85] Howden (iv, 121) in his account of the dissension between the citizens of Paris and the German scholars, refers to Philip Augustus' desire to keep the scholars in his dominions.

Stripped of its literary extravagance, each of these reasons for the decadence of Normandy contains a profound truth.

1. The Normans were faced by a state which was steadily increasing in wealth, population and compactness. The resources of Henry II and Richard I were remarkable, and were perhaps greater in the bulk than those of Philip Augustus,[86] but the effective strength of the French monarchy was felt by Richard's ministers to be more than adequate to that which they could command.[87] If the barons of Aquitaine and Gascony had been consistently loyal, if the resources of Tours and Le Mans had been unreservedly at their lord's disposal, if the Bretons had never provoked a punitive expedition, and if the counts of Flanders, Boulogne, and Toulouse had never deserted the Angevin alliance, then there would have been no doubt as to Philip's inferiority. Men and treasure could have been diverted as necessity arose from any part of the empire to its threatened and vulnerable points. But these happy conditions did not prevail. The resources of the empire, with the exception of English treasure, were not readily available for general use. Even the wealth of England was very nearly exhausted in 1204. The heavy drain of specie had caused the currency to become seriously debased, so that Henry II's new coinage of 1180 had to be replaced by another in 1205.[88] The payment of the thirteenth in 1207 was the last great financial effort of the English people before the chaos of the next ten years.[89] Moreover, in comparing the position of Richard or John with that of Philip, it should be noted that a great deal of the formers' money found its way into the coffers of their enemies or of their very uncertain allies. The payment of Richard's ransom strained the resources of England and Normandy at the very beginning of the great war. Philip received large sums by the treaties of 1193 and 1200.[90] Otto and the princes of the Low Countries were maintained by large pensions. Expensive missions to Rome were constantly necessary. Towards the end of the wars the balance of money paid by each side in ransoms turned heavily against the subjects of John.[91] And, lastly, the needs of the Angevin governments

[86] See, for example, the comparison of their position in the French Chronicle edited by Delisle in the *Historiens de France*, xxiv, part ii, p. 758.

[87] See Archbishop Hubert's speech in 1197 at the Council at Oxford, *Vita Magni S. Hugonis*, p. 248. Richard, he said, needed money 'qui, sumptibus et militantium copiis inferior, contra regem dimicaret potentissimum, ad suam exhaeredationem et perniciem totis nisibus aspirantem'.

[88] Coggeshall, p. 151; *Annals of S. Edmund*, ii, 13. Cf. in corroboration of the statement that the coinage was clipped, the following entry in the *Rot. de Fin.*, 271: 'Rex mandavit thesaurario et camerario quod liberarent eidem Willelmo [Brewer] DCC marcas de thesauro suo qui fuit apud Wintoniam *de grossioribus et fortioribus denariis quas ei* comodavit ad redempcionem filii sui.'   [89] Above, p. 268.   [90] Above, pp. 99, 137.

[91] For some of the ransoms paid in 1204-5, see *Rot. de Lib.*, 103; *Rot.*

of Aquitaine and Gascony diverted a great deal of money from the main scene of conflict.[92]

2. Gerald of Wales rightly distinguished the absolutism of the Angevin rule in Normandy as a cause of Norman weakness in the struggle with France. As a strong upholder of the claims of the Welsh to independence, at least in ecclesiastical affairs, he was no doubt impressed by the decay of public spirit in England and Normandy. It was no tyranny of the ordinary kind that had prevailed in Normandy. The strong rule of Henry II was not a novelty, and must have found favour with the great majority of his subjects. He simply applied in more complicated conditions those principles of law and order which inspired the rule of the Conqueror and of Henry I. The chronicles only begin to speak of tyranny in the reign of John. The defect of Henry's rule lay in this, that under him Normandy was connected with an empire whose just and elaborate institutions were controlled by a body of officials, and by officials of whom half were not Normans. In the later twelfth century Normandy was brought through various causes—the Crusades, the wealth of the Rhenish cities, the connection between England and the south-west of France, and the growth of Paris—into intimate contact with the civilisation of Europe;[93] and during the same period she came under the control of a highly organised bureaucracy, which was drawn from many different quarters. At the same time a variety of influences changed the character of the baronage and diverted their interest from political to social ambitions. Hence there was a divorce between the baronage and the administration, and John bore the consequences.

This process becomes the more significant when we contrast the position of the Norman baronage at the end of the twelfth century with that which it occupied before the rebellion of 1173, or, again, after the settlement of the duchy by Philip Augustus. Before 1173 the Normans, rebellious and even treacherous though they might be, displayed a keen national consciousness. It is significant that in spite of their love for the heroic legends of Roland and William of Orange,

Pat., 41b (the Constable of Chester); Rot. de Fin., 271; Rot. Pat., 41b–42 (W. Brewer the younger); Salmon, Chroniques de Touraine, p. 150; Rot. Pat., 65 (for Girard of Athée).

[92] The culminating point is the enormous payment of 28,000 marks, said by Coggeshall (p. 147) to have been paid to the brother of the archbishop of Bordeaux in 1204 for raising an army in Gascony. The rolls show that money was sent to Gascony (Rot. de Lib., 102; Rot. de Fin., 271). Coggeshall states that the archbishop was hostage in England for the fulfilment of the bargain; and it is true that he was in England in 1204 (e.g., Rot Chart., 123; Rot. de Lib., 102; Pipe Roll, 6 John, 125, 212).

[93] In the custumal (Tardif, I, i, 37; ii, 33–34) essoins on account of absence in Spain, England, Germany, Ireland, Scotland, Denmark, are mentioned.

they do not seem to have naturalised the *chanson de geste*.[94] They adopted its form, but the matter of their own poetry was more severely historical or religious, and was frequently taken from a Latin original. Their literature satisfied the desire for knowledge, as their adventures took the form of stern practical enterprises. In Master Wace and the later historians in the vernacular they produced an historical school of a sort. Henry II was sympathetic and imaginative enough to avail himself of this movement. He was the patron of Wace, and the friend of the chief Norman chronicler, Robert of Torigni. For a short time Norman patriotism seemed to be merged in the wider patriotism of the Angevin empire. In his savage satire, the *Roman des Franceis*, Andrew of Coutances professes to speak for English, Bretons, Angevins, Manceaux, Poitevins and Gascons as well as for his fellow countrymen: they all look to Arthur as their national hero, to the beer-drinking Arflet of Northumberland as their leader.[95] Unfortunately the self-consciousness of the Normans was not often capable of such flights. A faculty for powerful criticism, derived perhaps from the heavy satire of their Scandinavian ancestors, was certainly bound up with their practicality, but it was as easily directed against their own rulers as against the outside world.[96] In 1173 the barons rebelled, as they had rebelled against earlier dukes. They were crushed, and Henry II was free to develop the customs and institutions of Normandy unhindered.[97]

The dukes of the house of Anjou were not aliens in Normandy; their rule had caused no break in the forms of government. The duchy was not a subject or conquered state, but the centre of a great feudal dominion.[98] Hence there could be no provincial opposition to Henry's rule, and no ground of appeal from his legislation as opposed to the customs of Normandy.[99] The effect of his policy was simply that the

[94] Gaston Paris, *La Littérature Normande avant l'annexion* (Paris, 1899), a lecture read to the Société des Antiquaires de Normandie on December 1, 1898.

[95] *Ibid.*, pp. 46–52. In his *Estoire de la Guerre Sainte*, the poet Ambroise mentions that during the third Crusade the Angevins, Manceaux, Poitevins and Bretons marched together; but the Normans do not seem to have marched with them.

[96] Orderic Vitalis, has a story, quoted by G. Paris (*op. cit.*, p. 39), of a certain Luke of La Barre, near Pont de l'Arche, who so exasperated Henry I by his rimes, which were of a personal nature, that the king condemned him to have his eyes torn out, 'a punishment which the unfortunate man evaded by dashing his head against a wall'.

[97] The young king Henry was at the head of this rebellion, but the causes were not merely personal. He availed himself of the opposition, as the Prince of Wales did in the reign of George III.

[98] See Haskins, 'Normandy under Geoffrey Plantagenet' in the *English Historical Review*, for July, 1912 (xxvii, 417); reprinted in a revised form in *Norman Institutions*, pp. 123–155.

[99] There was some popular indignation in Brittany against Geoffrey's assize,

baronage as a class lost political influence. But after Normandy had been added to the French king's demesne, the society of the duchy was linked to that of a state with different traditions and customs, a society, moreover, which would naturally claim to be superior to the descendants of Danish pirates. Within a comparatively short time the political sense of Normandy was aroused from the trance into which Henry II had thrown it. Even the Norman Exchequer, largely composed though it was of French officials, felt its influence, and asserted the independence of Norman law by decisions contrary to the *Ordonnances* of the French kings. In 1315 the Normans received their charter, by which the privileges of classes were preserved and the right of appeal from the exchequer to the parlement of Paris was taken away.[100] The next step, derived from the charter, was the insistence by the Normans on their rights to meet together and to discuss questions of taxation in the assemblies of the estates.[101] The provincial institutions of Normandy were developed, the political aptitude of her inhabitants in their various ranks displayed, and the virility of her customs made manifest,[102] not when the duchy was the centre of the Angevin empire, but only after its annexation to France. The stubborn resistance which the Normans made against the English during the Hundred Years' War need cause no surprise if this development is remembered.

3. The third reason suggested by Gerald of Wales for the success of the French was that, at the French court, the pursuit of arms was accompanied by devotion to the Muses. This is not the place for the examination of the general principle which underlies Gerald's contention. But there is nothing fanciful in the view that the social interests and literary impulses of the time were all in favour of French supremacy. The court of Philip Augustus was the natural home of a literary tradition, and from his boyhood Philip had learned to associate the great theme of the *matière de France*, the exploits

on the ground that primogeniture, being opposed to natural justice, should be confined to those countries in which it was customary. See the chronicle of Saint-Brieuc, as quoted by A. de la Borderie, *Histoire de Bretagne*, iii, 284.

[100] Viollet, *Histoire des institutions politiques*, ii, 246. The same scholar has pointed out, in the *Histoire litteraire*, xxxiii, 83, 121, that the thirteenth century custumal (c. 1258) is strongly Norman in tone: 'cette affectation singulière qui consiste à envisager, avec une sorte d'entêtement patriotique, un duc de Normandie qui n'existe plus et qui s'est fondu dans le roi de France.' This obstinacy was justified by events.

[101] Coville, *Les états de Normandie, leurs origines et leurs développement au xive siècle* (1894).

[102] The tenacity of Norman custom may be studied in the law of the Channel Islands. In the sixteenth century Norman customs still prevailed in a few parishes of the Beauvaisis which had formed part of the honour of Gournai three or four hundred years before; above, p. 109.

of Charlemagne and his knights, with the political ambitions of his own race. The habits of the French and the intellectual tendencies of the twelfth century gave emphasis to this claim. The frugality and good taste of the French, the fastidious taste which they showed in their luxury, are frequent topics in contemporary literature; and the foreigner who began by despising them, ended in the discovery that they were essential to the chivalrous refinements which were then in fashion. And the conditions which made the French such an illuminating force in the thirteenth century were already present. They were the main force of the Cistercian influence in art. The students of their great university were destined to become prelates in all the lands of western Europe and to send to the Ile de France for the artists, carpenters and masons whom they required.[103] Only a very powerful and brilliant court, such as Henry II gathered together in his best days, or only a man of great personal force, as was Richard I, could counteract the influence of the French king and of French ideas.

It is probable that Richard's career did more than Henry's statecraft to rally the chivalry of north-western Europe against Philip. The new chivalry of the twelfth century was not necessarily a political force. It became such in France and learned during the campaign of 1214 that it was an integral part of the French nation. But there is sufficient evidence to show that in England and Normandy the knightly class had few political interests. The growth of a bureaucratic system combined with economic and legal changes[104] to create a class of idle gentlemen with cosmopolitan tastes. Their thoughts were not of law courts or bailiffs, but of tournaments and adventures in vast forests, of fair castles and launds, of hermitages where one could pray and rest. The young king Henry, not his father, was their model. He had 'made chivalry live again,' says John of Early, 'when she was dead, or nearly dead. . . . In those days the great did nothing for young men; he set an example and kept the men of worth by his side. And when the men of high degree saw how he brought together all men of worth they were amazed at his wisdom and followed his lead.'[105] Yet they were not dilettanti in their pursuits. Their associations were managed on business lines. The Marshal's practical ability, as well as his moral code, was developed in the following of the young king. There was no reason why this

[103] See Anthyme Saint-Paul, 'L'architecture française et la guerre de Cent Ans', in the *Bulletin Monumental* (1908).

[104] On the effect of Henry II's insistence upon primogeniture in forming class distinctions, see the *English Historical Review*, xxii, 39.

[105] *Guillaume le Maréchal*, iii, 37. In this paragraph I have adopted some sentences from the *English Historical Review*, xxii, 40–1.

energy should not have been trained in the service of the state. And for a short time chivalry found a royal leader in Richard. His taste for music, literature and building must have appealed to his generation. His strength and courage made it possible to join his name without absurdity with those of the heroes of chivalry, with Alexander, 'that king who conquered Darius', and with Charlemagne and Arthur.[106] His captivity had made him doubly interesting: it was due, said William the Breton, no friend of his, to a kingliness which could not be hid. Under his guidance politics could be exciting and for a few years French and Norman were engaged as in a tournament. But with John all was changed, and the sympathy between the French and the Normans was no longer suppressed. Political unity joined two peoples who already had the same speech, manners and ideas.[107]

After the annexation Normandy became a province. As a result of the separation England became a kingdom. The loss of Normandy hastened the twofold development of the English state. The king strengthened his position as the source of justice; the people, under the leadership of the baronage, gradually acquired the power of making the law. [According to the pleadings in a case of the year 1220, the 'consilium domini regis et tocius regni' had provided that 'nullus de potestate regis Francie', *i.e.*, resident in France, should be replied to in England until Englishmen could plead their right in the land of the king of France.][108]

It is now a commonplace with historians that the disaster of 1204 was the direct cause of the Great Charter. The greater barons, having surrendered their Norman lands were free to devote themselves to English affairs, while the less important men, amongst whom those of the north were conspicuous, denied that their feudal obligations extended any longer to service upon the continent, and insisted upon reforms at home. The change came none too soon, for during the later years of the twelfth century the attractions of the continental lands had given a serious shock to the growth of an English public opinion. For those intent upon knightly occupations England offered no delights,[109] and even if the sons of the feudal gentry had held no property in Normandy they would, like the Marshal, have sought their fortunes across the Channel. The effect of primogeniture, however, had been to make the greater families as much at home in Normandy as in England. In the period which immediately succeeded

[106] See the song composed after Richard's death by Gaucelin Faidit, the son of a burgess of Uzerche, in *Bibliothèque le l'Ecole des Chartes*, i, 362.

[107] Gaston Paris, *La littérature Normande avant l'annexion*, p. 53.

[108] *Curia Regis Rolls*, 3–4 Henry III (1938), p. 343.

[109] As the chamberlain of Tancarville genially remarked to the young Marshal, England was not a land for those who would go tourneying; it was fit only for vavasors and stay-at-homes (*Hist. de Guill. le Maréchal*, ll. 1530–50).

the Conquest, the Norman kings had encouraged the division of
Norman and English lands between different branches of the holder's
family.[110] The Conqueror applied this principle to his own family,
when he left Normandy to Duke Robert and England to William
Rufus. But Henry I had set aside this precedent, which does not
appear to have been followed by many families. When his grandson
declared that baronies were indivisible, he stereotyped a practice
which seems to have been applied to those baronies which included
fiefs in both countries no less than to those which were confined to
England or Normandy.[111] In consequence many baronial families
grew up without feeling the force of any local ties, and the younger
sons, having no hope of succeeding to their fathers' estates, roamed
at large. In 1204 the earls of Chester and Warenne and Leicester, in
spite of their noble patrimony in England, and great lords of the
Welsh marches like the Marshal and William of Briouze, had in all

[110] Stubbs, *Constitutional History*, i, 394.

[111] This point is illustrated by a dispute between Henry of Tilly and his
brother William, which was settled in 1200 (*Rot. Norm.*, 8. Cf. 7, 42). William
had disputed Henry's right to succeed to the English and Norman lands of
his father and mother, but finally agreed to receive certain lands in England
to be held of his brother by homage. This result shows that the estates as a
whole were regarded as an inclusive barony, and that there was no question
of parage. The question whether a succession was impartible or not was raised
in this year in the case of William de Merle (*Rot. Norm.*, 41; *Rot. Chart.*, 76b):
William gave £500 in Angevin money 'pro habenda carta domini Regis de
terris suis tam in Normannia quam in Anglia. Ita si terra ipsius tam in Normannia quam in Anglia nunquam partita fuit inter fratres vel antecessores
suos, qui antiquitus fuerunt, inter quos terra illa partiri debuerit si partiri
debuisset; quod et heredes sui terram illam habeant omnibus diebus vite sue
sine particia.' In the case of female succession the lands were, of course,
divided. The chief instances are the division of the Giffard inheritance between
the Marshal and Richard de Clare, earl of Hertford, in 1191 (Stapleton, II,
cxxxviii, and John's confirmation in 1200, *Rot. Chart.*, 47) and of the
Trossebot inheritance in 1196 (Stapleton, II, lxxvii). In the former of these
cases the Marshal received the Norman *caput* of the barony, and earl Richard
the English. The other lands were divided between them. It is worthy of
notice that after the separation of Normandy, the Marshal's son made a con-
ditional grant of his Norman lands to his brother (*Cart. Norm.*, no. 285; p. 43).

A curious case is mentioned in the *Querimoniae Normannorum*, no. 54.
Nicholas Malesmains had, with royal consent, assigned his Norman and
English lands to his two daughters respectively; after his death the bailiffs
seized the Norman lands 'pro custodia'. John of Bruecort, whose son was
betrothed to the heiress of the Norman property, bought the wardship, but
before he had raised the money, the bailiffs seized the lands again, and afterwards only surrendered half, on the ground that the other half was held by the
king as belonging to the heiress, who being in England had not made her
peace with the king. This case is of special interest as relating to events which
occurred some time after 1204. Nicholas Malesmains held some of the Tillières
lands in England and Normandy. See below, pp. 353–5.

probability spent the greater part of their lives out of England.[112] Hence the contrasts between the rare ineffective protests against royal exactions before 1204 on the part of a few bishops and earls—protests which have been made to play far too important a part in our constitutional history[113]—and the outburst of indignation which began in 1213.

At the same time, if the loss of Normandy led directly to the Great Charter, it also helped to establish the relation between the king and the common law which is a peculiarity of the medieval constitution of England. John was the first king of foreign stock to penetrate again and again into all parts of England and to leave his mark upon her local traditions. Under the guidance of his successors English law grew with a rapidity and comprehensiveness as no body of provincial custom could have done. The nation, united and self-contained, did not look beyond the king to any other source of justice. Their charter was interpreted in favour of the royal prerogative and of the authority of the courts. Process by royal writs continued to increase through the thirteenth century, and when the parliament threw up a barrier against this development, the king's council and the chancellor continued the work of the common law by providing equitable remedies for unforeseen abuses. It is curious to notice how powerless the barons and even the commons were to direct the course of royal justice. The barons successfully withstood the influence of the canon law, but they could not check the royal courts. Parliament, with the help of the common lawyers, contrived to save cases of freehold from the encroachment of the council, but this was almost the limit of its success.[114] The judicial supremacy of the crown was undoubtedly one of the main factors in the development of the English constitution. If judicial immunities, privileges of peerage and independent corporations had flourished in England instead of existing, so far as they did exist, upon sufferance; if, in other words, the king and the king's court had not remained supreme in the interpretation of the law, it is very unlikely that the English people would, from the thirteenth century onwards, have gradually secured the right to make the law. The separation from Normandy was largely responsible for this development. Had England been, not an independent kingdom, but the province of a larger empire, it is more than probable that the English would have sought to establish their liberties by means of immunities and privileges, of class distinctions and estates.

If the loss of Normandy was a gain to the cause of constitutionalism, it occurred too late to take away the most serious disadvantage which

[112] This was especially true of the earl of Leicester, who succeeded his father in 1191, and was the son of Petronilla of Grandmesnil.
[113] e.g., the protest of the bishop of Lincoln in 1198. Above, p. 215.
[114] Baldwin, in the *American Historical Review* (1910), xv, 748–9.

x

the connection between England and Normandy had involved. Had the separation between the two countries, which followed the death of the Conqueror, been a permanent one, it may reasonably be supposed that the complete conquest of Ireland and of the Scottish Lowlands would only have been a question of time. The absorption of Henry I and his successors in Norman affairs, and especially in the wars with the kings of France, distracted them from this natural sequel to the conquest of England. Before 1204 only a very inadequate attempt to combine the various communities of the British Isles had been made. After that date the task was too difficult. John's thoughts turned more than ever to the project; but the anarchy of his later years, and the prolonged continental difficulties of Henry III made progress impossible. Edward I and his successors had to choose between a remnant of the Angevin inheritance and Ireland.[115] They chose the former and left the Irish question to posterity.

Still wider issues of the events described in these pages might be pursued by the philosophical historian. The contest between Philip and the sons of Henry II provoked some of Innocent III's most far-reaching utterances. The Pope drew a clear distinction between feudal law and the higher code of right and wrong. His letters contain one of the earliest applications of the law of nature by what was, in the middle ages, the nearest approach to an international tribunal.[116] Philip, on his side, fastened upon the papal admission that problems of secular law were beyond the cognisance of Rome. The assembly of Mantes, in which the bishops and barons of France asserted his right to disregard papal injunctions, was a turning point in the history of the French state. Or, again, the adventurous enquirer might try to estimate the importance of the conquest of Normandy in the history of private rights in international law. For the first time in the modern world one highly organised state had annexed another. In spite of his claims as a suzerain, who was unlawfully resisted by the Normans on behalf of a disinherited lord, Philip made no attempt at widespread confiscation. The Normans did not suffer as the English had suffered after 1066. Are we not at the beginning of all those conventions about rights of property, and municipal custom, which protect the vanquished even against the right of conquest? If so, the loss of Normandy helped to lay down precedents which might establish international custom during the transition from medieval to modern warfare.[117] Or, again, one might raise that vague and elusive subject,

---

[115] Edward I had also to choose between Ireland and Scotland.

[116] Above, p. 83. Cf. Figgis, *From Gerson to Grotius*, pp. 4, 220.

[117] See Wheaton's *International Law*, part iv, chapter ii, § 346, and notes (8th edition, pp. 432 *seqq.*). For later medieval literature upon this subject, see Walker, *A History of the Law of Nations*, vol. i (1899), *e.g.*, p. 230.

the origin of England's claim to the narrow seas, and ask—not very profitably—whether John did or did not order foreign ships to lower their flag to his ships, and, if he did, whether it was before or after he ceased to rule both sides of the English Channel.[118] But it is sufficient to remind ourself that when the Normans became French they did a great deal more than bring their national epic to a close. They permitted the English once more to become a nation, and they established the French state for all time.

[118] For John's alleged ordinance of March 30, 1201, see the *Black Book of the Admiralty*, I, xix, and Fulton, *The Sovereignty of the Sea* (1911), pp. 39–43.

APPENDICES

I. KING JOHN AND ARTHUR OF BRITTANY

FEW references have been made in the preceding work to the murder of Arthur in 1203 as a cause of the loss of Normandy. It is clear, I think that Philip, rightly or wrongly, attacked Normandy in pursuance of the condemnation of John by the royal court in 1202. It is also fairly certain that Philip was not convinced of Arthur's death and John's crime before the spring of 1204 (and probably not even then), when Normandy was more than half won. Yet, after studying, in the order of their composition, the authorities which refer to or discuss the alleged condemnation of King John by his peers in the French court after Arthur's death, I have been led to feel considerable doubt concerning the orthodox view on the subject. That view is the negative conclusion reached by M. Bémont in his well-known thesis a quarter of a century ago.[1]

M. Bémont rests his case upon the fact that no contemporary authority, official or unofficial, refers to King John's condemnation, until 1216 and later. In testing the value and importance of this fact, it is impossible to separate the evidence for Arthur's death from the evidence for John's trial at the French court. The conclusions to which a study of this evidence has brought me may be stated as follows:

1. The story of Arthur's death which is most likely to be true, and is corroborated by other evidence, is contained in the annals of Margam. The condemnation of John is an integral part of this story, which has no connection with the documents of 1216 and is probably due to William of Briouze.

2. Too much stress has been laid upon the argument from silence.

---

[1] For the literature of the whole subject, see Petit-Dutaillis, *Studies supplementary to Stubbs' 'Constitutional History'*, i, 108; Lot, *Fidèles ou Vassaux?* (Paris, 1904), p. 87, note. For a very sceptical criticism of the documents of 1216, not dealt with here, see Lehmann, *Johann ohne Land*, pp. 45–119. So I wrote in 1913: it is now necessary to emphasise the critical study by Petit-Dutaillis published in 1925, *Le déshéritement de Jean sans Terre et le meurtre d'Arthur de Bretagne* (109 pages), described by the author as the study of a legend. On the other side see a note by Barnaby C. Keeney in his *Judgment by Peers*, Harvard University Press, 1949, pp. 111–13, with the notes on pp. 182–3.

I

Within thirty or forty years of his death that great southerner
Richard the Lion Heart had become a peculiarly English hero of
English romance—romance full of confused reminiscences and pic-
turesque nonsense, which in its amplified anti-French form was used
by Shakespeare; and the notorious John suffered by comparison in
popular history.[2] Most of the popular version of John's misdeeds may
be put on one side; but the more critical narrative of Holinshed is a
suggestive starting-point for a study of the medieval tradition. Holinshed gives his authorities. The story of Arthur's interview with Hubert
is based on a contemporary Essex chronicle of Coggeshall. Holinshed
repeats the three or four rumours made current by Matthew Paris in
his *Historia Anglorum*,[3] that Arthur died of grief, or was drowned in
trying to escape from the tower of Rouen, or was killed by his uncle.
The most popular version of Arthur's death is unknown to Holinshed,
and therefore to Shakespeare. Hence in the famous play, the Hubert
scene naturally becomes the central theme.

There was a Breton tradition also, which was familiar in the fifteenth
century and was worked into the narrative of the learned Breton
historians of the seventeenth century.[4] According to this version the
barons and bishops of Brittany assembled in great numbers and
charged John with the murder fifteen days after it was committed.
On the strength of this charge King Philip of France condemned the
English king to lose all his possessions. So far as this story is true, it
can be traced, as M. Bémont pointed out, to the events described by
the Essex chronicle, to which I have referred.

King John captured Arthur at the castle of Mirebeau on August 1,
1202. Arthur was between fifteen and sixteen years of age—nearly a
man in those days—and had been invested by Philip with all the
Angevin lands outside Normandy. At the time of his capture he was
besieging his grandmother. He was taken to Falaise and imprisoned
in the tower. John is said to have promised that if, with the aid of
William des Roches, the most powerful baron and official in Maine
and Anjou, he succeeded in defeating Arthur, he would act on
William's advice. His trickery after the successful march on Mirebeau
and his cruelty to the prisoners cost him the allegiance of William and

[2] See G. Paris in *Romania*, xxvi, 357, 387. Compare Bishop Bale's long
since forgotten play about King John, which Shakespeare is said to have used.
[3] Ed. Madden, ii, 95.
[4] See Bémont, *Revue Historique*, xxxii (1886), 290–300; Stubbs, Introduction to the so-called *Memoriale of Walter of Coventry*, ii, p. xxxii. Several
continental chroniclers refer to the rumour of Arthur's murder, but their
evidence throws no light on the facts.

of the barons of the west. They joined with the Bretons and the rebels of Poitou. Some of the Normans were won over.[5]

The Coggeshall chronicle is the sole authority for what happened at Falaise.[6] John's counsellors saw that so long as Arthur was kept in Falaise, away from his followers, yet safe and well, John was in danger. It must be remembered that the king was already under sentence of deprivation by the French court, on account of the appeal of the Poitevin barons. If the alliance was not to be overwhelming Arthur ought either to be handed over to William des Roches or to be put out of the way. Some of John's friends suggested mutilation. In his anger at failure, after the only brilliant military achievement of his life, John agreed, and sent two servants to Falaise, where, his feet fettered by a triple chain, the young man was guarded by Hubert de Burgh, the chamberlain. Hubert, moved partly by the agony of Arthur, partly by the folly of the deed, prevented John's agents from accomplishing the royal command. Yet he felt also that the only way to coerce the Bretons was to convince them of Arthur's death. What folly there might be in mutilation or murder lay in the fact that John's subjects, especially his knights, would refuse to serve a parricide. Hubert announced that Arthur had died. For fifteen days (we see here the fifteen days of the Breton story) the rumour spread. The place of Arthur's burial was known also. Then the Bretons, fully roused, swore that they would never cease their attacks on the king of England after this atrocious deed. They believed that Arthur had been murdered. It is not at all unlikely that they held a solemn assembly; the Coggeshall narrative rather implies common action. In this case the chief facts of the Breton version would be true, and the fifteenth-century and later writers were following veracious but obviously independent annals in their detailed account of the gathering at Vannes. The error simply lay in this, that Arthur was not yet dead.

This explanation is the more probable because from that time Arthur disappeared. Hubert, when the danger increased rather than diminished, announced that he was alive, but the Bretons could have no proof of this. They would naturally prefer to believe that Arthur was dead, if he was not handed over. Philip and they clamoured for his release and offered hostages in vain. Their scepticism is expressed distinctly in the charter of King Philip in which he refers to Arthur 'if he still lives'.[7] Till the spring of 1204 this scepticism was maintained; then it became certainty that Arthur was dead; but there was

[5] *Vie de Guillaume le Maréchal*, iii, 167–70; Coggeshall, p. 139. Above, p. 157.
[6] *Ibid.*, pp. 139–41.
[7] Delisle, *Catalogue des Actes de Philippe-Augustus*, no. 783, p. 177, October, 1203, before Château Gaillard, charter for Guy of Thouars; Bémont, *Revue Hist.*, xxxii, 42.

no proof. The semi-official chronicler Rigord of St. Denis, who lived till about 1206, makes no mention of it. A few chroniclers tell us that Arthur was removed to Rouen; and no doubt, as time went on, this fact became common knowledge. But after that all was darkness and vague rumour. Only here and there—*e.g.*, by the chronicler of Tours[8] —was Arthur supposed to have been killed. In 1204 Philip refused peace, partly because he was confident of success in war, partly, according to the Coggeshall chronicler, because he had heard that Arthur had been drowned in the Seine.[9] Many years later even Matthew Paris, who was not exactly friendly to John, can only give the various stories of his death and hope doubtfully that the story of murder is not true. Gradually, in popular talk Arthur's fate became subject to the variations of time and place and incident which control all mysteries.

Such was the main historical tradition concerning the relations between John and his nephew. Putting aside other evidence as valueless, M. Bémont has urged that it is sufficient to disprove the story that John was condemned, a second time, for the death of Arthur. It certainly does not prove it, but it is hard to see how it can be said to do more. The condemnation of John ought to be considered together with the question, When did Philip become morally certain of Arthur's death by murder? The orthodox view is as follows: John must have been condemned, if at all, in 1203; and, as Philip was uncertain of Arthur's fate in April, 1204, John could not have been condemned at all. Now the only serious reason for the statement that John must have been condemned, if at all, in 1203 is that Philip continued the war in 1203, and sentence must come before the punishment.[10] This in its turn seems to imply that Philip would not have invaded Normandy in 1203, if John had not been condemned. It is true that the later writers, looking back, are so much impressed by the crime that they say it caused the loss of Normandy, as indeed it did to a large extent. Philip was urged on by indignation.[11] One or two witnesses, as we shall see, imply that Normandy was escheated because of the sentence. Indeed, if sentence was passed, this must have been true also. But all these considerations are irrelevant to the fact that Philip, while still uncertain or ignorant of Arthur's fate, invaded Normandy in 1203, and would have done so in any case. The evidence

[8] *Historiens de France*, xviii, 295.

[9] *Saeviebat autem permaxime pro nece Arturi, quem in Sequana submersum fuisse audierat*: Coggeshall, p. 145.

[10] *Revue Historique*, xxxii, 55.

[11] The anonymous chronicler of Laon, who is especially interested in Anglo-Norman history, puts the case exactly from the retrospective standpoint: 1203, *Iohannes rex Anglie Arturum . . . crudelissime iugulavit. . . . Guera inter regem Francie et regem Anglie fit solito gravior* (ed. Cartellieri, p. 61).

for the condemnation is not invalidated because some of the witnesses thought that it caused a war already in progress. The truth is that Philip and John were at war and that there was no break. It is certain that Philip regarded Normandy as escheated in 1202, together with Poitou and the other possessions of King John.[12] There is no hint that the military operations from the opening of war in 1202 to the surrender of Rouen in June, 1204, were not regarded as continuous. Rigord says explicitly that there was no truce at the end of 1202;[13] and there was certainly no break at the end of 1203. Hence it is impossible to connect the operations of 1203 exclusively with Arthur's death or the condemnation of John. So far as this argument goes, it shows that the condemnation might have been passed in 1203 or 1204 or 1205, or any other year. At the same time Philip, who had been urging on war all the more fiercely because of his suspicions, became convinced that Arthur was dead. In reply to every suggestion of peace he said, 'Either produce Arthur, or, if you have killed him, surrender all your continental possessions.' At last he felt sure. He had heard, says the Coggeshall chronicler, that he was drowned. This was in the spring of 1204, and the condemnation, if it was passed, would most naturally follow then. Philip did not know the exact details, nor do I think that he knew them until some years had gone by.

Our chief authority for this summary has been the chronicle of Coggeshall. All historians, except Miss Norgate, are convinced of the value of this source.[14] The narrative is at bottom annalistic, embroidered by tales of visitors and neighbours. There is no attempt at continuous history, but, mixed with jejune summaries, we find two kinds of story, both of which show the sort of authority upon which they are based. One of them is the religious marvel, the other the striking political incident. We do not need the writer's explicit statement to know that a special source—a visitor, a monk who has been on business, a neighbouring baron—has produced these stories. The vivid narrative of Richard's capture was related by the royal chaplain, Anselm.[15] Another eye-witness, Hugh de Nevill, brought back a story of the crusade.[16] In spite of Miss Norgate's criticism the account of the first condemnation of John in 1202 has been amply verified by French scholars; nor is there any reason to disbelieve the circumstantial relation of the events at Falaise, though they are not

[12] This seems to follow from the papal letters of 1203 taken with Arthur's letters of July, 1202 (*Layettes*, i, 236, no. 647).

[13] Rigord, ed. Delaborde, i, 153. *Superveniente vero hyeme uterque sine pace et treuga, marchiis munitis, a bello cessavit.* This is the more significant, since John attempted to bring about a truce. Above, p. 163.

[14] See Petit-Dutaillis, *Le déshéritement*, pp. 7–8, where the share of Abbot Ralph seems to me under-estimated; cf. my article in *English Historical Review*, xxi (1906), 286 ff.   [15] Coggeshall, p. 54.   [16] *Ibid.*, p. 45.

mentioned by any other writer. Now it seems to me to be a valid
argument that, if the widespread tale of Arthur's supposed death at
Falaise has only come down in one chronicle, his mysterious fate
would be still more likely to pass unchronicled, or would only be
revealed accidentally through the gossip of the few people who knew
what had happened. It is only when a chance discovery, like that of
the biography of the Marshal, brings some unknown authority to
light that we can realise faintly what a vast story lies untold. By
accident or good fortune a chronicler here and there heard one thing
out of a hundred, or a rhyming biographer put down the reminiscences
of his hero. Except in rare and definite cases the argument *e silentio*
is invalid for the medieval historian. Further, when there is reason
for secrecy, the chances of truth are of course less. Arthur *subito
evanuit*, said Roger of Wendover. We must not think of Arthur at
this time as a popular hero, except in Brittany. When John's crime
was made a political question by Philip and Louis in 1216, the pope
did not trouble himself to deny it. He made little of it. The chronicles,
he said, tell us of the murder of innocent persons by many princes,
the kings of France as well as others, but we do not read that the
murderers were ever condemned to death. Arthur was no innocent
victim; he was captured at Mirebeau, a traitor to his lord, to whom
he had sworn homage (*cui homagium et liganciam fecerat*), and he
could rightly be condemned without a formal trial to die the most
shameful of deaths.[17]

In the spring, then, of 1204 Philip was becoming convinced that
Arthur was dead. If the Breton tradition be correct—and we have
seen reason to believe that it is based on truth—he had long been
urged to condemn John for the murder. If and when he condemned
him is, so far as this body of evidence goes, uncertain. If he did, the
natural date would be early in 1204, before the last campaign and the
fall of Rouen. Those writers who state or imply that the condemnation
took place in 1203 are either late, like the chronicle of Lanercost, or
are joining several events together in the usual medieval way. Nothing
is more common in the historical writing of all ages than to anticipate
events for the sake of clearness or through the natural association of
ideas, and in the medieval chronicles, with their short annalistic
entries, events are often transferred to a wrong date for the same
reason. There is an excellent illustration of this in an important
reference to Arthur in a chronicle of Rouen. The chief of three small
chronicles of Rouen, which were first thrown into one in 1546, was the
chronicle of St. Catherine. Part of this was, according to M. Chéruel,

[17] Matt. Paris, *Chron. Mai.*, ii, 659 (from Wendover). For remarks on the
effect of Arthur's disappearance see above, p. 167. The papal view of treason
was evidently more comprehensive than the feudal view (above, p. 285).

written in the first half of the thirteenth century. Its local character lends it value. Under the year 1201—an entirely wrong date—after referring to the death of Arthur, the chronicler says of John *super quo a baronibus apud regem Franciae, cuius vassallus erat, quum comparere nollet, post multas citationes per iudicium parium exhaeredatus est.*[18]

The authorities with which I have dealt hitherto may be regarded as contemporary, or as going back to a contemporary source. The Coggeshall chronicle was written up from time to time. The portion comprising the years 1202–1205 is a coherent and separate fragment, possibly written in, or at least derived from John's court in Normandy. The Breton tradition is largely borne out by Coggeshall and shows when suspicion was first aroused. The charters are of course contemporary. On the strength of this evidence I think we might assume that Philip had sufficient cause for calling his court together to condemn John, but we could not be certain whether he did so or not.[19]

II

Twelve years later the English barons urged Louis of France to come over and help them. King Philip had twice before been baulked in an attempt to invade England, and he was not prepared to let this third chance slip. Both in France and at Rome the French case was justified—in France before the legate Guala, in Rome before the pope himself. One argument upon which great stress was laid was thus expounded by Louis' proctor a fortnight after Easter at Laon, before king and legate and all the assembled barons and clergy: 'My lord king, it is well known (*res notissima*) to all that John, styled king of England, was condemned to death in your court by the judgment of his peers for his treachery to his nephew Arthur, whom he slew with his own hands, and that afterwards, because of his many crimes, he was repudiated by his barons in England,' etc.[20] It is round this

[18] *Normanniae nova Chronica e tribus chronicis MSS. Sancti Laudi, Sanctae Catharinae, et Maioris Ecclesiae Rothomagensium collecta,* nunc primum edidit e ms. codice Bibliothecae publicae Rothomagensis A. Chéruel (*Mém de la Société des Antiq. de Normandie* (1850), xviii, 156, separately paged, published under the final editorship of MM. Charma and Delisle).

[19] Petit-Dutaillis argues with much force, that King Philip was not really sure of Arthur's death until 1206, and that the conclusion of a truce for two years on October 26, 1206, precludes a condemnation of John in the French king's court (*Le déshéritement,* pp. 56–63). Both Petit-Dutaillis and Keeney, who takes a different view of the evidence in 1203–5, seem to agree that some kind of action took place, but the former would confine it to sworn declarations of vengeance.

[20] The documents of 1216 are preserved by the St. Albans chronicle of Roger of Wendover, and are best seen in Matthew Paris, *Chron. Mai.*, ii, 647.

316   THE LOSS OF NORMANDY

text that a famous literary controversy has been fought. M. Bémont, arguing from the silence of most authorities, from the late date of others, and from the charters of Philip Augustus, declared that Philip and Louis told a bold lie in 1216, and that it was on the strength of this assertion, and not upon other evidence, that later chroniclers believed in the condemnation of John. Unless the proof be very positive this view is hard to maintain. It seems such a stupid lie, so easily refuted. Unless we put aside as fabrications all the documents preserved by Roger of Wendover which deal with the negotiations, it is clear that the pope and everybody else believed the story. Innocent's view was that the condemnation was not justified. The argument that these documents, somehow preserved at St. Albans, are the source of the other evidence upon the subject can only be considered when we have examined this evidence. The evidence is twofold—a marginal commentary in Matthew Paris (who follows Wendover for these years) and a rather long bit of narrative in the annals of Margam, a Cistercian abbey in Glamorganshire. Let us consider the latter first.

Like the Coggleshall chronicle, the chronicle of Margam is a brief record amplified by narrative passages. It exists in a manuscript of Trinity College, Cambridge (O. 2. 4, no. 1108). The chronicle ends abruptly and imperfectly in 1232; the manuscript belongs to about 1240. It does not seem to be the original,[21] and there is little evidence as to the dates of the original composition, but the part with which we are concerned was put together after 1210.[22] This is noteworthy, since it reminds us that the narrative of what happened in 1203 could be connected with later events. The monks of Margam had heard, circumstantially, how John had killed Arthur in a drunken fury, on a certain day, in a certain place, at a certain time (*in turre tandem Rothomagensi, feria quinta ante Pascha, post prandium, ebrius et daemonio plenus, propria manu interfecit*). He had tied a stone to the body and thrown it into the Seine. It was discovered by a fisherman, recognised, and, for fear of John, buried secretly in Sainte-Marie-de-Pré, one of the priories of Bec. When Philip was convinced that Arthur was dead he summoned John to the French court to answer the charge of murder, for Arthur was a very important man. He never came, and was condemned *per iudicium curie regis et principum Francorum* to lose all the lands held of the French crown. And it was a righteous judgment.[23] There may be faults of chronology in the

[21] There is a similar MS. with the same diagram of parhelia, ending at the same date, in the library of Trinity College, Dublin. For the Cambridge MS., see M. R. James, *The Western Manuscripts in the Library of Trinity College, Cambridge*, iii, 83, 84.

[22] Under the year 1199 reference is made to the exile and death of William of Briouze in 1211; *Ann. Monastici*, ed. Luard, i, 24.

[23] *Ann. Mon.*, i, 27, 28.

story, though it should be noted that the interval between murder and trial is not stated. There is the erroneous implication that the king of France had not already got possession of John's territories—not so very erroneous, however, for Rouen held out till June, 1204, and Chinon till the following year, and there was local fighting after that. It is all the same significant that, as a story, the narrative hangs together. It is just the kind of story that a man who knew the facts but had no particular interest in giving every detail correctly would tell to a curious listener. The chronicler is by no means interested only in the horror of the murder; that was dreadful, but after all murders are common. Arthur was a great man, the rightful heir of England, count of Brittany, brother-in-law of the French king. We should remember that we are on Celtic ground, though in an Anglo-Norman honour. A few years before, the bones of King Arthur had been found at Glastonbury: the monks of Margam knew all about that.[24] Modern scholars believe that Henry II was responsible for the semi-official reception of the Arthurian legend; it marked the fusion of Norman and Celtic. At one time Henry's grandson, the new Arthur, had been accepted by King Richard as his heir, and after Richard's return John had been disinherited by solemn decision of the royal council for his treachery. The Margam chronicler insisted on this also.[25] And now the new Arthur was gone; and it was indeed a righteous judgment— *fixum et iustum indicium hoc*—which the court of the French king had uttered.

This seems to be valuable testimony. But, in his essay, M. Bémont put it aside as valueless for three reasons. In the first place the chronicle was written after the expedition of 1216; secondly, the dates are wrong; thirdly, Margam was an obscure monastery in South Wales, and cannot have acquired information which was unknown to the other annalists of England and France.[26] The second of these reasons is of little or no value unless the others are made good. The first contention is that the chronicle was composed too late to have much authority, especially since Louis' invasion had presumably given currency to the story of John's second condemnation. In reply to this it may be urged that, unless we know how the annals were compiled, it is impossible to decide one way or the other. The chronicle was written up after 1210, and possibly after 1221;[27] but notes were always followed, and some parts were often written before others. It

---

[24] *Ann. Mon.*, i, 21, a. 1191.

[25] *Ibid.*, i, 24; Rog. Howden, iii, 241, 242; Miss Norgate, ii, 329.

[26] *Revue Historique*, xxxii, 59.

[27] M. Bémont lays stress on the fact that, under the year 1200, Hugh of Lincoln is described as St. Hugh, although he was not canonised till 1221. But any copyist writing after 1221 would insert the word 'sanctus' before the words 'Hugo Lincolniae episcopus' as a matter of course.

is true that the difference between this narrative and most of the
chronicle is marked. M. Bémont is obliged to suppose that the compiler used two different sources; but with the example of Coggeshall
before us we need only see the usual dry record of a scriptorium with
the addition of a few vivid stories, like the story told by the chaplain
Anselm to the abbot of Coggeshall. Now, if this story in the Margam
annals came from a definite source it has great value. It is just a story
of this kind upon which we rely when we accept the Coggeshall account
of John's first condemnation. But might it not have come by way of
Louis in 1216? In making this suggestion M. Bémont has failed to
observe that there is not a single reference to Louis in the chronicle.
His invasion is ignored; we are told simply that John died and Henry
succeeded him and was crowned by the legate Guala. There is therefore no evidence at all for this view.

It is erroneous, in reply to the third objection against the chronicle,
to suggest that the abbey of Margam was too obscure to be well
informed. Just as Coggeshall was in a land of royal forest and manors,
near London, just as St. Albans was on one of the great roads, so
Margam had special advantages for hearing strange information.
Gerald of Wales speaks of its importance, its hospitality, its connection, when scarcity of corn made connection useful, with Bristol.[28]
When we turn to the Margam records we find no ignorant and secluded
community, but a powerful house, favoured and harassed alternately
by great neighbours who were some of the greatest barons in England
and the Marches,[29] an abbey which lay on the road from England to
Ireland, and was twice visited by King John himself[30]—at one time
under the king's special protection, favoured almost as much as his
peculiar foundation, the Cistercian house of Beaulieu.[31] The delightful
studies of M. Bédier have shown us that the information and influence
of a monastery depended not so much upon its general position as
upon the road on which it lay, or upon what friends the abbot had.
He has demonstrated that the isolated and obscure house of Saint-
Guilhem-du-Désert could mould the history of a great epic cycle,
because it was visited by pilgrims on their way to Compostella.[32]
Conversely special information could make a chronicle of the most
meagre and unpretentious range a very valuable authority. The
monks of Coggeshall knew a great deal more about Richard's cap-

[28] *Opera* (Rolls Series), vi, 67, 68.

[29] G. T. Clark, *Cartae et alia Munimenta quae ad Dominium de Glamorgan
pertinent*, especially vol. iii, *passim* (Cardiff, 1891).

[30] *Rot. de Liberate*, 172, 229; *Annales Monastici*, i, 10. In his *History of
Margam* (London, 1877) Mr. W. de Gray Birch suggested that there was some
connection between John's presence at and favours to the abbey, and its
chronicler's knowledge of Arthur's death (pp. 176–80).

[31] *Ann. Mon.*, i, 30.　　　[32] *Les Légendes Epiques*, vol. i (Paris, 1908).

tivity than did many great abbeys, because Anselm, the king's chaplain, 'told us all these things as he saw and heard them'. Now is it possible to suggest the chief channel of communication open to the monks of Margam?

In reading the chronicle one or two suggestions occur to mind which must be put aside. It might be observed that the compiler seems to have been interested in Bec. He knows that Sainte-Marie-de-Pré is a priory of Bec; he notes that Hugh of Nonant, bishop of Coventry, died at Bec in 1198. Again, it is worthy of mention that in November, 1203, Margam had an agent at Rome, who was engaged in securing lengthy privileges and confirmations from Pope Innocent III.[33] On his journey to and from Rome the person entrusted with the business of the abbey, whether a monk or not, could acquire information which might interest his employers. But it is not very likely that this would be of unique importance. Let us approach the problem from the other direction and ask who was likely to know what happened before and after the murder of Arthur. Ralph of Coggeshall says that Arthur was entrusted to the care of Robert of Vieuxpont at Rouen; but Robert was a north-country magnate, nor does he appear in the story of the murder. He was a busy official who probably did not live constantly at Rouen.[34] Two of John's companions and counsellors however were very conspicuous in Glamorgan, and both of them probably knew a good deal more than they cared to say. William the Marshal, earl of Pembroke, and William of Briouze (de Braosa) granted privileges to or attested the charters of Margam more than once. The Marshal kept absolute silence. It is difficult to say to what extent he knew how Arthur died. He was certainly acquainted with the course of the negotiations which followed the murder during 1204–5, since he was one of the embassy. I think that his biographer knew a good deal, and hints at Arthur's fate, but there is not a word of explicit reference to the matter in the poem which tells us so many new things.[35] Nor were the Marshal's lands in South Wales near the abbey of Margam. But William of Briouze was in a very different position. The story of his life would, if it were thoroughly known, be the most important record we could have of the personal history of John and his baronage during the first part of the reign. He was the king's

[33] Clark, *op. cit.*, iii, 225–34.

[34] Coggeshall, p. 143. He was bailiff of Caen and the Roumois in 1203, and is identified by Stapleton with the Robert of Vieuxpont who was lord of Westmorland, and clung to John in 1216, while his brother joined the rebels (Stapleton, II, cclxiv–cclxvii; cf. Farrer, *Lancashire Pipe Rolls*, p. 258). After the loss of Normandy, Robert got some of Ralph Tesson's lands in Kent (*Rot. Norm.*, p. 140). Below, p. 357.

[35] There are possible hints in ii, 81, 145. For the Marshal's embassies, see vol. iii, pp. 176–8, with Meyer's notes.

constant companion during the Norman campaigns. It is well known
that the official records reveal the presence of John near Rouen just
about the time when, according to the Margam annals, the murder
was committed.[36] William of Briouze was with him at the time. About
1207 he lost the king's favour, and in 1210 John tried to exterminate
him and his family. His wife, Matilda, is said to have refused to hand
over her children as hostages to the murderer of Arthur, and John
pursued her thereafter with a ferocity unusual even in him. The grisly
story of her and her son's death by starvation in Windsor is the most
awful of many awful tales.[37] It is impossible to believe that the debts
of William of Briouze were, as John said in the official account, the
cause of this persecution.[38] The natural supposition is that this chosen
companion knew too much to be allowed to live after he and so many
others had quarrelled with the king. In 1210 he managed to escape
to France; in 1211 he died and he was buried at Corbeil on the eve
of St. Lawrence.[39] All this we know apart from the evidence of
Margam.

Now by far the most conspicuous person in the annals of Margam,
and one of the most important figures in its records, is this William of
Briouze. He was lord of Brecon, Radnor, and Gower. Between 1202
and 1207 he was responsible for the administration of Glamorgan,
in which Margam lay.[40] He attests the charters of local benefactors to
the abbey.[41] In the annals we are told how William of Briouze was
chiefly responsible for John's accession to the throne in spite of his
previous condemnation. Except the great semi-official chronicler,
Roger of Howden, the Margam annalist is the only writer to mention
this condemnation of John at the court of King Richard.[42] He is
interested in William's life and alone tells us that after his death in
France he was buried by the exile Stephen Langton, archbishop of

[36] See the itinerary appended to Sir T. D. Hardy's introduction to *Rot. Litt.
Patent.* (1835); cf. Miss Norgate, ii, 430. That William of Briouze was present
is clear from the attestations; *e.g.*, *Rot. Norm.*, p. 86.

[37] See Meyer's long note in *Hist. de Guillaume le Maréchal*, iii, 156; *Dict. of
Nat. Biogr.*, *s.v.* 'Braose', for authorities; *e.g.*, Rog. Wendover, ii, 49 (Rolls
Series).

[38] *Calendar of Documents relating to Ireland*, i, no. 408.

[39] Rog. Wendover, ii, 59; Matthew Paris, *Chron. Mai.*, ii, 532; *Annales
Monastici*, v. 40, and index.

[40] See John's charter of June 3, 1200, in Clark (iii, 177), and the extent of
1235 (iii, 381); also *Rot. Litt. Pat.*, p. 19 (October 23, 1202), and p. 68b
(1207).

[41] Clark, iii, 144, 217. In 1193 William attested a charter of John, then count
of Mortain, at Cardiff (i, 33). An interesting charter of Robert, son of Wian,
granted to the abbey a lease of land for six years from Michaelmas, 1197, 'que
videlicet festivitas Sancti Michaelis tercia secuta est captionem castelli de
Sancto Claro *factam per Willelmum de Brausa*' (iii, 169).

[42] *Ann. Monast.*, i, 24.

Canterbury. Finally, the relations of John and William were a theme of popular tradition in South Wales nearly eighty years after the death of Arthur. In February, 1203, John had granted the land of Gower to William. In 1279 the earl of Warwick contested the right of William's descendant to this honour, and especially to the castle of Swansea, on several grounds, including the significant plea that William had extorted the original charter from John when the king was in a panic and feared that his companion was going to leave him.[43] In short, the man who was most in John's confidence was William of Briouze, and if any chronicler was likely to hear about the death of Arthur and its consequences it was the chronicler of Margam.

There is another significant fact which, so far as I know, has never been noticed, but which adds an element of certainty to this view. It has often been observed that the Margam story only reappears in one place—and there with some variation—in the epic, *Philippid*, of King Philip's chaplain William the Breton. The variations are not great, and show that the chaplain was giving the same story independently. Now it is very curious that he singles out William of Briouze, who is not mentioned elsewhere in the poem, as the spokesman of those barons who were with John near Rouen at the time of Arthur's death. John brought Arthur to Rouen (I summarise the flowery verses) and aroused the suspicions of the barons. William of Briouze declared that he would be responsible for him no longer, and that he handed him over safe and sound. After a moody seclusion at the royal manor of Moulineux, John did away with his nephew at Rouen by night.[44] This comes in book vi., which with the beginning of book vii. has been shown with some probability to have been composed before 1214.[45] Now part of this story at least had been well known or suspected at the French court for a long time. The Coggeshall chronicler tells us that Philip heard in 1204 that Arthur had been drowned. On the other hand, as William the Breton wrote his poem in three years, this part could not have been composed much earlier than 1214, in any case after the flight of William of Briouze to France. He was in almost constant attendance upon Philip, and likely to hear what was going on. He would be interested in the famous fugitive who had experienced such a turn of fortune and fled like a beggar from the English coast. Is it not possible that at last the full story of the murder

[43] P.R.O., K.R. Miscell. Books, vol. i, p. 478b, 8 Edw. I.; printed in Clark, iii, 532.

[44] *Philippid*, vi, 470–564.

[45] Delaborde, *Notice sur Rigord et Guillaume le Breton* (prefixed to his edition), pp. 70 *seqq*. The references to Arthur's death in William's Continuation of Rigord are brief and casual, though emphatic (ed. Delaborde, i, 253, 293).

Y

was known at the French court, and that in the *Philippid* we get the tale—naturally favourable to William of Briouze—which is found elsewhere only in the chronicle of a Welsh abbey? This would partly account for the terror and atrocities of John during these years, for the alliance between Philip and the English barons, and for the projected invasion. It would be tempting to suggest that it was then that Philip summoned John to appear for his crime; but this is impossible.

This analysis has, I think, enabled us to form a juster idea of the value of the Margam chronicle, and to trace to some extent the origin of the most detailed account which has come down to us of Arthur's death. I have maintained that the Margam narrative is to be regarded as a whole, and therefore, unless very serious evidence were brought against it, we are forced to the belief that Philip's court probably did condemn John a second time. Louis' proctor in 1216 said he was condemned to death; the Margam chronicle and later tradition are content to say that he was sentenced to lose all his continental possessions. It is quite possible that, after the revelations and awful crimes of 1210, when John was excommunicated, and Philip had been urged by the pope to deprive him entirely, Philip's court had proceeded to a sentence of death. The language used in 1216 suggests that the repudiation of allegiance by the English barons followed the French judgment after no very long interval. Still, this is only possible. What seems to me unlikely is that Louis told a lie in 1216 and that the annals of Margam, the tradition in Brittany, and the independent testimony of Matthew Paris are at fault. With the argument that the condemnation must have taken place in 1203 I have dealt already; it depends on the partly erroneous belief of our authorities that it caused the loss of Normandy. Yet everybody would agree that the death of Arthur gave strength to the French king, and if so a formal sentence of confiscation, as soon as he was sure of Arthur's death, would strengthen him much more. The other arguments against the condemnation are negative —the late and unsatisfactory nature of the authorities and the silence of the chief records and chronicles. But we have seen that the annals of Margam are not so very unsatisfactory after all.[46]

[46] I omit the conclusion of this section, as it appears in the first edition; this dealt with the marginal note by Matthew Paris on the documents preserved by Roger of Wendover (*Chron. Mai.*, ii, 658). Although I am not convinced by it, the essay of Petit-Dutaillis, *Le Déshéritement*, is now the best introduction to the evidence as a whole. My own view, for what it is worth, is that Philip, though he may well have sworn to avenge Arthur even to the death of John, confined any legal extension of the sentence of 1202 to the conquest of England.

III

I should say a word about the last important argument used by M. Bémont and his followers, the argument from silence. It may be admitted that this is invalid so far as the chroniclers were concerned; if the murder passed unrecorded, the condemnation obviously would also; but what about the French registers and the papal registers; and why did not William the Breton, who says so much about Arthur, enlarge upon the condemnation? But the French registers were not kept systematically like the English records, and there is no mention of *any* condemnation upon them or in Philip's charters. Philip wrote about the first trial to the pope, but our only authority is the pope's answer; no official record would tell us anything. The French court of 'peers' was like the English *curia regis*—in its broadest sense—in this, that its proceedings could pass unnoticed by the ordinary man if they were not recorded. John's trial after Richard's return passed almost unnoticed in England. Everything was very informal, and the trial of John is really of importance to the French historian and jurist because it seems to suggest the beginnings of something a little more formal.[47] I have purposely avoided all the juridical arguments of M. Guilhiermoz; if the historical evidence is lacking, the judicial can hardly be adduced; but although I think the historical evidence is sufficient to allow us to believe in the condemnation, I would also urge that these semi-legal, semi-political, proceedings would easily escape the attention of contemporaries. They hardly form a theme for the chaplain's epic. He was content to say that Philip hastened to take vengeance, that *Iohanni retribui possit pro morte nepotis,* and this is not altogether unjuridical.[48] Since John did not appear, the trial would be short, and all the more easily disregarded.

Great stress, again, has been laid on the silence of the papal letters of 1203. As the trial, if there was a second trial, took place later, papal silence in 1203 is not surprising.[49] It is not hard to see why Innocent should refrain from mentioning the subject. The point is that he does not mention the disappearance of Arthur, of which he must have heard. It is certain that Arthur disappeared, yet there is no allusion to him; surely then it is rather illogical to say that John was not tried for the death of Arthur, because the pope does not refer to the trial.

[47] How relatively unimportant the undeniable (first) trial was is seen from any consecutive account of the French court, *e.g.*, Viollet, *Hist. des Institutions Politiques*, iii, 301–2.   [48] v. 16 (Delaborde, ii, 177).
[49] Innocent, in his well known letter to the Norman bishops in 1205, refers to the sentence of Philip's court as Philip's plea in justification of his attack on Normandy (above, p. 276), but it is probable that the pope was referring to the condemnation of 1202. Keeney takes a different view in his *Judgment by Peers*, p. 111.

At this time Innocent was anxious to bring about peace between Philip and John in the interests of the king of the Romans, Otto. He was also in the midst of his efforts to rescue the unfortunate wife of Philip, Ingeborg, from her imprisonment. So far as he took sides he was certainly supporting John rather than Philip.[50] One English chronicler, who was in the way of knowing, states definitely that it was part of the papal legate's duty to find out exactly what had happened to Arthur.[51] The documents of 1216 show that the pope had got some information, and professed to think that John's action was justified. After his quarrel with John he doubtless may have made much of the death of Arthur; but here a significant fact appears to show us how vain is this argument from silence. On October 31, 1213, he wrote to Nicholas, bishop of Tusculum, his legate in France, ordering him to collect and destroy by fire every letter which he had written against John to the English bishops, whether before or after the interdict of March 1208, and especially one letter which had been distributed through France, England, Scotland, Ireland, and in the bishoprics of Liége and Utrecht.[52] Surely we can no longer wonder that Innocent's letters tell us nothing of the fate of Arthur. It is a curious and noteworthy fact that the chancery rolls for the very years when John was busiest in his furious attacks on the clergy and barons have also been destroyed.

IV

In the previous inquiry I have taken up and examined the arguments used by M. Bémont to controvert the statements that King John was condemned for the death of Arthur by the court of Philip of France. The whole evidence with regard to the murder of Arthur has in this way been brought before the reader, and we have seen that the chronicle of Margam, which is most explicit in affirming the trial of the murderer, is also best informed on the details of the murder. Setting on one side the problem of the trial, I will, in conclusion, bring together the scattered evidence which tends to confirm the story of the crime as told by the annalist of Margam and William the Breton.

The date given by the annalist is *feria quinta ante Pascha, post prandium*, that is, on Thursday, 3rd April, since in 1203 Easter Day fell on 6th April. On this day, according to the itinerary drawn up

[50] Scheffer-Boichorst in *Forschungen zur deutschen Geschichte*, viii (1868), 511–16.

[51] Gervase of Canterbury, ii, 95.

[52] See *Epist.*, xvi, 133, in Migne, *Patrol. Lat.*, ccxvi, 926. Potthast, no. 4837. Also edited with a translation in Cheney and Semple, *Selected Letters*, p. 164.

by Duffus Hardy, John was in Rouen.[53] Easter is also given by
Matthew Paris as the time of year to which French gossip ascribed
the murder.[54]

A few days later, John sent a letter from Falaise to his mother and
the distinguished men of the south, in which M. Richard has seen,
I think with much probability, a veiled allusion to the fate of Arthur.[55]
It is worth giving in full:

> Rex ete. Regine matri et domino Burdegalensi archiepiscopo
> et R. de Thornham senescallo Pictavie et M. Algeis senescallo
> Wasconie et Petragorum et B. senescallo Andegavie et H. de
> Burgo camerario et fratri Petro de Vernolio et Willelmo Maingo
> et Willelmo Coco salutem. Mittimus ad vos fratrem Johannem de
> Valerant qui vidit ea que circa nos geruntur et qui vos de statu
> nostro poterit certificare cui fidem habeatis in hiis que inde vobis
> dixerit *et tamen gratia Dei melius stat nobis quam ille vobis dicere
> possit* et de missione quam vobis fecimus fidem habeatis eidem
> Johanni in hiis que inde vobis dicet. Et vobis R. de Thornham
> mandamus quod pecuniam quam vobis transmittimus non dividatis
> nisi per visum et consilium matris nostre et Willelmi Coci. Teste
> Willelmo de Braosa apud Faleis xvj die Aprilis.[56]

The business of the court at Easter had been important, and John
may have been encouraged to broach the question of Arthur's fate,
as the story in William the Breton rather implies, and finally to have
taken the matter into his own hands. Geoffrey Fitz Peter, the English
justiciar, was with the king at Moulineaux on the Wednesday:[57] his
rare and fleeting visits were doubtless the occasion of conference upon
public affairs. On the same day John confirmed the administrative
measures taken by Guy of Thouars, late count of Brittany, in the
honor of Richmond.[58] Moreover, about the same time the king heard
that negotiations for an understanding with Castile had been successful.[59] It throws some light on the man's character, that he should

[53] As Miss Norgate has pointed out, William the Breton errs in saying that
John spent three days at Moulineaux, a ducal manor a few miles down the
river, before the murder; but it is noteworthy that he was at Moulineaux on
the day before (April 2) and also on the 7th and 8th (*Angevin Kings*, II, 430).
Minor discrepancies between the two authorities are to be noted: according
to the Margam annalist the murder was committed in the castle (*in turre
Rothomagensi*) and the body was afterwards taken to the boat; according to
William the Breton, John slew Arthur by night in the boat.
[54] *Hist. Anglorum*, ii, 95.   [55] *Comtes de Poitou*, ii, 425.   [56] *Rot. Pat.*, 28b.
[57] *Ibid.*, 27b. He attests a confirmation of a judgment which had been
delivered in the court at Westminster.   [58] *Rot. Pat.*, 27.
[59] Letter to the archbishop of Bordeaux and others of April 5 (*Rot. Pat.*,
27b, 28). Compare the references to arrangements with the count of Nevers
and the chamberlain of Flanders on the 4th and 7th of April, in *Rotuli de
Liberate*, p. 29.

steal away from the consideration of such high matters on the eve of Good Friday, to commit the crime which, more than any other, was to bring about his ruin.

NOTE A. ARTHUR'S HOMAGE, 1202

I. March 27, 1202, Andeli. Letter from King John to Arthur demanding his presence and service (*Rot. Pat.*, 7b).

Rex dilecto nepoti suo Arturo etc. Mandamus vobis summonentes vos quod sitis ad nos apud Argentan in octabis Pasche, facturi nobis quod facere debetis ligio domino vestro. Nos autem libenter faciemus vobis quod fecere debemus caro nepoti nostro et ligio homini nostro. Teste me ipso apud Andeliacum, xxvij die Marcii.

II. July, 1202, Gournai. Letters of Arthur announcing that he has done homage to King Philip, and entered into an agreement with him.
(Original, sealed with Arthur's seal, in Trésor des chartes, J. 241, Brittany; edit. Teulet, *Layettes du trésor des chartes*, i, p. 236, No. 647).

Arturus dux Britannie et Aquitanie, comes Andegavie et Cenomannie, universis ad quos littere presentes pervenerint salutem. Noveritis quod ego feci karissimo domino meo Philippo regi Francie illustri hominagium ligium, contra omnes qui possunt vivere vel mori, de feodo Britannie, et de Andegavensi, et de Cenomannensi, et de Turonensi, quando, Deo volente, ipse vel ego predicta acquisierimus, salvis omnibus teneamentis de quibus ipse dominus rex et homines sui tenentes erant eo die quo ipse diffiduciavit Johannem regem Anglie pro interceptionibus quas ei fecerat de hac ultima guerra, de qua ipse obsedit Botavant, tali modo quod, quando ego recipiam hominagia de Andegavia, et de Cenomannia et de Turonia, ego recipiam hominagia illa, salvis conventionibus inter ipsum et me factis; ita quod, si ego resilierim a conventionibus inter ipsum et me factis, ipsi cum feodis suis ibunt ad dominum regem et ipsum juvabunt contra me. Insuper autem de dominio Pictavie feci eidem domino meo regi hominagium ligium, si Deus dederit quod ipse vel ego eam quocumque modo acquisierimus. Barones vero Pictavie, qui imprisii domini regis sunt, et alii quos ipse voluerit, facient ei hominagium ligium de terris suis contra omnes qui possunt vivere vel mori, et de precepto ipsius facient mihi hominagium ligium, salva fide ejus.[60] Si autem illustris rex Castelle in terra aliquid juris clamaverit, per judicium curie domini nostri regis Francie diffinietur, si ipse dominus noster rex Francie predictum regem Castelle et me de utriusque nostrûm assensu non poterit pacificare. De Normannia sic erit: quod ipse dominus noster rex Francie hoc quod acquisivit et de eo quod Deus ipse dabit acquirere, ad opus suum retinebit quantum sibi placuerit, et hominibus suis, qui pro ipso terras suas amiserunt, dabit id quod sibi placuerit de terra Normannie. Actum apud Gornacum, anno Domini M° CC° secundo, mense julio.

[60] This is a clear case of 'two liege lords' (above, p. 294, note 74) and distinguishes the action of Philip in Poitou from practice elsewhere.

Note B. John's Letters of February, 1204, to the Clergy
and Laity in Ireland

The following letter, which was endorsed upon the Charter Roll,
5 Joh. m. 15, (*Rotuli Chartarum*, ed. Hardy, 133b–134) was sent from
Nottingham on February 10, 1204, to the clergy and laity in Ireland. It
is important as giving an official version of the political situation after
the king's return from Normandy. John calls upon the inhabitants of
Ireland, not as a right (*non consuetudinarie sed amicabiliter*), to join
the English in offering aid against the king of France. The following
points in the letter should be noted. First, John refers with gratification
to his reception in England and to the efforts which were made by the
English on his behalf (see above, p. 266). Secondly, he emphasises the
critical nature of the situation; he is not despondent but his needs are
urgent. Other evidence shows that John was in no hurry, but, so far
as this letter goes, it strengthens the view that he was planning a serious
campaign in Normandy, and that his plans were interrupted by Philip's
rapid and unexpected success. Thirdly, John speaks in general terms of
his *exhereditatio*.[61] The reference throws some light upon the problems
discussed in this Appendix. The words used by the king, namely, that
Philip, contrary to his charter and oath, continued to seek his deprivation, recall the similar words used on July 7, 1202, to the Cistercian
abbots (*Rot. Pat.*, 14; above, p. 149). John had written to the Cistercians
immediately after Philip had broken the treaty of 1200 in pursuance of a
judgment given against John by the French court. In this later letter,
of February, 1204, John implies that Philip's campaign in 1203–4 was
simply a continuation of his policy in 1202; in other words, it strengthens
M. Bémont's contention that Normandy was included in the condemnation of 1202, and also my view that it is useless to look for evidence
for or against the second condemnation in the records of 1203. Fourthly,
John suggests a distinction in this letter between the service owed by
the English across the English Channel and the voluntary aid which he
hoped to receive from the clergy and laity of Ireland.

Rex, etc, archiepiscopis, episcopis, abbatibus, prioribus, archi-
diaconis et universo clero per Hiberniam constitutis salutem. Satis
nostis sicut et totus mundas qualiter Rex Francie contra Deum
et rationem et contra cartam suam et juramentum nos warrare et
exhereditationem nostram querere non cessat. Nos autem propter hoc
venimus in Angliam gratia Dei sani et incolumes, ubi omnes de regno
Anglie nos honorifice receperunt sicut dominum, qui liberaliter et
benigne habita consideratione ad urgentissimum negotium nostrum
nobis efficax faciunt auxilium, tam in veniendo corporaliter in servicium nostrum quam de militibus et pecunia. Quia igitur instat ista

[61] It should be noted, on the other hand, that the word *exhereditatio* had a
very general measure, as in the *Vita S. Hugonis*, p. 248, where the Archbishop of Canterbury is reported to have said in 1197 that Philip aimed at
the *exhereditatio* of Richard. The word, however, is very rare in official
correspondence, and seems to me to be used in a more judicial sense by John.
See also above, p. 315, the phrase 'per judicium exheredatus'.

necessitas, qua nunquam nobis major emersit aut emergere poterit, vos non consuetudinarie sed amicabiliter rogamus quatinus sicut de vobis confidimus, et sicut nos et honorem nostrum diligitis, efficax nobis auxilium faciatis in hoc necessitatis nostre articulo sicut dilecti et fideles nostri justiciarius Hibernie, W. de Lascy, archidiaconus Staffordie,[62] et alii nuncii nostri cum eis ad vos venientes vobis dicent ex parte nostra vel aliquis de illis, si omnes interesse non possint, et tantum inde facientes quod vobis perpetuo teneamur obnoxiores, et quod debeamus vos merito exaudire in negociis vestris cum nos requisieritis; et certissime sciatis quod nunquam nobis ab illo auxilium fieri postulabimus qui nobis in hac tanta necessitate auxilium denegabit. Teste me ipso apud Notingham x die Februarii.

Sub eadem forma scribitur comitibus, baronibus, justiciariis, vice-comitibus, militibus, civibus, mercatoribus, burgensibus et libere-tenentibus et omnibus aliis fidelibus suis per Hiberniam constitutis.

II. THE DIVISION OF THE NORMAN BARONAGE

A DETAILED study of Philip's confiscations in Normandy and of the *Terrae Normannorum* in England would demand a separate volume. Its author would require to be familiar with the records and chartu-laries of England and France, and also to be a trained genealogist and topographer. In this appendix I have only attempted to com-pare the lists of 1172 with the feodaries contained in the registers of Philip Augustus, and to reduce some order out of Stapleton's valu-able *Observations*. The justification for a tentative inquiry may be found (1) in the fact that no methodical list of the barons who followed John and Philip respectively in 1204 has ever been attempted, and (2) in the interest which such a list may possess for the general student. For example, the history of the fiefs of Eu, Harcourt, Fon-tenai (Marmion), L'Aigle and Tillières illustrates the survival of double tenancy in England and Normandy after 1204. The history of some families, Hommet, Préaux, Tournebu, Traci, Vernon and Vieuxpont shows how the Anglo-Norman families fell apart after 1204, just as, in so many cases, they had fallen apart in the eleventh and early twelfth centuries, into English and Norman lines.

The feodaries which are included in the Registers of Philip Augustus are exceedingly important. Register A contains a copy of the state-ment of knight service drawn up in 1172, with later additions; also a valuable list of *Feoda Normanniae* which was compiled between

---

[62] Cf. *Rot. Pat.*, 41b, for the presence of this favourite clerk in Ireland early in 1204.

1204 and 1208.[1] Register C contains a detailed list of knights' fees of
the Côtentin[2] and Register E incorporates this in the most important
document of all, the complete *Scripta de feodis ad regem spectanti-
bus*.[3] This last list presents a survey of Norman society as it was
between 1210 and 1220.[4]

All these documents, with several others of less interest, are edited
in the twenty-third volume of the *Recueil des historiens de France*.
Of other documents the most important are Philip's declaration of
the lands added to his demesne in 1204 (*Cartulaire Normand*, No.
113), and the inquiry into the rights of the duke in ecclesiastical affairs,
which contains a list of the Norman barons who formed the jury, and
who were therefore adherents of Philip in 1205 (*ibid.*, No. 124). The
articles of surrender which were drawn up at Rouen in 1204 (Teulet,
Layettes, i, 250) certain lists of pledges (*e.g.*, *Cartulaire Normand*,
Nos. 204–6) and the lists of barons who took part in important
judgments, such as the division of the lands of Ralph Tesson in
1214 (*ibid.*, No. 230), are also useful. A great deal of scattered information is to be found in Delisle's *Cartulaire Normand* and *Actes
de Philippe Auguste*; also, for the period before 1204, in Round's
Calendar of Documents preserved in France.

On the English side, the *valor* of certain lands of the Normans in
1204 (*Rotuli Normanniae*, p. 122), the list of fees drawn up in 1212,
and the Fine Rolls are especially valuable. For the history of the
English baronies, however, the student should turn to the other
records of the thirteenth century, the Chancery and plea rolls, the
inquisitions *post mortem*, the Hundred Rolls; also to the more important county histories and peerages, and to the family histories,
such as Gurney's *Record of the House of Gournay*, and Mr. Watson's
papers in the *Genealogist*.

In the following list I have taken the chief fiefs of 1172 as a basis,
and have started as a rule from the entry in the *Red Book of the
Exchequer*, which contains the list of 1172. I have added the fiefs of
some important officials, such as Richard of Fontenai, and Geoffrey
of Sai.

Delisle compiled a useful list of the more important baronies,
arranged according to dioceses (*Bibliothèque de l'Ecole des Chartes*,
xi, 400). I have found this helpful in making my selection.

---

[1] *Historiens de France*, xxiii, 705–14. The entries relating to Guérin of
Glapion show that it was compiled before Guérin's disgrace in 1208.

[2] *Ibid.*, 608g–612d. Register C was compiled 1211–20.

[3] *Ibid.*, 608–81.

[4] See Delisle's *Actes de Philippe Auguste*, pp. vi–xxv, for the Registers. In
the following pages I have for the sake of convenience treated the *scripta de
feodis* as though they presented the state of society in 1220; but it should be
remembered that this is the date of the register, not of the entries.

* William the Marshal, earl of Pembroke, did homage to Philip Augustus for his lands, but did not join him.

ABBREVIATIONS

B. of F. = Book of Fees; H. de F. = *Recueil des Historiens de France*, vol. xxiii; R.N. = *Rotuli Normanniae*; C.N. = *Cartulaire Normand*; R.B. = *Red Book of the Exchequer*; V.C.H. = *Victoria County Histories*; G.E.C. = G.E.C(okayne's) *Complete Peerage* (new edition); *Anglo-Norman Families* = Lewis C. Lloyd, *The Origins of Some Anglo-Norman Families*, edited by C. T. Clay and D. C. Douglas for the Harleian Society (Leeds, 1951).

L'AIGLE. The land of Gilbert of L'Aigle in Dorset was among the *Terrae Normannorum* in 1204 (R.N., 124). The lord of L'Aigle, Gilbert, or his successor, appears in lists of pledges after 1204 in Normandy (C.N., nos. 206, 366). For their charters, compare C.N., no. 366, note, and Stapleton, II, xlviii, note.

For the genealogy of the house cf. Round, *Calendar*, pp. 218, 225, 511. For the Norman barony, see the return of Richer of L'Aigle in R.B., ii, 629, H. de F., 709a (Crepon, Calvados, arr. Bayeux); and *ibid.*, 678 b.c. (L'Aigle).

The honour of *Aquila* in England was centred in Sussex. By 1212 it was confiscated (B. of F., 65, 71). The honour was granted to Gilbert Marshal in 1234 (*Cal. of Charter Rolls*, Henry III, i, 191).

ALENÇON. For the defection of Count Robert of Alençon or Séez, see above, p. 158. The count played a prominent part in Norman politics until his death (*Actes de Philippe-Auguste, passim*). In January, 1221, his heirs, the viscount of Châtellerault, Ella, the count's sister, and Robin Malet (his nephew) surrendered Alençon and other lands to Philip Augustus (*Actes*, no. 2028; C.N., no. 1126, p. 306).

The counts of Alençon, according to the return made by Robert III's father, John, in 1172, owed the service of 20 knights to the duke, and received the service of 111 knights (R.B., ii, 626). In the later part of the twelfth century Alençon and its castle were the seat of a bailiwick (above, p. 73, but the lordship of the counts within and without the town and bailiwick was very extensive: see C.N., nos. 122, 283, 340, 1126.

ARGENCES, Richard of. Richard, who had farmed the honour of Evreux in 1198, had joined Philip Augustus in 1202 (above, pp. 206, 174–5). He figures in the court of the Exchequer between 1209 and 1215 (*Jugements*, p. 251, note, and no. 153; see also C.N., nos. 124, 230). In May, 1205, Philip endowed him with the important fief of Ollonde (*q.v.*) and with other lands, including those of the Earl of Arundel at 'Buevilla' (C.N., no. 121; cf. H. de F., 620).

ARUNDEL, the earl of. The fiefs held by the earl of Arundel in Normandy were added to the ducal demesne by Philip Augustus (C.N., no. 113).

See Argences.

AUFFAI. In 1172 Richard of Auffai owed the service of 5 knights, and had 16 knights in his own service (R.B., ii, 627). In 1198, John of Auffai accounted at the Exchequer for the residue of his relief (*Rot. Scacc.*, ii, 422). The barony was divided between the king and William Martel after the conquest (see H. de F., 707j, 708a).

John died in or shortly before 1204, leaving a daughter as heiress of his English lands, the chief of which was the manor of Norton Ferris in Somerset (*Rot. Fin.*, 224). See B. of F., p. 81 and *Anglo-Norman Families*, p. 8.

AUMALE. The town and castle of Aumâle were occupied two or three times by Philip Augustus between 1193 and 1204 (above, pp. 97, 110 and notes). On the last occasion it was entrusted to Renaud of Boulogne who was afterwards invested with the county (*Actes*, nos. 884, 1217; C.N., no. 1155). On the title see G.E.C., i, 350 ff., and *Anglo-Norman Families*, p. 9.

Baldwin of Béthune, the last count of Aumâle to hold of the independent Norman dukes, was one of John's most faithful friends. See above, pp. 109–10, 296.

AUNOU. In 1172 Fulk of Aunou (Aunou-le-Faucon, south-east of Argentan) owed the service of 4 knights and had 34½ in his service.[5] His son, Fulk, succeeded him about 1195 (Stapleton, II, lxxxvii), and, after remaining loyal to John up to the last (cf. R.N., 106) submitted to Philip (H. de F., 619f; C.N., no. 326).

For the extensive lands of his family, which included places near Séez, in Auge and the Lieuvin, as well as near Argentan, see Round, *Calendar*, pp. 148, 155, 210, 243; and Stapleton, I, lxxv, II, cxxxix.

The Somerset family was different. See B. of F., 81; Collinson, *History of Somerset*, ii, 421, *s.v.* Compton-Dando.

BAQUEVILLE. This fief (Seine-Inferieure, arr. Dieppe) was held by the family of Martel. See Round, *Calendar*, p. 356; cf. *Geoffrey de Mandeville*, pp. 146, 416. In 1172 Geoffrey Martel owed the service of 2 knights and had 8⅓ in his service (R.B., ii, 629). In 1180 his fief was in the king's hands (*Rot. Scacc.*, i, 92), probably by reason of his heir's minority. William Martel, one of John's officials in 1203 and for a time Constable of Arques (*Rot. Pat.*, 22) joined Philip (C.N., no. 124), and his successors are found as lords of Baqueville (*ibid.*, no. 1216).[6] See also *Anglo-Norman Families*, *s.v.* Martel, pp. 60, 61.

BEAUFOU. In 1172 Richard of Beaufou (*Belfagus, Bellafagus*) owed the service of 2 knights and had in his service 6¾ (R.B., ii, 630). The

---

[5] This is the reading of Register A. The R.B. has 24½ knights (ii, 641).

[6] Cf. Anselme, *Histoire Genealogique de France*, viii, 209. On the other hand, the fief was for a time in the king's hands at a date after 1204, according to an addition in Register A to the list of 1172.

fief was held by Henry of Beaufou at the time of the conquest of Normandy (H. de F., 635e; R. N., 97).

For the fief in Norfolk granted by Henry I to Ralph de Beaufou, see B. of F., p. 129; cf. Blomefield and Parkin, *History of the County of Norfolk*, v. 1199).

BOHUN. There were two branches of this family. See *Anglo-Norman Families*, p. 16. Both families held extensive lands in England and Normandy, and both chose to remain in England after 1204. For their genealogy see Stapleton, II, xxii–xxxvi, and Round, *Calendar*, p. xlvi.

Bohun. The elder branch of the family owed the service of $2\frac{6}{7}$ knights and had in its service 7 knights (R.B., ii, 627). Saint-Georges de Bohon lies in the marshy district south of Carentan (Manche). In 1204 the barony was held by Engelger II, in virtue of a very complicated ancestry. His barony of Midhurst, in Sussex, was the main source of his family's importance in England (G.E.C., ii, 199).

Carentan. The younger or Carentan branch of the family owed the service of $2\frac{1}{7}$ knights in 1172, and had that of 2 knights (R.B., ii, 628). Henry, its representative in 1204, was created earl of Hereford by John.

In 1220 Bohon and Carentan were in the hands of Philip Augustus (H. de F., 608d, 611b, g).

BRICQUEBEC. According to Stapleton (I, xcii) the family of Bertram had its seat in Auge, at Roncheville-le-Bertrand, not at Bricquebec in the Cotentin. In 1180 Robert Bertram farmed the viscounty of Auge, apparently by hereditary right (*Rot. Scacc.*, i, 40). But the main strength of the barony lay in the Cotentin, where in 1172 Robert Bertram had $34\frac{1}{2}$ knights in his service, and owed the service of 5 knights (R.B., ii, 629). In 1202 his son, Robert, was a minor. Robert of Thibouville bought the wardship for £6,000 of Anjou (above, p. 238 n). This caused some confusion in 1204, for whereas Philip Augustus seized Robert's lands on the ground that he was in England with John (Round, *Calendar*, p. 528; C.N., no. 113), John seized his English lands on the ground that Robert of Thibouville, who held the heir, had deserted (R.N., 129).[7] In 1207, however, it is clear from the judgments of the Norman Exchequer (*Jugements*, no. 13) that Philip was respecting the boy's rights. For the state of the fief in 1220, revealing by the royal grants the effects of Robert's minority, see H. de F., 608–9. Later, as the husband of Joan, the daughter of Ralph Tesson, he became lord of Thury (Stapleton, II, lvi, ccx). See also Breard, *Cartulaire de Saint-Ymer-en-Auge et de Briquebec* (Soc. de l'hist. de Normandie, 1908), p. 183; Stapleton (I, xcii–iii, II, xxviii), and the charters in Round's *Calendar*, pp. 120, 341, 347, 423, 456.

Robert Bertram's English lands were confiscated (R.B., ii, 805;

---

[7] Robert of Thibouville lost his English lands (R.N., 125; *Rot. de Fin.*, 279).

Excerpta e Finibus, Henry III, p. 288). The Bertrams of the north of England, amongst whom the Christian name Robert was common, must be distinguished from the Norman family (G.E.C., ii, 159). The Robert Bertram with whom we have been concerned is described as 'Normannus' by the English records.

BRIOUZE. In 1172 William of Briouze owed the service of 3 knights for the honour (R.B., ii, 631). In Register A there is no comment upon this entry (H. de F., 695g), but Philip Augustus granted fees of the fief of Briouze in 1222 (C.N., no. 307; cf. no. 283). Briouze (*Braosa*) between Falaise and Domfront (Orne) was the *caput* of the Norman fief of the well-known William of Briouze, who is mentioned so frequently in these pages. His history is inextricably connected with that of John. For the genealogy of his family see Round, *Calendar*, especially pp. xlii–iii, 37–40, 395 *seqq.*; cf. *Anglo-Norman Families*, p. 20.

CAILLY. The history of this fief before and after 1204 is complicated, and is involved with the history of Baudemont, and the families of Longchamp, du Bois, and Vere. Cailly is between Saint-Saens and Rouen (Seine Inferieure). For a separate English family settled in Norfolk, see *Anglo-Norman Families*, p. 22, citing Farrer, *Honors and Knights' Fees*, iii, 382–4.

In 1172 Osbert, son of Roger of Cailly, owed the service of 2 knights (not 12, as in R.B., ii, 628) and also held 2 knights' fees in the barony of Saint-Saens (*ibid.*, p. 641, *English Historical Review*, xxvi, 92). In right of his wife he was lord of Baudemont, a castle in the châtellenie of Vernon, in the Vexin (Stapleton, II, cxii). Osbert died between 1189 and 1198.[8] He left two daughters, one of whom, Petronilla, was married to Stephen Longchamp, the other, Matilda, to Henry de Vere. It appears that Stephen received Baudemont as well as a share of the honour of Cailly, for in the treaty of Louviers in January, 1196, his actual or future possession is secured (C.N., no. 1057, p. 276); but the rights of Matilda were recognised later (Stapleton, II, cxvii, note). Henry de Vere died early, and Matilda was in 1204 the wife of Reginald du Bois.

The English lands attached to Baudemont which came to Osbert of Cailly through his wife, formed the manor and half hundred of Mutford in Suffolk (*ibid.*, II, cxii, and the passages there quoted).

In 1204 Reginald du Bois took the side of Philip and consequently lost his English lands at Lothingland in Suffolk (*ibid.*, II, cxiv–v). On the other hand Stephen Longchamp, except for a brief interval in November, 1205, retained his lands in England.[9] For a short time

[8] A charter of his, dated 1189, is mentioned by Stapleton (II, cxiii). On the exchequer roll of 1198 (ii, 418) Henry de Vere is stated to owe £100 'de relevio terre Osberti de Quaillie'.

[9] The conflicting writs relating to Stephen which are collected by Stapleton (II, cxv–vi) proves this. On November 13, 1205, he was at Rouen (C.N., no. 124; *Actes*, no. 961).

Reginald apparently got possession of the Cailly lands in Normandy (Register A; H. de F., 694j), while Stephen received Reginald's English lands and his share of the Baudemont inheritance at Mutford. The other half of Mutford was secured for Henry de Vere's son by Matilda, who was under age (Stapleton, II, cxv). But before 1213 Stephen had definitely attached himself to Normandy; he was present at the judgment upon the Tesson inheritance in that year (C.N., no. 230). He is said to have fallen on the French side at Bouvines. In the *Scripta* his son, Baudri, is said to be in possession of his lands and also of his share in the Cailly inheritance.[10] Baudri died before 1223 (see the necrology of the priory of Longueville; H. de F., 434c and note; *Jugements*, no. 358). The last survivor of these tangled events seems to have been Matilda, who describes herself in 1231 as 'vidua, domina de Cailli et de Baudemont' (C.N., no. 1146; p. 313).

The heir of Henry de Vere died young without heirs, and Mutford came back to the crown (Stapleton, II, cxvi). For Stephen of Longchamp's share see B. of F., 392, 403; *Rot. Claus.*, i, 448.

On the public career of Stephen of Longchamp see Stubbs, *Chronica Rogeri de Hoveden*, iii, p. xl; *Vie de Guillaume le Maréchal*, ed. Meyer, iii, 173, note; *L'Estoire de la Guerre Sainte*, ed. G. Paris, Index, *s.v.*; and above, p. 164, note 228 and p. 166, note 236.

I add a genealogical table:

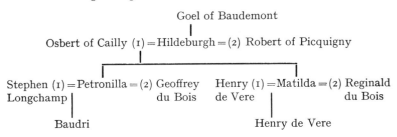

Goel of Baudemont

Osbert of Cailly (1) = Hildeburgh = (2) Robert of Picquigny

Stephen (1) = Petronilla = (2) Geoffrey   Henry (1) = Matilda = (2) Reginald
Longchamp   du Bois   de Vere   du Bois

Baudri   Henry de Vere

CHESTER, the Earl of: The earl owed the service of 10 knights for his honour, of which the chief seats were Briquessart, a few miles southwest of Bayeux, and Saint-Sever near Vire (Calvados). He had in his service $51\frac{7}{8}$ knights (R.B., ii, 626). After the conquest Philip Augustus laid hold of his lands (H. de F., 706f, j, 707a, d, 709b). He

---

[10] H. de F., 615a; cf. 717c. In the document entitled *Feoda Normanniae*, which is found in Registers A, B, C, D of Philip Augustus (*ibid.*, 705), and which obviously dates from the years immediately after the conquest, Stephen Longchamp and Reginald du Bois are said to hold Cailly (707 g, cf. 708j), and Baudemont is an escheat, in the hands of Robert of Picquigni, a baron of the honour of Vernon (711g, 714b). Robert was the second husband of Hildeburgh of Baudemont, the widow of Osbert of Cailly (Stapleton, II, cxiii, note). This document represents a transitory state of things after 1204. In another list Baudri of Longchamp appears as lord of fiefs near Vernon, which would be his in virtue of the Baudemont inheritance (H. de F., 717c).

gave Saint-Sever to André of Vitré and his brother (*Actes*, no. 1000). For other references to the earl's lands see C.N., no. 536, and *Jugements*, no. 232.

The earl of Chester was hereditary viscount of the Bessin, the Avranchin and the Vau de Vire. His scattered fiefs in Normandy deserve elaborate study. A great deal of material has been collected by Stapleton and Round. A description of his fiefs in 1220 in H. de F., 611e, 612e, 620g, 633h, 636g, h.

See Fougères.

CLARE, fiefs of Richard, earl of Clare or Hertford: Philip Augustus confiscated these in 1204 (C.N., no. 113). They consisted apparently of those Norman lands which had come to him in 1191 when the honour of the Earl Giffard was divided (*see* Longueville, and Stapleton, II, cxxxix). A list of fiefs of the honour of the earl is contained in the feodary drawn up shortly after the conquest (H. de F., 708, cf. 641 *passim*). Stapleton thinks that the 'terra Comitis Ricardi', which was situated in Saint-Saens and the neighbouring Omonville, and was in 1180 farmed by ducal agents, belonged to this earl of Hertford (*Rot. Scacc.*, i, 59; Stapleton, II, cxxxvii). But Richard had succeeded to the earldom in 1173, and no reason has been alleged for the confiscation of his Norman lands by Henry II. It is more probable that the lands at Saint-Saens had belonged to his cousin, Richard, earl of Pembroke, who had been involved in the civil war in the middle of the century.

See Montfort.

CLEVILLE. In 1172 Jordan du Hommet owed the service of 3 knights for *Clivilla*, and had the service of 13 knights. After 1204 this fief became ducal demesne (R.B., ii, 630; H. de F., 707a, 621a). Cleville is in Auge (Calvados, arr. Caen).

Jordan, who was constable of Séez, died in Palestine in 1192 (*Estoire de la Guerre Sainte*, ll. 4714–5, 10994). King Richard, in a letter to Tancred, November, 1190, calls Jordan 'constabularium nostrum' (*Ben. Pet.*, ii, 134).

In 1198 John, son of Jordan du Hommet, was an accomptant in the bailiwick of Lieuvin (*Rot. Scacc.*, ii, 374). Again, in 1203 the king ordered the bailiff of the Lieuvin to allow John du Hommet the tallage of his men in the bailiwick (R.N., 82).

Jordan, the brother of the constable William, is identified by Stapleton with the baron of 1172.

In 1204 John du Hommet had land at Sherringham in Norfolk (*Rot. Claus.*, i, 7); at this time it was apparently in the king's hands (September 5, 1204), but he had fined for his lands before the following June (*ibid.*, 38b; *Rot. Fin.*, 259). Though they were certainly in royal hands in 1207 (*Rot. Claus.*, 79b) John appears again in possession later (*Rot. Fin.*, 503, 586; R.B., ii, 533, 539, 552).

COLOMBIERES, fief of Philip of: In June 1204, Philip Augustus gave

Gérard de Merc the land of Philip of Colombières up to the annual value of £100 of Anjou (C.N., no. 88; *Recueil des actes de Philippe Auguste*, ii, 387, no. 808). For this baron see above, p. 166, note. His Norman lands were situated near Roumare, and were probably part of the fief of William of Roumare (Stapleton, II, clx).

Delisle notes that members of this family, bearing the same name, held lands in Normandy in the thirteenth century (C.N., no. 88, note; cf. H. de F., 736e). For the English barony of Philip, see B. of F., iii, 160 (Index., *s.v.* Columbers), and above, p. 166, note 235. As an opponent of John in 1215 he for a time lost his lands (*Rot. Claus.*, i, 231b, 237, 277, 308).

COURCI. The Norman honour of Courci was centred in the valley of the Dive (Calvados) at Courci and Ecajeul-sur-Dive. In 1172 William of Courci owed the service of 5 knights for the former and of 3 knights for the latter. In his own service he had 50 knights (R.B., ii, 627). In 1204 the honour was held by Robert of Courci, who stayed in Normandy (H. de F., 706d). He appears in various inquisitions and charters between 1205 and 1226 (C.N., nos. 124, 326, 1140). On the Norman lands see the charters in Round, *Calendar*, pp. 430–3, from the chartulary of Marmoutier, mostly in favour of the priory of Saint Vigor at Perrières, near Courci. Robert's English lands were situated at Bilsington in Kent (R.N., 140), and at Warblington and Emsworth in Hampshire. Bilsington was granted in 1207 to the earl of Arundel; Warblington and Emsworth to William Aguillun (Stapleton, *De antiquis legibus*, pp. xxxix–xl and notes). In the reign of Edward I, the latter fiefs came in touch again (through the Aguillun family) with the great English honour of Courci (*ibid.*), on which see Farrer, *Honors and Knights' Fees*, i, 103.

In his *Introduction* to the acts of Henry II (p. 440) Delisle distinguishes the Robert of Courci, who attests so many of Henry's charters, from the subject of this note.

CREULLY. This place, on the river Seulc to the east of Bayeux (Calvados),[11] was the seat of the honour which was held in 1172 by Richard, son of the earl of Gloucester (above, p. 183, note 27). The return of his service was omitted from the roll included in the *Red Book*, but is preserved by the Register A of Philip Augustus. He owed the service of 3 knights and had that of 11. His heir, Philip of Creully, died between 1198 and 1202. Geoffrey des Roches had the custody of his heir until he deserted John in 1202 (R.N., 62; *Rot. Pat.*, 23, 24, 25). John gave the office to Richard of Reviers, but after the loss of Normandy, Geoffrey des Roches regained possession (H. de F., 694h). In 1219 the lord of Tillières, once ward of Philip of Creully, had the honour, probably as the brother of Philip's wife. (See V.C.H., Surrey, iii, 291.) In 1220, Philip's younger brother Richard held Monthuchon (Manche), which was part of the honour,

---

[11] Perhaps the place which gave the name to the old *pagus Corilisus* (Stapleton, I, xlii).

z

of the lord of Tillières (Stapleton, II, xlv, note, lv, clxxvi). In 1272 Ralph of Creully held the fief (H. de F., 755c).

For the antecedents and extent of the honour see the charters in Round, *Calendar*, pp. 164, 336–8, 521, 535.

See Tillières.

ESNEVAL. In 1172 Robert of Esneval (Seine-Inferieure) owed the service of 3 knights and had that of 12¼ (R.B., ii, 630). In 1204 his son, Robert, was one of the Norman barons who signed the capitulation of Rouen and afterwards joined Philip Augustus (above, p. 261; C.N., no. 124; H. de F., 643d, 707h).

EU. The history of the county of Eu and of its count, Ralph of Exoudun, has frequently detained us (cf. above, p. 147, note). Ralph held the honour in right of his wife Alice, and was a Poitevin who did not long remain loyal to Philip, in spite of the precautions taken by the king (*Actes*, nos. 966, 1182, edited pp. 510, 515). He died in 1219, when his widow received the greater part of her honour of Eu from Philip (C.N., no. 276, p. 304). Owing no doubt to the services rendered to John and Henry III by Ralph of Exoudun, the countess of Eu retained possession of the vast English possessions of the honour until 1242, a few years before her death (see the valuable discussion in Stapleton, II, ccxxxii–ccxxxvi).[12] Alfonse of Brienne, the husband of her granddaughter, and his son John, made the well-known claim to possess Hastings and Tickhill in the years 1259 and 1290. See Stapleton, II, ccxxxvi and cf. above, p. 288.

FERRIERES. The Norman family of Ferrières, which must be distinguished from the English branch which had the earldom of Derby, had its seat at Ferrières-St. Hilaire in Eure, canton Broglie: see *Anglo-Norman Families*, pp. 10, 42 and Index, *s.v.* Ferrers. In 1172 Walchelin of Ferrières owed the service of 5 knights and had 42¾ in his service (R.B., ii, 630). He was with Richard during his captivity in January, 1194, at Speyer (Round, *Calendar*, p. 469), having been sent with treasure from Normandy (*Rot. Scacc.*, i, 249). He died in 1201 and was succeeded by his son Henry (*Rot. de Fin.*, 178; Stapleton, II, lxix). Henry joined Philip (C.N., no. 124; H. de F., 684e, 710c).

The English lands of this house included the manors of Oakham in Rutland and of Lechlade in Gloucestershire. Walchelin of Ferrières had given the latter to his other son Hugh. His daughter, Isabella, wife of Roger Mortimer of Wigmore, was after 1204 allowed a life interest in both manors (*Rot. Claus.*, i, 390b; Stapleton, II, cxxii–v, and the authorities there quoted). After her death they escheated to the crown as *terrae Normannorum*. See Banks, *Dormant and Extinct Baronage*, i, 75.

[12] She died in 1245 according to the chronicle of the Counts of Eu, H. de F., 442.

FONTENAI. Fontenai-le-Marmion (Calvados) is situated above the valley of the Laize, south of Caen, and was apparently held of the honour of Beaumont-le-Roger by Robert Marmion (H. de F., 710h). After 1204 Robert Marmion stayed in England, but his eldest son Robert, remained in Normandy (see his charters quoted by Delisle, C.N., no. 273, note, and no. 378, note, and Stapleton, II, civ). The latter's son, Philip, left Normandy for England, and in 1256 Joan, daughter of Ralph Tesson, had the disposition of the Norman fief in virtue of some relationship (Stapleton, II, cvii).

The circumstances under which Philip Marmion came to England are significant. Robert Marmion the elder died in 1218 leaving, in addition to Robert of Fontenai, another son Robert, by a second wife. In May, 1218, after his father's death, this second son Robert, made an elaborate fine with Henry III, whereby he was to hold the extensive English lands of his father 'until the lands of the English and Normans should be common to both' again.[13] On his elder brother's return, he would retire to the lands already granted to him by his father. Robert, the eldest son, availed himself of this arrangement in 1220 and, in spite of his tenure in Normandy, contrived to hold Tamworth and Scrivelsby of Henry III (*Rot. Claus.*, i, 442b; Stapleton, II, ciii–civ). This is one of the most striking cases of double tenure (above, p. 296). Both sons died shortly after 1240, and were succeeded by their sons Philip and William. Philip came to England in 1242. The cousins took opposite sides during the civil wars, Philip fighting for the king and William being an adherent of Simon de Montfort.

For more particulars see Stapleton, Banks, *op. cit.*, i, 129–31; D.N.B., xxxvi, 190. Through Philip Marmion's daughters, Tamworth and Scrivelsby passed ultimately to the families of Freville and Dymoke. The descendants of William, son of Robert Marmion, junior, were the lords of Witringham in Lincoln, and of West Tanfield in Yorkshire.

FONTENAI, Richard of: Richard was perhaps the most important local official in Normandy during the last year of John's rule (above, pp. 248, 253). His connection with the family of Marmion is not stated, but it is curious that he was connected with the same family by marriage as was Robert Marmion, the elder son of Robert the elder.[14]

---

[13] *Excerpta e rotulis finium*, i, 9, 10. 'Robertus Marmiun junior finem fecit cum domino Rege per quingentas libras pro habenda custodia castri de Tameworth et terrarum que fuerunt Roberti patris sui, unde fuit saisitus die quo obiit *quousque terre Anglie et Normannie sint communes, ita quod Anglici habeant terram suam in Normannia et Normanni terras suas in Anglia*, et si forte antequam terre predicte sint communes supradicto modo, Robertus frater ejus senior veniat ad pacem domini Regis,' etc.

[14] Robert Marmion married Juliana, and the son of Richard of Fontenai married Matilda, both daughters of Philip of Vassy (Stapleton, II, civ; Lechaudé d'Anisy in *Mémoires de la Société des Antiquaires du Normandie*, viii, part 2, p. 56).

340   THE LOSS OF NORMANDY

In 1204–5 Philip Augustus endowed him with lands in the Côtentin (*Recueil des actes de Philippe Auguste*, ii, no. 881; cf. H. de F., 611h), and he appears constantly in the records of the Norman Exchequer after the conquest (*Jugements*, nos. 233, 244, 299, 352; and notes to pp. 267, 291).

FOUGERES, fiefs of William of: For the confiscation of William's lands in Normandy by John see above, p. 166. In right of his wife Clementia, the grand-niece of William, Randle, earl of Chester claimed Ipplepen (in Devon) and other possessions of the house of Fougères in England. They were granted, but with the qualification that they were 'not of just right annexed to his honour' (Stapleton, II, cc).

GACE. The honour of Gacé, near Argentan (Orne), was held in 1172 by Amauri of Sablé by the service of 3 knights. He had 11½ in his service (R.B., ii, 629). He was succeeded by Lisiard and by Peter of Sablé, who died in 1195 and 1203 respectively (Stapleton, II, lii). In 1203 Reginald du Bois had the custody of the heirs (R.N., 114). The family remained in Normandy. According to Register A, Guy of Sablé had the honour shortly after the conquest (H. de F., 695b) perhaps as guardian of the 'heres de Gaci' (*ibid.*, 684g). In 1227 Amauri was lord of Gacé (C.N., no. 366).

GISORS, fief of John of: The baron held an extensive honour in the French and Norman Vexin near Gisors (see the list of his fiefs in 1220, H. de F., 630, and the inquest into the fiefs of the archbishop of Rouen, in C.N., no. 202). After the loss of the Vexin, or rather the valley of the Epte, in Richard's reign, John's Norman lands escheated, so far as they were in the duke's power (cf. *Rot. Scacc.*, ii, 306, 'firma terre Johannis de Gisorz' (1198), and above, p. 176). See Stapleton, II, xxxvi–viii, for his family and lands; also C.N., no. 517, note. His Sussex lands ultimately went to Hugh of Gournai (B. of F., 618; and see *Anglo-Norman Families*, pp. 45–6).

GLOUCESTER, fiefs of the earl of: The Norman fief of the Earl of Gloucester had its centre at Sainte-Scolasse (Orne, arr. Alençon), the chief tenant being the lord of le Mesle-sur-Sarthe (H. de F., 618e; cf. also 611j, 619k, 620d, 715c). The fief came to King John in right of his wife, but a great part of it, together with the title of earl, went to Amauri, count of Evreux, after the loss of Evreux (C.N., no. 54; R.N., 92). Amauri's father had married the eldest daughter of Earl William. On his career see Stapleton, II, clxiii.

GOURNAI. Hugh of Gournai and his father before him held the honour of Gournai by the service of 12 knights and with the duty of defending the March with their other knights (R.B., ii, 628; cf. *Rot. Scacc.*, ii, 416, 551). In Register A the entry on the list of fees is subpuncted for deletion, and in later registers of Philip Augustus it is omitted

(R.B., ii, 628, note; H. de F., 694, note). After its conquest in 1202 Gournai became a royal castle (C.N., no. 209). Saint Louis refers in one of his charters (March, 1248) to his palace at Gournai (*ibid.*, no. 1180). Ecouché, near Argentan, is stated by Stapleton (II, lxxxv) to have been part of the honour, and seems to have been in royal hands in 1220 (C.N., nos. 283, 284, 307).

For Hugh of Gournai see above, pp. 108, 285. For the extent of his honour on the borders of Normandy in the valleys of the Epte and Bresle, and in the dioceses of Amiens and Beauvais, see Stapleton, I, cii, clxxix; and the authorities named in Tardif, *Coutumiers*, I, ii, p. lii, note. The distribution of his Norman lands outside Brai, which had been commenced by John in 1203 (R.N., 82, 94, 95) was continued by the French kings (C.N. nos. 134, 771).

In May, 1203, the lands of Hugh in Norfolk and Suffolk had been granted to John the Marshal (R. N., 92), and in June, Wendover was granted to Ralph of Tilly (*Rot. de Liberate*, 45, 74). After his reconciliation with John in 1206 (*Rot. Pat.*, 57b) Hugh was reinstated, as the inquisition of 1212 shows (R.B., ii, 477, 537). In 1208 he appears in possession of the soke of Waltham (*Rot. Pat.*, 85; R.B., ii, 523) formerly held by Alan FitzCount. In Sussex, of the lands of the Normans, he had the manor of Berlinges, once the land of John of Gisors, *extraneus* (*ibid.*, ii, 803).

Mapledurham and Petersfield were the dowry of his daughter on her marriage with Amauri, earl of Gloucester (Stapleton, I, cxliv).

GRAVENCHON-EN-CAUX (Seine-Inferieure) was an honour of the counts of Evreux, and remained to the counts after the loss of Evreux until 1204, when Philip Augustus added it to his demesne (C.N., 113). For its content see H. de F., 705h.

GRAVILLE. Graville, *Geraudeville, Girardivilla*, near Harfleur (Seine-Inferieure), was the *caput* of the Malet barony in Normandy: for the early history of the family in Normandy and England, see *Anglo-Norman Families*, pp. 29, 30, 40, 56. In 1172 Matthew of Graville [*i.e.*, Matthew Malet?] held Graville by the service of 4 knights. He had 12½ knights in his service (R.B., ii, 629). In 1204 William Malet was the lord of Graville. His wife was Philippa, daughter of the count of Alençon, and when he died, soon after the conquest, he left her with a son Robin or Robert. This Robert Malet was, through his mother, one of the heirs to the honour of Alençon (C.N., nos. 284, 1126, 1140, 1149). On his father's death, he was a minor, and Graville was for some time in the custody of his mother's third husband, William of Préaux, brother of Peter of Préaux (H. de F., 695c, 708c, g). On the Norman and English lands of William Malet and his successors see Stapleton, II, cxli–cxlvii *passim*.

The history of the English fiefs of the honour of Graville is interesting. In 1204, Lilley in Hertfordshire and Coleby in Lincolnshire were seized as *terrae Normannorum*, which belonged to William Malet (R.N., 129; cf. B. of F., 14, 124, 188; *Rot. Claus.*, i, 283b; Stapleton,

II, cxlii). William of Préaux, who had at first stayed in Normandy (cf. R. N., 126) came to England late in John's reign and received seisin of Coleby in right of his wife Philippa (cf. *Rot. Claus.*, i, 233). He thus maintained for a time a connection between the English and Norman fiefs of the honour of Graville. Robert Malet, who had lived in Normandy (C.N., nos. 416, 426) is said by Stapleton to have done homage to Henry III for his ancestral lands at Lilley and Coleby in 1242 (II, cxlvi). This statement is not borne out by the records. In 1242 Robert Malet *lost* Coleby, which had previously been restored to him (*Cal. of Patent Rolls*, 1232–47, p. 336. Cf. *Charter Rolls*, Henry III, i, 276, 338).

This family must be distinguished from the Malets of Somersetshire.

LA HAIE-DU-PUITS. La Haie was the *caput* of the honour of Plessis in the Côtentin, which was held in 1172 by Ralph of la Haie by the service of 2½ knights. He also owed the service of a knight for the fief of Créances, near La Haie-du-Puits, which belonged to the honour of Mortain. He had 6½ knights in his service (R.B., ii, 632). In 1204 Robert of La Haie left Normandy and settled on his English lands, of which the honour of Burwell in Lincolnshire was the chief (*Rot. de Fin.*, 286; B. of F., 166, 175; Stapleton, II, ccxxxix). In consequence the honour of La Haie or Plessis was added to the ducal demesne (H. de F., 695j).

The charters in Round's *Calendar* contain some information upon the earlier history of the family. See also *Anglo-Norman Families*, p. 51.

HAMBYE. Hambye (Manche, arr. Coutances) and Bréhal (*ibid.*) were the chief fiefs of Fulk Paynel. His large honour in the Côtentin, partly held of the abbot of Mont-Saint-Michel, is described at length in the feodary of 1220 (H. de F., 610c). In spite of their vacillation, he and his son Fulk retained their Norman lands. In 1205 Fulk had joined Philip (C.N., no. 124); his English lands at Bingham in Nottinghamshire appear in the list of *terrae Normannorum* in 1204 (R.N., 141; B. of F., 152, 230; *Rot. Claus.*, i, 6, 7b).

See Round, *Calendar*, pp. 325, 444, 537; Stapleton, II, xlvi, note. *See* Saint-Sauveur.

HARCOURT. The lord of Harcourt, near Brionne (Eure) owed service to the honour of Beaumont-le-Roger, and held only 1 knight's fee in chief of the duke (R.B., ii, 641; H. de F., 710k). In 1204 Robert of Harcourt was still living, but he was succeeded by his son Richard before 1208 (Stapleton, II, ccix). Richard, as the husband of Matilda, the youngest daughter of Ralph Tesson, was, after 1213, lord of Saint-Sauveur-le-Vicomte (H. de F., 609d; Stapleton, II, lv, ccx, cclxxx). He died between 1236 and 1242 (H. de F., 725g, 728d).

Richard of Harcourt's relations with England are important. In 1204 his father had possessed the manors of Sileby and Burstall (Leicestershire), Sherston (Wiltshire), Wellingborough (Northamptonshire), Ludham (Suffolk), Ilmington (Warwickshire), and Bensington (Oxfordshire). In 1204 these lands were confiscated (R.N., 132, 135, 138, 139, 140). His son John held Rothley in Leicestershire, and this also was confiscated (R.N., 139). Both Richard and John of Harcourt made overtures to the king in 1206 (*Rot. Pat.*, 57b; Stapleton, II, cciv), but only John returned to England and received possession of his own and the ancestral lands between 1211 and 1215 (*ibid.*, ccvi; *Rot. Claus.*, i, 115b, 210). He died before Damietta in 1219 (*Rot. Claus.*, i, 402b). In the following year Richard, the elder brother who lived in Normandy, got seisin of the Harcourt lands in England for £500 (*Excerpta e rotulis finium*, i, 58; Rot. Claus., i, 445), and retained them until 1236 (Stapleton, II, ccvii) when he lost them, owing perhaps to his share in the campaign undertaken by Saint Louis in that year (H. de F., 725g). His son John succeeded for a time in securing Ilmington, which had gone to Simon de Montfort: he defended Simon in 1260 against the charge of treason.[15] This is an interesting illustration of the effect produced by the civil wars upon the *terrae Normannorum*. Ilmington afterwards came to the Montforts; Dugdale, *Warwickshire* (ed.1730), i, 629; cf. ii, 799.

The Norman family here described must be distinguished from the English family of Harcourt.

See Saint-Sauveur.

LE HOMMET. In 1172 Richard du Hommet owed the service of 3½ knights, and had the service of 18 knights (R.B., ii, 630). His eldest son William, who succeeded him as constable of Normandy, joined Philip and was living in possession of this honour in 1220 (H. de F., 609j). His English lands in Northamptonshire were confiscated in 1204 (R.N., 134; cf. *Rot. Claus.*, i, 28b; and for other lands B. de F., Index).[16] Stamford, which had been granted to his father in 1173, went to Earl Warenne (above, p. 296, *Rot. Claus.*, i, 37).

Through his mother William and his brother Enguerrand succeeded to the honour of Remilly (Manche). This was held by Enguerrand in parage (H. de F., 609k).

The various connections of the members of this family with each other and with other families are too complicated to be dealt with here.

LEICESTER, honour of the earls of: In 1204 the honour included Breteuil and, through Petronilla, the mother of Robert IV, Grandmésnil (Calvados, arr. Lisieux). It had been stripped of Paci-sur-Eure in 1194 (above, p. 107) but was still of vast extent. In 1172 it had contained 121 knights (R.B., ii, 627). According to the life of the Marshal, Robert IV was prepared to come to an arrangement about his Norman fiefs in 1204 (above, p. 294), but he died in October

[15] See a chronicle, probably of Evesham, in Leland, *Collectanea*, ed. Hearne (1715), i, 245—an interesting passage.
[16] His loyalty to Philip was not above suspicion, for he had to find pledges (C.N., no. 204).

(Bémont, *Simon de Montfort*, p. 2). Philip Augustus added his lands to the demesne (C.N., Nos. 99, 100, 113, 209). See the full entries in the Registers and the *Feoda Normanniæ* (H. de F., 616–17, 705–6, 714–15).

LITTEHAIRE. Under this heading the 'honor de Luthare et de Oireval' (*Rot. Scacc.*, ii, 521) may be treated. It belonged in 1172 to William of Orval (Manche) and was held by the service of 2½ knights (R.B., ii, 628). Through Mabilia of Orval the honour came to her husband Adam of Port and their son, William of Port, or as he is called afterwards, of Saint-Jean (*Rot. Scacc.*, ii, 530; Stapleton, I, clx, II, xii). Adam and his son followed John to England, and the honour came into Philip's hands. In Register A, the words 'Rex et comes Bolonie habent'[17] are inserted after the entry relating to William of Orval (H. de F., 694h). In the feodary of 1220 it is given as part of the demesne (*ibid.*, 610k).

For further references to Adam of Port *see* Saint-Jean-le-Thomas.

LONGUEVILLE. Longueville (Seine-Inferieure, arr. Dieppe) was the *caput* in Normandy of the honour of Earl Giffard. The division of the lands of Earl Walter in 1191 has already been mentioned (above, p. 304, note). William the Marshal retained possession of Longueville after 1204 (above, p. 260; H. de F., 708d), and the place was in the hands of his widow and sons in 1219 (C.N., no. 1120, p. 304). The honour of Earl Giffard had comprised nearly 100 knights in 1172 (R.B., ii, 633; for a somewhat different statement *see* H. de F., 696b).

See also Clare, Orbec.

MEULAN. The history of the count of Meulan in 1204 and the next few years suggests a story of great misfortune. Owing to the fact that they were vassals of the king of France his predecessors had never been able to retain uninterrupted possession of their Norman lands (cf. above, pp. 71, 181). They were closely connected with the greatest Norman families (Delisle, *Robert de Torigni, passim*, Stapleton, II, cxcvii–viii) and some of their vassals, as the Marmions and Harcourts, were among the most powerful feudatories in the duchy. The honour stretched along the valley of the Risle, at Pont-Audemer, Brionne and Beaumont-le-Roger. Count Robert was so unfortunate as to become reconciled with John for the last time in April, 1203 (*Rot. Pat.*, 27). A month later his son Peter betrayed Beaumont-le-Roger to Philip Augustus, and lost his Norman lands and English benefices (above, p. 161). Robert was obliged by his circumstances to pledge his Norman lands for 5000 marks and to retain only a contingent interest in them (*Rot. Chart.*, 105; Stapleton, II, cci). On May 1, 1204, the count, who was an old man, divested himself

---

[17] The Court of Boulogne's share in the honour was perhaps due to a connection between it and his honour of Mortain.

of all his lands in France, Normandy and England in favour of his daughter Mabiria, wife of William, earl of the Isle of Wight (*ibid.*). This act apparently took place at Préaux, near Rouen. Neither Philip nor John was disposed to pay any heed to this attempt on the part of the count to transmit his honour intact. The eldest son, Waleran, had been killed during a pilgrimage (*ibid.*, II, cxcix), Peter, the traitor, was dead, Mabiria a woman. Philip Augustus excluded the count from his peace proposals (Teulet, *Layettes*, i, 250)[18] and John's officials enrolled Stourminster, the *caput* of his English lands, among the *terrae Normannorum* (R.N., 141; cf. *Rot. de Fin.*, 279, for Lincolnshire lands). In France and Normandy all knowledge of him was lost (Stapleton, II, cciii). He lived for a few years, dependent on John's charity. His wife Matilda was rather more fortunate, since she possessed lands in Cornwall in right of her father, Reginald, earl of Cornwall. Her attempt in 1219 to recover Stourminster in right of dower led to an interesting suit: see *Curia Regis Rolls*, 3–4 Henry III (1938), 116, 266. 'Apparently Mabiria . . . alone of their issue, left posterity, and through her the representation of the *Comtes* de Meulan will have ultimately vested in the family of Courtenay.'

The Norman honour owed the service of 15 knights and comprised 63 (R.B., ii, 626; Register A reads 73). It was added to the demesne (C.N., no. 113).[19] Its contents are specified in the *Feoda Normanniae* (H. de F., 712–13. King Philip did not admit the claims of Ralph of Meulan, son of Waleran and nephew of Peter, to succeed to Beaumont-le-Roger and Brionne, but assigned him Courseulles-sur-mer (Calvados) This recompense was confirmed and enlarged by King Louis in August, 1255, 'in consideration of his noble ancestry'.[20]

MONTBRAI [in this period Monbrei or Molbrai]. In 1172 Nigel of Montbrai owed the service of 5 knights for Montbrai (Manche, arr.

[18] This receives confirmation from an inquisition of 1230, 'quomodo boscus de Pomeria, quem Johannes de Bosco petit, venit ad manum domini regis' (C.N., no. 1143). One witness said that the wood had been given to Osbert, the father of the petitioner, by the count of Meulan. This was one of many gifts, and later the count 'recessit in Angliam cum rege Johanne. Rex antem Philippus *inhibuit quod dona que dictus comes facerat tempore dicti J. regis nullatenus tenerentur*, excepto dono quod fecerat dicto Johanni de Pratellis et Guillelmo de Hoxeia', and, we may add, the lands given to Richard of Harcourt; see the next note.

[19] Elboeuf, which Count Robert had granted to Richard of Harcourt was excepted. (*Rot. Chart.*, i, 104; C.N., no. 371).

[20] C.N., nos. 536, 537. In a letter dated August 25, 1925, the late Lewis C. Loyd pointed out to me that the details of Ralph's ancestry and claims, as son of the brother of Peter (whereas Gui de la Roche, whom King Philip had favoured in 1203, was the son of a sister of Peter), are contained in a *querimonia* made by Ralph in 1247: see *Recueil des Historiens de France*, xxiv, p. 38, no. 286. Ralph's descendants in the male line continued at Courseulles until 1463.

St. Lo) and Chateau-Gontier (Mayenne) and had $11 + \frac{1}{4} + \frac{1}{7}$ knights in his service (R.B., ii, 629). William of Monbrai left Normandy in 1204, and the honour came to the king (H. de F., 707b, e). Philip still held it in 1220 (*ibid.*, p. 619k), but Andrew of Vitré got it in 1231 (C.N., no. 1147; cf. H. de F., 737a).

For William of Mowbray's English lands see *Rot. de Fin.*, 102, 174; R.B., ii, 490, 551. For his origin and descendants, see G.E.C., v, 410, ix, 368. Cf. *Anglo-Norman Families, s.v.* Mowbray, p. 71.

MONTFORT, honour of Hugh of: In 1172 Robert of Montfort owed the service of 6 knights for Coquainvilliers (Calvados) and $2\frac{1}{2}$ for Orbec (q.v.), and in the former he had in his service $33 + \frac{1}{3} + \frac{1}{4}$ knights' fees (R.B., ii, 627). Robert died in 1179 and his wife paid a heavy fine for the custody of the lands and her children (Stapleton, I, xc). In 1204 Coquainvilliers was held by Hugh of Montfort (*Rot. Chart.*, 34). Hugh was in John's favour up to the last (cf. R.N., 121; Stapleton, II, lxvii), but disappears from the records after the middle of 1204.[21] In 1207 Philip assigned rents to the value of £100 in the land which Hugh had held at Coquainvilliers to Guy of Auteuil (*Actes*, no. 1027; cf. C.N., nos. 160, 403, 611). For a statement of his fiefs see H. de F., 634g, 711a.

The house of Montfort took its name from Montfort-sur-Risle, one of the fiefs of the count of Meulan. It should be noted that the honour of Montfort was quite distinct from that of Coquainvilliers and came to the duke in 1161 (*Robert of Torigni*, ed. Delisle, ii, 38, 77). Robert of Montfort and Hugh his son were castellans of Montfort several times before and after 1180, but 'solius nomine custodiae' (Stapleton, I, cxviii; above, p. 181). On the relation between the families of Meulan and Montfort see Delisle's notes to his edition of Robert of Torigni (i, 163, 224, 282). Montfort was of course annexed to the demesne in 1204 (C.N., no. 209; the phrase in no. 113 'honor de Montforti qui fuit Hugonis de Montforti' refers to Coquainvilliers). On its service see R.B., ii, 642–3; H. de F., 710d; and above, p. 219, note.

MONTPINÇON. In 1172 Hugh of Montpinçon (Calvados, arr. Lisieux) held the honour by the service of 3 knights; he had in his service 12 knights (R.B., ii, 628). In 1204 Philip Augustus gave the honour to Guérin of Glapion (*Recueil des Actes de Philippe Auguste*, ii, no. 793; H. de F., 707b). In 1220 it was an escheat (*ibid.*, 620d).

In 1236 a Fulk de Monte Pinzin was tenant of the barony of Valoines in Essex and Norfolk (B. of F., 579; cf. Giles de Munpincham, pp. 903, 904, 911).

MORTAIN. The county was granted by Philip to Renaud of Dammartin, count of Boulogne (C.N., no. 107), and came to Philip's son, Philip

---

[21] There is a reference in *Rot. Claus.*, i, 50 (September, 1205), to lands which he had held in Kent.

Hurepel through the latter's marriage with Renaud's daughter Matilda (*Actes*, nos. 1217, 2158; C.N., no. 1121). On the younger Philip's death in 1235, the honour was divided into three lots (C.N., no. 412) of which the king took two, while Matilda was left in possession of one, including Mortain without the castle. Renaud had lost control of the castle in 1211 (*Actes*, nos. 1299–1301).

MORTEMER. The castle of Mortemer (Seine-Inferieure, arr. Neufchâtel) had been taken from the family of Mortemer by the Conqueror and given to William of Warenne (Stapleton, II, cxx–cxxi). It remained one of the chief seats of the honour of Warenne in Normandy until 1202, when it was taken by Philip and given to Renaud of Boulogne (above, p. 149). In 1204 Philip resumed possession of it (C.N., no. 93; *Actes*, no. 884; above, p. 275), and it became part of the demesne (C.N., no. 209). On June 4, 1202, John gave to the young Earl Warenne as much of Renaud of Boulogne's land at Lillebonne, as Renaud possessed of his (R.N., 47).

The other fiefs of the Earl Warenne were confiscated by Philip in 1204 (C.N., no. 113). They comprised Bellencombre and various lands in Caux and other districts of Normandy (cf. H. de F., 643a, 714h). Varenne, which gave its name to this great Anglo-Norman family, is situated near Bellencombre (arr. Dieppe).

On the Earl Warenne of 1204, see above, pp. 152, 296.

See Saint-Victor.

MORTEMER, William of: This great official, who had defended Verneuil in 1194 and Arques in 1202 (above, pp. 101, 152) and was in 1203 bailiff of La Londe and of Caux (Stapleton, II, cclx) joined Philip Augustus after the capitulation of Arques in 1204 (C.N., nos. 124, 230). He was alive in 1217 (*Jugements*, p. 291, note). He was a tenant of the honour of Montfort (Stapleton, II, cclx) and of Breteuil (H. de F., 714f) as well as in Caux. See H. de F., 644m, 645l, 710e.

MOUTIERS-HUBERT. Moutiers-Hubert (Calvados) lies just on the border of the department in the old archdeaconry of Gacé (Stapleton, I, cxxi). It was the *caput* of the honour of Hugh Paynel, who in 1172 owed the service of 5 knights and had 6 in his service (R.B., ii, 627). In 1180 his son Peter was a debtor for a fine of £500 'pro terra patris sui' (*Rot. Scacc.*, i, 89). Hugh, according to Stapleton (l.c.) had taken the vows of a monk. By 1204 Peter had apparently been succeeded by another Hugh. Philip Augustus added the honour to his demesne (C.N., no. 113). References to the fiefs of Hugh Paynel are to be found in the list of 1220 (H. de F., 616g, 621d), and in earlier documents (*ibid.*, 706b, h, 709d, 710c, d, 715b).

For Hugh Paynel and his English lands at West Rasen, *see* Loyd, *Anglo-Norman Families*, p. 77.

MOYON. In 1172 William of Moyon (Manche, arr. St. Lô) owed the service of 5 knights and had 11 knights in his service (R.B., ii, 629).

In 1204 Reginald of Moyon remained with John, and Moyon was granted to Guérin of Glapion (*Recueil des actes de Philippe Auguste,* ii, no. 793). After Guérin's disgrace, the king had the honour (H. de F., 611g).

The seat of the English honour of Mohun was at Dunster in Somerset (B. of F., 83, 262; G.E.C., ix, 17 ff.).

Moyon charters in Round, *Calendar,* pp. 173–8, 282–3.

NEGREVILLE. Négreville (Manche, arr. Valognes) was the seat of the Norman honour of the Wake family. According to the *Scripta de feodis,* it was held about 1220 by the count of Ponthieu (H. de F., 608h. 612d; Stapleton, II, clxxxi). In 1204 the heir was Baldwin Wake, whose mother was the daughter of William du Hommet, the constable. The constable had bought the wardship of the English and Norman lands for 1000 marks in 1201 (*Rot. de Fin.,* 169; Stapleton, II, clxxx).

Baldwin's English lands lay in Lincolnshire (B. of F., 182, 187, etc.). He chose to stay in England after 1204 (cf. *Rot. Claus.,* i, 6).

NEHOU. Néhou (Manche) had come to a Vernon branch of the family of Réviers or Redvers (Round, *Calendar,* p. 314; Stapleton, II, cclxix–cclxxx *passim*). In 1172 Richard of Vernon, in addition to his honour of Vernon held Néhou by the service of 10 knights and had 30 knights in his service (R.B., ii, 630). His grandson Richard, who lost Vernon in 1195 (above, pp. 107, 108), retained Néhou after the loss of Normandy (H. de F., 609h; cf. C.N., no. 204). For later charters of his family see C.N., no. 520n.

The name Vernon was used also by some members of the Redvers family in England. Cf. *Anglo-Norman Families,* p. 75 and Stapleton, II, cxlv, note.

Distinguish the Norman Richard of Vernon from the Richard of Vernon who held lands in Derbyshire and Buckinghamshire (R.B., ii, 584).

NEUBOURG. In 1172 Henry of Neubourg owed the service of 10 knights and had 15 $\frac{1}{16}$ in his service (R.B., ii, 630). His heir is mentioned on the exchequer roll of 1198 (*Rot. Scacc.,* ii, 462). This Henry of Neubourg joined Philip) cf. C.N., nos. 205, 230). In B. of F., 1416 (a, 1248), there is a reference to lands in Berkshire which had once belonged to a Norman of this name.

In 1220 the lord of Neubourg held only 2$\frac{1}{2}$ knights' fees at Neubourg (H. de F., 636a). The main strength of Henry lay at Annebecq (Calvados, arr. Vire).[22] In 1220 he stated that he owed the service of 2$\frac{1}{2}$ knights and possessed 22$\frac{3}{4}$ knights' fees at Annebecq (H. de F., 618m). In 1195, perhaps in the minority of the lord of Neubourg, this land seems to have been in the hands of Guérin of Glapion (*Rot.*

[22] Stapleton erroneously identifies it with St. Georges-d'Annebecq (Orne, near Briouze).

Scacc., i, 246); and in the year 1202 the honour of Neubourg was also at King John's disposal, either through the minority or the young lord's defection (see the references to Neubourg and Annebecq in Stapleton, I, clxix; II, lxx; R.N., 56; 52, 53, 60).

NONANT. In 1172 two members of the family of Nonant (Orne, arr. Argentan) held fiefs of the duke (R.B., ii, 630, 632; H. de F., 695d, j).[23] The more important of these was Guy who held 11¼ fees by the service of one knight. In the *Feoda Normanniae*, compiled shortly after 1204, Henry of Nonant, Guy's successor, is said to have held 6 fees by the service of 1, and Renaud 4½ by the same service (*ibid.*, 706e). The king had the barony of Henry, but Guérin of Glapion had received some of his outlying lands to the extent of 4⅔ fiefs (*ibid.*, 620b, c).[24] All these, with the exception of Renaud's lands, were in the king's hands in 1220 (*ibid.*, 620b, 636e, f). Renaud apparently handed on his fief to the barons of Nonant who are found in Normandy during the thirteenth century (*e.g., ibid.*, 756j).

Henry of Nonant's ancestors were lords of Totnes in Devonshire. Henry stayed in England. The English honour was divided between him and Reginald of Briouze. Henry was apparently dead in 1207 (*Rot. Claus.*, i, 80). See also V.C.H., Devon, i, 559. In 1212 Henry FitzCount had Totnes (B. of F., 98).

OLLONDE. Ollonde (Manche, arr. Coutances) was the seat of the honour of the Norman family of Mandeville (*Magnavilla*). For their ancestry see Stapleton, II, clxxxviii–cxc; and the Montebourg charters in Round, *Calendar*, pp. 313 *seqq.*; also *Anglo-Norman Families*, for corrections, pp. 57–8.

In 1172 Roger of Mandeville owed the service of 2½ knights and had the service of 3 (R.B., ii, 635). His son William died between 1195 and 1198 (*Rot. Scacc.*, i, 144; ii, 476, 479). William's daughter and heiress, Joan, was given in marriage with her lands to Matthew FitzHerbert (R.N., 51, 96; cf. Round, *Calendar*, p. 316). After the separation Matthew FitzHerbert and his successors became lords of the English lands, of which the *caput* was Earl's Stoke in Wiltshire. Ollonde was given by Philip Augustus to Richard of Argences (C.N., no. 121 and *Recueil des Actes de Philippe Auguste*, ii, no. 903) and was held in 1220 by William of Argences (H. de F., 608d, 609a, j, 611f).

[23] According to the Red Book (ii, 630, 632) three persons of this name held fiefs. Roger held 11¼, John 3½ and Guy 11¼ fees, each by the service of one knight. But in the text preserved by Register A, the entry concerning John is omitted, and Roger's 11¼ fees are given as 3½. It looks as though the Red Book had confused the entries, and that Guy and Roger were the only tenants.

[24] If Henry's six fees near Nonant (detailed, p. 636f, g) are added to the 4⅔ fees which are detailed as having gone to Guérin of Glapion, and to the extra fee (4½ instead of 3½) which had gone between 1172 and 1204 to Renaud of Nonant (cf. 636e) we have 11⅔, approximately the 11¼ which belonged to Guy in 1172. This calculation assumes that Renaud was Roger's successor, and that Roger had held only 3½ fees. See the last note.

ORBEC. In 1172 the honour of Orbec (Calvados, arr. Lisieux) was held by Robert of Montfort (*see* Montfort), but it was originally in the possession of the family of Clare, and came back to the family in the reign of Henry II. It was the seat of William the Marshal's honour in Normandy, and was retained by him in 1204–5 (C.N., no. 74; H. de F., 708e; above, p. 260).

PAVILLY. In 1172 Roger of Pavilly (Seine Inferieure, arr. Rouen) owed the service of 2 knights (R.B., ii, 632). He also owed service at Lions (p. 636). His successor, in 1204, was Thomas of Pavilly, who after joining in the capitulation of Rouen (Teulet, *Layettes*, i, 250) remained in Normandy (C.N., no. 124). On his fief see H. de F., 615h, 707g.

The Wiltshire family of this name was by this time distinct. It was connected, however, with the Malets of Graville (Stapleton, II, cxliii, note; *Rot. Fin.*, 49).

See, further, *Anglo-Norman Families*, p. 77.

PREAUX. In 1204 John of Préaux was lord of Préaux (Seine-Inferieure, arr. Rouen). He was the eldest of a large family of brothers, the sons of Osbert of Préaux, and he often appears in official records before and after 1204 (cf. C.N., nos. 124, 167, 204, 230; H. de F., 684f, 707h; Stapleton, II, Index, *s.v.*). In 1220, the fief was held by Peter, presumably the son of John; also 3 knights' fees. The description of his fief shows that, apart from his demesne, 7 knights' fees were held of him (H. de F., p. 614j).

John's English lands were confiscated (R.N., 135, 138, 140, 142; cf. *Rot. Claus.*, i, 6.) In 1218 he received favours from Henry III, but perhaps only as Philip Augustus's envoy (*Rot. Claus.*, i, 227b, 272, 285b; cf. *Rot. Pat.*, 140b).

Peter of Préaux, the best known of John's brothers, as a friend of King John, was one of the most important persons in Normandy in 1204 after the seneschal. See above, pp. 221–22, 261–63. He died between 1207 and 1212, and apparently joined John in England in the former year if not earlier (*Rot. Pat.*, 68, 69b; *Rot. Claus.*, i, 51b, 79b, 89b, 96; Stapleton, II, ccxxxi).

For William of Préaux, *see* Graville.

ROUMARE. In 1172 William of Roumare owed the service of 14 knights for his various fiefs in the Roumois. This service was given at the castle of Neufmarché; 'et si Dux mandaverit eum alibi, ibit cum iii militibus vel cum iiii' (R.B., ii, 628). This definition of William's service was due to the fact that the Conqueror had granted a moiety of the custody of Neufmarché to his ancestor, Gerold the Dapifer (Stapleton, II, clii). William died before 1198 (*ibid.*, p. clix). His heir is mentioned on the exchequer roll for 1203 (*Rot. Scacc.*, ii, 551), and the *Feoda Normanniae*, after the Conquest, repeats the statement of service without comment (H. de F., 707h). It would appear, therefore, that no change resulted from the loss of Normandy. The family, however, does not seem to have survived.

The English lands of William of Roumare remained in the custody of the crown. In 1205 his inheritance in Dorset and Somerset, which had come through his grandmother, Hawisia de Redvers, was assigned to Gilbert of Clare (Stapleton, II, clix); while in 1217 Earl Randle of Chester established a claim to the earldom of Lincoln, which had been held jointly by the families of Roumare and Ghent (Gand). On this and the ancestry of William of Roumare, see Stapleton, II, cli–clx; Round, *Geoffrey de Mandeville*; D.N.B., v, 269; G.E.C., vii, 667, note.

SAI, ficf of Geoffrey of: In 1180 Geoffrey had land in the neighbourhood of Arques by reason of his marriage with the widow of Hugh of Periers (*Rot. Scacc.*, i, 90).[25] In 1198 he was bailiff of Arques. He gathered together a property of several knights' fees, which was confiscated by Philip Augustus in 1204 (C.N., no. 113).[26] It is possible to reconstruct his fief from the documents contained in Philip's registers. In the *Feoda Normanniae* (H. de F., 705e, 708n; cf. 714f) he is stated to have held a knight's fee at Bellencombre and another, of the honour of Breteuil, at Til and Thieville (Thil and Thiedeville, between Yvetot and Arques?). In 1220 (*ibid.*, pp. 614c, 640b, 621f) half a fee at Fresnay-le-Long and Humesnil is mentioned, and another half at Quesnai—these places are near Bellencombre and Saint-Saens, and may have constituted the fee mentioned above —also half a fee at 'Estoupefos' and 'Estarvilla', which owed its aid in the bailiwick of the castle of Gaillon. The last-named places are Eterville and Fontaine-Etoupefour, just south-west of Caen, and were held in 1220 by Alan of Falaise. Geoffrey of Sai had also possessed the manor of Les Moulineaux in this neighbourhood, which was given in May 1204 to Pain of Meheudin (C.N., no. 1071; see H. de F., 621a).

On his English lands and descendants see G.E.C., xi, 466 ff. He received some of the Tesson lands in Kent (B. of F., 270).

SAINT-HILAIRE. The family of Saint-Hilaire-du-Harcouet (Manche) owed the service of 2½ knights, of which that of 1½ was due in the honour of Mortain, and 1 in the Avranchin (R.B., ii, 637). Hasculf of Saint-Hilaire died before 1180, and his rights descended to his daughter and her husband Frederick or Fraeric Malesmains. The lands of the honour lay between Saint-Hilaire and Pontorson, on either side of Saint-James-de-Beuvron. A certain Peter of Saint-Hilaire, who had joined Philip during Richard's captivity, and afterwards returned, had rights in Lapenty and Les Loges, near

[25] A 'Hue de Periers' is mentioned in a fourteenth-century list of fiefs held of Saint-Ouen (H. de F., 615, note).
[26] Geoffrey of Sai, *junior*, is mentioned in R.N. 63, in a roll of 1202. He may have succeeded his father by this date.

Saint-Hilaire, for which he strove with more or less success in the reigns of Richard, John and Philip Augustus (R.N., 39;[27] *Rot. Scacc.*, ii, 545; *Jugements* (1216–1219), nos. 163, 249). Peter seems to have gone to England in 1220 and made fine for his English lands at Corfton, in Somerset (R.N., 126; *Rot. Claus.*, i, 12; *Excerpta e Rotulis finium*, i, 52; Stapleton, I, lxvii), leaving Fraeric in possession of his Norman claims. Fraeric's fief as tenant of the honour of Mortain, is of course not entered upon the Registers of Philip Augustus, for the honour was in the possession of the counts of Boulogne; but he is named first in a list of knights of the honour (H. de F., 716f). He appears as a tenant-in-chief of the fief in the Avranchin, which lay at Sacey and Vessey, south of Pontorson (H. de F., 612h, cf. 729d; Stapleton, I, clxxx).

SAINT-JEAN-LE-THOMAS. This honour was held of the abbot of Mont-Saint-Michel (H. de F., 703–4). Its lord, William of Saint-Jean, farmed the viscounty of Coutances for more than forty years, 1160–1203 (Tardif, *Coutumiers*, I, i, pp. 111–12; Stapleton, I, xi, lxviii, clviii, cx; II, ix, ccxxxvii). He died about this time, for his name was taken by William, the son of Adam of Port (cf. *Rot. de Fin.*, 259). Adam had married the niece of William of Saint-Jean. Philip Augustus confiscated his land (C.N., no. 113; H. de F., 612g, h), and the castle at Saint-Jean-le-Thomas was destroyed (see Gerville, in *Mémoires de la société des antiquaires de Normandie*, 1827–8, pp. 100–2). The King held it and made deduction for it from the service due from the abbot of Mont-Saint-Michel.

The son of Adam of Port succeeded to the Sussex estates, at Halnecker and Mundham, of William of Saint-Jean. For the history of these lands see Round, *Calendar*, pp. 281, 331; G.E.C., xi, 320–1. Through descent from Adam of Port, the family held Basing in Hampshire (see V.C.H., Hampshire, iv, 116).

SAINT-SAUVEUR-LE-VICOMTE. On the early history of this important honour (Manche) see Delisle's *Histoire de Saint-Sauveur*. It came in the middle of the twelfth century to Jordan Taisson or Tesson, the lord of Thury (now Thury-Harcourt, on the Orne, Calvados, arr. Falaise). In 1172 Jordan owed the service of 10 knights for Thury and of 5 for Saint-Sauveur, and had in them 30½ and 15 fees respectively (R.B., ii, 628). His son, Ralph Tesson, who was for a time seneschal of Normandy in John's reign, joined Philip Augustus (C.N., no. 124). In 1213 his possessions were divided between his three daughters and their husbands. Petronilla, who married William Paynel, the son of Fulk Paynel, got Percy and

---

[27] a. 1200—'Petrus de Sancto Hylario dat domino Rege cc. libras Andegavenses et j equum, quem Domino Regi pacavit, pro habenda tali saisina de terra de Leges et del (*sic*) Apentico qualem habuit quando ivit in Franciam, unde Rex Ricardus frater Domini Regis fecit partiam irrationabilem postea, ut dicet, inter eum et Fraticum Malemans et J. uxorem ejus occasione servicii domini Regis.'

other lands in the Côtentin. Joan, wife of Robert Bertram, got Thury, and Matilda, wife of Richard of Harcourt, got the rest of the honour of Saint-Sauveur (Stapleton, II, lv; C.N., no. 230; H. de F., 609d, e, f; 610e, f, g; 618m).

Ralph Tesson's English lands lay in Kent, Gloucestershire and Nottinghamshire (R.N., 140, 141, 142; Stapleton, II, lv). They were confiscated in 1204; cf. *Pipe Roll, 6 John*, 87–8.

SAINT-VICTOR-EN-CAUX. This place, now Saint-Victor-l'Abbaye, near Tôtes (Seine-Inferieure) was the seat of the Norman honour of Roger of Mortemer, lord of Wigmore. In 1172 Hugh of Mortemer, his father, owed the service of 5 knights and had 13½ (R.B., ii, 631). The family of Mortemer also held Saint-Riquier (arr. Neufchatel) and certain fiefs of the honour of Mortemer (H. de F., 640m, 641a). After 1204 the fiefs of Roger of Mortemer came into the hands of the king (*ibid.*, p. 707g). For some interesting details on the services owing to Roger before 1204 see *ibid.*, 714a, b, c.

It is not necessary to dwell upon the important part played by Roger's descendants in English history. For his defence of Dieppe, see above, p. 264.

See Mortemer.

TANCARVILLE. The lord of Tancarville (Seine-Inferieure) hereditary chamberlain of Normandy, owed the service of 10 knights and held 94¾ knights' fees (R.B., ii, 629; H. de F., 644–5). William of Tancarville joined Philip Augustus (C.N., nos. 124, 125). His land at Hailes, in Gloucestershire, was confiscated (R.N., 142). It is described as an escheat in the *Book of Fees*, 51; cf. *Rot. Claus.*, i, 12.

See G.E.C., x, 47–54.

TILLIERES. The succession to this honour brings out several interesting points. In 1172 Tillières-sur-Avre (Eure) was held by Gilbert of Tillières for the service of 3 knights (R.B., ii, 631. A. reads 4 knights). He died during the third Crusade and his heir was still under age in 1198 (*Rot. Scacc.*, ii, 311). This heir, Gilbert the younger, died between 1220 and 1227 since he was succeeded by his sister Juliana, who was dead in the latter year (Stapleton, II, xlvi, note).[28] By this time, if not before, the rights of a second sister, Joanna, the wife of Thomas Malesmains, had been recognised also, although she and her husband lived in England (see below). The co-heirs in 1228 were Hilaria, the daughter of Juliana, and Nicholas Malesmains, the son of Joanna (Stapleton, II, xlviii). Hilaria's husband, James of Bavelingham, did homage to the king of France for the whole honour, and, *tanquam antenatus*, secured by judgment of the exchequer in 1234 the right to the whole *auxilium exercitus*,

[28] It is possible that the fief of Tillières had been divided after 1172, perhaps in the minority of Gilbert, since the 'Dominus de Tileriis' held only two fiefs in 1220 (H. de F., 618b).

AA

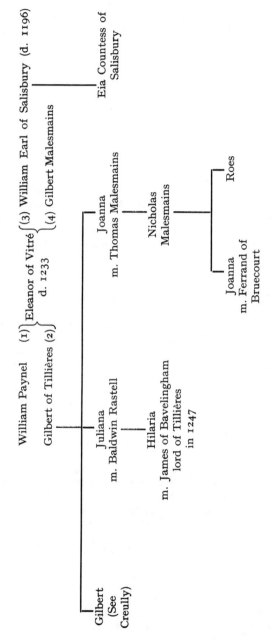

Note. The English lands of Gilbert of Tillières and Eleanor of Vitré came (1) to the crown, *e.g.*, Wootton; (2) to the successor of Roes, *e.g.*, Hadleigh; (3) to Eia and her successors, *e.g.*, Burton in Northamptonshire. Ferrand of Bruecourt claimed lands in the honour of Tillières.

from the lands of Nicholas as well as from his own.[29] (*Jugements*, no. 546; *Querimoniae*, no. 247). A few years later Nicholas died, leaving his Norman lands to his daughter Joanna, and his English lands to his daughter Roes, but in 1247 Joanna's husband had still failed to get possession of them from the royal bailiffs (*Querimoniae*, no. 54; above, p. 304, note).

The English lands of the honour of Tillières lay at Hadleigh and Westcote in Surrey and at Compton in Berkshire; also, in right of his wife Eleanor of Vitré, afterwards Countess of Salisbury, Gilbert the elder had lands in several counties. On the story of these lands see Stapleton (II, xlv *seqq.*). Hadleigh had come to Joanna and her husband, Thomas Malesmains, and fell into the king's hands for a short time in 1204; but Thomas recovered it in 1206 after his return from pilgrimage (R.N., 133; *Rot. Claus.*, i, 90). Most of the English lands were divided in 1233, after the death of Eleanor, between the co-heirs, Hilaria and Nicholas (*Excerpta e rotulis finium*, i, 246; *Close Rolls*, Henry III (1231–4), pp. 244, 261, 283), but Hilaria's husband, when the time of choice came, decided to stay in France. He was alive in 1247 (*Querimoniae*, no. 247). His English lands went in part to the crown. Hadleigh, though not of his share, was for a time annexed, but was afterwards recovered by the heirs of Nicholas Malesmains (Stapleton, II, xlix; V.C.H., Surrey, iii, 291).

The history of the Countess of Salisbury is connected with that of the house of Tillières. Her fourth and last husband was Gilbert Malesmains, who had some of her lands as dowry. The chief of these was Wootton in Oxfordshire. In 1204 these were confiscated as the lands of Gilbert Malesmains (R.N., 129) but they were afterwards allowed to Eleanor, who continued until her death in 1233 to enjoy her dower in England and Normandy (Stapleton, II, xlvii–viii).

TOURNEBU. In 1172 Thomas of Tournebu (Eure, arr. Louviers) owed the service of 3 knights for his 17. His successor appears to have been Amauri, whose fief at Saint-Sulpice, near Bayeux, was farmed by the duke in 1198 (*Rot. Scacc.*, ii, 376). Richard of Tournebu was in Normandy in and before 1212 (B. of F., 88) and had been deprived of his lands in England (cf. Stapleton, II, ccv–ccvi). A Richard of Tournebu, the same or another, was granted the Tournebu manor of Charborough in Dorset in 1215 (*Rot. Claus.*, i, 186b). In 1220 the lord of Tournebu was John, who said that he held 16 fees by the service of 2 (H. de F., 619a; cf. 684f, 772h).

On the family see also Tardif, *Coutumiers*, I, i, 104–5.

TOSNY. Roger of Tosny (Eure, arr. Louviers) held lands on either side of the Seine near Andeli, and also in the honour of Bellencombre (*Rot. Scacc.*, ii, 431). Tosny was given to Cadoc (C.N., nos. 118, 119, 363; *Actes*, no. 1790); the lands on the right bank of the river,

[29] Nicholas held him in parage, and his lands lay at Les Barils, Bourth and other vills in the neighbourhood of Tillières (c. Verneuil).

at Heuqueville and elsewhere went in 1218 to Walter the young, the chamberlain (C.N., no. 271).

For the hostility of Philip Augustus towards Roger, and for other references, see above, pp. 134, note 42, 294.

Roger is mentioned in the English records as in possession of some English lands, but the head of the English family was Ralph, whose ancestors had held their honour since the eleventh century. See *Book of Fees*, Index, *s.v.* Tosny and, for his Tosny connections with Norman and English families, *Anglo-Norman Families*, Index, *s.v.* Todeni and Tosny.

TRACY. Three distinct fiefs are mentioned in the list of 1172, those, namely, of Oliver, William and Turgil of Tracy.

Turgil of Tracy (Tracy-sur-Mer,[30] arr. Bayeux) owed in 1172 the service of 2 knights, and had the service of 8 (R.B., ii, 628). He was succeeded by a William of Tracy who died before 1200. In that year William of Pirou fined with John for his lands (R.N., 38; H. de F., 694j; Stapleton, II, ccxxxviii). From the marginal reference in the Norman rolls and from the later lists of knights and knights' fees (see H. de F., 619e, 707f, 736h) it appears that the fief of Turgil had been held partly of the castle of Vire, and lay in part of the Côtentin (cf. Stapleton, I, clxxx; *Rot. Scacc.*, ii, 536). William of Pirou and his descendants continued to hold the fief.

Oliver of Tracy in 1172 owed the service of 4 knights to the count of Mortain (R.B., ii, 635). In England he held a moiety of the honour of Barnstaple. After his death in 1210, Henry of Tracy got his English lands (*Rot. Pat.*, 101) and, in 1213, he was granted the entire Barnstaple honour, Tavistock, etc. (*Rot. Claus.*, i, 137). The Norman fief is not mentioned in the lists subsequent to 1204.

William of Tracy in 1172 owed the services of a knight in the bailiwick of le Passeis (R.B., ii, 639). He appears to have died about the same time as his namesake mentioned above (*Rot. de Finibus*, 15). He was succeeded by his son Henry, the Henry mentioned above, who united the English lands of the Tracy family.

TROISGOTS. The fief of Troisgots (Manche, arr. Saint-Lô) was held in 1172 by William of Tresgoz (R.B., ii, 633). In 1220 it was an escheat in the king's hands (H. de F., 612d), although by a grant of 1218 Milo of Lévis had the usufruct of the land which William's successor Robert had held at Troisgots and the neighbouring Favarches and Saint-Romphaire (C.N., no. 265). In 1231 St. Louis gave these lands to Andrew of Vitré (C.N., no. 1147). This Robert of Troisgots or Tresgoz was an important bailiff and official in the reigns of Richard and John (Stapleton, I, clxxiv). In England he was lord of Ewyas

[30] So the Index, H. de F. There is a Tracy between Vire and Caen. On this doubtful matter and on the early history of the family of Tracy in England and Normandy see *Anglo-Norman Families*, pp. 106–7, also Stapleton, II, ccxxxviii–xli, for the tangled story in the reign of King John.

Harold in right of his wife (*Rot. de finibus*, pp. 219, 528, compared with *Excerpta e Rotulis finium*, i, 307 (a. 1236). For his lands and descendants see *Book of Fees* (index) and G.E.C., xii, part ii, 16–18).

VASSY. Vassy (Vaaceium) is in Calvados (arr. Vire) between Condé and Vire. In 1172 Juliana of Vassy held the honour by the service of 4 knights (R.B., ii, 629). In 1220 Philip of Vassy held by the service of 2 knights (H. de F., 619a). He had succeeded to his lands in 1198 (*Rot. Scacc.*, ii, 471, see also H. de F., 695c, 707c).

See Fontenai (above, p. 339, note 14).

VIEUXPONT. On the roll of 1172 two families of Vieuxpont are mentioned.

1. William of Vieuxpont is stated to owe the service of 2 knights and to have 11¼ in his service (R.B., ii, 631). Register A adds the words 'in ballia Sagiensi' (H. de F., 695h), and this fief would therefore seem to be identical with that mentioned in the *Feoda Normanniae* and the register of 1220 as in the bailiwick of Exmes (*ibid.*, 706e, 636e). There is a Vieuxpont south of Ecouché near Argentan. Now fees of William of Vieuxpont are mentioned at Ecouché (C.N., no. 283) and at Nonant, in the same district, south of Exmes (H. de F., 636e). This William, who was alive in 1224 (C.N., no. 326, in connection with an inquiry concerning Domfront), was probably the grandson of the William of Vieuxpont who was alive in 1172; in 1198, the land of Robert of Vieuxpont at Chaioullé, north of Séez, was in the king's hand (*Rot. Scacc.*, ii, 389), and it is reasonable to suppose that this land belonged to the same fief and that the lord was recently deceased.

2. The relationship, if any, between William of Vieuxpont and Fulk of Vieuxpont is obscure. In 1172 Fulk owed the service of 2 knights and had that of 10¼ (R.B., ii, 629). He was alive in 1198 (*Rot. Scacc.*, ii, 402, 407). In John's reign the lord of Vieuxpont (Vieuxpont-en-Auge, Calvados, arr. Lisieux) was Robert of Vieuxpont, who was lord of Courville in France (Eure-et-Loir). In 1202, after the outbreak of war between Philip and John, he went into France, and his lands at Vieuxpont were granted to his brother William and afterwards to his nephew Robert (R.N., 49, 55, 91). This Robert last-mentioned was very active in John's service during 1203; he was bailiff in the Roumois, with charge of the king's interest at Rouen, and also in Caen. After the separation he was equally active, as lord of Westmoreland, in England. His father, William, apparently died between the 13th July, 1202, when Vieuxpont was granted to him (R.N., 55) and the 6th May, 1203, when it was granted to Robert (*ibid.*, 91). William's eldest son, Ivo, succeeded to his English lands, Hardingstone in Northamptonshire, and Alston in Tyndale (Stapleton, II, cclxv–vii). But in the civil war Ivo took sides against the king, and Robert was, as John's adherent, granted Hardingstone in 1217 (cf. Farrer, *Lancashire Pipe Rolls*, p. 258).

In the meantime Vieuxpont was held by the widow of Robert the elder.[31] She brought up the heir in France (H. de F., 619j; cf. the reference, 684h). See Stapleton, II, cclxvi.

[31] For a time, unless the addition in Register A is misleading, William of Vieuxpont had the honour after 1204 (H. de F., p. 695b). This could not be the English baron, the brother of Robert, who was dead; he was perhaps the baron mentioned in the early part of this discussion, who lived in the bailiwick of Séez.

INDEX

Bourges, *cont.*—

archbishopric of, 23; viscounty of, 12, 21, 87; viscount of, 'king of', 10. *See* Berri, Charles VII, Philip I

Bourth (c. Verneuil), 355 n.

Boury (*Burriz*, arr. Beauvais) captured by Richard, 121

Boutavant (*Boteavant, Buteavant*), 136, 148 and n., 326; site of disputed, 122 n.; built by Richard, 122, 194; relation of Château Gaillard to, 198; meeting place between le Goulet and, 133, 147; taken by Philip (1202), 148; a place of same name in Ireland, 194 n.

Bouteilles, *i.e.*, Roux-Mesnil-Bouteilles (*Botellae*, Seine-Inferieure, arr. Dieppe), manor of, given to the archbishop of Rouen in part exchange for Andeli, 116 and n.

Bouvines, battle of, 94, 109, 117

Bowes (Yorkshire), castle of, 166 n.

Brabançons, 178, 226, 228 and n.; riot with the Welsh at Portsmouth, 228. *See* mercenaries

Brabant, 88, 90; recruiting among knights of, 221; dukes of, *see* Godfrey, Henry of Louvain

Branchart (Hugh)

Brandin, mercenary, 150 and notes, 184 n., 231; seneschal of La Marche, 33 n., 150 and n., 229, 230 n.; his son, 150 n.

Braosa, 191 n.; *see* Briouze

Bray, district of, 84, 234, 251; bailiwick of, 69; viscounty of, 77; *ministerium* of, 69; works of Henry II in, 187; bailiff of, 53 n.; *see* Alvered of Saint-Martin

Breauté (Fawkes)

Brecon, lord of, 320; *see* William of Briouze

Bréhal (arr. Coutances), fief of Fulk Paynell (*q.v.*), 342

Bresle, river, 109, 341; part of Norman frontier, 184, 185

Bretêche, la (Geoffrey)

Breteuil (*Britolium*, arr. Evreux), honour of earls of Leicester, 185, 252, 343, 347, 351; exempted from *fouage*, 36 n.; privileges granted by Philip to burgesses of, 273 n.; roads from Rouen and Lisieux to, 165 n., 197; road to Bonmoulins from, 103 n.

Bretons, the, 156 and n., 157, 165–6, 167; understanding between Richard and (1196), 111, 118; and the death of Arthur, 310–11; Philip Augustus and, 156, 159; advance of (1204), 253, 257–9; the fair of Montmartin and, 179, 238–9. *See* Brittany

Bretteville (*Bretevilla*, arr. Falaise), 176

Brewer (William)

Brézolles (*Bruerolae*, arr. Dreux), honour of, and Tillières, 171, 179, 182 n.; lord of, 171, 179; John at (1203), 165 and n.

Bricavilla, see Bricqueville-sur-mer

Brice the chamberlain, seneschal of Anjou, 154 and n., 160 and n., 325; castellan of Mortain and Tenchebrai (1203), 258 n.

Bricquebec (Erchenbold)

Bricquebec (arr. Valognes), fief of, 333; *see* Bertram

Bricqueville-sur-mer (Hugh)

Brienne (Alfonse, John)

Brigantes, the, found Bordeaux, 24

Brigstock (Northants), 199 n.

Brikestok, see Brigstock

Brionne (*Briona*, arr. Bernay), 180 n., 253 n.; counts of, succeeded by counts of Meulan, 45, 344, 345; viscounts of, 45

Brioude, county of, 22

Briouze (Reginald, William)

Briouze (*Braosa*, arr. Argentan), fief of, 334

Briquebec, see Bricquebec

Briquessart (arr. Bayeux, c. Livry), fief of earls of Chester, 180 n., 335

Bristol, the abbey of Margam and, 318

Britannia, regio, 154 n.; see Brittany

Brittany, dioceses of, and the archbishop of Tours, 124 and n.; peasant rising in, 48–9 n.; legislation of Henry II and count Geoffrey for, regarding succession, 25, 50, 51 n., 300–1 n.; barons of, 51 n., 156, 275; clergy of, 51 n.; Philip acknowledges Richard's rights in, 87; Richard and, 111 and notes; Mercadier in, 232; adjudged to John by the French court (1200), 135, 292; held of John by Arthur, 135 and n.; Arthur does homage to

Edward I, *cont.*—
130 n., 249, 289, 306 and n.;
Gascon inquest of, 33
Edward III, king of England, 94
Eia, countess of Salisbury, 354 and n.
Eleanor, queen of England, duchess
of Aquitaine, 141, 232, 325; the
marriage of Louis VII of France
with, 21 n.; marries Henry of Anjou, afterwards king of England,
8, 11, 16, 82 n.; revenues of, from
Falaise, 56 and n.; does homage
to Philip after Richard's death,
131 n., 132, 133 n.; Constance of
Brittany and, 132; at Fontevrault,
142 and n., 143; besieged by
Arthur at Mirebeau, 27, 151, 310
Eleanor of Barneville, and her sisters,
283 n.
Eleanor, sister of Arthur of Brittany,
159, 260; suggested as wife of the
son of the duke of Austria, 93, 106;
sent to Austria and brought back,
110; suggested marriage between
Louis of France and, 106; im-
prisoned at Corfe, 258
Eleanor of Vitré, countess of Salis-
bury (d. 1233), 354–5; *see* Tillières
Elias, Master, 190 n.
Elias of *Bouelles*, 175 and n.
Elias of Carville, 175 n.
Elias *de Chigehan*, leader of Welsh
mercenaries, 227 n.
Elias *de Elemosina*, 112 n.
Elias of Malmort, archbishop of Bor-
deaux, 299 n., 325 and n.
Elias V, count of Périgord, 265; rebel-
lion of (1192), 98
Elias *de Wimblevill*, 280 n.
Ella, sister of Robert III of Alençon,
331
Ely, bishops of; *see* William Long-
champ, Eustace
emprumenta, 235 n.
Emsworth (Hampshire), 337
Enard, Matthew, son of; *see*
Matthew, Everd
Engelger of Bohon, lawsuit of (1199),
51 n.; honour of, 333; joins John
(*ibid.*). *See* Midhurst
Engineers, the, 224 and n.
Engine makers, 224
enginneor, see Engineers
England, 168; bishops of, 324; inter-
dict in (1208), *ibid.*; Henry II and,

34–5; knight-service in, 40 n.;
Henry II and the castles of, 186;
rebellion of 1173 in, 202–4; development of constitution of, after 1204,
305–6; primogeniture in, 43, 44;
forest law in, 66 n.; law of treason
and aliens in, 82, 286–90
— administrative districts of the continental parts of the empire and of,
26 and n., 38; connection between
Normandy and, in Henry II's
reign, 54–5; social unity of Normandy and, 303–5; administrative
inquiries in Normandy and in,
52 n., 77; comparison of forest
administration in Normandy and
in, 57–8; Norman judicial reforms
applied in, 63, 66; assimilation of
financial systems in Normandy
and, 235; treasure from, 188, 235
and notes, 260, 298; cheeses from,
189, 208
— Philip plans invasion of (1193),
95; John checked in, *ibid.*;
Richard's preparations in (1194),
98; military preparations in,
111–12, 121, 144; military organisation of, 218—19; John's flight to
(1203), 168–9; help given to John
by (1204), 327–8; plans for French
invasions of, 265–6; preparations
against invasion in (1204–7), 209
and n., 266–8; separation from
Normandy of, 280; consequences
of separation of, 303–6; lands of
Norman deserters in, 174–7, 328
seqq.
English, in Normandy, 162; in
Château Gaillard, 254; in Poitou
(1206), 267 and n.
Engolismae, Engolismum, see Angoulême
Enguerrand, son of Richard du Hommet, 343
Enguerrand of Montigny, 176
Enguerrand the Porter, farmer of
Bray, and castellan of Beauvoir,
69, 187
Epte, river, 84–5 and n., 109, 133,
150, 283, 340, 341; part of the
Norman frontier, 184, 185; for-
tresses on the, 69; Château Gaillard
and the castles on, 194; fighting
in the valley of (1198), 120–2;
French garrisons on (1199), 200

Guala, the papal legate, 315, 318

Guérin of Cierrez, bishop of Evreux, 98, 114 n.

Guérin of Glapion, seneschal of Normandy, 140 and n., 146 and n., 173–4, 176, 229 and n.; receipts and expenditure of (1201–2), 52, 223 n., 229 and n., 249; Norman estates of, 173, 174 and n.; joins Philip, 173–4, 262; seneschal under Philip, 272 and n.; receives lands from Philip, 346, 348, 349 and n.; suspected of relations with the emperor Otto, 174, 269, 283

Guernsey, farm of, 76; John receives revenues of, 100 n.

Gueroldus Lailier, 217 n.

Guines (Gisnae, etc., arr. Boulogne), 89; count of, 139 n.

Guiomarc'h IV, viscount of Leon, 246 n.

Guiomarc'h V, viscount of Leon, 246 and n.; Conan, his son, 245–6

Guitebo, see Quitteboeuf

Guletum, see le Goulet

Gunfrid of Choques, 289 n.

Guy of Auteuil, 346

Guy of Dive, 209 n., 281

Guy Geoffrey, duke of Aquitaine, 24

Guy of Laval, 156 n., 177

Guy, viscount of Limoges, 140 and n., 141, 145

Guy of Nonant, knight service of, 349 and notes

Guy of La Roche, 161 n., 269 n., 283

Guy of Sablé, in possession of Gacé after 1204, 340

Guy of Thouars, brother of Aimeri, viscount of Thouars, 153 n., 154, 167, 177, 258, 311 n.; captured at Aumâle (1196), 110 n.; marries Constance of Brittany, 139; administers honour of Richmond, 325; recognised by Philip as count of Brittany, 143 and n.; joins Philip, 165 and n.; loses his English lands, 160 n., 177; leads the Bretons into Normandy (1204), 257; position of, in 1204, 258; sent by Philip to reduce western Normandy, 259

H

Hadleigh (Surrey), 354 n., 355

Haia, see La Haie

Haie, le (Nicolaa, Ralph, Robert)

Haie-du-Puits, la (Haia Putei, arr. Coutances), honour of, 342; see Burwell

Hailes (Gloucestershire), 353

Hainault, 88 seqq.; recruiting among knights of, 221; count of, 144 n.; see Baldwin

Halnecker (Sussex), 352

Hambye (Hambia, arr. Coutances), fief of Fulk Paynel (q.v.), 342

Hamo Pincerna, bailiff of the Bessin, 59, 72; styles himself seneschal of Bayeux, 59 n., 72, 271 n.

Harcourt (John, Richard, Robert)

Harcourt (Harecurt, Haricuria, arr. Bernay), fief of honour of Beaumont-le-Roger, 328, 343; Norman and English families of, 343–4

Hardingstone (Northants), 357

Harecurt, see Harcourt

Harfleur (Harefluctus, Harefluvius, arr. le Havre), revenues of, 68; commune of, 149 n., 211 n.

Hasculf Paynel, 290

Hasculf of Saint-Hilaire, 351; his daughter, ibid.; see Frederick Malesmains

Hastings (Sussex) claimed by the counts of Eu, 288, 338

haute justice, 39

Hauteville (Tancred)

Haveret (Simon)

Hawisia of Réviers or Redvers, English lands of, 351

Haye, see Haie

Haye-de-Herce (arr. Mantes), 197 n.

Haye-Malherbe, La (Haia Malherbe, arr. Louviers), 107 n.

Hebertot, i.e., Saint-André d'Hebertot, (arr. Pont l'Evêque), 167

Helyas, see Elias

Henry (Richard, son of)

Henry VI, emperor, 135; Richard and, 90; intrigue of Philip Augustus with, 91–2; causes of alliance between Richard and, 92–4; Italian policy of, 104; foments war between Richard and Philip (1195), 105–6; death of (Sept., 1197), 117; Henry I, king of France, 15, 16

Henry I, king of England, duke of Normandy, 181, 238, 299, 304, 306; as count of the Côtentin, 185;

coronation of, 142; isolated at Chinon, 157; brought to Le Mans, 158

Isabella, d. of Baldwin V of Hainault, wife of Philip Augustus, 88; her dowry, 89–90; treaties concerning dowry of, *ibid.* and notes; *see* Artois

Isabella of Ferrières, d. of Walchelin of Ferrières, wife of Roger Mortimer, has life interest in the English lands of her father and brothers after 1204, 338

Isabella of Gloucester, first wife of king John, 141, 173

Isabella of Vermandois, wife of Philip of Alsace, count of Flanders, 89, 90 n.; death of (1182), 89; Philip Augustus seizes part of dowry of (1185), *ibid.*; *see* Vermandois, Valois, Amiens, Montdidier

Isoldun, see Issoudun

Issoudun (Ralph)

Issoudun (*Exoldunum, Isoldun, Issoldunum,* Indre), lordship of, in Poitevin Berri, 21, 22; ceded by Richard to Philip (1191), 87; Richard at, in July, 1195, 107 n.; Philip besieges (Nov.), 106–7; Richard relieves, *ibid.* and n., 218 n.; terms made at (Dec.), *ibid.*, 135 and n.; ceded by John, 137; other references to, 171, 195

Italy, politics of (1194), 104; inquiries into baronial service of south, 34 and n.

Itun, river, 103 n., 136, 170 and n., 171 and n., 172 n., 251, 252; John promises to fix Norman frontier at (1194), 97; becomes part of the frontier, 185

Ivo the Balistarius, founder of the house of Bellême, 185, 225n.

Ivo, Master, the *balistarius* or engineer, in the service of Richard and John, 163 n., 196, 225–6

Ivo of Vieuxpont, elder son of William (I) of Vieuxpont, inherits Hardingstone and Alston, 357; fights against John in 1216, *ibid.*

Ivon (Renaud)

Ivry (*Ibriacum, Ivriacum,* arr. Evreux), occupied by Philip (1193), 97; retained in 1196, 108; other references to, 124 n., 136, 182, 184

J

James of Bavelingham, husband of Hilaria, co-heiress to the honour of Tillières, 353–5; becomes lord of Tillières, 354, 355

James *de Jhota,* Italian financier, 233 n.

Jarnac (Charente, arr. Cognac), 33

Jersey, 149 n.; *ministeria* in, 76

Jerusalem (Baldoin)

Jerusalem, kingdom of, 295. *See* Crusade, Crusaders, Pilgrims

Jew, the, who helped the constable of Chester at Château Gaillard, 254 n.

Jews, 77, 202; charter of the, 241 n.; the king and the bonds of, 240 n.; John and the Norman, 240–1 and notes; warden of the Norman, 77, 241 n.; tallage of the Norman, 241 n., 253; Philip Augustus and, 274; release by king of debts owing to, 157 n., 213 n., 240 n.

Jhota (James)

Joachim of Flora, 90

Joan of Arc, 10

Joan, d. of Henry II, king of England, wife of William II, king of Sicily, and afterwards wife of Raymond VI, count of Toulouse (1196), 86

Joan, d. of William of Mandeville, wife of Matthew fitzHerbert, 349

Joan, d. of Ralph Tesson, wife of Robert Bertram, 333; inherits Thury, 353; in control of Fontenaile-Marmion (1256), 339

Joanna, d. of Nicholas Malesmains, wife of Ferrand of Bruecourt, 354

Joanna, d. of Gilbert of Tillières (1), her claims to the honour of Tillières in England and Normandy, 353–5; wife of Thomas Malesmains, and mother of Nicholas Malesmains, *ibid.*

John, count of Mortain, king of England, character of, 128; destructiveness of, 128 n.; lethargy of, 158, 162–3; financial unscrupulousness of, 233 and n.; tyranny of, 299; as a negotiator, 238 n.; journeys of, in England, 305; in Ireland, 166 n., 306

DD

Pont Audemer (*Pons Audomari, Alde-mari*, Eure), fief of honour of Meulan, 176, 177, 181 n., 231, 252, 344; annexed by Richard, 71; baili-wick of, 71, 272; strengthened by John, 253; loan raised in, 208 n.; Jews of, 241 n.; commune of, 261. See Auge, Cadoc

Ponte (William *de*)

Ponthieu, counts of, *see* John, William

Pontorson (*Pons Ursonis*, arr. Avran-ches), 184 and n., 186 n., 248, 252, 275, 352; built by Henry I, 186; castle and *prepositura* of, 75, 76; privileges of, 212; earl of Salisbury and, 76, 258 and n.; loss of, 259

Port (Adam, William)

Portes (Roger)

Portes (arr. Evreux), 170, 171 and n.

Portjoie (*Portus Gaudii*, cant. Pont de l'Arche), bridge over Seine at, 106, 193

Portmort (arr. Les Andelys), 137 and n.

Portsmouth, forces gathered at, 98, 213, 214, 216, 266 and n., 267

Portugal, John and, 141 and n.; Moors and, 104

Possession, *see* assize, recognition

potestas, 25

Potigny (*Postenny, Postigneium*, arr. Falaise), 177

Pouchin (Thomas)

Poupeville (arr. Valognes, c. Sainte-Marie-du-Mont), farm of, 75, 78

Praeriis, see Presles

Pratella. see Préaux

Préaux (John, Osbert, Peter, William)

Préaux (*Pratella*, arr. Rouen), 262 n., 345, 350; family of, 328, 350

Préaux (arr. Pont-Audemer), abbot of, 290 n.; abbess of, *ibid.*

Preez (Herveus)

prepositura, in Normandy, 45, 47, 53 and n., 55 and n., 68–78, 206 n., 274; in Poitou, 31

prepositus, prepositi, 59 n.; in Anjou, 20, 28; in Normandy, *see preposi-tura*

Presles (Robert)

Prices, 208 and notes, 223

Primogeniture, 43–5, 50–1 and n.; social effect of, 302 n.; political effects of, 303–4 and notes

principes, 44

prisia servientum, 220 and n.

Prisoners, details concerning, 243–6; taken at Mirebeau, 151 and n., 167

Private jurisdiction, 61, 63 and n.

Private warfare, 67 and n.

Procedure, in England and Nor-mandy, 62–4 and notes

proceres, 44

procurator, used in special sense, 96 n.

Provins (Seine-et-Marne), 195

Prudhoe (Northumberland), 204

Punishment, severity in, 209

Puteac (Henry)

Puy-en-Velay (Haute-Loire), associa-tion against mercenaries formed at (1182), 22, 230

Puy (Bartholomew)

Q

Quaillia, see Cailly

Quesnai (arr. Neufchâtel), 351

Queu (William)

Querci, added to Toulouse, 22; seized by Richard (1188), 86; Philip Augustus acknowledges to be part of Aquitaine, *ibid.*; restored to Toulouse by Richard (1196), *ibid.*

Quevilli (*Chivilleium*, arr. Rouen), park of Henry II at, 186 and n.

Quinci (Saer)

Quitteboeuf (*Guitebo, Quittebeuf, Witebo,* arr. Evreux), 170, 171 and n.

R

rachimburdi, 28 n.

Radepont (*Radepons*, arr. Les An-delys), 161, 185, 251; repaired, 190 n.; garrison in, 256; taken by Philip, 164 and n., 166 n.; granted to P. de Moret, 164 n., 252, 275

Radnor, 320

Ralf, *see* Ralph

Ralph the Archer, 243 n.

Ralph of Arden, 51 n.

Ralph of Argences, 175

Ralph of Beaufou, 333

Ralph, viscount of Beaumont-sur-Sarthe, 158 n.

Ralph of Cailly, 167 n.

Ralph, abbot of Coggeshall, 313 n.

Ralph of Creully, 338

Ralph, viscount of Déols, 87 n.; Denise, d. of, *ibid.*

*

This index contains critical and the first or more important references.

William of the Paraclete, 92
Wykes, 130 n.

MODERN

Adigard, J., 36
D'Aguesseau, 286 n.
Amira, Karl von, 2 n., 43 n.
Anisy, Lechaudé d', 3, 58 n., 339 n.
Anselme, 332 n.
Arbellot, 125 n.
Audouin, E., 249
Baldwin, J. F., on scutage, 216 notes,
  221 n.; on the chancery, 305 n.
Baluze, 14 n.
Banks, 338, 339
Bardonnet, 25 n., 31 n., 191 n., 200 n.
Barrau-Dihigo, 23 n.
Bateson, Mary, 211 n., 246 n.
Beautemps-Beaupré, 18 n, 154 n.
Bédier, 43 n., 297 n., 318
Bédier and Aubry, 246 n.
Bémont, C., on confiscation of Nor-
  mandy, 148 n.; on the condemna-
  tion of Arthur, 309–24 passim; on
  Robert IV, earl of Leicester, 344
Berger, E., 269 notes
Bessin, G., 277 n.
Bigelow, 63 n.
Birch, W. de Gray, 318 n.
Bloch, M., 14, 94 n.
Blosseville, 172 n.
Boehmer, 2
Boissonade, 32, 99, 141, 142, 143
Bolin, S., 48
Bonnard, 184
Borderie, A. de la, 49 n., 166 n.,
  246 n., 301 n.
Borrelli de Serres, on Philip Augustus
  and Artois, 89 n.; on the communal
  militia, 211 n.; on the French
  military system, 220 n., 249 n.
Boussard, J., 1, 5, 9 n., 21, 23, 25,
  32, etc.; on mercenaries, 129 n.
Boutaric, E., 227 n.
Bréard, 333
Bréhier, 246 n.
Brette, Armand, 284 n.
Brooks, E. St. John, 227 n.
Brown, R. A., 180 n., 194
Brunner, H., 2, 3; on the Norman
  viscounts, 47 n.
Brussel, 9 n., 36 n., 273 n.
Cam, H., 61
Canel, 67 n.
Cartellieri, A., 1 and passim; on Philip

Augustus and Flanders, 90 n.; on
  Richard's itinerary, 107; on Otto
  of Brunswick, as count of Poitou,
  118 n.; on Boutavant, 122 n.; on
  the scheme of the legate, 124 n.;
  on Mercadier, 228 n.; on Philip
  Augustus and the Jews, 249 n.
Cazel, A., 141
Chadwick, H. M., 38 n.
Chaplais, E., 33
Charpillon, 171 n., 173 n.
Chartrou, J., 5
Cheney, C. R. and Semple, W. H.,
  Selected Letters of Pope Innocent
  III, 95 n. and passim
Chéruel, P. A., 117 n., 261 n.; on the
  composite chronicle of Rouen,
  314–5
Chew, H. M., 216
Clark, G. T., 318–20 notes
Clay, C. T., 49
Cokayne, G. E., see Complete Peerage
Collinson, 332
Complete Peerage, 331
Courson, 258 n.
Coutil, L., 184, 206 n. etc.
Coville, 35 n., 44 n., 301 n.
Cuttino, G., 84 n.
Davis, H. W. C., 62 n., 211 n.
Degert, 23 n.
Delaborde, H. F., on the treaty of
  January 1194, 97 n.; on the scheme
  of the legate, 124 n.; on the death
  of Richard, 127; on the grant made
  by Philip and John for the relief
  of the Holy Land, 145 n.; on John
  in Brittany, 166 n.; on William
  the Breton and Gerald of Wales,
  227 n.; on the date of the Philippid, 321 n.; his edition of Rigord
  etc., and of acts of Philip II
  passim
Delisle, Léopold, Etudes sur la condition de la classe agricole, 5, 57 and
  passim
— Des revenus publics en Normandie, 5 and passim; on the distribution of families, 46, 329; on aids
  and tallages, 234 n.; on Philip's
  ordinance concerning money, 264 n.,
  279 n.
— Cartulaire Normand (q. v.), 4,
  164 n., 329;
— Catalogues des actes de Philippe-
  Auguste (q .v.), 4, 145 n., 164 n.,

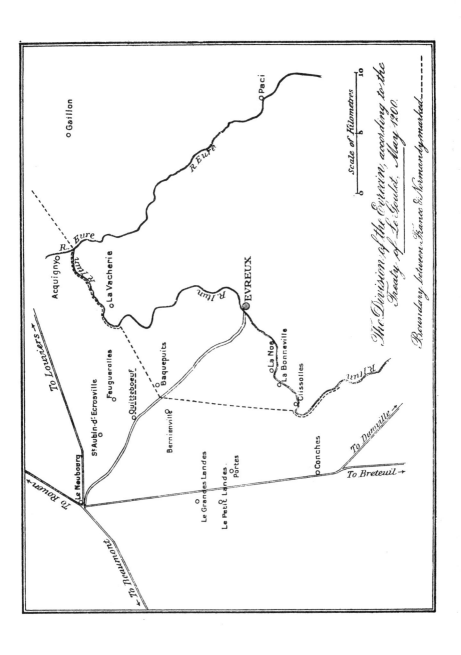

The Division of the Evrecin, according to the Treaty of Le Goulet, May 1200.

Boundary between France & Normandy marked

Scale of Kilometres

o Gaillon

R. Eure

R. Eure

Acquigny o

o La Vacherie

R. Iton

R. Iton

EVREUX

Paci

To Louviers

St Aubin d' Ecrosville o

Feuguerolles o

Quitteboeuf o

Baquepuits o

La Noe o

La Bonneville o

Cissolles o

R. Iton

Bernienville o

Le Neubourg o

To Rouen

Le Grandes Landes o

Le Petit Landes o

Portes o

Conches o

To Dumville

To Breteuil

To Beaumont

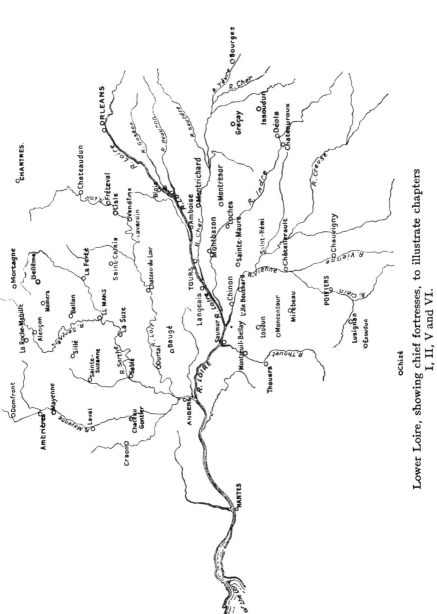

Lower Loire, showing chief fortresses, to illustrate chapters I, II, V and VI.

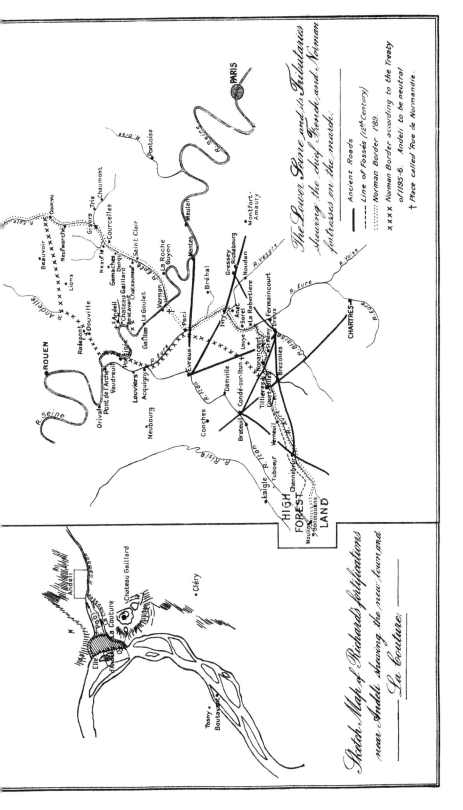

The Lower Seine and its Tributaries
shewing the chief French and Norman
fortresses on the march.

Ancient Roads
Line of Fossés (12th Century)
Norman Border
× × × × Norman Border according to the Treaty
of 1195–6. Andeli to be neutral
† Place called 'Rive de Normandie.

PARIS

ROUEN

CHARTRES

R. Seine

R. Eure

R. Epte

R. Andelle

R. Risle

R. Iton

R. Vesgre

R. Voise

R. Blaise

R. Oise

Beauvoir
Courvil
Gisors
Trie
Chaumont
Neufmarché
Lions
Courcelles
Saint Clair
Neaufle
La Roche Guyon
Gamaches
Danqu
Château Gaillard
Boutavant
Châteauneuf
Le Goulet
Gaillon
Vernon
Paci
Bréhal
Gressey
Richebourg
Houdan
Montfort-Amaury
Andeli
Douville
Radepont
Orival
Pont de l'Arche
Vaudreuil
Louviers
Acquigny
Evreux
Ivry
Nonancourt
Anet
Sorel
La Robertière
Fermaincourt
Dreux
Brezolles
St Rémy
Louye
Neubourg
Conches
Damville
Condé-sur-Iton
Tillières
Court Villé
Breteuil
Verneuil
Aigle
Tuboeuf
Chennebrun
Moulins
Bonmoulins
HIGH FOREST LAND
Pontoise

Sketch Map of Richard's fortifications
near Andeli: shewing the new town and
La Couture.

Château Gaillard
Andeli
Cléry
L'Ile
Tool
La Couture
Tosny
Boutavant
R. Gambon
R. Seine